# Women's Legal Guide

# Women's Legal Guide

Barbara R. Hauser, Editor
with Julie A. Tigges

Fulcrum Publishing
Golden, Colorado

Library of Congress Cataloging-in-Publication Data
Women's legal guide / edited by Barbara R. Hauser with Julie A. Tigges.
　　　　p.　　cm.
　　Includes bibliographical references and index.
　　ISBN 1-55591-913-8 (hardcover). — ISBN 1-55591-303-2 (pbk.)
　　1. Women—Legal status, laws, etc.—United States. I. Hauser, Barbara R.
II. Tigges, Julie A.
KF478.W674　　1996
346.7301'34—dc20　　　　　　　　　　　　　　　　　　　　95–46893
[347.306134]　　　　　　　　　　　　　　　　　　　　　　　　CIP

Printed in the United States of America
0　9　8　7　6　5　4　3　2　1

Fulcrum Publishing
350 Indiana Street, Suite 350
Golden, Colorado 80401-5093
(800) 992-2908

*Dedicated to my dear husband, Douglas Cameron,*
*who first suggested law*

*and to Wellesley College,*
*where this book began.*

# Contents

# *Foreword*

Women have special legal needs. There are times when dealing appropriately with the issues and events of our lives—from reproductive rights to real estate to retirement planning—may mean calling on the help of a lawyer.

But how do you know when you need a lawyer? And what should you expect from your attorney? For many women (and men!) who have never hired a lawyer, the prospect can be intimidating. That's why I strongly recommend this book as a valuable resource for women of all ages.

*Women's Legal Guide* takes the mystery out of standing up for your legal rights. Each of the 29 women lawyers who contributed to the book had one purpose in mind: to help you make informed decisions on the legal issues facing you.

In some cases, you may find you don't need a lawyer at all. But when you do, the information in this book can help you choose an attorney equipped to handle your legal needs; and help you work effectively with your lawyer.

You may have purchased this book for help with a specific legal problem—such as divorce or adoption. But I encourage you to look over the other chapters as well. This can be a reference book you'll return to many times in the years ahead.

I applaud the efforts of editor Barbara Hauser, as well as the 29 women lawyers who contributed to this valuable reference book; and I congratulate them on behalf of the American Bar Association for a job well done.

—Roberta Cooper Ramo
President, American Bar Association

# *Preface*

"Sunshine Class, ready to line up; the almanae parade is going to begin!" We were waiting obediently, wearing our yellow hats and prescribed white outfits. Twenty-five years earlier we had not known each other, but we were enjoying visiting while we waited for the parade to begin. "I work with a publisher," she said. "Interesting," I said. "I am a lawyer." "Interesting," she said. "You know we have been thinking about a book explaining the law—especially for women." "That's a good idea, and I would be glad to help."

Three years later we have this book for you. It turned out to be a big project, but an intriguing and satisfying one. We hope you like it.

**Purpose of the Book**

There is an increasing need for women to know more about the law. In the past, it was often true that the men in the family took care of all forms of business, including dealing with the lawyers. Even one generation ago, women did not even have many of the rights that men had. Fortunately, that has changed dramatically since then. For many women today there are increasing reasons to contact lawyers and coordinate legal matters. With divorce having become increasingly common, women want to understand their property rights. In addition, they have become single parents, with the responsibility of dealing with all legal matters that can affect them and their children. Many women are also choosing not to marry and must coordinate their own investments, real estate, and business interests. With the aging of our society, it is often daughters who are assuming responsibility for their parents, which again includes many legal matters, including health care rights and decisions, disability planning, estate tax and probate issues, and handling the estate after death. As working women, there are additional legal issues that arise in the workplace. For women starting or continuing their own business, there is a need to know the best legal structure to use, ways to protect intangible interests, and rules that apply to employers.

Law is a highly technical and difficult-to-understand field. There are myriad rules that apply; they have been interpreted by courts and agencies; they are increasingly subject to change. In addition to the federal system of law, there are also fifty independent state jurisdictions with their own bodies of law.

### The Benefit for the Reader

This book contains a wealth of information. It will give you an overview of all of the areas of the law that seem to be of the most interest, and the most needed. You will become acquainted with a specialized vocabulary (and a practical glossary). Cautions are included in each area (to warn you of areas of risk), so that you can avoid many common pitfalls. You will acquire a good understanding of when you do need to consult with a lawyer, and learn how to receive the most benefit from hiring a lawyer. You will know when money will be well-spent, and when not having legal advice could be extremely expensive.

### Why This Book Is Special

There are other guides to the law, but they are usually limited to a very specific subject. The general works that are available are not put together with women in mind and are not as comprehensive. We all felt that this book covers a real need. It should be the first item you reach for when you need to know something—from background information to specific alternatives—about the law.

### Authority

Each chapter has been written by a woman who is an attorney specializing in the field, or who has extensive personal knowledge of the field. A number of these attorneys have not only practiced the kind of law that they write about but also teach it in law school. Two are judges. One is an organization made up of many lawyers. Every one of these authors cares deeply about her subject. Every one has made a tremendous effort to write about her specialty in clear, precise language to help you understand not only the law, but also the reasons behind the law. Wherever legal "terms of art" are used, they are clearly defined. Each chapter ends with a bibliography for further reading and a list of organizations that can provide more information and assistance.

## Organization and Scope of the Book

The book begins with a chapter on selecting a lawyer; how to find one, hire one, and communicate with one. It gives low-cost alternatives for those who cannot afford an attorney and explains the different bases for fees that are charged. The rest of the chapters are arranged in broad sections, beginning with personal/body issues such as health care, patient rights, reproductive rights, and sexual assault. The next group of chapters deals with family law, including children's rights, marriage and divorce, adopting a child, and placing your child for adoption. The third section covers your rights more generally—including both school and the workplace; sexual harassment or discrimination, women in sports, the rights of lesbian women, and the rights of disabled women. The fourth section, Business Law, provides information about the woman as employer, how to start your own business, intellectual property rights, real estate, bankruptcy, and consumer rights. The fifth section covers issues that will affect us as we move toward the end of our careers and lives and as we care for aging parents. It deals with planning for retirement, planning the administration of an estate, and the legal aspects of dealing with a death. The final chapter and afterword move to a broader arena and spotlight issues of refugee women and the impact the law can have to improve the equality of women on a global basis.

## Audience

This is a useful reference source for every woman. It is designed for women with families, women who are single, women who work, women who are retired. Occasionally a chapter author takes a position with regard to a particular issue, but generally the aim of the book is to provide a balanced overview of the law as it is today and of the way it affects us at home and out in the world.

## To the Reader

You can browse through this book, as you would browse through any other reference manual in a new field. You can use it only to look up particular questions. You can, and probably will, do both. We put this information together for you. Mark it up, turn down the pages, share it with your lawyer, with your family and friends.

Let us know how this book has helped you. Let us know if you have any other questions. We would love to hear from you.

Barbara R. Hauser
June 1995

# *Acknowledgments*

---

Each author deserves tremendous thanks. Thanks also to the review board: Jeannette Walker Kornreich, J.D.; Susan J. Tyburski, J.D.; and Martha B. Taylor, J.D. Special assistance was received from: Gina M. Calabrese, J.D.; NOW Legal Defense and Education Fund; and Dara Klassel, J.D., Director of Legal Affairs, Planned Parenthood Federation of America.

It was very satisfying to contact so many top lawyers to write about each separate field, and to hear and see their enthusiasm for the goal of providing a very "user-friendly" reference guide to so many complex areas of the law.

This book would not exist without the initial and ongoing enthusiasm, support, and assistance of Shirley Lambert. As I worked through the process of putting this project together, Shirley was invaluable. I also would not have been able to finish this without the additional assistance of Julie A. Tigges, a talented lawyer who helped with all the follow-up and editing (and then had twins!). My secretary Jim Blum began with the project, an able and astute believer in the book, and my secretary, Zhenya Stone, finished the project with relish and persistence. Finally, thanks to all my partners at Gray, Plant, Mooty, Mooty & Bennett, an outstanding firm.

Chapter 1

# Selecting a Lawyer

Andrea Williams

Chapter Outline

**Introduction**

**When a Lawyer Is Needed**

**Determining If Legal Assistance Is Needed**
Organizations

**Lawyers**
The Importance of Lawyer Selection • Generalists and Specialists

**Finding a Lawyer**
Recommendations • Professional or Service Organizations • Legal
Directories • Lawyer Referral Services • Pro Bono Legal Services •
Law Schools

**Important Attorney Attributes**
Ability to Communicate With the Client • Subject Matter Expertise •
Ethics and Judgment • Clear Roles and Reasonable Fees

**Special Considerations for Women**
Office Hours • Collaborative Interaction • Extralegal Considerations
• Wait Time • Participation of Others

**Determining If a Lawyer Meets the Criteria**
Making Inquiries • Conducting Interviews • Contacting Clients

**The Initial Interview**
Background and Expertise • Handling of the Matter • Fees and Billing Procedures

**Attorneys' Fees**
Estimates • Statements • Fee Increases • Written Agreements • Retainers • Expenses • Payment Schedule • Interest • Interview Questions

**Maintaining the Relationship**
Communication and Quality of Service • Client Assistance • Confidentiality • Fees and Billings

**Terminating the Relationship**

**Conclusion**

## Introduction

The law sets the framework and boundaries for most of our interactions. Most of the time, these are invisible contours. When is a lawyer needed to understand and negotiate those contours? What avenues are available for identifying lawyers? What qualities are important in a lawyer? Are there options about how the lawyer will handle the matter? What fosters a positive attorney-client relationship? When is termination of the representation appropriate? How do you know when you need a lawyer? Where do you find one who will work best for you? This chapter addresses these issues about the attorney-client relationship.

## When a Lawyer Is Needed

Sometimes it is apparent that a lawyer is needed; in other situations, the need for legal advice is unclear. It is advisable to consider retaining a lawyer in the following circumstances:

1. When there is opposing representation. When others involved in a transaction or dispute have retained counsel, it is appropriate to consult an attorney. A lawyer's participation is valuable in describing and assisting the parties in following established procedure and identifying and addressing significant legal issues. A lawyer's role is to understand her client's interests and act to maximize them, not to represent all parties. If several lawyers are involved, each lawyer need not redo every piece of legal work. One lawyer can review the documents the opposing lawyer has prepared and initiate only necessary additional legal work. So, while the representation of other parties may suggest retaining a lawyer, the legal work required may be minimal.

2. In an adversarial proceeding. Legal representation should be considered in any adversarial proceeding, such as a civil court case, a proceeding before a zoning board, an administrative hearing deciding workers' compensation or unemployment compensation, or a contested proceeding in probate court. While an individual may represent herself before these bodies, the process is laden with intricate procedures that often confuse and intimidate the layperson (the legal term for a nonlawyer). The presiding authority is often unsympathetic to the oversights and procedural mistakes of a party appearing *pro se* (the Latin term meaning "for himself," used to describe a party not represented by counsel). If counsel is retained, she can be most helpful at the matter's inception. During prehearing procedures, the lawyer can often shape the proceeding and enhance the client's position.

3. When legal principles shape the issue. There are legal parameters in almost every issue. In some, they are remote, for example, a personality conflict with a coworker. In others, such as being terminated from employment, the law provides a person with a specific range of options. In those situations, retaining a lawyer to describe the law applicable to the situation is particularly helpful.

4. When the legal implications are unknown. One may be embroiled in a complicated and difficult problem and be unsure if it has legal dimensions or implications. Consulting with a lawyer will clarify the legal issues that can or should be considered in resolving the problem.

## Determining If Legal Assistance Is Needed

An array of community and public services are available in many communities to aid a person in determining if legal assistance is needed.

### Organizations

The following types of organizations usually provide focused, meaningful help:

1. State and local bar associations.* Often state or local bar associations have programs providing responses to general inquiries, which direct the public to the appropriate person or agency. Generally, the bar association does not give specific legal advice to an individual. The kinds of programs sponsored include:

    • Audiotapes explaining the basic procedures and options in subject areas that most affect the public, such as holding real and

---

*The bar association is an organization of lawyers. In some states, membership is voluntary; in others, admission to practice brings with it automatic admission to the bar association. The name is taken from the physical layout of the courtroom where judges sit on the bench and lawyers stand in front of a bar, separating them from the public.

other property in joint tenancy, bankruptcy, and child custody. Often these tapes are offered in conjunction with the Better Business Bureau.

- Call-in programs, either on the radio or in private conversations, staffed by lawyers who volunteer their time. Although specific legal advice is generally not given, the nature of the problem is explored. Usually, these calls lead to recommendations to a specific social service agency or governmental department for further information; for example, a consumer credit counselor or the consumer fraud division of the state or municipal attorney's office. If a lawyer is clearly needed, the volunteer lawyer would identify organizations that locate lawyers.

- Clinics, either free or for a nominal fee, on subjects such as divorce, child support enforcement, bankruptcy (debtor and creditor), unemployment compensation, small claims, and collections. These clinics are typically given in the evening. The participant is exposed to the basic concepts and procedures and can then ascertain whether she can maneuver through the required steps on her own or needs assistance of counsel.

2. Women's legal groups. In some communities, female lawyers have formed their own bar associations or similar groups. These voluntary organizations focus on issues important to women lawyers and, more generally, to women. They do not duplicate the routine work of the existing bar association. They do not give legal advice, but they can identify organizations that evaluate whether a lawyer is needed and suggest how to identify appropriate candidates. If the women's bar association is not listed in the telephone book, the general bar association will know if there is a local women's bar association in the area and how to reach it.

3. YWCA (Young Women's Christian Association). The YWCA often has a legal information center typically staffed at certain hours by local lawyers. General responses to questions posed are given, but matters needing detailed and specific legal advice are referred to an organization that can assist in locating a lawyer. Often these programs are operated in conjunction with the clinics described previously. If the information needed relates to handling a matter *pro se,* the caller is referred to the clinic.

4. Women's support organizations. Organizations committed to women's issues often provide general legal advice, hold legal clinics, or make

referrals to organizations that can locate a lawyer. These organizations can be identified through the bar association or through local nonprofit or other community activist groups dealing with the general subject matter of women's concerns, for example, groups that assist women who are victims of domestic abuse may counsel about obtaining divorces and/or custody of children. The local battered women's shelter and Planned Parenthood are two examples of sources for identifying the projects and organizations rendering legal assistance to women.

5. Women's resource centers. Many communities have women's resource centers, often associated with a public college or university, that provide information about counseling and educational opportunities. They assist clients in finding appropriate public resources and, if necessary, refer these women to an organization that can provide legal assistance. Typically, they do not give legal advice.

## Lawyers

Another method of determining if legal assistance is needed is to ask a lawyer. In ambiguous instances, most lawyers will recommend retaining a lawyer, but they will not do so in every case. Having a lawyer explain how she, as an attorney, could assist, you will be able to better assess whether or not you need an attorney. If the purpose of this conference is to ascertain whether legal counsel is needed, it is appropriate to request that this short conference be a no-charge exploratory meeting.

### The Importance of Lawyer Selection

While all lawyers must meet certain criteria, their knowledge, skill, and experience vary. An able lawyer can make the difference between a satisfactory and an unsatisfactory experience and result. The process of finding a lawyer is time-consuming. The extra effort and energy invested initially enhances the likelihood of engaging a lawyer who can achieve the legal goals and work successfully with the client.

### Generalists and Specialists

Lawyers are usually generalists or specialists. Generalists deal with legal problems in a wide range of legal areas. Lawyers in practice by themselves, in small firms, or in smaller communities may be generalists. They may handle divorces, prepare wills, try civil and criminal cases, and advise on real estate transactions. If multiple and far-reaching legal needs are anticipated, a generalist may be appropriate, as the lawyer will know the client and her business or family situation, and be poised to assist as each legal issue arises.

In today's increasingly complex and legalistic world, lawyers tend to specialize in one or a limited number of related fields of practice. A lawyer may specialize in family law, taking cases involving divorce, child support, and child custody. Other lawyers will specialize in trusts and estates—the creating of instruments to pass real and personal property from one generation to another and the administration of the property of the deceased. Others specialize in corporate and partnership law.

There are advantages to selecting a specialist:

- The lawyer will be knowledgeable about the field and can give immediate feedback. While many legal problems include issues that even the most astute lawyer will need to ponder or research, the specialist will be able to frame the basic parameters.

- The specialist will usually need to invest less time in learning the legal rules applicable to any particular situation.

- The specialist will likely have well-honed skills appropriate for use in that field.

There are also possible disadvantages:

- A specialist may charge more for legal services.

- A specialist may be so focused on the issue within her area of expertise that she fails to identify another important issue in a different field.

- With each new problem, the client starts with another lawyer and must educate the new lawyer about her background and develop a personal relationship with the new lawyer.

## Finding a Lawyer

Once a prospective client has determined that legal counsel is advisable, there are a variety of methods for locating a lawyer.

### Recommendations

A common and effective method is to ask someone in the legal community for a recommendation. One approach is to ask a lawyer in any field for recommendations. If the lawyer does not know lawyers who practice in the involved field, she can identify several with a phone call or two. Most lawyers are happy to respond to referral requests, even if they do not know the caller. It is customary to ask for the names of several lawyers who could handle the problem. If the lawyer being asked for recommendations self-volunteers, it is acceptable to renew the request for the names of other lawyers while also inquiring about the lawyer who is providing the information.

Another approach is to ask a nonlawyer who works in a law firm. Whatever his or her position in the firm, he or she will likely be willing to ask a lawyer in the firm for a referral. The prospective client should speak to the firm lawyer, either by telephone or in person, rather than having the friend describe the problem and convey the referral. There may be special concerns of which the friend is unaware. This will also give the prospective client an opportunity to assess the lawyer making the recommendation.

## Professional or Service Organizations

Another recommended approach is to contact appropriate professional or service organizations. The same organizations that have services directing callers to appropriate social service agencies will guide callers to organizations that identify lawyers or give legal assistance if the problem described suggests that assistance of counsel is needed. The organizations to contact include:

1. Statewide and local bar associations. Usually the bar association will have a specific procedure. In many communities, the bar association will suggest that the caller contact a lawyer referral service or Legal Services (see page 8). Some bar associations have programs that put a client in contact with a lawyer who has agreed to handle legal matters on a no-fee or reduced-fee basis. In addition, the bar association will have committees or sections of lawyers in specialty areas—family law, litigation, trusts and estates, and so on. The committee chair in the area of concern could identify several lawyers who could handle a legal matter. If the caller does not know which field is involved, there will likely be someone associated with the bar association who can listen to a brief description of the problem and recommend the appropriate area.

2. Women's bar associations. Through the officers, board, committee structure, or executive director of the women's bar association, the caller should be able to speak with an attorney who can recommend several lawyers.

## Legal Directories

Legal directories list lawyers and their credentials. A widely used resource is *Martindale Hubbell*, published annually by Martindale Hubbell, a Reed Reference Publishing Company (121 Chanlon Road, New Providence, NJ 07974, 908/464-6800), which can be found in most public libraries. It contains a state-by-state alphabetical listing of individual law-yers and a list of firms organized by state and then by city. The informa-tion is limited to firm size, age and education of its lawyers, and a de-scription of areas of practice. Lawyers pay a minimal fee to be listed in the individual geographical section and a more substantial fee to have their firms listed. Many other directories exist and generally are useful as a starting point to identify lawyers about whom further inquiry can be made. Public libraries, courthouse libraries, and the bar association of-fices are likely repositories of these volumes.

## Lawyer Referral Services

Many communities have lawyer referral services, often created by the bar association. The attorneys request inclusion and are listed by specialty, for example, family law, criminal, general business, and so on. They complete an application and are approved by the bar asso-ciation without an independent verification of the attorney's compe-tence. A referral is based on the attorney's declared specialty and office location. The client will be given only the lawyer's name, ad-dress, and level of experience. Typically, the first half hour of consul-tation is free or at a minimal charge. If the lawyer is retained, addi-tional time will be based on the lawyer's regular fee arrangement.

## Pro Bono Legal Services

If legal counsel is needed but the client cannot afford to pay for a lawyer, many communities have organizations that provide legal ser-vices without cost. Generally, these organizations operate under the auspices of the federal Legal Services Corporation and serve individu-als and families who fall within the federal poverty guidelines. Typi-cally, they handle only civil cases (family law; public entitlement—Social Security, welfare, Aid to Dependent Children; housing; con-cerns of the elderly—wills, disability, and retirement; and consumer matters such as garnishments). Legal Services does not handle any cases that may generate substantial recoveries, such as a personal injury claim, from which attorneys' fees could be paid. However, Le-gal Services does accept representation of cases where federal or state statutes provide for the recovery of attorneys' fees.

## Law Schools

Many law schools include clinical programs in their curricula. These clinics provide free legal services and are staffed by law students supervised by practicing attorneys or faculty members. Clinic legal services, however, are available on a limited basis and clients are carefully screened.

Regardless of the issue being addressed, a lawyer should have the following important attributes.

### Ability to Communicate With the Client

The most critical attribute is the lawyer's ability to communicate *with the client*. The law is filled with technical words, but the underlying concepts are easily understood. They are based on general, simple principles, evolved over time through the stories of ordinary people that can be used to explain the most obtuse concept. An able lawyer explains the legal world without condescension and allows the client to evaluate and participate in the actions or positions being taken. An effective lawyer also appreciates and recognizes the emotional concerns a client experiences, whether the legal issue relates to family or business issues.

### Subject Matter Expertise

Knowledge of the relevant area of law is also essential. This encompasses (1) substantive law, consisting of statutes, case law (the written decisions from previous cases), and regulations, and (2) procedure, the protocol by which one asserts and pursues legal rights under the substantive law. Detailed knowledge of the laws, their interaction, and how to move with them rather than against them comes only from experience. Some substantive areas are more complicated than others and more expertise is desirable. A client should look for an indication that the lawyer is thorough and attentive in her preparation and will use that expertise.

Both the lawyer's knowledge of the legal field and her ability to communicate are equally essential. If a lawyer knows the law but cannot or will not explain it and the choices to the client, the client does not benefit from that expertise. Conversely, if the lawyer excels in talking with the client about the law and how her situation fits into it, listening to the client, her concerns, and feelings, but is not adept at working within the relevant legal framework, the client's self-esteem will remain intact, but she may not achieve her desired legal goals.

### Ethics and Judgment

Generally, ethical rules governing the legal profession concern who a lawyer may represent and how, not the substance of the legal dispute. There is no certain method to test a lawyer's sensitivity to general ethical issues, but the client's relationship with the lawyer will progress more smoothly if they share similar perspectives. For example, is the lawyer's inclination to take advantage of an opposing party or is it to seek a workable resolution through negotiation and conciliation? The ethical perspective informs a lawyer's judgment—

the practical and overarching advice given on what course is recommended, given the legal parameters and uncertainties. Most lawyers can recite the legal requirements. Able lawyers offer insights into what the client might do given the law and her circumstances.

### Clear Roles and Reasonable Fees

Different roles for lawyers and clients are possible even on the same types of legal problems. Sometimes a lawyer will agree to minimize legal fees by limiting her work strictly to those legal matters only she can do or can do most efficiently. Many problems combine overlapping legal considerations with business and personal considerations. The lawyer typically segregates the legal issues, leaving the decision affecting business or personal circumstances to the client who will experience the consequences of the decision. Some lawyers are more accustomed than others to splitting responsibilities with clients.

An active, participatory role by the client has several advantages. First, this interaction saves money. For example, if the client organizes her own records and prepares explanatory statements, attorneys and paralegals will not need to review and organize records with which they are unfamiliar. Second, the client will have a better sense of what is involved in the legal process and why progress has been delayed or additional concerns have arisen. Third, the client will be better able to participate in strategy decisions if she has participated in the step-by-step development of her matter. A client should look for a lawyer who will allow her to play as active a role as she chooses and whose fees are reasonable for the value of the work to be performed. Fee disputes sour many attorney-client relationships. The reasonableness of the fee should be considered initially to forestall later problems (see discussion beginning on page 16).

## Special Considerations for Women

Social scientists continue to study differences between men and women. Many researchers contend that men value independence and autonomy, while women emphasize the importance of connection and relationship. Consequently, women tend to shoulder more family responsibilities. Women with full-time jobs outside the home often have a second full-time job in the home. These special circumstances suggest additional considerations for women who are selecting a lawyer.

### Office Hours

A client's employment situation may preclude her from meeting with a lawyer during normal business hours, 8 or 9 A.M. to 5 or 6 P.M. Perhaps one or two visits during the regular work week can be arranged; however, if the legal issue requires extended in-person consultation with the lawyer, the client may need to arrange alternative meeting times. Some lawyers will willingly arrange to meet a client on weekends, early in the morning, or in the early evening. If that is an important consideration, it is critical to ask a lawyer when she will be able to schedule meetings.

### Collaborative Interaction

Some lawyers are thoughtful, good listeners; others are arrogant and condescending. Working with a lawyer who treats the client as though she is ignorant and inappropriately taking up the attorney's time adds stress to an already stressful process. The client may then find herself making decisions just to conclude the legal matter and avoid further contact with the lawyer. In many instances, the client will spend a significant amount of time with the lawyer and share private information with her. The relationship and the legal outcome are enhanced if the client and lawyer share a relationship of trust and respect.

### Extralegal Considerations

The line between legal and personal or business advice is a blurry one. The lawyer usually will not advise the client on nonlegal issues which are related to legal issues; for example, what to tell the child who is the subject of a custody dispute. Yet, the client wants someone who will listen and who recognizes that these issues are as important to resolving her problems as are the legal issues. The lawyer should understand the client's other needs and be willing to recommend other professionals who can help the client meet them.

### Wait Time

Women sometimes need "wait time" before responding to problems and choices, so that they can collect both analytical and emotional responses. Interactions grounded in rapid question and response, without time for processing, cause some women to respond without fully considering important ramifications. The client's thought process must be valued and allowed to function. The legal process can accommodate different ways of thinking and responding, but not all lawyers recognize that different people assess ideas and communicate differently.

### Participation of Others

Legal problems are often laced with emotional issues. To facilitate interaction with the attorney, some clients wish to have a close friend or family member accompany them to meetings, to provide emotional support and be a resource in reviewing the lawyer's advice. She should discuss the lawyer's willingness to have others participate in their meetings. Some lawyers welcome the participation of others. Other lawyers feel that having to explain the law and available options to two people will complicate the representation. The privilege of confidentiality that is usually attached to communications between lawyer and client may be waived by the presence of another person. This is an issue the client should discuss with the lawyer if she wants someone else to participate in the discussions.

## Determining If a Lawyer Meets the Criteria

The three most accessible and useful methods for evaluating potential counsel are talking with others in the community, interviewing prospective counsel, and talking with other clients.

### Making Inquiries

Asking others in the community is an important avenue for assessing lawyer candidates. As the prospective client makes contacts looking for lawyer candidates, she can ask about the criteria important to her. Many criteria can be addressed directly; people expect to answer questions about expertise. Other areas do not lend themselves to such direct questioning. For example, it would likely not be fruitful to ask directly about a lawyer candidate's sense of ethics. Most people would only recommend a lawyer whom they feel is ethical. Yet, a few open-ended questions may disclose information about the lawyer's manner and way of thinking: "What have you found most rewarding in dealing with this lawyer?" or "What has been difficult for you in working through your problem?"

### Conducting Interviews

A second and critically important basis of evaluation is the client's own interaction with the lawyer candidates. A client should interview any lawyer she is considering hiring. Even if she has received multiple recommendations for one lawyer, the client should contact that lawyer to assess retaining her. Although a client can retain a lawyer, work with her for any length of time, and then terminate the relationship, a face-to-face interview can often foretell if the working relationship will be satisfactory. An initial arrogant attitude displayed by potential counsel may be a warning of similar future behavior. The client should be prepared to pay for an initial interview, although the charge may be waived.

More than one lawyer should be interviewed. A client may think she does not know what she is looking for in a lawyer or cannot tell whether a particular lawyer meets the criteria. The contrast of interactions alone may assist the client in determining what is most important to her. To obtain a sense of how a lawyer operates and how well the client and the lawyer are likely to interact, an in-person interview is necessary. Nonverbal behavior is revealing. Little of that comes across in a telephone interview. Sometimes a client may need an attorney in a distant location, however, and only a telephone interview is available. If an attorney refuses an introductory interview and is the only lawyer in the community familiar with the field of law in which help is needed, the client may decide to retain her anyway.

## Contacting Clients

A third method of evaluation is through other clients. Lawyers will typically provide an overview of the kind of work they have done and the clients they have represented. In some instances, they may identify specific clients and the prospective client can call them as references. While other lawyers will be important sources of information about the lawyer's competence and experience, they may not be as sensitive about working with the lawyer. Other clients can provide that perspective.

The considerations in retaining a lawyer should be used to conduct the first meeting with the attorney. Even if research has answered many questions, it is advisable to confirm the information with the lawyer herself. Typically, an exploratory interview will last thirty to sixty minutes. Figure 1 shows a checklist of suggested topics for the initial interview. The following is a descriptive summary of these subjects:

## The Initial Interview

## Background and Expertise

Appropriate questions about the lawyer's general background include: How long has the lawyer been in practice? Where did she receive her training? How long has she been with this firm? What is her employment history? Although lawyers tend to specialize in one or more areas of the law, the legal profession does not have a certification process. A lawyer merely declares her area of specialization. In the assessment interview, it is appropriate to ask about the lawyer's specialization, how long she has worked in the area in which the problem exists, what kind of matters she has handled in that area, her normal objective (for example, settlement or court determination), what results she has obtained, and whether she has taught or written on the subject. It is informative to ask if the lawyer can discern something unique in the client's situation. If so, has the lawyer handled matters with that dimension. A lawyer usually cannot discuss pending matters but can give information about completed cases or transactions and can describe pending matters in a general way.

Attorney's general background
- Description of firm
- Length of time attorney in practice
- Education
- Employment history

Specialization
- Area(s)
- Length of time working in this area
- Examples of matters handled
- Typical objective
- Results obtained
- Teaching or writing on subject

Handling of the matter
- Identification of legal issues and considerations
- What the matter entails
- Typical time for completion
- Use of other attorneys
- Form and frequency of communications
- Office hours and meeting times
- Client role
- Potential conflicts of interest

Fees and billing procedures
- Fee arrangements available
- Fee estimate
- Type and frequency of statements
- Fee increases
- Written fee agreement
- Retainer
- Expenses
- Payment schedule
- Interest

*Figure 1*
*Initial Interview*
*Checklist*

## Handling of the Matter

Discuss how the lawyer would proceed on the prospective client's particular legal matter.

1. General discussion of the legal work needed. Generally, the prospective client describes her perceived need for a lawyer. Because the client has not yet retained this lawyer and because she may not be paying for this time, she should not ask for or expect to receive detailed legal analysis or advice relating to the situation. It is appropriate to ask what kinds of issues and complexities

the lawyer sees in the situation presented: What are the legal considerations involved? What does a matter like this entail? How quickly should action be taken? Is the lawyer available to meet that deadline?

2. Other attorneys. Another area to probe is how the legal work will actually be done. What portion of the work will this lawyer be doing personally? Who else will likely work on this matter?. What responsibilities will they have? What are their backgrounds and experience? What procedure does the lawyer use to oversee their work? Does this add to the lawyer's fee? If so, how much?

3. Role of the client. Varying client roles can be explored with open-ended questions. What information will the client need to furnish? What are the legal steps? What role does the attorney anticipate the client will play? Are there other ways in which the client might assist the attorney? Would the lawyer want the client to collect information or documents? Would the lawyer ask the client to find witnesses? Would the client review the correspondence or other documents the lawyer prepares? Would the client sit in at sessions in court or with other attorneys?

4. Communication. Communication is at the heart of a viable attorney-client relationship. Will the client and counsel communicate primarily by telephone, in person, or by letter? Will the client communicate primarily with the lawyer or with the assisting lawyers? Can meetings be scheduled to fit the client's availability? If the client has a question when the lawyer is not available, (for example, the lawyer is on vacation), what procedure will the client follow to have the question answered? What should the client do if she has an urgent question after normal business hours? What kind of information will the lawyer send to the client as work progresses on the matter?

From the answers to the interview questions, the client should be able to determine if the lawyer's communication approach will be comfortable and if it will provide the client with sufficient explanation about the legal process to allow her to understand and participate in the legal events as they unfold.

5. Conflict of interest. The client will be asked to identify all the persons or entities who have a role in the situation. The lawyer will then conduct a conflict of interest check to determine if she is representing or has represented someone involved in the dispute or situation. If so, it is necessary to determine if she received any confidential information that could compromise or jeopardize her

representation of the other party or of the prospective client. The conflict of interest check may not be accomplished during the assessment interview, but the information necessary for conducting such a check should be provided if the prospective client is considering retaining this lawyer.

## Fees and Billing Procedures

Fees and billing procedures are important subjects for the initial interview. Interview questions are included at the end of the following section, which sets out the common arrangements.

## Attorneys' Fees

Attorneys' fees are a central issue to consider in retaining counsel. Lawyers are surprisingly reluctant to discuss their fees—some feel uncomfortable discussing financial matters. The law is supposed to be an honorable *profession* where money is not the primary objective of a lawyer's service. Focusing on the pecuniary aspects of the relationship may send the client a message that financial remuneration is more important than solving the client's problem. Other lawyers feel uncomfortable because the amount they charge is large compared to other services a client may purchase. It is critical that the client take the initiative to inquire about the lawyer's intended fee arrangement. It is also critical to obtain a written fee agreement at the outset to avoid misunderstanding. A description of typical legal fee arrangements follows.

1. **Time-based rates.** Hourly or other time-based fee arrangements are the most common. The lawyer has a fixed hourly rate and calculates the total fee based on the number of hours spent on the matter. Lawyers will have different rates reflecting how long they have practiced and their expertise. Many firms employ paralegals to assist the lawyers by doing specialized detail work. Their hourly rates are usually substantially lower than those of the lawyer. Many lawyers charge one rate regardless of the service they are providing. Others have an office rate and a slightly higher rate for court appearances or other specialized work. Other lawyers have a standard rate and an enhanced rate for work within their area of particular expertise.

    An important consideration is the amount of time people at different levels are likely to spend working on the matter and what activities will be billable. Does the lawyer employ less experienced lawyers, charging lower rates, to do research or investigation work? How will that time be evaluated? Will the bill be adjusted so that the client is billed only for the value of the work produced by the less experienced lawyer or will the client be billed for all the time spent? Will the conferences during which the less experienced lawyer reports to the more senior lawyer be billed? Will the time the senior lawyer spends revising the less experienced lawyer's work be fully charged? Will the attorney's time spent traveling be billed? At what rate?

Attorneys generally bill their time in tenths of an hour, that is, in six-minute increments. Some bill a preset minimum for phone calls. For example, even if a phone call lasts only three minutes, it will be billed at 0.2 hours. Some lawyers round time to quarter- or half-hour increments.

2. **Contingency agreements.** Another form of fee arrangement is a contingency agreement. The lawyer is only paid for her services out of what she recovers on the claim. This type of arrangement is available only in situations where the client is seeking financial recovery. Contingency fees are typical in personal injury claims, employment contract claims (for example, a claim for wrongful termination of employment), discrimination claims, and antitrust claims. A lawyer may work for years before receiving any compensation. If the client does not prevail, the lawyer receives no compensation. Therefore, before undertaking a contingency matter, the lawyer will carefully review the claim. She has a genuine incentive to take on only those matters with a good chance of a significant recovery. Contingency percentages vary among kinds of matters and in different regions of the country. The attorney's percentage may depend on the stage of the proceeding when the claim is concluded. Some attorneys will take cases for 25 percent of the recovery if the case is resolved before a lawsuit is filed. The percent will increase to 33 percent if the case if taken through trial and 40 percent if the case is taken through an appeal. Generally, agreeing to share 25 to 45 percent of the proceeds with the attorney is typical.

Some lawyers have a mixed hourly and contingent fee agreement. They charge less than the going hourly rate, which is paid throughout the matter regardless of whether the client prevails, plus a percentage (usually less than the going percentage) which is paid only if the client prevails. Some lawyers set off the amount paid hourly against the percentage; others collect the hourly fee and the full percent of the award. Some attorneys have a mixed fee whereby both the hourly rate and the percentage slide depending on the stage of the case at resolution. Usually, the hourly fee will decline and the percent will increase. The variations are limited only by the lawyer's creativity. It is critical that the client question the lawyer until the agreement is understood. This takes time. Using numerical examples often clarifies the situation. Some states require the attorney to provide a disclosure statement about the contingency fee (see Figure 2). Even if this document is not required, this form can be used as a checklist. In many jurisdictions, lawyers are required by the applicable court rules to have a written fee agreement to cover contingency arrangements. A standard form of contingency fee agreement is shown in Figure 3. The client is advised to take the documents about the contingency fee arrangements home and study them before signing them.

3. **Statutory fees.** A third type of fee arrangement relates to attorney fees awarded pursuant to federal or state law. For example, Title VII of the 1964 Civil Rights Act provides that the court may award the prevailing party a reasonable attorney fee (including expert witness fees). Claims for race or sex discrimination, including for sexual harassment, are brought under this law. Lawyers generally treat these claims as contingency fees, with the lawyer expecting payment only if the claim is successful. The lawyer and the client still must agree on how the lawyer's fee will be calculated. Generally, the client and the lawyer agree on a formula. The most common approach is to combine the damage award and the fee award and take a percentage of the total recovery. Sometimes the attorney will compare this combination award to the amount of attorney fees awarded and take whichever is larger. Infrequently, attorneys will take a percent of the damage award plus whatever fees are awarded. The court has considerable discretion in setting attorney fees. They are almost always less than the lawyer's accrued fee.

4. **Project fee.** Another fee arrangement is the project fee. In this type of arrangement the attorney sets a specific fee for completing certain specified work (for example, filing a bankruptcy petition, a home purchase, or a divorce proceeding where there is no custody issue). This fee arrangement is generally applicable to standardized legal matters. It is critical to define the scope of the project and what will happen if unexpected circumstances occur.

## Estimates

Ask for a fee estimate for the work. In some matters, it is difficult to gauge what the work will cost. Often, the cost is not completely within the control of the attorney. Nonetheless, it is useful to request an estimate for the entire matter or each of its distinct pieces. Because estimates of legal fees are so uncertain, it is advisable to make an arrangement with the attorney about what will happen if the fees exceed the estimate. If it is a long-term project, the client can ask for updated estimates on a periodic basis. The lawyer should be directed to seek specific authorization before undertaking additional or particularly costly work. If the work is to be completed in a concentrated period of time, the client can request that the attorney advise if the amount of time she or her firm is spending on the matter is greater than estimated. The client may adjust the scope of work being undertaken, renegotiate the fee, or renegotiate the payment schedule.

## Statements

The client needs to know how much is being accrued in fees. Most attorneys will agree to send a bill each month for the time accrued during the prior month so the client is informed what the services are costing. Each day, lawyers enter the amount of time spent on each matter, together with a description of the work done. Many lawyers have computerized billing systems that compile the information for each client matter, automatically totaling the amount of time spent during the period multiplied by the hourly rate to arrive at the total dollar value of the services. Lawyers can provide bills with varying amount of detail about the work performed and their fees. The client should discuss with the attorney what information will be contained in a statement. Information may include the following:

- The date each work item was performed

- A description of the work performed on each day

- Who performed each item of work

- The amount of time spent by each attorney and paralegal each day on the matter

- The dollar cost of the work performed each day (the number of hours times the rate)

- A summary of all professionals (usually lawyers and paralegals) who worked on the matter during the billing period, their hourly rates, and the number of hours spent on your project during the billing period

A sample of a statement containing this information is shown in Figure 4.

There are several reasons for receiving such detailed bills. The first is so the client has a cogent summary of the work done. The bills provide a concise, chronological record of what is happening (or not happening). The second is so that fees can be monitored. The purpose of

STEWART AND MILES
Attorneys at Law
1600 King Street
Cambridge, MA 02138

Contingency Fee Disclosure Statement

**Type of Attorney Fee Arrangements:** I have been informed and understand that there are several types of attorney fee arrangements: (1) time based, (2) fixed, or (3) contingent. "Time based" means a fee that is determined by the amount of time involved such as so much per hour, day, or week. "Fixed" means a fee that is based on an agreed amount regardless of the time or effort involved or the result obtained. "Contingent" means a certain agreed percentage or amount that is payable only upon attaining a recovery regardless of the time or effort involved. I understand I have the right to choose the type of attorney fee arrangement.

**Specially Awarded Attorney Fees:** I have been informed and understand that the court or an arbitrator may sometimes award fees in addition to the amount of recovery being claimed. I understand that the fee arrangement I enter into with my attorney should contain a provision as to how any specially awarded attorney fees will be accounted for and handled.

**Expenses:** I have been informed and understand that there may be expenses (aside from any attorney fee) in pursuing my claim. Examples of such expenses are: fees payable to the court, the cost of serving process, fees charged by expert witnesses, fees of investigators, fees of court reporters to take and prepare transcripts of depositions, and expenses involved in preparing exhibits. I understand that an attorney is required to provide me with an estimate of such expenses before I enter into an attorney fee arrangement and that my attorney fee arrangement should include a provision as to how and when such expenses will be paid. I understand that the fee arrangement should tell me whether a fee payable from the proceeds of the amount collected on my behalf will be based on the "net" or "gross" recovery. "Net recovery" means the amount remaining after expenses and deductions. "Gross recovery" means the total amount of the recovery before any deductions. The estimated amount of the expenses to handle my case will be set forth in the contingent fee agreement.

*Figure 2*
*Sample Contingency*
*Fee Disclosure*
*Statement*

**The Potential of Costs and Attorney Fees Being Awarded to the Opposing Party:** I have been informed and understand that a court or arbitrator sometimes awards costs and attorney fees to the opposing party. I have been informed and understand that should that happen in my case, I will be responsible to pay such award. I understand that the fee arrangement I enter into with my attorney should provide whether an award against me will be paid out of the proceeds of any amount collected on my behalf. I also understand that the agreement should provide whether the fee I am obligated to pay my attorney will be based on the amount of the recovery *before* or *after* payment of the awarded costs and attorney fees to an opposing party.

**Associated Counsel:** I have been informed and understand that my attorney may sometimes hire another attorney to assist in the handling of a case. That other attorney is called an "associated counsel." I understand that the attorney fee arrangement should tell me how the fees of associated counsel will be handled.

**Subrogation:** I have been informed and understand that other persons or entities may have a subrogation right in what I recover in pursuing my claim. "Subrogation" means the right to be paid back. I understand that the subrogation right may arise in various ways such as when an insurer or a federal or state agency pays money to or on behalf of a claiming party like me in situations such as Medicare, Medicaid, workers' compensation, medical/health insurance, no-fault insurance, uninsured/underinsured motorist insurance, and property insurance situations. I understand that sometimes a hospital, physician, or attorney will assert a "lien" (a priority right) on a claim such as the one I am pursuing. *Subrogation rights* and *liens* need to be considered and provided for in the fee agreement I reach with my attorney. The fee agreement should tell me whether the subrogation right or lien is being paid by my attorney out of the proceeds of the recovery made on my behalf and whether the fee I am obligated to pay my attorney will be based on the amount of recovery *before* or *after* payment of the subrogation right or lien.

I acknowledge that I received a complete copy of this Disclosure Statement and read it this _____ of _____, 19____.


_____
        (Signature)

STEWART AND MILES
Attorneys at Law
1600 King Street
Cambridge, MA 02138


Contingent Fee Agreement
(To Be Executed in Duplicate)

Dated _____, 19____

The Client _____
                    (Name)    (Street and Number)    (City or Town)

retains the Attorney _____
                        (Name)    (Street and Number)    (City or Town)

to perform the legal services mentioned in paragraph (1) below. The attorney agrees to perform them faithfully and with due diligence.

(1) The claim, controversy, and other matters with reference to which the services are to be performed are: _____

(2) The contingency upon which compensation is to be paid is: _____

(3) The client is not to be liable to pay compensation otherwise than from amounts collected for the client by the attorney, except as follows:
_____

(4) The client will pay the attorney (including any associated counsel) ____* percent of the gross amount collected. ["Gross amount collected" means the amount collected before any subtraction of expenses and disbursements.]

(5) Costs and attorney fees awarded to an opposing party against the client before completion of the case will be paid (by the client) (by the attorney) **[indicate which]** when ordered. Any award of costs or attorney fees, regardless of when awarded, (will) (will not) **[indicate which]** be

*Here insert the percentages to be charge in the event of collection. These may be on a flat basis or on a descending scale in relation to amount collected. "Net amount collected" can be used here instead. "Net amount collected" means the amount of the collection remaining after subtraction of expenses and disbursements and may or may not include court-awarded costs or attorney fees. The amount collected may or may not include specially awarded attorney fees and costs awarded to the client. If "Net amount collected" is selected, the agreement should specify how these amounts will be treated.

*Figure 3
Sample
Contingency Fee
Agreement*

subtracted from the amount collected before computing the amount of the contingent fee under this agreement.

(6) The client is in any event to be liable to the attorney for her reasonable expenses and disbursements. Such expenses and disbursements are estimated to be $_____. Authority is given to the attorney to incur expenses and make disbursements up to a maximum of $_____ which limitation will not be exceeded without the client's further written authority. The client will reimburse the attorney for such expenditures (upon receipt of a billing), (in specified installments), (upon final resolution), (etc.) **[indicate which]**.

(7) **[if applicable]** The client (authorizes) (does not authorize) **[indicate which]** the attorney to pay from the amount collected the following: (e.g., all physicians, hospitals, subrogation claims and liens, etc.). Any amounts so paid (will) (will not) **[indicate which]** be subtracted from the amount collected before computing the amount of the contingent fee under this agreement.

WE HAVE EACH READ THE ABOVE AGREEMENT BEFORE SIGNING IT.

Witnesses to Signatures:


_____          _____
(witness to client's signature)          (signature of client)



_____          _____
(witness to attorney's signature)          (signature of attorney)

STEWART AND MILES
Attorneys at Law
1600 King Street
Cambridge, MA 02138

Invoice no. 1632

March 10, 1995

Jayne Simon
14 Ogden Street
Sommerville, MA 02144

**For professional services** rendered in connection with Simon v. Simon, District Court, No. 93-125

| | | | | |
|---|---|---|---|---|
| 02/01/95 | C. Dagny | Conference with client about dissolution of marriage | 1.0 | 150.00 |
| 02/03/95 | D. Peters | Draft petition | 2.0 | 140.00 |
| 02/06/95 | C. Dagny | Revise petition; call with client about financial affidavit | 2.0 | 300.00 |
| 02/16/95 | C. Dagny | Conference with client to review petition and discuss issues relating to dissolution | 2.0 | 300.00 |

|  |  |  |
|---|---|---|
| **Hours total** | 7.0 | |
| **Services total** | | $890.00 |

Disbursements and other charges
    Photocopying     $3.00
    Long distance telephone     6.31
    Copies of governmental documents     8.00

**Disbursements and other charges total**     $17.31

**This statement total**     **$907.31**

| Hours summary | C. Dagny | 5 hours @ $150.00/hour |
|---|---|---|
| | D. Peters | 2 hours @ $70.00/hour |

*Figure 4*
*Sample Invoice*

reviewing detailed bills is to clarify what an entry refers to or the amount being charged for particular work. A lawyer is accustomed to being asked questions about these items. While the estimate is not a guarantee, it does provide the basis of inquiring about the statement if the amount charged for a specific item is significantly different than estimated. The client should review the bills carefully before paying them. Lawyers generally do not charge for their time preparing the bill, unless a client has exceptional or onerous requirements.

### Fee Increases

If the legal work is likely to take the lawyer a number of months to complete, the client should inquire whether her quoted hourly rate will be subject to increase during that time. Normally, a lawyer will reevaluate her standard hourly rate annually. The lawyer will usually notify the client of a rate increase and apply it to all future work. The client should discuss the possibility of rate increases and agree with counsel about how they will be handled.

### Written Agreements

It is advisable to have a written engagement agreement so that the pivotal parts of the representation are clearly agreed to by the client and the lawyer. The agreement is generally in the form of a letter prepared by the attorney (see Figure 5). The main elements will be the scope of the work and the billing and payment details.

### Retainers

Some lawyers require the client to pay a retainer at the commencement of the representation. As fees accrue, they are billed against the retainer. In other words, the client prepays the bill. Under most state rules, lawyers receiving advance monies from the client are obligated to put them in a separate agency account and not commingle them with the attorney's operating business funds. An attorney might ask for a retainer if she does not know the client. Or, if the attorney represented the client previously and the client had difficulty paying her bills, a retainer might be required to avoid a repetition of that problem. The amount of the retainer is negotiated between the attorney and the client. It may cover the work anticipated for the first month or two or for all legal work requested. Once the retainer is depleted, the lawyer may submit bills to the client on a monthly or other periodic basis or require the client to replenish the retainer to cover future bills. Paying a retainer is not usually in the client's interest because it commits funds before they are needed. Typically, the retainer does not earn interest for the benefit of the client. If it will help the client to set aside the payment for the services requested, however, then it

STEWART AND MILES
Attorneys at Law
1600 King Street
Cambridge, MA 02138

January 12, 1995

Jayne Simon
14 Ogden Street
Sommerville MA 02144

Re:  Engagement letter

Dear Ms. Simon:

This letter is to welcome you as a client of Stewart and Miles and to con-firm our discussions regarding your engagement of this firm. Your satisfac-tion with our services is the key to a successful professional relationship. Please let me know promptly if you have any questions regarding any aspect of the matters the firm is handling for you.

You have asked us to represent you in the dissolution of your 15-year marriage to Edward Simon. Our fees will be based primarily on the amount of time spent by lawyers and paralegals. I would expect to do most of the work on this matter. My rate is $175 per hour. My legal assistant may assist me in preparing the documentation and collecting certain information. His rate is $55 per hour. We may adjust the charge downward or upward based on other factors such as the novelty or complexity of the issues and prob-lems encountered, the extent of the responsibility involved, the results achieved, the efficiency of our work, the customary fees for similar legal services, and other factors that will enable us to arrive at a fair fee. We have estimated that the legal fees and disbursements would be in the range of $8,000 to $10,000. The actual cost could be substantially lower or higher than we estimated, depending on changes in the anticipated work the parties request or cause, additional complexity or difficulties, or changes in facts or circumstances.

*Figure 5
Sample
Engagement
Letter*

Statements will normally be sent monthly for work done in the previous month, covering and identifying services rendered as well as disbursements and other charges. These disbursements and charges include items incurred and paid for by us on your behalf, such as long distance telephone charges, special postage, delivery charges, telex or telecopy charges, travel, photocopying, and use of other service providers such as printers or experts, if needed. We also make separate charges for use of Lexis or Westlaw, which are computerized legal research systems that, in our experience, significantly reduce lawyer research time.

Payment will be due 30 days after the date of our statement. Statements unpaid within 30 days are subject to a late charge of 1.5 percent per month (18 percent per year) on the unpaid balance commencing from the date of the original statement and continuing until paid.

An important consideration in accepting an engagement is whether it will put us in conflict with any existing client interest. If such a conflict is discovered after we have commenced work, we may be disqualified from continuing our representation in your matter. It is, therefore, very important that you reconsider all of the interests that are involved to be certain that you have advised us fully. If, in our judgment, we determine that a conflict of interest does exist, we will notify all affected clients and will proceed in a manner consistent with the ethical standards contained in the Rules of Professional Conduct.

I appreciate your retaining us for this work. If at any time you have questions, please contact me immediately.

Sincerely yours,


Carole Elaine Dagny
for STEWART AND MILES

may be in the client's interest to establish a retainer. Any unused amount left in the deposited retainer will be returned to the client at the end of the engagement. All of these considerations should be reflected in the written agreement that establishes the retainer.

### Expenses

Fee discussions usually focus on the attorney's rate and the rates of other professionals who may work on the matter. Other costs may be incurred; it is important to understand what they are and how much they may total. Some expenses reimburse the lawyer for the internal costs of running her operation. Will the client be charged for long distance telephone calls? This is likely and is typical. Will the client be charged for local faxes as well as long distance faxes? Will the client be charged for copying of documents? If so, at what rate? Will the client be charged for the use of the automobile when the attorney travels on the client's behalf? How is that calculated? Some firms charge the client on an hourly or document basis for the word processing specialists' work on each client document.

Other expenses relate to fees and costs paid to other professionals or to governmental offices. The lawyer can estimate these costs in the same manner as the fees for her services. They can be significant, so they are worth inquiring about. The client should specify how much can be spent on the account without specific prior authorization. Some firms ask the client to advance these costs or they impose a service charge for advancing the money.

These expenses are the client's responsibility even on a contingency fee basis. In some contingency agreements, the lawyer expects the client to pay the costs as they are accrued. In others, the lawyer understands that even payment of the costs will depend on the outcome of the case. The arrangement should clearly spell out how the costs will be assessed against the recovery—whether they will be subtracted before the attorney's percentage is applied or whether they will come only from the client's recovery.

### Payment Schedule

If the client cannot pay for needed work now, she should discuss a payment arrangement with the attorney. Some lawyers will agree to a payment schedule. If requested, they will send monthly statements listing the payment due under the schedule. In some instances, the lawyer will request the same type of security that one would give a bank. She may ask for a guarantee of payment from a financially responsible person. In that case, the guarantor's financial statement may be requested. She may ask for a promissory note, particularly if the client has a long-overdue statement. In some instances, the firm might request a security interest in property to secure the promissory note.

A client's failure to pay legal bills strains the attorney-client relationship. A court may require a lawyer to continue her representation in the matter, even if the client is not paying for the services, but the attorney will lack the incentive to be forceful and creative. If the client believes that she may have difficulty paying for the services needed, the best approach is to advise the lawyer as soon as possible. It may be during the initial interview or after the work has begun. Some lawyers take work on a *pro bono publico* basis. This Latin term means that the lawyer does work without charge for the "good of the public." Other lawyers may be willing to work at a reduced rate or with the understanding that the client will pay when and if she is able. Some lawyers will refuse the work. It is important to be open about financial capacity and work with the lawyer to create an arrangement satisfactory to both lawyer and client.

## Interest

Some law firms charge interest if the statement is not paid within a set period of time, usually 30 days. The client should know what procedure the lawyer follows. Often interest charges are added to the bill, but can be waived. The firm is principally concerned about having its bills paid. Assessing interest gives the client an incentive to pay the bill promptly.

## Interview Questions

The following questions should be asked during the initial interview about fees. The first question is, how will the lawyer charge for her services? Depending on the answer, different additional questions are appropriate.

1. If the lawyer charges the client on an hourly basis, what is the lawyer's hourly rate? Does the rate differ depending on the kind of work being done? What are the assistants' rates? Is all of their time billed or is it evaluated to see if their work was done efficiently? Does the lawyer charge for time spent reviewing or revising their work? How frequently will the lawyer send a statement? What information is included on a statement? Will the lawyer prepare a written agreement to describe the fee arrangement? What is the fee estimate for these services? Will the lawyer let the client know if these estimates are low? If there are divisible parts to the work, what is the fee estimate for each portion? Will there be other costs associated with preparing this matter? How much are they likely to be?

2. If the lawyer charges the client on a contingency basis, what percentage of the recovery will be paid to the attorney? Will that percent be the same if the matter is concluded in a preliminary stage? Is there a possibility of recovering attorney fees from the other parties? If so, how would that affect the payment to the attorney? Will there be other costs associated with preparing this matter? How much are they likely to be? When would payment be expected? Would any payment be expected if the case is lost?

3. If the client will be paying the attorney on a project basis, what is the charge for the project described? What if the project becomes more complicated than originally imagined? What kinds of complications could arise in this type of situation? Will there be other costs associated with preparing this matter? How much are they likely to be?

4. Whatever the fee basis, questions should be asked about payment arrangements. How soon after receipt of the bill is payment expected? Is there an interest charge if payment is not submitted by that time? How much is the interest? If difficulty is anticipated in making the payments, what payment schedule can be arranged?

## Maintaining the Relationship

A lawyer is retained to *help* the client through a situation. Clients sometimes assume they can escape the stress of dealing with a problem's emotional aspect by turning it over to an attorney. The lawyer can give counsel; she can implement the client's wishes and directions, but the client is not relieved of the problem once she hires an attorney. The lawyer will need additional information and instructions as the matter proceeds. A client-attorney relationship requires work like all other relationships. The following issues need attention throughout the relationship:

### Communication and Quality of Service

The most important part of the relationship is the client's comfort with it. Although the client lacks expertise and experience in the substantive area, she will know if she understands what is happening and why, and whether she feels comfortable with it. A lawyer's principal responsibility is to serve her client. If the client does not feel well served, she needs to discuss this with her attorney.

### Client Assistance

A client hires a lawyer because she needs advice on the law and how it applies to her situation. With a little guidance from the attorney, the client often can provide the lawyer with pertinent information in a form that will reduce the lawyer's work. For example, the client may be able to assist the lawyer in a pending dispute by obtaining governmental records or by writing down all the dates of communications and a summary of what was said. By undertaking these tasks, the client stays involved and substitutes her work for attorney fees. The client should inquire if the tasks completed were useful to counsel. Lawyers may be hesitant to let a client know if her assistance was not helpful. Unless the client ascertains that information, however, she cannot alter her efforts to be more effective.

### Confidentiality

Oral or written communications between a client and her lawyer are confidential under the attorney-client privilege. The attorney cannot divulge what they discuss. This privilege is intended to encourage clients to tell their lawyers their story, fully and honestly. Only with full knowledge can a lawyer adequately advise her client of her rights and obligations, and offer sound advice. To maintain the privilege, the information must remain in confidence. If a client discusses her communications with her attorney with others, she may jeopardize the attorney-client privilege. The client should discuss with her lawyer what communications with others relating to the legal matter are appropriate. Can the client discuss what she has told the lawyer? Should the client discuss the lawyer's explanation of the legal requirements and implications of the matter? With whom?

### Fees and Billings

The client should pay conscious attention to the lawyer's compliance with the client's needs and expressed wishes about those requests. If they are not met, the client should let the lawyer know.

## Terminating the Relationship

Women who strive to develop and maintain relationships may be uncomfortable with the concept of terminating the relationship with their attorney. All clients, however, should be aware of this option. If the relationship with the attorney is not working out as the client wishes, she may terminate the relationship and retain another lawyer.

One reason to terminate a relationship with an attorney is that the lawyer does not do what she says she will when she says she will. Another reason is a growing discomfort with a lawyer's failure or inability to explain what is occurring so that the client can meaningfully participate in making the vital decisions. A client might terminate the relationship if she feels the lawyer has acted unethically. Unsatisfactory results are probably the most common reason a lawyer is terminated. An adverse result does not necessarily justify changing lawyers.

An analysis of whether the representation has been appropriate is necessary. Another reason for terminating the relationship with counsel relates to fee disputes. If a client disputes the amount charged for certain legal work and the attorney and the client cannot reach a mutually agreeable settlement, the client may wish to look elsewhere.

In switching counsel, it is important to assess the practical consequences of this action. How much of the information provided to the first attorney and how much of her work will be transferable to the second attorney? Lawyers have an ethical obligation to assist new counsel in taking over a matter, although fees will be charged for this time. Yet, it can be expected that much of the work will be revisited. If the client is uncomfortable with the attorney and has decided to make a switch, she may wish to evaluate the status of pending matters. It may make sense for the first lawyer to finish certain projects or tasks. The client can retain another lawyer to start new matters. Some legal issues are affected by externally imposed requirements or time schedules. When changing counsel, the client cannot be assured that any legally imposed time deadlines will be extended because of the counsel change.

## Conclusion

Selecting a lawyer who can effectively and meaningfully represent a client takes energy, time, and focus. Often, a client needs to retain a lawyer to assist with an emotional and stressful situation. Undertaking a thorough and thoughtful selection process may only increase the stress. Commitment to that process is critical to achieving an ultimately satisfactory resolution of the legal matter.

### Bibliography

Numerous resources list lawyers in a particular state; others list lawyers by specialty. Check your local library or call the local or state branch of the Bar Association. Reference books listed below are broad in scope and would be a good starting point in searching for the kind of lawyer you need.

*Butterworth's Law Directory 1993*. New Providence, NJ: Martindale-Hubbell, 1993.

*Directory of Associations of Women Lawyers*. Chicago: American Bar Association, 1993.

*Directory of Lawyer Referral Services*. Chicago: American Bar Association, 1994.

Martindale-Hubbell Staff, editor. *Martindale-Hubbell Bar Register of Preeminent Lawyers 1995 (annual)*. New Providence, NJ: Martindale-Hubbell, 1995.

Martindale-Hubbell Staff, editor. *Martindale-Hubbell Law Directory, 126 ed.* New Providence, NJ: Martindale-Hubbell, 1995.

Wasserman. *Encyclopedia of Legal Information Sources, 2d ed.* Detroit: Gale Research, 1992.

**Andrea Williams** was a trial lawyer specializing in commercial disputes for twenty years in Denver, Colorado. Currently, she consults about gender issues in the workplace. She is active on a committee of the Colorado Bar Association that is studying the dynamics of the legal system. She also chairs a working group of the American Arbitration Association which has developed a claims resolution process for sexual harassment claims.

Chapter 2

# Health: Patient Rights and Policing the Quality of Health Care

Linda W. Rohman and Penny L. Huber

Chapter Outline

**Introduction**

**Informed Consent and the Right to Refuse Treatment**
Duty to Obtain Informed Consent • Adequacy of Disclosures • Must a Practitioner Disclose Her HIV Status? • Refusal of Treatment

**The Right to Die—Euthanasia and Assisted Suicide**

**Competency to Consent to or Refuse Treatment**
Documenting Consents and Refusals of Treatment

**Confidentiality and Disclosure of Medical Records**
Purposes and Content of Patient Medical Records • Ownership of Medical Records and Patient Access • Confidentiality and Disclosure of Medical Records • The Physician-Patient Privilege

**Scope and Extent of the Physician-Patient Privilege**
Assertion and Waiver of the Privilege

**Policing the Quality of Health Care**
Regulation of Health Care Professionals • The Food and Drug Administration

**Product Liability**

**Conclusion**

Health care is currently the fastest growing industry in the United States and accounts for what is perhaps the largest single segment of the country's gross national product. On an individual level, all of us pay more of our income for health care than ever before. It appears, however, that health care reform is imminent. Because reform is in the air, much of what can be included under the heading of "health law" may change in the near future. The reform movement is so strong and promises to be so drastic and far-reaching, that the pace of change in health law will certainly be accelerated beyond what practitioners in the field have ever known.

What follows in this chapter and the next is a detailed discussion of five topics that are basic to many encounters with the health care industry: informed consent and the right to refuse treatment, confidentiality and disclosure of medical records, reproduction and the law, property rights and the human body, and a section we have chosen to call "policing" the quality of health care.

Health care is undergoing a radical transformation, both in terms of improved technology and paying for health care. This chapter discusses basic rights that patients may exercise when seeking medical treatment. Because of the extreme state of flux in health care, however, matters of payment and coverage are not discussed, and technological advances may cause abrupt changes in other aspects of health care that are covered here.

## Introduction

The basic principle underlying the consent requirement is the belief that "[e]very human being of adult years and sound mind has a right to determine what shall be done with his [or her] own body."[1] An historical basis for the law concerning consent to medical treatment can be found in the tort of battery. Battery is a legal offense defined as "nonconsensual touching." If a health care professional physically touches a patient without her permission, the professional commits battery and, under the law of battery, is responsible to the patient for any ill effects she experienced as a result of the battery.

Until the late 1950s and early 1960s, the law focused almost exclusively on the requirement that a patient's consent be obtained before a physician rendered treatment. Beginning at that time, the focus shifted to the *type* of information a health care provider must give a patient in order to ensure that her consent to treatment is adequately informed. The concept of "informed consent" was born. Although it has not been uniformly adopted in the fifty states, informed consent to medical treatment is currently required as a matter of law in most of them.

## Informed Consent and the Right to Refuse Treatment

## Duty to Obtain Informed Consent

A health care provider must obtain a patient's informed consent when a proposed treatment or procedure will have an ascertainable impact on the patient, or when the proposed treatment or procedure entails more than a minimal risk. Clearly, the health care provider must exercise her professional judgment in determining whether a particular treatment or procedure meets one or both of these criteria. As a practical matter, physicians routinely make disclosures and require patients to sign detailed consent forms.

The treating physician often chooses to make the required disclosures to the patient and secure her consent, although practical considerations may justify a physician's delegation of this function to others. Regardless of who makes the required disclosures to the patient, however, the physician bears the ultimate risk of liability should the patient's informed consent not be obtained.

## Adequacy of Disclosures

State laws set the standard determining whether a physician's disclosures about a procedure or treatment are adequate to ensure that the patient's consent, if obtained, is truly "informed." The majority of states have adopted one of two different standards to measure the adequacy of disclosures.

In most states, a health care provider must disclose information a "reasonable" physician would disclose under similar circumstances. This standard is known as the "reasonable physician (or professional practice) standard." It attempts to evaluate the adequacy of a particular physician's disclosures to her patient by what is considered acceptable among the physician's colleagues practicing in the same community.

In contrast, approximately one-third of the states have adopted a "reasonable patient standard." It requires a physician to disclose "material" information. Information is material if a reasonable person in the patient's position would likely attach significance to the information in deciding whether or not to accept the proposed therapy.

Regardless of which standard has been adopted in a particular state, patients should expect to be informed of the following:

- The diagnosis

- The nature and purpose of the proposed treatment

- The benefits of the proposed treatment

- The known consequences of the proposed treatment

- The possible risks of the proposed treatment (for example, death; brain damage; quadriplegia, paraplegia, or loss of function of any organ or limb; or disfiguring scars), together with the probability of each such risk, if reasonably determinable

- Alternatives to the proposed treatment

- The likelihood of success

- The risks and consequences inherent in refusing the proposed treatment

## Must a Practitioner Disclose Her HIV Status?

In response to the publicity surrounding the death from AIDS of Kimberly Bergalis of Florida, which she apparently contracted from her dentist, some people have begun to question whether their consent to be treated by a particular health care practitioner can be fully informed unless the practitioner discloses her AIDS/HIV status. Courts that have considered the question have rather uniformly concluded that health care professionals must disclose their AIDS/HIV status to patients before performing any invasive procedures.

## Refusal of Treatment

*In General.* After being fully informed, a legally competent adult patient has a recognized legal right to refuse treatment. Even recently, however, this has not always been the case. In the 1960s a series of inventions and refinements in medical science, enabling physicians to prolong life even when the patient's condition was terminal, took medical care into a new age. These inventions and refinements included increased sophistication of the respirator; the development of cardiac resuscitation technology; and advances in artificial feeding and hydration, enabling physicians to sustain comatose patients over long periods of time.

By the 1970s, as more patients and their families experienced the effects of these technological advancements in medical care, society began to question whether such care is always desirable. Attempts were made to distinguish situations in which medical technology should be fully applied from those in which such care should be withheld altogether. Not surprisingly, during that time, a series of cases involving the removal of respirators and, eventually, the removal of artificially administered food and water, began to find their way in to court.

In deciding *Cruzan v. Director, Missouri Department of Health* in 1990, the U.S. Supreme Court first acknowledged that a legally competent adult patient has a constitutional right to refuse treatment. According to *Cruzan,* individual states have an interest in preserving life, safeguarding the integrity of the medical profession, preventing suicide, and protecting innocent third parties. Consequently, individual states can enact laws limiting a patient's right to refuse treatment under certain circumstances.

Many states condition the withdrawal or withholding of life-sustaining treatment on the presence of a terminal illness or the threat of imminent death. These states may prevent the withdrawal of treatment for those patients who exist in a vegetative state that is permanent and irreversible. *Cruzan* suggests that the requirement a patient be terminally ill, or terminally ill and death imminent, as a precondition to refusing treatment may be unconstitutional. Until that question is resolved, however, the law implementing the right to refuse treatment will remain inconsistent.

*Advance Directives.* Shortly after the *Cruzan* decision was announced and, perhaps, in response to that decision, Congress passed a law known as the Patient Self-Determination Act. Since December 1, 1991, when the Act went into effect, all Medicare or Medicare-certified hospitals, nursing homes, hospices, home health agencies, and contracting Health Maintenance Organizations (HMOs) are required to provide certain information to patients. This information must be in writing, and it must spell out patients' rights to make decisions concerning medical care, including the right to accept or refuse medical or surgical treatment and the right to formulate advance directives.

An advance directive is a written statement summarizing an individual's wishes regarding medical care. It may also designate a particular person to accept or refuse medical or surgical treatment on the individual's behalf in the event the individual is prevented, by illness or incapacity, from being personally consulted. The following are the two most common forms of advance directives:

1. Living wills. This type of advance directive is a written declaration of a patient's decision regarding the administration or withdrawal of life-sustaining medical treatment under certain conditions. Such documents are called "living" wills because they become effective while the individual is still alive, but may be unable to make her wishes known. (See chapter 23 for additional information and an example of language that might be used in a Living Will.)

   More than forty states have enacted statutes giving patients the power to provide their families and physicians with such an advance directive regarding medical care.

2. Durable powers of attorney for health care. A power of attorney is a legal document authorizing one person, called an "agent" or "attorney-in-fact," to do something for another person, called the "principal." Under a "durable" power of attorney, the agent has the power to act on behalf of the principal even if the principal becomes incapacitated. In other words, the agent's authority to act and, consequently, the power of attorney itself, is "durable" because it survives even if the principal becomes legally incompetent after

appointing the agent. There are certain requirements for a durable power of attorney for health care. (See chapter 24, which covers estate planning.)

Under the Patient Self-Determination Act and state laws regarding living wills and powers of attorney for health care a health care provider is not required to follow a patient's advance directive if doing so would violate the provider's religious beliefs or sincerely held moral or ethical convictions. Those laws, however, do impose a duty upon health care providers to notify patients of the provider's beliefs and, ultimately, to transfer patients to a facility or to the care of an individual provider who will honor the patient's advance directive.

In some states a health care provider can be held liable for administering life-sustaining treatment if the provider has been notified of the patient's decision not to receive such treatment. Recently, an Ohio court confronted that question in a case involving the following facts: A patient was hospitalized for a heart condition and, upon hospitalization, requested a DNR order be entered on his medical chart (DNR means "Do Not Resuscitate"). Three days later, a nurse revived the patient after he had stopped breathing. The patient suffered a stroke two days after that, and lingered for two years before his death. His family sued the hospital for battery and requested damages for pain, suffering, emotional distress, disability, medical bills, and other expenses incurred by the patient from the date of his resuscitation to the date of his death.

The Ohio court denied the family's claim, rejecting their right to recover under a theory of "wrongful life" under the circumstances. This ruling does not mean that a recovery could not be had given other facts or under a different state's law. As advance directives become more common, the issues raised in the Ohio case may arise and be litigated more frequently and with various results.

If you decide to make an advance directive, regardless of the form used, it is imperative that you make at least two crucial decisions. The first task, of course, is to decide what extraordinary measures or life-sustaining treatment, if any, you wish to receive in the event you are terminally ill, death imminent, or in a persistent vegetative state. The second task is to choose an agent you can trust to carry out your wishes under circumstances that will probably be tragic and stressful for the agent. You have the responsibility of discussing your choice with your proposed agent, both to confirm that the agent is willing to accept the appointment and to assure yourself that the agent understands and will respect your wishes as expressed in the advance directive.

Although patients are encouraged to consider formulating an advance directive of some type, the Patient Self-Determination Act does not require them to do so. The ultimate goal of the law is to educate and inform, leaving the issue of whether or not to make an advance directive to the patient's discretion. However, if you don't have a living will, or other "clear and convincing evidence" of your wishes, many states will require that treatment be continued. It may be difficult, if not impossible, for a patient's physician, family, or friends to supply a court with "clear and convincing" evidence of the patient's wishes without a written document. It will certainly be impossible for them to do so if the patient does not discuss her wishes with them in advance.

## The Right to Die— Euthanasia and Assisted Suicide

Although there is strong legal support for a patient's right to refuse life-sustaining treatment, the law does not condone the taking of active steps to end life. Currently, few would disagree that a physician can ethically halt certain treatments to allow death to take its natural course. There is, however, a segment of modern society that advocates legal recognition of the right to accelerate the dying process and, as a necessary corollary to that right, the legalization of euthanasia and assisted suicide.

Euthanasia, also known as "mercy killing," is the act or practice of putting persons suffering from incurable or painful diseases to death. Each of the fifty states has laws prohibiting murder or manslaughter. In many states, suicide is also a criminal offense. Euthanasia is arguably contrary to each body of law: The "mercy killer" commits murder or manslaughter and the victim, if she seeks death and is, thus, a willing victim, essentially commits suicide.

In contrast, assisted suicide usually consists of an able-bodied person helping another individual who is catastrophically or terminally ill, but not necessarily in imminent peril of death, to end her life. Although assisted suicide is violative of laws proscribing suicide, unlike euthanasia, it may or may not be violative of the laws outlawing murder and manslaughter. If the "assistant" is careful not to do the deed herself, the "assistant" to a suicide may not commit murder or manslaughter. Traditionally, it is not a crime to be present when someone commits suicide, nor is it murder to make a means of suicide available to someone else, so long as the facilitator does not do the act that results in the death. Because of this "loophole" in the law, at least twenty-eight states have passed laws specifically making assisted suicide a crime.

Perhaps the most well-publicized representative of the right to die movement is Dr. Jack Kevorkian, a retired Michigan pathologist who, since 1990, has helped different individuals take their own lives by a variety of means. In 1993 the Michigan legislature, in an attempt to stop Kevorkian from assisting any more people to commit suicide, passed a temporary statute (which has now expired) specifically out-lawing assisted suicide in the state. The American Civil Liberties Union filed suit on behalf of a group of physicians, pharmacists, and advo-cates for the elderly challenging the law's constitutionality. The ACLU contends that it violates individual rights to privacy and is an illegal restraint upon the practice of medicine, particularly in the exercise of physicians' professional judgment concerning the relief of pain and suffering. In April 1995, the Supreme Court refused to hear the case. It did, however, uphold Michigan's right to prosecute Kevorkian in con-nection with aiding the suicides of terminally ill patients.

Clearly, Kevorkian and his supporters have raised disturbing ques-tions. Who has the right to choose death? Under what circumstances? What responsibility does a physician have to maintain a patient's life if, by doing so, the physician merely prolongs suffering? If it is legal and ethical for a physician to allow a patient to die by withholding or withdrawing life-sustaining treatment, including in many states with-holding food and water, should it also be permissible for a physician to help a patient to die through the administration of drugs or by other humane means?

Opponents of the right to die movement argue that the decision to commit suicide should be a difficult one. They contend that many, if not all, of the people assisted by Kevorkian were physically able to kill themselves—they simply lacked the moral power or conviction to do the deed alone. Commentators point out that the majority of the patients Kevorkian has assisted have been women. Although women may be equally to slightly less likely to attempt suicide than men, they are statistically less likely to succeed. These commentators, and other opponents of the right to die or "death with dignity" movement, con-tend that legalization of assisted suicide essentially gives people, par-ticularly women, the moral support they otherwise would not have in the endeavor to kill themselves.

Recent public opinion polls, conducted in Michigan and elsewhere, indicate that most people favor making physician-assisted suicide avail-able to the terminally ill. State legislatures in New Hampshire and Maine have recently considered bills that would legalize assisted suicide in those states. Voters in the states of California and Washington, however, rejected the idea in two separate referendums held in 1991 and 1992.

In the strict legal sense, the question of a person's "competency" to make decisions about health care goes to the person's ability and capacity to understand her medical condition, the consequences and risks of the proposed treatment, and the possible consequences should

## Competency to Consent to or Refuse Treatment

she decide to refuse that treatment. A person may be legally "incompetent" to make health care decisions for herself for a number of reasons. In the extreme, a patient may be rendered unconscious by an injury and may be expected to remain comatose or persist in a vegetative state indefinitely. Less extreme examples are the patient whose brain function is impaired, as in the case of a mentally retarded, senile, or brain-damaged individual; or the patient who may be mentally active and aware, but who has lost the physical ability to communicate with others effectively, as may be the case with stroke victims. Finally, minors are considered legally incompetent to make most health care decisions for themselves until they attain the age of majority. Depending on which state she lives in, a child legally becomes an adult, competent to make health care decisions for herself, somewhere between the ages of eighteen and twenty-one.

If the patient is incompetent, state law makes provisions for who may decide to accept or refuse medical treatment for her. Statutes in the fifty states make different provisions but, in general, the following persons may provide consent in the situations described:

- The parents, or either parent, for a minor

- An emancipated minor (that is, a child under the age of majority but considered an adult because she has married, or is otherwise self-supporting and living independently from her parents) can consent for herself

- A person legally appointed as the guardian of another person (the "ward") may consent to treatment on behalf of the ward

- In many states, a minor can consent on her own behalf in order to secure treatment for venereal disease, drug abuse, or pregnancy and the prevention thereof

- In many states, a person appointed in a living will or durable power of attorney for health care, may consent to or refuse treatment on behalf of the person making the appointment

- In some states, anyone standing *in loco parentis* (in the place of the parents) with respect to a minor may consent to treatment for that child

- In some states, the incompetent patient's next of kin[2] may consent on behalf of the patient

A patient has the right to refuse treatment, and it is the general rule that another person may not override her objections, unless the patient is a minor or is otherwise legally incapacitated. If, in the opinion of the health care provider, the patient clearly does not understand and appreciate the consequences of her refusal, the health care provider may, in most states, ask that a court authorize treatment for the patient.

## Documenting Consents and Refusals of Treatment

Most states have no general requirement that a consent for medical treatment be in writing in order to be valid. Because of the threat of legal liability, if a physician is unable to prove she satisfied informed consent requirements before treating a patient, most health care providers document patient consent in writing and make those forms part of the patient's medical records.

As a practical matter, a general consent to medical treatment is one of the conditions a hospital or clinic imposes before admitting a patient. Consequently, among the documents a person signs in the process of admitting herself to a hospital or clinic is a general consent to receive medical treatment. However, if the proposed treatment or procedure is significant in terms of its impact on the patient, or if it entails more than a minimal amount of risk, the patient's separate consent to that specific treatment or procedure is typically obtained as well. The forms used to document a patient's consent to invasive procedures or treatment entailing some degree of risk are sufficiently detailed to make a record of specific disclosures by the physician. The consent forms outline the nature of the procedure or treatment and include the risks involved, and statements by the patient that she understands the information provided and agrees to undergo the procedure or treatment in question.

Finally, if a patient opts to refuse recommended treatment, her physician must determine whether she is competent to do so. Ordinarily, this requires the physician to assure herself that the patient understands the nature of her medical condition and the consequences of her refusal. In addition, the physician must discover whether third parties might be jeopardized by the patient's decision. This includes an inquiry, if such information is not already a matter of record, into whether the patient has minor dependent children, is pregnant, or whether some other reason exists which, as a matter of public policy, limits the patient's right to refuse treatment. If not, the patient will typically be required to sign a form acknowledging that, although her physician recommended treatment, she refused it knowing the consequences she would suffer as a result of that decision.

Not very long ago health care was a rather uncomplicated system involving the patient and her family physician. Because most individuals paid their own medical bills, there was very little demand for the disclosure of medical information to persons other than the patient.

## Confidentiality and Disclosure of Medical Records

Today, the health care delivery system is increasingly complicated with a multiplicity of health care providers and third-party payers. Individual physicians, working in different specialty areas, must share information in order to treat the whole patient effectively. Health insurers and other third-party payers require access to medical information contained in patient files to verify their obligation to pay for the treatment received by the patient. The recognized need to computerize medical records for more efficient use, storage, and retrieval has arguably increased access, and, consequently, the chance of unauthorized access, to sensitive medical information.

Because of these and other trends in the delivery of health care, the confidentiality of medical records, and the circumstances in which such records can or must be disclosed, are important concerns. This discussion begins with a few general principles about the ownership and disclosure of medical records and the information contained in those records, and concludes with a discussion of the extent of a health care provider's legal duty to maintain patient confidences.

### Purposes and Content of Patient Medical Records

The primary purpose of a patient's medical record is to document and plan the course of a patient's treatment. Secondary objectives are:

- To facilitate evaluation of individual health care providers' performance and competence

- To provide information for third-party payers (for example, health insurance companies and government agencies responsible for administering Medicaid and Medicare programs)

- To satisfy legal and regulatory agencies' requirements, including but not limited to state and federal Medicare/Medicaid authorities

- To provide research data

- To provide information for utilization review

- To serve as evidence in medical malpractice and other legal actions involving the patient's treatment

At a minimum, medical records must contain sufficient information to identify the patient, support the health care provider's diagnosis, justify the treatment administered to the patient, and accurately document the course of the patient's recovery. As a practical matter, medical records usually consist of the following types of information:

- Patient identification data

- The medical history of the patient

- A summary of the patient's psychosocial needs

- Reports of relevant physical or psychological examinations

- Diagnostic and therapeutic orders

- Written evidence that appropriate informed consent was obtained from the patient or a proxy before treatment was rendered

- Clinical observations of medical staff members about the patient, including the results of therapy or treatment administered to the patient

- Reports of procedures and tests and their results

- Conclusions regarding the patient's status when she was released from the hospital or when evaluation and treatment were concluded

## Ownership of Medical Records and Patient Access

The health care provider, whether that be an individual (such as a particular doctor) or an institution (such as a hospital or clinic), owns the original of the physical record or file compiled in the process of treating a patient. The patient, however, owns the information contained in the record. The health care provider is merely the custodian of that information. Therefore, patients have a recognized legal right of access to the information contained in a provider's medical record.

A patient can be denied access to her medical record only if the health care provider can demonstrate that disclosure of the information contained in the medical record would be detrimental to the patient's health. This is called the "therapeutic" exception to the rules concerning patients' access to their own records.

Although a provider cannot usually deny a patient access to the information contained in her medical record, a health care provider can impose reasonable administrative regulations on a patient's access. Reasonable administrative regulations may include the following:

- Allowing access only during business hours of the office or health care facility

- Requiring patients to review files on-site

- Charging a fee for reproducing the records (such as duplication and labor costs)

- Permitting patient access only in the presence of medical personnel or hospital staff after first consulting the patient's physician

## Confidentiality and Disclosure of Medical Records

Protection of patient confidentiality has long been a hallmark of medical ethics. All major national medical, mental health, and counseling organizations recognize a general need to keep patient information confidential. Many states have incorporated ethical standards of confidentiality into licensing laws applicable to health care professionals.

The legal duty requiring a health care provider to keep patient medical information confidential may also arise from statutes protecting specific types of patient information. Special protection is afforded medical records of a sensitive nature. For example, under federal law, access to the records of alcohol and drug abuse patients in federally assisted drug and alcohol treatment programs is severely limited. Such laws are intended to encourage people to seek treatment by ensuring that neither their presence in treatment nor any information concerning that treatment will be disclosed, except in extraordinary circumstances.

In most states, the duty of a physician or related health care provider to maintain the confidentiality of patient information is reflected in a statutory physician-patient privilege. Some states, however, do not have specific statutes governing the confidentiality of medical records. In those states, health care providers' legal duty to keep patient records confidential may arise from the common law.[3]

### The Physician-Patient Privilege

Public policy generally requires full disclosure of relevant information in legal proceedings. Accordingly, no person or entity, absent a confidential relationship, can refuse to testify or to produce documents if ordered to do so in the context of a court proceeding. The physician-patient relationship is one example of such a confidential relation. The protection from disclosure or discovery the law gives to communications between a patient and her physician is called a "privilege." The law allows a patient the "privilege" to require her physician not to repeat or disclose information gained in the context of the physician-patient relationship, unless the patient is first consulted and consents to the disclosure.

Scope and
Extent of the
Physician-Patient
Privilege

The physician-patient privilege extends to confidential information a patient reveals to a physician, and to medical staff employed by the physician, for the purposes of diagnosis or treatment of the patient's physical, mental, or emotional condition. Although state laws may differ, confidential information in this context is usually defined as information that is not intended by the patient to be disclosed to third persons, other than those present, except to further the interest of the patient in obtaining treatment.

Clearly, the privilege does not cover everything a patient tells a health care provider. For example, incriminating statements regarding the cause of a traffic accident in which a patient was involved, made by the patient to an emergency room physician immediately after the accident, would not be necessary to enable the physician to render aid to the patient and, therefore, would not be privileged. Only confidential information that is necessary to enable the physician to diagnose and treat the patient's condition falls within the privilege.

There are, however, exceptions to this general rule. Under the following circumstances, confidential information is not considered privileged under the law:

1. The patient places her physical, mental, or emotional status in question in the context of a legal proceeding. For example, a patient places her health in question by filing a Workers' Compensation claim or a personal injury action. By pursuing a Workers' Compensation claim, a patient seeks to recover damages from her employer for on-the-job injuries. In the context of a personal injury action, a patient seeks to recover damages for personal injuries resulting from the negligence of a third party. In both types of cases, the patient must prove the extent of her injuries and the resulting damages, including the cost of medical care received by the patient. Consequently, the patient's physical condition is a central issue in either type of case and the patient cannot invoke the privilege to prevent her physician from revealing pertinent medical information.

2. The legal proceeding was initiated to determine whether the patient requires involuntary hospitalization. Perhaps the best example of this type of situation is the mental health commitment proceeding. If a person poses a danger to herself or to others, a court can commit that person to the custody and care of a mental health facility without her consent and against her wishes. In the context of a mental health commitment proceeding, a physician may reveal confidential communications between herself and a patient if the physician has determined that the patient needs to be hospitalized.

3. A court of law ordered the patient to submit to an examination by a particular physician retained by the court to evaluate the patient. A court may order an individual to submit to a physical and mental examination in the context of a variety of civil and criminal proceedings. If the court orders the examination and hires the physician to conduct the examination for the court, arguably no physician-patient relationship arises. The physician is obligated to report her findings to the court.

In addition, the law imposes an affirmative duty on physicians to report the following types of information that otherwise would fall within the scope of the physician-patient privilege:

1. Contagious diseases. Under the common law, a physician could warn third persons that a particular patient suffered from a dangerous and highly contagious disease. The physician's disclosure was condoned as long as she limited the disclosure to the release of information necessary to prevent the disease from spreading.

In modern times, many state legislatures have adopted statutes requiring physicians to report the incidence of particular contagious or infectious diseases, including sexually transmitted and other reportable diseases, illnesses, poisonings, or positive laboratory findings, to local and/or state health authorities. Many of these statutes require the physician to give the patient's name, address, and other identifying information. In most instances, the governmental entities receiving that information maintain the information in confidence (that is, the information is not subject to subpoena and is inadmissible in evidence in any legal proceeding). Statutes imposing the reporting requirement upon physicians usually grant the physicians immunity from suit for slander, libel, or breach of privileged communication.

In the case of AIDS and HIV diagnoses, there is a general consensus that state or local health departments, rather than health care providers, should have the obligation to notify third parties. In the case of an individual who is HIV positive, third parties at risk include current and future sexual partners and any person at risk of blood-to-blood exposure, like persons sharing hypodermic needles. A recent Presidential Commission Report on HIV suggests that health care providers should have the option, but not the obligation, to inform sexual partners of an infected patient who, after being counseled, refuses to make such notification herself. Legislation in many states formalizes this suggestion.

In addition, laws recently enacted in a number of states allow the disclosure of a patient's laboratory test results for certain diseases to "first responders" without the patient's prior informed consent. First responders are emergency medical personnel, police, or fire fighters. Under these state laws, if a first responder believes she was exposed to a contagious disease through interaction with a patient in an emergency situation, the first responder has the option to report the suspected exposure and, subsequently, be notified whether the patient suffers from hepatitis B, meningitis, or tuberculosis, or has tested positive for HIV or the AIDS virus. If the patient is tested for these diseases as part of the treatment rendered to the patient after the emergency situation, the results are reported directly to the first responder. If the patient is not tested voluntarily, the first responder can often compel the patient to submit to testing.

Clearly, statutes of this type narrow the scope and applicability of the physician-patient privilege when infectious, and potentially deadly, diseases are involved.

2. Patients' potential for self-destructive behavior and violence toward others.

Doctors have been held liable for the actions of dangerous patients resulting in injuries to other patients or occupants of a hospital. The physician's and health care facility's duty to control the behavior of inpatients arises in such cases from the physician's or the facility's custody of the patient. As such, the physician or hospital becomes legally responsible to control the inpatient's behavior.

Under certain conditions, a physician's or facility's duty to control a patient's behavior may extend into the outpatient setting. In addition, the duty to control the patient for the protection of others may, under certain circumstances, include a responsibility to warn third parties who may be physically harmed by the patient.

For example, in *Tarasoff v. Board of Regents of the University of California,*[4] two psychologists employed at the University's Health Center treated a patient who had told them of his intention to kill a former girlfriend. Believing the patient to be serious about his intentions, the psychologists asked the campus police to detain the patient. The police picked up the patient, but released him because he appeared rational. The psychologists took no other action to confine the patient, nor did they issue any warning to the woman he had threatened to kill or to her family. Approximately two months later, the patient killed the woman as he had threatened. The woman's family subsequently sued the university.

Because the psychologists knew their patient was at large and intended to kill the woman, the court held that their failure to warn her or others likely to apprise her of the danger constituted a breach of their duty to exercise reasonable care to protect her. Once a health care provider determines, or under applicable professional standards reasonably should have determined, that a patient poses a serious danger of violence to herself or others, the provider bears a duty to exercise reasonable care to protect the foreseeable victim of that danger.

Courts vary as to the extent of the obligation to protect. Some limit the requirement to a reasonable attempt to notify a readily identifiable victim. At least one court has ruled that whatever precautions are reasonably necessary to protect potential victims, even if they are not readily identifiable, must be taken to prevent a patient from doing physical harm.

Clearly, there is a tension between a physician's duty to protect third parties and a physician's duty to safeguard confidential patient information. In short, health care providers are in a classic catch-22 situation to which there is no clear, easy solution: They may be held liable to the patient for unauthorized releases of confidential medical information, but if they choose not to release certain kinds of information, they may be liable to persons who are harmed by the patient.

3. Abuse or neglect of a minor or vulnerable adult. Statutes in many states require health care professionals to report suspected cases of abuse or neglect of minors or of vulnerable adults, defined as elderly or incompetent individuals incapable of protecting or defending themselves. Abuse may involve physical injury, unreasonable confinement, sexual maltreatment, exploitation, and denial of essential services or material needs. Information communicated to a physician or other health care provider in the treatment context that is indicative of abuse or neglect is not subject to the privilege. Health care providers are required to report suspected cases of abuse or neglect to state health, welfare, and/or law enforcement authorities. In so doing, they are expected to reveal information received by them in the course of treating a patient which leads them to suspect that abuse or neglect has occurred.

4. Wounds. Many states require the reporting of certain wounds. Some jurisdictions specify that all wounds of certain types be reported (such as wounds inflicted by sharp instruments that may result in death and all gunshot wounds), while others limit the requirement to wounds that apparently resulted from a criminal act.

## Assertion and Waiver of the Privilege

The privilege belongs to the patient. Consequently, only the patient or the patient's representative (if the patient is a minor, is incompetent, or is otherwise incapable), has the power to assert the privilege. A physician may claim the privilege, but only on behalf of her patient. The physician's authority to claim the privilege is presumed in the absence of evidence to the contrary.

The issue of whether certain medical information concerning a particular patient is privileged typically arises when a third party attempts to discover the information for one of a variety of possible reasons. The third party might request the information directly from the health care provider. If the provider refuses to supply the information, as she should unless the patient has given consent, the third party might try to force the provider to disclose the information. This "force" often involves the authority of a court of law. For example, the third party might persuade a judge to issue a subpoena requiring the health care provider to produce the requested information or to appear in court to testify concerning the provider's treatment of the patient. The provider can attempt to resist by asserting the privilege on the patient's behalf. In all cases, the court has the ultimate authority to determine whether particular information falls within the privilege or is subject to disclosure.

A patient may waive, or lose the ability to claim, the privilege against disclosure of medical information if she voluntarily discloses part or all of the content of the confidential communication between her and her physician to someone with whom she does not share a confidential relation. For example, if an unmarried patient tells her physician that she has been sexually active and she makes that disclosure for the purpose of obtaining medical advice, that information is ordinarily subject to the privilege and, consequently, the physician cannot be compelled against the patient's wishes to disclose that information to a third party. However, if the patient makes the same revelation to a personal friend, the physician-patient privilege is waived, the patient can no longer assert the privilege and, consequently, the physician could be compelled by a third party to disclose that information.

## Liability for Improper Disclosure

A patient harmed by a health care provider's improper disclosure of medical information may have a variety of legal remedies available to her. In states that have incorporated the ethical standards of confidentiality into professional licensing laws, the patient can file a formal complaint against the provider's license, possibly subjecting the provider to disciplinary action for willful violation of a professional confidence. Disciplinary action against a health care professional's license may include the imposition of a fine, probation, or, ultimately, revocation of her license to practice within the state.

Depending on the facts and circumstances surrounding the particular disclosure involved, a patient may have the right to pursue one or more of a number of civil actions against the health care provider who made the improper disclosure. If the patient prevails in a civil suit, the patient will be able to recover her actual damages and, in some jurisdictions, punitive or exemplary damages as well.

Civil suits for improper disclosure of confidential information, however, are relatively rare because the trial itself causes further publication of the confidential information. Many patients feel the harm done to them by the additional publicity outweighs the personal and financial satisfaction that might be gained through prosecution of their claim against the health care provider.

## Policing the Quality of Health Care

There are a number of different ways in which our system of laws and government, both directly and indirectly, regulates the quality of health care. Regulation takes two general forms: regulation of individual practitioners and regulation of the use and sale of therapeutic drugs and medical devices.

### Regulation of Health Care Professionals
#### Licensure Laws

In most states, an individual who wants to practice one of the healing arts must get the state's permission to do so. A state gives its permission in the form of a professional license authorizing the person to work in a particular health profession. Professional licenses are awarded only to those who can meet the qualification standards set by state law. Ordinarily, a person applying for a professional license to provide health care services to others must show that she has graduated from an accredited school; has passed a qualifying test or series of tests administered by the state's Board of Examiners for the health care profession she seeks to practice; and has a certain amount of experience practicing under the supervision of another professional licensed in the field.

The laws in the fifty states are not uniform with respect to the various professions regulated by licensure law requirements. Some, but not necessarily all, of the various health professions listed below require a license in most states. The following health care professions are usually subject to licensure laws:

- Medicine and surgery

- Nursing

- Podiatry

- Dentistry, including dental hygiene

- Chiropractic

- Optometry

- Pharmacy

- Audiology and speech-language pathology

- Psychology

- Respiratory therapy

Clearly, licensure laws regulate the quality of health care by requiring people hoping to work in particular health care fields to meet certain minimum criteria before they can legally treat patients. In most states, licensure laws also define the scope of the particular health care professions regulated. For example, a pharmacist can fill prescriptions but cannot prescribe medications. Individuals licensed by the state to practice a particular health care profession are required to confine their professional activities to those falling within the statutorily defined scope of their licensed profession.

In many states, the law makes a distinction between state licensing and state certification of health care professionals. A license is a permit to engage in a particular health care profession. State licensure laws are mandatory. Without a license, a person cannot legally practice particular health care professions that have been made subject to a state licensing requirement.

In contrast, state certification is a voluntary process. It typically applies only to those health care professions that are not subject to state licensing requirements. In most states a person can work in the following types of health care fields without first obtaining a license:

- Social work

- Professional counseling

- Athletic trainer

- Physical or massage therapist

- Dietician and nutritionist

Unlike the licensing system, a state's certification system does not restrict the practice of these professions. Rather, a practitioner in these fields who voluntarily meets certain preset qualifications is granted state certification in recognition of that achievement. Practitioners who are state certified may use the term "certified" in their professional titles or in describing their professional activities. Practitioners who are not state certified may still practice, but they may not call themselves "certified" professionals.

## Complaints

Licensure and certification laws are designed to protect and to inform the consumer. It should come as no surprise that such laws also have a side to them dedicated to processing patient complaints about particular health care professionals. The typical state has an administrative agency, called the department of health or the department of public welfare, that coordinates the various licensing and certification boards for the individual health care professions. A patient dissatisfied with the quality of care provided to her by a licensed or certified health care professional, particularly if the patient has reason to question the professional's competence, should contact the state health care authority to lodge a complaint about that professional.

State health care authorities have the power to investigate complaints received from patients and others, to bring charges against individual practitioners, to hold hearings, and to take action against the practitioner's license or certificate if such action is warranted. The following are some examples of acts or offenses that would warrant disciplinary action under the licensing laws in most states:

- Fraud, forgery, or misrepresentation of facts in obtaining a professional license

- Grossly immoral or dishonorable conduct evidencing an unfitness or lack of proficiency to practice

- Habitual intoxication or drug dependency

- Practice of the profession fraudulently, beyond its authorized scope, with manifest incapacity, or with gross incompetence or gross negligence

A state health authority finding an individual professional guilty of these or other offenses typically has the authority to impose one or more of the following types of sanctions upon the professional:

- A monetary fine

- Probation, requiring the professional to practice only under the supervision of the agency or another licensed professional for a period of time

- Denial, refused renewal, limitation, revocation, or suspension of the professional's certificate or license to practice

## Medical Malpractice

A patient harmed by the incompetence or negligence of a health care provider can ensure that the provider is held accountable to the state by lodging a complaint with the state licensing authority. If the patient wishes to hold the provider personally accountable for damages done to her due to the provider's incompetence or negligence the patient must file a lawsuit charging the provider with malpractice. Malpractice, as applied to medical practitioners, is bad, wrong, or injudicious treatment of a patient, resulting in injury, unnecessary suffering, or death to the patient, and is caused by the practitioner's ignorance, carelessness, lack of proper professional skill, disregard of established rules or principles, neglect, or malicious or criminal intent.

In order to prosecute a malpractice claim against a health care provider successfully, a patient must ordinarily prove the following five elements:

- The provider owed a duty of care to the patient

- The level or scope of the duty owed, called the "standard of care"

- The provider deviated from the appropriate standard of care in treating the patient

- The patient was injured or damaged in some way

- The injury or damage suffered by the patient was the direct result of the provider's wrongful conduct

A duty of care arises as a result of a relationship imposing a special responsibility on one person to protect, or at least to act in the best interests of, another person. In the typical medical malpractice case, such a relationship arises when the doctor-patient or hospital-patient relationship is established.

The scope of the duty owed by a health care provider to a patient is generally to do what a reasonably prudent health care practitioner engaged in a similar practice would have done for the patient under similar circumstances. Consequently, the patient pursuing a malpractice claim proves that her physician breached the duty of care owed to her by proving, usually through the testimony of other physicians, that her doctor did not do what a reasonably prudent physician would have done under similar circumstances. The standard of care is based on whether the treatment rendered was reasonable under the circumstances, and it does not ensure every patient a favorable healthy outcome.

Next, the patient must prove damages. Negligence without injury or damage does not support a cause of action for malpractice. A patient's injury may be physical, emotional, psychological, or wholly financial in nature.

Perhaps the most difficult element to prove is causation (that is, that the patient's injury resulted directly from the health care provider's breach of the duty of care). A wrongful act is the legal cause of a patient's injury if the patient can demonstrate that "but for" the wrongful act, the patient would not have suffered harm. If the patient does something wrong that contributes to her injury, like disobeying her doctor's orders or failing to take prescribed medication, the doctor may be able to escape liability by arguing that it was the patient's behavior, not the doctor's failure to satisfy the applicable standard of care, that was the primary or moving cause behind the patient's injury.

Statutes in most states establish a time period within which a patient must file a medical malpractice action or lose the right to do so. Such laws are called "statutes of limitations." The length of the time period varies from state to state, but is typically a matter of years. The limitations period begins to run in most states when the patient discovers, or as a reasonably prudent person should have discovered, her injury and its cause.

A patient who wins a malpractice action can recover damages from the health care provider for the following:

- Costs and expenses incurred as a result of the patient's injury, including charges for medical care necessitated by the injury

- Future medical care, if necessitated by the injury

- Pain and suffering

- Lost earnings and lost earning capacity resulting from any residual disability

A patient's survivors can recover for wrongful death if the patient's death results from the physician's malpractice. In some, but not all, states, a patient can also recover punitive or exemplary damages in a professional malpractice action. Punitive or exemplary damages are damages awarded to a patient, not for the purpose of compensating the patient for her loss, but for the purpose of punishing or penalizing the health care practitioner for the wrongdoing.

Over the last twenty years, the volume of medical malpractice claims filed in the various state courts has increased dramatically. The costs incurred by the medical profession in insuring and defending against and in paying such claims has contributed to spiraling health care costs during the same time period. This "malpractice crisis" has led many people to call for reform. Although various reforms have been suggested, the most common reform measure advocated today is a limit on the amount of money a jury can award to a patient who wins a malpractice case. A number of states have this type of measure and others designed to alleviate the perceived "crisis." Evidence does suggest that the incidence of medical malpractice claims is beginning to stabilize and, in some jurisdictions, even decrease. It is not known, and perhaps can never be known, whether this trend is the result of reform measures or is simply an independent and unpredictable fluctuation.

## Regulation of Therapeutic Drugs and Medical Devices

Therapeutic drugs are the medicines prescribed by our physicians and those found on drugstore shelves (over-the-counter drugs). Medical devices are instruments, machines, or implants intended for use in the diagnosis or treatment of a disease or intended to affect the structure or any function of the body. A medical device's effect on the body is not chemical. Unlike a drug, a medical device is not dependent on being consumed and metabolized by the body in order to have an effect. Some examples of medical devices include defibrillators, pacemakers, heart valves, contact lenses, hearing aids, tampons, and breast implants.

## The Food and Drug Administration

The Food and Drug Administration (FDA) is an agency of the federal government. It is part of the Department of Health and Human Services. The primary purposes of the FDA are to protect the public health and, at the same time, provide the public access to important new drugs and medical devices. It attempts to do so by regulating the manufacture, packaging, labeling, advertising, sale, and use of therapeutic drugs and medical devices in the United States.

The agency originated with passage of the Food and Drug Act of 1906, enacted by Congress to regulate questionable advertising claims made by patent medicine companies and to prevent drugs sold in the United States from being mislabeled or adulterated.

In 1938, shortly after more than one hundred people died as a result of taking "Elixir Sulfanilamide," a solution consisting of an antibiotic in a poisonous solvent, Congress passed the Food, Drug and Cosmetic Act. Under the Act, drug manufacturers were, for the first time, required to notify the FDA before placing new drugs on the market so the FDA could assess their safety. The measure also authorized the FDA to take action against adulterated or misbranded medical devices, as the agency had been authorized to do since 1906 with respect to drugs.

The first major amendment to the 1938 Food, Drug and Cosmetic Act came in 1962 in response to the tragedy surrounding the use of the drug thalidomide in Europe. The drug, it was discovered, caused birth defects. Unfortunately, the link between the drug and birth defects was not realized until literally thousands of deformed babies were born in Europe, the sons and daughters of women who had taken the medication. A similar tragedy was avoided in the United States because the FDA had not approved use of the drug. In light of the tragedy, however, Congress changed the premarket-notification-of-safety requirement in the Food, Drug and Cosmetic Act. The FDA was given premarket approval of the safety and effectiveness of every new drug proposed to be sold in the United States.

Subsequent amendments to the Act have primarily addressed the FDA's authority with respect to medical devices. In 1976 Congress gave the FDA the power of premarket approval over certain types of medical devices. In 1990 the FDA was granted the authority to recall medical devices from the marketplace. Prior to that time, the FDA had to negotiate with a medical device's manufacturer to remove a product from the market. Finally, also in 1990, Congress passed an amendment to the Act requiring health care facilities using medical devices to report to the FDA incidents in which it is reasonably probable that a medical device caused or contributed to the death, serious illness, or serious injury of a patient.

The FDA's authority to determine the safety and effectiveness of all new drugs, and certain types of medical devices, and to grant or deny a manufacturer the right to market them in the United States is, perhaps, the FDA's most important power. The FDA will deny a manufacturer's application for premarket approval of a new drug if, in the opinion of the agency, (1) the testing summarized in the application is inadequate to show that the drug is safe for use under the conditions recommended in its labeling, or (2) the manufacturer fails to provide substantial evidence that the drug will have the effect it is represented to have under the conditions of use suggested in the proposed labeling.

Only medical devices that are life-supporting or -sustaining or that potentially pose an unreasonable risk of illness or injury to patients require preapproval. Like the manufacturer of a new drug, the manufacturer of a new medical device must prove to the FDA that the device is safe and effective. In recognition of differences between drugs and medical devices that pose practical obstacles to large-scale clinical testing of the latter, however, the FDA may not require controlled clinical studies to document the safety and effectiveness of medical devices. The medical device manufacturer need only provide the FDA reasonable assurance of the device's safety.

Some people question whether the FDA's regulations regarding new drugs and new medical devices indicate that the agency considers it more important to protect the public health than to ensure that new drugs and devices are made available. The process manufacturers must go through to obtain FDA approval of new drugs and devices often takes years. During that process, drug and medical device developers and manufacturers bear the cost of the required animal research and clinical trials. Moreover, even if a drug or device is approved by the FDA, its manufacturer can still be held liable to persons who experience an adverse reaction. FDA standards only serve as a minimum floor below which a manufacturer's product cannot fall. Consequently, juries have decided warnings given by a drug manufacturer were deficient and have held the drug manufacturer liable, even though the FDA mandated the precise wording of the warnings. One drug manufacturer was found liable for providing an inadequate warning concerning a drug even though the manufacturer had requested the FDA to allow it to change the warning and the FDA had denied the manufacturer's request.

## RU-486

It is no coincidence that the most publicized advance in human reproductive medicine, RU-486, was developed by a French company. RU-486, also known as mifepristone, can be used as a "morning-after" birth control pill and is capable of inducing an abortion within the first trimester of pregnancy. Although it is available in France, the United Kingdom, Sweden, and China, the French manufacturer of the drug has declined, to date, to request FDA approval to market the drug in the United States.

The French manufacturer's reluctance to attempt to break into the American market is traceable to a number of factors. One of the company's primary concerns is the reaction of pro-life constituencies, including the possibility that other drugs made by the company and sold in the United States may be boycotted by pro-life adherents. Another concern is certainly the fact that, even though more than 100,000 women have already used RU-486, the Food, Drug and Cosmetic Act and the regulations relating to premarket approval of new drugs by the FDA would require the manufacturer to begin the FDA's approval process at square one—with animal studies. Even if the process were to begin immediately, the company could not hope to begin marketing the drug for years.

At the same time, there is a great deal of interest and demand among American women for access to the drug. Approximately a million and a half abortions are performed in the United States every year. Reports by women of their experiences using RU-486, as compared with the experience of an abortion by traditional surgical methods, indicates a preference for RU-486. Women report that it is less painful and more private than a surgical abortion. RU-486 is also significantly less expensive than traditional procedures. Statistics compiled to date indicate that the drug is at least as safe as a surgical abortion. Moreover, in a recent poll approximately 90 percent of physicians who currently perform abortions indicated they would administer RU-486 to their patients instead of performing surgical abortions, if the drug were available.

## Breast Implants

If the situation involving RU-486 is an example of the FDA's emphasis on protecting the public health at the expense of making drugs available, the current controversy concerning silicone gel-filled breast implants serves as an example of the agency's inability to act quickly enough to remove what may be a dangerous product from the marketplace. Case studies and research reports in the news over the last twenty years describe a litany of health problems that may be associated with silicone gel implants, including skin rashes, swollen breasts, hardened breasts, severe joint pain, chronic fatigue, and disorders of the immune system. These, and other health problems are thought to result from the tendency of implants to leak or burst, releasing silicone which may then migrate to other parts of the body. In addition, many oncologists contend that breast implants make mammograms difficult, if not impossible to read, impairing physicians' ability to detect tumors in breast tissue at an early stage when breast cancer is most treatable.

Between 1916 and 1960, various substances were tried and discarded in the quest to find a material suitable for use in reconstruction or augmentation of the female breast. Physicians tried body fat; glass balls; transformer coolant, a kind of liquid silicone which was the forerunner of "Silly Putty"; polyurethane, polyethylene, and spongelike materials. Each material produced an unnatural feel and form, along with medical side-effects and other physical complications. Silicone gel-filled breast implants were first used in the early 1960s.

Dow Corning was the first company to experiment with liquid silicone. It received permission from the FDA to conduct studies using animals and human beings in 1965. Due to concern for safety, the FDA revoked Dow's permission to conduct the research in 1967, but reinstated permission in 1969 when Dow agreed to stop injecting liquid silicone directly into women's breasts.

When the FDA was first authorized to regulate and preapprove new medical devices in 1976, silicone gel-filled breast implants were already on the market. Although, beginning in 1976, the FDA had the power to require breast implant devices to be tested and proven safe and effective, it exempted implants from testing because they were in widespread use and were, at that time, extremely popular.

Dow apparently had some evidence linking silicone breast implants to autoimmune system disease as early as 1978. These findings were reported to the FDA, but the agency did nothing to require further study or to require manufacturers of breast implants to provide the agency with safety data until the 1980s.

In 1988, the FDA ordered manufacturers of silicone gel breast implants to submit detailed scientific data by 1991 proving product safety, in order to keep implants on the market. After receiving and reviewing the data submitted by implant manufacturers, and after holding hearings concerning the issue of product safety, the FDA ordered a moratorium on silicone gel breast implants in April of 1992. Currently, only women participating in clinical trials and women requiring reconstructive surgery, due to breast cancer, for example, have access to silicone gel breast implants.

The publicity surrounding the silicone gel breast implant controversy has led some people to suggest that medical product safety testing should not be left in the hands of product manufacturers. Rather, they argue, the FDA's authority should be expanded to enable the agency to conduct clinical trials, or to use objective research consultants to perform that task. Short of that, many commentators advocate giving the FDA the power to compel drug manufacturers, by subpoena, to disclose to the agency all documents in the manufacturers' possession relating to a particular drug or device that is suspected of being unsafe.

Like the individual patient harmed by the negligence of her **Product Liability**
physician, the patient who has an adverse reaction from a defective or unreasonably dangerous drug or medical device can sue to
recover damages. In many cases, such a patient has a malpractice
claim against the health care provider who prescribed the drug in
question or who applied or implanted the particular medical device in treating the patient. But the patient harmed by a defective
drug or medical device may also have a claim against the manufacturer of the drug or device. The type of lawsuit typically filed
by a patient against the maker of a therapeutic drug or medical
device is called a product liability action.

The history and development of the law relating to product liability is complex and impossible to summarize in a few sentences. The
essential idea behind the law of product liability is that a manufacturer
is liable when a product it places on the market proves to have a
defect that causes damage to human beings. A product liability action
requires proof that the product was defective, and it may or may not
require proof of the manufacturer's negligence.

Product defects generally fall into one of three categories:

- A product flaw resulting from the manufacturer's failure to make
  the product according to specifications

- A design defect rendering the product unsafe even though it
  meets the manufacturer's specifications

- A defect in the warnings or instructions given by the manufacturer concerning the potential dangers inherent in each of the
  foreseeable uses to which the product can be put

If state law requires a patient to prove a manufacturer's negligence, the patient has to demonstrate each of the elements of negligence (see the section of this chapter discussing malpractice actions).
Generally, the manufacturer of a drug or medical device has a duty to
the public as a whole to produce products that are reasonably safe.
The following factors should be taken into account:

- The foreseeable uses of the product

- The potential for harm that the product may cause

- The usefulness of the product to consumers

If a manufacturer breaches that duty and, as a direct result of its breach,
a patient is harmed, the manufacturer is liable to the patient in damages.

Some states hold product manufacturers strictly liable if a person
is harmed by a defective product. Strict liability means that the manufacturer is liable, regardless of the degree of care it exercises or whether

it knew, or could not have known, of the defect during the manufacturing process.

A patient who wins a product liability action can recover compensatory damages and, in some states, punitive damages from the manufacturer of a defective drug or medical device. Damage awards in product liability cases are often very large. One manufacturer of a childhood vaccine was ordered to pay a punitive damage award of more than two hundred times the company's annual revenue generated by sales of the vaccine. The damages awarded to tens of thousands of patients who used the Dalkon Shield, an intrauterine contraceptive device that caused, among other health problems, pelvic inflammatory disease, infertility, and sterility, exceeded $2.3 billion and bankrupted the manufacturer of the device, the A. H. Robins company.

A more recent example, which promises to assume the proportions of the Dalkon Shield case, is the increasing number of lawsuits against manufacturers of silicone gel breast implants. Implant makers were sued prior to 1990, but patients complaining that the implants caused their health problems seldom prevailed in court. The first big damage award in a breast implant case was obtained from a San Francisco federal court jury in December of 1991. The $7.3 million verdict was based upon the jury's conclusion that the implant manufacturer, Dow Corning, was aware of, but actively concealed, evidence linking ruptures of the implants to immune disorders. Almost exactly one year later, a Houston woman won a $25 million verdict against Bristol-Myers Squibb Co., another silicone gel breast implant manufacturer. Another company, Mentor Corporation, was recently reported to have paid a total of $24 million to women suing it for damages caused by breast implants marketed by the company, and agreed, as part of the settlement, to stop making breast implants.

Literally thousands of the one million women who are estimated to have had silicone gel breast implant surgery since the early 1960s have filed lawsuits in courts all over the United States. There is little doubt that, given the severity of the problems many women have experienced and the size of recent damage awards, the number of lawsuits will continue to grow.

Although such awards are intended to punish the manufacturers of defective products, they also have the effects of decreasing the availability of drugs and medical devices and increasing their cost. For example, as a result of the high frequency of product liability actions, the number of companies making childhood vaccines has declined to the point where, for some vaccines, only a single supplier remains. At the same time, the cost per dose of such vaccines has increased dramatically. Between 1982 and 1986, the cost per dose of the diphtheria-tetanus-pertussis vaccine increased from eleven cents to eleven dollars and forty cents. Eight dollars of the cost increase reportedly reflects the cost of the company's liability insurance.

Health care laws touch and affect the most intimate and personal ethical, moral, and religious issues facing us individually and collectively: birth, life, and death. Clearly, we as a society have not reached a consensus concerning whether the right to self-determination should have limits and, if so, where those limits should begin and end. Health care law, like most bodies of law, is reactive. As technology improves and as societal values change and evolve, health law must adapt if it is to remain relevant.

**Conclusion**

## Notes

1. *Schloendorff v. Society of New York Hospital,* 211 N.Y. 125, 105 N.E. 92, 95 (1914).
2. A minor's next-of-kin are her family members. In their order of priority, after the parents, a minor's next-of-kin are her adult brothers and sisters, her grandparents, and her aunts and uncles. An adult patient's next-of-kin, in order of priority after her husband, are her adult sons and daughters, her parents, her adult brothers and sisters, her grandparents, and her aunts and uncles.
3. The common law is the body of law and legal theory that originated and developed in England prior to the 1700s. It is a body of principles derived from decisions made from courts. The "common law" can be contrasted with laws passed by legislatures. Most of the individual states in the United States recognize "common law" principles and incorporate them into modern law and legal codes.
4. 551 P.2d 334 (Cal. 1976).

## Bibliography

(See also the resource list at the end of chapter 3.)

Doukas, David. *Planning for Uncertainty: Wills and Other Advance Directives for Health Care.* Baltimore: Johns Hopkins University Press, 1993.

DuBoff, Leonard D. *The Law (in Plain English) for Health Care Professionals.* New York: John Wiley & Sons, 1993.

Eisenstein, Zilla R. *The Female Body and the Law.* Berkeley: University of California Press, 1989.

Hall, Mark A., and Ira M. Ellman. *Health Care Law and Bioethics in a Nutshell.* Denver: West Publishing, 1992.

Isaacs, Stephen L., and Ava C. Swartz. *The Consumer's Legal Guide to Today's Health Care: Your Medical Rights and How to Assert Them.* Boston: Houghton Mifflin, 1992.

Rees, Alan M. *Consumer Health USA: Essential Information from the Federal Health Network*. Phoenix: Oryx Press, 1995. Reprints 151 federal government publications that provide answers to health questions most frequently asked by the general public. Comprehensive listing of documents available to the public, as well as agencies, with addresses and phone numbers.

Rozovsky, Fay A. *Consent to Treatment: A Practical Guide, 2d ed.* New York: Little, Brown, 1989.

### Organizational Resources
(See chapter 3.)

---

**Linda W. Rohman** received a B.A. degree in 1976 from the University of Missouri at Columbia, graduating magna cum laude with honors in psychology. She received her J.D. from the University of Nebraska at Lincoln in 1982 and a Ph.D. in psychology from that university in 1987. Rohman is a member of the Lincoln, Nebraska, and American Bar Associations. She is an attorney in practice with Erickson & Sederstrom, P.C., a law firm in Lincoln, where her main emphasis is in litigation with a concentration in health and utilities law.

**Penny L. Huber** graduated cum laude with a B.A. from the University of South Dakota in 1991. She received her J.D. from the University of Nebraska in 1994 and currently resides in Denver, Colorado, where she is a Westlaw Account Representative for West Publishing Company.

Chapter 3

# Reproduction and the Law

Linda W. Rohman and Penny L. Huber

Chapter Outline

**Introduction**      Women have the unique ability to bear children and consequently may be faced with the decision of how, if, and when to have a child. Relatively recent legalization of contraception and abortion, as well as technological advances in infertility treatment, highlight a woman's decision-making responsibility.

**Contraception**      Before the mid-1960s, it was not unusual for state law to prohibit or restrict the use of contraceptives. In 1965, for example, it was still a crime in the state of Connecticut for any person to use "any drug, medicinal article or instrument for the purpose of preventing conception." The U.S. Supreme Court made history when, in *Griswold v. Connecticut*,[1] it struck down the Connecticut statute as an unconstitutional invasion of the right to privacy.

Today a state cannot restrict the use of contraceptives by married or unmarried adults. Many states expressly authorize minors to obtain contraceptives without the prior knowledge or consent of their parents. In addition, certain federally funded family planning programs mandate confidential services to teens. The U.S. Supreme Court has held that minors have a consitutional right to purchase over-the-counter contraceptives.

**Abortion**      Abortion is a medical procedure which is intended to terminate a woman's pregnancy and to produce a nonviable fetus at any stage of gestation. (This is the definition according to the Centers for Disease Control. Note that abortion methods *extract* as well as *expel* the fetus and may be performed *after* the fetus would be viable *if* born.) There is a great deal of controversy concerning the moral and ethical aspects of the procedure. There are those who argue that, at the point of conception, a human life is created and, consequently, abortion is equivalent to murder. This "pro-life" contingent advocates making abortion illegal except, possibly, in cases of rape or incest or in cases where the pregnancy poses a threat to the mother's life.

Others insist that a fetus is not legally a "person" until some later stage of its development, for example, at viability, the point it becomes capable of surviving outside the womb, or at birth. This "pro-choice" group advocates keeping abortion legal and leaving the choice of continuing or terminating a pregnancy to the woman.

The U.S. Supreme Court decisions shaping the law as it applies to abortion have not decided the moral issues dividing the pro-life and pro-choice viewpoints. The Court has not determined when life begins. It has held, however, that a fetus is not a person for constitutional purposes. Historically, the Court's approach has been to balance the interest each woman has in her own self-determination, her "right to privacy," with the interests society has in protecting public health and in preserving potential human life.

In 1973 the U.S. Supreme Court decided the landmark case *Roe v. Wade.*[2] In *Roe,* an unmarried pregnant woman challenged the validity of a Texas state law prohibiting abortions except in cases where the procedure was necessary to save the life of the mother. She argued, and the Court agreed, that a law preventing a woman from obtaining an abortion violated her right of privacy as guaranteed by the U.S. Constitution.

Although not specifically provided for in the Constitution, the "right of privacy" is viewed as part of the liberty guaranteed by the Fourteenth Amendment, prohibiting the states from making any laws which "deprive any person of life, liberty, or property without due process of law." In cases decided before *Roe,* the Court had recognized that certain aspects of an individual's life are so intimate and personal that state intrusion amounts to a violation of a person's right to liberty. In *Roe,* the Court concluded that the matter of deciding whether or not to carry a pregnancy to term is one of those intimate and personal issues.

However, the right of privacy is not absolute. It must be balanced against states' legitimate interests in regulation including, in the case of abortion, protecting the health of the mother and protecting the potential for human life represented by the fetus. According to the Court in *Roe,* the importance of states' interests varies, depending on how far pregnancy has progressed. Pregnancy was broken down into three trimesters and a different ruled applied to each.

During the first trimester of pregnancy, the chances that a pregnant woman would suffer serious health problems or death were greater if the woman carried the fetus to term than if she obtains an abortion.* For that reason, the *Roe* Court concluded that a state's interest in protecting the health of the mother could not justify restricting her access to abortion during the first three months of her pregnancy. Because the fetus is not sufficiently developed during the first trimester to exist independently from the mother, even with artificial support, the states' interest in protecting the potential for human life represented by the fetus could not, in the opinion of the court, support the restriction either.

Because abortion involves more risk to a woman after the first trimester of her pregnancy, the *Roe* Court considered the states' interest in protecting women's health to be stronger, justifying some regulation of women's access to abortion. On that basis, the *Roe* Court concluded that states could pass laws whose purpose was to protect women's health during and after the second trimester. For example, a state could require that abortions performed at a certain point in the second trimester of pregnancy be performed at certain facilities, such

---

*Today abortion is safer than childbirth at *all* stages of pregnancy.

as ambulatory surgi-centers or hospitals, rather than in a clinic if the state could show such restrictions are necessary to protect maternal health. (Note that hospitalization for *all* second trimester abortions was ruled unconstitutional in *City of Akron v. Akron Center for Reproductive Health, Inc.*) However, during the second trimester, protection of the fetus continued to be viewed as an inadequate basis for imposing restrictions on a woman's right to terminate a pregnancy, and states could not bar abortions during that period.

The Court in *Roe* felt that the states' interests outweighed the individual woman's interest in self-determination when a fetus becomes viable, at some point during the third trimester of pregnancy. In the opinion of the *Roe* Court, at viability the states' interest in protecting the fetus becomes very strong because the fetus is capable of living apart from its mother. Consequently, after viability, a state could legally prohibit abortions, except when abortion is necessary for the woman's health.

For nearly twenty years the landmark case of *Roe v. Wade* provided the basis for the laws relating to the regulation of and access to legal abortion. According to the *Roe* Court, the extent to which a state could regulate abortion depended upon how far the pregnancy had progressed. During the first trimester, the state could impose no restrictions on access to abortion. Some regulations were permissible during and after the second trimester to protect the woman's health. Finally, a state could prohibit abortions entirely when the fetus is viable, approximately the last three months of pregnancy, but may never prohibit abortions necessary to preserve the woman's health.

Then, in 1992, the U.S. Supreme Court decided *Planned Parenthood of Southeastern Pennsylvania v. Casey*[3] and, in doing so, abandoned the trimester approach it had so carefully developed in *Roe,* replacing that approach with the "undue burden" standard.

Under this standard, a state may not enact any law which unduly burdens a woman's ability to abort a nonviable fetus. A state's law constitutes an undue burden if the law's purpose or effect is to place "a substantial obstacle in the path" of a woman who wants to have an abortion prior to viability. However, most laws that merely make obtaining an abortion more costly and time-consuming are not considered unduly burdensome. Rather, the Court views such laws as "structural mechanisms" that further the state's profound interest in human life.

The following are examples of laws that various state legislatures have enacted, or may be considering, which do not "unduly burden" access to abortion:

1. Parental notification and/or consent. Laws requiring that one or both of the parents of a woman under the age of eighteen be notified before she can obtain an abortion were valid, even before *Casey.* In

*Casey,* the Supreme Court approved a law requiring a minor to get the prior consent of one of her parents. However, laws requiring parental notification or consent must also make a "judicial bypass" available for those young women who choose not to, or cannot, notify their parents or obtain consent. A "judicial bypass" is a process young women can use to obtain a court order waiving the parental notice or consent requirement if she can persuade a judge that she is mature enough to give an informed consent to the procedure for herself and that an abortion is in her best interests. In addition, parental notice and consent requirements must be suspended in the case of a medical emergency. (State courts in California and Florida have ruled such laws violative of state consitutions.)

2. Informed consent/waiting period. The Pennsylvania statute approved in *Casey* provided that no abortion could be performed, except in the case of a medical emergency, unless the woman's physician, at least twenty-four hours prior to the abortion, had supplied her with information regarding the nature of the procedure, the approximate gestational age of the fetus, the health risks of both abortion and childbirth, and the availability of printed materials describing the fetus and listing alternatives to abortion.

3. Record-keeping and reporting requirements. States can require facilities that perform abortions to file certain reports, listing items such as the identity of the doctor, the woman's age, the number of prior pregnancies and prior abortions she has had, gestational age of the fetus at the time of the abortion, and other medical information. The names of the women who obtain the abortions are not included. Laws requiring such reports are considered valid because the information aids medical research, but confidentiality must be maintained, so that the woman's identity is not revealed to the public.

4. Prohibiting the use of state funds to pay for abortions. Federal Medicaid funds are currently prohibited from being used to pay for abortions unless the procedure is necessary to protect the life of the mother or in cases of rape and incest. The individual states can similarly prohibit the use of state funds, and most do, but they are not required to do so. (Recently, some state courts have struck down such funding bans because they are held to violate state constitutions.)

5. Viability testing. A Missouri law requiring a woman to undergo tests to determine the viability of the fetus if the gestational stage is suspected to be twenty weeks or more has been upheld.

A state, however, cannot pass a law requiring a married woman to obtain her husband's consent or notify him before having an abortion. A woman does not lose her constitutionally based liberty to make choices for herself simply because she marries. Although the father of an unborn child has an interest in the life of the fetus, his interest is not considered equal to the mother's, because she bears the physical responsibility of pregnancy. Moreover, a spousal notice or consent law could prevent a woman involved in an abusive marriage from obtaining an abortion out of fear for her own physical safety.

In summary, the primary focus continues to be on the point of viability, that stage in the pregnancy where the fetus is able to survive outside the mother's body, with either natural or artificial support systems. States have the ability to enact laws providing for a ban on all abortions after the fetus reaches viability, but an exception must be provided where the health of the mother is at stake. Although *Casey* has increased the ability of individual states to enact laws placing limits on a woman's access to a legal abortion, women continue to have the constitutional right to make the ultimate decision.

## Sterilization

Sterilization refers to the various surgical procedures used to incapacitate the human reproductive system. Male sterilization is usually achieved by a vasectomy, severing the ducts between the gonads and the genitourinary tract that the sperm flows through. Female sterilization is typically accomplished through one of two different surgical procedures: salpingectomy and hysterectomy. A salpingectomy, or tubal ligation, involves severing the fallopian tubes between the ovaries and the uterus. A hysterectomy is a more radical procedure, involving the removal of the uterus.

Sterilizations historically have been performed for three general reasons:

1. Involuntary sterilization performed on certain individuals including mentally incompetent persons and, in some states, habitual criminals, particularly sex offenders.

2. Therapeutic sterilization performed when the risk of pregnancy is a threat to a woman's health.

3. Voluntary sterilizations performed at the request of the patients, usually as a form of contraception.

Historically, most of the litigation involving sterilization involved involuntary or "eugenic" sterilization of mental incompetence and habitual sex offenders. Under modern law, involuntary sterilization of criminal sex offenders is unconstitutional. However, the procedure is authorized by statute in approximately twenty states and permitted under the common law in a few others. In the other half of the fifty states, involuntary sterilization of any person is not legal and would subject the persons performing the procedure to criminal and civil liability.

Where it is legal, involuntary sterilization is strictly governed by law. A request, often initiated by next-of-kin or the person's guardian, usually must be accompanied by a physician's certification regarding the need for the surgery. The request is reviewed by a court or special administrative body, with a right to appeal to a higher court to contest the initial ruling.

Recently, as voluntary sterilization has become a more common method of birth control, a number of cases have reached the courts involving claims against physicians for performing sterilizations that prove ineffective. These cases are characterized as "wrongful conception," "wrongful pregnancy," or "wrongful birth" claims. In each case, one member of a couple underwent an operation to render him or her sterile, but the female partner became pregnant at some point after the surgery. The couple's claim against the surgeon is usually prosecuted in an effort by the couple to recover damages for the costs of raising a child they did not want.

Although the courts have treated such claims differently, depending on the factual circumstances involved in each case and depending on state law, in general, couples able to prove negligence on the part of the surgeon have obtained damage awards. However, courts typically do not require the surgeon to pay the entire cost for the couple to raise the child. Most courts consider the benefits derived by the couple from being the parents of a healthy child to outweigh child-rearing costs.

## Genetic Screening and Counseling

A medical procedure called "amniocentesis" was developed during the 1960s and 1970s. The procedure involves the insertion of a long, hollow needle into the uterus. A sample of the amniotic fluid surrounding the fetus is extracted. The fluid contains fetal cells. Those cells can be studied to see whether the fetus has any genetic abnormalities. The test results are extremely accurate and the risk of any significant complications to the pregnancy as a result of the procedure is very low. The procedure is recommended for women age thirty-five and over, women with a history of multiple miscarriages, and women with certain genetic indications.

Before the *Roe* decision in 1973, in most states, physicians who detected genetic defects through the use of amniocentesis could offer their patients no legal alternative to carrying the pregnancy to term. Legalization of abortion in 1973 eliminated this dilemma, at least for previable fetuses.

It is not unusual for couples who know they are, or suspect they might be, at risk of bearing children with genetic defects to request assurance, through genetic testing, that their child is developing normally in the womb. If the testing is done negligently, or the results are misinterpreted, and prospective parents are informed the fetus is normal when it is not, the parents may have a legal claim against the physician who performed the test or interpreted the results.

Three different types of claims have been asserted by parents in lawsuits against doctors who provided inadequate or inaccurate information to women at risk of bearing children with genetic defects:

1. "Wrongful birth" claims by parents who would not have conceived or carried the pregnancy to term had they known of the possibility they would have a baby with a genetic defect.

2. Emotional distress claims by parents who must witness their child's suffering and, often, death.

3. "Wrongful life" claims asserted by the parents on behalf of the child, contending that the child would not have been born but for the negligence of the physician.

Courts in most states have recognized "wrongful birth" and emotional distress claims by parents. In those cases, parents have been able to recover damages measured by medical expenses incurred, and to be incurred during the child's expected lifetime, over and above those that would be expected for a normal, healthy child. In a few cases, parents have been able to recover damages for their own emotional anguish.

No state has recognized a child's "wrongful life" claim. They reason that it is never better for the individual not to have been born than to have been born with handicaps. In fact, statutes in several states expressly prohibit cases grounded on the argument that, but for the negligence of a physician, the fetus would have been aborted, thus eliminating both wrongful birth and wrongful life claims.

## Substance Abuse During Pregnancy

Most states have laws proscribing child abuse or neglect, child endangerment, and delivery of controlled substances, such as marijuana or cocaine, to minors. Prosecutors in several states have recently begun to charge women who abuse drugs during their pregnancies with violations of these and other laws. These laws aim to control behaviors during pregnancy that may be harmful to women's babies.

The majority of cases tried to date have involved cocaine addicts. Some courts have held that babies born addicted to cocaine or heroin are "abused" and that their mothers are guilty of child abuse. In other instances, women who use illicit drugs during pregnancy have been charged with child neglect. Moreover, evidence of substance abuse during pregnancy may be the sole basis of a court's order terminating the parental rights of the addict/mother.

Certain states have accused and prosecuted women who use a drug shortly before giving birth for "delivering a controlled substance" to their child. In one such case, a woman who had ingested cocaine the night before she gave birth was charged with violating a state law prohibiting the delivery of a controlled substance to a minor. The prosecutor contended that the woman had "delivered" cocaine or a cocaine derivative to her baby through the blood flowing in the umbilical cord during the thirty to ninety seconds after birth but before the cord was clamped. The Florida Supreme Court reversed the woman's conviction, stating that the law prohibiting delivery of drugs to a minor was never intended to apply to such a situation.

Similarly, an Ohio court refused to find a woman guilty of child endangerment based on her cocaine use during the last trimester of pregnancy, stating that such a ruling would "mean that every expectant mother who ingested a substance with the potential of harm to her child, e.g., alcohol or nicotine, would be criminally liable under [the child endangering statute]."

Opponents of the trend predict that bringing criminal charges against women who use drugs during pregnancy will have an adverse impact on the overall welfare of the family. Health care professionals fear that addicted pregnant women will be deterred from seeking prenatal care. Similarly, criminal prosecution may discourage those women who do consult a doctor from providing the doctor accurate information. The mother's failure to disclose all pertinent information to her doctor may jeopardize both her and the baby's health. Finally, women who use drugs may abort their pregnancies in order to avoid the possibility of criminal prosecution.

Many argue that the imposition of criminal sanctions on these women is misplaced since mothers rarely, if ever, ingest drugs with the purpose of harming their fetus. Rather, any harm done to the fetus occurs as a result of the mother's need to satisfy her addiction. As stated by the American Medical Association Board of Trustees, "If a pregnant woman suffers from a substance dependency, it is the physical impossibility of avoiding an impact on fetal health that causes severe damage to the fetus, not an intentional or malicious wish to cause harm." These women are arguably unable to make rational decisions about their drug use and its possible effects on their unborn children. Consequently, prosecuting and punishing such women may not actually deter them from abusing substances during pregnancy because, by definition, addicts lack the ability to resist, on their own, the urge to feed their addiction.

## Surrogacy Contracts

Recent advancements in reproductive technology have led couples unable to conceive children to enlist the aid of other women who function as surrogates. The term "surrogate" is used to refer to a woman who becomes pregnant and gives birth to a baby for the purpose of providing a couple, of which the surrogate is not a member, with a child. Typically, the arrangement occurs when one woman and her partner are unable to have children due to the woman's infertility or inability to carry a pregnancy to term.

A variety of organizations are currently in the business of bringing childless couples and surrogate mothers together. After matching infertile couples and surrogates, these businesses explain the surrogacy procedure to the parties and provide form contracts that set out the terms of the surrogacy agreement. The content of such an agreement varies, depending on the context in which it arises. In most cases, however, surrogates are compensated for their services; the couples pay the surrogates' medical expenses; and the businesses receive a fee for brokering the arrangement.

The use of surrogacy agreements has raised interesting legal and ethical questions regarding the definition of "parenthood." Disputes arise when the surrogate has a change of heart during her pregnancy or after the birth of the child and refuses to relinquish the child to the couple who "hired" her as a surrogate.

The American public became aware of the practice of surrogacy and the potential problems associated with its use through the publicity surrounding the case of "Baby M." The Baby M[4] case involved William and Elizabeth Stern, a married couple who were unable to have a child due to the wife's infertility. The Sterns became acquainted with Mary Beth Whitehead through the Infertility Center of New York (ICNY), an organization that solicited women to become surrogate mothers and informed infertile couples about the option of surrogacy.

With the aid of ICNY, Mr. Stern and Mrs. Whitehead entered into a contract, agreeing that Mrs. Whitehead would become pregnant through artificial insemination using Stern's sperm. Whitehead agreed to carry the fetus, give birth to the baby, and then relinquish her parental rights to the child enabling Mrs. Stern to become the child's legal parent through adoption. Under the surrogacy contract, Stern was obligated to pay Whitehead ten thousand dollars after the baby's birth, upon her surrender of the baby to him. In addition, Stern paid ICNY seventy-five hundred dollars.

After undergoing artificial insemination, Whitehead became pregnant, and on March 27, 1986, she gave birth to a baby girl. Three days later she gave the baby to the Sterns. The following day, however, an emotionally distraught Whitehead went to the Sterns' home and begged them to let her have the baby for one week. The Sterns granted her request, believing that Whitehead would return the baby within a week. Whitehead, however, fled the state, taking the baby with her. The Sterns were not reunited with the child until four months later, after the police forcibly removed the child from the home of Whitehead's parents in Florida. The Sterns filed a lawsuit, asking for legal custody of the child and asking the court to order Whitehead to relinquish all parental rights to the child as she had promised to do when she signed the surrogacy contract.

The court ruled that surrogacy contracts are invalid and unenforceable in the state of New Jersey, because they conflict with the state's adoption laws and violate public policy. Before a legal adoption can take place, the biological parent's rights to the child have to be terminated. According to New Jersey law at the time, however, parental rights could not be terminated unless (1) the parent(s) (in this case Mrs. Whitehead) voluntarily surrendered the child to an approved agency, or (2) there was a showing of parental abandonment or unfitness.

Because Whitehead did not voluntarily surrender the child to an approved agency and there was no indication she was an unfit parent, her parental rights could not legally be terminated. Consequently, Mrs. Stern could not adopt the child. The court, however, determined that it was in the best interest of the child for custody to be granted to Mr. Stern. Whitehead, as the child's biological mother, was granted liberal visitation rights.

A decisive consideration in the Baby M case was the fact that the surrogacy contract between the Sterns and Whitehead violated laws proscribing the exchange of money in adoptions. New Jersey's laws prohibited the use of money in adoptions, except for payment of approved agency fees and medical expenses. Thus, a surrogacy contract, like the Sterns' with Whitehead, requiring the payment of money to a woman on the condition that she relinquish her parental rights and allow her child to be adopted, was illegal. The court specifically stated that its opinion should not be construed to prohibit a woman from voluntarily serving as a surrogate mother, as long as no payment was involved and she was not bound to an agreement that forced her to give up her parental rights.

The legal question in Baby M turned on the fact that Whitehead was biologically related to the child born pursuant to the surrogacy agreement. But there is no biological relationship between a surrogate and the child she bears if the surrogate does not contribute the egg for fertilization. How docs this affect the legal outcome?

In *Johnson v. Calvert,*[5] a surrogate agreed to allow an embryo, formed from the husband's sperm and the wife's egg, to be implanted in her uterus. The agreement provided that the surrogate carry the fetus to term, give birth, and turn the baby over to the couple, to be raised as their child. Such an arrangement is often referred to as gestational surrogacy. In exchange for the surrogate's services, the couple was to pay her ten thousand dollars and provide her with a two-hundred-thousand-dollar life insurance policy. A month after the embryo was implanted in the surrogate, tests confirmed that she was indeed pregnant.

Approximately six months into the pregnancy, a dispute arose between the parties. Even though the husband and wife were clearly the genetic parents of the baby, the surrogate contended she should be regarded as the child's mother because she carried and would give birth to the child. The court ruled that in a situation where the genetic mother and the birth mother are not the same, California law dictates that the woman who intended to bring about the birth of the child and raise it as her own is the "natural mother." Thus, the wife, who had entered into the surrogacy agreement with the intent of raising the baby as her own was held to be the child's legal and natural mother.

The Calvert court rejected the argument that surrogacy contracts violate California's laws prohibiting the payment of money in adoptions. It contrasted gestational surrogacy with adoption, stating that a gestational surrogate is not paid for the termination of her parental rights, but for the services she provides in carrying the fetus and going through labor (renting her womb, if you will).

Surrogacy agreements are widely criticized as being harmful to children and exploitative of women. Many critics of surrogacy contracts argue that paying a woman to bear a child, and then give it away, is analogous to buying and selling the child. The fear is that babies will become mere commodities in commercial transactions brokered by businesses that coordinate the matching of infertile couples and surrogate mothers for high fees. One court has referred to such organizations as "a middle man, propelled by profit" who "promotes the sale."

An additional concern is that couples may obtain custody of babies through surrogacy without any real determination of what is in the best interest of the child. Rather, the terms of the surrogacy agreement are based solely on the wants and desires of the contracting parties. The fear is that, regardless of the relative fitness of two or more infertile couples to be parents, babies will go to the couple who can pay the highest price. Additionally, little regard is given for the possible effects of a child's discovery, in later years, that a woman gave birth to him or her for the purpose of financial gain.

Some people contend that surrogacy contracts exploit women, reducing them to mere "breeding machines" who are paid for their reproductive services. As one Kentucky justice stated in a dissenting opinion, "...the consequences which could arise from the opening of the human uterus to commercial medical technology does not contribute to the emancipation of women." Another concern is that widespread use of such agreements would affect poor women disproportionately. Financially insecure women may be induced to become pregnant and surrender their maternal rights for money.

The opposite view is that women are more than capable of making decisions regarding their bodies, and any effort to outlaw surrogacy agreements only perpetuates the antiquated notion that women need someone else to decide what is best for them.

## Property Rights and the Human Body

Advancements in medical technology have raised new questions about the nature of each person's interest in her own body, both the individual organs and tissues that make up the body and genetic material, such as ova, sperm, embryos, and fetuses, produced by the body. Legal disputes have arisen between people competing for custody and control (ownership, if you will) of the body, bodily organs, or genetic products of a deceased human being. At least one couple has vied, in the context of divorce proceedings, for custody of embryos formed from genetic material taken from each of their bodies. At the heart of these legal controversies are the following questions:

- Is the human body, its parts, and its products property?

- If so, whose property is it?

- Who can make a legally effective gift of a human body, its parts or products?

- For what purposes can such gifts be made?

- If vital organs are to be donated upon a person's death, when is a person legally dead?

## Cryogenically Preserved Sperm and Embryos

One Tennessee couple recently went to court to battle over which of them should receive "custody" of several frozen embryos after their divorce. While still married, Junior and Mary Davis unsuccessfully attempted to conceive a child together through in vitro fertilization. Such a process involves the harvesting of ova from a woman's ovaries, which are then fertilized in a petri dish by the sperm provided by the man. After fertilization takes place, the product is transferred into the uterus of the woman, in hopes that implantation will occur. If more ova than needed at the time are harvested and fertilized, the surplus material may be frozen for use by the couple at a later date. When Junior and Mary divorced, seven of the couple's frozen embryos remained in storage.

The major obstacle the court faced in the Davises' custody dispute was determining whether such material constituted a "person" or "property." The court noted three major positions asserted in the debate over the status of frozen embryos. One view holds that a frozen embryo is a "person," entitled to all the rights associated with that status. At the time of this writing, Louisiana is the only state that has adopted this view, and it has enacted a law that regulates how embryos may be treated. Louisiana's statute states that any disputes that arise between parties should be decided in the "best interest" of the embryo.

An opposite view is that the material is just like any other form of human tissue. The Tennessee court espoused a third view, however, and held that its status is somewhere between a person and mere tissue. Because an embryo may never actually reach its biologic potential, the court ruled that it could not be properly characterized as a person. Yet it deserved more respect than that given to human tissue because of its potential to develop into an individual human being.

Although the frozen embryos were not viewed as "pure property," the court did state that the Davises, as the gamete providers, had "an interest in the nature of ownership, to the extent that they have decision-making authority concerning disposition of the preembryos...." The court recommended that progenitors, before undertaking the in vitro procedure, should enter into agreements providing for the disposition of excess embryos in the event of a death or divorce. Unfortunately, Junior and Mary Davis never entered into, or even discussed, such an agreement. Thus, the court had to decide which spouse possessed the greater interest in disposition of the embryos—Mary, who wanted to donate the embryos to another couple for implantation, or Junior, who wished to have them destroyed. The court ruled that Mary's interest in donation was not as significant as Junior's right to avoid becoming a parent against his wishes. The court indicated that any disputes arising between gamete providers should ordinarily be resolved in favor of the party wishing to avoid procreation. However, it acknowledged that a different outcome might be appropriate if the party opposing destruction has no other means available to achieve parenthood other than through the existing frozen embryos.

It appears that a party can sue for damages that result from the improper "care" of embryonic material. A New York woman, undergoing in vitro fertilization, succeeded in recovering $50 thousand for emotional distress in a lawsuit against a doctor who intentionally destroyed a petri dish containing her egg and her husband's sperm.

In contrast, courts have generally been more willing to consider reproductive material (that is, a woman's egg or a man's sperm) as "property" than a human embryo. A dispute involving the disposition of frozen sperm was recently decided in California. In *Hecht v. Superior Court of California*,[6] a man deposited several vials of sperm in a Cryobank in Los Angeles. When doing so, the donor signed a specimen storage agreement, stating that he authorized the sperm bank to release the specimens to his girlfriend. In addition, in his will, he included a clause bequeathing all his interest in the sperm to the girlfriend upon his death.

After the sperm donor's death, an intense feud arose between his children and his girlfriend. The children sought to keep the girlfriend from obtaining possession and control of their deceased father's sperm. The court ruled that the sperm was a "unique type of property," part of the decedent's estate and subject to the rules of probate.

The situation of a man who deposits his sperm in a bank for future personal use should be distinguished from that in which a man donates sperm. While one who stores his sperm for personal use retains a property interest in the specimens, mere donors normally sign agreements acknowledging their waiver of rights to the sperm or potential offspring.

## Anatomical Gifts and Organ Transplants

Beginning with the first recorded kidney transplant in 1950, organ transplant technology has become one of the most rapidly expanding areas of medical science. Expansion of the field in recent years is largely due to the advent of powerful new drugs used to suppress the body's immune system, thus decreasing the likelihood a patient's body will reject the transplanted organ.

A national task force created to study organ transplantation published its report in 1986. It made the following conclusions:

- Ninety-three percent of Americans surveyed knew about organ transplantation and, of these, 75 percent approved of the concept.

- Only 27 percent indicated that they would be very likely to donate their own organs.

- Only 17 percent had actually completed donor cards.

- Among those who were very likely to donate, nearly half had not told family members of their wishes.

- Despite substantial support for transplantation and a general willingness to donate organs and tissues after death, demand far exceeds supply with an estimated eight thousand to ten thousand people waiting at any one time for a donor organ.

The Uniform Anatomical Gift Act has made the laws in the fifty states concerning organ donations substantially consistent. Although each of the states has varied the individual sections of the Anatomical Gift Act, customizing it to local law, the act has been adopted in each of the fifty states.

Under the Anatomical Gift Act, any competent adult can make an anatomical gift, which can be all or any part of a human body, including the body of a stillborn infant or a fetus. In addition, at a person's death, her spouse, adult children, parents, adult siblings, grandparents, or guardian at the time of death, in that order, can make a gift of all or part of the decedent's body. Anatomical gifts can be used for transplantation, therapy, research, or education. The donor can specify the uses to which the gift can be put by the donee. Donations can be made to universities, organ banks, hospitals, or particular physicians or surgeons.

Anatomical gifts can be made in various ways. Many of the state statutes include suggested forms a person can use if she wishes to make arrangements to donate organs after her death or forms a surviving family member might use to donate organs of a deceased relative. Other states have passed laws requiring space on the reverse side of drivers' licenses to be set aside for making and recording anatomical gifts. Of course, organs can be donated by will under the laws in most states. Given the legal acceptance of advance directives and their association with terminal medical conditions, it may become common to discuss and make provision for organ donations in the text of such documents.

The Uniform Act, as a matter of public policy, absolutely forbids the sale of human organs or tissue. Some people, however, have suggested that the purchase and sale of organs would be much more efficient than the current system. In particular, advocates of the market approach predict that more organs would be available if they were treated as a commercial commodity, eliminating the shortage and the consequent need for thousands of individuals to wait for organs to become available. This view has not yet prevailed in any state to date.

To encourage people to consider making a voluntary donation, the Uniform Act requires hospitals to inquire, upon a patient's admission, whether she has considered the issue. The hospital is then required to obtain copies of any statement the patient has made regarding donating organs in the event of her death, and to make that statement a part of the patient's medical record. The Act also includes a provision requiring health care professionals treating a patient who is at or near death to inquire of the patient's family concerning their feelings about donating the patient's organs and to discuss that option with them.

Because there is only a short time following a person's death for organs to be harvested if subsequent transplants of the organs are to be successful, the transplant team must remove the organs as soon as possible. Given advances in medical technology, however, the time of death is not always clear. Generally, state statutes and common law consider a person legally dead when one or more physicians determine, in accordance with the usual and customary standards of medical practice, that the person has suffered a total and irreversible cessation of all brain function. This means the person's heart and lungs cannot function and are not functioning without artificial support.

In an increasing number of states, there are statutes authorizing medical examiners or coroners to remove eyes or corneal tissue of a decedent if no objection was made to the procedure by the decedent during her life or by her next-of-kin after her death. A Georgia woman, however, challenged the constitutionality of a such a law when her deceased child's corneas were removed without prior notice to her and without giving her any realistic opportunity to object to the procedure.

Under Georgia law, as in most states, the family of a decedent has only a "quasi-property" interest in the decedent's body. The family has a right to possession of the corpse, but only for the purpose of giving it a proper burial. In the opinion of the court, this interest is not one of constitutional proportions and, consequently, does *not* outweigh the state's interest in protecting and fostering public health. The Georgia statute was upheld. Subsequently, statistics indicate that the law has contributed to a significant increase in the number of corneal tissues available for transplant in the state.

## Human Tissue

The status of human tissue was recently debated in a California court. In *Moore v. Regents of the University of California,* a man suffering from hairy-cell leukemia underwent an operation for the removal of his spleen. After removal, his doctor used the cells from the spleen to develop a profitable cell-line, which he (the doctor) later patented. At no time during Moore's treatment did the doctor inform him of the proposed use of the cells. Moore sued his doctor, asserting that he had committed conversion and breached his fiduciary duty to Moore. The tort of conversion is the unauthorized use or assumption of another's property. In this case, Moore's spleen and the cells within were the purported property, and the doctor's patenting of the resulting cell-line was the "assumption."

While the court acknowledged that Moore may have a claim against the doctor for breach of fiduciary duty, it held that there could be no recovery for conversion since a patient retains no ownership interest in his tissue after it leaves the body. According to the *Moore* court, people simply do not have any property rights to their body tissue.

Property interests, however, *have* been found to exist in tissue that is capable of being reproduced, such as blood and sperm. Both are frequently sold to hospitals by various collecting banks. One man who discovered that he had an extremely rare type of blood actually began selling it by the pint for large sums of money.

Another concern is the disposition of fetal tissue. Like other types of tissue, fetal tissue contains certain qualities that may provide physical benefits to others. For example, fetal tissue transplantation has recently been used to treat persons suffering from Parkinson's disease. The fetal tissue, which grows quickly and is less likely to be rejected than other tissue, is transplanted to repair the brain and spinal cord. Although such transplants are legal, a moratorium issued in 1988 prohibits federal funds to be used in any research involving the transplantation of tissue from an aborted fetus (fetal tissue from an ectopic pregnancy or spontaneous abortion, however, is exempted from the ban).

Many states currently have laws that restrict the use of aborted fetuses. Among these are laws that make it illegal to sell fetal tissue or use the material to conduct research unless it is for the performance of an autopsy. Other states allow fetal research, but only after receiving the mother's consent. The consent provision may imply that the mother has some type of ownership interest in the fetus, although it may simply be an extension of the quasi-property right relating to dead bodies. Some laws prohibit the performance of an abortion if the only compensation the doctor receives is her right to use the fetus for research purposes.

Two states have enacted laws that relate directly to the issue of fetal tissue transplantation: Missouri prohibits a doctor from performing an abortion if she knows that the mother conceived the fetus for the purpose of providing transplant tissue. In Pennsylvania, a woman who obtains an abortion is prohibited from designating a recipient for transplantation of the fetal tissue.

The laws regulating the use of fetal tissue are based on the fear that women will conceive and then abort fetuses for the specific purpose of selling the tissue or donating it to an ailing relative. As with other body tissue, there is little to indicate that a woman retains any sort of ownership interest in fetal tissue after it leaves her body.

## Notes
1. 381 U.S. 479 (1965).
2. 410 U.S. 113 (1973).
3. 120 L.Ed.2d 674, 112 S.Ct. 2791 (1992).
4. 537 A.2d 1227 (N.J. 1988).
5. 851 P.2d 776 (Cal. 1993).
6. 20 Cal.Rptr.2d 275 (1993).

## Bibliography
Many organizations publish newsletters and pamphlets on pro-choice or pro-life issues. Several are listed in the resources section. The local public library will also be able to recommend current books and articles on this subject—there are far too many to provide even a representative list here.

Bowers, James R. *Pro-Choice and Anti-Abortion: Constitutional Theory and Public Policy*. New York: Praeger Publishing, 1994.

Chalker, Rebecca, and Carol Downer. *A Woman's Book of Choices*. New York: Four Walls, Eight Windows, 1992.

Craig, Barbara H., and David M. Craig. *Abortion and American Politics*. Chatham, NJ: Chatham House, 1993.

Cusine, Douglas J. *New Reproductive Techniques: A Legal Perspective*. Brookfield, VT: Ashgate, 1990.

Harrison, Maureen, ed. *Abortion Decisions of the United States Supreme Court*. (There are three volumes, each covering a decade: the 1970s, 1980s, and 1990s). San Diego: Excellent Books, 1993.

Hood, Howard A., ed. *Abortion in the United States: A Compilation of State Legislation, 1992 Supp*. Buffalo, NY: Wm. S. Hein, 1993.

*Midwifery and the Law*. Mothering Magazine, Santa Fe, 1990.

Whitney, Catherine. *Whose Life*. New York: William Morrow, 1991.

## Organizational Resources
Many of these organizations provide referrals or information for specific health problems, as well as information on legal questions. For an excellent list of resources, see the *1995 Information Please Women's Sourcebook* (Boston: Houghton Mifflin, 1994).

ACCESS
25 Taylor Street, #702
San Francisco, CA 94102
(415) 441-4434

Center for Medical Consumers
237 Thompson Street
New York, NY 10012
(212) 674-7105

Jacobs Institute of Women's Health
409 12th Street SW
Washington, DC 20024
(202) 863-4990

Menninger Clinic: The Women's Program
5800 S.W. Sixth Avenue
P.O. Box 829
Topeka, KS 66601
(800) 351-9058

National Women's Health Network
1325 G Street NW
Washington, DC 20005
(202) 347-1140

National Women's Health Resource Center
2440 M Street NW, Suite 325
Washington, DC 20037
(202) 293-6045

Office of Minority Health Resource Center
Department of Health and Human Services
P.O. Box 37338
Washington, DC 20013
(800) 444-6472

Planned Parenthood
810 Seventh Avenue
New York, NY 10019
(212) 603-4600
(800) 248-7797

Women's Health Education Project
2271 Second Avenue
New York, NY 20035
(212) 987-0066

---

**Linda W. Rohman** received a B.A. degree in 1976 from the University of Missouri at Columbia, graduating magna cum laude with honors in psychology. She received her J.D. degree from the University of Nebraska at Lincoln in 1982 and a Ph.D. in psychology from that university in 1987. Rohman is a member of the Lincoln, Nebraska, and American Bar Associations. She is an attorney in practice with Erickson & Sederstrom, P.C., a law firm in Lincoln, where her main emphasis is in litigation with a concentration in health and utilities law.

**Penny L. Huber** graduated cum laude with a B.A. from the University of South Dakota in 1991. She received her J.D. from the University of Nebraska in 1994 and currently resides in Denver, Colorado, where she is a Westlaw Account Representative for West Publishing Company.

Chapter 4

# *Sexual Assault*

Kathryn Quaintance

## Chapter Outline

**Introduction**

A forcible rape occurs every 1.3 minutes.[1] One in three American women will be a victim of sexual assault in her lifetime.[2] Most sexual assaults are perpetrated by someone known to the victim.[3] On the average, there are seven victims per rapist.[4] Rape is the fastest growing violent crime in the United States and remains the most underreported. Rape is probably the crime dreaded and feared most by women. This chapter addresses the legal aspects of sexual assault. It is also designed to answer the question, "What should I do if I or someone close to me is the victim of sexual assault?"

## What Is Sexual Assault?

The legal definition of the crime of sexual assault varies from state to state. What sexual assault is called even varies from state to state; it may be called criminal sexual conduct, sexual battery, indecent conduct, or rape. A general definition of sexual assault against adult women is unwanted touch of the genitals and/or breasts, and, in some cases, the thighs or buttocks. It also includes being forced to touch the genitals of an assailant.

Sexual assault may take the form of sexual penetration. The definition of sexual penetration depends on the law of the state, but it generally includes intercourse and may include anal penetration and/or oral sex. Oral sex is defined as the victim being forced to put the assailant's penis in her mouth, as well as contact between the mouth of the assailant and the genitals of the victim.

Sexual assault can also refer to nonconsensual sexual touching of the intimate parts of the victim. Attempted sexual assault is also a crime and usually requires that the assailant take some steps to accomplish the assault beyond verbal threats.

The assailant is often known to the victim of sexual assault. He may be a friend, neighbor, coworker, or relative. This is commonly referred to as acquaintance rape. Date rape or marital rape refers to rapes that are committed by assailants who are in romantic relationships with the victim.

Sexual touching of children under a certain age is criminal regardless of whether the child agreed to the touching or not. This is what is commonly referred to as "statutory rape." The "age of consent" and the particulars of what constitutes the crime vary from jurisdiction to jurisdiction.

### Elements of the Crime

There are a number of factors, called elements of the crime, that police and prosecutors need to know to determine what, if any, crime has been committed. A list of these elements follows:

- Did the assault involve sexual penetration? Sexual penetration can include anal or vaginal intercourse, cunnilingus (the assailant putting his mouth on the genitals of the victim), or fellatio (the assailant forcing the victim to put her mouth on his penis). It may also include penetration of the victim's anus or vagina with another body part or a foreign object.

- Did the assault include sexual contact or fondling but not sexual penetration? Fondling may be criminal even though it occurs over the clothing of the victim.

- What are the ages of the victim and the assailant? There are different laws governing sexual assault against children and teenagers and adults. Whether the assailant was an adult or a juvenile will also make a difference as to whether he is prosecuted in juvenile court, and it may affect what sentence he can receive. In some states the difference in the age of the victim and perpetrator may be significant.

- Was a weapon used in the assault?

- Was there injury to the victim? What was the nature and extent of that injury?

- What was the nature and extent of the force used by the assailant?

- What was the relationship between the victim and the assailant? Whether the parties were married makes a difference in some states. Some states have special provisions for sexual misconduct occurring in the context of doctor-patient, counselor-client, clergy-parishioner, or teacher-student relationships. When the victim is a young person, it may be important if the assailant is a relative (uncle, stepfather, grandfather) or is in a position of authority (employer, coach).

- Was the victim in any way mentally incapacitated or physically helpless as a result of drugs or alcohol, physical or mental disability, or mental illness? There may be special provisions in the laws to take into account particularly vulnerable victims.

## Sexual Harassment

It is important to note the difference between sexual assault and sexual harassment. Sexual harassment may include sexual assault, but it does not necessarily involve any touching of the victim at all. A lawsuit for sexual harassment is brought in civil court rather than criminal court and seeks money damages as opposed to jail time, probation, or other punishment (see chapter 12). A civil lawsuit for damages may also be brought for sexual assault. This kind of suit is litigated by a private attorney hired by the victim, not a prosecutor who works for the state or county. The private attorney's client is the individual victim. The prosecutor's client is the citizenry of the state whose law has been violated.

## What If You Are a Victim of Sexual Assault?

It is the victim of sexual assault who ultimately makes the decision whether the assailant, assuming one is identified, is successfully prosecuted. Practically speaking, it is virtually impossible for a prosecution to go forward without the cooperation of the victim. What you do within the first few minutes and hours of a sexual assault can be very important and may determine whether or not your case can be prosecuted at all. Be aware that the victim of sexual assault may always decide later that prosecution is not important to her or does not serve her needs. She can always decide later to pursue a healing process through counseling or a civil lawsuit. But the failure to take immediate steps to collect evidence of a crime will mean that evidence that could make or break your criminal case is lost forever.

In order to convict an assailant of rape, the prosecutor must prove to the jury *beyond a reasonable doubt* that the crime occurred and that the person charged committed it. "Beyond a reasonable doubt" is a very high standard of proof. Juries take this standard seriously because they know that their verdict will have a major impact, not only on the life of the victim, but also on the defendant. In order to meet that burden of proof, the prosecutor needs not only your testimony, but any and all other evidence that will corroborate your account of what happened. Without that additional evidence the case may come down to your word against the word of the defendant. In many jurors' minds, that alone creates a reasonable doubt because there is no other evidence to prove who is telling the truth. Therefore, other witnesses and physical evidence can be very important in supporting your testimony. Ultimately, the decision whether to charge the case will be up to the prosecutor.

It may seem very unfair that anyone would question that you are telling the truth about what happened to you. The basis of our adversarial system of justice, however, favors the criminal defendant by presuming him innocent until proven guilty. Our system was formulated partly to prevent individuals from being convicted simply on the accusation of another, an accusation that might be based on unjust motives. It may seem that these safeguards create a disadvantage to the victim of rape. But the people who make up juries are becoming more and more educated to the dynamics of sexual assault through the media and by hearing the stories of people they know who have been victims.

When a rape has occurred, it is extremely important to report the crime to police as soon afterward as possible. This will allow police to begin gathering evidence immediately, before any is destroyed, and to apprehend the assailant as soon as possible.

The following is a checklist to assist in the initial response to a sexual assault:

1. Call 911 or another emergency number as soon as possible and report the rape. Give as many details about the identity of the assailant as you can. Describe what you smelled, heard, and felt, as well as what you saw about the assailant. If you could not see because of darkness or disability, but *felt* a rough beard, suede clothing, or frizzy hair, those details will be of particular importance to police in identifying the rapist. Information about scars or tattoos is especially valuable since those parts of a person's appearance cannot be changed readily.

2. Call a friend, relative, or rape crisis center. You will need a support person to help you cope with how you feel and what you need to do to be safe. Many rape crisis centers can talk you through the first steps you should take and give you advice that will ultimately help your case.

3. Get a medical exam as soon as possible. Do not shower or bathe before getting a physical exam. Keep the clothes you were wearing at the time of the assault and give them to the police or hospital. The sooner after the assault that the medical exam is performed, the greater the likelihood that useful evidence can be collected. In order to be useful, the exam must be conducted within thirty-six to seventy-two hours but preferably sooner. Remember that if you get an exam, you can always decide not to proceed with prosecution, but if you do not get an exam, the evidence is lost forever.

   The sexual assault exam will include a pelvic examination during which samples are collected from the vagina and surrounding area. These samples will be tested to discover whether there is any semen present that could be matched with any potential suspect. The exam will also include cultures for sexually transmitted disease and HIV testing. Photos should be taken of any injuries. Pubic hair and fingernail scrapings will also be collected if indicated by the nature of the assault. You may be offered oral or another type of postcoital contraceptive to help ensure that you do not become pregnant as a result of the rape.

   Larger metropolitan areas may have locations where specially trained medical personnel perform sexual assault exams. The police or rape crisis center will know about their availability. If these exist in your area, you will want to take advantage of them because the exam will be more thorough and the doctors and nurses will be trained to assist you with emotional and psychological needs.

4. Give a statement to the police. If you wish to press charges, or sometimes even if you don't, a police investigator will interview you

about the assault. Give as many details as you can remember. Tell the officer what you felt, heard, smelled, saw, even tasted. Tell the truth, even if you think it may hurt your case. For example, if you were drinking before the rape, you may think it is better to underestimate the number of drinks you had. But if it later comes out through a witness that you lied about how many drinks you had, that will hurt the case far more than the fact that you may have been a bit tipsy.

You may be insulted, offended, or annoyed by some of the questions you are asked. Often rape victims are appalled to be asked what they were wearing at the time of the assault because of the inference that their dress somehow provoked the rape. But the question may be asked because the clothes are physical evidence and might show tears or stains. Ultimately, the question will be asked again by the prosecutor, if the case goes to court, to show the victim's clear recollection of the details of the event. Some officers are insensitive, but others may just be asking questions now that you will inevitably be asked if the case proceeds further. This is their opportunity to get the most detailed description you can give. The statement you give the police will be helpful to you later should you have to refresh your recollection before testifying.

5. Remind yourself as often as necessary, and find a support person to do the same: This is not your fault. You are the victim of a crime. You did nothing wrong. You did not make this happen to you. You did nothing to deserve this. It is not your fault.

6. Do everything you can to assist in the gathering of witnesses and evidence:

- Identify anyone who saw you immediately or shortly after the assault and saw your physical and emotional state.

- Identify anyone you told about what had happened to you.

- Give a complete description of the assailant.

- Advise medical and police personnel of any injuries or bruises. Be aware that bruises sometimes do not surface until days later. Get the police or someone else to take pictures of the injuries. (Avoid Polaroids—they decay over time and may be discolored and useless by the trial date.)

- Return to the scene with police if you are up to it and point out to them exactly where and how the assault occurred. This may assist in collecting evidence such as hairs, fibers, fingerprints, buttons popped off clothing, and so on. If you left anything at the scene, advise police so that they may recover those items as evidence.

7. Know your rights. As a victim you have rights; some states have enacted laws to protect your rights. A rape crisis center, crime victim's assistance, or victim's advocate program will be able to assist you in this area.

## What You Can Expect If Your Case Goes to Trial

Most criminal cases are resolved before trial by plea bargaining. A plea bargain means that the prosecutor offers the defendant the opportunity to plead guilty to a lesser charge or to the same charge for a lesser sentence. Usually this is done after consulting with the victim and getting her input about what she would like to happen with the case. The prosecutor makes the ultimate decision whether or not to settle the case and under what terms. Some states now require by law, however, that the victim be consulted about any negotiation. Often plea bargains come about because the victim wishes to avoid a trial.

If the prosecutor does not offer any plea bargain or if the defendant does not take the offer, the case will go to trial. The prosecutor should meet with you prior to trial to prepare you for your testimony. This does not mean telling you what to say on the witness stand but to let you know what will be asked and to make sure that the jury will understand what you have to tell them. It should also include giving you some idea what the defense attorney will ask you when you are cross-examined. Many prosecutor's offices have victim advocates who can stay with you while you meet with the prosecutor and who will keep you up to date on the progress of your case. You have a right to request that a friend, family member, or advocate be present with you while you meet with the prosecutor. Often the prosecutor may not know until the day of trial whether or not the defendant will plead guilty. This is extremely stressful for the vicitm, but, unfortunately, it sometimes cannot be avoided.

When you testify, friends or relatives who are also potential witnesses in the case will probably not be allowed in the courtroom. But you may bring a support person who is not a witness in the case to sit through your testimony. It is often helpful for victims to have a friendly and caring face to look at when the going gets tough.

The prosecutor will be the first to ask you questions and will lead you through the story of what happened. This is called direct testimony. Then it is the defense attorney's turn. This is cross-examination and is the most scary and anxiety-producing part of the experience for many people. Rape victims are very vigorously cross-examined and often end up feeling as if they are the ones being put on trial because the defense attorney is trying to make them feel as if they have done something wrong. This is where you will again need to remind yourself over and over again, "I have done nothing wrong. I am the victim of a crime. I am not on trial. This was not my fault." This is also where the presence of a friendly and supportive person can be very helpful.

The defense attorney has a right to ask you any question she thinks has a bearing on your credibility or believability. The prosecutor may make a legal objection to questions that are inappropriate, but it is ultimately up to the judge whether to allow the question or not. What kinds of questions you have to answer and what kind of tone the defense attorney is allowed to use depends on the knowledge and sensitivity of the judge, as well as the rules of evidence.

There are laws called Rape Shield Statutes that prohibit the defense attorney from asking you about your previous sexual conduct with anyone other than the defendant. The defense is allowed to question you about your sexual relationship with the defendant if he is claiming that the rape was consensual sex. You may also be asked about other partners if you are saying that you became pregnant or got a sexually transmitted disease as a result of the rape. The defense can then try to prove that there was some other possible source of the pregnancy or disease. These laws may be more strict or lenient in the questioning that is allowed, depending on the state. These laws may also be more strictly or leniently enforced depending on the judge.

Usually you will not be allowed to sit through the rest of the trial either before or after your testimony. In most cases, all witnesses are "sequestered," which means they are not allowed to hear the others' testimony, which might cause them to consciously or unconsciously change their own. You may be permitted to return to hear the closing arguments of each attorney. Be aware that listening to what the defense attorney says about you, in an effort to help his client, may be unfair and may make you very angry or upset.

You and the prosecutor will have to make arrangements so that you can be notified when the jury reaches a verdict. You may choose to be present for the reading of the verdict, or not. Some states have a provision giving the victim the right to make a statement to the judge at the time of sentencing, if the defendant is convicted.

You must always prepare for the possibility that the defendant will be found "not guilty." If this happens, keep in mind that it does not mean that the jury did not believe you, but that perhaps they wanted some other evidence, which was not in the case, in order to be convinced "beyond a reasonable doubt."

## Civil Suits

Many victims of sexual assault do not wish to prosecute because of concern over the toll the legal system will take on them personally. Others are not able to prosecute because too much time has passed since the assault and evidence and/or witnesses are no longer available. Each state has a statute of limitations that sets a legal limit on how long after the event a criminal or civil lawsuit can be brought. Usually the time expires for the criminal case before it expires for the civil case, so that even if the case cannot be prosecuted criminally, the victim may still proceed with a civil suit. This option is often helpful to those who do not discover or are not able to tell of the assault until long after the fact, for example, childhood abuse.

A civil suit is often an alternative even in cases where the criminal case cannot proceed because there is not enough evidence. The standard of proof in civil suits is "by a preponderance of the evidence." This means that it is more likely than not that the rape occurred and that the defendant committed it. This standard is lower than the criminal standard of "beyond a reasonable doubt" so evidence that is not sufficient for a criminal case may be adequate for a civil case. A "not guilty" verdict in a criminal case, however, may make the civil case much more difficult to prove.

To initiate a civil suit, you need to find and hire your own lawyer. Many communities have lawyer referral services that can help you find someone who specializes in this area. The attorney may require a retainer and an hourly fee or may be willing to proceed with the lawsuit for a percentage of the recovery. Keep in mind that a civil suit is for money damages and is not worthwhile unless the assailant has assets or insurance.

## Counseling

Counseling is helpful to most victims, regardless of what legal choices are made. If a victim receives counseling in connection with a criminal or civil suit, a request can be made as part of the legal proceeding that the defendant reimburse the victim for the cost of counseling. Some states have victim reimbursement funds that can be used to cover uninsured medical or counseling costs for victims of crimes. In some instances, counseling is available on a sliding-fee basis or at no cost.

Referrals for counseling services may be available through the hospital that does the medical exam, the prosecutor's office, a rape crisis center, women's resource centers, or culturally specific resource centers. You may prefer a one-to-one or group setting or a combination of both. Many rape crisis centers offer peer counseling for crisis situations. You may also find it helpful to be in a group with other women who have experienced sexual assault.

**Alternatives to Criminal Prosecution**

There is always some chance that the records of the counseling session may be made available to the other side in the course of litigation, whether criminal or civil. Your conversations with your counselor are legally "privileged communications" and, therefore, presumed to be confidential. There are cases, however, in which the defense attorney is able to convince the judge that what occurred in counseling is relevant to the case and helpful to the defense. The records are more likely to be available to the other side in a civil suit when part of the claim has to do with the emotional distress suffered by the victim.

## When the Victim Is a Child

Sexual assault has essentially the same definition when the victim is a child, with one major exception: Sexual assault against children below an age set by statute is a crime regardless of whether or not the child consented to the sexual activity. The law presumes that children are not competent to give consent; the law also takes into account the fact that children may consent because an authority figure is telling them that the sexual abuse is all right.

A child's failure to report the abuse immediately is not as likely to have an impact on the case as it would if an adult victim had delayed in contacting the police. It is generally recognized that there are reasons, such as fear, shame, or lack of understanding, why a child might not tell anyone what has happened. While those same reasons might also explain why an adult woman failed to report immediately, society generally considers children less likely to have any reason to lie about sexual matters. (See Chapter 6 for a longer discussion of children and the court system.)

The first concern of many caretakers is that the investigation and court process will unduly traumatize the child. Indeed, there have been some highly publicized cases of children apparently being manipulated by parents, lawyers, police, and psychologists. These cases are the exception. Most major metropolitan areas have developed a protocol in this area that is specifically designed to be "child friendly" and to eliminate any suggestive or coercive interviewing. Police forces have investigators who are specially trained in child abuse investigation. Some jurisdictions have provisions for the child to be interviewed by a psychologist or social worker. These interviews are sometimes videotaped, thus eliminating the need for the child to be reinterviewed by police, prosecutors, or child-protection workers. (See chapter 6 for a longer discussion of children and the court system.)

Should the case go to trial, many district attorney's offices have prosecutors who specialize in this area, assisted by victim advocates whose job it is to make sure that the child is not unduly traumatized by the experience and understands what is happening. Judges are also receiving training in how to make the courtroom a safe place for children.

The past ten years have seen tremendous advances in this area. Law enforcement and court personnel have made a lot of progress toward accommodating the specific needs of children who are victims and witnesses.

## What to Do When a Child Tells You of Abuse

1. Listen. At the earliest convenience, write down what the child said; use the child's words and be as specific as possible.

2. Do not interrogate. Once the child has disclosed and you have a basic idea of who, what, when, and where, do not raise the issue again with the child. But if the child brings it up, continue to keep a record of what the child says about the abuse. These statements made to you may become crucial evidence, therefore it is important to remember and record the time and circumstances of everything the child tells you about the abuse. If you question the child, the argument can be made later that you were suggesting what the child should tell you by the nature of your questions.

3. Call the police or child-protection as soon as possible. Report what you know.

4. Make sure the child is safe. If the abuser is living in the same home as the child, make the necessary arrangements for the child or the abuser to be living elsewhere. If the abuser is your husband or boyfriend and you want to keep living with him, send the child to a relative or arrange with child-protection for foster care.

5. If the abuse involved sexual penetration of any kind (see definition above) arrange for a medical exam. This should be done at a local hospital and again, doctors specializing in this area should be used if available. The police will know which is the best place to go. Your regular pediatrician is most likely *not* the appropriate person to do this examination. On rare occasions it is necessary to sedate the child in order to complete the examination without undue trauma. The presence or absence of particular medical findings does not necessarily indicate that abuse has or has not occurred. For example, the idea that a doctor can tell whether the hymen of a girl is intact and therefore whether she has been sexually penetrated is a myth. On the other hand, the presence of venereal disease in a small child is a clear indicator of abuse since there is virtually no other possible explanation. Discuss any findings with the doctor in order to understand their significance.

6. Get some counseling for the child. Prosecutors or doctors may be able to refer you to a child psychologist with the appropriate expertise. This is where your pediatrician may be of assistance.

7. Assist the police in collecting any physical evidence (clothing, bedclothes, diaries of the child, etc.) and in identifying any other witnesses. The police may wish to find out whether other children had any knowledge of the abuse. They will also want to know whether the child discussed the abuse with any other adults (grandparents, teachers, other family members). If you are aware of any other victims of the same abuser, the police will need to have that information.

8. Get support for yourself. Depending on your relationship to the abuser and to the child, the allegations may cause you extreme stress. If you are a victim yourself, all kinds of feelings may come flooding forward. You may need assistance to keep separate your own feelings about what has happened from your role as comforter and supporter for the child.

## Conclusion

Sexual assault is devastating to its victims and debilitating to those close to them. Too often experiences with law enforcement and the legal system are frustrating and unsatisfactory, resulting in further pain and insult. Some progress has been made to insure that these systems better serve victims of sexual assault and their friends and family. But in many courtrooms it still feels as if the victim is on trial. More must be done to offer support and empowerment to women and children who have been sexually assaulted. It is hoped that the information and the action steps set forth in this chapter can assist in the transition from victim to survivor.

### Notes
1. National Victim Center & Crime Victims Research and Treatment Center, 1992
2. Russell and Howell, 1983
3. National Victim Center & Crime Victims Research and Treatment Center, 1992
4. Id.

### Bibliography
The NOW Legal Defense and Education Fund has a Legal Resource Kit on violence against women (available for a nominal fee) that contains a list of national and state hotlines and crisis centers, as

well as a selected annotated bibliography of materials. Contact them at 99 Hudson Street, New York, NY 10013.

Benedict, Helen. *Recovery: How to Survive Sexual Assault for Women, Men, Teenagers, Their Friends, and Families, rev. and expanded ed*. New York: Columbia University Press, 1994.

Bohmer, Carrol, and Andrea Parrot. *Sexual Assault on Campus: The Problem and the Solution*. New York: The Free Press, 1993.

Brownmiller, Susan. *Against Our Wills: Men, Women, and Rape, rev. ed*. New York: Bantam, 1988.

Fairstein, Linda. *Sexual Violence: Our War Against Rape*. New York: William Morrow, 1993.

Kelly, Liz. *Surviving Sexual Violence*. Minneapolis: University of Minnesota Press, 1989.

Ledray, Linda E. *Recovering From Rape*. New York: Henry Holt, 1986.

Martin, Laura. *Life Without Fear: A Guide to Preventing Sexual Assault*. Nashville: Rutledge Hill Press, 1992.

Mauro-Cochrane, Jeanette. *Self Respect and Sexual Assault: Before, During and After*. New York: McGraw-Hill, 1993.

*Rape in America: A Report to the Nation*. National Victim Center and Crime Victims Research Center. (Available from the National Victim Center, 2111 Wilson Boulevard, Suite 300, Arlington, VA 22201.)

Parrot, Andrea. *Sexual Assault on Campus*. Lexington, MA: Lexington Books, 1993.

Warshaw, Robin. *I Never Called It Rape: The Ms. Report on Recognizing, Fighting, and Surviving Date and Acquaintance Rape*. New York: Harper and Row, 1988.

## Organizational Resources

National Clearinghouse on Marital and Date Rape
2325 Oak Street
Berkeley, CA 94708
(510) 524-1582

National Coalition Against Sexual Assault
P.O. Box 21378
Washington, DC 20009
(202) 483-7165

National Victim Center
2111 Wilson Boulevard, Suite 300
Arlington, VA 22201
(703) 276-2880
(800) 877-3355 (referrals)

NOW Legal Defense and Education Fund
99 Hudson Street
New York, NY 10013

Rape Crisis Center Hotline
(202) 333-7273
*This national center will provide referrals to local centers.*

---

**Kathryn Quaintance** is a prosecutor with the Major Offender unit of the Hennepin County Attorney's Office in Minneapolis, Minnesota. She specializes in the prosecution of child abuse and sex crime cases. She serves on the boards of the Sexual Violence Center, a rape crisis center, and the Minnesota chapter of the American Professional Society on the Abuse of Children. She teaches trial advocacy at Hamline Law School and has lectured at the University of Minnesota Law School on topics relating to sex crimes. She has trained judges, lawyers, law enforcement officers, and victim advocates in the areas of child abuse and rape. She is a graduate of Smith College and Rutgers School of Law, Newark.

Chapter 5

# *Spousal and Family Violence*

Pamela Jo Lewis

## Chapter Outline

### Introduction

### Definition of Domestic Violence

### Why Domestic Violence Occurs

### Legal Options
Before an Attack Occurs • During an Attack • After an Attack

### Conclusion

Once hidden from public view, family violence is now front-page news. Nearly one out of every four women has been physically abused by her boyfriend or husband. Almost 35 percent of the women who are treated at hospital emergency rooms have been injured by someone with whom they have an intimate relationship. Despite the fact that it has been against the law for almost one hundred years in this country, domestic violence is one of the leading causes of death for women and accounts for one-third of all female homicides. In this chapter, we will attempt to define the scope and basis of the violence, in addition to offering

**Introduction**

advice on how the legal system can protect a victim from an abusive relationship.

## Definition of Domestic Violence

Domestic violence is a *pattern* of assaulting and controlling behavior that one adult in a relationship inflicts on another. Domestic violence occurs between people of the opposite sex as well as people of the same sex who are intimate. Abusive behavior between people who are currently living together, who have cohabited in the recent past, or who have children in common also constitutes domestic violence. It generally does not include abuse to children (this is characterized as child abuse), although many children are also victims of domestic violence. Certainly they are emotionally scarred by the violence that they see, and studies show that most abusive parents come from abusive homes themselves.

Most domestic violence is against women. Ninety-five percent of the victims are women. Victims are of all races, ages, and economic classes. Due to the controlling nature of domestic violence, vicitms feel that they are alone, they are the only ones in this situation, and that somehow they must handle and deal with it. Even more peculiar to domestic violence is the fact that the person who commits the violence continues to have a relationship with the victim after the incident occurs. In addition to dealing with the trauma of being the victim of the crime, each victim still is under the control and watchful eye of the person who committed the offense. The victim may be further threatened if she seeks help. The confusion and fear that this creates often makes the victim want to retreat, to forget about the whole thing, to refuse to cooperate with the court system, or to refuse to listen to friends. This allows the batterer to continue to control and batter, and no one knows and no one intervenes and no one stops the violence.

Domestic violence is not the problem of minorities or of uneducated, unemployed, nonreligious, unmarried families. When the criminal justice system is evenly applied, the number of domestic violence cases are evenly distributed throughout the population. A well-to-do woman may simply have more resources available to her to deal with the violence. She may be able to fly to a friend's home to hide out for awhile, or she may have a psychiatrist who is counseling her. The poor woman may be more directly tied into the network of government agencies. The violence may be more noticeable when her caseworker comes and sees the bruises on her face. Unfortunately, when there is not a law that requires arrest (mandatory arrest law), the police more frequently arrest poor, unmarried, minority males than wealthy, white executives.

Domestic violence runs the gamut from verbal abuse (that is, name calling and slanderous comments) to stalking, bodily injury, rape, and murder. It includes crimes against property, such as trespassing, criminal mischief, vandalism, and arson. Domestic violence is also violence that is directed at an outside person or the children in an attempt to control the adult. It is not uncommon for victims of domestic violence to be threatened with the death of their children, families, or friends.

Although each state defines its crimes differently, the following are general definitions:

*Assault.* Any intentional physical contact that causes pain or injury or, in some states, anything the victim considers offensive is a criminal assault. A push, shove, slap, or spitting is a criminal activity if the intent is to harm. An assault can also be the credible threat of physical injury or contact. A police officer or the prosecuting attorney for the area should be able to identify if the contact was criminal.

*Stalking.* This is a very new area of the law. Most states require a pattern of repeated unwanted behavior; some states require a credible threat of physical injury. Many states do not consider this a crime. In those states it may be possible to use harassment as the crime to punish and prevent the behavior. The crime of harassment occurs when there is the intent to annoy and may involve the telephone or mail.

*Sexual assault.* The majority of the states have recognized that a rape (or sexual assault) can occur between persons who are or have been cohabiting. If any sexual act is done by force or against the will of the participant, it is sexual assault. In the case of marital partner rape, some states require injuries and insist upon immediate reporting. (See chapter 4.)

*Trespassing.* When a person comes onto your property after being told to leave, that person is trespassing. This sometimes causes difficulty for married couples in that some jurisdictions consider the property to be jointly owned until a divorce is final. So the spouse in possession may not be able to charge the absent spouse with trespass.

*Criminal mischief/vandalism/arson.* These property crimes have the same difficulty as trespassing. Some states have ruled that you cannot be criminally charged with destroying your own property. So until the divorce is final, it is best to clarify with the prosecuting attorney if a spouse can be charged with damaging joint marital property.

Other forms of controlling behavior may also be present. There may never have been any physical contact, but, by sheer difference in size or by verbal threats, the woman is terrified that she will be hurt. The man may try to control the following:

- How the woman looks

- How the woman acts and thinks

- How the woman spends her money

- How frequently she sees her family

- Who the woman's friends are

- Where the woman goes and with whom

- What kind of job she has, if any

- What kind of education she has

Women in abusive relationships often feel as though they are walking on eggshells just to keep their partner from getting upset. Abusive men frequently blame the woman when something goes wrong, or they may accuse the woman of being crazy. Men in these relationships tend to be extremely jealous and are always suspicious. To understand and deal with domestic violence, one must understand both the legal definition as well as the behavior associated with it.

## Why Domestic Violence Occurs

Domestic violence is not a new behavior. Records of it exist in early recorded history. Sometimes it was openly approved. The "rule of thumb" originally referred to the fact that it was okay to beat your wife as long as you didn't use a stick bigger than your thumb. Today, approval is more subtle. Women are encouraged to stay in the relationship "for the children." The media still portrays the macho male as the man who is always in "control." Until recently most courts and police stayed clear of domestic disputes, insisting that they were "family problems." The legal system referred men and women to mediation or marriage counselors. Women were told that if they would only try harder, the abuse would not happen. Unless these counselors were trained in the dynamics of domestic violence, the women were victimized again.

Most experts agree that domestic violence is learned behavior. The woman who keeps the marriage together "for the children" is giving her children a chance to learn domestic violence. Her little boys will often grow up to be batterers, and her daughters will frequently marry abusive men. This perpetuates the abuse with each generation.

Once the behavior is learned, it continues, because it is effective and reinforces itself. The man beats his wife or girlfriend to get her under his control. She becomes submissive to avoid further violence. Most women do not want to end the relationship, only the violence. Clearly these women believe the way to keep the relationship and end the violence is to give the man what he wants. What women eventually realize is that this does not end the violence. For an abusive man, the woman can never be good enough or submissive enough.

This leads the batterer to tell his victim that she is in control: "It is your fault that I hit you," or "You made me hit you." In truth, the victim is never in control of this situation. The batterer is simply denying reality; to him the situation has become normal.

Victims are often accused of being combative and "asking for the abuse." This attitude simply reinforces the batterer. The fact that a woman may refuse to do exactly as the abuser demands or may in fact fight back or attempt to protect herself does not negate the fact that the batterer is still in control and is still the one who is causing the violence.

Even more frightening is the fact that all studies show that the violence will probably get worse. A study in Kansas City found that in 85 percent of domestic abuse homicides, the police had been called to the home at least once in the prior two years. It may start with an insult, controlling access to money, or an occasional shove. From there it will escalate to more serious bodily injury unless someone intervenes.

It is also important to understand what does not cause domestic violence. It is not an out-of-control temper or stress. Batterers choose to abuse their partners even when they are angry at others. They destroy only the possessions that belong to their partners. They selectively hit certain areas of the body where the bruises don't show. All of these are choices that are made. They are not the actions of someone who has lost control of his temper or who is simply under a lot of stress.

Current research shows that domestic violence is not caused by drugs or alcohol, although abuse of these substances can aggravate the problem. Many people use a variety of substances and never abuse anyone. There are also many batterers who never touch drugs. Some batterers do suffer from substance abuse problems, but substance abuse must not be used to justify the violence. It constitutes another problem that must be dealt with.

Domestic violence is a problem that touches the lives of everybody. If you are not the batterer, if you are not the victim, then you are the friend, the relative, or the coworker of someone who is in an abusive relationship. It poses a danger and a threat to each and every one of us, because if the batterer does finally kill, he kills not only his wife, but he may also kill his children, neighbors, coworkers, friends, or his children's friends. Each year, according to the National Crime Survey, domestic violence results in $44 million worth of medical costs and an estimated 175,000 days of missed work. Obviously, this is a problem that must be solved and must be stopped.

**Legal Options**     The general legal theories described in this section have been adopted by most of the states, and although the terms and specific procedures may vary from state to state, the general law set forth here is fairly uniform throughout the United States. The first step, however, is for the victim to decide she must end the violence.

### Before an Attack Occurs
### Temporary Order for Protection

Legally there is only one option available to a victim before an attack occurs. That option involves the civil department of the law. Every state offers a person who believes that she is in imminent danger the right to request a court order that will restrain or stop the violence. This comes under various names. It may be called an injunction, a restraining order, an order for protection, a stay-away order, or a no-contact order.

The first step is to get a temporary version of this order. This temporary order can be applied for generally with just an affidavit or a sworn statement in which the victim states why she feels she must be protected. It should be filed with the Clerk of the Civil Department. If there is a filing fee, the victim has the right to request that the fee be waived. A judge then reviews the application and issues a temporary order based on that application. It is not always necessary to have a hearing, and the batterer is generally not notified. The temporary ruling for protection should be made on the day that the application is made. In the order the judge will also set a hearing date for a permanent version of the order, usually within a very short time.

The batterer must then be served with notice of the temporary protective order and the hearing date. The temporary order may simply order the batterer to stay away from the victim, or it may go so far as to divide property or grant temporary custody of the children and set visitation. The application for the temporary order should ask for everything. If you don't ask for something, it can't be given it to you. If you ask for too much, the court can limit what is given. Usually within a week to ten days the hearing on the permanent order is held. At that hearing the victim will have to give sworn testimony as to why she feels she needs permanent court protection. This is the time to bring in witnesses, hospital bills, or anything that will support the victim's claim of danger. The batterer will also be given a chance to present evidence. He may attempt to get the court to give him possession of the house and the children. The judge will rule and issue an order either granting the permanent order or denying it. In some states the permanent order may be valid for a certain length of time. Even if the application is denied the first time, additional circumstances can justify reapplying.

This entire procedure may be pursued as an action by itself, or it may, in some states, be joined with a divorce petition. In either case, what the victim acquires is a piece of paper in which the court orders the batterer to stay away from the victim. It is only a piece of paper, and it may not give the victim any protection if the batterer chooses to ignore it; however, it does give the police additional reason to intervene.

## Violation of a Protective Order

If the order is violated, it is often up to the victim to go back to court to prove that the batterer has acted in contempt of a court order. Of course, the police should be called. Sometimes police are reluctant to get involved in civil matters. Consequently, several states have enacted special laws to assist victims of domestic violence when the protection order has been violated. These provisions include mandatory arrests or mandatory sentencing for violation of court orders. If the police will not assist, then the prosecuting attorney for criminal matters should be contacted. If she refuses to assist, then the victim must prepare another affidavit in which she states how the batterer has violated the order and ask that the same court that issued the order set another hearing to determine if the order has been violated. In some states a warrant may be issued for the batterer's arrest. In any event, the victim is creating a record that may be useful in the future even if she is unsuccessful initially.

In some cases, violation of a protective order issued to people in an intimate relationship may also be a federal law violation, and the U.S. Attorney for the district would prosecute the violator. Persons in an intimate relationship are those who cohabit or have cohabited with the abuser as a spouse, or, if not married, they may qualify under this law if they are included under their own state's class of protected people.

Under recently enacted federal law it is a crime to cross a state line with the intent to engage in conduct that violates a protective order and then to engage in the prohibited contact. The protective order must state that it protects against "credible threats of violence, harassment, or bodily injury." It does not matter if the violation occurs in the jurisdiction in which the order was issued. Whenever a protective order is requested in a state court, it should contain the language mentioned above to ensure the additional federal protection.

The penalty under federal law for violating an order can be as harsh as life in prison, and it requires mandatory restitution for expenses incurred by the victim, including medical, psychiatric, physical and occupational therapy, transportation, temporary housing, child care, loss of income, and attorney's fees. This same federal law also prohibits subjects of restraining orders from possessing firearms and contains a penalty for anyone who knowingly gives or sells a firearm to a person subject to a restraining order.

Most important is that the woman is in real danger during this period when a restraining order is in effect and when she is in the process of trying to end her relationship with her husband or boyfriend. A study in Chicago indicates that over 28 percent of the women killed by their boyfriends or husbands were attempting to end the relationship at the time they were murdered. For this reason victims must not be too complacent or too dependent upon protection under the law. At this point, victims must consider other remedies.

### Planning an Escape

The first step is to make a conscious decision to end the violence. It may be necessary to plan an escape. Keeping aside some money for such an emergency, possibly with a trusted friend, is a good precaution. Some advocates recommend that an extra set of car keys and house keys also be kept with a friend or relative. Important papers, including birth certificates, marriage license, bank books, immunization records for the children, immigration papers, food stamp cards, medication needed by you and your children, and prescriptions should be kept in a safe place away from the batterer. Finally, a suitcase should be packed for the victim and the children.

Some women plan their escape for years. In a sense, it is the one time when they have some control. They are in control as to when they will leave, how they will leave, and where they will go. They are also determining at which point they are willing to involve outside agencies as well as the court system. This is a time when victims need not only the support of the court but also the support of their friends and family.

Although the law may allow a judge to award you use of the house, use of the car, and custody of the children, some judges are reluctant to make those decisions on a temporary order. If there is a dissolution pending, they may be reluctant to allow attorneys to gain the upper hand by getting an early distribution of property. The victims may often feel disillusioned by a court system that has not allowed them to receive everything to which they feel they are entitled. It is also important to remember that, just like assets, debts can be considered marital property. It is essential that a woman who is planning an escape not sign any documents for loans, taxes, credit cards, and so on, without fully understanding that she may be assuming full liability for these debts, even if the husband uses the credit cards to buy things for himself.

If the victim is unable to stay in her home or fears that a protective order from the court will not give her sufficient protection, a shelter for battered women may be the best and safest alternative. It may only be necessary for a few days or until the protective orders have been entered, the batterer has been served, or until after the hearing. It is extremely important that all precautions be made during this time period when the victim has moved out to ensure her safety and that of her children. Approximately 75 percent of all spousal abuse reported in a national survey was of people who were divorced or separated. This is an extremely dangerous time period.

A shelter will offer more than a roof, food, and safe haven. Some have counselors on staff and most have access to a wide variety of support services. A shelter will have information on applying for welfare, Aid for Families with Dependent Children (AFDC), jobs, finding an alternative place to live, and so forth. Talking to other victims will help the woman realize that she is not the only one facing this problem; joining a support group may help her make what will probably be difficult decisions. A support network is extremely critical at this time.

## Log of Events

One of the most helpful items that any victim can provide the legal system is a log of events. Not only will it substantiate claims when the victim makes application for protective orders, it also provides a basis for showing violations of those orders. The individual judge has the discretion to determine the extent of a violation. Some judges may find that annoying phone calls at all hours of the night are not sufficient to show a willful violation of the court order. Keeping a log will enable the court to consider the cumulative effect and may even give rise to an additional charge such as harassment or stalking.

## During an Attack

When an attack occurs the victim will probably be alone. The judges, attorneys, counselors, police, and advocates will not be there to give legal advice or protection. The decisions that will need to be made on an immediate basis can have long-range legal impact, however. But at this point the victim has only three choices. She can stick it out and take the abuse, she can attempt to leave, or she can fight back.

If the decision is to stay and accept the abuse, then, of course, the victim must do everything she can to protect herself and her family. She must attempt to minimize the abuse and try to defuse the situation. She might consider locking herself and the children in a room that is safe and waiting until the violence has de-escalated. If she has a current protective order, she should attempt to contact the police to let them know that a violation is occurring. (Even if the victim has chosen to stay and accept the abuse, the court system may still intervene.) A neighbor may hear the violence and call the police. The batterer may be arrested. The victim may plead with the police not to arrest the batterer; however, many states have adopted mandatory arrest laws, and, in those states, the choice to arrest is not up to the victim or the police. Arrest is mandatory.

If a victim decides to leave, the legal system is generally supportive of that decision. If the victim is married to the batterer, she cannot be charged with stealing the car if it is joint marital property. She may find it difficult to get back into the house to get her personal belongings. The other danger is if the victim does not take the children with her; some courts may look at this as abandoning the children. Deciding to leave does not necessarily mean that the crime must be reported, however; that is a separate decision that can be made once the victim and her children are safe.

If the woman decides to fight back, several legal risks can occur. These include the danger that she may be charged with assault, or worse. Most states recognize self-defense, but self-defense is limited to the amount of force necessary to protect yourself *at the time*. Women who have fought back and killed their abusers have been prosecuted for murder. Courts have also been slow to recognize "battered woman syndrome" as a defense. If a woman waits and plots an attack later, she will very likely be prosecuted for assault. If there is a mandatory arrest law that requires arrest upon visible signs of injury and the victim is successful in defending herself physically, the batterer may also have injuries. The victim may find herself thrown in jail along with the batterer.

### After an Attack

When an attack has occurred, a crime has been committed. The crime may be called assault, domestic abuse, or domestic violence. Whatever its title, it is a crime and there are criminal penalties. Whether the victim stays, leaves, or fights back, a decision must be made about whether to report the crime. Some states have enacted mandatory arrest laws. Those laws require that if the police have probable cause to believe that domestic violence has occurred, they must arrest the batterer and take him to jail. In most states the batterer cannot post bond and be released until he has been brought before a judge. This prevents a batterer from getting out of jail and immediately reassaulting the victim. It also gives the victim time to make decisions.

If the batterer has not been arrested at the time of the attack, the victim can go to the police and file a report of the crime. The prosecuting attorney will decide how or if it should be pursued. A warrant may be issued at that time. The batterer who is arrested is brought before the judge; the judge will have the option to set terms and conditions of release from jail. Among the terms and conditions that can be set, a judge may order a batterer not to have any contact with the victim. This is a criminal protective order, which is very similar to the civil protective order. Violation of this order would result in violation of terms and conditions of release from jail and could mean that the batterer would be required to stay in jail until a trial date. Some states have special provisions for these types of orders and special penalties when they are violated.

It is essential that the victim notify the prosecuting attorney if she wants one of these criminal protective orders. Generally these orders do not decide the division of property or custody but the victim can ask that the batterer be ordered away from a certain address. A victim should never assume that she will get this protection without asking for it. The prosecuting attorney should also be notified if there is a serious threat that the batterer will do further injuries. Any person charged with a crime can be kept in jail if his or her release is a "threat to the safety of the community."

In any event, the fact that the attack has now occurred brings the criminal judicial system into the picture. It also means that the batterer now has the right to be represented by an attorney, and if he cannot afford one, he can have one appointed for him. His attorney's job is to be a zealous advocate for the batterer. This includes using all of the information and skill at the attorney's disposal to discredit the victim and her story. Some states have attempted to balance this by hiring victim advocates who work at the prosecutor's office. They not only provide support, they also give the victims valuable information about court procedures. Because the victim is often the only witness to the violence, her testimony is essential. If the victim can be convinced not to testify or simply does not show up, the case will be dismissed.

The trial will be set at a later date, and the victim will receive a subpoena to testify at that trial. A subpoena is a court order. If the victim does not appear for the trial, she could be found in contempt of court and go to jail. Any evidence of the abuse, including photos, logs, testimony of neighbors or the testimony of children should be preserved to assist in the prosecution. The criminal penalties for domestic abuse vary depending upon the state and upon the level of abuse. The more serious the injuries, the greater the possible penalties. The sentences may vary from a few days to months. There may be a fine imposed or the sentence may be suspended for a period of time. Some states now order batterers to go to special education groups in an effort to change their behavior.

The greatest complaint of prosecuting attorneys and judges is that the victims do not follow through with the prosecution. Victims often don't show up for trials or have "forgotten" everything that occurred. Twenty years ago the legal system turned victims away and would not help. Today most courtrooms are available to provide assistance to women in abusive relationships. The women, however, must want help, and they must assist in the procedure.

Although legal procedures may be in progress after an attack, victims must consider that they may be in greater danger than before. If the batterer has been arrested, he may be extremely angry. While the batter is being held in jail may be the best time to escape to a friend's house or to a domestic violence shelter. The victim may want to look for a battered woman's support group. It may also be a good time to consult with an attorney about a divorce or to consider a civil tort action for the damage done to you. Interspousal immunity in tort actions has been eliminated in all states. This means that a victim can file suit against her spouse for any injuries she may have received. Homeowner's insurance may even cover the claim. Although most of the cases that have gone to trial have not been successful, it is still an option to consider and discuss with an attorney.

In the hours and days following the attack it is not always a good time to make permanent decisions. The victim may find herself under a lot of pressure from the batterer, his and her families, friends, and other well-meaning people. Especially if there is a trial pending, a major decision at this time may later be regretted. The victim should meet with an attorney, discuss the options, consider the consequences but wait to make important decisions.

## Conclusion

Twenty years ago it was the commonly held belief that if you left domestic violence alone, it would go away. Then society went through a stage where it was believed that mediation and counseling were the answer. Today most experts recognize that an active community response, including arrest and prosecution, significantly reduces the incidence of domestic violence.

The legal system is not the ultimate answer, however. The legal system is made up of people whose job it is to protect everyone's rights within the narrow confines of a written rule. It does not have the power to change batterers, and it cannot solve all the problems of a society that has created them. By combining other remedies with the legal ones, victims have the best hope. They have the chance to stop being victims of domestic violence and to start being survivors. Perhaps even more important, they may be able to save their children from following in their footsteps.

### Bibliography

The NOW Legal Defense Fund (address below in Organizational Resources) will provide an Attorney Referral Services List (cost is $1.00) if you write to their New York address. They also have a Legal Resource

Kit ($5.00) that has a list of national and state hotlines and crisis centers, as well as an annotated bibliography and list of organizations. Their Fact-Pack contains facts on rape, facts on self-defense, facts on domestic violence, and facts on liability for the police if they fail to intervene.

Barnett, Ola W., and LaViolette, Alyce D. *It Could Happen to Anyone: Why Battered Women Stay.* Newbury Park, CA: Sage Publications, 1993.

Brown, A. *When Battered Women Kill,* New York: Free Press, 1987.

Dutton, G. *The Domestic Assault of Women.* Boston: Allyn and Bacon, 1988.

Hawker, Lynn. *End the Pain: Solutions for Stopping Domestic Violence.* Excelsior, MN: Excelsior Music Publishing, 1994.

Hoff, Lee A. *Battered Women As Survivors.* NY: Routledge, 1990.

Jaffe, P., Wolfe, D., and Wilson, S. *Children of Battered Women.* Newbury Park, CA: Sage Publications, 1990.

Jones, Ann. *Next Time, She'll Be Dead: Battering and How to Stop It.* Boston: Beacon Press, 1994.

Jones, Ann R., and Schechter, Susan. *When Love Goes Wrong: What to Do When You Can't Do Anything Right: Strategies for Women with Controlling Partners.* NY: HarperCollins, 1992

Loeb, Leonore, ed. *Violence and the Prevention of Violence.* Westport, CT: Praeger Publishers, 1995.

Pence, E. and Paymar, M. *Educational Groups for Men Who Batter: The Duluth Model.* New York: Springer, 1993.

Roy, M., ed. *Battered Women: A Psychological Study of Domestic Violence.* New York: Van Nostrand Reinhold, 1977.

Walker, L. *The Battered Women's Syndrome.* New York: Springer, 1984.

## Organizational Resources

(See also the listings in chapter 8.)

AYUDA
1736 Columbia Road NW
Washington, DC 20008
(202) 387-0434

Battered Women's Law Project
National Center for Women and
  Family Law
799 Broadway, Room 402
New York, NY 10003
(212) 674-8200

Center for Battered Women's Legal Services
105 Chambers Street, Suite 5A
New York, NY 10007
(212) 349-6009

Center for the Prevention of
  Sexual and Domestic Violence
1914 N. 34th Street, Suite 105
Seattle, WA 98103
(206) 634-1903

Crossroads
3945 Rivers Avenue
North Charleston, SC 29405
(803) 747-6500

CUNY Battered Women's Clinic
1867 ACP Jr. Blvd.
New York, NY 10026
(212) 662-7509

Family Violence Prevention Fund
383 Rhode Island Street, Suite 304
San Francisco, CA 94103-5133
(415) 252-8900

Family Violence Project
1001 Portero Avenue
Building One, Ste 200
San Francisco, CA 94110
(415) 821-4553

Gay Youth Community Switchboard
P.O. Box 846
San Francisco, CA 94104
(415) 387-6193

Haven House, Inc.
P.O. Box 50007
Pasadena, CA 91105-0007
(213) 681-2626

National Assault Prevention Center
P.O. Box 0205
Columbus, OH 43202
(614) 291-2540

National Clearinghouse for the
   Defense of Battered Women
125 S. Ninth Street, Suite 302
Philadelphia, PA 19107
(215) 351-0010

National Clearinghouse on Domestic Violence
P.O. Box 2309
Rockville, MD 20852
(301) 251-5172

National Clearinghouse on Marital Rape
2325 Oak Street
Berkeley, CA 94708
(415) 548-1770

National Coalition Against Domestic Violence
(202) 638-6388
(800) 333-SAFE (7233) (Hotline)

National Council on Child Abuse
   and Family Violence
1155 Connecticut Avenue NW,
   Suite 400
Washington, DC 20036
(202) 429-6695

National Family Violence HelpLine
(800) 222-2000

National Gay and Lesbian Crisis
   Center
666 Broadway, 4th Floor
New York, NY 10012
(212) 529-1604

National Organization for Victim
   Assistance
1757 Park Road NW
Washington, DC 20010
(202) 232-6682
(800) 879-6682

National Runaway Switchboard
(800) 621-4000 (Hotline)

National Women Abuse Prevention
   Project
1112 16th Street NW, #920
Washington, DC 20036
(202) 857-0216

New York Asian Women's Center
39 Bowery Street, #375
New York, NY 10002
(212) 941-1192

Sanctuary for Families
P.O. Box 413
Times Square Station
New York, NY 10108
(212) 582-2091

San Francisco Neighborhood Legal
   Assistance Federation
49 Powell Street
San Francisco, CA 94102
(415) 627-0240

Violence Intervention Project
515 W. 135th Street, #1C
New York, NY 10031
(212) 368-4596

---

**Pamela Jo Lewis** became involved in the area of domestic violence nearly 25 years ago, when she helped set up one of the first crisis lines in Iowa. While in law school at the University of Iowa, Iowa City, she did extensive work in the area of marital rape and presented programs at the National Women and Law Conference as well as at the Midwest Women in the Law Conference. She helped draft the first mandatory arrest laws in Iowa (for domestic violence). She currently serves as Magistrate for Linn County, Iowa, and is a judicial representative on the Linn County Coalition Against Domestic Violence. She has taught a section on domestic violence at each of the State Magistrate Schools for the last six years. In 1993, Lewis served on the Iowa Supreme Court Committee on Domestic Violence and is one of the coauthors of a bench manual on the subject for all judges in the state.

Chapter 6

# Children's Rights
## Part I: Sexual Abuse

Connie Bauman

Part I Outline

**Introduction**

**The Decision to Report**

**The Investigation**

**Charging Decisions**

**The Court System**

**Preparing for Trial**

**The Trial**

**Conclusion**

Introduction   Over the past two decades there has been a steady increase in the number of children who appear as witnesses in criminal court. The vast majority of these children are victims of sexual assault. However, children may also appear in criminal court as victims of assault, neglect, or child endangerment, or they may be witnesses to violent crimes, including homicide. The legal process and the process of preparing the children are essentially the same for all of them. Part I of this chapter focuses on sexual abuse, since it is the crime that brings the most child victims into court.

Since the 1970s criminal courts have changed substantially in how child abuse cases are handled. During the 1970s women set up a network of rape centers across the country and began to talk about their adult and childhood experiences. These discussions led to public education on the subject of child abuse, which led to new laws to deal with it. Groups were also formed which began to educate children in schools about sexual abuse, such as what kind of touching is appropriate. The number of reported incidents of sexual abuse greatly increased. As reports increased, child protective services and police investigators needed training not only on investigative techniques and coordinating investigative efforts, but also on how to talk to children about sexual abuse. Lawyers and judges have been slower to recognize the need for specialized training and treatment of children in the court process.

Learning that your child has been abused is a nightmare for parents. Adding to the dilemma is the fact that the majority of suspects is someone the child knows. Most parents hope that their child would come directly to them if something was wrong. Unfortunately, this is rarely the case with sexual abuse. A child may tell a classmate, sibling, or diary; a child may tell a teacher, draw a disturbing picture, or repeat something inappropriate that a suspect had told them. If your child does not tell you immediately it does not mean you are a bad parent. Children interpret sexual abuse in a varieties of ways, all of which generally make it difficult for children to talk about.

Parents assume that if they talk to their children about abuse, their children will know what to do if it happens. One mother was puzzled because her eight-year-old daughter did not tell her that her father was touching her, even after the mother had spent considerable energy educating her daughter. When she asked her daughter why she had not told her she replied, "You never told me what to do if daddy touched me. You only told me what to do if it was a stranger." There are as many reasons why a child does not tell as there are children. The only way to understand the child's reasoning is to ask him or her and to listen very carefully to the child's explanation. Many children feel that it's their own fault and that their parents will blame them. If the abuser is a parent, family friend, or other relative, children may worry about causing a conflict between adults. In many situations the abuser is very kind, which causes the child more confusion. The child may even have liked the special treatment, special presents, or physical enjoyment. The child should be given permission to acknowledge the pleasure and reject the loss of control. Overt violence is rarely involved in these cases.

Parents, too, react in a range of ways. Some want to take the law into their own hands; others become immobilized with fear and anger. Some despair and say their child's life is ruined when, in fact, it is not. For those who were abused as children themselves, their child's disclosure triggers painful memories of the past. If the abuser is a spouse, close friend, or relative the report can spur a conflict of loyalty for the nonabusive parent; there exists a feeling of having to choose between the child and another significant relationship.

Amidst the emotional turmoil of both parent and child, decisions need to be made. Trusted friends and relatives can be a great support. Most communities have sexual assault centers, women's centers, crime victims centers, crisis lines, or other organizations that are staffed with trained people who can assist you. Pediatricians, school counselors, and ministers may also be of assistance. Seek support for your child and yourself. This is not a time to do it alone. No parent is generally prepared for this type of disclosure by her child. Do not be afraid to ask for help.

## The Decision to Report

In most states the decision to report abuse to the authorities is not necessarily left up to the parents. Any professional who has knowledge of a child being abused must report. If you seek assistance from a medical doctor, counselor, or school personnel in most states they are required to report the incident immediately.

If the incident has not been reported, then the parent or guardian must make that decision. If the suspect is the child's parent or caretaker there will be severe consequences to the child for not reporting; the child will be with the abuser with no intervention. If a nonoffending parent knows that the other parent is abusive but does not report it, there can be serious consequences for both parents. Most professionals recommend that all abuse be reported. Even if no legal action can be taken, at least the report is on record and may be useful if a subsequent report is received.

In most communities reports of child abuse are made either to the police or child protection services. Reports must be made in the jurisdiction where the incident happened. It is best to make the report as soon as possible after learning of the incident. As time passes it becomes more difficult to obtain evidence and to locate witnesses. Be sure to indicate if you feel the child is in immediate danger.

Most suspected child abusers are not arrested immediately, which is often very frustrating for parents. However, a careful investigation must occur and evidence must be gathered first. Remember that even though you may be convinced of a suspect's guilt, the suspect has constitutional rights that cannot be violated. The suspect remains innocent in the eyes of the law until proven guilty.

## The Investigation

Investigations that can result in criminal charges are conducted by a police officer. The purpose is to gather as much specific information from the child as possible. The interview with the child is often videotaped. The interviewer generally asks the parents to wait in a separate area to avoid there being any suggestion that the parents told the child what to say. Also, for many children, it is easier to talk about the graphic details without their parents being present. In preparing your child for the interview, it is best to simply explain what is going to happen and to give your child permission to tell the police the truth. Never suggest to the child how to answer any questions. A simple instruction to tell the truth is best. Never ask the child questions that would suggest a type of behavior by the suspect such as, "Did he touch your breast?" Say instead, "And then what happened?" Let children explain in their own words and in their own way. How adults question a child is always scrutinized during the investigation, and some children, particularly very young children, can be susceptible to suggestions.[1]

Remember that it is the police's role to conduct the investigation; it is not your responsibility. Cooperate by providing them with all the information you have as well as names of other potential witnesses. Do not attempt to investigate yourself. This could result in a faulty investigation which could jeopardize the case. Police may request that your child have a medical examination to determine if there is physical evidence. The investigation may take days, weeks, even months. The police may also keep some evidence from you to protect your reliability as a witness should the case go to trial. Parents become very frustrated and impatient during this process. Sometimes knowing this is the normal process can help relieve some of the anxiety. Once the investigation is complete, the information is sent to the prosecutor's office to be reviewed for possible charging.

## Charging Decisions

The decision whether to charge a suspect is made by the district attorney after reviewing the investigation. It is not you against the suspect; the state brings the charges. The district attorney represents the state and is technically not your attorney. You do not need to hire your own attorney.

Not all cases presented to the prosecutor are charged. The district attorney generally must ask herself if she believes a crime was committed and if she feels she can prove it. There are cases where no one is sure what happened. There are cases where the prosecutor believes a crime was committed but sees no way to prove it. However, there are cases where it is believed a crime was committed and there is evidence to prove it. These are cases that are charged and enter the court system.

If your child's case is not charged, the police or the prosecutor's office can provide you with an explanation. This explanation will often be a technical legal reason; it will probably be frustrating to you. This decision does not mean your child was not abused; it means the legal system will not attempt to hold the suspect accountable. There are still many steps you can take to help your child. You can keep your child safe. You can get counseling for your child and yourself. You can get a court order to keep the suspect away from your child. If the suspect is the child's parent, legal action may be taken in juvenile court or family court to keep the suspect away from the child. Another option is to contact a private attorney to discuss filing a civil suit against the suspect.

## The Court System

For most adults, and especially for children, entering the court system is like entering a foreign culture with its own language, rules, and ethics. As a parent, your first step should be to find a guide who has experience with child witnesses and with your local court system and who can walk you and your child through the process. These guides can be found in a number of places. Many district attorney's offices now have programs for victims and many have staff who work specifically with children. They can explain the process, as well as your rights. If your district attorney does not have such a person, ask if she is aware of anyone in the community who can fulfill this function. Most communities have a rape center, women's center, or crime victim's center that may have advocates available. In some areas the child welfare department may be able to provide this service. If your child is in counseling, perhaps the therapist would make herself available. You need someone who can translate for you and advocate for your child's needs in this system. Don't assume that the system will automatically look out for your child's needs.

The court process will take a very long time; a minimum of many months, possibly a year, and in the worst cases two years. Some states now have laws that child cases have priority in scheduling, but there continue to be enormous delays. It's important to go on with your life during this time. You need to separate the things you can do from those over which you have no control. You will most likely not be involved in the routine legal procedures of this case. Most of the decisions will be made by the district attorney.

The laws in your state will determine what rights you have as a victim. In most states you have the right to be kept informed of the case status, the right to be informed of and to object to any plea bargain, and the right to make a statement at the time of sentencing. Most victims view these rights as minimal compared to the defendant's rights. But remember that the system is referred to as the "criminal justice system," not the "victim justice system." It was established to protect the rights of defendants, and those rights are important. It is only in the last decade that victims have had any rights at all. Many now believe that it is possible to provide rights for both defendants and victims.

The vast majority of cases will be settled by plea negotiations. These are meetings between the defendant's attorney, the district attorney, and the judge to see if there is a way to settle the case without going to trial. Plea bargaining often receives bad press, but it is a necessary part of the system. There are often good reasons on both sides to avoid a trial. If the defendant goes to trial and is found guilty, he or she may risk a stiffer sentence. The prosecutor may want to spare the child having to testify, or she may want a guaranteed conviction rather than risk an acquittal. Parents often assume that going to trial will bring a conviction. This is not true. There is always a risk when going to trial. Plea negotiations are a balancing act. If a good outcome can be achieved without a trial the prosecutor may be in agreement. In most states this decision will not be made without discussing the options with the child's family.

If the defendant accepts the plea bargain and pleads guilty, the next step will be the sentencing. If the defendant pleads not guilty the next step will be to prepare for trial.

## Preparing for Trial

Preparation is the key to bringing a child into a courtroom. From the beginning it is important to tell children—in age-appropriate language—the truth about what may happen. What they imagine may be worse than what is reality. Some children believe that the judge might put them in jail. Others may think they have to sit and talk to the defendant. Some children worry about weapons in the courtroom, or they fear being on TV and having their friends see them.

The most important way anyone can help a child prepare to go to court is to listen. Provide the child with some very basic information and listen carefully to his or her responses. Children respond in such a multitude of ways that there is no one prescription for helping kids through this process. Children who have been treated violently or threatened with weapons are generally the most fearful. Convincing these children of the safety of the courtroom is often difficult. Kids who have been sexually abused are often shameful when talking about the actual events. For them, actually saying the words is the most difficult. For each child the hurdles will be different and will require different remedies.

In some communities, staff in the victim/witness unit will do much of the pretrial preparation, and the child will meet the prosecutor shortly before the trial. It is important that your child meet with the prosecutor sometime before trial. Although the prosecutor is more than likely overwhelmed with cases, that is no excuse for your child not to get the preparation he or she needs. No child should go into a courtroom without being prepared. Parents should insist on meeting the prosecutor ahead of time. Provide the prosecutor with information about your child and how your child is handling the aftermath of the abuse. Get all of your questions answered.

The prosecutor should discuss with the child what she intends to ask in court. The prosecutor will try to determine the best way to question the child so that the child is able to tell what happened. Prosecutors vary in their ability and comfort level in talking with children. If your child expresses concerns about the attorney or the questions being asked you should be assertive and discuss this with the prosecutor.

Children also need a tour of the courtroom. They need to know who will be in the courtroom when they testify and what that person's job is. They need to know that the defendant will be present during their testimony. This is often frightening and/or embarrassing for the child. It is a good time to strategize with the child regarding different things he or she can do to handle seeing the defendant. Children often suggest their own best strategies. Some children often enjoy playing the different roles in the courtroom: judge, juror, bailiff, court reporter. The more mystery that can be taken out of the process the better. In some communities judges may be receptive to meeting a child prior to trial. Some children are afraid of the judge and this may help to calm their fears.

During the tour is a good time to talk about the oath and what it means. Children should never be told what to say other than to tell them that they should listen to the questions and just tell the truth. Children also need to be told that it is okay if they don't know the answer to a question they are asked. Because children may be penalized in school for not knowing the answer, they may feel that the same is true for court. They need to be reassured that in this instance it is okay if they don't know all the answers.

The courtroom tour usually allows misconceptions about the trial process to surface. For example, some children may believe that the verdict is randomly pulled from a hat. Others may believe that the jurors are all the friends and relatives of the defendant. Some children might think that the court reporter is writing letters to the defendant. It is important that every role performed in the courtroom be understood by the child before the trial begins. What they wrongly believe may cause them unneeded anxiety at the time of trial.

## The Trial

No two criminal trials are alike. Although the legal rules are the same, the courtroom atmosphere varies greatly according to what judge hears the case and the personalities and styles of the prosecutor and defense attorney. It is an adversarial system and often a hostile environment, especially for children.

Since a traumatized child is not a good witness, there are steps that some judges take to minimize the trauma for children. In many states the judge may keep all spectators (other than a support person for the child) from the courtroom while the child testifies. Some judges will allow a trusted adult to sit by a very young child while he or she testifies. A handful of judges will try to reassure the child and say something like, "This is my courtroom and you are safe here. I just want you to tell the truth." Unfortunately, many judges treat the child as a miniature adult and make no special provisions unless the child cries or is frozen in fear. Even then some judges do nothing. By the time a child gets to this emotional point he or she may have lost the ability to testify. Thus, it is important to make the courtroom a safe environment before the child enters.

Some states are beginning to pass laws on alternative ways to admit children's testimony. Some states allow videotaping or closed-circuit TV. But the states and situations in which alternative means can be used are rare. In the vast majority of cases the child must testify. Check with the prosecutor to learn what the rules are in your state.

Language is a huge barrier for children in court. They cannot answer what they do not understand. There are no special rules that take into account the cognitive and linguistic development of children:

> Children's apparent lack of credibility has as much to do with the competence of adults to relate to and communicate with children as it does with children's abilities to remember and relate their experiences accurately. The communicative competence of adults and children is an often overlooked determinant of credibility. Broadly defined, communicative competence in the forensic context is the ability of adults to elicit and of children to provide reliable information in a questions–answer format about a potentially traumatic autobiographical event, an event of which the adult has no firsthand knowledge but

likely does have preconceived notions based on information provided by others.

The adult questioner's communicative competence depends on the ability to communicate in a non-biased manner at the child's level of understanding of conversational rules and concept, accounting for the child's age, vocabulary, and linguistic skill. Children's communicative competence depends on a host of skills required of witnesses, including the ability to translate memories into language, to deal with non-comprehension, to reason, and to distinguish fact from fantasy. Also germane is their knowledge of the legal system and their ability to cope with the stress of testifying. Successful communication entails all these skills. It advances the fact-finding process and the course of justice, protecting children from danger and adults from false accusations. Communication failures obscure the fact-finding process and derail the course of justice, with cases dismissed because of concerns over children's competence and credibility.[2]

This is not to say that there are not attempts on the part of some prosecutors, defense attorneys, and judges to modify their languages in order to communicate effectively with the children. But there are no rules to modify the court process to take into account emotional, cognitive, and linguistic development of a child. Children can testify and can tell the truth, but they can only tell in a child's way, not a lawyer's way. If the trial is indeed a truth-determining process, then it seems that the process itself should be designed to ensure that the truth is determined. For children to explain their experiences they need to feel safe; they need to be asked questions that they understand. Judges and lawyers vary greatly in their ability or willingness to ensure this type of environment. The system does not guarantee this environment for the child. It is entirely at the discretion of the judge and lawyers. More often than not they do not provide it.

In spite of many barriers, children can and do testify in criminal trials. After the child testifies, the prosecutor will call to the witness stand any other witnesses that corroborate what the child has said. These witnesses may be police officers, doctors, counselors, other children, parents, teachers, or social workers. Although the child's testimony is critical, the case does not rest on the child's testimony alone. After the prosecution's case is complete, the defense will then call its witnesses. The defendant may testify but is not required to do so.

At the close of the trial each lawyer will give a closing statement. The judge will explain the law to the jurors, who will then deliberate. If the jury reaches a guilty verdict, it will be up to the judge to sentence the defendant. In many states the victim or victim's family has a right to make a statement at the time of sentencing. Each state has different laws, however, so the prosecutor needs to be consulted regarding the sentencing guidelines in your state.

A not guilty verdict is very difficult to explain to children. Many children feel that they were not believed. This is usually not the case. Jurors often report that they believe the child but wanted more evidence. The quality of the investigation may also be an issue. Sometimes the jury is confused by the judge's instructions. If this happens, it is important to reassure the child that he or she is safe and that the child did his or her best. The prosecutor should take responsibility for the verdict so that the child does not feel that the burden rested on the child's shoulders. And remember that there are still options for keeping your child safe even if the defendant is not held accountable.

## Conclusion

The criminal justice system is neither easy nor perfect for children, but it remains the only peaceful vehicle in our society to stop the victimization of children. No matter what the system does or does not do, children can heal from abuse with love, support, counseling, and time. Many parents despair that their children's recovery depends on what the system does. Although everyone works and hopes for a conviction, the child's recovery is not dependent on it. If a perpetrator is convicted and sent to prison a family must still heal its pain, just as the child whose case was not charged must. Do not allow yourself or your child to be a victim to this system or to your beliefs of what the system will do for you and your child. Even if the defendant is convicted and punished, it will not take away your pain or restore your child to innocence. Take steps whenever possible to protect and support your child. Get counseling, ask for help, and obtain information. Do what you can but realize when you are powerless. Remember that the system will not determine your child's ultimate recovery—that is up to you.

## Notes

1. S. J. Ceci, D. R. Ross, and M. P. Toglia. "Age Difference in Suggestibility: Narrowing the Uncertainties." In S. J. Ceci, M. P. Toglia, and D. R. Ross (eds.). *Children's Eyewitness Memory*. New York: Springer–Verlag, 1987.
2. K. Saywitz, R. Nathanson, and L. Snyder. "Credibility of Child Witnesses: The Role of Communication Competence." *Language Disorders* (August 1993): 59–78.

## Bibliography

Byerly, Carolyn M. *The Mother's Book: How to Survive the Molestation of Your Child, 2d ed.* Dubuque, IA: Kendall/Hunt Publishing, 1992. (To purchase a copy, contact the publisher at (319) 589-1000.)

Crewdson, John. *By Silence Betrayed: Sexual Abuse of Children in America.* Boston: Little, Brown, 1988.

Crowley, Patricia. *Not My Child: A Mother Confronts her Child's Sexual Abuse.* New York: Doubleday, 1990.

Hagans, Kathryn, and Joyce Case. *When Your Child Has Been Molested: A Parent's Guide to Healing and Recovery.* Lexington, MA: Lexington Books, 1988

Dziech, Billie Wright, and Judge Charles B. Schuydon. *On Trial: American Courts and Their Treatment of Sexually Abused Children.* Boston: Beacon Press, 1989.

Finkelhor, David. *A Sourcebook on Child Sexual Abuse.* Beverly Hills: Sage Publications, 1986.

Iverson, Timothy J., and Marilyn Segal. *Child Abuse and Neglect: An Information and Resource Guide.* New York: Garland Publishing, 1990.

Mithers, Carol Lynn. "Incest and the Law." *New York Times Magazine,* October 21, 1990.

National Center on Women and Family Law. *Legal Issues and Legal Options in Civil Child Sexual Abuse Cases: Representing the Protective Parent.* New York, 1990. (To obtain a copy contact the organization at 799 Broadway, Room 402, New York, NY 10003.)

Webster, Linda. *Sexual Assault and Child Sexual Abuse: A National Directory of Victim/Survivor Services and Prevention Programs.* Phoenix: Oryx Press, 1989.

"Young Victims of Sex Abuse Go Unheard." *Washington Post,* March 15, 1992. Families of children who have been molested are filing civil suits far more frequently, because the burden of proof is lower. The problem of very young victims on the witness stand is also covered.

## Organizational Resources

These national organizations can refer you to local resources:

ACLU—Children's Rights Project
132 W. 43rd Street, 6th Floor
New York, NY 10036
(212) 944-9800

Boys Town
(800) 448-3000
Offers nationwide referrals to a variety of social service agencies geared toward issues including abuse, suicide, runaways, school problems, and drug and alcohol problems.

Children's Defense Fund
122 C Street NW
Washington, DC 20001
(202) 628-8787

Covenant House
(800) 999-9999 ("Nineline")
One of the largest privately funded
child care agencies in the country
provides shelter, counseling, food,
and other necessities to youth under the age of twenty-one. It has
shelters in a number of cities and
the Nineline provides referral information.

National Center for Missing and
    Exploited Children
(800) 843-5678

National Clearinghouse on Run-
    away and Homeless Youth
P.O. Box 13505
Silver Spring, MD 20911-3505
(301) 608-8098

National Council on Child Abuse
    and Family Violence
(800) 222-2000
Monday through Friday only.

National Network of Runaway and
    Homeless Youth Services
1319 F Street NW, Suite 201
Washington, DC 20004

National Organization of Victim
    Assistance (NOVA)
1757 Park Road NW
Washington, DC 20010
(202) 232-6682

National Victim Center
307 West Seventh Street, Suite 1001
Fort Worth, TX 76102
(817) 877-3355

Naitonal Victim Resource Center
U.S. Department of Justice
Box 6000-AJE
Rockville, MD 20850
(800) 627-6872
(301) 251-5525

**Connie Bauman** has provided advocacy for children within the
Hennepin County Attorney's Office in Minneapolis since 1984.
She previously was on the staff of the Minnesota Program for
Victims of Sexual Assault, which provided funding and technical
assistance to the thirty rape centers throughout Minnesota.

Chapter 6

# Children's Rights
## Part II: Families in Juvenile Court

I. Fay Nosow

Part II Outline

**Introduction**

**Juvenile Delinquency Proceedings**

**Welfare Proceedings**

**Conclusion**

Introduction

In the 1990s, the problems of juveniles have attracted the attention of society as never before. The lower educational standards and greater dropout rates have troubled educators and parents. The rapid increase in pregnancies among teenagers is a key factor propelling welfare reform. The trend toward more violent crimes being committed by younger and younger offenders has led to harsher treatment of juveniles through changes in juvenile statutes. Juvenile courts often are called upon to deal with these and similar problems faced by young people and their families.

A family can come into contact with juvenile court in two ways. First, a child can be charged with an offense. An offense that would be a crime if committed by an adult is called a "delinquency." An offense that only a minor can commit, for example, truancy, running away from home, or underage drinking, is called a "status offense." In either type of case, the child is the "respondent" who must answer the allegations of the petition.

The second way in which a family can be brought to juvenile court is when a petition is brought against the parents of a child for neglect or abuse. The parents are the respondents in these child protection or welfare cases, and the children are named as the subjects to be protected. The first part of this portion of the chapter will discuss the procedures and rights of juveniles in delinquency and status cases. The second part will discuss the procedures and rights in welfare cases.

Juvenile courts have jurisdiction over any person charged with the commission of an offense while the person is a minor. In most states, minors are defined as those under the age of eighteen. Some states have lowered the age from eighteen to seventeen or sixteen for an accused to be subject to juvenile court jurisdiction. Even where the jurisdiction of juvenile court extends to the age of eighteen, juveniles may be tried in adult court if they are charged with serious felonies, such as murder, rape, and some drug offenses. The transfer of a case to adult court may be automatic, given the nature of the crime and the age of the accused, or following a process known as certification or reference. This process will be discussed further below. Normally, children must be at least ten years old before they are charged with a delinquency. Younger children who commit criminal acts are considered to be children in need of protection rather than delinquent.

Juveniles charged with delinquencies have most of the rights and protections of adults charged with crimes. When a youth first comes in contact with the police, the youth is protected by the constitutional guards against unlawful searches, arrests, and questioning. For example, a young person cannot be stopped by the police and searched without a reasonable suspicion that the youth is carrying a weapon. The youth cannot be arrested and then searched unless the police have probable cause to believe that the youth is committing or has committed a crime. On the other hand, searches at school may be conducted by school personnel without the same requirements. School authorities may search student lockers for drugs, weapons, and so forth.

If a juvenile is a suspect in a case, the police will usually seek to question him or her. Before questioning can begin, a juvenile must be advised of his or her "Miranda" rights if the youth is under arrest. Police in many communities routinely advise juveniles of their Miranda rights even if they are not in custody. The Miranda rights include the right to remain silent, that is, not to answer any questions other than

**Juvenile Delinquency Proceedings**

those relating to identification. The Miranda rights also include the right to consult with an attorney before questioning and to have the attorney present during questioning. Though the court will appoint an attorney for a juvenile who cannot afford an attorney, an attorney will not normally be available until the juvenile is charged and makes her first appearance in court. Finally, the child should be told that what she says can and will be used against her in court. Anything the juvenile says can be used in court, even if it is not recorded and even if it is not said in court under oath.

Some states require a parent or guardian to be present during questioning. The presence of a parent is not a substitute for an attorney, however. A parent can make sure that a child is treated fairly, but parents rarely understand the full implications of the child's situation. What may seem like fairly minor conduct on the part of a juvenile may lead to serious delinquency charges. For instance, a youth and her companions may get involved in a fight with another youth. If one of the companions then takes the victim's money, the youth could be charged with participating in a felony robbery even though her role was only a simple assault.

The parent's view of a situation, too, is often different from that of a lawyer. Many parents want their children to take responsibility for their actions and encourage their children to talk to the police. By contrast, an attorney would advise a juvenile not to talk to the police until the attorney has had a chance to discuss the case with the juvenile and to learn about the nature of the charges. Regardless of whether the parent can be present during questioning, an attorney should be consulted before a juvenile speaks with the police about the incident. Police often suggest to suspects that they can help themselves by talking to the police, or that they can go home if they give a statement. This may or may not be true. The police are not in a position to offer promises to an accused; only the prosecutor can do that. In the rare instances where it is in the juvenile's best interest to give a statement to the police, this is best arranged through the juvenile's attorney.

A juvenile has a right to a court-appointed attorney if the juvenile cannot afford one.[1] Courts may vary as to what standards are applied. Parents may be expected to hire an attorney for their child or help pay the costs of a court-appointed attorney if they can afford to do so. Even if the child's parents hire an attorney to represent the child, the child is the client, not the parents. The attorney will keep communications with the child confidential, unless the child authorizes the attorney to share information with the parents. The parents may not agree with the way the attorney is handling the case, but, in cases of conflict, the attorney must protect the interests of the child as she sees fit. The child has the right to make the decisions any client would make, not the parents.

Following an arrest, a juvenile may be detained in order for new charges to be filed or because the juvenile has a warrant for an old charge or a probation violation. If a juvenile is detained, the juvenile will be brought to court as soon as possible for a hearing. This will usually take place within thirty-six hours of arrest. Parents will be notified of the time, place, and nature of the hearing. At this hearing, the court will decide whether to detain or release the juvenile. Juvenile courts have much more leeway to detain respondents than do adult courts. Bail is not required to be set. Instead, juveniles may be held in detention centers or shelters, or they may be released to their parents with or without strict conditions, including, in some communities, electronic monitoring.

The juvenile may be arraigned at the initial hearing or at a subsequent hearing. If the juvenile is not charged with a delinquency immediately and is released after arrest, the juvenile and her parents will receive notice of the arraignment and a copy of the petition before the first court date. At the arraignment, the juvenile admits or denies the charges in the petition. If the case is not resolved at the arraignment, a pretrial conference will be held a few days or a few weeks later.

One of the functions of the defense attorney is to try to resolve the case without a trial. This process, known as "plea bargaining," occurs in most cases. After discussing the case with the client and reviewing the police reports, the attorney will assess the strength of the prosecutor's case and advise the client. The defense attorney will try to minimize the risk to the client, by seeking an agreement to reduce the number or severity of the charges and to limit the penalties. The plea bargaining may occur at any stage of the proceedings, depending upon the practice in a given court system. Families may be unhappy about having to return to court, but often the best results can only be reached with several appearances.

In order to admit a charge, a juvenile must give up her trial rights. A juvenile has all of the same rights at trial as an adult, except the right to a jury trial. A few states provide for jury trials in some juvenile cases, but most juvenile trials are decided by a judge. At a trial, a juvenile is presumed innocent until proven guilty beyond a reasonable doubt. The prosecutor must call witnesses, whom both the prosecutor and the defense attorney may question. The defense also has a right to call witnesses and to have witnesses ordered to appear in court by subpoena. The juvenile, like an adult defendant, decides whether or not to testify at trial. A juvenile cannot be forced to testify or be penalized for remaining silent at trial.

A concept that both juveniles and their parents often do not fully grasp is that the U.S. Constitution gives the juvenile an absolute right to trial and to make the state prove its case, even if the juvenile is guilty of committing the offense charged. Sometimes the prosecutor does not have the evidence necessary to prove the case and sometimes the evidence against the juvenile is inadmissible because it was obtained unlawfully. If such is the case, it may be best for the juvenile to demand a trial to avoid a juvenile record and the penalties that follow a finding of guilt ("adjudication of delinquency"). Again, this may come into conflict with the parents' or child's belief that the child should take responsibility for her actions. The ultimate decision as to whether to have a trial or admit the offense is that of the juvenile.

If the juvenile is found to have committed the offense charged after a trial or upon her own admission, the juvenile will be adjudicated delinquent. A disposition hearing will be scheduled or will be conducted at the same time, depending upon whether the court needs a report from a probation officer, social worker, psychologist, or similar professional before deciding what to order. The disposition, equivalent of a sentence in adult court, may range from probation to incarceration in a juvenile facility. First-time offenders and those charged with minor offenses may be ordered to perform community service, to attend informational or counseling programs, or merely to obey the law and rules at home. Options for those charged with more serious offenses or who have prior juvenile records may include placement at a group home, a residential treatment center, or a juvenile correctional facility. In deciding what type of disposition to order, the court will consider the juvenile's age, prior history, the nature of the offense, and any special circumstances, such as chemical abuse, mental illness, or child protection issues in the juvenile's family.

The disposition options available to the court depend upon the resources in the community and whether the law requires particular punishments for particular crimes. The trend is to mandate commitments to juvenile correctional facilities for specified serious crimes. The juvenile justice system's traditional purpose to rehabilitate juveniles is giving way to the goals of punishment and incapacitation by locking up juveniles in secure facilities.

This trend is most evident in the expanded application of juvenile reference or certification statutes, which allow juveniles to be tried in adult court. Some reference statutes provide for certain cases to proceed automatically in adult court, based on the age of the accused and the nature of the charge. Other cases can be transferred to adult court only after a hearing to determine whether probable cause exists to believe the youth committed the crime charged and whether the youth can be treated in the juvenile justice system, without an undue risk to public safety. The court may consider such factors as the youth's personal, family, and court histories; any psychological profile and diagnosis; and the treatment options available in the juvenile system. If the court decides the juvenile meets the criteria for prosecution in adult court, an adult prosecution will commence. If not, the case proceeds in juvenile court like any other juvenile case.

A hybrid of the juvenile and adult systems is "dual jurisdiction," by which a juvenile may be sent to a juvenile treatment facility while having an adult sentence hanging over her head. For example, a new law in Minnesota allows for the imposition of both a juvenile disposition and an adult probationary sentence after a jury trial in juvenile court. At the same time, the juvenile remains on probation in juvenile court until the age of twenty-one instead of nineteen.[2]

At the other extreme of juvenile offenses are the status offenses. These cases often begin with attempted intervention by school social workers or social services workers. If the behavior continues, a juvenile may be brought to juvenile court. There the procedures are the same as for a delinquency, but the right to a court-appointed attorney may not always apply. Though status cases may seem insignificant, they often signal that the youth has serious individual or family problems. Court action may eventually lead to out-of-home placement in a foster home, group home, or treatment facility. It is, therefore, advisable for a juvenile to obtain legal representation, particularly when out-of-home placement is being contemplated.

## Welfare Proceedings

Sometimes the same problems that can be brought into court as status offenses are instead brought into court as welfare cases. The focus is on the parents instead of the child. For example, the prosecutor may decide that the reason children in a family are not attending school is that the parent's depression is preventing the parent from getting the children to school. Instead of bringing truancy charges against the children, the prosecutor may file a petition charging the parent with educational neglect. This would allow the court to order the parent to get appropriate help, if the petition were proven or admitted.

Welfare cases are all aimed at protecting children. In some cases, the welfare authorities are attempting to force parents to receive treatment or services they have resisted. In such instances, the authorities may not seek removal of the children, but rather protective supervision, that is, the ability to check on the welfare of the children. A welfare case might be brought when a child has special needs the parents cannot meet without court-ordered assistance. Most commonly, however, welfare cases are begun when children are removed from the home due to immediate danger caused by abuse or neglect.

If children are removed from the home, the parents have the right to have a hearing to determine if the removal was justified and should continue. That hearing must take place promptly and after notice to the parents. If the children continue to be held, the parents will be informed of what they are expected to do before the children can be returned. The most frequent requirements include a chemical dependency evaluation and appropriate treatment, a psychological evaluation, and counseling and parenting courses. If an abusive relationship exists between the adults in the home, they may be required to obtain domestic abuse counseling. The court cannot order anyone to do any of these things until the case is proven against the parents, or as a condition of having the children return home pending final resolution of the case.

If the case is not resolved within a reasonable period of time, which may be months or years, the state may seek to terminate parental rights. Termination of parental rights severs all ties between the parent and child and frees a child for adoption.

Parents in welfare cases have certain procedural protections, but they have fewer protections than a defendant would have in a criminal trial or a juvenile would have in a delinquency case. For example, the standard of proof may be much less.[3] Also, parents have the right to be represented by counsel in a welfare or termination case, but they may not be entitled to a court-appointed attorney. If that is so, the parent should try to obtain a lawyer through legal services or legal aid offices, battered women's shelters, or the local bar association. A parent should not attempt to proceed without a lawyer, because a finding that children are neglected or abused can lead to an attempt to terminate parental rights.

Because both welfare and termination cases are civil rather than criminal, the parents can be called as witnesses by the state. The parent could be made to answer questions about the allegations of abuse so long as those allegations do not involve actual or potential criminal charges. The possibility of related criminal charges being brought is another reason people involved in welfare cases should have legal advice.

Children who are the subjects of a welfare or termination petition may have the right to participate. Depending on the child's age, an attorney or a guardian ad litem may be appointed. Unlike a legal guardian, a guardian ad litem's duties and powers are limited to the particular court proceeding. The guardian ad litem's duty is to report to the court what the guardian believes to be the best interests of the child and to take appropriate legal steps on behalf of the child. Unless the child's attorney is also appointed to act as guardian, the attorney is not expected to evaluate and act upon the child's best interests. Instead, the attorney must represent the child's position to the court, regardless of the attorney's view as to what the best interests of the child might be. Therefore, even if a child has an attorney, a guardian may play an important role in a child welfare case.

With more and more juveniles becoming involved in—and being charged with—criminal activity, we can expect to see change in this area of the law. Attorneys who are familiar with juvenile law will be able to advise families of their child's rights and help guide families through the court process.

**Conclusion**

## Notes

1. Jurisdictions may vary as to when an attorney will be appointed. A general rule is that an attorney should be appointed when the juvenile is charged with a felony level offense or faces the possibility of out-of-home placement.
2. The law took effect January 1, 1995, and is now being challenged in the courts.
3. This varies by jurisdiction. Termination must be proven at least by clear and convincing evidence. Federal law mandates that termination of parental rights in cases covered by the Indian Child Welfare Act can only occur where the state proves beyond a reasonable doubt that termination is in the child's best interest. This law applies to cases involving children who are enrolled or are eligible for enrollment in Indian tribes.

## Bibliography

Bernard, Thomas J. *The Cycle of Juvenile Justice*. New York: Oxford University Press, 1991.

Champion, Dean J. *The Juvenile Justice System: Delinquency, Processing, and the Law*. New York: MacMillan Publishing, 1992.

Chesney-Lind, Meda, and Randall G. Shelden. *Girls, Delinquency, and Juvenile Justice*. Belmont, CA: Wadsworth Publishing, 1992.

Fox, Ken. *Everything You Need to Know About Your Legal Rights*. New York: Rosen Publishing, 1992. (For grades seven through twelve.)

Jasper, Margaret C. *Juvenile Justice and Children's Law*. Dobbs Ferry, NY: Oceana Publishing, 1994.

Krisberg, Barry, and James F. Austin. *Reinventing Juvenile Justice*. Newbury Park, CA: Sage Publications, 1993.

Schwartz, Ira M., ed. *Juvenile Justice and Public Policy: Toward a National Agenda*. New York: MacMillan Publishing, 1992.

Siegel, Larry J., and Joseph J. Senna. *Juvenile Delinquency: Theory, Practice, and Law, 5th ed*. St. Paul, MN: West Publishing, 1994.

## Organizational Resources

ACLU—Children's Rights Project
132 W. 43rd Street, 6th Floor
New York, NY 10036
(213) 944-9800

National Center for Juvenile Justice
701 Forbes Avenue
Pittsburgh, PA 15219
(412) 227-6950

*Research division for National Council of Juvenile and Family Court judges. Publishes a number of reports, maintains statistics, databases, and a major research library.*

National Center for Youth Law
  (NCYL) (Family Law)
1663 Mission Street, 5th Floor
San Francisco, CA 94103
(415) 543-3307

National Runaway Switchboard
(312) 880-9860 (business)
(800) 621-4000 (hotline)

Runaway Hotline
(512) 463-2000 (business)
(800) 231-6946 (hotline)

---

**I. Fay Nosow** is an Assistant Hennepin County Public Defender, specializing in juvenile law. She has taught juvenile justice courses at William Mitchell College of Law. In addition to a J.D. from Georgetown University Law Center, she holds a B.A. from the University of Michigan and an M. Phil. from the University of Edinburgh.

Chapter 7

# Premarital Agreements and Cohabitation Arrangements

Jacqueline Miller

Chapter Outline

**Premarital Agreements**

**Cohabitation Arrangements**

Premarital (sometimes called prenuptial or antenuptial) agreements are contracts signed by a couple before they marry. These contracts traditionally covered the rights a husband and wife would have in each other's property during the marriage and upon the death of one of them. In practice, this usually meant that a wife would agree to accept a certain sum of money in return for waiving any interest she might have in her husband's estate after his death; or a husband might waive lifetime rights he might have in his wife's property. There has never been much controversy surrounding these types of premarital agreements, and all fifty states recognize and will enforce valid premarital agreements which are limited in scope to property rights during marriage and after death.

However, premarital agreements that attempt to define the rights a husband and wife will have in each other's property in the case of divorce or the right each one will have to alimony have been less unanimously enforced. In past years, such agreements were held to

## Premarital Agreements

be against public policy since they "encouraged" divorce. This view is now the minority viewpoint and most courts today will enforce a valid premarital agreement dealing with property in a divorce proceeding. Provisions fixing the amount of alimony or doing away with it entirely are not as widely enforced. Only twenty-nine states have laws that clearly allow a couple to include alimony as part of a premarital agreement. But a woman should not sign a premarital agreement which limits her right to alimony if there is a divorce under the belief that it will not be enforced.

The law is moving in the direction of allowing couples to preplan their financial affairs. Even in those states that currently do not rigidly enforce alimony provisions in premarital agreements, the court may at least use the fact of signing as evidence of the party's intent. While some states do not automatically prohibit terms about child custody or support in premarital agreements, no state allows the couple to bargain away a parent's obligation to support his or her children or usurp the judge's job of deciding what custody and visitation arrangements are in the best interest of children.

The question of what makes a premarital agreement a valid one that the court will enforce differs from state to state and from one factual situation to another. Therefore, a woman should consult an attorney in the place where she is getting married to be sure of the effect of a premarital agreement she is being asked to sign. There are some basic considerations that apply to most premarital agreements. Almost all states require that the premarital agreement be in writing; many states also require that the parties personally sign the agreement. Premarital agreements must be voluntarily and freely entered into and a court will refuse to enforce one if there has been fraud, duress, coercion, or undue influence applied to one party. Complete disclosure of each party's assets and income is generally required, and there is an overall requirement that the premarital agreement be fair when made. The general trend is to interpret the condition of fairness being satisfied if both sides were represented by their own attorneys and there has been a full and frank disclosure of all income sources, assets, and debts on the part of both parties. Judges, however, are sometimes willing to set aside a low alimony provision as unfair if a long period of time has elapsed between the original agreement and the time of the divorce.

A woman who is asked to sign a premarital agreement should always consult a lawyer before doing so to make sure her rights are protected. Men sometimes tell their future wives that the premarital agreement just says each person gets whatever they brought into the marriage free and clear of all claims from the other. Many agreements, however, say more than that; often there are provisions that determine the fate of the property which is acquired during the marriage. For instance, a provision dealing with stocks may provide that the man receives not only the shares which he already owned at the time of the marriage, but also any additional shares acquired during the marriage. A provision dealing with a house one of the parties owns at the time of the marriage may not take into account the increase in the home's value over the course of years due to improvements and maintenance made to the property by the other party. A woman should also be concerned about provisions that purport to release all her claims in the man's property since this can be interpreted to mean she has released probate claims, such as a widow's allowance, the spouse's elective share, and homestead rights in the event that her husband dies.

A couple is not necessarily bound for all time by the terms of a premarital agreement. Specific terms in the premarital agreement can be made inapplicable by lifetime gifts and provisions in a will. In other words, even if a premarital agreement states that a husband will have no claim to the wife's house, she can give him the house by signing a deed during the marriage and he will own the house at the time of divorce or death. Likewise, a husband can bequeath his wife stock in his will even if the premarital agreement says she shall have no claim to his stock. Couples who have been married many years should review their premarital agreement and determine if it still expresses their property wishes. It may be that at the time of the marriage the couple were focused on "saving" property for children of a prior marriage, but by the time the second marriage has lasted thirty years, the couple feels more obligation to provide for the surviving spouse than to leave an inheritance for scattered children. Some states have specific procedures which need to be followed to formally revoke a premarital agreement; however, the couple may be able to undo the effects of the agreement by lifetime gifts and/or bequests in wills.

## Cohabitation Arrangements

In recent years, more women are becoming involved in cohabitation situations. Cohabitation, or living together, does not have the institutionalized status of marriage, and therefore the law that applies to the situation is not generally codified in statutes or spelled out clearly in case law. Legal principles that are applied to cohabitation arrangements also vary widely from state to state and even from county to county. As a basic principle, it is important to realize that any law that applies to "spouses" or "wives" generally does not apply to a cohabiting woman. This is unfortunate for the cohabiting woman since these "spouse's rights" laws were often passed in recognition of the bad situations married women endured because of unilateral actions on the part of their husbands. For the cohabiting woman, these bad situations remain a very real possibility since she is not covered by the laws and so does not receive the protection provided to married women. For instance, there is a federal law that requires a wife's consent by signature if her employee husband wants to take all of his pension benefits up front and leave nothing for her when he dies. In a cohabitation situation, the man can make all the decisions about retirement payout, survivor benefits, etc. totally on his own and there is no requirement that his unmarried mate of many years even be informed, let alone have any input into the decision making. Likewise, health insurance policies that cover a spouse will not cover the unmarried partner.

There is a growing trend for cohabiting couples to enter into written cohabitation agreements. These agreements can be fairly complex and cover how the partners intend to handle finances, household chores, and general living arrangements. It is doubtful that a couple could get a court to enforce provisions concerning who does the housework or even who owns the property as long as the relationship remains intact. However, courts have been willing to enforce the financial and property terms when the couple splits up. If a woman is going to live with a man without being married she might want to check her state law and see if a cohabitation agreement would be in her best interest.

One area where marriage and cohabitation are being treated more and more the same is child custody and child support. Equity actions for the custody of children can be filed when the cohabiting couple breaks up. These actions are used to determine the legal and physical custody of children and the visitation rights of the noncustodial parent. In the past, it was standard for states to have laws providing that an unmarried mother was the sole custodian of a child born out of wedlock; therefore, hardly any unmarried fathers were awarded physical custody of their child. However, the modern trend is to apply the custody standards used in divorce cases to the equity custody actions, including presumptions favoring joint legal custody and liberal contact between the child and both parents, particularly in those cases where the father, mother, and child have cohabited. Therefore, a woman who is hesitant to marry her child's father should think twice before she agrees to live with him, if one of her concerns is possible disputes over the care and raising of the child. She may have a better chance of retaining control of those issues in a custody action if she has never resided together with her child's father as a family.

The laws on child support pretty much disregard the marital status of a child's parents. In other words, the parent/child relationship is what triggers the obligation for support and brings parents into the provisions of state child support statutes that lead to orders for child support from the noncustodial parent. Most states have adopted the

Uniform Child Support law which authorizes child support collection agencies and county attorneys to bring actions for child support against noncustodial parents. These support actions establish a child's paternity and order support, but typically do not include any provisions for custody or visitation. Most jurisdictions will have public officials "represent" a woman for the purposes of the child support action, but will require her to retain her own counsel to deal with custody/visitation issues. The passage of the Uniform Reciprocal Support Act by all fifty states means there is a mechanism for collecting child support from the noncustodial parent wherever resident.

Property distribution is one area where a cohabiting partner may be much worse off than a married partner. Modern divorce laws specifically provide for a more or less even division of the couple's joint property, no matter who it technically belongs to. However, these laws do not apply to the cohabitation couple who is breaking up; regular personal property law is usually applied to the disposition of the couple's assets. Typically the first problem is that there may not be a clearly defined cause of action for getting the property dispute in front of a judge. A woman who is part of a splitting couple who cannot agree on the distribution of their assets will probably have to consult an attorney to determine if she should file a partition action or declaratory judgment action or even some of the old common law property actions like replevin or conversion. Whatever the name of the action, ownership of property is usually determined by who paid for it and/or the name on the title. A woman who has not worked outside the home will have a difficult time arguing that any of the property acquired during the time she and her partner have lived together belongs to her. His proof that he paid for it all will usually be enough to give him the victory in court. Some modern courts are beginning to recognize that the body of law from the property dispute actions of the past is not completely applicable to the splitting cohabiting couple and are starting to use more equitable concepts which can give a woman some relief from the harshest consequences in the question of ownership.

Likewise, a woman who has signed a written cohabitation agreement can look to the courts to enforce the property distribution terms contained in the agreement. As for support, or palimony, the only way to collect it is through an agreement between the parties. In other words, there is no right for the unmarried woman to get support from the man; any right she may have is derived totally from whatever agreement she and her partner entered into. Many women, including the celebrities, have tried to get courts to enforce oral agreements for support. There is no question that the courts are much more likely to find an agreement exists and to enforce it if it is in writing.

## Bibliography

See also chapter 8.

Ihara, Toni, and Ralph Warner. *The Living Together Kit,* 7th ed. Berkeley, CA: Nolo Press, 1994.

Zwack, Joseph P. *Premarital Agreements: When, Why, & How to Write Them.* New York: Harper Collins, 1987.

## Organizational Resources

Consult your local bar association or women's bar association.

---

**Jacqueline Miller** earned her Juris Doctor at the University of Iowa College of Law in 1984 and has worked as a solo practitioner since then. She has taught family law in the paralegal program at Kirkwood Community College, Cedar Rapids, Iowa (1988) and cofounded a domestic violence project, also in Iowa. Her particular areas of expertise include family law, juvenile law, discrimination in employment, assault, and domestic assault. She was the winning attorney for the birth parents in the highly publicized Baby Jessica case. She currently practices law in Minneapolis, Minnesota, where she also does legal research on a variety of topics at the Legal Research Center and is a volunteer attorney for the Legal Advice Clinic.

Chapter 8

# *Divorce*

Jacqueline Miller

Chapter Outline

**Introduction**

**The Marriage Contract**

**When Is a Lawyer Needed?**

**Divorce Law**
Procedural Issues • Substantive Law Issues • Child Custody • Child
Support • Alimony • Property Distribution

**Annulments, Separate Maintenance, and Separations**
Separate Maintenance • Trial Separation

**Conclusion**

For many women, their first contact with the legal system occurs
when their marriage breaks up. Important issues affecting the future
well-being of a woman and her children need to be addressed at a time
when a woman's energy and emotional strength is frequently taxed to
the maximum by the events surrounding the breakup of her marriage.
Unfortunately, a woman often has to live with the consequences of

**Introduction**

choices made under those stressful conditions for many years. A basic understanding of divorce law and procedure can help a woman make decisions that will be in her best interest over the long term.

## The Marriage Contract

Most of us focus on the personal relationship aspect of marriage in today's society and pay little attention to the fact that marriage is a legal contract. Just like a regular contract, rights and obligations flow to each side from the contract of marriage. Spouses have legally recognized property rights in each other's real estate, they may have to pay each other's medical bills, they have rights in each other's pensions or retirement funds, and they may have a duty to support each other financially. Because the marriage contract has traditionally been considered vital to the functioning of society, laws regulating the formation and dissolution of the contract exist in every state. State laws governing the formation of the marriage contract are usually fairly minimal.

The couple contemplating marriage generally obtains a marriage license from the clerk of vital statistics by filling out a simple form. Some states require the couple to have blood tests for venereal diseases, and the couple may have to wait a few days before the license will be issued. States are much more heavily involved in the dissolving of the marriage contract and have detailed and comprehensive laws that must be followed in order to declare the marriage over. The laws governing divorce not only lead to the end of the marriage and the restoration of the parties to single status, but also to court orders on the issues of child custody and support, alimony, and property division.

## When Is a Lawyer Needed?

A threshold issue for each woman involved in a divorce is whether she needs the assistance of a lawyer and if so, when to get it. In terms of the mechanics of getting the divorce, a woman may or may not need a lawyer. Some states have specific streamlined procedures for getting a divorce that are designed to be used by nonlawyers in certain circumstances. Most often those circumstances are limited to couples with no children and/or no property. Absent a specific procedure designed for people to use without an attorney, most people have difficulty preparing and filing documents on their own with all the right "magic words." Perseverance, self-help manuals or groups, and friendly court clerks can enable a woman to handle her own dissolution paperwork, particularly if her husband is not contesting the divorce.

In terms of the substance of the divorce, every woman owes it to herself to at least talk to a lawyer about her particular situation. Many women are told about divorce law by their husbands, and much of that information may be slanted in a way most beneficial to him or even completely wrong. A woman often gets advice from friends and family who have gone through a divorce. Since divorce law is very fact specific, what is true in one state or for one situation or judge will probably not be fully applicable to another person. The only way a woman can be sure of the issues she needs to be concerned about is to explain her situation in detail to an experienced attorney who has no other connection with the case. Her husband's attorney should *never* be used and, in many cases, neither should the family attorney. Once she does that, she may decide she does not need to hire the lawyer at all, or only for a limited purpose such as reviewing a settlement proposal prepared by her husband's attorney. If a woman decides not to use a lawyer, she should always feel free to change her mind at any point and bring a lawyer into the case. It is often difficult to predict at the start of a dissolution action exactly what issues will become a problem; a man who says he does not want custody of the children may suddenly decide he will ask for it anyway, or a woman who thought she wanted to live in the house forever may decide she would rather have it sold and the proceeds split.

Three common scenarios illustrate some of these considerations.

*Scenario 1.* The man and woman have been married one year, and she knows it was a mistake from the beginning. They have no children, no house, no car. Their only possessions are the wedding presents and a joint checking account with one hundred dollars in it. The woman does not expect her husband to fight the divorce. If this woman lives in a state with a streamlined procedure designed for nonlawyers to use, she probably can do her own divorce. To make sure she has not overlooked anything, she should have at least one appointment with a divorce attorney. For instance, if scenario #1 remains the same except the couple have been married ten years and the wife has worked the whole time putting her husband through medical school, she may have a claim against his future income. In some states, professional degrees are treated as marital property if acquired during marriage, and in others this fact pattern would at least generate a claim for temporary alimony.

*Scenario 2.* The man and woman have been married for twelve years and have three children, ages three, six, and ten. She works part-time, and he is a car salesperson making between $40 and $60 thousand a year in salary and commissions. They have ordinary savings and checking accounts, a retirement account, and certificates of deposit in the children's names. He has been having an affair and charging large amounts for entertainment on their joint credit cards. She is on an emotional roller coaster, sometimes trying to get him to marriage counseling and sometimes determined to take the children and move back to her home state. She is thinking of filing for divorce. This woman needs to see a lawyer immediately. She needs to know what the law says about joint debts, about child support, about custody and visitation if one party moves out of state, and whether her state has court-ordered marriage counseling available.

*Scenario 3.* The man and woman have been married for twenty years and have two children, one in college and one a high school senior. He is a minister, and she is a dental hygienist. The marriage has not been good for several years, and he has hired a lawyer and filed for divorce. The woman agrees that a divorce is necessary, and he tells her that his lawyer can handle all the paperwork for both of them. He gives her various documents to sign plus an explanation as to what each one is. This woman should not sign anything until she understands thoroughly the terms of each document and its purpose. If one of the documents is a settlement agreement which contains provisions for property settlement, child support (including provisions for the older child's college tuition, and so on), she should take the proposal to her own attorney for review. Her attorney can help make sure she is getting the settlement she thinks she is getting and also give her advice as to what else she may be entitled. The woman may not need to hire the attorney to put in a general appearance in the case, since the man's attorney can take care of the paperwork as long as they agree on the terms.

## Divorce Law

The law on divorce can be broken into two basic categories: (1) laws that describe the necessary procedures which must be followed, and (2) laws that govern the actual terms of the divorce. For example, a waiting period before a decree is final is a procedural law (category 1), and a requirement that joint marital property be equitably divided is a substantive law (category 2).

Procedurally, all states require the initial filing of a legal document to get the divorce (or dissolution, as it is called in some states) process started. This document may be called a Petition for Dissolution or a Complaint or something else, but its basic function is to request that the marriage be declared legally over and to furnish the legal system with information it needs in order to grant that request. The petition must state the legal grounds or reasons that will allow the court to declare a marriage over and also must request the court to enter orders disposing of the issues of property distribution, support, and child custody, if necessary. The Petition must be filed with the court, and both the husband and wife must receive a copy of it. Many states require a waiting period before the divorce can be granted. At the end of that period, a judge will issue an order dissolving the marriage. The final order will also contain any necessary terms governing property distribution, support, and child custody. In most states, the parties are free to remarry immediately.

## Procedural Issues

Sometimes the procedural requirements for getting a divorce can present problems. Usually it is clear where the divorce action should be filed, and it is easy to make sure the other side receives the required notice and copy of the divorce petition. The choice of the proper court can present a problem if the parties live in different counties or states, especially if children are involved. Most venue rules require that the action be filed in the county of the defendant's residence, and the Uniform Child Custody Jurisdiction Act requires that actions affecting the custody of children be filed in the children's home state.

The home state of a child is defined as where the child has been living for at least six months, provided she was not brought to that state by some sort of child snatching or deceit. A woman will spend less money if she can litigate her divorce in her local court system, so it is often worth her while to resolve any disputes in her favor at the outset. Other problems getting the divorce action filed can arise because some states have a residency requirement before a dissolution action can be filed. There are usually exceptions to these requirements, but anyone who wishes to file a divorce action and is new in a state needs to check out residency requirements.

"Serve the petition" means that the other side must receive a copy of the petition for dissolution at roughly the same time it is filed with the court. If relations between the man and woman are friendly, the other side can accept service of the papers by picking them up and signing a document that says "I received the papers." If relations are not so good, the sheriff or a private process server will have to be hired to find the other side and hand the paperwork to him or her. Sheriffs are often cheaper, but slower. Private process servers can be expensive, but may be worth the extra money, particularly if a woman needs to know exactly when the other side was served (often a good idea if he is a batterer). The paperwork will tell the other side how long he or she has to answer or respond to the dissolution petition, and it is a good idea to meet that deadline.

While it is true that most judges will allow late filings in dissolution actions or set aside default judgments fairly easily, there is no sense in taking that risk. If a woman cannot get to a lawyer before the deadline, she should copy the heading from the paperwork she received, make a statement of her intention to participate in the dissolution action, sign her name, and file it with the court.

Other procedural matters to be aware of concern temporary orders and required paperwork. Most states make some provision for temporary orders concerning child custody and support after a divorce action is filed, but before it becomes final. Some states also allow temporary orders concerning property distribution or occupancy of the family home. Basically, a party requests that the court enter these temporary orders at the start of the action. Some states provide for in-person hearings which can be quite elaborate in terms of evidence and testimony presented. Other states provide that the temporary orders will be issued only on the basis of paperwork submitted by the parties. Some states require that both sides file a financial statement showing their assets and debts. Some states also require statements showing both sides' incomes, particularly if child support or alimony are at issue. Other states may require proof of mediation, marriage counseling, or custody counseling. All of these required papers must be filed before the final divorce decree can be granted.

If the divorce is contested it will be assigned a trial date before a judge; there are generally no juries in dissolution trials. After the trial, the judge will issue a written Finding of Facts, Order and Decree, in which she will tell the parties what the terms of their divorce will be. If neither side appeals, the judge's decree will be final. If the parties can work out a settlement agreement on their own, no trial will be scheduled. Some states still require the presence of at least one party in front of a judge for a five-minute hearing before the judge signs a decree prepared by the party's lawyer. Many states, however, do not require the physical presences of either side if there is a signed settlement agreement. It should be noted that a fairly large number of people who file for divorce do not complete the action. In many states, the petitioner can voluntarily dismiss the action before the other side has submitted any paperwork; if the other side has responded, both sides must join in a voluntary dismissal of the action. Most states also have automatic dismissal rules that will end an old divorce case that was filed but never completed due to the parties' reconciliation.

Any divorce decree can be appealed within the proper time limit, usually fifteen to thirty days. If it is not appealed it becomes final and the parties must live with it until and unless it is modified by later court action. Under the proper circumstances, a court will modify child support, child custody orders, and alimony. Property settlements are usually not modifiable at a later date.

### Substantive Law Issues

Every state requires a person seeking a divorce to plead and prove a legal reason why the court should declare the marriage over. In past years, these legal reasons or grounds were adultery, desertion, and mental or physical cruelty. Most states have discarded the so-called "fault" based grounds and now allow a court to end a marriage if there has been a breakdown of the marital relationship. Sometimes this is described as incompatibility or irreconcilable differences, but the basic idea behind all of these terms is that the point of the marriage can no longer be fulfilled, and so it should be ended. Obviously if one party is swearing under oath that the marriage has broken down and there is no possible way it can continue, a judge has little choice but to find that the ground of irreconcilable differences has been proved, even if the other party swears he or she is sure the marriage can continue. This has led to what some people call "no-fault" divorce, which basically means that if one side is determined to get a divorce there is little the other side can do to prevent it. The most the reluctant party can do is slow the process, more in some states than in others, but the divorce will be granted in the end.

A woman should be aware that some states do retain the old "fault" based grounds along with the irreconcilable differences ground for seeking a divorce. Sometimes it is to a woman's advantage to plead one of the fault grounds since proving fault on the husband's part may increase her property distribution or alimony amount. Both fault and no-fault grounds are usually pled together, so the divorce will be granted even if a judge determines that the woman has failed to prove fault.

Sometimes women will encounter the question of whether there is a marriage to dissolve. Many women who cohabited with a man are under the mistaken impression that they have a common-law marriage. Marriage by the common law is a holdover from pioneer days when it could take months for a minister or judge to get to an isolated settlement and perform wedding ceremonies. Therefore, the law recognized as married couples who met the following criteria but who had not actually gone through a formal ceremony:

1. The man and woman each had the subjective intent to be married;

2. The couple held themselves out to the community as husband and wife; and

3. The couple lived together.

Only a few states still recognize common-law marriages as legal marriages that must be ended by divorce. In those states, a common-law divorce petitioner sometimes must prove at the outset that the marriage exists before he or she can get to the question of divorce. Often it is to one side's advantage to deny a marriage and claim that the couple was only living together. Couples who are only living to-gether typically do not have the subjective intent to be married and usually correct community members who mistakenly call them Mr. or Mrs. Separating nonmarried couples often have less claim on each other's property and income than do divorcing couples, but some states, nota-bly California, have recognized "palimony" claims to a varying degree.

## Child Custody

Almost every divorce between a couple with children involves issues of child custody. Child custody encompasses three main con-cepts. The first of these is the child's *legal* custody; which parent is legally required to support the child and entitled to know about the child. For example, the parent with legal custody is entitled to see medical and school records and to participate in major decisions con-cerning the health and welfare of the child. It is uncommon for either parent to be denied legal custody of his or her child. Different states express this idea differently, but the basic premise is that unless grounds exist to terminate a parent's rights to a child (such as repeated or severe physical abuse), the divorce is not going to change the basic legal nature of the parent/child relationship. Therefore, most courts award divorcing parents joint *legal* custody of a child.

The so-called "custody" battle is usually over the second compo-nent of custody, *physical care* or *physical custody* of the child. The child will live with the parent who is awarded physical care on a day-to-day basis, and that parent will be responsible for making ordinary daily decisions like bedtime and curfew. The third component of child custody is *visitation*. The visitation award determines when and un-der what circumstances the parent who does not have day-to-day physical care of the child will see and care for the child.

The overarching legal principle which is used by courts in deter-mining custody of children is usually phrased as a custody arrange-ment that will be "in the best interest of the child." The problem with this formulation is that it does not have a precise meaning, although most state legal codes contain a list of factors that the judge is sup-posed to consider in making a determination of what custodial ar-rangements would be in the best interest of the child in each specific divorce case. Because different judges can give different levels of im-portance to these factors, it is critical to get specific custody advice from an attorney who has experience with the judges who will be deciding a contested custody claim. Some factors typically receive more weight than others.

Continuity of care often weighs heavily in a judge's determination of the best parent to have the day-to-day physical custody of the children. Many states presume, either explicitly or implicitly, that it will be in the best interest of the child to reside with the parent who has been the child's primary caretaker during the marriage. In some states, this presumption is specifically articulated, and each of the parties in a contested custody case attempts to prove that each one was the primary caretaker. In other states, the presumption is not part of the law, but because it impacts so heavily on continuity of care, the court spends considerable time establishing who did the major portion of the child care during the marriage. Women often have an advantage on this issue because they have generally done the major share of diapering, feeding, washing, taking care of the sick, transporting, attending parent-teacher conferences, and meeting emotional needs. A woman needs to be aware, however, that often there is an unarticulated assumption that women will provide most of the day-to-day care for children, so that her hours of care are often taken for granted, whereas her husband's few instances of fixing dinner or changing a diaper are accorded great weight.

Another reality is that women are often judged more harshly if they leave their children when they leave their husbands than men who move out of the family home. Once again, it seems that many judges have a stereotypical view about maternal behavior that says that mothers who really love their children will never leave them. Stereotypes about paternal affection do not seem to be affected by the man's willingness to leave his children behind when he separates from his wife. In the future this view may change, particularly for women who must flee domestic assault and are unable to get their children out when they first leave. Currently, a woman should consult an attorney about her particular situation if she wants physical care of her children, but thinks she may have to leave them with someone else, including her husband, during the divorce.

Another important factor to many judges in determining the best interest of the child is one parent's willingness to facilitate the child's relationship with the other parent. Many state codes state explicitly that maximum contact with both parents is presumed to be in the child's best interest, and most judges strongly embrace that concept.

Thus, if both parents want physical care of the child, and one parent has interfered with the other parent's attempts to maintain a relationship with a child, this fact alone may be enough for a judge to grant the noninterfering parent physical care. What this means for some women is the necessity of allowing their children's father to have more contact with their children than they really think is good for them. Because of the risk of losing physical care of a child if a woman refuses to allow visitation by the father, any woman who believes her situation justifies such action *must* contact an attorney as soon as possible to find out how to protect her custodial rights.

Some women have concerns that their husband may have physically abused or sexually molested their children. Other women are concerned that the children will not be safe with their father because of his substance abuse or other lifestyle choices. A judge will protect the children from harm in these situations *if* she is convinced that the woman's claims are true. If a father has been found by a court to be abusive to his child, a judge will usually restrict his access to the child. (Unless there has been a complete termination of the father's parental rights to a child, it is rare for a judge to order no visitation at all.) The problem for many women is that there is no juvenile court or police involvement; she may be the only witness to his acts of cruelty to the children. If there are other witnesses they may be her friends or family, whom the court could consider biased, or his friends or family who refuse to testify against him. An attorney can help the woman determine the best balance between risking an unfavorable permanent custody decision and protecting her children.

One factor that is generally not as important as it once was to a custody decision is that one or both of the parents has an extramarital relationship. A woman should listen to her lawyer on this subject because there are old-fashioned judges who will condemn her (perhaps more so than they would a man) for an extramarital relationship, but most do not find the mere fact that a parent is dating to be enough to conclude that the parent should not have physical care of the child. A pattern of sexual relationships with different partners or exposing the children to a new partner with problems (such as substance abuse, unemployment, criminal record) can lead a judge to conclude that the parent is not as morally fit to have physical care of the children as the other parent. Another factor that is usually not of overwhelming importance to the award of physical care is the relative income of the parents. The courts, generally, take the view that child support from the other parent can smooth out income disparities, thereby eliminating relative income of the parties as a major consideration.

True fifty-fifty physical care of a child is not common today. At one point fifteen or twenty years ago, split physical care (the child is with each parent three and one-half days a week, or two weeks a month, or six months a year) was looked upon as the best possible arrangement for children. Subsequent research showed that many of these arrangements were very hard on the children involved and were often abandoned. The modern trend is to award primary physical care to one parent who will maintain the child's principal home and to award visitation rights to the other parent. Most judges will award "liberal" visitation between the child and the non-physical care parent. Many variations of visitation plans are possible. At the outset, a woman needs to determine if specific, spelled-out dates and times fit her and her children's needs best or if a more general statement that the father shall have visitation at such times and places as is mutually agreed upon is better. Detailed visitation specifics can avoid arguments and the necessity for frequent communication between the parties, but they can also impose a rigidity to family life that may be uncomfortable. Other visitation issues include who is responsible for providing transportation to and from visitation, and who pays the cost of air travel. Also to be considered is what happens to visitation if one of the parties moves a significant distance from the other.

Parties are almost always happier with a visitation plan they negotiate and agree to, even if it is not perfect, than they are with a visitation plan the judge orders. Unfortunately, many court systems are so clogged with cases that often judges do not spend the time needed to work out detailed visitation orders that take into account all of the limitations and restrictions that occur in each family's life. The parties often end up with a standard scheme that may not fit their lives or the lives of their children.

## Child Support

Federal law mandates that all states have specific guidelines that judges must follow in awarding child support. These usually take the form of a chart that takes into account the income of the parties and the number of children entitled to support. Typically, the guidelines start with the gross income of the parent who does not have physical custody of the child, and they specify what may be deducted to arrive at an income figure to fit into the chart. Adjustments for ordinary living expenses of the person paying support and the family receiving support are built into the chart. The income of the parent with whom the child lives may be plugged into the chart, or it may be built into the chart along with living expenses. The chart will give either a specific payment amount or a percentage. If the percentage is used, it is then applied to the payor's income to determine the actual payment amount. A person usually needs to prove some kind of extraordinary circumstance before a judge is authorized to depart from the child support guidelines.

Child support must be paid through the legal system; some districts have separate agencies that handle support while others use the clerk of court's office. Most states have an automatic process that will garnish the child support right out of the payor's paycheck. Sometimes this process cannot be used until or unless the payor is at least one month behind in support payments. In the future, federal law may require automatic payroll deductions for child support in every case. Every state requires that child support be paid until the children are eighteen years of age or graduate from high school. Most states also have a provision for a continuing duty to pay child support for a child between the ages of eighteen and twenty-two years if he or she is a full-time college student. If a child support order has been entered in a divorce case, it is important for parties who reconcile and live together again to notify the court of their status and do what is necessary to remove the child support order. If the order is not changed, it will continue to be in effect even during the period in which the family is living together and could result in the seizure of income tax refunds or in liens on property.

One of the most common child support problems women encounter is determining the income of a self-employed husband. Without a paycheck from an outside employer, the man's own records must be relied on to determine income. Sometimes he falsifies the records deliberately, but more often they are just poorly kept or complicated. Tax returns may contain all kinds of "paper" deductions, such as depreciation, which lead to an artificially low taxable income. Self-employed income is more likely to fluctuate, which makes it harder to determine what the payor's income actually will be in the future. A woman faced with this situation usually must incur the expense of hiring an accountant to sort through the records and arrive at an income figure. She may also spend more time than other women in court over the years in child support modification actions, either because she wants the child support increased since his income has gone up or because he wants it decreased since his income has gone down.

Another common child support problem is actually receiving the court-ordered support. If the parent who must pay child support has a steady, well-paid job, the system will usually make him pay support for his child, even if he does not want to. It may take a few months, or the woman may need to hire her own attorney, but eventually the employer will be required to withhold the support from the payor's paycheck and send it directly to the agency that handles support payments; however, the system seems to break down when the man who does not want to pay is self-employed, unemployed, changes jobs often, or moves from state to state. There is a legal "solution" for all these situations, but the reality is that a woman can face months of legal actions, often at her own expense, only to end up without the support payments to which she is entitled. Federal law *does* require child support agencies to offer help in collecting child support to all women who are owed such support. A woman must be assertive with child support agencies and demand the services to which she is entitled because the agencies usually have many more cases than they can handle and often focus on the cases in which the woman and her children receive AFDC.

Federal law also requires all states to make responsibility for the children's medical expenses part of child support orders. The goal of the medical provision of the child support order is to ensure that the payor parent covers his or her share of medical bills. Often a child support order will require the working payor parent to carry medical insurance for the children. Problems can arise because the insurance company usually requires some action (signatures on forms, authorizations to send payments directly to doctors) from the payor. If he is unwilling to meet these requirements, the woman can end up paying medical bills out of her own pocket in order to make sure her sick children see the doctor and then spending months (or years!) trying to collect from the payor. Another problem can arise when the payor's employment is terminated. Often he will not purchase a private insurance policy with the same scope of coverage. Once again, the woman ends up paying the medical bills up front and then trying to use the legal system to collect from the payor.

Problems are created when child support payments are not made through child support agencies or under the terms of a support order. Many men, especially when they first move out of the house, tell their wives that they will voluntarily send them money for food and expenses. Often the women, either because they want to try to reconcile or want to show good faith, agree to the voluntary arrangement and do not seek a court order for child support. Within a few months the voluntary payments may have dwindled to a fraction of the original amount or ceased altogether. It may take months for the woman to go through the process, obtain a child support order, and have it enforced; if she had done all the legal groundwork at the beginning she would have been less likely to suffer a gap in support. Sometimes men offer to pay a woman directly rather than go through the child support agency. Most states will not give credit for any payments that are not made through an agency, so this is not really in his best interest and may lead to unnecessary interaction between the parties over support payments.

## Alimony

Alimony, or spousal maintenance, is support money paid for the support and maintenance of a spouse. Alimony can be awarded either to women or men and can be permanent (until the receiving spouse dies or remarries) or temporary (for a set period after the divorce is final). Most state divorce codes authorize a judge to grant alimony, but do not require her to do so. Typically, the judge is to consider such factors as the length of the marriage, the education and work history of each spouse, the physical and mental ability of each spouse to work, the relative incomes of the parties, property distribution, and the child support award. Alimony is being awarded less frequently than it was in the past. More married women stay in the work force during marriage and have the skills and abilities to support themselves after divorce. Alimony is still a consideration if the marriage is of long duration and there is a large difference in the incomes or income potential of the parties. If a woman lives in one of the states that still has fault based grounds for divorce, her chances of receiving alimony may be increased if the divorce is granted due to the fault of the husband. For most divorces, the spouses' behavior has no formal effect on whether alimony is granted and, if so, how much.

Temporary or rehabilitative alimony is more common today than permanent alimony. The idea behind the temporary award is to give the disadvantaged spouse the ability to support herself in the long run. Some typical temporary alimony awards are for a monthly sum to be paid for two years, or until a woman finishes college, or until the youngest child is in school full time. Unlike child support, alimony must be declared as income for income tax purposes by the person who receives it and can be declared as a deduction from income by the person who pays it.

## Property Distribution

In years past, women suffered greatly when it came to splitting up property in a divorce because the title theory of ownership was usually followed. The judge determined who owned the property by looking at the actual title (for real estate and cars) or figuring out who paid for the item. Since married women were generally not in the work force, almost all property ended up being awarded to the husband on the assumption that he owned it since he paid for it. Fortunately, the law has changed, and in most states (other than the eight community property states), the law calls for equitable division of property with due consideration given to the contributions, both paid and unpaid, of both spouses. In practice this often leads to a fifty-fifty split of marital property.

The first step in determining the property distribution is to determine what is marital property. Most states define marital property as the property acquired during the marriage by either spouse, except property that one spouse inherited or received as a sole gift. Therefore, the property that each spouse brought into the marriage is usually not marital property, and each spouse gets that property back at the time of the divorce.

Problems arise when the spouse used his or her separate property to contribute to a joint marital asset; for instance, a woman cashes in her ten-thousand-dollar certificate of deposit at the start of the marriage and uses it as a down payment on the couple's house. Generally if the specific property can be traced it will still be considered separate property; in the example above the woman would get her ten thousand dollars back. If the separate property has been mixed into the family accounts so that it is indistinguishable, it will usually be found to have lost its identity as separate property, and the spouse who brought it into the marriage will get not credit for it at the time of divorce. For instance, if the woman who cashed in her ten-thousand-dollar CD used the money to buy some food, pay some utilities, pay for the wedding photographs, buy a couch that was destroyed three years later, and buy baby clothes, she probably will not receive a ten-thousand-dollar "credit" for separate property.

Exactly which spouse inherited property is usually clear, but sometimes gifts can cause confusion. Did her parents give the washer and dryer to the couple or just to her? If it was a gift to both of them, then it is marital property and must be divided as part of the assets of the marriage. If it was just to her, it is often characterized as separate property and will not be part of the overall property distribution. Often the nature of the gift must be established by testimony of those involved, and a party's parents are hardly the most unbiased witnesses.

Another component of the marital property settlement is marital debts. These are debts that were acquired during the marriage by either or both of the parties. An argument can be made that some kinds of debts acquired during the marriage are so purely personal that they should be regarded as separate property. This argument works best for school loans and business debts, but it is also sometimes applied to entertainment debts (vacations or hobbies such as race cars, boats, guns) incurred by only one person. Generally, it is a good idea for debts associated with specific items of property to be awarded to the person who receives the property. For example, the person who receives the car should also be required to make the car payments; many women have had their cars repossessed because their ex-husbands quit making the monthly payments even though the divorce order required them to make the payments. In this case the woman is legally entitled to be reimbursed by her ex-husband, but she may have trouble collecting from him.

Pension and retirement benefits are also marital property, provided they were accumulated during the marriage. Many people are surprised to learn this, because the benefits seem so tied to their own personal efforts at work. Federal law allows pension plans to be split pursuant to a divorce decree, and they are routinely treated as marital property by most judges. The biggest issue for most parties becomes the valuation of pension and retirement benefits. Some plans give participants a statement of the current value of their plans, but many do not. Therefore, valuing a pension/retirement plan may require the assistance of an expert, since many plans contain not only pension benefits, but also stock options, investments, and savings components.

A woman also needs to be aware of the tax consequences of splitting pension and retirement benefits. Under current law, a person who receives a share of retirement plan benefits because of a divorce will have to pay taxes and penalties if she actually takes possession of the money. If her share of the benefits is deposited directly into an approved retirement account, she will not have to pay any taxes or penalties.

Once the marital assets are identified, they must be divided. In a typical fifty-fifty distribution scheme, each party receives assets equal to roughly one-half of the total value of marital assets. This may mean that one party receives the house, and the other receives everything else. Alternatively, one party may keep the bulk of the physical assets and pay the other party in cash for his or her share. Debts are divided between the parties and may be used to offset assets so that one party may keep most of the assets and most of the debts.

Due to recognition that even with a fifty-fifty split of assets women often end up with a lower standard of living after a divorce while men have a higher standard of living, some lawyers are arguing that the proper frame of reference for determining an equitable distribution of property is the lifetimes of the parties. Under this argument, the "equitable" property distribution may be sixty percent for the woman and forty percent for the man because the assets she is taking will earn less over the years than the ones he is taking. This argument has had some limited success in certain states and may be worth looking into when a significant amount of property will be divided.

Most people are better off if they reach their own agreement on how to divide up their assets. Judges will resolve competing claims to valuable assets, but may simply order that everything else be sold and the proceeds split. Likewise, the parties can incur huge attorney fees if the lawyers have to argue about who gets the Tupperware. Physical objects sometimes take on symbolic importance to people involved in divorces, and a woman is urged to do her best to keep her perspective.

One problem area for property distribution concerns location of and use of property during the pendency of the divorce. Possession should not be nine-tenths of the law in divorce property distribution, but in reality it is often very significant. Negative legal consequences such as those that flow from leaving children do not occur if a woman leaves property. In other words, a woman does not lose any of her right to claim the house or furniture if she moves out; however, untitled items of personal property such as couches, desks, sports equipment, etc., can be sold or given away by either spouse during the divorce action. The *value* of the item will have to be taken into account when the property is split up, but the item itself will be gone. Thus, a woman may want to plan to take certain items of personal property with her when she moves out of the house if the objects themselves are important to her. Some states authorize a judge to make a temporary order concerning the use and location of property when the divorce action is first filed. In other states, a judge will enter an injunction forbidding either party to dispose of joint marital assets. In the absence of such court orders, a woman will usually not be penalized for taking all of her personal possessions, such as clothing and jewelry, all of her separate property, and approximately half of the joint marital assets at the time of the separation. A woman should be careful not to take anything that is her husband's separate property. If a woman believes she needs to "clean out" savings and checking accounts in order to support herself and her children until temporary or permanent support is ordered, she should consult with a lawyer first. Likewise, a woman who wants to lock her husband out of the house should talk to a lawyer about the law in her state regarding occupancy of the homestead during the divorce.

It is important to remember that whatever is worked out between the divorcing couple in terms of payment of the marital debts does not apply to creditors. For instance, if both the husband and wife signed the waterbed loan, and he takes the waterbed and agrees to make the loan payments and then stops, the creditor may come after the wife for payment. It is no defense for her to claim that her ex-husband is responsible for the loan according to the terms of her divorce; the creditor has a right to get the money from her, because she also signed the loan document. Her only recourse may be to sue the ex-husband for the extra money she had to pay, but her victory may be hollow if he has no wages or other money for her to garnish to satisfy her judgment. Sometimes a woman may be able to "get her name off" a joint loan, but often creditors will refuse to refinance in the husband's name alone unless he has an outstanding job and perfect credit. Some women who recognize that their ex-husbands are unlikely to pay any debts believe they are better off agreeing to pay the debts themselves as long as they receive a larger share of the marital assets.

Other property distribution problems can arise due to family debts. Sometimes parents give the married couple money without being clear whether it is a loan that must be repaid or a gift. Years may go by with no mention made of the sum of money, but at the time of the couple's divorce, it is suddenly characterized as a marital debt by one of the parties. If each side is ordered to repay one-half of the debt, the reality is that the spouse who is the child of the parent lenders may pay nothing, while the other spouse pays his or her share. Other times the lender parents may simply wait until the divorce is final and then sue the ex-spouse for collection of the "loan." Therefore, it is a good idea to get agreement between the parties as to the nature of any sums of money that the couple received during marriage from family members. Generally, transactions between family members are presumed to be gifts if there is no written documentation.

The family home can present the biggest property distribution problem for many women. Many times the divorcing couple owns a house with substantial equity. The woman and children want to continue living in the house, so she does not want to sell it. It may be tempting to continue some kind of joint ownership with the ex-husband for a period of years before selling the house. Continued joint ownership is almost always a bad idea because it ties a divorced couple together financially, thereby creating the potential for conflict. The arrangement in which one spouse lives in the house and the other makes house payments is particularly bad. If the man quits making the payments, he will not be the one thrown out of the house by foreclosure, even if he does suffer monetarily. Likewise, if the occupier of the house lets it run down, the person making the payments may end up with nothing to show for his or her investment. Terms that require one spouse to pay the other a set sum for his or her share of the house when it is sold some years in the future can cause severe hardship if housing prices drop. In the best case, ownership of the house should be transferred completely at the time of the divorce; however, many times there are not enough other assets to compensate the party who does not receive the house, and less than the best outcome must be accepted. A lawyer can help a woman devise the best possible plan for dealing with this thorny problem under the circumstances of her case.

## Annulments, Separate Maintenance, and Separations

In certain circumstances it may be appropriate to end a marriage by some legal mechanism other than divorce. Legal annulments are not the same as religious annulments. A person seeking a legal annulment must petition the court in the same way as a person seeking a divorce. The grounds for annulment are different from those for divorce; therefore, different allegations must be made and proved in order for a judge to grant an annulment of the marriage. Generally, the grounds for annulment are that one or both of the parties were under the legal age for a valid marriage; one of the parties was already married at the time of the marriage; there has been no consummation of the marriage; or the parties are related to each other in a way that violates their state's incest statute. In the past, legal annulment meant that the marriage had never taken place so there were no awards of alimony, and any children born of the marriage were illegitimate. These old-fashioned consequences of annulment have been abolished, and child custody, support, and property distribution are all part of annulment actions today.

## Separate Maintenance

Most states allow a married party to file an action for separate maintenance. This action results in final orders concerning child custody, support, and property distribution, but does not end the marriage. It is used most often by people who have religious reasons for not wanting a divorce decree, but who are separated and living apart. Typically, an action for separate maintenance requires the same kind of paperwork and procedures that a petition for divorce requires, so it should not be seen as a quick alternative to divorce. In addition, since the marriage has not been declared over, the parties are not free to remarry and will continue to have legal responsibilities for each other.

## Trial Separation

Sometimes a couple facing a breakup of a marriage will decide to undergo a trial separation period. Usually there is some discussion and agreement as to child custody, living arrangements, and monetary issues before the couple separates. Many women wonder if their husbands will live up to the terms of the agreement after they separate. Some states do have provisions for court-enforced separation agreements that are not part of a divorce action, but many do not. In those states that sanction such agreements, there is usually a statute that requires the separation agreement to meet certain requirements before it will be enforced by a court. If one side fails to follow through on the promises made in the separation agreement, the other side can resort to the legal system for enforcement of the agreement under general contract principles. Judges are more likely to set aside separation agreements because of fraud, duress, or misrepresentation than they are ordinary business contracts.

If a state has no authorization for separation agreements that are not part of a divorce action, the agreements (even those in writing with notarized signatures) will not be enforced by a judge in court. Instead, the couple will be told to file a divorce action if they want a judge to settle their dispute as to child custody, support, and so on. Most states allow the couple to incorporate their agreement into a divorce action if they do file for divorce.

## Conclusion

It is uncommon for any person to be completely happy with every aspect of a divorce. Nonetheless, if a woman understands the limitations of the legal system and obtains the appropriate assistance from an attorney, she need not feel like a victim who has no control over what happens to her.

## Bibliography

Briles, Judith. *The Dollars and Sense Guide to Divorce: The Financial Guide for Women.* New York: Ballantine Books, 1991.

Chesler, P. *Mothers on Trial: The Battle for Children and Custody.* New York: McGraw-Hill, 1986.

Harwood, Norma. *A Woman's Legal Guide to Separation and Divorce in All 50 States.* New York: Macmillan Publishing, 1985. This guide is somewhat dated, but the information is basic. Consult a local attorney for specifics of recent changes in the law.

Jereski, L. "Managing a Divorce like a Business." *Working Woman* (February 1993). Helpful tips on how to avoid being manipulated financially by your partner during a divorce and custody proceeding. Tips on keeping legal costs under control.

Joselow, Beth. *Life Lessons: Fifty Things I Learned from My Divorce.* New York: Avon Books, 1994.

Maclean, Mavis. *Surviving Divorce: Women's Resources after Separation.* New York: New York University Press, 1991.

Sack, S. M. *The Complete Guide to Marriage, Divorce, Custody and Living Together.* New York: McGraw-Hill, 1987.

Takas, M. *Child Custody: A Complete Guide for Concerned Mothers.* New York: Harper and Row, 1987.

Wilson, Carol, and Edwin Schilling. *The Survival Manual for Women in Divorce.* New York: Kendall/Hunt Publishing, 1994.

## Organizational Resources

These organizations can provide divorce information, publications, referrals, and occasionally, legal help. Several have affiliates in other locations. Also check your telephone directory for the local chapter of the Women's Bar Association and the Legal Aid Society.

National Center on Women and
   Family Law, Inc.
799 Broadway, Room 402
New York, NY 10003
(212) 674-8200

Women's Legal Defense Fund
1875 Connecticut Avenue, NW
Suite 710
Washington, DC 20009
(202) 986-2600

### Groups with a specialized focus:

Displaced Homemakers Network,
   Inc.
1411 K Street, NW, Suite 930
Washington, DC 20005
(202) 628-6767

Mothers Without Custody
P.O. Box 27418
Houston, TX 77227-7418

Older Women's League
730 11th Street, NW, Suite 300
Washington, DC 20001
(202) 783-6686

Parents Without Partners
8807 Colesville Road
Silver Spring, MD 20910
(301) 588-9354

---

**Jacqueline Miller** earned her Juris Doctor at the University of Iowa College of Law in 1984 and has worked as a solo practitioner since then. She has taught family law in the paralegal program at Kirkwood Community College, Cedar Rapids, Iowa (1988) and cofounded a domestic violence project, also in Iowa. Her particular areas of expertise include family law, juvenile law, discrimination in employment, assault, and domestic assault. She was the winning attorney for the birth parents in the highly publicized Baby Jessica case. She currently practices law in Minneapolis, Minnesota, where she also does legal research on a variety of topics at the Legal Research Center and is a volunteer attorney for the Legal Advice Clinic.

Chapter 9

# *Placing Your Child for Adoption*

Carole J. Anderson

Chapter Outline

**Introduction**

**Avoiding a Hasty Decision**

**The Adoption Process**

**The Effects of Adoption**

**Arranging Adoption**
Private Adoption • Unlicensed Agencies • Licensed Adoption Agencies • Multiservice Family Agency • Placement With Extended Family

**Conclusion**

Introduction    People often ask whether a woman with an unplanned pregnancy is ready to be a mother at this time in her life. They may claim adoption means she can choose not to be a mother now. But, however she feels during the worry and stress of an unplanned pregnancy, a woman who gives birth to a child is profoundly and permanently changed. She cannot choose *whether* to be her son's or daughter's mother, only *what kind* of mother. Will she be the only mother, or only the birth mother?

If you continue your unplanned pregnancy to term, you must decide whether to raise your child or to seek a substitute caregiver who will temporarily or permanently take your place and fulfill your legal responsibilities for raising your child. Relatives may care for your child without a formal agreement. Nonrelatives typically provide temporary care only under a foster care agreement. Adoption is the legal procedure in which all of the rights and responsibilities of parenthood are permanently transferred from a child's parents to another individual or couple.

A decision to place a child for adoption should never be made before the birth. No one can predict what being a parent will feel like until after the child's birth. This is true even of married couples with planned pregnancies. To better understand the feelings and problems a birth mother and her child might face in the years ahead if that child were adopted, the mother might consider contacting a birth parent support group such as Concerned United Birthparents, Inc., 2000 Walker Street, Des Moines, IA 50317. There are also books available on the subject, such as, *Birth Bond* by Judith S. Gediman and Linda P. Brown (New Horizon Press, 1989); *The Primal Wound: Understanding the Adopted Child* by adoptive parent Nancy Newton Verrier (Gateway Press, 1993); *Lost and Found* by adoptee Betty Jean Lifton (Dial Press, 1979); and *The Other Mother*, by birth mother Carol Schaefer (Soho Press, 1991).

## Avoiding a Hasty Decision

Even mothers who do not feel maternal during the worry and stress of an unplanned pregnancy will be changed by the experience of creating and giving birth, whether or not they raise their children. The social, family, and financial pressures faced by a woman are usually obvious, but an unplanned pregnancy may also be accompanied by guilt, lowered self-esteem, confusion, and doubt about a mother's ability to provide for her child. These stresses may lead to denial or a delay in a mother's normal feelings for her baby. Those around her may focus on the pregnancy as a problem or as a mistake that must be corrected. The mother may become vulnerable to those around her telling her that her baby would be better off adopted. She may be told that if she gives up her child for adoption, she will not develop motherly feelings for her child. She may be told that her life after placing the baby for adoption will be just like it was before she became pregnant.

There are far fewer newborn babies placed for adoption than there are people who want to adopt them. As a result, adoption arrangers and people who want to adopt are becoming increasingly sophisticated at pressuring pregnant women to consider adoption. They may appear very friendly and concerned, telling a pregnant woman what they think she wants to hear and offering to help her during her pregnancy. They may help her with housing and expenses; they may even accompany her to the delivery room. This help is often effective in obtaining babies for adoption because a mother who has accepted such help may not seek independent counseling or learn about alternatives. She may come to feel she owes her helpers her baby.

A professional counselor who has no personal or financial stake in the mother's decision may be helpful in exploring the alternatives open to her and the long-term consequences of those alternatives for both her and her child. She may be disadvantaged by youth, lack of education, unemployment or underemployment, or housing limitations. She may have little or no emotional or financial support from her family or her baby's father. While these problems are serious, with effective planning they can be temporary. There are counselors experienced in assisting mothers to resolve such problems whether their children are not yet born or are five or ten years old. Obtaining professional counseling from people who have nothing to gain if she decides to place her baby, educating herself about the adoption process, and refusing before the birth to make any commitment about placing her child will protect the rights of a mother while she decides what will be best for her and her baby in the long term.

## The Adoption Process

If a mother is considering placing her child for legal adoption, she needs to understand the adoption process. Each state has its own laws about adoption and uses its own terms to discuss the participants and the process, so you will need to check on laws in your state. Most adoptions are of children, although some states also allow adults to be adopted (see chapter 14).

Before a child can be adopted, a court must first terminate the rights of the natural parents. In a voluntary termination, the parent signs a document permanently surrendering parental rights and responsibilities for her child and agreeing to allow someone else, usually not named in the surrender document, to assume those rights and responsibilities. This document may be called a surrender or relinquishment of parental rights, consent to adoption, consent to placement, release of custody, or some other term. *It may not be obvious from the title of this document that the woman is giving up all rights to her baby forever, so she should be careful about what she signs.*

In many states, a parent cannot sign a surrender until a specific number of hours or days have elapsed after the birth. In others, parents can sign immediately upon the birth, or even before. Usually, as soon as the surrender is signed, the child is placed with an individual or couple wishing to adopt the child. In some instances the child temporarily remains in the hospital or is placed in foster care.

A new mother should sign a surrender only if she is absolutely certain that adoption is the right choice for her and her child. If she is not positive, she can take her baby home, live with her baby in a group care home, or live with relatives or friends. Allowing someone else to care for her baby while she makes up her mind carries the risk that the baby's caregiver will refuse to return her baby.

In some states, there is a grace period of a specified number of hours, days, or months in which a parent can revoke, or take back, the surrender and recover her child. In others, there is no revocation period at all. Before a surrender is signed, the mother should find out whether there is a revocation period in her state and what the revocation requirements are. Even when there is a revocation period, those periods are short. If a mother asks for her child's return within the revocation period, she may not recover her child if she did not use the specific form required, sign it properly (which often means before a notary public), and file it with the court or deliver it to the correct person. There is also a strong possibility that the individual or couple with whom her baby was placed may challenge the revocation or even move to another jurisdiction. A mother may not have the financial resources needed to pay for a lawyer and for expenses necessary to enforce her right to recover her child. Because of the uncertainty of whether she will be allowed to revoke a surrender, a mother should not sign a surrender unless she is sure she does not want to raise her child.

A court presented with a voluntary surrender after expiration of the revocation period, if any, may then terminate the parent's rights and responsibilities for her child. Termination means that the court ends the parent's legal relationship to her child. The law will then regard the birth parent as a stranger to her child, and the birth parent will have no legal right to knowledge of or contact with her child, and no legal responsibility for further financial support. A court may refuse to terminate parental rights if the court is concerned that there will not be an adoption and that the parent's financial support is needed.

If only one parent's rights are terminated, the other parent may still have parental rights and responsibilities. If the mother is married to the child's father and only one parent surrenders, the other will be permitted to raise the child unless his or her rights are involuntarily terminated for unfitness.

Single mothers generally are allowed to raise their children unless it can be demonstrated to a court that they are unfit. The rights of single fathers are not as clear. State laws vary widely on whether a father who is not married to the mother has rights to his child, what legal steps a father must take to establish his rights, and what those rights will be. This is a dynamic area of the law. Your child probably cannot be adopted without the father's consent unless there is cause for his rights to be involuntarily terminated. If your child's father does not agree to an adoption and can establish paternity, he may be able to block an adoption. If your rights have already been terminated, it is possible that sole custody may be awarded to the father while you will have no rights. Talking to your child's father and obtaining his agreement to your decision can avoid a prolonged custody battle.

In most states, after the rights of both parents are terminated, a temporary custodian or guardian, who may be an agency or prospective adoptive parent, is named for the child; this guardian makes parental decisions until the child is adopted. The individual or couple wishing to adopt a child must petition the court to be appointed the child's legal parents. There is usually a period of about six months from the time of placement until an adoption can be finalized. This period allows the adopting individual or couple to be sure that they really want to adopt the child. Birth parents typically are not told when an adoption is finalized and may not be informed of whether or not it is finalized.

If the individual or couple with whom the child was placed does not complete the adoption, there is no legal obligation that the child's birth parents be notified of the placement disruption. The child may be placed with others who want to adopt, or the child may be placed in foster care without the birth parents' knowledge.

In some states, there are no fixed time lines for the process of surrender, termination, and adoption. Parental rights can be terminated and an adoption can become final in the same court proceeding, which may be held almost immediately after the birth. The birth parents cannot change their minds and recover their child. However, if the adopting individual or couple later change their minds, they may petition the court to annul the adoption or they may voluntarily surrender their parental rights.

After a court has ordered that the individual or couple wishing to adopt are to be given all the legal rights and responsibilities of parents, the law will treat an adoptive parent as a natural parent and will treat the adopted child as if the child had been born to the adoptive parent. Usually, though not always, an adoption means that the adopted person then inherits from the adopting family and loses all rights to inherit from the birth family. Any birth or adoptive relatives who do not want this result must each execute a will specifying any contrary arrangements.

After finalization of an adoption a substitute birth certificate is issued in place of the original birth certificate, upon presentation of the adoption decree to the vital statistics office or other governmental unit with responsibility for birth certificates. Usually, the adopting individual or couple changes the child's name, and the names of the adopting individual or couple appear in place of the names of the birth parents. Sometimes the date, time, and place of birth are changed on the certificate as well.

In most states, the true birth certificate and any agency and court documents concerning the adoption are "sealed," either permanently or until the adoptee reaches a specified age. The identifying information contained in these records is not released to anyone, including the adopted person and the birth parents, without a court order. While records are sealed, the adopted person will have access only to the amended birth certificate which states that the adoptive parent gave birth; the birth mother will not have access to any birth certificate for her child. The adoptive parent, however, may have identifying information concerning the birth parents. In an increasing number of states, access is permitted at a specified age of the adoptee, or there is a registry or intermediary system that permits the release of names and other information with the agreement of the party sought. Further, a court may allow access if it finds "good cause." Courts vary widely in what they consider to be good cause for the opening of records.

A mother who surrenders her child without knowing the names of the adopting individual or couple cannot be sure of whether or not she or her child will have access to information about each other in the future. Laws imposing confidentiality or allowing access may be changed at any time. If it is important to you that you have ongoing information about your child, or if it is important to you that your child's adoptive parent or parents have access to changing medical and social information concerning you and your family, you may prefer an open adoption in which you and the adoptive parent meet and exchange identifying information such as names, addresses, and birth dates before records are sealed. Although you may make an agreement with the individual or couple adopting your child concerning the exchange of pictures and information or visits, such agreements are not enforceable. If your child's adoptive parent does not honor such an agreement, you will have no legal recourse because a termination of parental rights ends all of your rights with regard to your child. The law will treat you as a stranger having no relationship to your child and no legitimate interest in your child's welfare.

## The Effects of Adoption

Adoption cannot guarantee a better life for your child than you can provide, only a different life. People seeking to adopt cannot guarantee that they will not divorce, die, or become ill or alcoholics, nor can they guarantee that they will maintain the same income and lifestyle they have now. Like other people, adoptive parents come in all varieties.

Adoptive parents may or may not come to love your child as if he or she were their own. Although some people who already have children adopt, most adopt because they cannot conceive and bear their own children because of infertility, because they waited until they were too old, or because of lifestyle choices such as homosexuality or preferring not to marry. Adopting your child is probably a second choice to raising the natural child the adoptive parent could not have.

Adoption guarantees that a mother loses forever her right to raise her child; and the child loses forever his or her right to be raised by his or her natural mother. Much like children living in blended families due to divorce and remarriage, an adoptee has two sets of parents and grows up with a dual identity, whether or not the adoptee knows his or her birth parents. Adopted people eventually understand that before they were adopted they were first surrendered. Many believe that their birth parents neither loved nor wanted them, and they may view the surrender as abandonment. The certain losses involved in adoption must be carefully weighed against the possible gains.

## Arranging Adoption

There are five major alternatives for arranging your child's adoption; all involve some risks for you and your child:

1. An adoption arranged independently

2. An adoption arranged by a pregnancy counseling service or unlicensed adoption agency

3. An adoption arranged by a licensed adoption agency

4. An adoption arranged by a licensed multiservice family agency

5. An adoption by a relative or other person you already know, trust, and respect

### Private Adoption

A private adoption, also called independent or nonagency adoption, may be suggested by a doctor, lawyer, or some other person and must be handled by a lawyer. Some lawyers who specialize in arranging adoptions place ads in newspapers, on bulletin boards at college campuses, in doctors' offices, and so forth. Lawyers are not trained in the psychological and social needs or welfare of children and families or in the long-term emotional consequences of adoption for you or your child. In most private adoptions, only the individual or couple wishing to adopt is represented by a lawyer, whose only obligations are to the client, not to you or your child.

Nonagency adoption has fewer protections for you and your child than an adoption through a licensed agency. Often the child is placed with an adopting individual or couple that has not yet been screened or determined suitable to adopt. It is the individual or couple that selects and pays the person who will make a home study report to the court. This can mean that people with serious problems who would not be approved by a licensed agency can still adopt privately.

Some mothers decide on a private adoption so that they can screen and select the individuals or couples who will raise their children. In these instances, it is especially important that the mother obtain counseling to assist her in that process and that she retain her own lawyer to represent her interests.

## Unlicensed Agencies

Some pregnancy counseling services function as unlicensed adoption agencies, often with an antiabortion agenda. The September/October 1993 issue of *Ms.* magazine describes the coercion sometimes used by such services. There are also unlicensed adoption agencies that specialize in obtaining babies for people wanting to adopt. They have the same disadvantages as independent adoptions.

## Licensed Adoption Agencies

Like nonagency adoption arrangers, licensed adoption agencies may focus on obtaining babies for people who want to adopt rather than on helping mothers explore all of their alternatives. Their funding may depend heavily on arranging adoptions. Counseling you may be motivated by the prospect of obtaining a placement fee for your baby. An agency should be willing to explain fully the following:

- The percentage of mothers it counsels who actually place their babies

- The application process for those seeking to adopt

- The agency's criteria for those seeking to adopt

- The counseling provided to prospective adoptive parents

- The agency's policies on whether you can select the individual or couple to adopt your child

Ask whether you can meet individuals or couples after your child's birth but before you decide whether or not to place your child with them. Ask about the types of adoptions the agency arranges: Does the agency arrange open adoptions in which you will know the adoptive parent and occasionally visit while your child is growing up? Does it offer semi-open adoptions in which pictures and information are exchanged? Would such contact be only for a limited period or until the child is an adult? What percentage of the agency's adoptive parents honor agreements for contact and the exchange of pictures and information?

### Multiservice Family Agency

A licensed multiservice family agency accredited by the Child Welfare League of America (see the resource section) offers the most protections for the mother and her child. Most have counselors who are trained in the entire range of services available to help the mother raise her child or to arrange for her child's adoption. Many multiservice family agencies offer parenting classes and sponsor support groups for single parents. The agency should be willing to work not only with the mother, but also with her parents and the child's father. Again, mothers should ask about the application process for adopters, criteria for adoptive parents, the counseling provided to adoptive parents, selection procedures, whether she can meet individuals or couples after the birth and before she decides whether to place her child with them, and the types of adoptions the agency arranges.

### Placement With Extended Family

Another adoption possibility is arranging for a family member the mother respects and trusts to adopt her baby. If a mother wants to explore this alternative, she should strongly consider seeking counseling from a multiservice family agency that can help both sides explore whether this is what they want, what the consequences might be, and how it could be arranged. The agency can help work out the kind of adoption with which both parties will be comfortable. The mother and the relative or friend who will adopt should each obtain legal advice and representation from separate lawyers. The adoption would then be processed by the adopting relative's lawyer as an independent adoption.

## Conclusion

Emotionally, adoption is not a one-time event but a lifelong process. A mother never forgets her child. Nothing that is irrevocable and has permanent consequences should be entered into without serious consideration and without all alternatives being explored. A number of groups exist for the purpose of helping mothers make an informed decision; a representative sample of these organizations is listed in the resource section.

### Bibliography

These books are available from Concerned United Birthparents (see following for address):

Gediman, Judith S., and Linda P. Bond. *Birth Bond*.
Jones, Merry Bloch. *Birthmothers: Women Who Have Relinquished Babies for Adoption Tell Their Stories*.
Lifton, Betty Jean. *Lost and Found*.
Schaefer, Carol. *The Other Mother*.
Verrier, Nancy. *The Primal Wound*.

The following books are available from the American Adoption Congress (see below for address):
Burgess, Linda Cannon. *Adoption: How It Works*.
Kirk, David. *Adoptive Kinship*.
Melina, Lois R., and Sharon K. Roszia. *The Open Adoption Experience*.
Severson, Randolph W. *Adoption: Philosophy and Experience*.
Silver, Kathleen, and Patricia M. Dorner. *Children of Open Adoption*.

In addition, Concerned United Birthparents (CUB) has a number of booklets and papers at nominal prices. See address below.

## Organizational Resources

ALMA (Adoptees Liberty Movement Association)
P.O. Box 727
Radio City Station
New York, NY 10101-0727
(212) 581-1568
*Begun in 1971, ALMA has the largest registry in the world for adoptees searching for their birth parents and for birth parents searching for their children.*

American Adoption Congress
1000 Connecticut Avenue NW #9
Washington, DC 20036
(202) 483-3399

Child Welfare League of America
440 First Street NW, Suite 310
Washington, DC 20001
(202) 638-2952

Concerned United Birthparents, Inc.
2000 Walker Street
Des Moines, IA
(515) 263-9558

Council for Equal Rights in Adoption
401 East 7th Street
New York, NY 10021
(212) 988-0110

---

**Carole J. Anderson** was a social worker and is currently a litigation partner in the law firm of Lane & Waterman, Davenport, Iowa. For the past eighteen years she has been active in adoption reform and in efforts to assist families at risk of unnecessary separation. She has been reunited with the child she lost to adoption when she was a teenager. She is a former president of Concerned United Birthparents (CUB) and edited the *CUB Communicator* for twelve years.

Chapter 10

# *Adopting a Child*

Amy M. Silberberg

Chapter Outline

**Introduction**

**Agency Versus Independent Adoption**
Adoption Agencies • Independent Adoption • Choosing the Right Attorney

**Deciding What Kind of Child You Want to Adopt**
U.S.–Born Infant Adoptions • Stepparent and Relative Adoptions • Children with Special Needs Adoptions • Transracial Adoption • International Adoption

**Minimizing Your Legal Risk**
Be a Good Adoption Consumer • Make Sure That You and the Birth Parents Have Separate Attorneys • If You Adopt a Child From Another State, Know the Law

**The Adoption Process**
The Home Study • Consent to Adoption • Direct Placement Versus Foster Care • Finalizing the Adoption

**Open Adoption**

**Conclusion**

Adoption can be a wonderful and emotionally rewarding way to build your family. This chapter will introduce you to the legal challenges involved in adopting a child and warn you of the problems you may encounter along the way. Recent well-publicized cases have illustrated the tragedy of adoptions gone wrong. In response, states are changing their laws, and new alternatives to traditional adoption are appearing. This chapter presents the various options available to parents who wish to adopt. It will help to minimize the emotional and financial risks so that the process of becoming a parent is an enjoyable one. This is an introduction only, however. An attorney should always be consulted before adoption procedures begin.

## Introduction

Once you have made the decision to adopt, your journey has just begun. Next you must decide what kind of adoption is right for you, agency adoption or independent adoption.

An agency adoption is usually one in which the birth parents give legal control of their child to the adoption agency. Agency social workers then select an adoptive family for the child based on criteria set by the agency such as religious background, age, or educational background. The adoption agency usually involves the birth parents in the selection process. Agencies also will facilitate designated adoptions (also called identified adoptions). A designated adoption is an adoption in which the birth parents choose the adoptive parents without the help of an adoption agency. Together the birth parents and the adoptive parents approach an adoption agency about providing a home study, counseling, and any other services required to help them to finalize the adoption.

There are hundreds of adoption agencies from which to choose. Because of the expense involved you will probably have to select just one of them. Choosing the one that is right for you can be very difficult. Most of the adoption agencies and adoption facilitators and some of the adoption attorneys have brochures describing their programs. Call or write to them and ask them to send you their brochures. Most of the agencies also offer orientation meetings to describe their programs. After you have read the brochures, attend orientation meetings at the agencies that seem to best fit your needs. If the agency does not hold orientation meetings in your area, call them and ask your questions over the phone.

An independent adoption is an adoption in which the birth parents and the adoptive parents choose each other independently of an adoption agency. They make contact with each other through mutual friends or relatives, through advertising, or by other means. Independent adoption is sometimes called private adoption. Sometimes it also

## Agency Versus Independent Adoption

refers to identified or designated adoption, in which birth parents have chosen adoptive parents and an agency has agreed to work with them to meet the legal requirements of finalizing the adoption.

To learn more about independent adoption, visit your public library or local bookstore. There are many good books on independent adoption, such as *Beating the Adoption Game*, by Cynthia D. Martin, Ph.D., and *There are Babies to Adopt*, by Christine A. Adamec.

Adoptive parent support groups are another excellent way to obtain accurate, current information about independent adoption in your area. Contact an attorney specializing in independent adoption in your state. Some attorneys offer a free initial consultation that will give you enough information to decide whether independent adoption is for you. Be careful. The law can change quickly. As of publication of this book, forty-six states allow independent adoption, but four states do not. The four states include Colorado, Connecticut, Delaware, and Massachusetts. In Connecticut and Delaware, you may adopt independently after receiving permission from the court. Your attorney will have to ask the court to give its permission on the basis that an independent adoption is in the child's best interests.

## Adoption Agencies

Many people choose to work with an adoption agency rather than to adopt independently because the idea of having experienced agency workers screening birth parents and providing counseling makes them feel safer. It may also be appealing because in an agency adoption, while you cooperate with the agency home study and wait for your baby, the agency does much of the work of the adoption for you.

### Choosing the Right Adoption Agency

Adoption agencies are either private or state agencies. Although both private and state adoption agencies are licensed by the states in which they are located, the licensing requirements are minimal standards and do not provide much protection for you. Among licensed agencies, some are very good and some are very bad. Most fall somewhere between the two extremes. It is important that you do everything you can to protect yourself from the exploitation or incompetence you could suffer at the hands of a bad adoption agency.

The philosophical biases of adoption agencies vary widely, and it is important that before you decide to work with a particular agency, you find out as much as you can about it to make sure that it is the right agency for you. Does the agency offer the kind of adoption that you want? Ask what types of children are available. For example, if the sex of the child is important to you, make sure that the agency will allow you to select the child's sex.

In an agency adoption a prospective adoptive family pays a fee to the agency to cover the agency's administrative costs, a home study, the cost of counseling for the birth parents and the adoptive parents, foster care for the child, and supervising the adoptive placement of the child. These costs can be minimal, or they may be as high as $20,000 or more. Make sure that you ask the agency to itemize its fees and find out what fees, if any, are refundable if things do not work out. Does the agency have a sliding fee scale? Ask to see a copy of the contract they use. If your state allows adoptive parents to pay the birth mother's expenses, ask the agency what it expects you to pay. Does the fee include legal expenses or are they extra?

Typically, the birth parents voluntarily give legal control of their child to the adoption agency after counseling by agency social workers. The quality of the counseling will depend, to a certain extent, on the type of agency. If an agency does nothing but adoptions, it has a strong interest in the birth mother choosing to place the baby for adoption and it is less likely to explore the options of abortion and parenting with her. Next, the agency may involve the birth parents in the process of choosing adoptive parents for the baby, or the agency may choose the parents on its own. Many agencies place the baby in foster care until the birth parents' legal agreements to place the baby for adoption have become irrevocable. This practice greatly reduces the risk that the birth parents will disrupt the adoption after placement. But remember, the risk is only reduced and never eliminated. Ask the agency about its experience with adoption disruptions.

Nationwide, adoption agencies place mostly older, foreign born, or children with special needs. Since most families adopt infants through independent adoptions, an agency adoption may not be the best way to adopt a healthy infant. Because there are so many people who want to adopt, prospective adoptive parents may wait many years to adopt even an older child from an agency. Some people become discouraged by the adoption agencies' complicated and seemingly arbitrary selection criteria. For example, there are agencies that will not allow smokers, those with biological children, overweight people, single people, diabetics, working mothers, or divorced people to adopt. Some agencies will only work with born-again Christian couples. It is critical that you learn what the agency's restrictions are for prospective adoptive parents before you commit to working with them.

## Independent Adoption

Generally, an independent adoption is a faster process than an agency adoption. Because you are actively involved in the adoption, you have more control over the pace of the process. And because most birth mothers place their infants for adoption independently, it is a more effective way to adopt an infant.

Independent adoption is a way to avoid the arbitrary criteria that the adoption agencies often impose on who can adopt. It allows the birth parents themselves to choose who will parent their children. Another reason that a birth mother might choose independent adoption is that it may allow her to control the amount of contact that she has with the baby after the adoption is finalized. Some agencies have policies or philosophies that restrict the amount of contact that the adoptive parents and the birth parents will have after the birth of the baby. Many birth mothers want to have more control over the process and resent the interference by the adoption agency. Some agencies require that the baby go into foster care until the baby is legally freed for adoption (that is, when the birth parents' legal consents to the adoption become irrevocable). Many birth parents are uncomfortable with this arrangement and choose to place the baby directly with the adoptive parents through an independent adoption.

In deciding whether to adopt independently, you should also consider whether you are willing to do much of the work yourself. An independent adoption will take more effort on your part. You will have to actively look for birth parents and develop and implement a strategy to find a child to adopt. But along with the effort and responsibility comes more control over the process. If you want a completely anonymous adoption, independent adoption is not a good choice for you. Most of the birth mothers choosing to place a child in an independent adoption want to have some amount of contact with the baby after the adoption is finalized. The contact may be as little as photographs and letters once a year to as much as face-to-face visits. Another reason that birth mothers plan independent adoptions is so that the baby will not go into foster care but will go directly into the adoptive parents' home. These placements are called legal risk adoptions because there is usually a period of time after the placement of the baby in the adoptive parents' home during which the birth parents can still change their minds about the adoption. There is always a risk the birth parents will reclaim the child within the legal time limits.

### Choosing the Right Attorney

Do not hire a general practitioner to handle an adoption. Because adoption is a highly specialized area of the law, you should hire an attorney who is an expert in adoption. The best way to find an adoption attorney is to talk to other people who have recently adopted. Find out whether they were satisfied with their representation. If that does not work, look in the yellow pages under "Adoption Attorneys"; ask your adoption agency to give you their list of referral attorneys; consult the

American Academy of Adoption Attorney Directory (available from AAAA, P.O. Box 33053, Washington, DC 20033-0053); ask AFA (Adoptive Families of America, 612/535-4829) and Resolve (617/623-0744) who they would recommend; or contact your local bar association for the names of attorneys in your area who specialize in adoption.

Once you have the names of one or more adoption attorneys, call them and interview them over the phone before you hire them. Ultimately, whoever you decide to hire depends on how comfortable you are with the attorney. Consider the following:

- What kind of experience does the attorney have? Since adoption law is changing rapidly, it is important to know how many and what kinds of adoptions the attorney has done within the past year.

- How long has the attorney been handling adoptions?

- Is the attorney a member of the American Academy of Adoption Attorneys?

- What will the attorney's role be in the adoption?

- Feel free to ask for references. Does the attorney have any former clients who would be willing to talk to you?

- How much does the attorney charge? Does she charge an hourly fee or a flat rate? On the average, what will a case like yours cost? What services are included?

- In some states attorneys are prohibited from matching you with a birth mother. Will the attorney help you to find a child to adopt as well as providing you with the legal services necessary to finalize the adoption?

- Are you considering working with birth parents in another state? If so, make sure that the attorney has contacts in the other state or states and understands the complexities of adopting from another state.

- Does the attorney approve of the type of adoption you are planning?

- How does the attorney feel about openness in adoption? Does the attorney's attitude about adoption match your own?

## Deciding What Kind of Child You Want to Adopt

The type of child you can adopt will depend to a large extent on who you are. Factors such as your age, religion, marital status, weight, health, sexual preference, ethnic background, and your budget will determine which adoption agency or country or birth parents (biological parents) will work with you. Your temperament, understanding of other cultures, and personal preferences will also help to steer you in the direction of the right adoption for you.

### U.S.–Born Infant Adoptions

Healthy, U.S.–born infants probably account for only 20 to 30 percent of all adoptions in the United States. While many people would like to adopt an infant, there are just not enough infants available for adoption. Some people adopt healthy infants through agencies, but most adopt healthy infants independently (that is, privately). Many decide to adopt internationally or to adopt an older child or a child with special needs when they realize how few infants are available for adoption in the United States and that it might take years.

### Stepparent and Relative Adoptions

Most adoptions in the United States are adoptions of children by close blood relatives or by stepparents. These children may become available for adoption after the death of a parent or parents, through the juvenile court system after the parents' relationship with the child is ended because of abuse or neglect, because of the parents' divorce and remarriage, or for a variety of other reasons. Usually state laws make it easy for relatives or stepparents to adopt by simplifying the adoption process for them. If no parent or other relative objects, they may not need to have a home study done, wait to finalize the adoption, or provide an accounting of adoption related expenses—all of which would usually be required in a nonrelative adoption.

### Children With Special Needs Adoptions

Adoption of children with "special needs" refers to any adoption of a child who is considered hard to place. These children may be older (two years old or older), be nonwhite, or have significant emotional, physical, or intellectual handicaps.

There are many reasons why you might choose to adopt a child with special needs. You may not fit the agency criteria to qualify to adopt an infant and a child with special needs may be the only child that the agency will consider placing with you. You may have been a foster parent to a particular child and have come to love the child while he or she lived in your home. You may have special expertise or training and feel that you and your family are strong enough and have the resources to provide a home to a child who might otherwise remain in long-term foster care.

Before you adopt a child with special needs, make sure that you are well prepared. Do not allow yourself to be pushed into a decision that may not be right for you and do not make a decision motivated by guilt feelings. Some things to consider include:

- Are you prepared for the extra time and effort it may take to parent a child with special needs?

- Are you patient, tolerant, and flexible? Do you have a good sense of humor?

- Are your spouse and other children enthusiastic about the adoption plan? Are your extended family members and your community supportive of your decision?

- Have you identified professionals who will be able to help you with the difficult periods you will undoubtedly experience?

- If your child will require medical or psychological help, do you understand the extent of financial help that will be available to you in the form of state or federal adoption subsidies? Can you be a fierce advocate for the child when he or she does not receive the services that are deserved?

State agencies and social workers have a mandate to try to find adoptive homes for these hard to place children. If you express an interest in adopting a child with special needs, it is their job to help you to find the child who will fit into your family. Agencies maintain national adoption exchange books with pictures and descriptions of children with special needs who are available for adoption. This book is available for you to review. You can find out where to view it by calling your local social service agency.

If you are considering adoption of a child with special needs, a good place to start is by contacting the NACAC (North American Council on Adoptable Children, 1821 University Avenue West, St. Paul, MN 55104; 612/644-3036). The NACAC is an organization dedicated to providing education and support for families who have adopted or are thinking about adopting special needs children in the United States.

## Transracial Adoption

Transracial adoption refers to the adoption of a child of one race by a family of another race. Usually the adoptive family is white, while the child could be Native American, Black, Hispanic, or Asian. Transracial adoption is very controversial. Many people feel that children should be raised within their own culture by people who share the same ethnic and racial traits. This view has been enacted into law in some states. For example, in Minnesota it may be difficult to adopt transracially. The law there requires that adoption agencies and the courts must place children in adoptive placements according to certain preferences. First, the child must be placed with a relative if one is available. If no relative is available, the child must be placed with a family of the same racial or ethnic heritage. If no family of the same background is available, the child may be placed with a family of a different background that is knowledgeable and appreciative of the child's racial and ethnic heritage.

Many oppose same-race placement requirements in adoption, and in response, the U.S. Congress enacted the 1994 Multiethnic Placement Act. The Act penalizes states by denying them federal assistance if they delay or deny placement of a child into foster or adoptive homes based on color, race, or national origin. This law has been very controversial, and an act to repeal it is currently under consideration.

Native American children are protected by a special federal law that applies only to them: the Indian Child Welfare Act. This law was enacted to protect Indian children from being adopted by those outside their culture and to promote survival of Indian tribes. Like the Minnesota law, it sets preferences for adoptive placements of children. Indian children must be placed first with a member of the child's extended family, then with members of the child's tribe, and finally with other Indian families. The legal requirements for freeing a child for adoption are stricter than in many other adoptions, and the tribe must be notified and involved in the adoption process. While it may be possible for a non-Indian to adopt an Indian child, it is always a high-risk situation that depends to a large extent on the wishes of the child's tribe.

## International Adoption

Children are available for adoption from India, Colombia, and many other countries. Because countries and their requirements change frequently in response to current events, it is important to keep up with the political and economic trends within these countries that can affect adoption. There are many risks to adopting a child from another country. To minimize those risks and because of language barriers and cultural differences, make sure that you are working with a knowledgeable and reputable adoption agency or adoption facilitator. Satisfy yourself that the agency or individual has a strong history of recent successful adoptive placements from a particular country. Even a well-meaning agency or facilitator can make costly and emotionally draining mistakes if they have not yet solidified an adoption program in a particular country.

When you are trying to choose an agency, a facilitator, or a country with which to work, ask a lot of questions. How long will it take? How much will it cost? Get a breakdown of the fees. How old will the child be? Make sure that you understand the legal process in the foreign country. Talk to adoptive parents who have recently worked with the agency or facilitator.

In deciding to adopt a child from another country, look at yourself first. Are you the right person? Can you provide the racial and cultural ties this child will need to develop healthy self-esteem? Will your family and friends be supportive? Do you understand what it means to raise a child who is from a different culture and possibly of a different race? Are you prepared for the challenges that being an interracial family will present? Do you already have cultural contacts and a support network? If not, start to develop them before you adopt.

When you adopt internationally, the country of the child's origin requires that you meet its own criteria for adoption. The requirements may be very restrictive and sometimes seem unreasonable. For example, some countries require that you make two separate trips to the country before they will finalize the adoption and allow you to bring your child home. Make sure that before you commit to adopting from a particular country, you know that you fit the adoption criteria.

A brave minority of people choose to handle their international adoption on their own. While this is possible, it is not for the faint of heart. The paperwork can be overwhelming, and one small mistake can slow the process to a crawl. With some countries, an independent, international adoption is more feasible if you speak the language or if you have the right translator and have ties to the country (for example, family or friends who live there).

Some choose to adopt children from poor or war-torn countries out of a desire to provide these children with opportunities that they will never have in their home country. Others choose to adopt from a foreign country when they find out how difficult it can be to adopt a healthy American-born infant. Compared to adopting within the United States, international adoption can be a relatively quick process. You may also find that because of your age or marital status it will be more difficult for you to adopt a newborn child in the United States, but you may qualify to adopt a very young child from another country.

Some are motivated to adopt internationally because they are opposed to the idea of an open adoption. They believe that adopting internationally is the only sure way to cut off contact with the birth parents altogether. If you choose this strategy, it may backfire on you. Many of the adult adoptees who were adopted internationally are now returning to their home countries to search for their birth parents. Some of them have been successful in finding their birth parents.

Those who have not found their birth parents are often resentful of a process that has stripped them of their birthright. In recent international adoptions it has become more and more common for the adoptive parents to meet the birth parents and to share identifying information to make it easier for the children and the birth parents to stay in contact after the adoption. In the future, there may not be any anonymous adoptions, even in international adoptions.

Adopting internationally can present many challenges. Be aware that you will not be adopting a newborn. The child, who will probably be several months to several years old, may be very sad on arrival. He or she has had to leave trusted caregivers at the orphanage or foster home. It will take time for the child to feel comfortable with you in his or her new home. You may receive very sketchy health and social history, and the information that you have may not be correct. For example, sometimes the age of the child will not be correct. It can be difficult to get reliable medical information about children from other countries, and the health risks can be great.

## Minimizing Your Legal Risk

Watching legal battles over adoption on television and reading about them in the newspaper has made us all aware that adoption can be risky. While there is no way to eliminate the risk, there are steps that you can take to minimize the danger.

### Be a Good Adoption Consumer

One of the most important things that you can do is to educate yourself about adoption. Often, by the time that people begin to think about adoption, they have been through years of medical treatment for infertility. They feel vulnerable, and it may be tempting to be passive and to allow adoption professionals to take the more active role in the adoption. The more knowledgeable you are and the more actively involved you are in your adoption, the less risk you will be taking.

A good first step is to contact AFA (Adoptive Families of America, 3333 Highway 100 North, Golden Valley, MN 55422; 612/535-4829). AFA can provide you with a packet of general information about adoption to get you started with many of the decisions that you will have to make initially. Another good resource is Resolve, a national organization providing education and support for infertile people (1310 Broadway, Sommerville, MA 02144; 617/623-0744). Resolve also has local chapters throughout the United States. Your local library is another good resource. If you are trying to decide what kind of child to adopt, whether to adopt privately or through an agency, or want to learn about open adoption, you can find books and magazine articles that will help you sort through all of the confusion. If you have questions on very specific topics, you may want to contact the National Adoption Information Clearinghouse (11426 Rockville Pike, Suite 410, Rockville, MD 20852; 301/231-6512). This organization can provide you with a bibliography of specific adoption-related topics, information about your state's adoption laws, and fact sheets on adoption-related areas of more general interest.

### Make Sure That You and the Birth Parents Have Separate Attorneys

Hire a good adoption lawyer for yourself and make sure that the birth parents are represented by a separate adoption attorney who can give them quality legal advice and representation. If the birth parents are not able to pay for an attorney, ask your attorney for advice about paying for the attorney for them. It is in your best interests that the birth parents are represented by a lawyer. Birth parents who have gone into the process with their eyes open and who are knowledgeable about the process will be much less likely to change their minds. And if they do change their minds, it will probably be before the baby is placed with you.

### If You Adopt a Child From Another State, Know the Law

Each state has a separate set of laws governing adoption. In addition, all of the states have enacted a law called the Interstate Compact on the Placement of Children (ICPC). If you live in one state but are adopting a child from another state, you must follow the laws in your state and the child's state as well as the ICPC. Each state has an Interstate Compact Administrator (ICA) who reviews the adoption home study, medical and social histories, and other adoption paperwork before allowing the child to go to the adopting parents' state for the purpose of adoption. The ICAs in both the sending and the receiving states must give approval before the child goes to the adopting parents' state. If the child is moved without approval of the ICAs, there is a strong likelihood that the adoption will not be granted by the courts. Generally, it is somewhat more expensive to adopt across state lines. There will be additional expense because of the ICPC paperwork required and because of the additional time required to process the paperwork. You may also incur some additional expense if the child has to stay in foster care in the home state during the time that the paperwork is being processed.

### The Home Study

When you file an adoption petition, you are asking the court to decide whether the adoption is in the best interests of the child to be adopted. Generally the courts are not in a position to judge whether a

**The Adoption Process**

particular adoptive placement is in the best interests of the child without some assistance. In most cases, state law requires an adoption agency or other adoption professional to provide the court with an evaluation of the prospective adoptive family. The evaluation is called a home study or an adoption study.

A home study is an evaluation of whether a family is a suitable adoptive family. In some states the home study must be completed before a child may be placed in your home and in almost all states it must be completed before an adoption can be finalized in the courts. When the study is done, who completes it and what it includes varies a great deal from state to state, within states, and even from agency to agency.

A typical home study includes criminal background checks; personal references; a history of birth, marriage, and death; employment history; financial information; and psychological interviewing or testing. In some states the study may be completed by a qualified person, such as a social worker, while in other states the study must be done by an adoption agency or by the state Department of Human Services.

### Consent to Adoption

In a voluntary adoption, whoever has legal responsibility for the child to be adopted must give consent. This person or persons must sign a written document consenting to the adoption. The form of the document, who must sign it, how it is signed, and when it may be signed varies significantly from state to state. Most of the adoption cases that have been sensationalized in the news media have been cases in which adoption agencies or attorneys made mistakes when the birth parents signed the consent forms. The complicated legal requirements for the consent to the adoption are good reasons to make certain that both you and the birth parents are represented by lawyers.

In almost every adoption, the birth mother is required to sign a form consenting to the adoption. The birth father may be required to sign also or he may only be entitled to notification of the adoption proceedings, depending on the state. Sometimes it is difficult to determine exactly who the birth father is. For example, a man who fathers a child by a woman who is married to another man is the biological father, but the husband is the "presumed" or legal father.

If the birth parents are minors, their parents, and in some states a guardian *ad litem,* will also have to sign a form consenting to the adoption. If the adoptee is of a certain age or level of maturity, depending on the state, he or she may also be required to consent to the adoption.

The timing for signing the consent is critical and is governed by state law. In most states the consent form cannot be signed prior to the baby's birth. Even in those states that allow a prebirth consent by the birth mother, the consent does not become irrevocable until after the baby is born. In some states, however, the birth father is allowed to sign an irrevocable prebirth waiver of consent. There may be a waiting period after the baby's birth during which time the birth mother may not validly sign a consent form. Usually there is a period of time during which a birth mother can revoke her consent after the consent to adoption is signed.

The formal requirements for how the consent form is signed also vary a great deal from state to state. Some states have minimal requirements and others specify that there have to be witnesses and a notary. Others require that the consent be signed in front of a judge or that a particular form be used. Even in those states with very minimal requirements, the safest method is to be more formal, even if it's not legally required. Some states mandate that birth parents be represented by attorneys. In any adoption, making sure that the birth parents are represented by attorneys when they sign the consent forms improves the integrity of the process and makes the adoption safer for you.

If a birth mother changes her mind within the revocation period, you must return the baby to her. Experts estimate that anywhere from 1 to 10 percent of birth mothers change their minds about adoption. The actual numbers are impossible to determine because no record is kept of disrupted adoptions. While there is no way to completely eliminate this risk, your risk will be minimized if the birth mother has good preadoption counseling and if she has been well prepared by her attorney.

If a consent to adoption is taken according to all of the legal requirements, and if the legal time limit in which the birth parents can revoke their consent has passed, the adoption can be disrupted by the birth parents only on the grounds that the consent was taken fraudulently or as a result of duress or other wrongful conduct.

## Direct Placement Versus Foster Care

Direct adoptive placement of a child is the process in which the birth parents give the child to the adoptive parents without using an adoption agency as an intermediary. In the case of a newborn, for example, the baby would go directly from being at the hospital with the birth mother to the home of the prospective adoptive parents. Many adoptive parents and birth parents prefer direct placement because they want to have the baby in a safe, secure, and permanent place as soon as possible. In order for direct placement to work, you must be willing to take the risk that a baby who is placed with you before he or she is legally available to be adopted may be reclaimed by the birth parents. For example, if there is a ten-day period in your state in which the birth mother can revoke her consent to the adoption, and the baby is placed with you on day two, you will have to wait eight days before you know that the baby will be legally available for you to adopt. During that ten-day interim, the birth parents can reclaim the baby.

While direct placement is a common occurrence today, it was rarely done even five years ago. For many years adoption agency wisdom was that prospective adoptive parents should be protected from the risk of a baby being reclaimed. Agencies also wanted to protect birth parents. Many felt and some still are of the opinion that a birth parent will not feel comfortable about reclaiming a child if they know the prospective adoptive parents. Adoption agencies try to protect birth parents and adoptive parents by placing the baby in foster care immediately after birth and releasing the baby to the adoptive parents only after the time period for the birth parents to change their minds has expired. Because the adoptive parents are usually responsible for paying for the foster care placement, this process is more expensive than a direct placement.

In an independent adoption, whether you opt for a direct placement or temporary foster care is a highly personal decision that you and the birth parents must make together. If you are going through an adoption agency, you may not have a choice. You may be restricted by agency policies. If you are working with a more enlightened agency, it may be flexible enough to structure the initial placement the way that you and the birth parents want.

### Finalizing the Adoption

Once your home study has been completed, the baby has been placed in your home, and the birth parents' consents to adoption are irrevocable, the last step in the adoption process is to finalize the adoption. Because so much of the work of adoption is done in advance by you, the birth parents, social workers, and attorneys, the final adoption hearing is largely ceremonial. All of the paperwork of the adoption, the preadoption counseling, the labor and delivery have already happened. If everything is in order, the hearing will be brief (fifteen minutes or less). The adopting parents and the baby appear with their lawyer in front of a judge. You will swear under oath to the facts in your adoption petition and agree that you will raise this child as your own, that you will be legally and emotionally responsible for the child, and that from now on the child's name will be the name you have chosen. Many judges will allow you to take pictures at the end of the hearing, so remember to bring your camera.

## Open Adoption

Until recently, anonymous adoptions were the rule. When a birth mother made an adoption plan, she had little choice but to allow the adoption agency to choose the adoptive family for her baby.

Nonidentifying information was exchanged between the birth parents and the adoptive parents using the adoption agency as an intermediary. But careful measures were taken to make sure that the birth mother would not be able to discover where or with whom her baby had been placed. Face-to-face meetings were not allowed.

The trend now is toward open adoption. An open adoption is an adoption in which the adoptive parents and birth parents share information with each other or maintain contact with each other after the adoption is finalized. In an open adoption the contact may be as limited as the adoptive parents sending letters and pictures on an annual basis to the birth parents, or it may expand to include more regular contact and visitation by the birth parents.

Open adoption is becoming more widely accepted now, primarily because birth parents are insisting on it. Birth parents are no longer willing to drop their children into the black hole of anonymous adoption. They want more control over deciding who is going to parent their children. Adoptive parents who are unwilling to consider an open adoption are limiting their chances to adopt. There are far more people wanting to adopt than there are babies to adopt, and this means that birth parents' choices about adoption are being considered much more seriously and respectfully than ever before. Almost all independent adoptions and many agency adoptions are open adoptions because that is what the birth parents and many adoptive parents want.

Open adoption sounds frightening at first. If you are concerned, read about it and consider talking to an adoption professional with experience in open adoption. A social worker may be able to put your mind at ease. Talk to adoptive parents who have open adoptions. Find out what they think are the good and the bad aspects of openness. Most people worry that if a birth mother knows where her child is she will try to reclaim the child, even though that very rarely happens. In my professional experience, openness in adoption seems to ease the anxiety of birth parents so that they are less likely to change their minds.

Later in the adoption process, if you have identified a birth mother who wants to place her baby with you in an open adoption, you will have to work out an agreement about the extent of the openness. There are examples of these agreements in some of the books that have been written on open adoption. An adoption professional can help you to develop a contract with the birth mother outlining your understanding. While openness agreements are not legally enforceable in most states, they are an important road map to understanding what each of you expects from your relationship. This is a relationship based on trust. In most states after the adoption is finalized, the birth parents will not be able to petition the court to enforce the openness agreement, but it is critical and ethical that you promise only what you can comfortably deliver. It may be a good idea to agree in advance to a mechanism for resolving any disagreements that may develop over time. Be aware that in many adoptions, the relationship tends to become more open over time. So you should be prepared for your relationship to evolve toward more openness.

Many adoption professionals feel that openness is in the best interests of the child. It is good for the child to have easy access to first-hand medical and social history. In addition, children of open adoption do not worry about the missing puzzle piece of their birth family. It also is good for the birth parents, who in the past had to worry about where their children were and whether they were safe or even alive. Adoptive parents can also benefit from open adoption. By knowing and respecting the birth family, they can gain insight into genetically related personality traits and can also give their child a better sense of identity and a positive feeling about their adoption. By getting to know and trust the birth family, they will feel more secure as the adoptive parents and stop worrying about the unknown.

## Conclusion

Although the trend is for more open adoptions, it has become a very controversial issue within adoption agencies. If you are interested in an open adoption and the agency you are considering is philosophically opposed to open adoption, find another agency.

To learn more about open adoption, these books may be a good place to start: *The Open Adoption Experience*, by Lois R. Melina and Sharon K Roszia; and *Open Adoption: A Caring Option*, by Jean Warren Lindsay.

### Bibliography

Adamec, Christine A. *There are Babies to Adopt: A Resource Guide for Prospective Parents,* Mills and Sanderson, Bedford, MA 1987.

*American Academy of Adoption Attorneys Directory*. Washington, DC: American Academy of Adoption Attorneys. Available from AAAA, P.O. Box 33053, Washington, DC, 20033-0053.

Caplan, Lincoln. *An Open Adoption.* New York: Farrar, Strauss & Giroux, 1990.

Dunn, Linda, ed. *Adopting Children with Special Needs: A Sequel.* Washington, DC: North American Council on Adoptable Children, 1983.

Gilman, Lois. *The Adoption Resource Book.* New York: Harper & Row, 1984.

Gitlin, H. Joseph. *Adoptions: An Attorney's Guide to Helping Adoptive Parents*. Wilmette, IL: Callaghan and Co., 1987.

Lindsay, Jeanne Warren. *Open Adoption: A Caring Option.* Buena Park, CA: Morning Glory Press, 1988.

Martin, Cynthia D. *Beating the Adoption Game*. Harcourt, Brace, Jovanovich, San Diego, New York, London, 1988.

McKelvey, Carole A., and Dr. JoEllen Stevens. *Adoption Crisis: The Truth Behind Adoption and Foster Care*. Golden, CO: Fulcrum, 1994. Analyzes the current adoption system in the United States, including the problems of foster care and special needs children. Resource list includes strategies for adoptive parents, a list of evaluative instruments, and a state-by-state list of organizations, as well as a list of international adoption agencies.

Melina, Lois, and Sharon Kaplan Rozia. *The Open Adoption Experience*. New York: Harper and Row, 1995.

Melina, Lois. *Making Sense of Adoption: A Parent's Guide*. New York: Harper & Row, 1989.

Michelman, Stanley B., et al. *The Private Adoption Handbook: A Step-by-Step Guide to the Legal, Emotional, and Practical Demands of Adopting a Baby*. New York: Dell Books, 1988.

Sifferman, Kelly Allen. *Adoption: A Legal Guide for Birth and Adoptive Parents, 2d ed*. Hawthorne, NJ: Career Press, 1994

## Organizational Resources

All states have state agencies that can provide information. Some are under the state's Department of Health, others under Human Services or Services for Children. Check your local directory. Many also have information on international adoptions.

Adoptive Families of America
3333 Highway 100 North
Golden Valley, MN 55422
(612) 535-4829
*This organization publishes a magazine.*

Child Welfare League of America
67 Irving Place
New York, NY 10003
(212) 254-7410

Committee for Single Adoptive
  Parents
P.O. Box 15084
Chevy Chase, MD 20815

International Concerns Committee
  for Children
911 Cypress Drive
Boulder, CO 80303
(303) 494-8333
*They publish "Report on Inter-Country Adoption" (annual, updated monthly) for $20. They also have an excellent list of books, newsletters, and magazine articles available.*

National Adoption Information
  Clearinghouse
11426 Rockville Pike, Suite 410
Rockville, MD 20852
(301) 231-6512

National Council for Adoption
(202) 328-8072
*The membership for this group is agencies; they promote adoption and serve as an advocate for their membership.*

North American Council on Adoptable Children (NACAC)
1821 University Avenue W
Suite N-498
St. Paul, MN 55104
(612) 744-3036
*Contact them for information if you are considering adopting a child with special needs.*

Resolve
1310 Broadway
Somerville, MA  02144
(617) 623-0744
*This organization has good resources for infertile people. They also have chapters throughout the United States.*

---

**Amy M. Silberberg** is on the board of directors of Adoptive Families of America. She is an attorney specializing in adoption who practices in St. Paul, Minnesota, and is a member of the American Academy of Adoption Attorneys. She and her husband adopted their five-year-old son Sam and one-year-old Maggie as newborns in open, independent adoptions.

Chapter 11

# Child Care Planning for Seriously Ill Mothers

Gina M. Calabrese

Chapter Outline

**Introduction**

**Mothers With Serious Illnesses, Including AIDS: The Problem of Child Care and Custody**

**The Legal Effect of a Guardianship**

**Making Guardianship Arrangements**

**Standby Guardianships: An Approach to Dealing With the Episodic Nature of AIDS and Other Serious Illnesses**

**Adoption**

**Conclusion**

Introduction

Women who are single parents face many problems, but the most tragic situation is when the mother is terminally ill. With the continued spread of AIDS, advance directives for the care of children are becoming more established. While this chapter is addressed to women in particular, custodial fathers with AIDS and custodial parents with other terminal illnesses face similar issues regarding the care of their children. This chapter outlines several options available to parents who need to plan for child care while they are incapacitated and for the future custody of their children.

## Mothers With Serious Illnesses, Including AIDS: The Problem of Child Care and Custody

The rate of HIV infection among American women of childbearing age is on the rise. Because many of these women are mothers, the AIDS epidemic has created another problem of social, yet intensely personal, consequence: the issue of AIDS orphans. By the year 2000, AIDS will have orphaned at least 82,000 American children.[1]

A mother who learns of an HIV-positive diagnosis faces all the issues that confront any other person with HIV: denial, impending illness, isolation, and mortality. As a mother, however, if she has the sole care responsibility for her children, she must also come to terms with the impact of AIDS on them. Arrangements must be made for someone to care for her children during her intermittent hospitalizations and, ultimately, after her death. The mother must hasten to make these arrangements while she is still well and before AIDS depletes her vitality. Mothers with other terminal illnesses will have the same concerns.

While informal arrangements with family or friends may work on a short-term basis, such arrangements can be detrimental to the child if they are not formalized. Potential complications of informal child care arrangements include the inability of the caretaker to register the child in school or consent to medical treatment; a claim to custody by an abusive or absentee father, and the inability of the caretaker to obtain social services aid for the child because of the informality of the relationship. Sadly, many children of HIV-positive mothers will end up in the foster care system, where they will not only have to cope with the loss of a parent, but also with the unfamiliar environment and possible separation from their siblings.

Fortunately, a mother with HIV or another terminal illness has at her disposal certain legal remedies to formalize child care arrangements and to designate the person or persons she wishes to have custody of her children after her death. By establishing a guardianship, she can arrange for the person of her choosing to be legally authorized to care for her children during periods of illness and eventually, after her death. In addition, she may begin the process of selecting the person or persons who will eventually adopt her children, thus diminishing the risk that the children will enter the foster care system, which often separates siblings.

A single mother who is ill could have her children taken away from her even if she is hospitalized only once if she does not make prior arrangements. Making prior guardianship arrangements empowers a terminally ill mother—who probably feels she has less control of other aspects of her life—because it allows her to choose her children's guardian and even their adoptive parent or parents. The selection of a guardian/adoptive parent is a legacy such mothers can leave to their children. Not only does it empower the mother, but it is also in the chidren's best interests. The children are comforted by being placed in the care of a familiar relative, close friend, or adoptive parents that they have gotten to know prior to the natural parent's death. Moreover, the child is spared the pain and insecurity of institutionalization.

## The Legal Effect of a Guardianship

Guardianship laws vary from state to state; this chapter is based on the guardianship law of California, where the author practices, except where the law of another state is specifically discussed. While some general principles may apply in many jurisdictions, the reader should consult the laws of her state of residence to learn what is required to establish a guardianship. The reader is also advised to consult an attorney or a legal services organization. Advocacy and support groups for people with HIV may be able to provide referrals to attorneys experienced with AIDS-related legal issues.

In a guardianship, the court appoints an adult other than the parent to be legally responsible for the care of a minor, who is referred to as the "ward." There are two types of guardianship: guardianship of the person and guardianship of the estate. A guardian of the person cares for the minor, while a guardian of the estate cares for the minor's property. It is possible to establish either or both types of guardianship and to have a different person be appointed guardian for each. This chapter addresses guardianship of the *person* only.

A guardian has "the care, custody and control of" the ward and is also in charge of the ward's education.[2] The guardian may determine the child's place of residence, but must obtain court permission to permit the child to live out of the state.[3] The guardian may authorize medical treatment for the ward, just as the parent would, with a few exceptions. The guardianship may also be made subject to special conditions.[4] In California, for example, before surgery can be performed on a ward age fourteen or over, either the ward must consent to the surgery or a court order must be obtained.[5] Also, a guardian is prohibited from involuntarily confining the ward to a mental health treatment facility and is prohibited from authorizing convulsive treatment, sterilization, or experimental drugs without a court order.

While a guardian has parentlike powers over the child's upbringing, a parent does not permanently lose her parental rights and obligations, as in an adoption. For example, the parent remains financially responsible for the child.

Guardianship has a great impact on eligibility for public assistance. Once the child no longer resides with the mother, the mother can no longer receive AFDC benefits on behalf of the child. If the guardian and child are related, the guardian can receive AFDC benefits on behalf of the child.[6] Depending on the circumstances, the guardian's income may be counted against the child for purposes of AFDC eligibility. If the guardian is unrelated to the child, however, neither the child nor the guardian will be eligible for AFDC benefits.[7] Other public assistance may be available from the state. California provides AFDC-FC benefits to foster parents on behalf of the children under their care. A guardian could obtain AFDC-FC benefits for the ward if the guardian became a licensed foster parent.

Guardians and minors may apply for food stamps together regardless of whether they are related. Unlike AFDC, eligibility for food stamps is determined by "household" and not by kinship.

## Making Guardianship Arrangements

Too often, a mother with AIDS or other terminal illness will delay the matter of beginning guardianship proceedings. Often, she sees the act of naming a guardian as the equivalent of an admission that she is going to die. The denial of the disease can lead to devastating circumstances for the family. The longer the guardianship process is delayed, the more likely it is that the mother will become unable to care for her children. Without a guardianship in place, the children are at risk of being placed in foster care[8] or in another care situation adverse to the mother's wishes or the children's interests, such as with an abusive relative. It may take several weeks to several months to complete the guardianship procedure. This is another reason why careful planning is important and why delay should be avoided. To avoid this, the procedure should be commenced as soon as possible.

Because the guardian will have parentlike powers over the children, the mother must carefully select the proposed guardian. The person selected must be trustworthy, stable, and well acquainted with the children. He or she should also be familiar with the complications of the mother's illness and be prepared to assume guardianship duties as the need arises.

Typically, a petition for guardianship is filed with the court. The person who initiates the proceeding is called the petitioner. The guardianship law designates the people who are eligible to petition the court for a guardianship. In California, for example, the parent, the proposed guardian, a relative, minor children over the age of twelve, or a friend of the minor may file the petition.[9]

It is a good idea for the mother to petition the court, depending on how healthy she is at the time of the petition. Petitioning the court indicates that the mother consents to and supports the guardianship. If there is a high probability that the mother's health will prevent her from participating in the proceeding, however, it is a better idea for someone else, such as the proposed guardian, to file the petition. Whether or not she is the petitioner, the mother should sign a written nomination of guardian, expressing her consent to the guardianship. California law allows for such a nomination to become effective only upon the incapacitation or death of the parent.[10] At that time, the nominated guardian would file the petition for guardianship.

If an emergency has already arisen, the petitioner may file for a temporary guardianship at the same time she or he files for the permanent guardianship. Temporary guardianships may be granted for "good cause," while the permanent guardianship petition is pending.[11] Examples of good cause are emergency and immediate needs relating to the child's health, education, or care.

The petitioner must pay a filing fee for the petition. Court filing fees are substantial. In 1995 in Los Angeles County, for example, the filing fee for a guardianship petition was $607, which includes $425 for the cost of a background investigation. If the mother is indigent, however, she may apply for a fee waiver. Some states refer to this document by its Latin name, *In Forma Pauperis.* In Los Angeles County, if the petitioner states under penalty of perjury that she receives AFDC, she will receive a fee waiver. Additionally, in California, if an eligible minor (twelve years of age or older) petitions for the guardianship, the minor may obtain a fee waiver if he or she lacks independent sources of income.

The petition names the proposed ward or wards and the proposed guardian and must include some basic biographical information, such as ages and addresses. Parents and relatives are also named in the petition.[12] The petition must also state the reason the guardianship is being sought and must contain facts that show the court that guardianship is in the best interests of the child.[13]

Guardianship laws provide that certain relatives must be notified of the proceeding and sent a copy of the petition.[14] Califonia, for example, requries notice to the proposed ward and to all relatives within the second degree—parents, grandparents, siblings, and half-siblings. Courts strictly enforce the notice requirements, but the law usually provides that notice may be waived where notice would be against the interests of justice.[15] For example, the court might waive notice to an absentee father with a proven history of child abuse. The burden and expense of notice may be avoided if the relatives entitled to notice sign a written waiver of notice. However, family members entitled to notice may oppose the guardianship, which can lengthen and impede the process.

Notice of the hearing and a copy of the petition must also be given to the state or local social services agency that handles child welfare matters.[16] The law requires the local social services agency to interview and investigate the proposed guardian. The agency will investigate whether the guardian has a record of criminal activity or of child abuse complaints. The agency will also conduct a home interview of the proposed guardian and make a recommendation on the appropriateness of the guardian. The agency may charge the petitioner an investigation fee, which can waived for hardship.

The mother (if she is able), the proposed guardian, and the ward (or wards) should attend the guardianship hearing. Some states may not require all of these people to attend, but attendance is a good idea, as the judge will probably want to hear how each person feels about the guardianship. In deciding whether to make the guardianship appointment, the court will be guided by the child's best interests.[17] In California, the court must consider the best interests of the child and may appoint a guardian if it appears "necessary and convenient." Upon approval, the court will issue Letters of Guardianship to the guardian. The Letters of Guardianship provide proof that the guardian has been appointed and has the authority that accompanies a guardianship appointment.[18] If the guardianship is unopposed, the hearing should be fairly short.

A guardianship terminates when the ward attains majority, marries, dies, or is adopted.[19] If it appears that the guardian is misusing authority, is not fulfilling responsibilities, or is not acting in the best interests of the child, the mother (or any other interested party such as a friend or relative of the child) may petition to have the guardian removed.[20]

## Standby Guardianships: An Approach to Dealing With the Episodic Nature of AIDS and Other Serious Illnesses

Unlike those with many other serious illnesses, people with AIDS often experience periods of illness interspersed with periods of health. The guardianship law of most states provides that once the mother relinquishes control over the children to the guardian, the mother cannot get this power back without petitioning for the removal of the guardian. Guardianship becomes an all-or-nothing proposition. These laws, therefore, do not address the episodic nature of AIDS or other illnesses, such as cancer or mental illness.

A mother with AIDS may delay the guardianship process out of reluctance to give up her right to care for her children until it is absolutely necessary. Unfortunately, when it is absolutely necessary, it is also too late.

The states of New York, Illinois, and California have changed their guardianship laws to address the cycles of wellness and debilitation that accompany AIDS. These states now enable a terminally ill parent to arrange for the appointment of a guardian to assume the care of her children only when she is unable, due to infirmity, to care for the children herself. She may also establish a guardianship that will come into effect only upon her permanent incapacitation or death. This new type of guardianship is being referred to as a standby guardianship.

Of all the standby guardianship laws, New York's appears to be best tailored for dealing with the cyclical nature of AIDS. The New York law provides for a standby guardian to assume guardianship authority upon the incapacitation *or* upon the debilitation and consent of the parent. A parent is incapacitated if she is unable to care for her child because of mental impairment. She is debilitated if she is unable to take care of her child because of a physical illness, disease, or injury. If the parent is debilitated, she must also consent to the guardianship. By activating the guardian's authority upon the mother's physical inability to care for her children, the New York law recognizes that a mother with AIDS may be mentally competent to care for her children, but physically unable to perform caretaking activities.

The New York law also makes it easy for a parent to designate a standby guardian without going to court. The parent may designate the standby guardian in writing before two adult witnesses, other than the proposed standby guardian. The standby guardian must also sign the designation.[21] The standby guardianship goes into effect when the guardian receives a copy of a determination by the mother's attending physician that she is incapacitated. It also goes into effect when the guardian receives the attending physician's determination that the mother is debilitated *and* a witnessed copy of the mother's written consent, which the guardian must also sign.[22]

The standby guardianship will expire after sixty days unless the guardian petitions the court to appoint him or her as standby guardian.[23] The parent may revoke the standby guardianship verbally or in writing. If the petition has already been filed, she must file a written revocation with the court and notify the standby guardian.[24]

Alternatively, the parent may petition the court to appoint a standby guardian whose authority becomes effective upon the parent's consent, incapacity, or death. The petition must be based on the existence of "a significant risk that the petitioner will become incapacitated or die" within two years of the filing of the petition.[25] It may be revoked by a writing filed with the court and notice to the guardian.

It may be comforting to a mother who needs to rely on the New York standby guardianship law to know that the law does not divest her of her parental rights as long as she is alive. Rather, the standby guardian and the mother share authority over the child.[26]

In Illinois, a standby guardianship "takes effect upon the incapacity or death of the minor's parent or parents."[27] Standby guardianship is not available if one of the child's parents is living and is willing and capable of exercising guardianship.[28] A parent may petition the court to appoint a standby guardian to automatically assume guardianship duties upon the parent's incapacitation or death. The guardian must obtain court approval within sixty days.

Alternatively, a parent may nominate a standby guardian by affidavit, without petitioning the court. However, if the period of guardianship exceeds sixty days, a Petition for Guardianship must be filed with the court.[29]

In contrast to the New York and Illinois laws, California's law[30] does not provide for the appointment of a standby guardian to take over only during periods of the mother's illness. Rather, it provides that the court may appoint the custodial parent and a person nominated by the custodial parent as joint guardians of the ward if the custodial parent has been diagnosed with a terminal condition. The mother and the guardian must both agree to exercise a guardianship power. If the mother dies, the guardian has power to act alone. If the mother is unable to act, however, the law seems to require a court order to allow the guardian to act without the consent of the mother.[31]

A noncustodial parent can prevent the appointment of a joint guardian. The appointment will be made, however, if the court finds that awarding custody to the noncustodial parent would be detrimental to the child.[32]

California's joint guardianship arrangement allows the mother to retain her parental rights as long as she is able to act. In theory, however, it could impede a mother's decision-making power because joint guardians must concur in all decisions. This may seem less desirable than the New York or Illinois options, under which the standby guardian has power only when the mother is debilitated or incapacitated. However, if the mother has chosen a trustworthy person to serve as guardian, the guardian is not likely to abuse the guardianship power.

Mothers with AIDS who do not reside in states that authorize standby guardianships may have other options for tailoring the guardianship to their needs. One traditional option has been for a parent to nominate a guardian in a will. While a will nomination allows a mother to express her wishes as to who will serve as guardian, such a guardianship would not take effect until after the parent's death. Therefore, it does not protect the children during the mother's hospitalizations. Another problem with testamentary nominations is that the children's caretaking arrangement will have an uncertain legal status during the long time it may take to probate the will.

Another option, which is available under California law, is for the mother to sign a written nomination of guardian, as would be filed with a guardianship petition. Such a nomination may provide that it will become effective only upon certain conditions, such as the subsequent legal incapacitation or death of the mother.[33] The proposed guardian should know where the original is kept, so that it is available when the need arises for him or her to petition the court for appointment as guardian.

Petitions for joint guardianship and petitions for a normal guardianship, with special conditions, are other options to explore. The California guardianship law, for example, has a provision that allows for additional conditions to be placed on the guardianship.[34] It may be possible to use this provision of the law to request that the guardianship be conditioned on the incapacitation of the mother.

If there seems to be no way of circumventing the state's "all or nothing" guardianship law, the only reasonable option may be to petition for a guardianship as provided under the laws of the state of residence. As long as the guardian is trusted, the guardian and parent may make an informal arrangement between themselves that the parent care for the children as long as she is able. Indeed, this may be consistent with a guardian's powers to make decisions concerning the child's care and residence. While a guardian has the power to decide where the child lives, she could certainly consent to the child living with his or her mother as long as the mother is capable of caring for the child. Of course, the guardian still has the legal power to change her mind about where the child lives. Once the guardianship is established, the parent would have to cooperate with the guardian's wishes.

## Adoption

In addition to a guardianship, it is a good idea for a mother with AIDS or another terminal illness to undertake the search for adoptive parents for her children. Again, this is a difficult emotional undertaking, because in searching for adoptive parents, a mother acknowledges her own impending death. She must also come to terms with the relinquishment of her parental rights.

Still, beginning the search while the mother is well is truly in the best interests of the children. The mother is able to have a voice in who will raise her children and even where they will be raised. She has the comfort of knowing the people who will be trusted with her child's upbringing. If she has more than one child, beginning an early search will increase the chances that the children will stay together as a family. Finally, selecting the adoptive parents while the mother is still well will allow for the mother, her children, and the adoptive parents to get to know each other before the adoption is finalized. Getting acquainted with the adoptive parents and having a sense that their mother approves of the adoption can help to reduce the distress that the children experience upon the loss of their mother and upon their subsequent adoption.

If a guardianship has been established, it will terminate upon the adoption of the children. However, another approach is to petition for the adoptive parents to be appointed as guardians of the children. Under this arrangement, a mother who is uneasy about formally terminating the parent-child relationship can avoid relinquishing her rights before she dies. Once she selects adoptive parents, however, she should sign a document stating that she nominates the adoptive parents and consents to the adoption. For further details about proceeding with an adoption, please see chapter 9 on giving your child up for adoption.

Recognizing the importance of finding a loving home for children, a Los Angeles mother who was dying of AIDS undertook a search for a family to adopt her daughters. During her search, she met other mothers confronting the same issue and founded an organization called Tanya's Children. Tanya's Children is a life-enhancement group for mothers with HIV and their children. Tanya's Children provides a myriad of support services for mothers and children, including counseling, family outings, and structuring quality time for both parents and children. Tanya's Children also assists mothers with adoption counseling and referrals. (The author is grateful to the dedicated members of Tanya's Children for their invaluable insights in meeting the needs of families confronting the consequences of AIDS and for the opportunity to work with them.)

## Conclusion

Unfortunately, most states do not yet have guardianship laws designed to deal with the cycles of infirmity and wellness that accompany AIDS and other terminal illnesses. In the meantime, it is important for a mother to use the laws of her state to make some formal arrangements for the care of her children. Establishing a guardianship and planning an adoption are essential to ensure that a mother with a terminal disease has a voice in structuring her children's lives and their future. Proper planning is also essential for the emotional well-being of her children.

### Notes

1. Nicholas, S. W., and Abrams, E. J. "The 'Silent' Legacy of AIDS. Children Who Survive Their Parents and Siblings." *Journal of the American Medical Association* (December 23/20, 1992): 3478.
2. California *Probate Code* § 2351 (a).
3. California *Probate Code* § 2352.
4. California *Probate Code* § 2358.
5. California *Probate Code* § 2353.
6. 42 U.S.C. § § 606 and 607.

7. *Curry v. Dempsey,* 701 F.2d 580 (6th Cir. 1983).
8. Duncan, Laura. "Standby Guardian Bills Advance in Legislature." *Chicago Daily Law Bulletin* (March 24, 1993): 1. The article notes that when parents with AIDS are hospitalized, the Department of Children and Family Services may be called in to care for the children.
9. California *Probate Code* § 1500.
10. California *Probate Code* § 1502 (b).
11. California *Probate Code* § 2250.
12. California *Probate Code* § 1510.
13. For example, California *Probate Code* § 1514 (b).
14. California *Probate Code* § 1511.
15. For example, California *Probate Code* § 1511.
16. California *Probate Code* § 1516 and § 1542.
17. For example, California *Probate Code* § 1514 and Illinois Revised Statutes Ch. 755 para. 11-5.2 (c).
18. For example, California *Probate Code* § 2310 and Illinois Revised Statutes ch. 755 para. 11-5.2 (a). Other states may use different nomenclature for this document.
19. California *Probate Code* § 1600.
20. California *Probate Code* § 2650.
21. New York *Surrogate's Court Procedure Act* § 1726 (4) (a).
22. New York *Surrogate's Court Procedure Act* § 1726 (4) (c).
23. New York *Surrogate's Court Procedure Act* § 1726 (4) (c).
24. New York *Surrogate's Court Procedure Act* § 1726 (4) (f).
25. New York *Surrogate's Court Procedure Act* § 1726 (3) (b) (ii).
26. New York *Surrogate's Court Procedure Act* § 1726 (7).
27. Illinois Revised Statutes Ch. 755 Para. 1-2.23. Illinois' standby guardianship law is effective as of January 1, 1994.
28. Illinois Revised Statutes Ch. 755 para. 11-5.2 (b).
29. Illinois Revised Statutes Ch. 755 para. 11-5.1
30. California's law is effective as of January 1, 1994.
31. California *Probate Code* § 2105 (e).
32. California *Probate Code* § 2105 (f).
33. California *Probate Code* § 1501 (b).
34. California *Probate Code* § 2358.

## Bibliography

The National Directory of Resources on HIV Infection/AIDS: The Professional's Reference. Alexandria, VA: National Directory Publishing Association.

## Organizational Resources

A number of local AIDS organizations (for example, AIDS Project-LA) can assist mothers with guardianship issues. Other organizations provide counseling services for terminally ill patients. Your doctor, hospital, or local library should be able to provide information on these services.

Tanya's Children
6167 Costello Avenue
Van Nuys, CA 91401
(213) 730-8202

---

**Gina M. Calabrese** earned her B.A. at Columbia University and her J.D. at Fordham University. As a litigation associate at a major Los Angeles law firm, she began to represent children through a pro bono program of Public Counsel, a legal services organization. A feminist who has been active in women's issues for twelve years, Ms. Calabrese saw that the interests of women and children were often intertwined. This was clearly demonstrated when, in her children's rights work, she represented three brothers whose mother had AIDS. Ms. Calabrese currently works as a full-time public interest attorney. She is a staff attorney and consumer advocate with the Proposition 103 Enforcement Project, a Los Angeles–based nonprofit orgaization that represents consumer interests in matters of insurance before regulators, legislators, and the courts.

Chapter 12

# *Sports*

Kathryn M. Reith

Chapter Outline

**Introduction**

**Title IX**
How Title IX Applies to Sports • Money • Opportunity

**Compliance**

**Financial Aid**

**Other Program Components**
Provision of Equipment and Supplies • Scheduling of Games and
Practice Times • Travel and Daily Allowance • Academic Tutoring •
Coaching • Locker Rooms, Practice, and Competitive Facilities •
Medical and Training Facilities and Services • Provision of Housing
and Dining Facilities and Services • Publicity • Recruitment of Stu-
dent Athletes • Provision of Support Services

**What to Do If Discrimination Is Suspected**

**Conclusion**

Introduction
　For years women and girls have been systematically denied access to organized sports. This has slowly changed, but parents must continue their vigilance so their daughters may reap the benefits of sports. This chapter offers guidance to those who wish to ensure opportunities for their daughters.

Title IX
　In 1972, a federal law created a revolution by opening high school and college sports to women. That law, Title IX of the Education Amendments of 1972, was aimed at ending sex discrimination in all educational institutions that receive federal funds, from kindergarten through post-graduate programs.

　Although Title IX is not the only law that affects women's access to sports opportunities, it is the most important. Title IX prohibits sex discrimination in educational institutions that receive federal funds. In brief, it states:

> No person in the United States shall, on the basis of sex, be excluded from participation in, be denied the benefits of, or be subjected to discrimination under any educational program or activity receiving Federal financial assistance.

　Most schools, from elementary schools through colleges, receive federal funds. Private colleges, for example, receive federal funding indirectly through financial aid programs, like the Pell grants, that go to their students. Private high schools, on the other hand, are not likely to be covered.

　The Office for Civil Rights (OCR) of the Department of Education enforces Title IX. Victims of discrimination can file administrative complaints with this office or they can choose to file a lawsuit in federal court.

　An educational institution that discriminates against women can lose its federal funding, although that penalty has never been applied to date. Institutions that have been found in violation of the law have agreed to specific plans to end the discrimination and comply with the law.

### How Title IX Applies to Sports

　Title IX applies generally to entire athletic programs rather than to specific teams. The men's and women's basketball teams, for example, would not be directly compared without looking at the rest of the program. Instead, the entire men's athletic program would be compared to the entire women's program.

　There are three major program areas involved in Title IX and athletics. The first is the effective accommodation of student interests and abilities—in other words, the opportunity to play sports. The second area concerns athletic financial aid. The final area includes all other program components. Determination of compliance in each of these areas includes an analysis of quantitative as well as qualitative factors.

The OCR looks for what it calls a "disparity" between men's and women's programs. Disparity is defined by the OCR as a difference in benefits or services that has a negative impact on athletes of one sex when compared with the benefits available to athletes of the other sex. There must be both a difference and a negative impact. As a result, some OCR investigations have found differences in the men's and women's programs, yet ruled that there was no violation of Title IX.

Both the federal courts and the OCR have generally allowed cases to focus on just one of the three major areas of Title IX. In other words, if a school violates the law in one of these three major areas, it doesn't matter if the school complies in the other two: it is still breaking the law. In high school complaints, the OCR will generally investigate only the area described in the written complaint. It will usually investigate all areas in college complaints.

## Money

The budgets for men's and women's sports do not have to be exactly the same under Title IX since different sports programs cost different amounts. A major difference in budget, however, can indicate a difference in the quantity and quality of the athletic programs. Sometimes, for example, budget limitations can cause unequal services. If women's team coaches have specific travel budgets that force them to house four athletes to a hotel room while men's team budgets are sufficient to sleep two to a room, these budgets have caused unequal travel arrangements.

Budgets can also affect the number of athletic opportunities. For example, a field hockey coach may carry only the minimum number of players on the team because the budget doesn't allow for the equipment and travel costs of additional players. On the other hand, the men's lacrosse team may carry many extra athletes because they can easily be paid for within the budget. This is a violation if only women's teams face this restriction of players because of budget.

The most important aspect of money and athletics is that the amount and source of funds cannot excuse discrimination. Many athletic departments use "We just don't have the money" as the excuse for maintaining discriminatory programs. That rationale, however, does not give the school permission to violate federal law. The school has several choices: raise more money to add services and opportunities for females; redistribute existing money and reduce services and opportunities for males; or a little of both.

In addition, goods and services paid for by booster clubs are included when considering budget disparities of entire athletic programs. Despite additional funds raised by these clubs or by alumni groups for specific teams or purposes, the school is still obligated to provide equivalent programs. The OCR's Investigator's Manual specifically notes that if booster clubs provide benefits and services to athletes of one sex, the school must act to ensure that benefits and services are equivalent for both sexes. The school could ask the booster club or other donor to provide equivalent benefits or it could even refuse the donation.

### Opportunity

Title IX requires that schools offer equivalent opportunities for males and females to play sports. In addition to the opportunity to play sports, the quantity and quality of opportunities are also considered, including the number of games or meets in which teams compete, plus the level of the competition. The programs do not have to be identical but instead must accommodate the interests and abilities of the male and female students. For example, very few schools would be able to find enough women who wanted to play football and few teams for them to play. On the other hand, finding capable players and competition for field hockey, soccer, or softball teams may be quite easy.

## Compliance

To determine compliance with Title IX's requirement of equivalent opportunities, there are three tests. If an institution can pass any one of the three tests, it has successfully offered equivalent opportunities.

The first test compares the male to female ratios of full-time male and female students (counting undergraduates only at the college level) with the male to female ratios of the athletic program participants. For example, if an institution has 53 percent female students and 48 percent male students and about 52 percent of the athletes are female and 48 precent male, then the school complies with this requirement of Title IX. Most institutions fail this test: At the average National Collegiate Athletic Association (NCAA) member school, 53 percent of college students are female but only 35 percent of the athletes are female.

The second test examines a school's history of expanding opportunities for females. The school's history of adding or dropping sports for both men and women must demonstrate a good faith effort to increase opportunities for women.

Finally, the last test concerns whether or not the interests and abilities of the underrepresented sex have been fully and effectively accommodated. Some administrators fail to accommodate women's interests and abilities because they assume women are not as interested in sports as men are, and therefore, the sports program will offer fewer opportunities for women.

Court cases are currently focusing on this last test. The most recent rulings have clarified that the words "fully and effectively" mean just that. Are there viable teams of women that are not getting the opportunity to play? For example, Brown University argued that a survey of students would show more male undergraduates than females to be interested in playing varsity sports, and therefore, the opportunities should be allocated in a similar ratio. In *Cohen v. Brown University,* the U.S. Court of Appeals for the First Circuit rejected Brown's argument, noting that this test would take the "full" out of "fully and effectively accommodate." It would also be very difficult to administer such a survey in an unbiased manner.

The requirement for accommodation often comes into question when schools add or drop teams. In *Kiechel v. Auburn University,* the women's club soccer team had repeatedly requested varsity status but the school turned down all requests. Only 25 percent of Auburn's varsity athletes were female. The soccer team had successfully competed on the club level for over five years, paying their own expenses and coaching themselves, but the institution maintained that it couldn't afford to add women's soccer as a varsity team. The university has settled this case out of court, agreeing to grant immediate varsity status, a new soccer field, scholarships, and repayment of the expenses that the plaintiffs incurred as members of the club team.

Other recent cases arise out of the elimination of existing varsity teams. At Colorado State University, for example, budget problems resulted in the elimination of the men's baseball and women's softball teams. But women constituted only 35 percent of all athletes at Colorado State. The judge ruled that Colorado State was in violation of Title IX before the cuts and should not have eliminated any women's opportunities until they reached parity with the men.

Although Title IX does not normally look at specific teams out of the entire program context, its policy interpretation defines when a school must offer a specific women's team. If a school offers a team in a contact sport for members of one sex, it must also offer a team in a contact sport for members of the opposite sex when 1) opportunities for the excluded sex have historically been limited, and 2) there is sufficient interest and ability to sustain a viable team with reasonable expectation of competition for that team. For noncontact sports, the establishment of a team for members of the excluded sex additionally requires that those members would not be likely to be selected for a coed team or compete actively if selected.

**Financial Aid**    Title IX requires colleges and universities to award athletic financial aid in the same proportion as the number of students of each sex that participate in athletics. That is why the opportunity to play sports is so important. A $179 million gender gap currently exists in athletic scholarships. Accordingly, more opportunities to play sports should result in more athletic scholarships for women.

For purposes of compliance with Title IX, athletes are counted if they participate in organized practices and team sessions on a regular basis, receive the kind of support that athletes normally receive, and are listed on the sport's squad lists. Each individual counts only once, even if they play for more than one team during a school year.

If the comparison between athlete male to female ratios and the scholarship money ratios are substantially equal, the institution is probably in compliance with Title IX. If, for example, 66 percent of the athletes at a particular college are male and 66 percent of scholarship dollars go to men, the college is probably in compliance. And some leeway is allowed: the OCR's statistical test allows approximately a 5 percent variance. Courts have been more stringent: at least one consent decree allowed only a 2 percent deviation.

**Other Program Components**    When examining athletic programs for Title IX violations, men's and women's programs are compared in their entirety. Some teams for men and some for women may get lesser levels of services and facilities so long as equal amounts of men and women are similarly inconvenienced. What should not happen is for only women's teams to receive those lower levels of service. This section examines various program areas and how Title IX problems may arise.

### Provision of Equipment and Supplies

In general, this area covers uniforms and apparel, sport-specific equipment and supplies, instructional devices, and conditioning and weight-training equipment. The factors to consider when comparing equipment and supplies are quality, amount, suitability, maintenance and replacement, and availability. The upkeep and condition of the equipment are also important, as well as whether it meets competition regulations. Uniforms are often a problem, especially when boys' teams in high schools get new uniforms much more frequently than girls' teams.

### Scheduling of Games and Practice Times

Boys' teams or girls' teams should not get preferential scheduling for practices. Consider that some times are clearly more convenient than others. If, for example, the gym is available right after school for a boys' basketball team while the girls always have to wait until the boys finish, that practice is discriminatory. It is also easily solved by having the teams alternate who gets the gym first. A team that is in its competitive season, however, may have scheduling priority over a team that is in preseason without running afoul of Title IX because the preference is not a gender-based criterion.

Scheduling of games is another potential problem, especially at the high school level. For example, some school districts schedule double-headers in basketball, with a girls' game taking place before the boys'. This scheduling can make it easier for parents and friends to attend the boys' game, and it sends the message that the boys' game is more important. Alternating the team that plays at the more preferred time is one solution.

Other aspects of scheduling to check for Title IX compliance are the number of competitive events per sport, the number and length of practices, and the number of preseason and postseason opportunities to compete.

## Travel and Daily Allowance

The factors to examine in this area include the method of transportation, housing furnished during travel, length of stay before and after competitive events, the daily allowance and the dining allowance provided to the teams. Nondiscriminatory differences may exist based on such factors as the size of the team, the amount of the equipment, or the distance traveled. For example, a larger team may require a full-sized bus while a smaller team may fit comfortably in a van. It is discriminatory, however, for a women's team to drive its own van while a men's team of similar size is driven in a full-sized bus by a professional driver to the same destination. Another example of discrimination occurs when women's teams drive to a site for competition while men's teams fly to the same location.

## Academic Tutoring

Many colleges and universities provide special academic tutoring to members of athletic teams. These services must be available on a nondiscriminatory basis. Factors to examine include the availability of tutoring, including the procedures and criteria used to get such help. The assignment of tutors is also a concern. Are the training, experience, and general qualifications of tutors for men's and women's teams comparable? Finally, the pay level and employment conditions of tutors should also be examined.

## Coaching

Title IX covers the opportunity to receive coaching, the assignment of coaches, and compensation of coaches. Individual coaches who believe they have suffered sex discrimination do not have a remedy under

Title IX. They may be covered, however, under other statutes that pertain to employment discrimination.

The opportunity to receive coaching focuses on the availability of coaches. Check the ratio of coaches to participants for the men's program versus the women's program. On the high school level, this ratio is  relatively easy to determine because nearly all coaches coach only part-time. Just add up the number of athletes and the number of coaches and compare the programs. On the college level, part-time coaches must be counted only as a fraction. A half-time coach is added as one-half when determining the coach-to-athlete ratio. Add up all the full-time coaches and add in fractions for part-time coaches, then divide into the number of athletes. Do the same for the men's and women's programs and compare these ratios.

The assignment of coaches indicates the quality of coaching. To be discriminatory, the institution must show a pattern of assigning less-qualified coaches to either the men's or women's programs. Heavy reliance on graduate assistants or volunteers may be a sign there is discrimination in this area. High schools sometimes hire a coach for the football team, which they are highly qualified to coach, and then assign them to coach a girls' team, like softball, in the spring, despite having few or no qualifications in that sport. Obviously, this results in a lower experience level for the girls' team coaches.

The coaches' compensation and conditions of employment should also be considered. Higher salaries may be permissible when nondiscriminatory reasons exist, such as the coach's experience or education level, additional work assignments, or an outstanding record. Contracting patterns may also provide evidence of discrimination. For example, signing men's team coaches to twelve-month contracts while hiring women's team coaches for only ten-month contracts could signal a Title IX violation.

### Locker Rooms, Practice, and Competitive Facilities

In each of these facility areas, look at quality, availability, and maintenance. Are boys' teams given exclusive use of locker rooms while girls' teams have to share with physical education classes? Does the men's basketball team always practice in the new gym, where they play their games, while the women's team practices in an auxiliary gym and then plays games in the new gym?

### Medical and Training Facilities and Services

The factors to consider here include the availability of medical personnel and assistance, availability and qualifications of athletic trainers, availability and quality of weight training and conditioning facilities, and the health, accident, and injury insurance coverage.

Check to see how trainers are assigned. Is it by nondiscriminatory factors, such as sport injury rates? Are the training facilities equally accessible to males and females? For example, reserving a weight room for the exclusive use of one or two men's teams would be a violation; assigning the most qualified trainers only to the men's teams would be another.

## Provision of Housing and Dining Facilities and Services

This category covers any special housing arrangements made by colleges for athletes and any services provided as part of those housing arrangements, such as special laundry facilities, parking spaces, and so on. Dining services may be included even when no special housing arrangements exist. Consider whether or not there are any differences in the treatment of men's and women's teams. Do only men's teams eat at a special training table? Is the food served to male athletes superior to that served to female athletes?

## Publicity

When looking at publicity, look at the quantity and quality of sports information personnel, access to other publicity resources, and the quantity and quality of publications and other promotional devices featuring men's and women's programs. Unique circumstances may create unique demands; for example, spending more time on a team that is in contention for a national championship is not a violation.

Other aspects of publicity include pep bands, assemblies, and cheerleaders. This is a particular problem with high school sports, which may provide cheerleaders for boys' football and basketball but not for any girls' teams. If cheerleading support is provided only for boys and never for girls, Title IX is violated.

## Recruitment of Student Athletes

Colleges and universities usually recruit the athletes who make up the bulk of their varsity teams. These athletes often receive preferential admissions treatment and possibly scholarships. Do men's or women's team coaches or other personnel have approximately the same opportunities to recruit? Or do budgets preclude women's coaches from extensive travel and from inviting potential recruits to visit? Do the financial resources available meet the needs of the respective programs? This area is a particular problem: An NCAA study showed that only about 18 percent of recruiting budgets go to recruiting female athletes.

## Provision of Support Services

This area includes administrative and clerical support. Quantity and quality of office space should also be examined.

## What to Do If Discrimination Is Suspected

If you believe that your school or your daughter's school discriminates against females in their athletic program, you have several options. You may want to consult an attorney or your regional office of the OCR to confirm your understanding of Title IX's requirements and to discuss your options.

It's a good idea to begin by finding others who agree with you concerning the school's discriminatory practices. A single individual may find it difficult to get the institution's attention or to be taken seriously. The school may also try to pressure the solitary individual or retaliate. A group of people is harder to ignore.

Sources for supporters include athletes, their parents, administrators, other students, women's groups, and alumni. Remember that coaches and athletic administrators have to worry about their jobs. Unfortunately, retaliation against coaches of women's teams who take an active role in lobbying for equal programs does happen. Coaches may serve as sources of information, but they may not feel comfortable in taking an active role.

Putting together a group also extends your information resources. Because Title IX applies to the athletic program as a whole, the experience of one athlete or one team may not accurately reflect the relative treatment of the entire women's program. If you can involve people from other women's teams, you can gather more accurate information.

Once you have put together as much information as you can, you must decide how to proceed. Options include:

- Contact your institution's Title IX officer and present the situation. (All schools must designate a Title IX officer: unfortunately, most do not have extensive knowledge of the law as it applies to athletics.)

- Ask a member of the athletic governing group, an athletic council, for example, to present the information to that group. Present it to the school board if you are at the high school level.

- Meet with members of the athletic department, noting areas where they may be out of compliance. Come prepared with suggestions for change. Document that these requests have been made: if the school turns you down, that evidence may be helpful in a later complaint or lawsuit.

- Suggest to the institution that the OCR can provide technical assistance in assessing whether or not the athletic program is in compliance with Title IX.

- File an administrative complaint with the OCR.

- Seek legal representation and file a lawsuit.

The last two options are the most serious. With either one, you have publicly alleged that an educational institution is violating federal law.

Anyone can file an administrative complaint with the Office for Civil Rights. You do not need a lawyer and it does not cost anything. Complainants can request confidentiality. The OCR, however, has a tendency to negotiate its way to a settlement.

A lawsuit is different: It must be filed in a court of law. You will need an attorney. Now that monetary damages are available in Title IX cases, more lawyers are willing to handle such cases with no payment up front, in the hope that they can receive part of any financial award.

A lawsuit can also provide immediate relief. An attorney can go to court and ask for a preliminary injunction, which can stop an athletic department from carrying out plans such as cutting a team. On the other hand, final settlement of lawsuits can take years as institutions exhaust all appeals. Consult an attorney for advice about any specific situation.

## Conclusion

Women have gained protection against discrimination in some areas of sports, particularly in high school and college sports. Many schools, however, still do not allow girls and women the same access to sports as they do to boys and men. Given the mental and physical health benefits of sports participation, discrimination in this area hurts girls and women. Effective enforcement of current laws and the extension of new laws into other areas, including access to recreational programs, is needed to provide truly equal opportunities for women and their daughters.

### Bibliography

Tokarz, Daren. *Women, Sports, and the Law: A Comprehensive Research Guide to Sex Discrimination in Sports.* William S. Hein, 1986.

### Organizational Resources

Women's Sports Foundation
342 Madison Avenue, Suite 728
New York, NY 10017
(800) 227-3988

See listing at the end of chapter 13, "Sexual Discrimination," for a complete list of regional OCR offices.

**Kathryn M. Reith** first became involved in women's sports as a member of the crew team at Brown University. Crew was added at Brown as an official sport in the spring of 1974 because of Title IX, and Reith joined in the fall. Later she became communications director of the U.S. Rowing Association. At the time of writing this article, she was assistant executive director of the Women's Sports Foundation, where she had responsibility for public relations, publications, and advocacy.

Chapter 13

# Sexual Discrimination
## Part I: In the Workplace

Susan L. Segal

## Chapter Outline

### Introduction

### Existing Legal Protection from Sexual Discrimination in the Workplace
Title VII of the Civil Rights Act of 1964 • Equal Pay Act • The Family and Medical Leave Act • Affirmative Action Requirements • Other Employment Discrimination Laws

### Employment Practices Affected by Fair Employment Laws
Prohibited Recruiting Practices • Prohibited Hiring Practices • Discrimination in Training and Promotion • Stereotype and Glass Ceiling Problems • Discrimination in Compensation • Discrimination in Employment Terminations and Discipline • Sexual Harassment Prohibited

### Conclusion

Introduction

Whether overt or subtle, sexual discrimination continues to be a significant issue in the workplace. The first major statute prohibiting sex discrimination in employment was enacted by the U.S. Congress in 1964 with the passage of Title VII of the Civil Rights Act (referred to as Title VII). In addition to prohibiting discrimination on the basis of gender, Title VII also prohibits discrimination against employees on account of race, color, religion, and national origin.

When Title VII was initially proposed, it failed to include sexual discrimination in its list of illegal employment practices. In fact, an opponent of the bill, southern Senator Howard Smith, proposed the amendment that would condemn sex discrimination, hoping that the addition of a provision guaranteeing equal employment rights for women would make the bill so controversial and radical that it would fail. Ironically, the bill's supporters spoke out against the amendment. Five female representatives did support the amendment, which one of them described as "this little crumb of equality."

Senator Smith's efforts to derail the civil rights bill failed and, instead, he unwittingly played an important role in the fight for equality for women in the workplace. Since the passage of Title VII, numerous state and local laws that ban employment discrimination based on sex have also been passed.

In the early 1980s, another major development in sex discrimination law occurred when the courts first recognized sexual harassment as an illegal form of sex discrimination under the employment discrimination laws. In recent years, the issue of sexual harassment has dramatically changed accepted standards of conduct in employment settings.

This chapter describes the laws prohibiting gender discrimination in the workplace. The chapter alerts employers to potential discrimination problems that can arise within their businesses, and apprises employees of the safeguards that the law provides to them. The focus of this chapter is sexual discrimination; however, other laws affecting women in the workplace are also briefly mentioned.

## Existing Legal Protection From Sexual Discrimination in the Workplace

### Title VII of the Civil Rights Act of 1964

The primary source of protection from sex discrimination under federal law is Title VII of the Civil Rights Act of 1964. Title VII has been amended several times over the years to expand and clarify its coverage. Generally, the Act forbids any form of discrimination in the employment relationship on the basis of race, national origin, color, religion, or sex. The protected classification of sex under Title VII is defined as being limited to gender, and does not include sexual activity. Consequently, Title VII does not proscribe discrimination based on sexual orientation.

### Who Is Covered by Title VII

An employer must comply with Title VII's requirements if it has fifteen or more employees and the business has an effect on interstate commerce. Federal, state, and local governmental employees are also protected by the Act.

Discriminatory practices of labor organizations and employment agencies are explicitly outlawed by Title VII. The safeguards provided by the Act also extend to American citizens who are employed by American companies in foreign countries.

## What Is Prohibited by Title VII

Title VII only proscribes discrimination that occurs in an employment relationship. If discrimination occurs outside of the context of an employment relationship, for example, between independent contractors, there is no violation of Title VII. Title VII, however, does affect every aspect of an employment relationship. Hiring decisions, training, promotions, benefits, compensation, and even job advertisements are subject to the requirements of Title VII. Moreover, Title VII also prohibits any retaliation by an employer against an employee for asserting rights under the Act. Unlawful retaliation could involve a transfer or assignment to "undesirable" duties, demotion, termination, or even the creation of a hostile work environment.

In 1978, Title VII was amended to include discrimination on the basis of pregnancy, childbirth, and related medical conditions as a form of sexual discrimination prohibited by the Act. The amendment requires that women affected by pregnancy, childbirth, and related medical conditions must be treated the same for all employment-related purposes as other persons not so affected but who are similar in their ability or inability to work.

There are very few statutory defenses for sex discrimination, and most lawsuits and administrative charges, therefore, turn on whether or not the discrimination did, in fact, occur. Title VII does provide that an employer may intentionally discriminate against an employee on the basis of sex when sex is a bona fide occupational qualification (commonly referred to as a BFOQ) that is reasonably necessary to the normal operation of a particular business or enterprise. For example, a theater's decision to hire only male actors for male roles is a valid BFOQ.

The BFOQ defense has been given limited application by the courts. For example, historically, airlines attempted to use the BFOQ defense to justify their employment policies of hiring only female flight attendants, because that was what their passengers supposedly desired. These arguments have been uniformly rejected. Customer preference is not a BFOQ. Therefore, a business's refusal to promote a woman to an important sales position due to concerns that customers, domestic or foreign, may respond to a woman negatively is not normally a valid BFOQ defense and, consequently, will violate Title VII.

BFOQ defenses have been allowed in only limited situations, typically where the presence of women implicates privacy concerns. The courts, for example, have permitted prisons to hire only male guards for positions that require contact with undressed male prisoners. When privacy concerns can be met using less discriminatory means (for example, giving women officers shifts that allow them to avoid situations where privacy rights may be intruded upon), the courts often require the use of the alternative means. If a reasonable alternative or other accommodation is available which would enable an employer to avoid discriminating against a particular sex, a BFOQ defense will not be available.

## The EEOC Charge—Filing Process

Title VII requires any person complaining of an unfair discriminatory practice to submit her claim to an administrative agency prior to bringing a lawsuit. A woman who believes that she has been illegally discriminated against in violation of Title VII must file a charge with the Equal Employment Opportunity Commission (EEOC) within 180 days of the occurrence of the unfair employment practice. In certain states that have a state or local fair employment practice agency empowered to review such charges, the charge generally must be filed within 300 days. An unfair employment practice is deemed to have "occurred" when the employee was made aware of the adverse effect of the discriminatory practice. In a limited number of circumstances, for example when a continuing Title VII violation is involved, an employee may have additional time to file a charge. The charge that is filed with the EEOC must be in writing, must identify the parties involved, should be under oath, and should generally describe the unfair practices that are the foundation for the charge.

Once the EEOC receives a charge, it will review the allegations and determine whether it believes reasonable cause exists, meaning it believes the charge is likely to be true and states a violation of the Act. If reasonable cause is found to be present, the EEOC will attempt conciliation with the employer to eliminate the practice and may eventually bring suit, itself, against the employer.

The victim of discrimination may file a private suit after receiving a notice of dismissal or a "right to sue" letter from the EEOC or responsible local governmental agency. After receiving either of these two notices, the employee has only ninety days in which to bring a lawsuit. A woman who has filed a charge with the EEOC, however, need not wait for the EEOC to exhaust its procedures before suing the employee individually under Title VII. She can bring suit individually after requesting and obtaining a notice of right to sue from the EEOC.

Remedies that are available to a woman who was the victim of discrimination in violation of Title VII include lost wages and benefits (both past and future), attorneys' fees, and, in some cases, emotional distress and punitive damages. Reinstatement to an employee's former position may also be appropriate in certain circumstances. Further-more, a court may grant a continuing injunction prohibiting an employer from engaging in discriminatory conduct in the future.

## Equal Pay Act

The Equal Pay Act outlaws any wage discrimination that is based on the sex of the employee. Of course, discrimination in wages and benefits is also prohibited by Title VII's general prohibition of sex discrimination. A violation of the Act occurs when an employer pays higher wages to a male employee than to a female employee (or vice versa) for doing equal work that requires equal skill, effort, and responsibility, and is being performed under similar working conditions. If such a situation exists, an employer can defend against a discrimination claim by showing that the pay differential is based upon a valid seniority system, a merit system, a system which bases earnings upon the quantity or quality of production, or any other non-gender-related factor. Non-gender-related factors can include differences in job content or working conditions, or any other difference which makes the work dissimilar.

"Comparable worth" claims, which argue that women who perform traditionally "female" jobs of comparable worth or value to the employer as higher paying jobs traditionally performed by males, even though the nature of the tasks are different should be paid similarly, generally have not been successful as yet. Many factors influence the determination of appropriate wages and it is, therefore, extremely difficult for a plaintiff to prove that two individuals should receive the same pay even though their jobs are not identical or substantially similar. "Comparable worth" claims have not generally gained acceptance with the courts even though it can be shown that certain traditional female jobs may pay less than traditional male jobs requiring similar levels of skill and effort. The language of the Equal Pay Act has been interpreted strictly by the courts as requiring a pay difference between males and females performing virtually identical jobs.

Unlike Title VII, the Equal Pay Act permits an individual to initiate a civil lawsuit for a violation without first submitting her claim to an administrative body. Such suit must be brought within two years of the alleged wrongdoing. Because Equal Pay violations often also involve claims of discrimination in violation of Title VII, an individual may pursue both claims jointly before the EEOC and in court. A successful plaintiff can recover wages that were illegally withheld, injunctive relief prohibiting future violations, and attorneys' fees for violations of the Equal Pay Act.

The EEOC can choose to initiate a lawsuit on its own claiming a violation of the Equal Pay Act against an employer, in which case an employee's right to sue is extinguished.

### The Family and Medical Leave Act

The Family and Medical Leave Act of 1993 (FMLA) provides employees with the right to obtain an unpaid leave of absence from employment for parenting and family health needs under certain limited circumstances. Although the Act applies to both men and women, the preamble to the Act recognizes that child care obligations still fall disproportionately on women, regardless of their employment status, and that mandated job protection, allowing leaves of absence to attend to family members, is necessary to protect women's employment opportunities.

Employers are subject to the requirements of the FMLA if they employ fifty or more employees. Employees are only eligible to receive the benefits of the FMLA if they have been employed for at least twelve months by the employer and have worked for at least 1,250 hours (approximately 24 hours per week without vacations) with their employer during the previous twelve-month period.

In general, the Act provides eligible employees the right to a total of twelve work weeks of unpaid leave during any twelve-month period for one or more of the following reasons:

1. The birth of a child and in order to care for such child.

2. The placement of a child with the employee for adoption or foster care.

3. To care for a seriously ill spouse, child, or parent.

4. Because a serious health condition prevents the employee from performing the duties of his or her position.

When leave is taken to care for a new child in the family, it must be taken in the twelve-month period immediately following the child's date of birth or placement with the employee.

The Act allows an employee to utilize the leave on an intermittent basis when the leave is taken due to a serious health condition of the employee or for the serious illness of a family member. Under the intermittent leave provision of the Act, an employee could work a reduced schedule or take off a day per week if needed for medical treatment, such as dialysis or other treatments performed on a periodic basis.

Employees are required to provide their employers with no less than thirty days' notice of the leave. If the leave was not foreseeable, the employee must provide as much notice as is practical.

When an employee returns to work following a leave, the employer is obligated to reinstate the employee to her former position unless the employee happens to be among the highest paid 10 percent of the employees employed by the employer within a seventymile area and only when denial of restoration is necessary to prevent a substantial and grievous economic injury to the employer. (The employee must be given an opportunity to return to work after notice from the employer.) Only then may the employer refuse to restore the employee to her former position. Employers must also continue employee health benefits during an FMLA leave on the same basis as if the employee was actively at work.

FMLA prohibits any person from interfering or retaliating against any person who has complained of a violation of the Act or with any right guaranteed by the Act. Eligible employees can bring a civil lawsuit against the employer for violations of the FMLA to recover lost compensation, interest, and injunctive relief (for example, possible reinstatement to their former job).

In addition to the FMLA, a number of states have family leave statutes that may provide additional rights.

## Affirmative Action Requirements

The federal government, along with many state and local governments, requires government contractors to engage in affirmative action to increase the participation of females and minorities in their workforces. The federal affirmative action program is administered by the Office of Federal Contract Compliance Programs of the Department of Labor. Under Executive Order 11246, contractors or subcontractors with $50,000 or more in contracts with the federal government must implement an affirmative action program establishing specific goals for the hiring and promotion of women and minorities to positions in which they are underrepresented. Affirmative action programs, while the subject of ongoing criticism, have had a substantial impact over the years on improving representation of women in nontraditional jobs.

## Other Employment Discrimination Laws

Other federal laws that prohibit discriminatory practices in employment relationships include the Age Discrimination in Employment Act of 1967 (ADEA), the Rehabilitation Act of 1973, and the Americans with Disabilities Act of 1990 (ADA). The ADEA makes it unlawful for employers to discriminate on the basis of age against employees or job applicants who are over forty and under sixty years of age. If an organization receives federal funding, age discrimination is unlawful regardless of the employees or applicant's age. The Rehabilitation Act prevents federal contractors or organizations that receive federal funds from discriminating against employee's or applicants with mental or physical disabilities. The ADA, in addition to provisions dealing with access for disabled persons, extends the protection found in the Rehabilitation Act to private employers. Any discrimination against a qualified individual with a disability in any part of the employment process by a state or private employer, employment agency, labor organization, or joint labor management committee is prohibited by the ADA.

Many states and municipalities also have enacted laws which prohibit discrimination. Such laws will vary between each state and city and, therefore, have to be inquired about at the local level. While many of these laws will contain similar or stricter prohibitions against discrimination on the basis of race, color, religion, sex, national origin, age, and physical or mental disability, others may prohibit additional types of employment discrimination such as unfair treatment due to an arrest record, political affiliation, marital status, unfavorable military discharge, or sexual orientation.

## Employment Practices Affected by Fair Employment Laws

### Prohibited Recruiting Practices

Title VII's protection extends to the interaction between employers and job applicants. Employers cannot use advertisements that express a preference for a certain sex or other protected class, unless a BFOQ will justify such a preference. An advertisement reading "Laborer Wanted—Male," therefore, is prohibited and is evidence of discriminatory hiring practices. Recruiting methods that perpetuate the hiring of males over females, such as word-of-mouth recruiting, may also be unlawful. If a business's workforce is predominantly composed of white males, such employment practices may tend to perpetuate the exclusion of other groups. Similarly, antinepotism policies often have an adverse impact on women, and can violate certain state laws which make marital status discrimination unlawful. Finally, employers who use employment agencies can be held liable for discrimination engaged in by the agencies in recruiting potential employees.

### Prohibited Hiring Practices

Violations of Title VII and other equal employment laws can occur during the hiring process when hiring decisions are based, at least in part, upon an applicant's gender. For example, questions pertaining to a woman's marital status, number of children, desire to have children, access to child care, or pregnancy all can raise red flags. Title VII does not expressly outlaw discrimination based upon marital status (although many state laws do) or these types of interview questions; however, if these inquiries are used to make employment decisions, it is discrimination. Reproductive decisions, according to the U.S. Supreme Court, are to be left to the woman herself and not to the employer.

## Discrimination in Training and Promotion

Generally, Title VII requires that training and promotions be provided to employees on a nondiscriminatory basis. If men are provided with training and work experience that is required or beneficial for career advancement and women are not, illegal and unfair discrimination is likely to exist. Similarly, if a woman was qualified and applied for a promotion, but the promotion was given instead to a man, she may have a viable discrimination claim. The employer can defend its training and hiring decisions by presenting valid business reasons for choosing the male over the female applicant, and if this is done, the woman must be able to show that the employer's offered justification is only a pretext to cover the discrimination. Without evidence of pretext, the employer's reason for selecting a male candidate over a qualified female applicant will normally be accepted.

For example, often an employer will defend its decision by explaining that a certain candidate for training or advancement was not chosen because the individual had not demonstrated a willingness or ability to perform the additional or new duties of the higher position. The employer will point to the employee's failure to volunteer for extra assignments, refusal to take on additional duties, poor work history, lack of educational requirements, or lack of experience as the reason for denying the employee's application. However, if the employer selects a male who also does not meet the criteria used to justify the disqualification of the female applicant, this suggests that the proffered explanation of the employer is merely a pretext. If a woman can show that she was actually more qualified for a position than the male applicant who received the promotion or training, she possesses strong evidence that unfair discrimination occurred.

Employers should try to avoid overly subjective methods of allocating promotions. Advancement and training opportunities should be posted to alert all employees of their existence and the requisite qualifications for a position listed.

## Stereotype and Glass Ceiling Problems

One of the primary purposes of antidiscrimination laws such as Title VII is to prevent employment decisions from being made on the basis of stereotypes of how men and women do act or should act. Rather, individuals should be judged upon their own qualifications and merit. For example, an employment decision not to hire women for a sales position based on a stereotype that women are not aggressive enough would violate Title VII.

Similarly, women should not be expected to conform to any type of female stereotype, where females may be rated negatively if they are aggressive, when males who are aggressive are rewarded for "demonstrating initiative." For example, in one case heard by the U.S. Supreme Court, a woman was denied admission to partnership in an accounting firm where she worked, despite having generated more business and having worked longer hours than the male candidates. The firm informed her that she had been rejected because of her difficulties in interpersonal skills, most particularly her aggressive, tough, and "macho" behavior. The woman was advised to act, talk, and dress more femininely in order to succeed at the firm The employer was found to be in violation of Title VII by discriminating against the woman because she did not conform to stereotyped notions of how women should behave in the workplace. Such criteria, comparing the woman accountant to some stereotype of femininity, is illegal and is a discriminatory method of making employment decisions.

Stereotypes also contribute to the so-called "glass ceiling." The term refers to an invisible barrier at companies for women and minorities that prevents them from obtaining upper-management positions. Stereotypes about females contribute to such barriers, for example, an assumption that females may not be "tough enough" to manage male employees. Other obstacles to promotions for top management positions can include informal mentoring and "grooming" of candidates that may tend to favor males over females.

The absence of women from upper management positions and positions which prepare an individual for future leadership opportunities are indicators of a glass ceiling problem. Employers then should examine career paths in their companies and identify any possible barriers to the advancement of females and minorities. The glass ceiling is an issue that is gaining attention, particularly from federal equal employment enforcement agencies.

### Discrimination in Compensation

Both Title VII and the Equal Pay Act prohibit differences in employee compensation that are based upon gender. If men and women are performing equal work in positions which require equal skill, effort, and responsibility and which are performed under similar working conditions, they should be receiving equal compensation. Disparities in pay must be based on relatively objective criteria related to job performance and not to the sex of the employee. Differences in the provision of benefits, such as health insurance, vacation time, overtime wages, retirement provisions, or profit sharing, also are illegal if based on sex and not job-related criteria.

As mentioned earlier, differences in compensation are valid if they are based upon criteria that have a direct relationship to the performance of the employee's job. If the work or skill required in two different positions is not essentially identical, equal pay is not mandated. However, jobs are not considered to be different solely on the basis of the job titles. Therefore, when, for example, male workers are classified as maintenance personnel and female workers are classified as service department employees and are performing essentially the same duties, discrimination may exist if the female employees receive less compensation unless a valid business justification exists for the pay differential.

Although federal law does not require an employer to provide employees with benefits for pregnancy-related conditions, other than that required by the FMLA, if the employer does choose to provide employees with health insurance and other income maintenance benefits during temporary periods of disability, such benefits must also cover female employees for pregnancy, childbirth, or related medical conditions. Pregnancy benefits for the wives of male employees must be comparable to benefits that are provided to husbands of female employees for other disabilities. Employers and employees should be aware that many state laws do require employers to provide employees with benefits for pregnancy-related conditions and child care.

## Discrimination in Employment Terminations and Discipline

Of course, an employer may not discharge or discipline an employee because of the gender of an employee. This does not mean, however, that the discharge of a woman who was unable to perform her duties and is replaced by a man is necessarily sex discrimination. If the reasons for termination are job-related, and not based on the gender of the employee, there is no violation. On the other hand, if a female employee can show a pattern of adverse treatment of females or that the employer's alleged reasons for a termination or disciplinary action are false, discrimination may exist.

A woman may be deemed to be discharged from employment even when she has left her employment of her own accord. This type of discharge is called a constructive discharge and it occurs when a woman resigns from work in order to escape intolerable discrimination as long as no other reasonable alternative to quitting was available.

An employer may not terminate a woman who is compelled to take a leave of absence because of pregnancy, childbirth, or related medical conditions. Moreover, employers cannot require women to start a leave of absence after a certain number of months of pregnancy or prohibit a woman from returning to work for a certain period of time following childbirth; such policies are discriminatory because they do not take into account the actual capabilities of individual workers, but rely on assumptions and stereotypes.

### Sexual Harassment Prohibited

Sexual harassment that occurs in the workplace is another form of sexual discrimination prohibited by Title VII. Sexual harassment has gained substantial attention in recent years. The risks and costs of litigation in this area are rewriting the rules of how employees are to behave in the workplace. Simply stated, sexual harassment includes unwelcome sexual advances, requests for sexual favors, or other verbal or physical conduct of a sexual nature where submitting to the conduct is made a term or condition of employment (for example, "Sleep with me or you're fired"); submitting to or rejecting the conduct is used as a basis for employment decisions ("Your refusal to go out with me will show up on your next review"); or the conduct unreasonably interferes with work performance or creates a hostile, intimidating, or offensive work environment. While sexual harassment violates the sex discrimination laws, it also can constitute criminal conduct, such as a rape or assault, and can also form the basis for a personal injury claim.

Sexual harassment claims are divided into two categories. The first category is called *"quid pro quo"* claims. *Quid pro quo* harassment occurs when an employee must submit to unwelcome sexual conduct in order to receive a tangible employment benefit or opportunity or when rejection of the conduct results in negative employment consequences. The classic *quid pro quo* case occurs when the employee must engage in sexual acts with her superior to retain her job or receive a promotion. *Quid pro quo* cases are characterized primarily by the fact that an exchange occurs. The employer offers the job benefit to the employee in exchange for sexual favors.

The second category is called a "hostile work environment claim." Hostile work environment claims are more common and involve sexually oriented words or conduct that are offensive and make a woman's workplace intolerable. A hostile work environment exists when:

- The employee is subjected to unwelcome harassment by a fellow employee or supervisor.

- The harassment interfered with her employment by creating an offensive work environment.

- If the harassment is by a fellow employee, the employer knew or should have known of the harassment.

Conduct that may constitute sexual harassment includes words of a sexual nature, including jokes, gestures, touching, pinching, grabbing, sexually oriented drawings, cartoons, or objects. Under certain circumstances, even such seemingly innocent conduct as repeated requests for dates may contribute to a hostile work environment.

An employer can defend against a claim of hostile work environment harassment by showing that it took prompt remedial action calculated to stop the harassment when it knew or should have known that harassment was occurring.

Increasingly, the courts are reviewing claims of hostile work environment from the perspective of the victim of the harassment. Initially, the courts asked whether a reasonable person would have found the conduct offensive in determining whether there was an offensive working environment. Many courts still follow this approach. In several jurisdictions, however, the courts have utilized the standard of "reasonable woman" to determine whether the conduct created an offensive environment. This approach recognizes that women may find certain conduct more offensive or threatening than most men. While this approach provides greater protection for women and recognizes current reality, it also perpetuates a view of women as being more vulnerable than men.

A woman who thinks she may have a valid claim for sexual harrassment should review it with an attorney who specializes in that area.

## Conclusion

Fair employment laws, such as Title VII, require employers to treat women employees as individuals without regard to their gender. Employment practices are unlawful if they intentionally discriminate against women or if they have disparate impact on women, unless a valid business justification exists. By understanding their rights, women can more effectively guarantee that they receive equal and unhindered access to employment and promotions.

## Bibliography

Anderson, Katherine. "Employer Liability Under Title VII for Sexual Harassment After *Meritor Savings Bank vs. Vinson.*" 87 *Columbia Law Review* 1258 (1987).

Bennett-Alexander, Dawn. "The Supreme Court Finally Speaks on the Issue of Sexual Harassment: What Did It Say?" 10 (1) *Women's Rights Law Reporter* 65, 1987.

Equal Employment Opportunity Commission (EEOC). "Guidelines on Sexual Harassment." EEOC Publications Unit, 2401 E Street NW, Washington, DC 20507, (202) 634-1947.

Gutek, Barbara. *Sex and the Workplace: The Impact of Sexual Behavior and Harassment on Women, Men, and Organizations.* San Francisco: Jossey-Bass, 1985.

Haimes Associates, Inc. *Sexual Harassment: A Handbook for Managers and Supervisors.* Haimes Associates, Inc., 708 South Washington Square, Philadelphia, PA 19106, (215) 922-1617. (Cost is $2.00)

NYC Commission on the Status of Women. *New York City Women's Advisors Committee on Preventing Sexual Harassment in the Workplace: A Guide to Resource Materials*. New York: NYC Commission on the Status of Women, 1987.

Omilian, Susan. *Sexual Harassment in Employment*. Deerfield, IL: Callaghan and Co., 1988.

Saltzman, Amy. "Hands Off at the Office." *U.S. News and World Report* (August 1, 1988): 56.

## Organizational Resources

Equal Opportunity Commission General information: (800) 669-4000 or (800) 800-3302 (hearing-impaired access). Check your local telephone directory for the office nearest you. Offices are located in many major cities across the country.

Business and Professional Women's Foundation
2012 Massachusetts Avenue, NW
Washington, DC 20036
(202) 293-1200

Equal Rights Advocates
1663 Mission Steet, Suite 550
San Francisco, CA 94103
(415) 621-0672

Institute on Women and Work
Cornell University
New York School of Industrial Labor Relations
16 East 34th Street, 4th Floor
New York, NY 10016
(212) 340-2800

National Committee on Pay Equity
1201 16th Street, NW, Suite 420
Washington, DC 20036
(202) 331-7343

National Employment Lawyers' Association
535 Pacific Avenue
San Fancisco, CA 94133
(415) 227-4655

9 to 5, National Association of Working Women
614 Superior Avenue, NW
Cleveland, OH 44113
(216) 566-9308
(800) 245-9865

NOW Legal Defense and Education Fund
99 Hudson Street
New York, NY 10013

Women's Bureau
Department of Labor
Washington, DC 20210
(202) 219-6652

Note that there are a number of firms that provide information to employers on combatting sexual discrimination and harassment. A list is available from NOW Legal Defense and Education Fund.

**Susan L. Segal** is the chair of the Labor & Employment Law Group of Gray, Plant, Mooty, Mooty & Bennett. She has been engaged in private practice since 1979, specializing in labor and employment law matters. She has advised clients on all aspects of employment law and personnel matters and has represented employers in employment litigation, NLRB matters, labor arbitrations, and related proceedings. She is a frequent lecturer on employment law and received the Author's Award from the Minnesota State Bar Association in 1989. She received her A.B. from the University of California at Berkeley and her J.D. *cum laude* from the University of Michigan.

Chapter 13

# Sexual Discrimination Part II: In the Schools

## NOW Legal Defense and Education Fund*

Chapter Outline

**Sexual Harassment in Schools: The Problem**

**Sexual Harassment: The Law**
How Students Can Use Title IX • Filing a Title IX Complaint With OCR

**Conclusion**

**Sexual Harassment in Schools: The Problem**

While sexual harassment in the workplace has recently come under greater scrutiny, the problem of sexual harassment in the schools has been largely ignored. Every day in schools across the country, harassment interferes with girls' educational opportunities. Sexual harassment is unwelcome sexual conduct (or other conduct based on sex) that interferes with a student's ability to learn in school. Sexual harassment encompasses a wide range of acts, including insulting

---

*Adapted from NOW Legal Defense and Education Fund's Legal Resources Kits "Sexual Harassment in Schools" and "Policies and Procedures on Sexual Harassment in Schools: A Guide for Administrators." Legal Resource Kits on various aspects of the law are available from the NOW Legal Defense and Education Fund (NOW LDEF) for a nominal fee. Contact them at 99 Hudson Street, 12th Floor, New York, New York 10013-2871, Attn: Intake Department. Used by permission.

remarks, leering, gesturing, touching, and sexual assault.[1] Sexual harassment is a form of discrimination, and it is against the law.

In many schools, girls, because they are girls, are the victims of verbal and physical harassment by their peers and sometimes by their teachers. In 1992 NOW Legal Defense and Education Fund and the Wellesley College Center for Research on Women sponsored a national survey on sexual harassment in schools.[2] Researchers surveyed over forty-two hundred girls, ranging in age from nine to nineteen years old, on their experiences of sexual harassment. The results, based on an analysis of two thousand randomly selected surveys, demonstrates that sexual harassment is a major problem for girls in elementary and secondary schools.

According to the survey, the majority of girls experience both verbal and physical sexual harassment: 89 percent reported receiving sexual comments, looks, or gestures, and 83 percent were touched, pinched, or grabbed. When harassment occurs, it is not a one-time-only event: 39 percent reported that they were sexually harassed at school on a daily basis in the last year. Also, harassment is a public event; other people were present at over two-thirds of the reported incidents. Girls are most often harassed by fellow students, but 4 percent of the girls reported harassment by teachers, administrators, and other school staff. Sexual harassment happens in all kinds of schools, to all kinds of girls—there are few differences by type of school or racial or ethnic background.

Another national study, commissioned by the American Association of University Women Educational Foundation and completed in June of 1993, found similarly alarming rates of sexual harassment in schools.[3] Based on a survey of more than sixteen hundred girls and boys in public schools in grades eight through eleven, the study revealed that four out of five (81 percent) students have experienced some form of sexual harassment in school.[4] Of those experiencing harassment, one in four reported being targeted "often." One of the most surprising findings of this study is that boys are often targets of sexual harassment as well as girls. Girls, however, reported experiencing harassment at a higher rate than boys.

The study also revealed that the educational, emotional, and behavioral impact of sexual harassment falls much more heavily on girls than it does on boys.[5] The most immediate effect often is retaliation—a teacher might lower a grade or refuse to write a college recommendation; a peer might sabotage the student's work or spread rumors about her.[6] These actions can also result in loss of self-confidence, lack of trust and belief in the educational system, a reduced ability to perform school work, excessive absenteeism, and even a transfer to another school. If boys are not punished or even reprimanded for harassing behavior, the message they get is that this is how they are supposed to act. Girls, in turn are taught that it is their role to accept and tolerate this humiliating conduct.[7] The law, however, says that girls have a right to an equal educational opportunity and schools have a responsibility to ensure that harassment doesn't prevent girls from getting the education they deserve.

## Sexual Harassment: The Law

Title IX of the Education Amendment of 1972[8] is the federal law that prohibits discrimination on the basis of gender in educational institutions receiving federal funds.[9] If a school violates Title IX it can lose its federal funding. Title IX also requires a school to have a grievance procedure providing for prompt resolution of sexual harassment complaints. The Office for Civil Rights (OCR) in the Department of Education is the federal administrative agency charged with enforcing Title IX.

Courts have recognized two forms of sexual harassment claims: the *quid pro quo* (this for that) claim and the hostile environment claim. *Quid pro quo* sexual harassment occurs when someone in a position of authority, such as a teacher, demands sexual conduct in exchange for an educational benefit, such as a grade. Hostile environment sexual harassment involves unwelcome sexual behavior that creates an intimidating, hostile, or offensive environment, or unreasonably interferes with a student's school performance, thus depriving the student of an educational benefit. The number of school sexual harassment cases litigated in court under Title IX has been small but is growing. Recently, some courts have recognized that sexual harassment in schools, including harassment by students, is a form of sex discrimination proscribed by Title IX. The law in this area is rapidly changing. Contact NOW Legal Defense and Education Fund (address listed above) if you feel that you have a sexual harassment claim or would like more information about the law.

In addition to the federal law, several states have passed laws specifically prohibiting gender discrimination and sexual harassment in schools. Some of the state laws provide more protection than Title IX. For example, a Minnesota law requires each school to post written sexual harassment policies throughout the school, to include the policies in the student handbook, and to teach students in grades kindergarten through twelve how to prevent sexual harassment and sexual assault.

### How Students Can Use Title IX

Students who are victims of harassment may file a complaint with the OCR or may file a private lawsuit for a violation of Title IX.[11] As the federal agency responsible for enforcing Title IX, the OCR investigates complaints submitted by individuals or by groups. The OCR can also initiate compliance reviews, which are broad-based investigations of school districts or universities.

If, after an investigation, the OCR finds that discrimination exists, it tries to achieve voluntary compliance by working with the institution to correct the Title IX violations. Failing this, the OCR may then conduct administrative hearings that could lead to termination of the school's federal financial assistance. The OCR can also refer the matter to the Department of Justice for federal prosecution or to state or local authorities for action under state or local laws. The primary purpose of filing a Title IX complaint is to get the school to change its procedures and/or policies. A student who has been harmed by these policies cannot recover money damages by filing a complaint with the OCR or as a result of an OCR investigation.

In addition to filing a complaint with the OCR, victims of harassment can file a civil lawsuit in court, in which case they may be entitled to monetary damages from the school district or a court order prohibiting the illegal conduct. In 1992, the Supreme Court heard a case called *Franklin v. Gwinnett County Public Schools* involving a teacher who created a sexually hostile environment for a high school student.[12] The Supreme Court held that Title IX provides students with a hostile environment sexual harassment claim and that students may receive monetary damages under Title IX. There are very strict deadlines filing a lawsuit. To find out about filing deadlines and other issues involved in a lawsuit, a student should discuss her case with an attorney.

## Filing a Title IX Complaint With OCR

If you believe your school (or your daughter's school) is treating students unfairly because of their sex, you might want to directly approach school authorities and ask them to remedy the situation. Strategies for identifying the best school official to talk to will vary with each situation, but you may consider speaking with the teacher, school counselor, principal, or assistant principal. Title IX requires each school to appoint a Title IX officer, who might be well-equipped to resolve the problem without OCR or judicial intervention. If that approach does not work, you may file a complaint with the OCR.

## Who Can File an OCR Title IX Complaint?

Anyone—an individual citizen or a group—can ask the OCR to investigate possible Title IX violations. Students, teachers, coaches, and administrators are directly protected by the law and can file charges known as "complaints." Parents, community organizations, and ordinary interested citizens may ask the OCR to investigate possible violations.

## Is There a Deadline?

Generally, you must file a Title IX complaint within 180 days after the discrimination occurs. If the discrimination is ongoing, for example, if your school has no harassment policy, you can file a complaint at any time.

## Is There a Required Form?

No. A letter to the OCR explaining why you believe your school or college is violating the law is sufficient. The letter must contain certain basic information (listed below) before the OCR will process your complaint. Your letter should describe the harassment as specifically and thoroughly as possible, so that the OCR can conduct a complete investigation. If there is a pattern of discrimination against girls or women throughout the school, school district or college, describe that in detail as well. Sometimes the OCR will send back a form for you to complete to provide that information, but nevertheless, your letter should include the following information:

1. The name and address of the school district, college, or other institution you believe is discriminating by sex.

2. A general description of the person or persons suffering from that discrimination. (You do not have to give the OCR names or addresses; although, if they are willing to be identified, it will assist the investigation.)

3. The approximate date(s) the discrimination occurred and whether it is continuing.

4. Your name and address, and, if possible, a telephone number where you can be reached during the day.

5. Enough information about the discrimination for the OCR to understand what happened.

In addition to the required information, it is a good idea to list the names, addresses, and telephone numbers of others who may have additional information about the charges. Explain why the OCR should talk with them. Also, if you know about written sources of information, such as student manuals or school board budget documents, written complaints by other students, or other relevant documents, you should call them to the OCR's attention.

If your complaint involves an emergency—if, for example, you or someone else is about to be expelled or suspended—ask the OCR to speed up the process. This does not always work, but knowing that prompt action could keep someone from serious academic injury might prod the government to respond more quickly. A sample letter including all these points is included on page 236.

## Where Do I Send the OCR Complaint?

The OCR should keep confidential the identity of the person or group who files a complaint, unless the information must be disclosed during the course of an investigation. You should, however, stress in your letter that you want to keep this matter confidential and ask the OCR to tell you in advance if there are plans to reveal your name.

In certain cases, particularly those that involve individual complaints, it is difficult to retain confidentiality. Keep in mind, however, that publicity may work to your advantage. Individuals and groups can sometimes pressure institutions into changing unfair practices simply by generating public interest in the issue. Sometimes those changes occur before the OCR has a chance to investigate.

If you are concerned that you might be harassed after you file a complaint, try to get an organization in your area to file for you. Local chapters of the National Organization for Women (NOW) and the American Association of University Women (AAUW) might be willing to file your case. In any event, harassment in retaliation for filing a complaint violates Title IX. You can add the retaliation charge to the complaint.

## Is It Worth Filing a Complaint?

You alone must decide whether you should file a complaint, but there are some very good reasons for doing so:

- If you have been pressuring a school district or college to end sex-biased practices and have met strong opposition to change, then the act of filing a complaint with the government may break the resistance.

- The OCR carries substantial weight when it handles an investigation. Although it has never done so, the OCR has the power to cut off federal dollars to a school or college that refuses to change.

- The OCR's estimates of the public demand for an end to sexual discrimination in education are based in large part on the number of Title IX complaints filed. The more complaints it receives, the more likely it is that the OCR will devote greater energy and resources to enforcing Title IX.

*Date*

Director
Office for Civil Rights, Region _____
U.S. Department of Education
*Address for your region*

Dear _____.

I am/We are filing a complaint of sex discrimination under Title IX of the Education Amendments of 1972 against (name and address of school district, college or other institution receiving federal education aid.)

(The next paragraph should explain what person or group of people you believe is being discriminated against. You need only identify them generally—"the girls in the sixth grade gym classes," for example—unless it's just one or two people who have been victims of specific acts of discrimination. In that case it would be helpful to give the Department of Education their names and addresses, although it is not required.)

(Follow this with as complete a description of the sex discrimination as you can. Make sure to tell what happened, when it happened and if the discrimination is still going on.)

The following people have agreed to provide further information to your staff. (Here list the people willing to tell what happened, when it happened and if the discrimination is still going on. Attach any evidence you may have which supports the complaint, such as letters, student handbooks, and so. Name any people you think were responsible for the discrimination and their position in the school.)

I/We ask that you investigate this complaint immediately and notify me/us when the investigation is complete. And please send me/us a copy of your findings as soon as they are sent to (name and school district or college). In addition, please send me/us copies of all correspondence with (name of institution).

Sincerely,


Name
Address
Daytime phone number

If you are sending copies of your complaint to other persons, list them below. For example:

cc: School Board
     Local Organizations
     National Organizations
     Newspapers

*Sample Letter for Filing*
*a Title IX Complaint*

Laws against sexual harassment merely establish a minimum level of conduct for schools. The ultimate solution to ending harassment is prevention and teaching boys and girls to treat each other with respect.

## Conclusion

## Notes

1. There is a distinction between sexually harassing conduct generally and legally actionable sexual harassment. For example, a stray comment does not constitute a viable legal claim for sexual harassment. However, constant abusive verbal attacks toward a student based on sex that go unaddressed by administrators after they have learned of them might make for a successful claim. In other words, the level of harassment must be significant before a claim will be legally actionable.

2. Nan Stein; Nancy L. Marshall; and Linda R. Tropp. *Secrets in Public: Sexual Harassment in Our Schools.* Co-sponsored by NOW Legal Defense and Education Fund and Wellesley College Center for Research on Women, 1992.

3. *Hostile Hallways: The AAUW Survey on Sexual Harassment in America's Schools*, researched by Louis Harris and Associates. Commissioned by the American Association of University Women Educational Foundation, 1993.

4. Researchers defined sexual harassment as "unwanted and unwelcome sexual behavior which interferes with your life." Students reported the following specific types of sexual harassment: sexual comments, jokes, gestures, or looks; touching, grabbing, and/or pinching in a sexual way; mooning or flashing; intentionally brushing up against in a sexual way; targeting with sexual rumors; pulling at clothes in a sexual way; showing, giving, or leaving unwanted sexual pictures or notes; blocking or cornering in a sexual way; targeting with written sexual messages/graffiti on bathroom walls, lockers, and so on; forced kissing; calling another gay or lesbian when he or she did not want to be called that; forcing another to do something sexual at school other than kissing.

5. While nearly half the students say they were "very upset" or "somewhat upset," 70 percent of girls responded this way, compared with only 24 percent of boys. One in four girls report that they were "very upset" by sexually harassing conduct.

6. *In Their Own Voices: Young Women Talk about Dropping Out.* NOW Legal Defense and Education Fund Project on Equal Education Rights, 1988.

7. Because more girls than boys are harassed and affected by harassment, girls are primarily referred to as targets or victims and boys as perpetrators in this chapter. However, schools should be aware that

the law makes no distinction and prohibits the harassment of boys as well as girls.

8. 20 U.S.C. §§1681-1686 (1988); Title IX Regulations, 34 C.F.R. §§106 et seq. (1992).

9. If any part of an educational institution receives federal money, then Title IX covers the entire institution. For example, a school is subject to Title IX if it accepts students on federal scholarship. Thus, even private schools may be subject to Title IX.

10. *See Cannon v. University of Chicago*, 441 U.S. 677 (1978) (establishing the right of a private party to sue under Title IX).

11. 503 U.S. 60 (1992).

12. Id.

### Bibliography*

"The Definition of Sexual Harassment Applies to Schools." In K. Swisher (ed.). *What Is Sexual Harassment?* San Diego: Greenhaven Press, 1995.

"It Happens Here, Too: Sexual Harassment and Child Sexual Abuse in Elementary and Secondary Schools." In S. K. Biklen, and D. Pollard (eds.). *Gender and Education*. Chicago, IL: National Society for the Study of Education, Yearbook 1993 (distributed by University of Chicago Press).

Lampher, Katherine. "Reading, 'Riting, and 'Rassment." *Ms. Magazine,* May/June 1992.

LeBlank, Adrian Nicole. "Harassment in the Halls." *Seventeen Magazine,* September 1992.

"Bitter Lessons for All: Sexual Harassment in Schools." Linn, Eleanor, and Jackie Young. In James T. Sears (ed.). *Sexuality and the Curriculum*. New York: Teachers College Press, 1992.

Sears, James T. *Sexuality and the Curriculum*. NY: Teacher's College Press, 1992.

Stein, Nan, and Lisa Sjostrom. *Flirting or Hurting? A Teacher's Guide on Student-to-Student Sexual Harassment in Schools (Grades 6 through 12)*. (To obtain a copy, write Center for Research on Women, 106 Central St., Wellesley, MA 02181-8259. The cost is $19.95.)

Strauss, Susan. *Sexual Harassment and Teens*. Minneapolis, MN: Free Spirit Press, 1992. (To obtain a copy, write the publisher at 400 First Avenue North, Minneapolis, MN 55401. The cost is $17.95.)

---

*Bibliography and resources are recommended by the editor, not NOW Legal Defense and Education Fund.

## Organizational Resources

Please note that some states have stricter laws against sexual harassment in the schools than those of the federal government. Contact your state department of education and ask to speak to the sex equity specialist. Many state departments of education provide films, books, speakers, or other resources.

American Association of Women in
   Community and Junior Colleges
8800 Grossmont College Drive
El Cajon, CA 92020
(619) 645-1700

Association of Black Women in
   Higher Education
c/o Professor Delores Smalls
Student Personnel Services
Nassau Community College
Building H
124 Education Drive
Garden City, NY 11530
(516) 222-7160

Center for Law and Education
Kathleen Boundy
Executive Director
955 Mass Ave.
Cambridge, MA 92139
(617) 876-6611

Center for Women's Policy Studies
2000 P Street NW, Suite 508
Washington, DC 20036
(202) 872-1770

Committee on the Role and Status of Women
William J. Russell, Executive Director
c/o American Educational Research
   Association
1230 17th Street NW
Washington, DC 20036
(202) 223-9485

National Coalition for Women and
   Girls in Education
c/o Girl Scouts of the U.S.A.
Carmen Delgado Votaw,
Chairwoman
1025 Connecticut Avenue, N.W.
Washington, D.C. 20036
(202) 659-3780

National Women Student's Coalition
Elizabeth Burpe, Co-Chair
c/o USSA
1012 14th Street NW, Suite 207
Washington, DC 20005
(202) 347-8772

NOW Legal Defense and Education
   Fund
99 Hudson Avenue, 12th Floor
New York, NY 10013
*NOW LDEF has two Legal Resource
Kits available on sexual harassment in the schools. One is written for students and the other for administrators, and both have excellent lists of resources.*

Organization for Equal Education
   of the Sexes
Lucy Picco Simpson, President
808 Union Street
Brooklyn, NY 11215
(718) 783-0332

Southern Coalition for Educational
    Equity
Winifred Green, President
P.O. Box 22904
Jackson, MS 39225
(601) 355-7398

Women Educators
c/o Melissa Keyes, Chair
Wisconsin Department of Public
    Instruction
P.O. Box 7841
Madison, WI 53707
(608) 267-9157

Chapter 14

# Legal Rights of Lesbian Women

Marcia Kuntz

Chapter Outline

**Introduction**

**Lesbian Women and Criminal Law**

**Lesbian Relationship Issues**
Access to Legally Recognized Institutions

**Legal Instruments**
Rights of Lesbian Couples in the Private Sector

**Children**
General Issues of Custody and Visitation • When People Other Than
Parents Seek Custody • Adoption and Foster Care • Second-Parent
Adoptions • Donor Insemination

**If the Relationship Ends**

**Other Discrimination—and the Bright Side**

**Conclusion**

**Introduction**

Whether you identify yourself as lesbian, are perceived to be a lesbian, engage in sexual acts with other women, or all of the above, you need to know what the law has in store for you and what you can do to ensure you are protected to the greatest extent possible. Lesbian women historically have been accorded no legal rights or protections; in fact, the law has sanctioned their persecution. This chapter discusses the law's evolution toward recognition of legal rights for lesbians.

**Lesbian Women and Criminal Law**

Whether or not your sexual practices are illegal depends on where you are and what you are doing. States in this country have a variety of sodomy laws that define particular sex acts as criminal. Some states prohibit oral or anal sex between any two people. This approximates what traditionally is considered to be sodomy. Other states prohibit only those acts of "sodomy" between people of the same sex. Still others prohibit more generally "crimes against nature," the definition of which is often left up to the particular prosecutor who decides to bring charges against a particular person, and up to the court that must decide what to do with those charges.[1] In some places, only those acts involving a penis are illegal. In some places, there must be penetration of sexual organs for any of the described activities to be illegal. In many states, no "non-commercial" sex acts between consenting, unrelated adults are illegal.

In *Bowers v. Hardwick,* the U.S. Supreme Court ruled that these laws do not unconstitutionally infringe on the right to privacy of gays and lesbians.[2] Because *Bowers* was the Court's first real statement on the constitutionality of sodomy laws, in the future the Court may decide that these laws are unconstitutional for other reasons, or the Court may decide that its decision was wrong. Until that happens, however, these laws will continue to hurt lesbian women and gay men. A prosecution for particular acts of private consensual sex is unlikely, but the threat of prosecution is a constant invasion of privacy and freedom.

Sodomy laws are more likely to impact in an even less direct way, however. If you are perceived to be a lesbian, you may be labeled by a judge, in an unrelated matter, as a "sodomite," and, consequently, a "felon." In the much-publicized recent case of *Bottoms v. Bottoms,* a judge in Virginia took custody of a two-year-old boy away from his mother in favor of his grandmother, in part because the judge noted that the mother, as a lesbian, was a felon under state law. Her allegedly felonious actions did not result in a criminal conviction, but they did provide the trial judge with powerful ammunition in his quest for justifications in denying custody to her. A Virginia appellate court[3] reversed the trial judge's decision, holding that the mother's lesbianism did not in itself constitute a justification for taking custody from her "in the absence of proof that such behavior or activity poses a substantial threat of harm to [the] child's well being." In April 1995, the state Supreme Court disagreed, upholding the original trial judge's decision and awarded custody to the grandmother, noting that one of the reasons for its determination was the likely deleterious effect on the child because of the mother's relationship with another woman.[4]

There are many other ways in which the perception that lesbians are felonious sodomites can be harmful. For example, lower federal courts have used the Supreme Court's decision in *Bowers v. Hardwick* to permit the federal government to discriminate against gay men and lesbian women in employment practices, reasoning, essentially, that a group of people that is defined by an activity that is a felony in many states is not entitled to constitutional protection.[5] Also, gays and lesbians can be declared unacceptable to adopt children because of their assumed sodomitical behavior.[6]

Whether your case is employment discrimination on the basis of your lesbianism; a custody battle; or one in which another set of rights is being asserted, if your state has a sodomy law, a judge may hold your "outlaw" status against you. It will be up to you and your lawyer to decide whether you can and should argue that you do not violate the sodomy statute. In making this decision, you and your lawyer should assess at least the following: whether you do in fact engage in criminal behavior under your state's sodomy law, whether you would be willing to make this an issue, and whether the particular judge would be receptive to introduction of evidence that you are not in fact a sodomite as defined by the relevant statute. Even more complicated an undertaking would be challenging the statute as being unconstitutional in your state. The factors involved in that assessment are beyond the scope of this chapter.

## Lesbian Relationship Issues

This country offers many benefits to people who marry: access to family health insurance plans, retirement benefits, tax breaks, workers' compensation benefits for family members, residency status for foreigners who marry American citizens, the ability to inherit under a spouse's will without susceptibility to challenge, the ability to inherit if one's spouse does not leave a will, preference in the appointment of a guardian, the right to have a court dispose of property in divorce, enforceability of spousal support, and so on. Whether the right to same-sex marriages would be worth fighting for, with the attendant investment of resources, is an interesting, often heated debate among lesbian and gay activists, and it is beyond the scope of this chapter. What follows is merely a discussion of where lesbian relationships now stand under the law and some suggestions for how to maximize your access to economic benefits that married couples enjoy.

## Access to Legally Recognized Institutions

One way for lesbian women and gay men to participate in rights given traditional, heterosexual married couples is to try to become a part of legally recognized institutions, such as marriage, domestic partnership, and adult adoption.

### Marriage for Lesbian Women and Gay Men

Marriage is an institution that is for the most part a creation of states, as opposed to the federal government or municipalities. States determine who can marry, except when courts step in and determine in particular cases how a state's marriage law should be enforced and whether its marriage laws are unconstitutional. At this writing, no state allows marriage between people of the same sex, although the Hawaii Supreme Court[7] has ordered a lower court to determine whether the state can provide a compelling reason for its prohibition of same-sex marriages. The state supreme court's decision is the first of its kind. Even if marriage is soon allowed in Hawaii for gays and lesbians, it is not clear whether other states will have to recognize a Hawaiian marriage, and it is not clear whether the federal government will confer to same-sex couples married in Hawaii those benefits received by heterosexual couples.

### Domestic Partnerships

Over the past ten years, several cities, including Los Angeles, San Francisco, Seattle, Minneapolis, and New York,[8] have made available to lesbian and gay couples, as well as heterosexual couples, the option of registering as domestic partners. If you are thinking about entering into a domestic partnership with your companion, you will want to consider several issues. Of course, you must first determine whether your city offers domestic partnership status to nonmarried couples, particularly to same-sex couples, and most particularly to someone in your and your lover's situation.

You will also want to determine what benefits accompany domestic partnership status. Domestic partnership ordinances vary widely in the benefits they allow participants. Benefits offered in some municipalities include health insurance coverage for the domestic partners of city employees, rights of visitation while one partner is in the hospital, and bereavement leave for the surviving partner in the event of the other's death, if the surviving partner is a city employee.

Then, research the responsibilities and obligations that attend domestic partnership status. These, too, vary among ordinances, but of particular note might be obligations you and your significant other would incur for your joint living expenses. You should also be aware of the possible tax consequences of receiving benefits such as health insurance coverage for your domestic partner. Finally, you will probably want to know what requirements the law places on couples who wish to dissolve their partnership.

## Adult Adoption

Some gay and lesbian couples have sought adoption as another form of legal recognition of their relationship. There are several reasons that some same-sex couples seek adoptions of one by the other, including wanting further to ensure that a court will recognize their wills as valid upon the death of one of the partners. Courts are far more likely to recognize a will or trust granting property to the "child" or "parent" of the deceased grantor than to her same-sex lover.

The availability of adoption of an adult by her same-sex lover varies from state to state.[9] In some states, adults simply cannot be adopted. In others, adults can be adopted only under certain circumstances. In some states whose statutes do not address adult adoptions explicitly, courts have permitted adult adoption even where the adoptive parent and adoptive "child" are sexually involved; courts in other states interpret state adoption law to prohibit this.

Aside from the legal difficulties you will likely encounter if you attempt to adopt your lover or she, you, there are drawbacks to entering into these relationships. Adoptions are final; if your relationship goes bad, you are still parent and child. Further, if you are the adoptive child, in some states you may lose the right to inherit from your natural parents, unless they provide for you by their own will. Also, there is the somewhat remote possibility that you or your partner will face charges of incest.

Talk to a lawyer who knows the law in your jurisdiction if you are considering this.[10]

## Legal Instruments

Same-sex partners often must create their own documents to attain any legal recognition as part of a couple who wants to care for her partner upon incapacitation, who wants to provide for her by a will or trust, and who wants to ensure that there is some method in place for the orderly resolution of financial affairs when and if the couple splits up.

## Planning for Incapacity

It is likely that you would want the person who knows you best to make financial and health decisions for you if you became unable to do so because of accident, illness, or other medical condition. To enhance the likelihood that such person—whether she is someone with whom you have a committed romantic relationship, friendship, or another kind of close relationship—will be given the exclusive right to make those decisions if you become incapacitated, you should consider executing a Durable Power of Attorney (for your financial issues) and a Health Care Power of Attorney, if one or both are available options in your state. Whereas standard powers of attorney terminate when the signer of the document becomes incapacitated,[11] a durable power of attorney becomes operative precisely at that point. It is not clear whether your attorney-in-fact can make highly personal decisions in states that do not provide for Health Care Powers of Attorney, but in states where these are recognized, these documents help avoid a protracted legal battle between that person whom you would want to make those decisions and your blood relatives (or spouse) who, in the absence of a power of attorney, would have these rights.

Unfortunately, not all states allow durable powers of attorney for nonrelative relationships. Also, durable powers of attorney are sometimes subject to challenge by those people who would have the right to make those decisions for you if the document did not exist. The states that do allow them generally have certain requirements of form that must be followed to allow the documents the best chance of surviving a court challenge.

Consult a lawyer or research your state law adequately before you execute these documents. Sometimes state statutes provide suggested forms for these documents, and there are several books out to help gays and lesbians create these documents.[12] General practice lawyers and family lawyers often have these forms on computer, which they can readily tailor to your needs.

### Wills and Trusts

If you and your partner want to leave property to each other at death, you should consider executing wills (see chapter 23). In the absence of a will (or other valid mechanism, discussed below, for disposing of your property upon your death), your property will go to your legally recognized family in an order of succession determined by state statute, and your lover will receive nothing.

Different states have different requirements for the forms that wills must take. You might prepare a will for yourself, and your partner for herself, by researching the law in your state and by using forms suggested in legal handbooks written for nonlawyers.[13] If, however, you have significant assets or complicated desires regarding how you want your property distributed, you should hire a lawyer to write your will. Will-writing is one area of law in which you can get a good estimate of the cost ahead of time, and your lawyer may even agree to a fixed price for your will. If you do write your own, you should ask a lawyer to review it, usually at a much lower cost.

Gifts to same-sex lovers in wills are not immune from challenge. Disgruntled relatives who would inherit from you by law in the absence of a will may challenge your decision, arguing that you were unduly influenced by your lover, or that you were not in a mentally sound position to sign the will.

There are several ways in which you can reduce the chances of success of such a challenge. First, make sure that you do everything required by the law of your state to write an effective will—have the required number of disinterested witnesses present, have it notarized if necessary, and so on. Second, you might consider including in your will a clause that provides anyone who legally challenges the will to forfeit his or her right to inherit under it. These clauses are not foolproof, however. Courts do not always enforce them, and they often do not deter the relative whose challenge you are trying to avoid, especially if the will leaves him or her little, such that a challenge to the will would involve little risk.

Another option to consider is an *inter vivos* trust, or living trust, which is a legal instrument providing a means to transfer your assets while you are still alive, and, presumably, able to exhibit independence and soundness of mind. You can place your assets, or those you intend to pass on to your lover, in trust for yourself during your life, and for your lover upon your death. If the trust is set up as "revocable," you can dissolve it at any time and convert the ownership of your assets back to you from the trust. There are no clear tax advantages to a revocable inter vivos trust, but such an instrument can be used to simplify your estate at the time of your death, avoiding the complicated court proceeding called "probate," and it is more likely to survive challenge by unhappy relatives.[14] Again, if you have significant assets or complex issues related to your estate, consult a lawyer with knowledge of issues concerning same-sex couples.

## Contracts

Like heterosexual relationships, lesbian relationships can end in nasty legal battles over money. Unlike heterosexuals, however, the institution of marriage is not available to these relationships, and so the law provides no means for any kind of orderly dissolution. Laws do not specifically address what to do with the income and property of unmarried persons who are breaking up. To fill this void, many people recommend that lesbian and gay couples enter into agreements that address who receives what if the couple splits up, or when one partner dies.

These contracts do have benefits. Couples who undertake the process of writing a contract often force themselves to focus on the relationship and to communicate with each other regarding difficult issues between them. They probably finish the process with a better sense of each other's feelings and ideas about the relationship. If the contract is enforceable, it can prevent long and expensive legal entanglements.

But these contracts are problematical. Just like prenuptial agreements executed by heterosexual couples, contracts that seek to solidify a lesbian relationship can have the opposite effect, especially when the party pushing the contract is in an emotionally dominant position in the relationship or, perhaps, is much better off financially than the other. Related to this problem, people contemplating a committed relationship might be at their most vulnerable and often do not act in their own best interest.

If you decide to enter into such a contract with your lover, there are steps you should take to make it more likely to be enforced by a court. Each of you should hire a separate lawyer to review it, which is the best evidence that coercion or misrepresentation did not figure into the execution of the agreement. The agreement should not mention your sexual relationship: A number of courts have invalidated agreements that state or imply that sex is part of the bargain. For example, if you are going to provide your lover with a monthly support payment, avoid language suggesting that this is being done because she has agreed to quit her job and "render her services as a lover, companion, homemaker."[15] Your agreement should also include a provision that if any part of the agreement is unenforceable, that part will be severable, and the rest of the agreement will remain in full force.[16]

## Rights of Lesbian Couples in the Private Sector

As discussed previously, married couples receive a number of benefits that are not available to unmarried couples, and particularly to lesbian women and gay men, who at this writing, still cannot marry in any state. Also, there are numerous areas of affirmative discrimination against couples who cannot marry. These include discrimination in the acquisition of housing through a variety of means, the unavailability of workers' compensation and Social Security benefits to partners of deceased employees, and the inability of someone to sue for emotional distress for the death of her lover.[17]

Some states and cities, however, prohibit discrimination in certain situations against people who are homosexual or are not legally married, resulting in certain limited rights for same-sex couples. Also, some private employers and businesses provide benefits to same-sex partners of employees in certain circumstances. Some of these rights and benefits may include the right to "inherit" a rent-controlled apartment upon the death of one's lover to whom the apartment was leased, health insurance benefits for the same-sex partner of an employee, and unpaid family leave. The variety and limitations of benefits are too numerous to address here. You might want to ask your employer if any such benefits are available, if you work in an environment where these questions would be safe to ask. You need to consult a lawyer who knows the law of your jurisdiction to determine what, if any, prohibitions are placed on discrimination against same-sex couples, and to determine what contractual obligations, if any, your employer has incurred and can be held to.

If you are a lesbian with children or with plans to adopt or bear or rear children, you will likely face at some point issues relating to custody, visitation, and, if relevant, your actual right to parent those children if you are attempting to adopt.

**Children**

## General Issues of Custody and Visitation
### Children From Heterosexual Relationships

In most divorces and other relationship breakups, a couple's property, child support, and child custody issues are resolved by the couple before a trial becomes necessary. Some couples are unable to reach an agreement, however, and must go to court.

If you are involved in a lawsuit with the biological father of your children over custody or visitation, a judge will likely consider your lesbianism in some way in his or her decision. In making this decision, the trial judge in most states is supposed to determine what custody and visitation arrangement would be in the "best interest" of your children. As a practical matter, however, there are few courts in which your lesbianism or your conduct as a lesbian will be absolutely ignored when you are battling custody with your children's heterosexual father.

If you are asking only for visitation with your children, your lesbianism will not likely prevent you from seeing them. Some courts, however, have placed severe restrictions on the conditions of visitation for homosexual parents. Some courts have prohibited overnight visits for homosexual parents. Some have ordered that visitation not occur in the presence of the parent's same-sex partner. Courts have placed many other equally invasive restrictions on visitation for homosexual parents.

It is beyond the scope of this chapter to address what you should do if you are involved in a lawsuit with your children's father over custody and visitation. What can be stated clearly is that you should hire the best lawyer you can find. That lawyer might well see fit to hire a psychiatrist or psychologist as an expert witness to testify that your orientation and way of life will not harm your children. There are organizations, identified at the end of this chapter, that can offer some guidance and information in litigating these cases, including references to lawyers in your area with some expertise in custody matters.

### When People Other Than Parents Seek Custody

Sometimes people other than the children's parent will sue for custody. In the case of *Bottoms v. Bottoms,* discussed earlier in the context of sodomy laws, the trial judge awarded a grandmother custody against her lesbian daughter of the daughter's two-year-old son, a decision upheld by the Virginia Supreme Court. The trial judge cited the daughter's lesbianism as creating a bad moral environment for the child, and the state Supreme Court agreed that the child may be harmed by her mother's lesbianism. The initial outcome cannot be dismissed as the backward view of one Virginia judge. In most states, courts will at least entertain a grandparent's challenge against a homosexual son or daughter for custody of his or her child, especially if other factors exist that the judge can rely upon in addition to the parent's homosexuality.

If a grandparent or another nonparent sues for custody of a child, he or she must prove to the court that the child's parent is unfit and that awarding custody to the grandparent would be in the child's best interest. These are ambiguous factors that confer considerable discretion on the judge deciding the case. Another decision like that of the *Bottoms v. Bottoms* court is possible. See a lawyer immediately if you are sued for custody.

### Adoption and Foster Care

The law recognizes other ways of becoming a parent, besides childbirth. When you adopt, you become the child's parent in all legal senses, as if you had given birth to that child. Except in the case of second-parent adoptions, discussed below, the child's birth parents forfeit all rights and are relieved of all obligations with respect to that child. All adoptions must be approved by a court. On the other hand, a foster parent arrangement is temporary, until the applicable state agency decides whether the child is better off with his or her biological parents.

Whether you can adopt or act as a foster parent depends on where you live. New Hampshire and Florida have laws that explicitly state that homosexual people cannot adopt children: New Hampshire prevents them from being foster parents as well. Prohibitions on adoption, however, are not limited to those states. Courts elsewhere have held homosexuals and bisexuals unfit to adopt, and some adoption agencies, both public and private, will not handle adoptions for lesbian women and gay men.

You might want to start the process by checking with a local gay and lesbian rights organization, or one of the national organizations listed at the end of this chapter. You will need a lawyer at some point in the process—perhaps at the beginning to help you determine whether and how you can arrange for an adoption, but definitely at the stage when a court must approve the adoption. If possible, you should find someone who is familiar with issues confronting gays and lesbians in adoption.

## Second-Parent Adoptions

The law of second-parent adoptions is likely to be relevant to more lesbian women than is that regarding traditional adoptions. In these, the partner of the biological mother adopts the child as her own, but the biological mother does not give up her legal status as parent. This enables the adoptive mother to have rights to visitation, and possibly custody, if the couple breaks up, and she will be the legally-recognized surviving parent if the biological mother dies. Without the legal status of adoptive parent, the nonbiological "mother" will very likely be left unrecognized by the law, with no right to raise, or even see, the children.

In granting the right for same-sex partners of biological parents to do this, a court must address two issues that arise in interpreting and applying a state's adoption statute: the court must determine whether the statute can be read to permit same-sex adoptions in this manner, and whether it can be read to permit an adoption in which the biological parent does not give up her rights. In the past few years, courts in the following states have decided that their state's adoption statute did not prevent second-parent adoptions: Alaska, California, Massachusetts, Minnesota, New York, Oregon, Vermont, Washington, and the District of Columbia.[18]

As with other adoptions, you must ask a court to approve your second-parent adoption petition. For this, you will need a lawyer. A lawyer is especially crucial if you live in a state that has not yet recognized second-parent adoptions.

Even without a second-parent legal adoption, the biological parent and nonbiological coparent can take certain steps to help protect the relationship of the nonbiological coparent with the child. Medical consent forms may authorize her to make decisions when the biological parent cannot be reached. The couple should also consider consulting a lawyer about executing coparenting contracts or guardianship forms for the nonbiological coparent to assume parenting responsibilities in the event of the biological mother's death or incapacity. Neither document is clearly recognized by state courts, but they do not hurt, and can make a difference.[19]

### Donor Insemination

You and your partner may want to have a child, where one of you wants to bear it. You need to decide what kind of sperm donor arrangement you want. Specifically, you must decide whether the donor is to be anonymous or someone you know. There are some advantages to selecting a known donor. In addition to your (and, later, your child's) knowing something about the father as a person, such as his health and disposition, you and he might actually share a desire that he be a part of your and your child's life.

You run the risk, however, that the donor will be more involved in the child's life than you would want. A known donor can ask a court to order visitation with the child and might even ask for joint or sole custody. He can prevent your partner from adopting the child through a second-parent adoption. There is no legally recognized relationship between his paying child support and his potential right to active involvement in the child's life. In other words, even if you refuse child support from him, a court may still grant him visitation with the child and even the right to help raise his child.

### Known Donor

If you want to select the donor, or if there is someone in particular whom you want to be the donor, and you do not want the donor to have rights as the father of the child, it is imperative that you determine what your state laws say regarding donor insemination. For example, some states require that in order for the biological mother to assert that the donor not be entitled to rights as a father, a licensed physician must act as intermediary, obtaining the semen from the donor to be used in the insemination.[20]

Whether or not you want the donor to be involved as a father, you should consider a formal agreement with him, setting out his rights and obligations with respect to the child. Be aware that a court does not have to enforce this agreement if the judge decides that it is not in the best interest of your child. For example, if your donor is a heterosexual man who enters into a relationship that a court would regard as stable, he might stand a particularly good chance of winning custody of your child from you, regardless of what you and he agreed to at the time of conception. Also, if the donor actually gets more involved in your child's life than the agreement contemplates, a judge could easily decide that it would be in the child's best interest for the donor to be recognized as the child's father, with all attendant rights and obligations. Any behavior of the parties to the agreement that does not strictly follow the agreement could justify a court in determining that the agreement has been modified or abandoned.

As a general matter, however, the agreement will at least give a court guidance as to the parents' intentions regarding the child. Also, hammering out the agreement helps to force you and the donor to confront difficult issues. There are many, such as what you will do if the child needs far more medical care than you anticipated.[21]

### Unknown Donor

If you want to minimize the risk of involvement by the donor in the child's life, you should opt for an anonymous donor. Talk to your doctor about contacting a sperm bank.

## If the Relationship Ends

You cannot marry someone of your same sex anywhere yet, so laws governing divorce in your state do not apply to your situation. (It is not clear what will happen if and when lesbian women and gay men start marrying in Hawaii, then divorcing in another state to which they have moved.) If you are registered as a domestic partner, you need to check with your state's domestic partnership law regarding dissolution of the partnership before you can enter into another one. But the domestic partnership laws will not tell you what happens to your children or your property if you and your lover are unable to agree.

If you and your lover had a contract addressing what happens if you break up, it may be enforced by a court, subject to the limitations and caveats discussed above. It is also possible that a court will rule that you and your lover had an unwritten or implied agreement regarding what is to become of your property if you break up. The law in this area is too undeveloped to permit predictions on what would happen if these arguments were made.

Rather than asking a judge to resolve disputes over your relationship agreement or over your property generally, for which there is little case precedent to guide him or her, you should consider trying to negotiate and work out an agreement regarding how to divide your property. The alternative could be a nasty and very expensive legal battle.[22]

Children add to the difficulty of breaking up. If you legally adopted your lover's biological child, you should have at least rights of visitation with the child (and obligations of child support, depending on your income and hers). It is better here, too, to reach agreement with your lover regarding the child's best interest, rather than having a judge do it after a trial that will certainly be expensive and traumatic for everyone involved. Even where you are both legally recognized parents, there is little guidance about what a court would do with custody, visitation, and two lesbian parents.

If you did not adopt your lover's biological child, you will likely be subject completely to your lover's decision about whether you should be able to spend time with the child. Here, again, for your sake and the child's, you should try to reach agreement regarding your rights to visitation and your obligations of support. Be aware, however, that a visitation agreement between a biological mother and someone with no legal recognition as a parent will probably not be enforced if the mother decides it was a bad idea, or dies. And you might still be obligated for the support to which you agreed.

## Other Discrimination— and the Bright Side

Advocates of lesbian and gay rights have seen some progress in the employment context. In public sector employment, up to now there have been some cases favorable to homosexual plaintiffs claiming discrimination or infringement of First Amendment rights to free speech, but as a general matter, little protection has been afforded lesbian women or gay men from discrimination on the job in government.

Very recently, we have seen some progress in the federal government. Changes in the law regarding homosexuals in the military, providing that one cannot be discharged merely for being gay and providing that investigations regarding conduct will not be undertaken as a result of mere rumor or unsubstantiated allegation, are arguably evidence of incremental steps forward. (It remains to be seen whether this new policy will be upheld in court as constitutional.)

Almost all executive branch agencies have issued formal policies prohibiting discrimination on the basis of sexual orientation. The Clinton Administration recently issued an Executive Order applying to all executive branch departments prohibiting the denial of security clearances on the basis of sexual orientation alone.

Unlike the federal government, private employers and local governments are not limited by federal agency regulations in their discrimination against lesbians and gays. Homosexuals, however, might find other forms of protection from employment discrimination. Some unions have supported gays and lesbians who have been the victims of discrimination, and union contracts requiring that an employer dismiss an employee only for just cause may provide further protection.[23]

Also, numerous municipalities and several states have recently passed laws or executive orders banning discrimination on the basis of sexual orientation. Some of these address discrimination in both private sector jobs and in local government. These laws may provide antidotes to a long and virtually relentless parade of cases in which courts found no protection from discrimination in either the private or public employment context, as well as to a number of other major and minor encroachments on the lives of lesbian women and gay men.

This is a time of flux for advocates of rights for lesbians and gays. As some localities quietly pass laws giving protection from discrimination, others are dealing, in some cases much more vocally, with initiatives to prevent lesbian women and gay men from receiving such protection. Whether they will withstand challenge on constitutional grounds by lesbian and gay activists is a question whose answer we await with great anticipation. There are others, many of which have been raised in this chapter. As our visibility grows at a revolutionary pace and the counterforces mobilize, we must hope that our successes, and not theirs, will render this chapter obsolete.

**Conclusion**

## Notes

1. Professor Ruthann Robson notes that sodomy laws in this country fall into one of these three categories in her inspired chapter "Crimes of Lesbian Sex," from Robson, *Lesbian (Out)Law*. Ithaca, NY: Firebrand Books, 1992.
2. 478 U.S. 186 (1986).
3. 444 SE 2d 276 (VA. App. 1994).
4. 457 SE 2d 102 (VA. 1995).
5. See, for example, *Padula v. Webster,* 822 F.2d 97 (D.C. Cir.1987).
6. See, for example, Appeal in Pine County Juvenile Action B-10489, 727 P2d 830 (Ariz. Ct. App. 1986).
7. 852 P.2d 44 (Haw. 1993).
8. William B. Rubenstein, ed. *Lesbians, Gay Men, and the Law*. New York: The New Press, 1993.
9. This summary is "adopted" from editors, Harvard Law Review, *Sexual Orientation and the Law*. Cambridge, MA: Harvard University Press, 1989.
10. There is at least one other possible way of having your relationship recognized by the law, if marriage continues to be unavailable, and domestic partnership or adoption are impossible or ill-advised. California has permitted families to register as private, nonprofit associations. See Rubenstein, *Lesbians, Gay Men, and the Law*.
11. Nondurable powers of attorney also have the distinct disadvantage in some states of being operative immediately upon their execution, giving the attorney-in-fact power to make the provided-for decisions at that time.
12. For example, see Curry et al. *A Legal Guide for Lesbian and Gay Couples*. Berkeley, CA: Nolo Press, 1993.
13. Curry et al. *A Legal Guide for Lesbian and Gay Couples*.
14. For more information on how to set this up and information on other ways to simplify your estate and avoid probate, including holding property with your partner as joint tenants, refer to Curry, et al. *A Legal Guide for Lesbian and Gay Couples*.

15. See *Jones v. Daly,* 176 Cal. Rptr. 130 (Ct. App. 1981).
16. Curry et al. *A Legal Guide for Lesbian and Gay Couples,* provides practical suggestions for creating a relationship contract.
17. Harvard Law Review. *Sexual Orientation and the Law.* Cambridge, MA: Harvard University Press, 1989.
18. Rubenstein, *Lesbians, Gay Men, and the Law.*
19. Achtenburg, R. *Sexual Orientation and the Law,* 1-04[3][a] (1993).
20. National Center for Lesbian Rights. *Lesbians Choosing Motherhood: Legal Implications of Donor Insemination and Co-Parenting.* 1991. NCLR's address is given below.
21. If you are contemplating insemination by a known donor, see Curry et al., *A Legal Guide for Lesbian and Gay Couples,* and get a copy of *Artificial Insemination: An Alternative Conception,* recommended in Curry et al. and available from the San Francisco Women's Center, 3543 18th Street, San Francisco, CA 94110.
22. Curry et al., *A Legal Guide for Lesbian and Gay Couples,* includes a form for a separation agreement, but if you have substantial property, or if your property issues are sensitive or otherwise complicated, you should each probably hire a lawyer to negotiate.
23. Harvard Law Review. *Sexual Orientation and the Law.*

## Bibliography

Curry, Hayden, et al. *A Legal Guide for Lesbian and Gay Couples, 8th ed.* Berkeley, CA: Nolo Press, 1994.

Harvard Law Review, Editors. *Sexual Orientation and the Law.* Cambridge, MA: Harvard University Press, 1989.

Hunter, Nan D. et al. *The Rights of Lesbians and Gay Men: The Basic ACLU Guide to a Gay Person's Rights.* Carbondale: Southern Illinois University Press, 1992.

*The Rights of Lesbians and Gay Men, 3d ed.* Carbondale: Southern Illinois University Press, 1992.

Rubenstein, William B. *Lesbians, Gay Men, and the Law: A Reader.* New York: The New Press, 1993.

Samar, Vincent J. *The Right to Privacy: Gays, Lesbians, and the Constitution.* Philadelphia: Temple University Press, 1992.

## Organizational Resources

In addition to these resources, there are many newsletters, as well as general resources directed to the lesbian community. Some are academic, some humorous; a good place to locate these resources is your local library. NOW Legal Defense and Education Fund also has an excellent list. Contact them at 99 Hudson Street, New York, NY 10013.

ACT UP
135 West 29th Street
New York, NY 10014
(212) 564-2437

ASTRAEA National Lesbian Action
   Foundation
666 Broadway, Suite 520
New York, NY 10012
(212) 529-8021

American Civil Liberties Union
Lesbian and Gay Rights Project
132 West 43rd Street
New York, NY 10036
(212) 944-9800, ext. 545

Asian Lesbians of the East Coast/
   Asian Pacific Lesbian Network
P.O. Box 850
New York, NY 10002
(212) 517-5598

Black Gay and Lesbian Leadership
   Forum
2538 Hyperion Avenue, Suite 7
Los Angeles, CA 90027-3305
(213) 666-5495

Gay and Lesbian Advocates and
   Defenders (GLAD)
P.O. Box 218
Boston, MA 02112
(617) 426-1350

Gay and Lesbian Alliance Against
   Defamation (GLAAD)
150 West 26th Street, Suite 503
New York, NY 10001
(212) 807-1700

Human Rights Campaign Fund
1012 14th Street NW, Suite 607
Washington, DC 20005
(202) 628-4160

International Gay and Lesbian
   Human Rights Commission
540 Castro Street
San Francisco, CA 94114
(415) 255-8680

Lambda Legal Defense and Education Fund
606 South Olive Street, Suite 580
Los Angeles, CA 90014
(213) 629-2728

Lesbian and Gay Community Services Center
208 West 13th Street
New York, NY 10011
(212) 620-7310

Lesbian Mothers National Defense
   Fund
P.O. Box 21567
Seattle, WA 98111
(206) 325-2643 (Voice and TTY)

Lesbian Switchboard
208 West 13th Street
New York, NY 10011
(212) 741-2610

National Center for Lesbian Rights
1663 Mission Street, 5th Floor
San Francisco, CA 94103
(415) 621-0674

National Gay and Lesbian Task Force
1734 14th Street, NW
Washington, DC 20009-4309
(202) 332-6483, TTY (202) 332-6219

National Hate Crime Reporting Hotline
Department of Justice
Community Relations Service
1-800-347-HATE

National Lawyers Guild Military Law Task Force
1168 Union Street, Suite 201
San Diego, CA 92101
(619) 233-1701

National Organization for Women
1000 16th Street NW, Suite 700
Washington, DC 20036
(202) 331-0066
*NOW has supported lesbian and gay rights for two decades. They suppport a lesbian rights action program and serve as a resource for state and local chapters. A Lesbian Rights Resource Kit and a Lesbian Rights Lobby Kit are available from NOW.*

NOW Legal Defense and Education Fund
99 Hudson Street, 12th Floor
New York, NY 10013
*In addition to making available the Legal Resource Kit, NOW LDEF has litigated cases involving lesbian rights in family law and employment discrimination issues.*

---

**Marcia Kuntz** is an attorney on the personal staff of a member of Congress. Before working in Congress, she was an associate with the law firm of Kuder, Smollar & Friedman, P.C., where she concentrated in domestic relations law and specific areas of health care law. She is a graduate of Princeton University with a B.A. in English and the University of Chicago with an M.A. and J.D. She teaches "Sexual Orientation and the Law" as an adjunct professor of law at Georgetown University.

Chapter 15

# *Disabilities*

Wendy Wilkinson and Laura Smith

Chapter Outline

**Introduction**

**Overview**
Definition of disability

**Title I: Employment**
Association • Insurance • Enforcement

**Title II: State and Local Government Services**
Grievance Procedures

**Title III: Public Accommodations and Commercial Facilities**
Transportation

**Title IV: Telecommunications**

**Exemptions From the ADA**

**Conclusion**

Introduction     This chapter of the book focuses on the Americans with Disabilties Act (ADA) and is taken completely from the statute and the regulations and analysis accompanying the regulations. All of the statutes, regulations and analysis, as well as other materials can be found in the ADA handbook published by the EEOC and Department of Justice that can be obtained at the Disability and Technical Assistance centers found in the bibliography.

Disability, though not gender-specific, is something that can profoundly affect women socially and economically. Much of the research conducted to date assumed that disability is a "unitary" concept. Little study has been directed to ascertaining what effect gender has on disability and what it means to be a woman with a disability. Studies conducted on people with disabilities have focused on males with disabilities. Furthermore, women with disabilities have also been largely ignored by women's groups. What little study has been done shows that women with disabilities are much worse off economically than males with disabilities. In 1981 the average income of males with disabilities was at $13,863 compared with $5,835 for women. The percentage of women with disabilities working was much lower than that of males with disabilities. All of these findings underline how vitally important it is for women to understand disability and especially to comprehend what it means to be a woman with a disability in our society.

The Americans with Disabilities Act (ADA) is the most important civil rights legislation to be passed in two decades. It did not spring from a vacuum. After years of piecemeal disability-related legislation, the ADA is the most comprehensive effort, ensuring access to all areas of society.

Overview     The ADA is divided into five Titles. Each Title covers a distinct area.

- Title I covers employment practices and went into effect for employers with 25 or more employees on July 26, 1992 and on July 26, 1994 for employers with 15 or more employees. Employers with fewer than 15 employees will never be covered by Title I.

- Title II prohibits discrimination in all programs and services of state and local governments. Discrimination in the employment practices of these governmental entities is also prohibited by this Title. All governmental employers are covered regardless of size. Title II went into effect on January 26, 1992. Public transportation is also covered by this Title.

- Private transportation, public accommodations, and commercial facilities are covered by Title III of the Act. In effect as of January 26, 1992, this Title contains the architectural guidelines for facilities covered by the ADA.

- Title IV, effective as of July 26, 1993, covers all telecommunication services.

- Title V, effective as of July 26, 1993, contains the miscellaneous provisions, which cover among other things, employer-provided insurance.

## Definition of Disability

The definition of disability in the act is divided into three parts. To be protected, an individual needs to be an individual with a "(1) physical or mental impairment that substantially limits one or more of the major life activities … ; (2) … have a record of such an impairment; or (3) being regarded as having such an impairment."

The determination as to coverage is, for the most part, made on a case by case basis. First, one should ascertain the existence of a physical or mental impairment. Physical impairments include any physiological condition which affects the functioning of a body system such as the respiratory system. The definition of mental impairment includes mental illness and learning disabilities. Impairments must be evaluated without regard to any devices or medicines that may mitigate the effect of the impairment. An individual with a hearing impairment would be covered even if she uses a hearing aid. Temporary conditions such as pregnancy are not considered to be impairments.

Next, one must consider whether the impairment affects a major life activity. Major life activities include things such as walking, hearing, breathing, sitting, and standing. Working is also considered a major life activity, so an individual who has an impairment that substantially limits her ability to work would be covered.

Finally, one must judge whether or not the major life activity identified is "substantially" limited by the impairment. In making this judgment several factors should considered, such as the "expected duration of the impairment," its nature, severity, and impact on the individual.

When assessing whether someone is covered by this first part of the definition, it is important to keep in mind that this is a functional, individualized determination. One should focus on the effect of the impairment on a particular individual. For instance, an individual with cerebral palsy may not automatically be covered under this part of the definition if she only experiences a slight tremor in her hands. On the other hand, if the individual has difficulty walking as a result of the palsy she would be covered.

If a person does not have an actual physical or mental impairment that impairs a major life activity, she will nonetheless be covered if she has a history of such an impairment. This part of the definition of disability protects, for example, persons who have recovered from cancer and are discriminated against because of their record of having had the cancer. This part also protects individuals who were misclassified as having a substantially limiting impairment, for instance, a person whose school record indicated she had a learning disability that she does not in fact have.

A person who is not covered under either of the first two parts of the definition may be covered by the third part of the definition if she is regarded as having a substantially limiting impairment. An individual will be covered if, for instance, her employer mistakenly believes that the individual's high blood pressure that is controlled with medication limits her ability to work in a certain position and transfers her to another less strenuous one because of this baseless fear. The woman with mild cerebral palsy may be covered under this part of the definition. Individuals who are not actually functionally limited in any way but are discriminated against because of the attitudes of others are also protected by this part. An employer moving an individual with a facial scar to a different position because of customers' negative reactions to the individual is an example of an impairment inflicted by attitudes. If an individual is discharged or demoted because her employer mistakenly believes that she has a substantially limiting impairment that she does not have, she would also be protected by this part.

To receive the protections of the Act an individual must fall into one of the three parts of the definition. Individuals who are receiving disability benefits or who are receiving workers' compensation benefits will not automatically be covered by the ADA, and must independently meet the ADA's definition of disability.

## Title I: Employment

The ADA prohibits discrimination in all aspects of the employment process. It asks that employers evaluate individuals for employment based on their ability to perform the essential functions of the position for which they are applying. Before the passage of the ADA, employers could ask questions about a person's disability that had nothing to do with her ability to perform the job. Individuals with disabilities could be given medical examinations when no other applicants were required to take them. Title I prohibits these discriminatory practices.

Specifically Title I prohibits discrimination against qualified individuals with disabilities. Employers may require that a disabled individual satisfy all the prerequisites for the position. If the individual does and is therefore found to be "otherwise qualified," the employer must then determine whether or not the individual can perform the "essential functions" of the job with or without a reasonable accommodation. In making this determination the employer must focus on the individual's capabilities at that particular point in time.

"Essential functions" are defined as, "the fundamental job duties of the employment position ... the term ... does not include the marginal functions of the position." The regulations list several factors as considerations in determining what job functions are essential. Such things as the amount of time spent performing a particular function, the number of employees available among whom a particular function may be delegated, the degree of specialization of a function, as well as the employer's judgment as to what is essential may all be considerations. The Act does not require written job descriptions but if an employer has a written job description prepared before the job application process then it may be evidence as to whether certain functions are essential.

Next, a determination must be made as to whether or not the individual can perform the essential functions of the position with or without a reasonable accommodation. An accommodation is any change in the employment environment that allows an individual equal access to all aspects of the job process. There are three stages at which employers must offer accommodations. First, during the job application process, the employer must provide accommodations which ensure that the individual with a disability can fill out the job application or that job tests be administered in a way that the applicant's abilities are fairly tested. Providing accommodations so an individual can perform the essential functions of the job itself is the second stage in which accommodation needs to be addressed. Finally, the employer must ensure that an individual has access to all benefits and privileges extending from the job itself.

Specific examples of reasonable accommodations are listed in the regulations and in the accompanying guidelines, but it is important to remember that these are only examples of possible accommodations. A reasonable accommodation is anything that will work for the individual and that the employer can provide without undue hardship. This is an individualized determination; for instance, not all individuals who use wheelchairs will need exactly the same type of accommodations. Possible accommodations mentioned include job restructuring, making facilities wheelchair accessible, acquiring special equipment, and providing qualified readers or interpreters.

An employer's obligation to provide an accommodation extends up to the point that provision of such accommodation causes an undue hardship. Undue hardship is any action which would cause "significant difficulty or expense." The regulations set out several factors that must be considered in this determination. Such things as the cost of the accommodation, the company's overall financial resources, and the impact a particular accommodation may have on the operation of a particular facility are appropriate considerations. In making this assessment the employer should consider the availability of tax credits, deductions, and any other available funding that could reduce the employer's cost in providing the accommodation. If there is no other funding assistance, then the individual with a disability must be given the opportunity to provide or pay for the accommodation herself.

Employers are required to accommodate only when they know that there is a need for an accommodation. Thus, unless the need is obvious, it is up to the individual who needs the accommodation to alert the employer. Once an employer has been alerted that there is a need for an accommodation it must make an effort to provide an appropriate one. "The ADA's guidelines suggest a "flexible, interactive process that involves both the employer and the qualified individual with a disability" to determine the appropriate accommodation. The "appropriate" accommodation is going to be the one that is effective. If there is more than one effective accommodation that would work then the employer should give preference to the one chosen by the individual. It is the employer, however, who has the final say in choosing between effective accommodations so that it may choose the least expensive among them.

Title I of the ADA also protects individuals with disabilities in the employment process by prohibiting employers from asking questions about an individual's disability before they have offered her a job. Sections 1630.13–1630.14(c) outline the inquiries that are appropriate at three identified stages of the employment process. Stage one is the pre-employment stage, which is the application and interview process before an offer of employment is made. An employer cannot make any inquiry about disability in the application or interview. The employer cannot give medical examinations at this stage or ask about an individual's workers' compensation history. Inquiry may be made into an individual's ability to perform the functions of the job. Employers may also ask an applicant to demonstrate or describe how she can perform job-related functions with or without reasonable accommodation, but only if they ask this of all applicants or where the known disability could interfere with the performance of a job function.

After an employer offers employment, it can require that the applicant be given a medical examination, ask about previous workers' compensation claims and make other inquiries as long as they are made of everyone in that job category. Medical examinations at this stage need not be related to the job and the offer of employment may be conditioned on the results of the medical examination. If, however, the offer of employment is withdrawn because the results of the medical examination show that the individual is not qualified to perform the job, the employer must show that the disqualifying standards are "job-related and consistent with business necessity" and that no reasonable accommodation would enable the individual to perform the essential functions of the job. If an employer believes that the results of the medical examination show that the individual poses a "direct threat" to the health and safety of herself or others, it must show that the individual does indeed pose a "significant risk of substantial harm" that cannot be eliminated or reduced through reasonable accommodation. This determination must be based on objective medical evidence and not on myths about disability.

At the third stage in the employment process, after an individual is employed, a medical examination may be conducted only to determine whether an employee can still perform the essential functions of her job. Thus, medical examinations may be conducted when an employee has demonstrated difficulty performing the job, or when required by Federal, state, or local law to determine fitness for duty or as necessary to the reasonable accommodation process. The medical examinations conducted here must be restricted to determining why the employee is having difficulty performing the job or what accommodation is necessary. Voluntary medical examinations may also be conducted as part of an employee health program.

Any medical information gathered at any of these stages must be kept in files separate from the employee's personnel records. The files should be kept confidential except to supervisors who may be informed of work restrictions and accommodations, first aid personnel who may be notified if emergency treatment may be necessary, or government officials investigating compliance with the Act.

## Association

Individuals who do not fall under the definition of disability will nonetheless be protected if they are discriminated against because of their relationship to a person with a disability. For example, an employer cannot refuse to hire a woman who has a child with a disability because of a fear that she will need to take time off to care for the child or because it is concerned about carrying the child on the company health insurance plan. Although an employer cannot discriminate against the woman, the ADA does not require that she be accommodated. So, the employer would not be required to give her more time off than other employees.

### Insurance

If employers provide any benefits they must provide them to everyone equally. Accordingly, employees must be given equal access to any insurance plan offered by the employer. Employers cannot refuse to cover certain employees because they have a disability nor can they refuse to hire an individual with a disability because their insurance premiums may increase. The ADA, however, does not prohibit pre-existing injury clauses or policies that limit coverage for certain procedures, types of drugs, or treatments even if these exclusions disparately impact people with disabilities. The ADA does prohibit policies that target a specific disability or that will not provide coverage to an individual because of their disability, unless it can be demonstrated that the exclusions are based on sound actuarial principles.

### Enforcement

The Equal Employment Opportunity Commission (EEOC) enforces the ADA. Individuals who have been discriminated against must file their complaints with the EEOC within 180 days, or within 300 days if there is a state or local agency that enforces the same type of law. The EEOC will investigate the complaint and, if discrimination is found, will first attempt to mediate the complaint. If this is not successful, the EEOC will file suit or issue a right to sue letter which allows the individual to file a lawsuit on her own. An individual may request a "right to sue" letter after the EEOC has not acted on the complaint for 180 days. Issuance of a "right to sue" letter does not mean that the EEOC has found discrimination, as it can be issued even though the EEOC eventually finds no discrimination.

If the individual prevails in court an employer may be ordered to accommodate, promote, or remedy whatever discrimination has occurred. Monetary damages may also be awarded if the court finds intentional discrimination. Punitive damages may be awarded where the employer has acted willfully or recklessly.

## Title II: State and Local Government Services

Title II of the ADA prohibits discrimination based on disability in the employment practices of state and local government and the provision of all governmental services. The employment practices and services of federal agencies and contractors are not covered by the ADA because they are already covered by the Rehabilitation Act of 1973. An individual is protected by Title II if she is a "qualified individual with a disability." An individual who meets the definition of disability is eligible for the program or service, and can participate in it with or without reasonable modifications in the program or facility or through the provision of auxiliary aids.

All programs, services, and employment practices are covered regardless of the size of the governmental entity. Activities carried out by governmental contractors are also covered. Town board meetings, social service programs, and city playgrounds are examples of some of the programs that are covered.

"Program accessibility" requires that " ... each service, program, or activity, when viewed in its entirety, be readily accessible to and usable by individuals with disabilities." This accessibility can be achieved by providing interpreters for individuals who are hearing impaired, through relocating services to facilities that are accessible, redesigning equipment, altering existing facilities, or building new facilities. The governmental entity must provide access to all programs and services in existing facilities unless such access would result in undue financial or administrative burdens. In determining whether providing access would cause an undue burden, the public entity has to look to all the resources it has available and document the reasons for its conclusion. If the action would result in an undue burden, access to the program or service must be provided through other means. Program access is a very strict requirement and must somehow always be provided. Structural changes in existing facilities do not always have to be made when access can be provided through other means, but if altering a facility is the only method through which access can be achieved then the alterations must be done.

In providing program access it is important that priority is given to methods which assure that services are provided in an integrated manner. Integration is a key aspect of nondiscrimination in the ADA. Historically, people with disabilities have been segregated, classified, and limited because of their disabilities. The ADA, however, requires that individuals with disabilities be given the opportunity to access the same things in the same manner that everyone else does. For example, a city museum may offer some guided tours with interpreters for individuals with hearing impairments. However, the individual with a disability does not have to participate in the special program if she chooses not to.

Public entities are required to document their plans to achieve "program accessibility." All state and local governments must evaluate all of their programs, services, activities, policies, and practices that may not be in compliance with the ADA. All written policies and operating practices should be reviewed and any discriminatory practices changed immediately. For example, a city day care policy requiring a child using a wheelchair to bring an attendant with him or her to the facility would be discriminatory and should be eliminated. Public licensing and certification programs are also covered and should be evaluated to assure that they do not impose discriminatory eligibility requirements. For example, a teacher certification program cannot require that applicants be able to hear, see, or walk.

If structural modifications will be required to achieve program access and the public entity has fifty or more employees, these changes must be addressed in a transition plan. The plan must identify all the physical changes that need to be made to governmental structures and set forth in detail a schedule of when and how these changes will be made. The deadline for these plans to be completed was July 26, 1992. The deadline for completing all structural modifications identified was January 26, 1995. Governmental entities with responsibility or authority over streets and sidewalks must include a schedule for providing curb ramps where pedestrian walks cross curbs. Individuals with disabilities and their representative organizations must be provided with an opportunity for comment.

When governmental entities make alterations or build new facilities they must build them according to designated accessibility guidelines. These guidelines contain the technical requirements for building ramps and installing accessible signage. Until the accessibility guidelines for Title II are issued, a public entity may choose to use the Uniform Federal Accessibility Standards or the ADA Accessibility Guidelines accompanying Title III of the ADA.

The employment practices of all governmental employers are subject to ADA requirements regardless of the number of persons a particular agency employs. In addition, all public entities with fifty or more employees must appoint an employee to be the ADA coordinator. This individual should have the ability and the authority to implement the regulations successfully. Her name, address, and phone number should be made available to the general public in a public notice or other appropriate means. Notice of the public entity's obligations under the ADA should be provided to employees, beneficiaries, and other interested parties on an ongoing basis. The notice can be provided in a variety of media and should be made available in alternative formats so that individuals with hearing and visual impairments can access it.

## Grievance Procedures

State and local governmental employers with fifty or more employees should also have grievance procedures in place so there is an available forum for resolution of ADA complaints. Grievance procedures already established may be used.

An individual who believes she has been discriminated against by a state or local governmental entity may not only use the internal grievance procedures, she may also file an administrative complaint or file suit in court. An administrative complaint should be filed with the appropriate federal agency within 180 days of the discriminatory act. If an individual can demonstrate good cause for not filing within the deadline then it may be extended. The administrative complaint should be filed with the entity's funding agency or with any of the eight agencies designated in the regulations to receive complaints. If it is an employment complaint it could be filed with the EEOC. Complaints filed with the wrong agency will be forwarded to the Department of Justice (DOJ) for proper referral. When in doubt, Title II complaints should be submitted to the DOJ.

A complaint is simply a written statement containing a detailed description of the incident, along with the complainant's name, address, and phone number. The appropriate agency will conduct an investigation. If an informal resolution is not successful, a Letter of Findings will be issued describing the outcome of the investigation. If the investigating agency finds discrimination, it will forward the Letter of Findings to the DOJ as it attempts to obtain voluntary compliance. If voluntary compliance fails, the DOJ may choose to file suit in federal district court. An individual may file suit in court at any time during this process on her own.

## Title III: Public Accommodations and Commercial Facilities

Many individuals take for granted their ability to easily access restaurants, hotels, movies, and doctor's offices. Many individuals with disabilities, however, have been denied the opportunity to visit these places with dignity because of the lack of a ramp or simply because the staff greeting the public treated individuals with disabilities in an inappropriate manner. Title III requires that places of public accommodation remove these barriers by installing ramps and modifying practices. In this context, it is important to remember that the most difficult, yet the least expensive barrier to remove is an attitudinal one. Successful implementation of the ADA requires that all of our societal myths and stereotypes about disability be addressed and eliminated.

A public accommodation is any private entity that

owns, leases (or leases to), or operates a place of public accommodation. Places of public accommodation are any facilities operated by a private entity that fall in any one of the following twelve categories:

1. ... an inn, hotel, motel, or other place of lodging (except for owner-occupied establishments renting fewer than six rooms);

2. ... a restaurant, bar, or other establishment serving food or drink;

3. ... a motion picture house, theater, concert hall, stadium, or other place of exhibition or entertainment;

4. ... an auditorium, convention center, lecture hall, union hall, or other place of public gathering;

5. ... a bakery, grocery store, clothing store, hardware store, shopping center, or the retail or wholesale sales or rental establishment;

6. ... a laundromat, dry-cleaner, bank, barber shop, beauty shop, travel service, shoe repair service, funeral parlor, gas station, office of an accountant or lawyer, pharmacy, insurance office, professional office of a health care provider, hospital, or other service establishment;

7. ... a terminal, depot, or station used for public transportation (other than air travel);

8. ... a museum, library, gallery, or other place of public display or collection;

9. ... a park, zoo, amusement park, or other place of recreation;

10. ... a nursery, elementary, secondary, undergraduate, or postgraduate private school, or other place of education;

11. ... a day care center, senior citizen center, homeless shelter, food bank, adoption agency, or other social service center establishment; and

12. ... a gymnasium, health spa, bowling alley, golf course, or other place of exercise or recreation. (These categories may be found at Title III Regulations 36.104 Definitions: Place of Public Accommodation 1–12, in ADA Handbook pages III-25 through 28.)

Title III also covers commercial facilities, which are basically places where employment occurs and are not public accommodations. An example of a commercial facility is a manufacturing plant. It is important to distinguish between public accommodations and commercial facilities because their owners have different obligations under Title III.

Since January 26, 1992, the ADA has required all public accommodations to remove barriers in existing facilities when it is readily achievable to do so. Both architectural and communication barriers that are structural in nature should be removed. Installing ramps, flashing alarm lights, rearranging display racks, and widening doors are examples of barrier removal steps. Title III only requires barrier removal in those areas open to the customers or clients of the establishment.

"Readily achievable" means "easily accomplishable and able to be carried out without much difficulty or expense." Measures that cannot be accomplished easily do not have to be carried out. Nevertheless, the obligation to remove barriers is an ongoing one: if an entity is unable at present to do any barrier removal, it must do so when it is able. The ADA suggests priorities for barrier removal in recognition that not all barriers can be addressed at once. A public accommodation should first take measures to assure access from public sidewalks, parking, and transportation. Addressed next should be access to the goods and services offered there. Access to rest rooms is the third priority. Finally, the public accommodation is to take steps to provide access to anything else offered there.

If a public accommodation cannot undertake appropriate readily achievable barrier removal measures then it must look at alternative methods to provide its services. Providing home delivery or offering curbside service are two of the methods suggested in the ADA's guidelines. These alternative ways of providing service must be offered if it is readily achievable to offer them. Whatever the means selected, the public accommodation must not pass on the costs of providing the alternative service to the individual with the disability.

Public accommodations also have to provide auxiliary aids and services to individuals with communication impairments. A business is obligated to provide the means for individuals with disabilities affecting their vision, hearing, or speech to communicate in an effective manner. The means of providing effective communication can include any number of things. In some instances, an interpreter may be required, in other cases communication can be effectively achieved through a note pad and paper. For those with visual impairments, brailled materials, taped texts, and qualified readers can be used to provide any "visual" materials that are offered. There is no requirement that the latest technology be used. What is required is that "effective communication" be achieved.

A public accommodation must provide auxiliary aids and services unless it can show that providing them would cause an undue burden, defined in the regulations as "significant difficulty or expense" or a fundamental alteration in the nature of the services offered. Any costs associated with providing these aids cannot be passed on to the individual with the disability. Thus, if a doctor provides an interpreter for a consultation to obtain informed consent for surgery from a woman who is deaf, the doctor may not incorporate the interpreter's cost into her doctor bill.

All the other nondiscrimination obligations apply to public accommodations. All the goods and services must be provided in an integrated setting. Eligibility criteria that screen out individuals with disabilities cannot be imposed unless it can be justified as necessary to the program. For example, day care centers cannot refuse to accept children who use wheelchairs by requiring all children to be able to walk to be eligible for admission into the day care. Public accommodations must also modify any practices, procedures, or policies that are discriminatory. For instance, restaurants must modify their "no animals" policies to allow service animals in their facilities for individuals with disabilities who need them.

Private entities offering licensing, certification, and testing for educational, professional, or trade purposes must also ensure that all of these activities are offered in a nondiscriminatory manner. Hence, testing should be offered at accessible locations and the examinations be administered in a way so that the ability of an individual with a disability is tested.

As with Title II of the ADA, Title III also anticipates an accessible future. Thus, the Act requires that all new construction of public accommodations and commercial facilities be built according to the ADA accessibility guidelines. These guidelines contain the technical requirements for building accessible facilities.

Title III complaints may be filed with the Department of Justice or an individual may proceed directly to court. Suit may be filed in federal, state, or local court. If an individual or organization files suit on their own, they are entitled to injunctive relief which means that the court may order the facility be made accessible. If the Attorney General joins the suit or brings suit then there is a possibility for fines and money damages. At this time it appears that the DOJ is only investigating cases where an issue of general importance is raised or where the discrimination alleged is part of a pattern and practice of discrimination.

### Transportation

An important aspect of ensuring individuals with disabilities full integration into society is providing equal access to transportation services. The ADA covers both private and public transportation services. Title II requires public transportation services to be accessible and Title III requires that those services provided by private providers be made accessible. The requirements for the services provided by each can be found in the Regulations published by the Department of Transportation on September 6, 1991 in 49 C.F.R Section 37.7.

### Title IV: Telecommunications

This Title of the ADA requires that all telecommunications services provide access to their services for individuals with communication impairments by July 26, 1993. Relay services provide this accessibility. This term is used in the statute and is commonly used by the systems in place that provide this service. These services enable individuals who cannot communicate by voice over the telephone to communicate through a relay operator. The operator, using a telecommunications device for the deaf, receives the communication from the hearing impaired person, then relays the message to the hearing person by voice. These services must be provided both instate and out of state at the same time and for the same price as the service offered to others. The statutory requirements for these services can be found at 42 USC, Section 225. This section also requires that all federally-funded public service announcements be closed-captioned for individuals with hearing impairments.

## Exemptions From the ADA

Private clubs are exempt from the ADA. Under Title III, however, if these clubs rent to a public accommodation such as a day care center, they become a public accommodation to the extent that they become a landlord to the day care center and assume the obligations of that relationship. Religious entities are also exempt from Title III but are covered by Title I with a caveat. They may require that an individual with a disability follow their religious tenets but they may not discriminate against the individual because of her disability.

## Conclusion

The ADA gives individuals with disabilities an important tool for them to use to access all that our society has to offer. It is an important civil rights statute and its mandate must be integrated into all societal activities. For it to be successfully implemented individuals with disabilities must educate themselves so they may fully understand its protections. An important part of successful implementation is the education of society about the ADA's mandate and disability in general. Enforcing one's rights under the Act is another important component in the process of implementation. Individuals with disabilities should no longer accept their status as second-class citizens.

### Bibliography

Americans with Disabilities Act, 43 USC, P.L. 101-336, 104 STAT.327,42 US 102.01 et seq.

Equal Employment Opportunity Commission and the U.S. Department of Justice. *Americans with Disabilities Act Handbook*. Washington, DC: U.S. Government Printing Office, 1991.

Fine M., and Asch A. eds. *Women with Disabilities: Essays in Psychology, Culture and Politics*. Philadelphia: Temple University Press, 1988.

Hillyer, Barbara. *Feminism and Disability*. Norman: University of Oklahoma Press, 1993.

Longdale, Susan. *Women and Disability: The Experience of Physical Disability Among Women*. Chicago: St. Martin's Press, 1990.

Rothstein, Laura. *Disability and the Law*. Colorado Springs: Shepard's/McGraw Hill, 1992.

Tucker, Bonnie P. *Federal Disability Law in a Nutshell*. St. Paul, MN: West Publishing, 1993.

### Organizational Resources

Specific organizations for each disability can also provide referrals and information. Check your local library for listings of organizations such as the Arthritis Foundation, National Hearing Association, National Association for the Physically Handicapped, National Center for Law and the Deaf, and so on.

The Center for Research on Women with Disabilities at Baylor College of Medicine
6910 Fannin, Suite 310 South
Houston, TX 77030
V (713) 797-6282
TDD (713) 797-0716
Fax (713) 797-6445
*The Center was founded in 1994 to conduct research on women with disabilities. A recent project of the center was an NIH-funded study that focused on psychosocial issues among women with physical disabilities.*

Independent Living Research Utilization (ILRU)
2323 South Shepherd, Suite 1000
Houston, TX 77019
*The ILRU program is a national center on information, training, and technical assistance in the field of disability and independent living. ILRU staff, a majority of whom are people with disabilities, serve, among others, independent living centers, consumer organizations, and educational institutions.*

Disability and Business Technical Assistance Centers
*There are ten federally funded centers located across the country, which provide materials, technical assistance, and training on the ADA. These centers have available for dissemination all the statutory, regulatory, and other materials produced with governmental funding. Some of the materials are available in Spanish. You may reach the center in your region by calling 1-800-949-4232.*

Center on Human Policy
724 Comstock Avenue
Syracuse University
Syracuse, NY 13244
(315) 443-3851

Disability Rights Center
2500 Q Street NW, Suite 121
Washington, DC 20007
(202) 337-4119

Disability Rights Education and Defense Fund (DREDF)
2212 Sixth Street
Berkeley, CA 94710
(415) 644-2555
*DREDF's Disabled Women's Education Project surveys the educational needs of disabled women and girls.*

Educational Equity Concepts
114 E. 32nd Street, Suite 306
New York, NY 10016
(212) 725-1803
*Conducts Women and Disability Awareness Project and maintains a computerized database, the National Clearinghouse on Women and Girls with Disabilities, that lists programs that provide services for women and girls with disabilities.*

Information Center for Individuals with Disabilities
Ft. Point Pl.
27-43 Wormwood Street
Boston, MA 02210
(617) 727-5540

National Association for Independent Living
878 Peachtree Street NE, Suite 18
Atlanta, GA 30309
(404) 894-5603

National Association of Protection and Advocacy Systems
2201 Eye Street NE, Suite 150
Washington, DC 20001
(202) 546-8202

**Wendy Wilkinson** is an attorney and coordinator of the Southwest Disability and Business Technical Assistance Center on the Americans With Disabilities Act (ADA). The Center, funded by a grant from the National Institute on Disability and Rehabilitation Research, provides information, assistance, and training on the ADA. It serves Texas, Louisiana, New Mexico, Arkansas, and Oklahoma. Ms. Wilkinson has experience in employment and personal injury law and is currently chairing the Texans with Disabilities Committee of the Texas Young Lawyers Association. Ms. Wilkinson is a graduate of the Florida State University School of Law, where she served on the Law Review.

**Laura Smith** is deputy project director for ILRU/Robert Wood Johnson Foundation program "Improving Service Systems for People with Disabilities." This national program develops and disseminates information and materials to the independent living, rehabilitation, and health care fields. She holds an M.S. in rehabilitation studies from North Texas State University, Denton.

Chapter 16

# The Woman as Employer (Or How to Hire a Nanny)

Sharon L. Reich

Chapter Outline

**Introduction**

**Are You an Employer?**
Examples • Hiring From Agencies • Hiring Family Members • References

**Federal Obligations of Employers**
Employer Identification Number • Verifying Employment Eligibility • Employee Social Security Number • Social Security and Medicare Taxes • Income Tax Withholding • Earned Income Credit • Federal Unemployment Tax • Year-End Recordkeeping

**State Obligations of Employers**

**Recordkeeping Tips**
Earnings Statements • Federal and State Tax Files • Expense Reimbursement File

**Special Information Regarding Aliens**

**Other Special Circumstances**

**Penalties for Noncompliance**

**General References**

Hiring domestic help is supposed to make life easier. But what about federal and state tax mandates and other recordkeeping requirements? Revelations in the media about the failure of some of President Clinton's nominees for various government posts to comply with laws regarding the hiring of domestic help have led to increased awareness of the laws and the potential sanctions for violating them. While violation of these laws may not cost the ordinary household employer a position as Attorney General, as it did Zoe Baird, laws regarding domestic workers are strict, and noncompliance may lead to substantial monetary penalties.

Fortunately, the laws are relatively straightforward, and compliance with them is not difficult once you have a good recordkeeping system in place. The purpose of this chapter is to outline the laws you should be aware of and the paperwork you need to maintain and file with the government. This should help minimize the time you need to spend in your role of "woman as employer."

## Introduction

The threshold question for anyone who uses domestic help is whether you are an employer or a customer. If you are an employer, you have paperwork and tax obligations as outlined in this chapter. If you are a customer, you do not have the same obligations. The difference hinges on whether your domestic help is an employee or an independent contractor. Independent contractors are considered self-employed and must take care of their own paperwork and taxes.

According to the Internal Revenue Service, whether a household worker qualifies as an employee or an independent contractor depends upon the degree of control the homeowner has a legal right to exercise over what must be done and how it must be done. The more control you exercise, the greater the likelihood that you qualify as an employer.

The IRS uses twenty factors to determine whether someone is an employee or an independent contractor, not all of which are applicable to the typical domestic worker situation. In general, if you provide the tools or supplies, if you control the compensation, if you control the hours worked, and if you control how the work must be done, the IRS will consider you an employer. If your domestic help comes into your home to perform a service, if they use their own tools, and if they determine when they will come and how much they must be paid, they can be considered independent contractors. The question boils down to whether you control not only *what* must be done, but also *how* it must be accomplished.

Specific factors that point to an independent contractor relationship include that the worker: negotiates dates and hours for the work;

## Are You an Employer?

is free to accept or decline particular assignments; works for a number of unrelated individuals at the same time; is paid on a per-job basis; is free to use assistants or to delegate the work to someone else; furnishes her own tools and supplies; makes her services available to the general public on a regular basis; is hired to produce a certain result (for example, a nicely groomed yard); and is free to determine the best way to achieve that result.

On the other hand, a worker is more likely to be considered an employee if the worker: must abide by work hours that you set; is required to complete all assignments of your choosing; maintains a continuing working relationship with you, even if the work is performed at irregular intervals; is paid on an hourly, weekly, or monthly basis; must personally render the services requested; uses tools and materials that you supply; and must follow your directions regarding how to accomplish a certain result.

No single factor is determinative, and it is not unusual to have some factors indicate an independent contractor relationship while others indicate an employer-employee relationship. As long as you have a good reason for treating a worker as an independent contractor, are consistent in treating the worker as an independent contractor, and file all required federal tax returns consistent with treating the worker as an independent contractor, the IRS must abide by your characterization of your work relationship. Once you treat the worker as an employee, however, you forfeit this protection. It is important, therefore, to determine your final, official view on whether your domestic worker is an employee or an independent contractor before you file any tax returns or other documents.

## Examples

Depending on individual circumstances, any of the following workers may be considered employees: babysitters, caretakers, cooks, drivers, gardeners, and housekeepers. This may be true regardless of whether the person works full time for you, and regardless of whether the person has reached the age of twenty-one. If you pay a nanny to care for your children and clean your house, and you have the right to tell her what needs to be done and how to do it, the nanny is your employee. At the other end of the spectrum, if you hire a lawn service that comes according to its own schedule and uses its own equipment, the service is performing as an independent contractor. A housekeeper may fall somewhere in the middle. If you pay someone to clean your house during a scheduled time and at a regular interval, using supplies and equipment that you provide, and pursuant to your instructions, the IRS considers that person to be an employee.

## Hiring From Agencies

If you hire a babysitter or other worker from an agency, that person is not your employee if the agency sets the fees and exercises control over the person, such as establishing rules of conduct and appearance. However, if you hire someone from an agency's list of individuals, and you pay the individual directly, that individual probably is your employee, even if you pay a fee to the agency.

## Hiring Family Members

Social security, Medicare, and federal unemployment taxes do not apply if you hire your spouse or your own child under the age of twenty-one to perform household services. If you hire your parents to perform such services, federal unemployment taxes do not apply, but social security and Medicare taxes do apply to wages you pay your parents if: (1) your parents care for your child, your child lives with you, and your child is under the age of eighteen or requires at least four continuous weeks of supervision due to a physical or mental condition; and (2) your parents care for your child because you do not have a spouse or because your spouse is unable to care for your child due to a physical or mental condition.

## References

The following IRS publications contain further explanations and examples of the IRS definition of "employer":

- IRS Publication 926, *Employment Taxes for Household Employers;*

- IRS Publication 15 (Circular E), *Employer's Tax Guide;* and

- IRS Publication 937, *Employment Taxes and Information Returns.*

If you want the IRS to determine whether your worker is an employee or an independent contractor, you may complete and file the following form:

- Form SS-8, Determination of Employee Work Status for Purposes of Federal Employment Taxes and Income Tax Withholding.

Filing this form is not, however, required. If you do have the IRS determine the status of your employee, you will be bound by that determination.

## Federal Obligations of Employers

If you are an employer of domestic help, your federal obligations are relatively straightforward:

1. You must verify your employee's eligibility to work, using an I-9 form from the Immigration and Naturalization Service.

2. You must pay social security and Medicare taxes on your employee's wages.

3. You must pay federal unemployment tax.

4. You must complete and maintain all appropriate paperwork.

### Employer Identification Number: Form SS-4

One of the first things you should do if you are going to hire a domestic employee is obtain an employer identification number, or EIN. The EIN is a nine-digit number the IRS uses to identify tax accounts of employers, just as the IRS uses social security numbers to identify individual taxpayers. You will use your EIN on all tax forms you send to the IRS and the Social Security Administration.

You may request an EIN by filing Form SS-4, *Application for Employer Identification Number.* The form is available from the IRS or the Social Security Administration. You may also obtain an EIN by telephone. Simply call the Tele-TIN telephone number for your state (the numbers are listed on Form SS-4) and an agent will assign you a number immediately. Alternatively, if your first tax form is due and you do not yet have an EIN, write "none" or "applied for" along with the date of your application in the space on the tax form that requests your Employer Identification Number, and the IRS will assign one to you automatically.

### Verifying Employment Eligibility: Form I-9

Once you decide to hire a particular individual, the first thing you must do is verify the person's eligibility to work in the United States. It is against the law to employ an illegal alien or someone who is in the United States on a visitor's visa. If you do, you are subject to fines of $250 to $2,000 for a first offense, plus additional amounts for poor recordkeeping. Ignorance of your employee's status is no excuse. Rather, the law requires you, as an employer, to verify the identity and employment eligibility of anyone you hire, even if you are certain that the employee is a U.S. citizen. The vehicle you must use is Form I-9.

Form I-9 is an Employment Eligibility Verification form that you may obtain from the Immigration and Naturalization Service. It is a single page, the first half of which the employee completes, the second half of which the employer completes. The instructions are contained on the face of the form, and require you, as employer, to certify that you have examined certain documents that establish your employee's identity and employment eligibility. You do not need to file Form I-9 with the government, but you must keep it in your records and be prepared to present it on demand.

Employees who cannot provide the certification required by the I-9 within three days must show that they have applied for appropriate documentation. If they cannot provide that documentation within ninety days, they must be fired in order for you to be in compliance with the immigration laws.

## Employee Social Security Number: Form SS-5

You should also be sure to get your employee's social security number and the spelling of the employee's name exactly as it appears on the social security card. You will need this information when you file certain tax documents, described later in this chapter. If your employee does not have a social security number, she should apply for one by completing Form SS-5, *Application for a Social Security Card.* You can get this form at a local Social Security Administration office or by calling 1-800-772-1213.

## Social Security and Medicare Taxes: Form 1040, Schedule H

You must pay social security and Medicare taxes on behalf of each employee to whom you pay wages of at least a certain threshold amount during the course of a year. Congress increased the threshold amount at the end of 1994 from $50 per quarter to $1,000 per year for household employees. If you meet the threshold, the following rules apply:

1. Social security and Medicare taxes apply only to cash wages paid. The value of in-kind benefits such as food and lodging is not subject to social security or Medicare tax.

2. You will find the current tax rates in IRS Publication 926, *Employment Taxes for Household Employers,* or in the Instructions for Schedule H of Form 1040. In 1994, the social security tax rate was 12.4 percent and the Medicare tax rate was 2.9 percent. Half of each tax due is chargeable to the employee. The employer must contribute the other half.

3. You must withhold the employee's portion of the social security and Medicare taxes from each paycheck. In 1994 that would have been 6.2 percent for social security taxes and 1.45 percent for

Medicare taxes. If you do not withhold these taxes from your employee's wages you must pay the total amount due out of your own pocket.

4. Some people decide voluntarily to pay the employee's share of these taxes without deducting them from the employee's wages. This is permissible, but then the amount of the taxes that you pay on your employee's behalf without deduction is counted as additional income to the employee for income tax purposes even though the employee does not receive any additional cash. For example, if you pay an employee $10,000 per year, the employee's share of social security and Medicare taxes totals $765 for the year. If you decide to pay that $765 on the employee's behalf without deducting it from her wages, the employee's total compensation for the year for income tax purposes is considered to be $10,765. Although the extra $765 is subject to federal income tax, it is not subject to additional social security or Medicare taxes.

5. You are responsible as the employer for depositing the entire social security and Medicare tax payment with the government. This is why you must withhold your employee's share from each paycheck if you expect the employee to contribute.

6. You must complete and file Schedule H with your IRS Form 1040 on an annual basis. You use this schedule to report your employee's gross wages for the year, the amount of social security and Medicare taxes you withheld from your employee's paychecks, and the total social security and Medicare taxes due to the government, including both the employee's share and your share as employer. To calculate wages for the year, include wages actually paid during the year. If you have a pay period that starts in one year and ends in the next, the wages for that pay period are counted during the year in which the wages were paid to the employee.

7. You should adjust your own income tax withholding to cover payment of your employee's year-end social security and Medicare taxes. Before 1995, household employers were required to report and pay social security and Medicare taxes on a quarterly basis using Form 942. In an effort to ease the paperwork requirements for such employers, Congress changed the law in October of 1994 to allow household employers to forego quarterly reporting and quarterly payments. However, because you will be paying your employer taxes on an annual basis with your Form 1040, you should consider increasing your federal income tax withholding from

your own paycheck or, if you make estimated tax payments, considering increasing the amount of those payments. Failure to do this may result in an unusually large balance due when you file your Form 1040, and may even result in estimated tax penalties for underpayment of estimated tax throughout the year. There is a grace period for underpayment of estimated tax if such underpayment is due to employment taxes reported on Form 1040 through 1997, but such penalties will begin to be levied in 1998. Use Form W-4 to increase your federal income tax withholding or Form 1040-ES to increase your estimated tax payments. Publication 505, *Tax Withholding and Estimated Tax,* contains additional information on how to do this.

8. School-age babysitters are exempt. Congress not only changed the reporting requirements beginning with the 1995 tax year, but also created a special exemption from the social security and Medicare tax requirements for household employees under the age of eighteen, unless household work is the employee's primary occupation. Household work does not constitute the employee's primary occupation if he or she is also a student. Thus, wages paid to a student under the age of eighteen are not subject to social security or Medicare taxes even if those wages total more than $1,000 for the year.

## Income Tax Withholding: W-4 and Form 1040, Schedule H

You are not required to withhold federal income tax from your employee's wages, but you may do so if your employee asks you to withhold, and you agree to do the necessary calculations and paperwork. You report and pay any income tax you withhold using the same Form 1040 schedule you must file for social security and Medicare tax purposes. Because of this, withholding federal income tax is not difficult, but you must follow several rules.

1. You must withhold the proper amount. The amount of withholding is based on your employee's number of withholding allowances and total compensation. Once you know the number of allowances and the total compensation, you use a grid contained in Publication 15 (Circular E), *Employer's Tax Guide* to determine the amount of money to withhold from each paycheck.

- To determine the number of allowances, have your employee complete a W-4 form, the *Employee's Withholding Allowance Certificate.* The number of allowances depends on whether your employee is married or single and whether she has any dependents. Once your employee completes this form, be sure to keep it in your files.

- Your employee's compensation for income tax withholding purposes may be different than your employee's compensation for social security and Medicare tax withholding. Income for social security and Medicare tax purposes includes cash compensation only. For federal income tax withholding purposes, income equals cash *and* noncash compensation, including salary, bonuses, meals (unless provided in your home and for your convenience), and lodging (unless provided in your home, for your convenience, and as a condition of employment). Generally, meals and lodging provided to live-in domestic help do not count as compensation for federal income tax withholding purposes.

2. If you withhold federal income tax for your employee, you must report the amount withheld on Schedule H of your annual Form 1040, which is the same schedule you must file for social security and Medicare tax withholding. You must then add to your annual tax bill the amount of income tax you withheld from your employee's paychecks.

### Earned Income Credit: Form W-5 and Form 1040, Schedule H

The earned income credit is a federal program to aid the working poor by paying back to them each pay period a portion of the social security, Medicare, and federal income tax you would otherwise withhold and pay to the IRS. If your employee supports a dependent child and earns less than a specified amount of income per year (the figure for employees with one child was $24,396 in 1994), then the employee may be eligible to claim an earned income credit.

As the employer, you are obligated to notify an employee that he or she may qualify for the credit if: (1) the employee does not have any federal income tax withheld; and (2) the employee does not claim to be exempt from federal income tax on Form W-4, the *Withholding Allowance Certificate*. You can meet this obligation by providing the employee with a copy of Notice 797, *Notice of a Possible Federal Tax Refund Due to the Earned Income Credit (EIC)*, or with a copy of the W-2 form, which explains the earned income credit on the back of Copy C. This notice requirement is an annual obligation. You should provide the first notice upon hire, and subsequent notices by February 7 of each year. If you provide your employee with a Form W-2 on a timely basis each year, this fulfills your notice requirement, unless you use a substitute W-2 that does not contain the required earned income statement on the back of the employee's Copy C. If you would like further information about this notice requirement, you should consult Publication 15 (Circular E), *Employer's Tax Guide,* or Notice 1015, *Employers—Have You Told Your Employees About the Earned Income Credit (EIC)?*

If your employee claims eligibility for the EIC and wants to take advantage of the program, the employee must present you with a Form W-5, *Earned Income Credit Advance Payment Certificate.* The employee must complete a new Form W-5 each year to verify his or her continuing eligibility. Once an employee does this, you are required to make earned income credit payments each payday. You may calculate the amount due using tables contained in Publication 15 (Circular E), *Employer's Tax Guide.* You report the total earned income credit payments for each year on Schedule H of your Form 1040. Earned income credit payments do not "cost" you anything; rather, you will deduct the EIC payments you make to your employee from the total social security, Medicare, and income tax withholding payments that otherwise would be due to the IRS, as calculated on Schedule H of your Form 1040.

## Federal Unemployment Tax: Form 1040, Schedule H

Federal unemployment tax paid under the Federal Unemployment Tax Act (FUTA) funds your employee's unemployment insurance. Most states also levy a state unemployment tax. You may take a credit against your federal tax for unemployment tax paid to the state, but your state tax will not exempt you from the federal tax. Following are guidelines that outline your FUTA responsibilities:

1. You are subject to FUTA tax if you paid cash wages of $1,000 or more to your household employees in any calendar quarter during the current or preceding year. Paying less than $1,000 in wages during any particular calendar quarter does not exempt you from FUTA taxes for that quarter. Rather, the tax still applies so long as you paid $1,000 in cash wages during any other quarter of the current or past year.

2. The FUTA tax does not apply to wages you pay to your spouse, your parents, or your children under the age of twenty-one.

3. The FUTA tax is imposed solely on the employer. That means you are not permitted to deduct it from your employee's wages, or otherwise charge the tax to your employee.

4. The FUTA tax rate in 1994 was 6.2 percent of the first $7,000 of cash wages paid to each employee during the calendar year. You

may get a credit, however, for your state unemployment taxes. With that credit, your federal rate can drop to 0.8 percent if you pay your state tax on time.

5. As with your social security and Medicare taxes, you must report your FUTA taxes once a year using Form 1040.

### Year-End Recordkeeping: W-2 and W-3

The W-2 is a Wage and Tax Statement that shows each employee's total compensation for the year and the taxes withheld. You must prepare a W-2 for each employee to whom you paid wages subject to social security and Medicare taxes. Even if your employee did not meet the $1,000 income threshold for social security and Medicare taxes, you must still file a Form W-2 if you either withheld income tax for the employee, or you paid advancements of the earned income credit to the employee. The W-3, *Transmittal of Income and Tax Statements,* aggregates the total wages and withholding for all of your employees. The W-3 applies only if you employed more than one person during the year.

The completed Form W-2 is due to the employee by January 31 of the year following the calendar year recorded on the W-2. If you had an employee who stopped working for you before the end of the year, you may give him or her a final W-2 any time between the end of the employment and the following January 31, unless the employee asks you to complete the form earlier. In that case, you must provide the W-2 within thirty days of the request or of the last wage payment, whichever is later.

In addition to giving the W-2 to your employee, you must also file Copy A of the form with the Social Security Administration by the last day of February. Do not file the form with the IRS; the Social Security Administration will forward it for you. You should also file the W-3 with the Social Security Administration by the last day of February, but only if you had more than one household employee. If you had a single household employee for the entire year, do not file the W-3.

## State Obligations of Employers

Your state tax and other obligations can vary quite dramatically, depending on where you live. It is, therefore, a good idea to contact your state tax office and your state employment office for information regarding your state obligations as soon as you decide you want to employ domestic help. For example, most states require the payment of unemployment tax. Some states also require employers of domestic help to pay into disability insurance programs and/or workers' compensation programs. You may want to check with the insurance agent who handles your homeowner's policy for information on the workers' compensation requirements in your state and also to explain what your homeowner's policy may or may not cover with respect to domestic employees. Finally, although federal law recently changed to require only annual reporting and payment of household employment taxes, your state may still require quarterly reports and tax deposits.

Compliance with federal and state tax and employment rules and completion of the required reporting forms is much easier if you keep good records throughout the year. As a general rule, you should retain your employment records for a period of four years. Also, check with your state tax and employment offices to see if there are any special state recordkeeping rules.

**Recordkeeping Tips**

### Earnings Statements

Although not required under federal law, it is helpful for you and your employee if you provide an earnings statement with each paycheck. The statement should provide the following information: the work days the pay period covered; the date you gave the paycheck to your employee; gross wages for the pay period; the amount of social security tax withheld; the amount of Medicare tax withheld; the amount of federal income tax withheld, if any; state income tax withheld, if any; and the net amount paid to the employee. A sample of a simple earnings statement is contained in Figure 2. You may also want to indicate on the statement the number of vacation or sick days covered by the pay period, and whether that time was paid or unpaid.

Provide a copy of each earnings statement to your employee, and keep a copy for yourself in an earnings statements file. Start a new file for each calendar year. The earnings statements are very helpful for completing your state and federal tax reporting forms.

### Federal and State Tax Files

In addition to earnings statements, it is helpful to keep a separate file for each type of federal and state tax form you file during the year, along with some general information files. Remember, you must keep records on employment taxes for at least four years after the due date of the return or after you pay the tax, whichever is later. One way to organize your tax information files is as follows:

- *EIN file,* containing your employer identification number and a copy of your Form SS-4.

- *Employee identification file* for each employee, containing the Form I-9, Form W-4, your employee's social security number or Form SS-5, your employee's name as it appears on the employee's social security card, your employee's current address, the beginning date of employment, and, if applicable, the ending date of employment.

- *Form 1040, Schedule H file,* with copies of your Schedule H for each calendar year.

- *A year-end file,* containing the W-2 and, if applicable, the W-3.

- *General federal information file,* containing useful federal publications for easy reference, such as Publication 926, *Employment Taxes for Household Employers* and Publication 15 (Circular E), Employer's Tax Guide.

- *State files.* Keep comparable files for your state tax and employment forms.

Regardless of how you decide to organize your records, the IRS directs that you keep the following information: your employer identification number; copies of tax returns and year-end statements you file (Schedule H of your Form 1040, Form W-2, and Form W-3); dates and amounts of any tax deposits or payments you make; each employee's name, address, and social security number; each employee's dates of employment; copies of each employee's *Withholding Allowance Certificate* (Form W-4); copies of each employee's *Earned Income Credit Advance Payment Certificate* (Form W-5), if applicable; dates and amounts of cash and noncash wage payments made to each employee; and dates and amounts of social security and Medicare taxes collected from each employee.

### Expense Reimbursement File

If your household employee incurs expenses on your behalf for which you reimburse your employee, it is a good idea to keep an expense reimbursement file with receipts to document that these reimbursements are for household expenses and are not an additional form of compensation. For example, if you have a nanny purchase groceries for you and your family, it is best to reimburse her with a separate check, rather than adding the cost of the groceries to her regular salary check. Then, write the date you reimbursed her on the receipt, and place the receipt in an expense reimbursement file.

## Special Information Regarding Aliens

As explained earlier, you must verify an alien's employment eligibility by using a Form I-9 from the Immigration and Naturalization Service. Generally speaking, you may lawfully employ an alien who is a permanent resident of the United States. In addition, you may hire a foreign au pair who has J-1 nonimmigrant status through one of several agencies that operate special exchange programs, but the au pair's employment is limited to one year. Domestic workers may also enter the country in an H-2B nonimmigrant status to fill a temporary need for one year if U.S. workers are unavailable. The H-2B status is extendable annually up to a maximum of three years.

If the alien you wish to hire does not have any of the documentation required by the Form I-9, you generally cannot legally hire that person, but you may want to see an immigration lawyer about applying for legal status for your prospective employee, or to see whether other special circumstances may exist that would allow you to legally hire the person. In the meantime, keep in mind that you are liable for social security and Medicare taxes even if your worker is here illegally. If the worker is not authorized to work in the United States then he or she probably will not have a social security number, so write "SSA 205(c)" in the spaces on federal forms where a social security number is requested. "SSA 205(c)" means the worker is not allowed to have a social security number.

If you were unaware of the immigration laws and have already hired someone who is a citizen of another country, your legal obligations depend on the date of hire. If you hired the person before November 6, 1986, you need not worry about it because at that point in time you had no obligation to check the legality of your employee's work status. If you hired the person after that date, you may, again, want to speak with an immigration attorney for help. To prevent a continuing recordkeeping violation, fill out the I-9 even though the employee has already been working for you. If the employee cannot produce the required documentation you cannot legally continue to employ him or her.

The penalties for failing to comply with the immigration laws include a $250 to $2,000 fine for the first hiring offense, and an additional $100 to $1,000 for failing to complete an I-9. The potential fines increase with each offense, up to a maximum of $10,000 per unauthorized worker. Under certain circumstances, criminal penalties may be invoked, including up to six months in jail.

## Other Special Circumstances

There may be other special circumstances or regulations that you can take advantage of as an employer. For example, you may be able to reimburse your employee for certain health insurance benefits without including the reimbursed amount in the employee's gross income for federal tax purposes. This presents certain financial advantages for both you and your employee. You may want to call the IRS for information on how to do this, or speak with an accountant or tax attorney for further information on this or other regulations that may present similar financial benefits.

## Penalties for Noncompliance

The IRS estimates that only 25 percent of the roughly 2 million households that employ domestic workers comply with the federal tax laws. Although the IRS has not specifically targeted its enforcement efforts against household employers in the past, household employers who violate the tax laws may be identified through random audits or when a worker applies for social security or unemployment compensation and the government finds no record of the appropriate taxes having been paid. If that happens, violators are subject to back taxes, interest, penalties, and payment of the employee's portion of the taxes owed.

In addition to the monetary cost to the employer for failure to comply with the tax laws, there may be a substantial cost to your employee. If you do not pay social security taxes, for example, your employee may not be able to collect social security benefits for which she otherwise would be eligible, or may be able to collect only a reduced amount. Despite the potential long-term harm to the employee, there may be instances when an employee asks you to ignore the federal tax requirements as a means of obtaining more cash up front. As the employer, however, you are liable for these taxes regardless of an employee's request for an exemption.

What happens if you discover after-the-fact that you should have paid taxes in the past? The IRS encourages those who discover past errors to come forward voluntarily. For those who do, the IRS may help you file your overdue returns, and may, where necessary, work out a payment plan. The IRS also says that those who come forward voluntarily to rectify honest mistakes made in the past need not fear criminal prosecution; only those who willfully keep failing to file will be subject to criminal charges. If you have some question about whether you are in compliance with the laws, you may want to discuss your concerns or questions with an attorney or accountant.

## General References

The IRS has a number of references available to assist household employers. The references are described in Figure 3. You can order any of these free publications as well as all required federal forms and instructions by calling the IRS toll-free at 1-800-TAX-FORM.

The IRS also provides individualized assistance. If you have questions about any of your federal tax obligations you may call 1-800-829-1040, or call or visit your local IRS office. Remember also to check with your state tax and employment offices for information regarding state and local laws. Once you get your system in place, hiring domestic help should still be a time-saver.

## Bibliography

"Avoid Nannygate!" from The Earnst & Young Tax Guide 1993: What to Do If You Employ Domestic Help. *Business Wire* (February 10, 1993): chapter 37. Available in LEXIS, Nexis Library, BWIRE File.

"Don't Forget to Withhold Taxes on Household Employees." *Business Wire* (April 6, 1993). Available in LEXIS, Nexis Library, BWIRE File.

"Employ Household Help? Here Are Some Rules on Taxes, Hiring." *Atlanta Journal and Constitution* (February 9, 1993): A7.

"Hiring Household Help—Who's the Boss?" *PR Newswire* (July 26, 1993). Available in LEXIS, Nexis Library, WIRES File.

"Key Questions and Answers About Household Employees." *Gannett News Service* (February 8, 1993). Available in LEXIS, Nexis Library, WIRES File.

"Line One." *Dallas Morning News* (April 1, 1993): 8C.

"Taxpayer Needs to Target SOS On Long-Overdue Refund." *Courier-Journal* (Louisville) (December 29, 1992): 3E.

Buck, Richard. "Many Now More Aware of Tax Laws on Hiring Help." *Seattle Times* (January 30, 1993): B8.

Caron, Paul L. "Nannygate and Dragons of the IRS." 59 *Tax Notes* (1993): 1849.

Crenshaw, Albert B. "To Ensure Domestic Tranquillity; Hiring Within Tax, Immigration Laws." *Washington Post* (January 24, 1993): H1.

Cushman, John H. Jr. "Taxes on Household Employment." *New York Times* (January 28, 1993): C6.

Durenberger, Dave. "Nannies and Taxes: A Solution." *The Washington Post* (May 21, 1993): A24.

I.R.S. Publication 15 (Circular E), *Employer's Tax Guide* (Rev. Jan. 1995).

I.R.S. Publication 926, *Employment Taxes for Household Employers* (Rev. Dec. 1994).

Immigration Reform & Control Act, Pub. L. No. 99-603, 100 Stat. 3359 (1986).

Internal Revenue Code, 26 U.S.C. § 1, et seq.

King, Ronette. "Household Help a Taxing Business." *Times-Picayune* (New Orleans) (February 10, 1993): A1.

Kistner, William G. "Payroll Tax Requirement for Child Care Providers." *Healthcare Financial Management* (April 1993): 99.

Kreiter, Marcella S. "The Nanny Tax." *UPI* (March 8, 1993). Available in LEXIS, Nexis Library, UPI File.

*MacNeil/Lehrer News Hour,* February 9, 1993. Transcript #4560. Available in LEXIS, Nexis Library, MACLEH File.

Mailman, Stanley. "The Zoe Baird Questions: Answers to Immigration Law Concerns." *New York Library Journal* (February 1, 1993): Outside Counsel 1.

McCormally, Kevin. "Uncle Sam Wants to Know What You Pay Household Help." *San Diego Union-Tribune* (February 17, 1992): E4.

Pratt, Katie. "In the Wake of Nannygate." *St. Louis Post-Dispatch* (March 18, 1993): 3C.

Rev. Rul. 87-41, 1987-1 C.B. 296.

Shanahan, Eileen. "IRS: 1 in 4 Have Taxing Problem." *St. Petersburg Times* (February 9, 1993): 1A.

Sommers, Robert L. "Nannygate Reconsidered: Do You Really Owe Taxes on Your Baby-Sitter?" 60 *Tax Notes* (1993): 359.

Stoeltje, Melissa Fletcher. "Am I Breaking the Law?" *Houston Chronicle* (February 10, 1993): Houston 1.

Stoll, Martin A. "Homegate: Social Security Tax Issue." *New York Library Journal* (March 2, 1993): Outside Counsel 1.

Treas. Reg. § 31.3506-1.

Weaver, Peter. "Tax Forms and Insurance for Household Employees." *Nation's Business* (January 1991): 65.

Yip, Pamela. "Illegal Hiring Causes Headaches From A to Zoe." *Houston Chronicle* (January 25, 1993): Business 1.

Zeidner, Rita L. "W&M 'Nanny Tax' Provision Answers Some Questions, Raises Others." 59 *Tax Notes* (1993): 1011

[12 Income Taxes] U.S. Tax Rep. ¶¶ 34,009.01, 35,064 (1993).

## Federal Forms and Due Dates[1]

SS-4 *Application for Employer Identification Number*

No specific due date. Complete one time, when you become a household employer.

SS-5 *Application for a Social Security Card*

No specific due date. Have employee complete the form upon hire if the employee does not have a social security card.

I-9 *Employment Eligibility Verification*

Does not need to be filed with the government but you are required to complete the form upon hire and retain it in your records.

Schedule H, Form 1040

April 15 following the calendar year for which your household employment taxes are due.

W-2 *Wage and Tax Statement*

January 31 to employee; last day of February to Social Security Administration.

W-3 *Transmittal of Income and Tax Statements*

Last day of February, along with W-2s. File this only if you had more than one employee for whom you filed a W-2.

W-4 *Employer's Withholding Allowance Certificate*

Employee should complete upon hire if you agree to withhold federal income tax.

W-5 *Earned Income Credit Advance Payment Certificate*

Notify employee of EIC program upon hire and each year thereafter by February 7. Use Notice 797 or the back of Copy C of a W-2 form. Employee responsible for filing W-5 with you, if applicable.

[1] If a due date falls on a Saturday, Sunday, or official federal holiday, the due date becomes the next business day.

*Figure 1*

**Sample Earnings Statement**

Statement Of Earnings And Deductions

Employee Name _____

Employee Social Security Number _____

Date: _____

Pay Period Covered:_____

**Gross pay:** _____

Deductions:

           Social Security Tax:   _____

               Medicare Tax:   _____

        Federal Income Tax:   _____

          State Income Tax:   _____

**Total Deductions:**   _____

Advance payment of Earned
Income Credit, if applicable:   _____

**Net Earnings:**[2]   _____

[2] Net earnings = gross pay *minus* total deductions *plus* advance payment of EIC.

*Figure 2*

## General References

| | |
|---|---|
| IRS Publication 926, *Employment Taxes for Household Employers* | Anyone who hires household help should get a copy of this free pamphlet, which is published by the IRS specifically for people who employ domestic help. |
| IRS Publication 15 (Circular E), *Employer's Tax Guide* | This is another useful publication that goes into a bit more detail than Publication 926. If you withhold federal income tax for your employee, or if your employee claims the earned income credit, you will need to refer to certain tables contained in Publication 15 that are not in Publication 926. |
| IRS Publication 937, *Employment Taxes and Information Returns* | This is intended primarily for small businesses, but it contains explanations of issues relevant to household employers such as the difference between independent contractors and employees. |
| IRS Publication 505, *Tax Withholding and Estimated Tax* | This publication contains information on how to adjust the federal tax withholding from your own paycheck or the estimated tax payments you otherwise make to cover the additional employment taxes you must pay on account of your household employee. |
| 1-800-TAX-FORM | Toll free number for ordering IRS publications and federal tax forms. |
| 1-800-TAX-1040 | Toll free number to call if you have questions about any of your federal tax obligations. |

*Figure 3*

**Sharon L. Reich** is Associate Dean for Administration and Director of Legal Writing and Trial Practice at the University of Minnesota Law School. She also serves as Special Counsel to the law firm of Faegre & Benson in the business litigation group. Ms. Reich graduated *summa cum laude* from Yale University with honors in economics. She received her J. D. from Stanford Law School, where she was a note editor for the *Stanford Law Review.* Following law school, Ms. Reich served as a clerk to the Honorable Harlington Wood, Jr., on the Seventh Circuit Court of Appeals in Chicago. She subsequently received an appointment as a Trial Attorney at the U.S. Department of Justice in Washington, D.C. and later moved to Minneapolis to work with the Faegre & Benson law firm. Ms. Reich was appointed by the Minnesota Supreme Court to a seat on the Lawyers Professional Responsibility Board in February 1995, and is an active member of the American Bar Association, as well as the Minnesota State Bar Association, Minnesota Women Lawyers, and a number of law school and university-wide governance and advisory committees. She and her husband have a young daughter and currently employ household help.

Chapter 17

# *Starting a Business*

Kathleen S. Tillotson

## Chapter Outline

The purpose of this chapter is to acquaint you with the practical legal aspects of starting a business. Before engaging in any significant business venture, you should consult a lawyer and an accountant. The information provided here merely supplements that advice and assistance.

Introduction

## Communicating and Protecting Your Business Idea

All business begins with an idea. "I want to set up a conference center with outdoor facilities." "I'd like to produce a catalog for the consignment resale of computer equipment." "I'm going to open a deli by the park." To start your business organize your idea in the form of a business plan. Doing this in writing is helpful, indeed necessary if you require financing from others. A business plan describes the company, product or service lines, legal structure, management and compensation, marketing analysis and strategy, operating plan, and financing sources and uses. If you have never written a business plan, borrow a how-to book from the public library. Once you know what a business plan is, go back to the library. The reference librarians there can assist you in finding much of the information needed for your business plan, such as information on your suppliers, your competition, and your market.

If the proprietary value of your business idea is itself an idea or knowledge, such as a software program or a chemical formula, you must commit that to writing as well. In fact, you should do this *before* you prepare a business plan.

No matter what your idea, its economic value to you rests in your ownership of it. Therefore, your first legal need is to protect the new idea, so that only you may capitalize on it. To protect ideas you may use intellectual property law or contract law or both. The law of patent, trademark or service mark, and copyright, collectively referred to as "intellectual property law," is discussed extensively in chapter 18.

Trade secrets, however, are not registered or patented. A trade secret is any valuable pattern, formula, device, or process not generally known to others. A trade secret loses its status if it can be revealed by inspection and analysis of the product. As long as a trade secret is kept secret, the courts will protect the owner's proprietary right to the information. Thus the keys to protecting trade secrets are safeguards like confidentiality agreements with employees and proprietary business workbooks.

As part of a plan to protect trade secrets, or as a direct way to protect ideas, a nondisclosure or confidentiality contract is useful prior to revealing information to a third party. Before you give your business plan to a prospective employee, partner, lender, or investor, ask that person to agree that she not divulge your ideas to any other person or use them for any purpose other than the immediate use contemplated by you. A lawyer can prepare a comprehensive nondisclosure or confidentiality agreement for you. In many cases, however, the following letter will suffice:

Dear [Prospective Business Associate]:

[Name of your business] has sole rights to certain confidential ideas and information relative to _____ hereinafter referred to as "Confidential Information." We wish to interest you in this Confidential Information. To generate such interest, we are willing to disclose in writing the Confidential Information to you under the following conditions:

1. You agree to hold in confidence all Confidential Information for a period of three years from the date hereof except:

    a. Confidential Information that, at the time of disclosure, is in the public domain or that, after disclosure, becomes part of the public domain by publication or otherwise; or

    b. Confidential Information that you can show is in your possession at the time of disclosure and was not acquired, directly or indirectly, from us; or

    c. Confidential Information that was received by you from a third party having the legal right to transmit it.

2. You agree that you will not, without our written permission, use or exploit, directly or indirectly, for a period of three years from the date hereof the Confidential Information for any reason other than to [describe contemplated use of the information].

Yours sincerely,

[Name of your business]


By:_____

Title:_____

Agreed:_____


_____
[Prospective Business Associate]

A concluding note on proprietary business information: you may possess it, but it may not be yours. Many new companies are started essentially as spin-offs of other companies. You believe that what you have learned on the job is yours, that it belongs to you because you worked on it. But if your employer or other source has taken steps to protect the information, and the information was developed specifically by and for that source, you may be prevented from using it for your own financial gain. Likewise, if your new business relates to your current business, make sure that you are not bound by a noncompetition agreement in favor of your employer. If you are a corporate officer or director of your current employer, a legal doctrine called "corporate opportunity" may also prevent you from exploiting for yourself a business opportunity that should be made available to your current firm. If necessary, talk to your employer or other information source about your plans; a compromise usually can be worked out.

## Organizing and Naming Your Business Enterprise

Once your business plan is drafted and your ideas are protected, consider how you will operate. Business organization is largely governed by state law, mainly by the laws of the state in which your headquarters are located. If the business will also operate in other states, a certificate of authority from that "foreign" state may be required. Care should be taken, however, not to subject your business unnecessarily to taxation by other states.

### Sole Proprietorship

Of the five basic forms of business organization, the sole proprietorship is the most common, least expensive, and simplest. The business is owned and controlled by one person—you. You alone receive the profits and are responsible for the debts of the business. You report the income and expenses of the business on your own income tax return. Profits are taxed at your personal income tax rate. There are no legal requirements unique to this form of organization. However, you must pay both the employer's and employees' share of social security tax.

### General Partnership

The second basic form of business organization is a general partnership, which is a commercial affiliation of two or more persons. Whether or not there is a partnership agreement, a general partnership has specific attributes. Partners share equally in the right to manage partnership affairs, and each partner is individually responsible for all of the obligations of the partnership. A written agreement is recommended to address issues like the purpose and powers of the partnership, capital contributions, managing the enterprise, division of profits and losses, distributions to owners, books and records, termination of the partnership, and division of the assets upon termination. A general partnership itself does not pay tax. You pay tax on your share of the partnership's profits at your personal income tax rate. A general partnership should, however, prepare and file an information tax return to report the income and expenses of the partnership.

A type of general partnership is a joint venture. A joint venture is a business owned by two or more persons who associate to carry on a specific enterprise, not an unlimited array of activities. Although a joint venture will be governed by the general partnership laws of a state, a contract between the joint venturers should be prepared to address the same issues that confront general partners.

### Limited Partnership

A third form of business organization is the limited partnership. A limited partnership has two types of partners, general partners and limited partners. A general partner controls the limited partnership and is individually responsible for the debts of the business. A limited partner shares in the partnership's liability only up to the amount of her individual investment in the partnership and, in exchange for limited liability, gives up her right to participate in the management of the business. A limited partnership must meet specific statutory requirements and, like a corporation, is subject to significant tax and securities laws.

### Corporation ("C" or "S")

A corporation is a separate legal person and, if properly formed and properly operated, is the entity that is liable for the debts of the business. However, if you guaranty any corporate loans, you will be personally liable under your guaranty. The corporation is owned by one or more shareholders. The shareholders elect a board of directors that has responsibility for management and control of the corporation. A corporation is a formal and complex form of organization. Failure to follow statutory requirements can result in loss of corporate status and imposition of personal liability on the shareholders.

A closely held corporation is a corporation whose shares are held by a small number of persons, generally fewer than thirty-five. Most small businesses will be closely held. In a closely held corporation, often all of the shareholders are also the directors and officers of the corporation. Many states make special provisions for closely held corporations, affirming the duty of all shareholders in a closely held corporation to act in an honest, fair, and reasonable manner in the operation of the corporation. A closely held corporation can be an advantageous form of organization because it provides limited liability for shareholders and S corporation status for tax purposes, while retaining many of the operating aspects of sole proprietorships and partnerships.

The corporation is a separate taxable entity. It may be taxed under chapter C of the Internal Revenue Code, a "C corporation," or chapter S, an "S corporation." A C corporation files its own income tax return and is taxed on its profits at corporate income tax rates. Profits are taxed before dividends are paid. Dividends, if paid, are taxed to shareholders at their individual income tax rate. As an expense of the business, however, salary may be paid without a double tax.

In general, an S corporation is taxed in a manner similar to a partnership. An S corporation must meet certain statutory requirements, which generally can be met by a small business enterprise. The income and expenses of the S corporation are passed through to shareholders, and profits are taxed to them at their individual tax rates.

### Limited Liability Company

A relatively new form of business organization is a limited liability company, a form of business organization that combines the tax treatment of a partnership with the limited liability characteristics of a corporation. A limited liability company is not subject to many of the restrictions that apply to an S corporation, such as a maximum of thirty-five shareholders and a single class of stock. Unlike a limited partnership, all members of a limited liability company may participate in the management of the company without risking loss of limited liability. In general, a limited liability company must have at least two members and be managed by a board of governors with at least two active managers.

As with a corporation, the procedures for forming a limited liability company are specified by statute. Because this form of organization is new in many states, and not currently recognized by others, there is little guidance in the operation of this company.

### Others

There are other forms of organization available to business ventures, but these forms, involving complex legal, financial, and accounting issues, exist to address a specific commercial need. For example, a business trust may be used to organize a mutual fund because mutual fund owners do not need the corporate governance rights required by business owners. A cooperative is designed for a business owned and managed by those who patronize the enterprise. Cooperatives are set up to serve their user-owners, like farmers or hardware retailers, not to make money for passive investors.

### Name

As you organize your business, carefully consider its name. For some purposes, naming your business may be more important than naming your child. Unlike a human being with tangible and intangible characteristics that readily identify the person, a business is a legal fiction, whose essence must be marked by a name. Before becoming emotionally committed to a name, however, call the office of the secretary of state to make sure the name is available to you. If you can, make sure, too, that there are no others who have perfected a prior federal trademark or common law right to the name. Most states require that the name be filed with the secretary of state.

By submitting a name reservation with the secretary of state, you may reserve a name for your business before proceeding with any other activity or state filing. A corporation, individual, or partnership may reserve the use of a name. A reservation may be effective for up to a year and may be renewed periodically.

To alert the public to the limited liability of the proprietors of a business, a corporate name must generally contain the words "Corporation," "Incorporated," or "Limited," or an abbreviation of one or more of these words, or the word "Company" or the abbreviation "Co." if "Company" or "Co." is not preceded by "and" or "&." A limited partnership name must include the words "limited partnership." The name of a limited liability company must include the words "limited liability" or the abbreviation "LLC" and may not contain the words "corporation" or "incorporation" or the abbreviations of either of those words.

The name of a business organization must also be distinguishable from a business name on file with the secretary of state. If the name you desire is not distinguishable from a name already on file, you have three choices. You may obtain consent from the person who has the prior right to the name; you may change your business name; or you may file a statement of dormant business with respect to the prior holder of the name.

Name filings do not protect you against a competing use of a business name, although you may be informed of subsequent filings relating to your name. You must take legal action to prevent undesired or unauthorized use of your business name.

Finally, if your store sign will read "Jane's Deli" not "Jane's Deli, Inc.," you may not be doing business under the actual name of your business. As a result, you may have to file with the secretary of state a certificate of assumed name. An assumed name filing is made to provide information to the consumer as to the identity and potential liability of the actual business owners.

No matter what form of business organization you choose for your enterprise, you will need to deal with government regulation. Your business is likely to be liable for federal and state income tax, state sales and use tax, social security tax, federal unemployment tax,

## Dealing With Government Regulation

and state unemployment tax. Most employers must also withhold federal and state income tax and the employees' share of the social security tax from their employees and pay those taxes to the federal and state government. Consequently, with the exception of certain sole proprietorships, your business will need a federal employer identification number, a state taxpayer identification number, and, generally, a state unemployment compensation employer identification number. The Internal Revenue Service presents workshops from time to time explaining the federal tax system to entrepreneurs. Information on state taxes is generally available from the state department of revenue. [See also Chapter 16, "The Woman as Employer"]

Many important issues for a business enterprise turn on whether the business is considered an "employer" of a worker. Certain tax responsibilities, minimum wage laws, workers' compensation laws, and human rights legislation apply only to employment relationships. An "employer" usually provides the tools and place to work and has the right to control, hire, and fire an "employee." In contrast, an independent contractor is not controlled by the person paying her. Generally, it is less expensive to use an independent contractor. If an employment relationship exists, however, the legal requirements placed on the employer will apply regardless of how the parties themselves label the arrangement. The nature of the employment relationship is discussed extensively in Chapter 16, "The Woman As Employer."

Starting a business may also involve securing one or more business, occupational, or environmental licenses or permits. Generally a state will have a bureau of business licenses that will provide information about federal, state, and local licensing requirements.

Prior to commencing operations, certain businesses may be required to obtain a bond. A bond is a contract, similar to an insurance policy, between a bonding company and the business that purchases the bond. Like a guaranty, the bond runs in favor of a third person to protect that person against loss caused by the bonded person. Companies operating in trust-related businesses, such as investment advisory firms and broker dealers, often are required to obtain bonds.

Offers and sales of limited partnership interests, corporate stock, and other securities, including in some cases memberships in a limited liability company, are subject to federal and state securities laws, which require either exemption or registration of the offering with the Securities and Exchange Commission and state securities regulators. Securities laws also forbid you to make reckless or fraudulent statements or omissions in connection with the offer or sale of a security. If such statements or omissions are made, the remedy usually is the return of all the investor's money plus interest and, perhaps, attorneys' fees.

Access to equity and debt financing in the formation of a business and the ability, when the company is ready, to have securities traded in the public markets, are critical factors in the growth of a small company. Yet, for all but the most fortunate, financing is the most troublesome, least understood aspect of starting a business. Obviously cash flow and profits are not financing alternatives for the new venture. The founder of a business must first turn to her own financial resources—a second mortgage on her home, a loan from her pension or profit sharing plan, her Visa card, or her own or family savings. After that, in need of capital, you face an uphill battle.

Sometimes you can borrow money, from someone besides your mother, but retail and service businesses are particularly difficult to finance with loans because the seed capital is usually used for working capital and inventory. Inventory and soft capital assets generally do not make good collateral from a lender's view because they are hard to resell. Consequently, retail and service operations are usually equity financed, discussed below.

The Small Business Administration (SBA) has lending programs that facilitate access to money from banks. Funding and eligibility for these programs change from time to time. You should check with your local SBA office as to guaranty availability and the current criteria for its programs. Your main contact, however, is with a bank loan officer. A bank actually provides the loan, which generally can be used to buy equipment or other property. The SBA's programs are not a source of funding for research and development, marketing, or other soft assets. All SBA eligible businesses need to have been in existence for at least a year and meet other specifications as to net worth, net profit, and annual revenues. Certain businesses, like publishers, broadcasters, movie companies, and gambling companies, are not eligible for SBA financing.

Another source of financing is a business partner. Corporate partnering—or strategic partnering, as it is also called—is a form of joint venture growing in popularity. Though there is no clear definition of business partnering, in general, the partners are a large corporation that provides the money and a small company that performs the work, usually research and development. The key for the small company is to have an idea, a research result, a technology lead or experience, or a particular skill, that is of special value in achieving ultimate product or technology. The advantages for the large corporation include speed of development, cost savings, risk reduction, and access to entrepreneurial talent.

Less traditional forms of partnering include bartering, licensing your property to be sold in geographic areas or used in industries in which you are not interested, or performing consulting services yourself to support your business in the early years.

# Financing Your Business

Franchising is a method of financing, as well as a way to market and distribute goods and services. Through franchising a company can add stores and expand its market presence with a small capital outlay. By becoming a franchisee, you receive the right to engage in the franchiser's business, using the same trade names, advertising, training manual, and often raw materials, in exchange for a franchise fee. Offers and sales of a franchise are subject to disclosure regulations by the Federal Trade Commission and to registration and other requirements in numerous states.

Occasionally financing is available from federal, state, or local governments. On the federal level, in addition to SBA programs, the Farmer's Home Administration offers loans to companies founded in rural communities. Some states encourage companies to operate in specific industries. For example, in Minnesota, a tourism loan program offers a low-interest revolving loan fund that lends money to resorts and campgrounds.

You can also turn to your vendors or suppliers for financing. For example, a lawyer may be willing to reduce her fees in exchange for an ownership interest in your new company. An experienced business executive might become your new chief financial officer in exchange for stock and options. If you are starting a retail business, ask your vendors if they will ship you merchandise on consignment or ship you inventory in installments. Either way, your vendor is agreeing to be paid when you are, thus significantly reducing your need for cash. If you require a particular asset, say a computer, a telephone system, or a copier, an equipment lease is a common financing technique. Over the long run, leasing property costs more than buying it, but you may be able to deduct the rental and avoid listing a liability on your balance sheet.

You might ask your customers for cash in the form of prepayments, even if you are a new company. If you want to start a valet parking firm, ask the hotel to prepay monthly. If you start a consulting business, charge your clients quarterly in advance.

One of the most commonly thought of, but less frequently available, means to raise money for a new venture is the sale of an ownership—or equity—interest in the enterprise. The success of raising private capital depends on your access to sophisticated, wealthy investors. If you are starting up a business, you will have to identify and persuade these parties to invest. As your company grows, a broker-dealer or an investment banker may find investors for you, for a fee ranging from 5 percent to 13 percent of all funds raised.

As previously mentioned, selling securities is a regulated activity. Generally, however, you can raise up to a million dollars every year with a minimum of expense, so long as you don't use a broker-dealer, and you sell securities to a very small number of nonqualified investors plus an unlimited number of qualified investors. A qualified investor would include a person with a net worth of a million dollars or income over $200,000 a year. If you are interested in selling securities, like limited partnership interests or corporate stock, you should consult a lawyer.

Venture capitalists are professionals who participate in a broad range of investments, from startup to more established companies. But they rarely make seed-capital investments. Venture capitalists are generally interested in companies with great potential growth and whose margins are 50 percent or better. They like to see the company's market growing at an annual rate of 20 percent or the company itself projecting growth to justify a three to five times return on the venture capitalists' money in three years. Cold calls to venture capitalists are accepted, but rarely result in an investment. Introductions by lawyers, accountants, or a successful venture capital–backed company receive more attention.

## Making Money

No business enterprise should begin without a clear idea of its profit potential. Roughly half of new ventures do not survive for five years, either because they do not make money or they do not generate cash. A pound of care will not pay an ounce of debt.

One of the most common ways to learn whether you can reasonably expect profits from your business is to determine, first, the amount of money you desire to receive from the business. In determining the revenue the business must generate, you must add up what you desire to withdraw from the company, what you need to pay on any borrowed money, and what you should reinvest in the company. If this revenue level cannot be reasonably supported by your business plan, you should reconsider the venture.

You should then test and verify your conclusions through market research. Market research is an inexact process, but can be performed by most prospective entrepreneurs. In addition to the library, other sources of market research are a personal network of colleagues, mentors, and other entrepreneurs; mail surveys; trade journals; focus groups; seminars and courses; colleges and universities; consulting or research firms; and the telephone book Yellow Pages to see how many other such businesses exist and where they are weak. Sound market knowledge will assist you in making rational decisions regarding your proposed business.

Another company which is doing what you want to do but in a location not competitive with yours is another good source of market and profit information.

A company may generate revenues and even earn a profit and yet have no cash to pay its bills. Although related to net income, cash flow is not equivalent. On a day-to-day basis, cash availability is more important than overall net income. So, in addition to a net income projection, a cash-flow analysis is an essential part of any business plan.

Once you decide to go ahead, keep score with frequent financial statements, which show you the overall financial picture. At a minimum, you should produce a monthly balance sheet and income statement. An income statement matches the amounts received from selling goods and services—revenues or sales—against the cost incurred in both producing the goods or services and operating the company. The result is either a net income or a net loss for the period. Financial statements may be prepared on an accrual or on a cash basis. The accrual method better matches revenues and expenses.

In addition to financial statements, at the end of each year or other period, based on its performance, the company should create a budget against which it should measure its performance through the succeeding year or period.

A personal computer and software allow efficient management of day-to-day business activities as well as financial reporting. Next to your time, it could be the single most valuable investment you make in your business.

## Bibliography

Abarbanel, Karin. *How to Succeed on Your Own: Overcoming Emotional Roadblocks on the Way from Cooperation to Cottage, from Employer to Entrepreneur.* New York: Henry Holt, Inc., 1994.

Hisrich, Robert D., and Brush, Candida G. *The Woman Entrepreneur: Starting, Financing, and Managing a Successful Business.* New York: The Free Press, 1990.

Jessup, Claudia, and Chipps, Genie. *The Woman's Guide to Starting a Business, 3d ed.* New York: Henry Holt and Co., 1991.

Milano, Carol. *Hers: The Wise Woman's Guide to Starting a Business on $2,000 or Less.* New York: Allworth Press, 1991.

Montgomery, Vickie. *Smart Woman's Guide to Starting a Business.* Hawthorne, NJ: Career Press, 1994.

Nelson, Carol. *Women's Market Handbook.* Detroit: Gale Research, 1994.

Sinclair, Carole. *Keys for Women Starting or Owning a Business.* Hauppauge, NY: Barron's Educational Series, 1991.

## Organizational Resources

Many women's organizations exist for specific occupations, such as travel agents, information processing, real estate, international trade, and so on. Consult your local library for directories of associations and of resources for women.

American Business Women's Association
9100 Ward Parkway
P.O. Box 8728
Kansas City, MO 64114
(816) 361-6621

American Woman's Economic Development Corporation
60 E. 42nd Street
New York, NY 10165
(212) 692-9100

Executive Women International
515 S. 700 East, Suite 2E
Salt Lake City, UT 84102
(801) 355-2800

Federation of Organizations for Professional Women
2001 S Street, NW, Suite 500
Washington, DC 20009
(202) 328-1415

The International Alliance
8600 LaSalle Road, Suite 617
Baltimore, MD 21286
(410) 472-4221

International Network for Women in Enterprise and Trade
P.O. Box 6178
McLean, VA 22106
(703) 893-8541

Latin Business and Professional Women
P.O. Box 45-0913
Miami, FL 33245
(305) 446-9222

National Association for Female Executives
127 W. 24th Street, 4th Flooor
New York, NY 10011
(212) 645-0770

National Association of Black Women Entrepreneurs
P.O. Box 1375
Detroit, MI 48231
(313) 559-9255

National Association of Minority Women in Business
906 Grand Avenue, Suite 200
Kansas City, MO 64106
(816) 421-3335

National Association of Negro Business and Professional Women
1806 New Hampshire Avenue NW
Washington, DC 20009
(202) 483-4206

National Association of Women Business Owners
600 S. Federal Street, Suite 400
Chicago, IL 60605
(312) 922-0465

National Chamber of Commerce for Women
10 Waterside Plaza, Suite 6H
New York NY 10010
(212) 685-3454
*Check your local telephone directory, or contact the national organization, for the location of the regional (state or city) Women's Chamber closest to you.*

National Federation of Business and Professional Women's Clubs
2012 Massachusetts Avenue, NW
Washington, DC 20036
(202) 293-1100

National Women's Economic Alliance
1440 New York Avenue, NW
Suite 300
Washington, DC 20005
(202) 393-5257

Organization of Pan Asian American Women
P.O. Box 39128
Washington, DC 20016
(202) 429-6824

Small Business Administration (SBA)
409 Third Street SW
Washington, DC 20416
(202) 606-4000
(800) 827-5722
*The SBA has regional offices all over the country. It services small businesses and may provide financing and consulting resources. SCORE (Service Corps of Retired Executives) is one of these. The SBA may also have information on international trade, technology, and local training programs.*

Women in Management
30 North Michigan Avenue
Suite 508
Chicago, IL 60602
(312) 263-3636

---

**Kathleen S. Tillotson** graduated *magna cum laude* from Tulane University School of Law in 1981. She specializes in the practice of corporate finance and securities law, handling such transactions as public offerings, private placements, and leveraged buyouts, and other business matters including investment management and securities litigation. She is the securities law author and editor of "Advising Small Business," published by Clark Boardman Callaghan.

Chapter 18

# *Intellectual Property Law*

Louise Nemschoff

Chapter Outline

**Introduction**

**What Are Copyrights, Trademarks, and Patents?**

**Protection of Ideas**

**Copyright Law**
How Are Copyrights Obtained? • Copyright Notice and Registration
• How Long Does Copyright Protection Last? • How Are Copyrights
Transferred? • Copyright Infringement

**Trademark Law**
How Are Trademark Rights Obtained? • Registration of Marks • How
Long Do Trademark Rights Last? • How Are Trademark Rights Trans-
ferred? • Trademark Infringement

**Patent Law**
How Are Patent Rights Obtained? • Patent Registration • How Long
Do Patent Rights Last?

**Conclusion**

**Introduction**     Certain types of property are protected by law, even though they are not physical objects, such as a house, a piece of land, or a car. Such intangible property is often described as "intellectual property," since it is created from the mental efforts of writers, artists, inventors, and the like. In the United States, the protection of such property stems from the Constitution, which authorizes Congress "To promote the progress of science and useful arts, by securing for limited time to authors and inventors the exclusive right to their respective writings and discoveries."

Congress has enacted three types of laws that create enforceable but limited legal monopolies in the form of copyrights, trademarks, and patents. This chapter will review the fundamentals of each of these forms of protection. However, copyright, trademark, and patent each represent an extremely broad and complicated area of the law. Many nuances are involved in applying the law to specific situations, which are beyond the scope of this chapter. Intellectual property law, dealing as it does with intangible property, is often very dependent on the specific facts, and so it is advisable to consult with an attorney with regard to any particular problems and questions you may encounter. Nonetheless, a basic knowledge of these areas of law may assist you in identifying potential problem areas and in selecting and working with a lawyer who is experienced in the relevant field.

**What Are Copyrights, Trademarks, and Patents?**     Generally speaking, copyrights protect works of expression. These include written works (such as books, newspaper articles, poems, plays, and movie scripts), musical works (including not only the music and lyrics of a musical composition but also a recording of that composition on vinyl, tape, compact disk, or other format), works of art (such as paintings, sculptures, photographs, drawings, lithographs, and architectural designs), audiovisual works (including all forms of motion pictures and television programs) and computer software (such as the source code, object code, and screen displays). Even the circuitry in semiconductor chips are protected as "mask works" under a variant of the copyright laws.

Trademark law protects words and symbols that identify the supplier of products or services. Protected marks can include single words, short slogans, brand names, musical sounds, shapes, designs, or logos that distinguish goods or services from competing offerings in the marketplace. Related areas of law provide protection for distinctive packaging as "trade dress."

Patent law, in general, protects invention. There are three types of patents available. A utility patent covers inventions such as new machines, articles, compositions and mechanical or chemical processes, and new uses for existing inventions. It is the functional aspects of the invention which are protected by the utility patent. Such patents have been issued for a wide variety of inventions, including different kinds of machinery, parts, tools, toys and game apparatus, vehicles, scientific testing equipment, abrasives, laminates, manufacturing processes, drugs, and even genetically altered animals. Design patents cover industrial or aesthetic design. They are available for unique ornamentation, shape, or design, as long as such ornamentation, shape, or design is an integral and inseparable part of the object. In most cases, surface design would be protected by copyright rather than a design patent, although there are exceptions such as the Spiro Agnew watch, which incorporated the image of a prominent political figure into the watch face and hands. Finally, plant patents are available for new forms of sexually or asexually reproduced plants.

In some instances, more than one form of protection may be available. For example, company logos may be eligible for both copyright and trademark protection. The design of a watch face or a lamp base may be eligible for both a copyright and a design patent. The on-screen displays and software for computer games may be eligible for copyright protection and also for utility patents, although this is a relatively new field which has been developing only over the last few years. It is useful to consult with an attorney to determine the best form of protection for your work. This decision should take into account not only the legal issues, but also the value of the work in relation to the cost of obtaining the protection and the various advantages, disadvantages, and risks inherent in each form of protection.

There are some additional methods of protecting intellectual property. These include trade secret protection and the law of unfair competition. These forms of protection are mentioned briefly below.

## Protection of Ideas

The question most commonly asked of intellectual property lawyers is "How do I protect my idea?" The short answer to this question is that it is difficult and often impossible to protect a mere idea. The First Amendment to the U.S. Constitution, in fact, is designed to protect and foster the marketplace of ideas. Therefore, it is often said that "ideas are free as the air." Once an idea has been reduced to some concrete form of expression, whether in the shape of a specific invention, a short story, a painting, a song, or some other form of expression, intellectual property law protection becomes available.

However, until that time, a mere idea can be protected only by keeping it a secret or by entering into a contract with any party to whom you disclose your idea. Such an agreement may be either express (that is, a written or oral contract to compensate the creator if the other party uses her idea) or implied from the circumstances. These are referred to as confidentiality or submission agreements, and they must be made prior to the submission itself. In general, such contracts provide for the party who will be accepting the submission to agree to treat it as confidential and to pay the submitting party at least the reasonable value of her idea if it is used.

Considerable caution should be exercised in dealing with submission agreements. First of all, the publishers, motion picture studios, manufacturers, and others to whom you are likely to submit your ideas often have their own form of submission agreements which are designed to *limit* rather than to protect your rights. Oral agreements are extremely difficult to enforce, or to use a singularly insightful malapropism generally attributed to Samuel Goldwyn, "An oral contract isn't worth the paper it's written on." At the very least, a letter should be sent, either prior to the submission or along with the submission itself, confirming that you are submitting your idea based on the other party's agreement to keep your idea confidential and to pay you if she uses your idea.

## Copyright Law

### How Are Copyrights Obtained?

Once an idea is "fixed in a tangible medium of expression," it is protected by copyright. The copyright comes into existence automatically at the moment of fixation—when a poem is put on paper or saved on a computer disk, an image is captured on still or moving photography, a painting is put on canvas, a sculpture carved from wood, dance choreography is recorded on film or on paper by means of Labanotation, a song is written on paper or sung and recorded on tape, or a fabric design drawn, to cite but a few examples. The work must have some degree of originality to qualify for copyright protection, but the required level is minimal. For example, a normal telephone directory would not be eligible for copyright, because the mere alphabetical listing of names, addresses, and telephone numbers is simply not original.

In most cases, the creator of a work is the author and initial owner of the copyright in the work. There is an important exception to this rule, however, known as the "work made for hire" doctrine. This can arise in two ways. First, when a work is created by an employee within the scope and course of her employment, it is considered a work made for hire and the employer is both the author and the initial copyright owner. Second, when certain specific types of works (including a translation, a textbook, a part of a motion picture or other audiovisual work, a test or test answer material, an atlas, and a contribution to a newspaper, magazine or other "collective work") are prepared on special order, the commissioning party rather than the creator will be the author and initial copyright owner, but only if there is a written agreement before creation of the work signed by both the creator and the commissioning party specifically saying that the end product is a "work made for hire."

Creators are well advised to be on the lookout for this phrase and should exercise extreme caution when it appears in contracts, on checks to be cashed, or any other document to be signed. While use of the "work for hire" doctrine is not always inappropriate, it should be undertaken only with adequate legal advice and complete understanding of the consequences. Not only does a work for hire deprive the creator of the initial copyright ownership, but it also eliminates the right to terminate assignments and licenses by giving written notice to the other party during a five year period beginning thirty-five years after the date of publication (or the date the agreement was signed, if earlier). This opportunity to recapture copyright interests sold early in the career of a writer or artist can prove very valuable in later years, when her work has presumably gained recognition and hence become more valuable.

When two or more authors prepare a single work with the intention that their respective contributions be merged into inseparable or interdependent parts of a unitary whole, they have created a joint work. This would occur, for example, when two people sit down and write a screenplay together. The creators of such a work are considered joint authors and co-owners of the copyright.

Coauthors, however, need not necessarily work together at the same time and place. A joint work may also be created when one person composes music and gives it to another to write the lyrics. The key is the intention of the parties at the time the work is created. If they intended for their respective contributions to become part of a single work, then it is considered a "joint work."

Absent an agreement between the creators to the contrary, the joint authors will each own an equal share in the copyright. Each author can enter into agreements with third parties for nonexclusive rights in the work, but she must pay her coauthors their share of the proceeds. The right to use a work on a nonexclusive basis may be valuable for some types of copyrightable works, such as songs which in large measure increase in value as more and more people perform and record them. However, for many types of works, such as a film script, it makes no sense for someone to invest a lot of money in its development and production, only to find that someone else has taken the same script and produced a competing film. To grant exclusive rights in a joint work, all of the coauthors must join in the transfer. For this reason, cocreators are well advised to enter into a collaboration agreement before beginning work on their project.

## Copyright Notice and Registration

Prior to 1978, U.S. copyright law required both copyright notices and registration of a work as a condition to protection. In recent years, primarily as the result of the U.S. decision to sign a major international copyright treaty known as the Berne Convention, these formalities have loosened, although there are still incentives for their use.

The basic form of the copyright notice is standard and set by law. It must include three elements: (1) the word "Copyright" or alternative © or "Copr." or on sound recordings ℗; (2) the year of publication; and (3) the name of the copyright owner. If the work is being or will be published outside the United States, it is a good idea to use only © or ℗ in the notice and to add the phrase "All rights reserved." The notice must be affixed to copies of the work in a place which gives reasonable notice of the copyright claim. For example, notices are typically placed on the back of the title page of a book or at the end of a motion picture.

For works published after March 1, 1989, the copyright notice is no longer required, but its continued use is strongly advised because it prevents an infringer from raising the defense of innocent infringement, should litigation be necessary to enforce your copyright. In addition, the copyright notice is still required for protection in certain countries of the world.

Similarly, for all works created on or after January 1, 1978, registration is no longer a condition of federal copyright protection, but there are substantial incentives for registration. First, although registration is not required to *create* copyrights, it is required before you can sue to *enforce* them. Second, and more important, registration before infringement is a precondition to the recovery of statutory damages and attorney's fees in copyright infringement litigation. Statutory damages allow the recovery of $500 to $20,000 (up to $100,000 in the case of willful infringement), without having to prove how much you were actually damaged by the infringing activities. Thus, statutory damages are particularly valuable in situations where it is difficult to place a monetary value on the infringed work or on the loss due to an infringement. The importance of recovering attorney's fees should not be underestimated, since copyright infringement litigation, like other types of litigation, can be quite costly.

Only registration of the work with the Copyright Office will provide these benefits. The so-called "poor (wo)man's copyright"—mailing a copy of your work to yourself—is of little or no value in most cases. At best, an unopened envelope with a clearly legible postmark may help to prove that the particular copy of the work was in your possession and that you claimed to be its author as of the date on the postmark. To institute a copyright infringement action, however, actual registration is still required. Given the simplicity, low cost, and the legal advantages of copyright registration, there is little or no reason to pursue any other course.

The basic registration forms (TX for textual material such as books, VA for visual arts, PA for performing arts such as screenplays and movies, SR for sound recordings, and SE for serial works such as newspapers and magazines) are available along with instruction sheets from the Copyright Office Forms Hotline at 202/707-9100. The registration fee is currently $20 per work. However, fees are subject to change and the amounts should be checked prior to filing. At the time of registration, copies of the work must be deposited with the Copyright Office—one copy of an unpublished work or two copies of the best edition for published works. For certain large, bulky or one-of-a-kind works of art, photographs may be deposited instead. The Copyright Office publishes a number of circulars explaining different aspects of copyright law and has a staff of information specialists to assist you in filing for copyright at 202/707-3000.

## How Long Does Copyright Protection Last?

For works created on or after January 1, 1978, copyright protects the work for the life of the author plus fifty years. For works made for hire and pseudonymous and anonymous works, the term of protection is the shorter of seventy-five years from the year of first publication or one hundred years from the year of creation. However, Congress is currently considering proposals to extend the basic term to life plus seventy years, to bring U.S. law into conformity with international practices.

For all works created before January 1, 1978, the initial term of copyright protection is twenty-eight years from the earlier of the year of publication or registration, with a renewal term of forty-seven years (for a total of up to seventy-five years).

Until 1992, renewals had to be filed within the specified time period by the copyright owner, or else all rights to the work fell into the public domain. However, if the author had assigned the work to a third party during her lifetime, but was dead at time the copyright came up for renewal, her heirs could recapture the copyright in the work by renewing it in their own names. This was intended as a protection for the widows and orphans of authors who may have sold their rights at an earlier time, before the ultimate value of the work was fully known.

This mechanism created a number of problems, particularly for owners of copyrights in movies based on short stories, songs, and other copyrightable works. If the author of the underlying work had died, her heirs could renew the copyright in their own names and prevent the owners of the motion picture from distributing it. This is, in fact, what happened with the well-known film *Rear Window,* and the movie was not available to the public for a number of years until litigation on the matter worked its way up to the Supreme Court which ruled in favor of the heirs. Ultimately, the film's distributor had to purchase the renewal rights to the underlying short story from a third party who had bought those rights from the author's heirs.

A new law regarding renewals took effect in 1992, making renewal of previously registered works automatic. The heirs of a deceased author may still recapture the rights by filing for renewal of the copyright. If they fail to do so, the rights will remain with the registered copyright owner. Nonetheless, questions regarding renewal of pre-1978 works can still be quite complex, particularly if the author is no longer alive or is a foreign national. Legal advice should be sought from someone knowledgeable in the field.

### How Are Copyrights Transferred?

Copyright should be thought of not merely as a single piece of property, but rather as a bundle of rights. It can be divided up in many ways—by territories (the right to publish the work throughout the universe or only in the United States, Canada, Japan, and so on), by language (the right to reproduce the work in one or more different language versions, such as English, German, and so on, or even in various computer or machine languages), by media (the right to distribute the work in all media now known or hereafter developed, or only in book form, in comic book form, in newspapers, in theaters, on videocassettes, over free, cable, or other forms of pay television, in CD-ROM format, and so on), and by time (the right to reproduce the work in perpetuity, or for one time only, for ten years, for the life of the copyright, and so on). Copyright includes the right not only to reproduce a work, but also to adapt it, as when a novel is adapted for television (called a *derivative work*).

The entire bundle of rights can be sold outright (known as an "assignment of copyright") or they can be licensed individually, in varying combinations. Each right can be licensed on an exclusive or nonexclusive basis. However, an assignment of all rights or an exclusive license is valid only if it is in writing. An oral or implied license will only be valid as a nonexclusive transfer of rights (that is, the same right may be sold to other parties). Sale of the physical embodiment of a copyrighted work (for example, the painting or original manuscript) does not convey any interest in the copyright, again unless there is a written agreement to that effect.

Copyrights can be assigned or licensed for a variety of different kinds of compensation, including a predetermined set fee, royalties from the use of the rights (for example, 10 percent of the suggested retail price of copies of a book or 6.61¢ per copy which is the new statutory mechanical royalty rate for audio recordings of songs), and/or a share of the profits from the exploitation of the work.

## Copyright Infringement

Technically, copyright infringement is subject to criminal penalties, but these are very seldom enforced. Civil litigation offers a number of remedies for copyright infringement. The rights owner may obtain an injunction against continuance of the infringement, have the infringing copies of the work seized and recover monetary damages, either in the amount of her actual losses or the amount of the profits which she has lost as a result of the infringing activity.

Copying need not be verbatim to constitute infringement. Since the copyright owner has the exclusive right not only to copy and reproduce the work, but also to change and adapt it, infringement could result from copying only portions of a work, from making a motion picture version of the work or from adapting it to other formats or media.

To prove infringement, you must demonstrate that the infringer had access to the copyrighted work and that the infringing work was substantially similar to the copyrighted work. The greater the proof of access, the less similarity is required. However, the similarity must go beyond a mere similarity of ideas. There must be substantial similarity in the *expression* of the ideas embodied in the copyrighted work.

Obviously, all creativity builds upon the body of work which has preceded it. Contemporary writers may be influenced by William Shakespeare, Aeschylus, Mark Twain, Isaac Asimov, Judith Krantz, and thousands of other authors, both past and present. Moreover, it would be impossible to write about certain subjects (for example, the music of Igor Stravinsky) without giving examples of their creative endeavors or quoting from other experts on the subject. Therefore, an exception has been carved out to protect scholarship, academic research, literary and other forms of criticism, satire, parody, comment, teaching, and news reporting.

This so-called "fair use" exception permits certain limited copying, but its application depends heavily on the specific facts of the situation. The courts will look at a number of factors, including the purpose and character of the use, the nature of the copied material, the amount and substantiality of the portion copied, and the effect of the use on the market for or value of the copied material. However, because "fair use" must be determined in each instance on a factual basis, it can be very risky to rely on this defense, and the area is full of potential pitfalls.

For example, the Supreme Court has decided that it is fair use to make a single videotaped copy of a program taken from free (as opposed to pay/cable) television for the purposes of viewing it at a later time. On the other hand, one appellate court has ruled that it is not a fair use for a scientist working in a for-profit corporation to photocopy articles from a scientific journal to keep in her files or use in the laboratory. Because this case was settled while on appeal to the Supreme Court, it is unclear whether the courts will ultimately come down on the side of the publishers of these copyrightable works or on the side of the scientists who conduct research for the benefit of their employers and ultimately the public who purchases their products.

## Trademark Law

### How Are Trademark Rights Obtained?

A trademark is a word, phrase, or symbol which identifies the source of goods, such as Exxon petroleum products or Macintosh computers. A mark which identifies the source of services (for example, H&R Block tax services or McDonald's for restaurant services) is technically called a service mark. For convenience, this chapter will refer to both types of marks as "trademarks" or "marks" unless the context requires otherwise. Federal and state trademark laws seek to protect the supplier's reputation and goodwill which attach to the mark during the course of its use. These laws are also designed to protect the public from confusion and deception in the marketplace.

In the United States, trademark rights are obtained from the actual use of the mark in connection with the sale of goods or services. Generally speaking, the first person to use the mark gains priority in claiming ownership. In most other parts of the world, however, trademark rights stem from registration of the mark, with priority going to the first person to register the mark with the appropriate authority. Use of the mark for U.S. trademark purposes requires placement of the mark on goods actually sold or transported for sale. The mark must be displayed on the goods themselves, on their containers, tags or labels, or on displays associated with the goods. Services must actually have been rendered, and the service mark must be used or displayed in the sale or advertising of those services.

In 1989, U.S. law for the first time began to recognize certain rights in marks not yet in use, by authorizing the filing of "intent to use" applications with the U.S. Patent and Trademark Office (PTO). Such an application may be filed only when there is a genuine intention to use the mark in connection with the sale of goods or services. The "intent to use" filing, in essence, reserves the mark for a period of up to one (1) year, but the trademark rights themselves accrue only on actual use of the mark.

To obtain protection, a name or logo must be used as a trademark, that is, as an *adjective* which describes the source of the goods or services. It should not be used as a noun to identify a business. Such usage constitutes a "trade name," which is not protected by federal or state trademark laws, although various other state laws provide some protection for trade names. A trademark should not be used as a noun or verb to identify the product or service itself. Thus, the Xerox Corporation is very careful to point out that the company sells Xerox brand photocopiers.

In fact, the uncontrolled usage of trademarks as either nouns or verbs has resulted in the loss of some very valuable trademarks, including the words "cellophane" and "aspirin." At one time, these words were brand names for a particular manufacturer's clear cellulose film and for a specific drug company's pain-killing medication (acetyl salicylic acid), but they became so commonly used by the public to describe the product itself that they became "generic" and lost all trademark protection. Now anyone can use these words, as part of our regular vocabulary.

Just as some words can lose their status as protected trademarks, others are not entitled to become trademarks at all. For example, immoral, deceptive, scandalous, or disparaging matter and certain government symbols may not be used as trademarks. Words that are purely descriptive, geographically descriptive (or misdescriptive) and personal names will not be recognized as trademarks unless the user can demonstrate that they have developed a "secondary meaning." This occurs when the mark achieves public recognition as a designation of the *source* of the goods or services, rather than a description of some other quality or feature.

The easiest marks to obtain and protect tend to be those that are purely arbitrary or even invented words. Kodak film, Crest toothpaste, Blue Cross health insurance, and Pepsi cola are examples of strong arbitrary or fanciful marks which would be given a wide scope of protection. Trademark protection is also available for "suggestive" marks such as COPPERTONE suntan lotion and SHEER ELEGANCE pantyhose, but the scope of protection for these marks is somewhat more limited than for arbitrary or fanciful marks.

Prior to selecting and using a mark, particularly one in which you plan to invest a lot of money or advertise heavily, it is a good idea to conduct first a trademark search. A search may be obtained from a trademark lawyer or from one of the nonlegal firms which specialize in performing such searches. The cost of such searches will range from $300 and up, depending on the type of mark, the nature of the intended use, and how quickly the search needs to be completed. Generally speaking, words are easier and less expensive to search than logos, where the search must be entirely performed by hand and the results will be substantially less conclusive due to the greater degree of subjectivity involved in analyzing logos.

## Registration of Marks

To obtain federal registration of a mark, it must first be used in interstate commerce. This means that the goods or services must be sold in more than one state. Goods that are shipped from one state to another for sale may also qualify, as well as services advertised in more than one state. A single interstate sale is sufficient, provided there is an intent to make continuous use of the mark in interstate commerce.

For marks not used in interstate commerce (for example, for a local restaurant or cleaners), each state has its own system for registration of marks. Although the requirements and fees vary somewhat, basically they all follow the same pattern as federal registration in terms of the use requirement and the elements of the application. Specific requirements of each state should be checked prior to filing.

The application form for federal trademark registration may seem simple, but in fact, it contains a number of terms of art and traps for the unwary. Legal counsel is strongly recommended in applying for trademark registration. Among other things, the applicant will be required to identify the goods or services involved according to an international classification system, as well as to provide a narrative description of the goods or services. Trademark protection may extend beyond the specific goods or services claimed, to include not only goods or services in the same class, but also certain closely related goods or services in other classes.

Along with the application, a typed or drawn sample of the mark must be provided. The form of the sample is dictated by strict PTO rules regarding such matters as the size, margins, and depiction of color through a black and white line code. In addition, five specimens are required, usually in the form of the actual labels, tags, or containers showing the mark in use. Filing fees are currently $245 per class, but they are subject to change and should be confirmed with the PTO prior to filing.

Each application is examined by a PTO attorney, to ensure that the application and the mark itself comply with pertinent provisions of federal law and that there is no likelihood of confusion with other previously registered marks. Frequently, the Examining Attorney will request amendments or disclaimers from the applicant as a condition to allowing registration. If the application is rejected, various appeal processes are available through the Trademark Trial and Appeal Board, the Commissioner of Patents and Trademarks, and the federal courts. Even after a trademark is allowed and/or registered, a prior user can successfully challenge the registration through opposition or cancellation proceedings in the PTO or through civil litigation.

Once registered, the owner is entitled to use the "circle R" symbol ® with the mark. This gives constructive notice of the registration and eliminates the possibility of an infringer claiming she used the mark in good faith, without actual knowledge of the registered owner's priority. Use of this symbol before issuance of the registration certificate is improper, since it constitutes false advertising, and it may be used to bar subsequent registration of the mark. Prior to registration, the superscript "TM" or "SM" symbols may be used to alert the public to your claim of trademark rights. Although these symbols have no formal legal effect, their use is recommended.

## How Long Do Trademark Rights Last?

For trademarks registered before November 16, 1989, the term of protection is twenty years. For marks registered on or after that date, the term is ten years. During the sixth year following registration, a declaration must be filed with the PTO showing that the mark is still in use. If this "Section 8 Affidavit" is not filed before the end of the sixth year, the registration of the mark is automatically canceled. Trademarks may be renewed repeatedly for additional periods of ten years, provided that the mark is still in use in interstate commerce.

If the mark has been in continuous use for any five-year period, the owner may also file a "Section 15 Affidavit" to obtain status for the mark as incontestable. The incontestability status does not preclude all challenges to the mark, but the mark will no longer be subject to an interference proceeding to set aside the registration on the grounds of likelihood of confusion with another mark.

## How Are Trademark Rights Transferred?

Trademarks cannot be sold outright (or assigned) apart from the good will they represent. Thus, they may be sold in conjunction with the sale of a business. However, the right to use a mark may also be transferred through a license agreement without conveying any ownership interest in the trademark itself, provided that the licensor maintains a sufficient degree of control over the quality of the goods or services to be sold by the licensee under the mark. If the license agreement fails to include adequate quality controls, the mark may be considered abandoned and the licensor can lose all trademark rights. On the other hand, extensive quality control provisions may subject the licensor to stringent federal and state laws regulating franchises and business opportunities. Therefore, legal counsel is extremely important in any transfer of trademark rights.

### Trademark Infringement

The test for trademark infringement is "likelihood of confusion." A mark is considered to infringe a previously used mark if the relevant group of consumers or potential consumers would probably be confused as to the source of a product. However, actual confusion is not necessary to make out a case for infringement.

Marks do not need to be absolutely identical to be infringing. Similarity in sight, sound, or meaning may be sufficient to infringe a protected mark. For example, the marks Datsun and Dotson have been found to be confusingly similar, as have S.O. and Esso; Steinway and Steinweg; Pledge and Promise; and Toro Rojo and RedBull. Likelihood of confusion is an issue of fact, which must be decided on a case by case basis.

Use of an infringing mark may be enjoined, and the infringer may be ordered to pay not only the trademark owners monetary damages (including lost profits), but also punitive damages and attorney's fees.

## Patent Law

### How Are Patent Rights Obtained?

Of the three types of patents issued, this chapter will focus primarily on utility patents, that is, patents that are available for a process (or method), machine, manufacture (or article of manufacture), composition (usually a chemical composition, but more recently including genetically altered life forms), or a "new use" of an invention falling into one of these four categories. Patent protection is not available for ideas per se, mental processes (such as speed reading or mathematical calculation), general scientific or mathematical principles in the abstract, or methods of doing business.

Although some ideas may ultimately be eligible for patent protection, they must be "reduced to practice," either by actually building and testing the invention which embodies the idea or by showing on paper, through written description and drawings, that the invention can be made and used.

To receive patent protection, an invention must also be useful, novel, and unobvious. To satisfy the usefulness or "utility" criteria, the invention must have some legitimate use, sometimes including use as a gag or amusement. It must also be workable, at least on paper. Thus, it is unlikely that a patent would be granted for a perpetual motion machine or a metaphysical process to turn straw into gold. In the case of a design patent, the invention must be ornamental rather than utilitarian.

"Novelty" and "unobviousness" are terms of art, with very specific meanings in patent law, and they apply to all three types of patents. These are among the most difficult concepts in patent law, and they require a comparison of the invention with the "prior art" in the field, that is, books, trade journals, technical journals, previously filed United States or foreign patents (including expired patents) and any prior public knowledge or use of the invention. A patent lawyer should be consulted in applying these concepts to your particular invention.

The actual inventor is entitled to apply for a patent on her invention, and if granted, she would be the owner of that patent. Invention, however, is rarely the result of the efforts of a single person.

When more than one individual contributes to the invention process, all are considered co-inventors who should join in the patent application and become joint owners of any patent which might issue. Absent an agreement to the contrary, each of the joint owners has the right to make, use, sell, or license the patented invention, without the consent of the other co-owners and without accounting to the other co-owners for the monies earned from the patent. Where more than one person is involved in the invention process, a written joint ownership agreement is, therefore, essential to prevent one of your co-inventors from depriving you of the income from your invention and from competing with you in the marketing and sales of the invention.

An invention created by an employee on company time or one created using company facilities or materials will be owned by the employee, but it will be subject to certain "shop rights" that the employer retains, again absent an agreement to the contrary. These "shop rights" permit the employer to use the invention for its own business and purposes, but not to transfer or assign these rights to a third party. Generally speaking, inventions made by an employee on her own time, using entirely her own materials and facilities, would belong entirely to the employee, again absent an agreement. However, as between employer and employee, questions of ownership can often be quite complicated, particularly where more than one individual participates in the invention process.

For this reason, companies that employ engineers, scientists, computer programmers, and other technical employees will often require employment agreements with such personnel. These agreements may extend the employer's rights considerably, often providing that all inventions made while the individual is employed with the company will belong to the employer, whether or not it was created on company time or with company resources, and whether or not it is outside the scope of the employee's job or the employer's line of business. Such agreements may also impose limitations on the employee's activities both before and after she leaves the company, especially with regard to the employer's trade secrets. Both employers and employees should proceed cautiously and seek legal counsel when entering into such an employment agreement.

### Patent Registration

In many ways, the first step in obtaining a patent begins before the invention itself is ever completed, by documenting the invention process itself from the outset. Detailed records of your invention, its purpose, how it works, how it was built, and how it was tested will assist you in obtaining and defending a patent, as well as providing evidence of the contributions made by each of the co-inventors, if any. The so-called "post office patent," that is, mailing yourself a description of your invention, whether by regular, certified, or registered mail, and keeping the unopened envelope is of little or no value.

Before making a utility or plant patent application, it is important to have a patent search conducted. Such a search should cover the "prior art" in the field, including previously filed patents and publications. First and perhaps foremost, a search will help you to determine if your invention is patentable. If not, other avenues can be explored, such as trade secret, copyright, and trademark protection, without spending more time and incurring further costs to pursue a patent which is ultimately unattainable. In addition, a search will assist in the preparation of your patent application. A patent search may be obtained through a patent attorney or patent agent.

In the United States, a patent application must be filed with the PTO within one year after you sell your invention, offer it for sale, or commercially or publicly use or describe it. However, it is normally not a good idea to take advantage of this so-called "one-year rule," because by doing so you may find yourself precluded from obtaining a patent in most other countries. In today's world, international exploitation and protection of patent rights is generally essential to realize the full financial benefits from an invention.

In most foreign countries, patent rights are granted to the first person to file for the patent, whereas in the United States, such rights are given on a "first to invent" basis. Under a major international patent treaty, known as the Paris Convention, most countries will recognize the date of filing of a U.S. patent application as the date of filing in that foreign country, provided that the foreign patent application is filed within one year after the U.S. application. However, in a few countries (most notably India, Taiwan, and Thailand) which have not signed this treaty, a patent application must be filed before the invention is made public.

The patent application itself consists of several components, including the patent specification, one or more drawings, the patent claim(s), an abstract or summary of the invention, a sworn declaration that the applicant is the true inventor, and a small entity declaration, where applicable. These should be accompanied by a written statement disclosing and providing copies of the prior art, a transmittal letter, and the basic filing fee (currently $730). Generally speaking, patent fees are relatively high, although for some fees, a reduction is available to those who qualify as "small entities." All fees are subject to change and current information should be obtained from the PTO at 703/305-HELP or 703/603-0465. The PTO also has detailed requirements with regard to the form of the application, including page numbering, top and bottom margins, side margins, punctuation, and claim numbering.

Patents, it should be remembered, are limited monopolies, giving their owners broad and exclusive rights to use the patented invention for a limited period of time. In exchange for this monopoly, the inventor is required to disclose her invention fully, so that once the patent has expired, it will be added to the general body of public knowledge and can be used by anyone. Thus, for certain types of inventions, it may be preferable for the inventor to keep the process a secret and manufacture the product herself, rather than disclose it in a patent. In fact, Coca-Cola has followed this practice with regard to the formula for its syrup base, and it remains one of the best-guarded and most valuable trade secrets in the world.

Once a patent application is complete and officially on file with the PTO, the phrase "Patent Pending" may be used in connection with the invention, either in promotional and other literature or on the invention itself. There are criminal penalties for the use of this phrase in advertising when no active patent application is officially on file. Although it is not possible to prevent infringement of an invention before a patent actually issues, use of "Patent Pending" helps to put others on notice of your claim and will discourage them from investing significant amounts of time or money to exploit your invention for what may turn out to be a limited period of time until the patent is issued. All applicants and their attorneys have a duty to disclose to the PTO all information which might influence the Examining Attorney. This includes both information known at the time the application is filed, as well as that which is discovered thereafter.

The patent application review can take six (6) months to over two (2) years to complete. If the patent is allowed, issuance fees must be paid and the "letters patent" will then issue. Once a patent has issued, products embodying the invention may be marked with the phrase "Pat." or "Patent" and the number assigned to the patent in connection with its issuance. Such marking is not required to maintain patent protection, but it does provide constructive notice to potential infringers. There are both advantages and disadvantages to the use of the marking, so consult with an attorney before proceeding.

### How Long Do Patent Rights Last?

The term of patent protection was changed effective June 8, 1995, to conform U.S. law to two newly accepted international trade treaties. Therefore, a utility patent filed on or after that date will protect against infringement for twenty years from the earliest effective filing date. However, according to information available from the PTO at the time of this writing, the term of protection will remain unchanged for a plant patent (seventeen years from the date of patent issue) and for a design patent (fourteen years from the date of issuance). Some patents already in existence or with applications pending on June 8, 1995, may also have their terms extended, but there may be some limitations on the remedies available for their enforcement. Legal advice should be sought to deal with the special problems these situations will present.

## Conclusion

If you are working as a writer, artist, musician, computer programmer, designer, inventor, or in any field to which these intellectual property laws apply, you will want to become as familiar as you can with the relevant legal principles. However, since the value in a piece of intellectual property may last over a long period of time and many of the legal issues are quite complex, you will probably want to develop a working relationship with a lawyer familiar with the appropriate field of law who can assist you. When you go to such an attorney, be sure to ask her about the nature and extent of her experience, not only with these different areas of law, but also with the specific industry in which you will be working. Intellectual property law is a highly specialized field, and a lawyer who is an expert in biological or electrical patents may know little or nothing about film or music law. In fact, a special bar examination and registration procedure is required for attorneys to handle patent, but not trademark, matters before the PTO. The right attorney can help you not only to protect your work, but also to evaluate it and exploit it to its fullest potential.

### Bibliography

Beil, Norman, editor and compiler. *The Writer's Legal and Business Guide*. New York: Arco Publishing, 1984.

Coleman, Bob, and Deborah Neville. *The Great American Idea Book: How to Make Money from Your Ideas for Movies, Music, Books, Inventions, Businesses, and Almost Anything Else!* New York: W.W. Norton and Co., 1993.

Crawford, Tad. *Legal Guide for the Visual Artist, 3d ed.* New York: Allworth Communications, 1990.

Halloran, Mark, Esq., editor and compiler. *The Musician's Business and Legal Guide*. Englewood Cliffs, NJ: Prentice-Hall, 1991.

Kirsch, Jonathan. *Kirsch's Handbook of Publishing Law for Authors, Publishers, Editors, and Agents.* Venice, CA: Acrobat Books, 1995.

Klavens, Kent J. *Protecting Your Songs and Yourself.* Cincinnati, OH: Writer's Digest Books, 1989

Krasilovsky, William M., and Sidney Shemel. *This Business of Music, 6th ed.* New York: Billboard Publications, 1990.

Pressman, David. *Patent It Yourself, 4th ed.* Berkeley, CA: Nolo Press, 1995.

Victoroff, Gregory T., ed. *Visual Artist's Business and Legal Guide.* Englewood Cliffs, NJ: Prentice-Hall, 1994.

## Organizational Resources
### General:

Copyright Office
Library of Congress
Washington, DC 20559
(202) 707-3000 (general information)
(202) 707-9100 (forms hotline)
*To use the forms hotline, you must be able to request forms by name (for example, Form TX, PA, VA, RE, etc.) and circulars by name and number.*

Patent and Trademark Office
Washington, DC 20231
*Some publications are available from the PTO as well, including "Basic Facts about Registering a Trademark" which includes trademark registration forms.*
Phone numbers at the PTO:
General Trademark or Patent Information: (703) 308-HELP
Recorded General Trademark or Patent Information: (703) 557-INFO
Automated Line for Status Information on Trademark Applications: (703) 305-8747
Trademark Trial and Appeal Board: (703) 308-9300
Assistant Commissioner for Trademarks: (703) 308-8900
Patent Enrollment and Discipline (for a list of registered patent attorneys and agents in your area: (703) 308-5316.)

Volunteer Lawyers for the Arts
1 East 53rd Street, 6th Floor
3rd Floor
New York, NY 10022
(212) 319-2787
*There are also a number of organizations like those listed below, located in major metropolitan areas. Some may be sponsored by state or local bar associations or may be independent entities. The state or local bar associations may also provide referrals.*

Business Volunteers for the Arts
200 South Biscayne Boulevard
Suite 4600
Miami, FL 33131
(305) 376-8674

California Lawyers for the Arts
San Francisco Office
Fort Mason Center
Building C, Room 255
San Francisco, CA 94123
(415) 775-7200

Los Angeles Office:
1549 11th Street, Suite 200
Santa Monica, CA 90401
(310) 395-8893

Colorado Lawyers for the Arts
200 Grant Street, Suite 303E
Denver, CO 80203
(303) 722-7994

Connecticut Volunteer Lawyers for
the Arts
Connecticut Commission on the Arts
227 Lawrence Street
Hartford, CT 06106
(203) 566-4770

Fund for the Arts
623 West Main Street, 2nd Floor
Louisville, KY 40202
(502) 582-0100

Georgia Volunteer Lawyers for the Arts
141 Pryor Street, Suite 2030
Atlanta, GA 30303
(404) 525-6046

Visual Artists and Galleries Association, Inc. (VAGA)
521 Fifth Avenue, Suite 800
New York, NY 10017
(212) 808-0616

Huntington Arts Council
213 Main Street
Huntington, NY 11743
(516) 271-8423

Lawyers for the Creative Arts
213 West Institute Place, Suite 411
Chicago, IL 60610
(312) 944-2787

Louisiana Volunteer Lawyers for
the Arts
c/o Arts Council of New Orleans
821 Gravier Street, Suite 600
New Orleans, LA 70112
(504) 523-1465

Maryland Lawyers for the Arts
Maryland Art Place
Baltimore, MD 21202
(410) 752-1633

North Carolina Volunteer Lawyers
for the Arts
City of Raleigh Arts Commission
P.O. Box 590
Raleigh, NC 27602
(919) 831-6234

Philadelphia Volunteer Lawyers for
the Arts
251 South 18th Street
Philadelphia, PA 19103
(215) 545-3385

St. Louis Volunteer Lawyers and
Accountants for the Arts
3540 Washington, 2nd Floor
St. Louis, MO 63103
(314) 652-2410

Texas Accountants and Lawyers
for the Arts
2917 Swiss Avenue
Dallas, TX 75204
(214) 821-1818

Texas Accountants and Lawyers
for the Arts
1540 Sul Ross
Houston, TX 77006
(713) 526-4876

Volunteer Lawyers for the Arts, DC
918 16th Street NW, Suite 503
Washington, DC 20006
(202) 429-0229

Volunteer lawyers for the Arts
  Program
Albany-Schenectady League of
  Arts, Inc.
19 Clinton Avenue
Albany, NY 12207
(518) 449-5380

Washington Area Lawyers for the
  Arts
1325 G Street, Lower Level
Washington, DC 20005
(202) 393-2826

### For Writers:

Author's Guild Inc. (book authors)
Robin Davis Miller, Executive
  Director
330 W. 42nd St.
New York, NY 10036
(212) 563-5904
*They have a book with a model
trade book contract with annota-
tions, which members get automatically; nonmembers must purchase.
To become a member, you must be
a published author or in the process.
Membership fees are on a sliding
scale, based on how much is earned
from a book. Membership is primarily national, but they have a number of international authors. They
hold conferences, provide advocacy,
and publish a quarterly bulletin.*

PEN International Center
568 Broadway, Room 101
New York, NY 10012
(212) 334-1660
*Domestic and international hu-
man rights work; advocacy for authors and support for freedom of
speech; literary awards. Approximately 2,800 members.*

PEN Center USA West
672 S. La Fayette Park Place
Suite 41
Los Angeles, CA 90057
(213) 365-8500

Society of Children's Book Writers and Illustrators (SCBWI)
22736 Vancouver Street, Suite 106
West Hills, CA 91307
*Creators of children's books find
this organization extremely helpful, but unfortunately they do not
seem to provide service by telephone.*

Writer's Guild of America, East
  (film and TV writers)
555 W. 57th Street, Suite 1230
New York, NY 10019
(212) 767-7800
*Union for radio, film, and televi-
sion writers.*

Writer's Guild of America, West
8955 Beverly Blvd.
Los Angeles, CA 90048
(310) 550-1000

## For the Performing Arts:

Director's Guild of America
7920 Sunset Blvd.
Hollywood, CA 90046
(213) 289-2000

Screen Actors' Guild
5757 Wilshire Boulevard
Los Angeles, CA 90036
(213) 954-1600

American Federation of Radio &
    Television Artists (actors)
260 Madison Avenue
New York, NY 10016
(212) 532-0800

Actors' Equity (stage)
165 W. 46th Street
New York, NY 10036
(212) 869-8530

Dramatists Guild (stage; NY only)
234 W. 44th Street
New York, NY 10036
(212) 398-9366

For many of these organizations
there are offices in New York, Los
Angeles, and other cities. Check
your local directory or call the
headquarters office.

## For Visual Artists:

Graphic Artists' Guild
11 West 20th Street, 8th Floor
New York, NY 10011
(212) 463-7730
*They publish a book called*
Graphic Artists' Guild Handbook:
Pricing and Ethical Guidelines,
*which is excellent.*

Society of Illustrators
128 E. 63rd Street
New York, NY 10021
(212) 838-2560
Offices in many other cities.

National Artists' Equity Association
P.O. Box 28068, Central Station
Washington, DC 20038
(202) 628-9633

Comic Book Legal Defense Fund
P.O. Box 693
Northampton, MA 01061
(413) 586-6967

Comic Book Professionals Association
    (CBPA)
P.O. Box 570850
Tarzania, CA 91357

## For Inventors:

American Association of Inventors
6562 E. Curtis Road
Bridgeport, MI 48722
(517) 799-8208

American Society of Inventors
P.O. Box 58426
Philadelphia, PA 19102
(215) 546-6601

Invention Marketing Institute (also
    headquarters for National In-
    ventors Foundation)
345 W. Cypress Street
Glendale, CA 91204
(818) 246-6540

Inventors Clubs of America
P.O. Box 450261
Atlanta, GA 30345
(404) 938-5089

## For Musicians:

American Federation of Musicians
Paramount Bldg.
1501 Broadway, Suite 600
New York, NY 10036
(212) 869-1330

American Society of Composers,
Authors and Publishers
(ASCAP)
One Lincoln Plaza
New York, NY 10023
(212) 595-3050

Broadcast Music, Inc. (BMI)
320 W. 57th Street
New York, NY 10019
(212) 586-2000

National Academy of Songwriters
(NAS)
6381 Hollywood Blvd., Suite 780
Hollywood, CA 90028
(213) 463-7178

Songwriters Guild of America
276 Fifth Avenue
New York, NY 10001
(212) 686-6820

## For Photographers:

Associated Photographers International
P.O. Box 2172
Chatsworth, CA 91313
(818) 700-0811

American Society of Media Photographers (ASMP)
14 Washington Road, Suite 502
Princeton, NJ 08550
(609) 799-8300
Call for local chapter.

## For Software Publishers:

Software Publishers Association
1101 Connecticut Avenue, NW
Suite 901
Washington, DC 20036
(202) 452-1600

---

**Louise Nemschoff** is a sole practitioner of entertainment and intellectual property law, with offices in Beverly Hills. She represents a wide range of parties in domestic and international transactions in film, television, the visual arts, and publishing. Ms. Nemschoff is a graduate of Harvard College and Yale Law School who has been in practice for over twenty years. She has published several articles and spoken extensively, both in the United States and Europe, on various aspects of copyright, trademark, and entertainment law. From 1993 to 1994 she chaired the Intellectual Property and Entertainment Law Section of the Los Angeles County Bar Association and currently sits on the Association's Board of Trustees.

Chapter 19

# *Real Estate*

Laura J. Schoenbauer

Chapter Outline

**Introduction**

**Buying a Home**
Making the Deal—Signing a Purchase Agreement • After Signing the Purchase Agreement • Title Insurance

**Selling Your Home**
For Sale by Owner • "For Sale By Owner" Services • Using a Real Estate Agent, Broker, or Realty Company

**Signing a Residential Lease**

**Real Estate Taxes**

**Conclusion**

Introduction
    A home is often the largest purchase a person will ever make. Most sales occur without any problems, but an informed buyer or seller should be able to overcome or avoid obstacles and costly errors. During their lives most people buy or sell real estate at least once. Few, however, understand all the implications of the documents they

sign when buying or selling a home or all of their options, rights, and potential liabilities. In many commercial transactions the options are so broad that expert assistance is often essential.

This chapter will discuss some of the issues to consider when involved in typical residential real estate transactions. Keep in mind, however, that this discussion does not consider unique practices in certain regions. Therefore, expert advice from someone in the state and/or county in which you are buying property is advised.

## Buying a Home

The real estate market has historically been one of "buyer beware." Thus, it is important that when you buy a home you understand what real estate agents will and will not do for you. Recently, there has been a movement toward protecting buyers initiated by consumer groups as well as professional associations.

Most people use a real estate agent when they want to purchase a home. In some states, the realtor can be a dual agent. If you, as buyer, have signed an agency agreement, the agent will typically then look out for your best interests and represent you solely as long as you only look at homes listed with other real estate companies. If, on the other hand, you decide to look into properties that the real estate agent or the agent's company has listed, the agent's first duty may be to the seller, not to you as the buyer. In this "dual agency situation"— where the agent represents two people—the real estate agent becomes the seller's agent and the buyer is the customer, not the agent's client. The agent would then have the obligation to reveal any confidences to the seller that you as the buyer have made to her.

In many states, dual agency is prohibited. Where allowed, the real estate agent is required by law to disclose this dual agency. Often the agency agreement will state that if you as the buyer look at one of the real estate agent's or her company's property, the exclusive agency relationship between you and the realtor terminates. The agent still must treat you honestly and fairly and must disclose any known defects about the property. However, the agent has an obligation to act in the best interests of the seller. In this situation, the buyer must keep in mind that the agent is no longer working for her and that she is unrepresented in the negotiations. A buyer should feel free to ask the agent at any time who the agent is representing and what conflicts there may be.

Many consumer groups and professional associations believe that the buyer, not only the seller, should have all of the benefits of a true agent, and these groups have been promoting single agency relationships between buyers and real estate agents. Across the country, many agents are becoming exclusive buyers' brokers, that is, have devoted themselves to single agency practice.

In a single agency relationship, the real estate agent works exclusively for the buyer or the seller and makes a full and clear disclosure of her agency relationship. This relationship is one of true agency in which the agent owes her client the fiduciary duties of loyalty and confidentiality, as well as her best efforts. The agent should be willing to sign a guaranty or an agreement stating and listing the agency duties the agent owes to the buyer. The agent will not just try to buy property for you but will counsel you and help find what is best for you. The agent has a duty to negotiate the best price for you and represent your interests only.

### Making the Deal—Signing a Purchase Agreement

Once you have decided you are interested in a house, you will make an offer to the seller. At this point, there will be negotiations over the price and other terms of the purchase agreement. You may want to obtain an independent appraisal of the home or at least look at other homes of comparable size, age, and condition to see if the asking price is reasonable.

All of the terms of the sale must be put into writing in the purchase agreement. Often, the seller's agent will have a preprinted standard purchase agreement drafted by the state or local realty association which contains terms most favorable to the seller and her agent. All terms are negotiable, however, and you should not hesitate to change anything on the preprinted form. You should also review the agreement with a lawyer.

You will want to include a section that describes any personal property that will be included in the sale of the real estate. If this is not spelled out, the seller can remove any personal property from the property.

The purchase agreement will state the price and terms of payment. The parties should stipulate whether the full cash amount will be required at the closing, or whether the seller will accept a down payment with later installments. The parties should also specify the method of payment required at closing: cash, certified check, or any other form of negotiable paper. With a certified check, the bank guarantees the check, but there is a time lag in getting the funds transferred through the bank; a federal reserve draw is guaranteed by the Federal Reserve Bank, and there is very little lag time in having the funds transferred.

The parties should also set out in the purchase agreement any earnest money which must be deposited. Earnest money is paid at the time the purchase agreement is signed to show the seller that you are "earnest" about your interest in the property. Depending on the terms of the purchase agreement, if you default on the contract the earnest money may be retained by the seller. The seller can also sue for actual damages which may be higher than the earnest money amount. You should require that the earnest money is held in an escrow account, by an independent third party. Then, if there is a default by the seller the earnest money can be returned to you without having to bring a legal action against the seller. Where the contract specifies that you are entitled to specific performance, you may be able to require the owner to sell the house to you.

If you are considering assuming a loan, you may want to include a clause in which the seller promises that the loan is not in default and states the amount due. Many loans, however, cannot be assumed.

The purchase agreement will specify the state of the title and the type of deed to be delivered to the buyer at closing. There are three types of deeds: general warranty deed, limited or special warranty deed, and quitclaim deed; and three levels of title quality: marketable title, insurable title, and good title. A warranty deed is the highest level of assurance for the buyer.

- A general warranty deed warrants that the seller has title to the property, that the seller has the right to convey the property, that there are no encumbrances on the property (except as set forth in the deed), and that the seller will be liable to the buyer for any loss if the title turns out to be defective or subject to any encumbrance.

- A limited warranty deed only warrants that the seller herself has not encumbered the title, but says nothing as to what her predecessors may have done affecting title.

- A quitclaim deed gives no warranties whatsoever. A quitclaim deed simply conveys any right that the seller may have in the property, if any. The buyer will usually want to receive a general warranty deed, but where there is title insurance, a special warranty deed may be acceptable. In some states, quitclaim deeds are customary, and title insurance is relied on instead. Also, in a divorce, the party who ends up with the house may only get a quitclaim from the other party.

- Marketable title means that the seller must be sure that there are no encumbrances or clouds on the title that would affect resale of the property at the time of conveyance.

- Insurable title means that a reputable title company would insure the property against defects.

- Good title means that the seller has the title to the property in fact. However, the seller may have to institute a lawsuit in order to get the title cleared.

The buyer does not want to agree to take good title; she will want marketable title. If the seller does not deliver the required state of title at the closing, the seller has breached the purchase agreement; and, depending on what the agreement provides, you, the buyer, may terminate the agreement and get back your earnest money or bring an action to enforce it and/or get damages.

It is best to require that the property be free of all encumbrances except those encumbrances specifically approved by the buyer. The seller may attempt to have the agreement provide that the seller will give marketable title, subject to "any and all encumbrances of record, if any." You should not agree to this. It means that you could be subject to mechanic's liens, tax liens, or any other interest people may have in the property and you will not be able to do anything about it.

The agreement will also spell out who will pay the real estate taxes and any special assessments. Typically, the parties will prorate any taxes as of the date of closing. In addition, it is common to ask the seller to pay all levied or pending special assessments against the property. (Special assessments are charged against property by either a city, county, or state, for the cost of such things as road improvements, utility installation, or curb cleaning.) Depending on the type of assessment, it can be paid in a lump sum or in installments (with interest charged) along with the real estate taxes.

The purchase agreement should also address what will happen if the property is damaged prior to the sale. If this is not included, you may be assuming that risk and may not be able to get out of the contract if the property is damaged before closing. You can stipulate that if the property is substantially damaged prior to closing, the agreement will terminate and the earnest money shall be refunded, at the Buyers option.

The parties will often include a clause regarding any warranties the seller makes about the condition of the property. As a general rule, sellers want to make no warranties and to sell the property "as is". On the other hand, you as the buyer should attempt to get as many warranties as possible. You might want the seller to warrant that all appliances, fixtures, heating and air conditioning equipment, wiring, and plumbing used in the property will be in good working order, as of the date of closing. You may also want the seller to make representations as to whether or not the basement has been wet or the roof has leaked. The seller may also disclose whether or not the property is connected to city water and sewer and whether it has cable television. Even with the above-described warranties, the sale should be contingent upon a favorable inspection of the property. You should consider hiring a home inspection company to examine the property. You may also want to have the purchase agreement contingent on a favorable environmental review of the property. Federal and state laws make the owner of the property potentially liable for any clean-up of toxic waste, regardless of whether the owner of the property put the toxic waste there.

If you currently own a home, you may want to make the sale contingent upon the sale of your current home. One of the most essential terms is that the purchase agreement is conditioned on your ability to to obtain financing for the home. It is very important to set out what are acceptable terms, including the interest rate, amount of the loan, and points. Frequently banks charge one or more points as an origination fee, and, depending on market conditions, may also add points to the mortgage loan to cover other fees. Whether the buyer pays all the points or the seller pays some or all is a matter of negotiation. Additional points may be charged by the lender in exchange for a lower interest rate on the mortgage loan. Often there is pressure to sign the purchase agreement quickly. If you feel that you must sign it before you can review it with a lawyer, you can add a clause that conditions the purchase agreement on being reviewed by an attorney within a certain time, with the right to cancel it if the attorney is not satisfied.

### After Signing the Purchase Agreement

There are several things you must do after signing the purchase agreement. You will want to have the property inspected by surveyors and home inspectors. All of these inspections are typically at the buyer's own cost. However, who pays this cost may be negotiated with the seller.

After obtaining the abstract of title or owner's title, the title should be reviewed by an attorney or by a title insurance company. Closely watch the time periods set forth in the purchase agreement for the time period in which you must make objections to title.

You may then have to obtain financing for the home. There are several ways the property may be financed: by obtaining your own mortgage; by assuming the mortgage of the seller; or by financing the sale with a contract for deed.

With a contract for deed the seller finances the sale. The buyer typically makes a down payment and then pays installments of principal and interest on the balance due. Although there are many variations to payment schedules, the contract may be set up so that equal installments are paid until the entire principal balance has been paid or a balloon payment may be required after a period of time. This arrangement is very beneficial at times when banks are charging very high mortgage interest rates and a seller is able to finance at a lower rate. If a buyer defaults in a contract for deed, and the seller cancels the contract, the buyer will typically lose all payments made to the seller up to date of cancellation. Depending on the language in the contract a seller may also be able to sue for damages.

A buyer may decide to assume or take the property subject to an existing mortgage. This option is attractive where the seller's mortgage is at a lower interest rate than the current market interest rates. This option is not always available and depends on the existing mortgage and lender. A buyer should review the seller's loan documents, including the mortgage, and contact the lender before considering this option. Most mortgages require a lender's consent prior to transferring the property. If consent is required, but not obtained, a buyer risks the lender foreclosing on the property. When a buyer assumes an existing loan, the buyer agrees to be personally liable to the lender for the mortgage debt. Whether the buyer assumes the mortgage or takes the property subject to the mortgage, unless the seller is specifically released by the lender, the seller remains personally liable for the mortgage debt.

As a seller it is very important to obtain the release from a lender or have some arrangement if the buyer assumes your loan. You need to be sure that the payments continue to be made, and, in the event the buyer defaults, you can reacquire the property. A seller should also be aware that remaining personally liable on a mortgage may affect the seller's ability to obtain other financing (as this remains a liability for the seller).

The most common type of residential real estate financing is a mortgage loan. The lender makes the proceeds available to pay the seller at closing. There are several different types of customary home loans; conventional loans, Federal Housing Administration (FHA) loans, and Veteran's Administration (VA) loans.

The FHA and VA loan programs are federal programs which insure mortgages, thus encouraging lenders to give loans to people who may not otherwise be able to qualify for loans. The FHA will examine and insure each loan individually. When the loan transaction is consummated by the private lending institution, the mortgage is then insured by FHA. Typically, FHA charges the purchaser a one time front end mortgage insurance premium which is a percentage of the loan amount. FHA guaranteed mortgages also typically only require a very low down payment.

VA loans are similar to FHA loans in that the VA guarantees the loans. Eligible borrowers are military veterans as well as veterans' widows who have not remarried. The VA's program differs from the FHA's in that the VA guarantees only a specific portion of the loan. If the lender's loss exceeds that amount, the lender must bear the remainder of the loss. The VA does charge the borrower a "funding fee," payable at closing, which is rather low, typically less than 2 percent of the loan amount. The VA does a careful review of the veteran borrower's credit and income before committing itself to guarantee a loan. However, it does not require a down payment, and many VA loans are made with no cash investment, or only a nominal cash investment by the borrower.

Another financing option is a conventional mortgage through a bank or mortgage company. Because these loans are not guaranteed, the mortgage company will often require a larger down payment than VA or FHA loans. If a person cannot make a large down payment, private mortgage insurance is sometimes available and required by a lender.

The mortgage company will do a thorough analysis of your credit history and will charge you the cost of doing the credit search. The mortgage company will give you a good faith estimate of the charges made in processing your loan application and any costs to be paid at closing. When reviewing your credit, the mortgage company will look at your current debt and your current income and the price of the home or amount of the mortgage and determine whether or not you can afford the mortgage payment. The mortgage company will let you know what percent of debt it will allow you to have in deciding whether to give you a mortgage.

There are many different structures for payments for residental loans including: conventional mortgage; adjustable rate mortgage; and buy-downs. A conventional mortgage typically has a set interest rate. Your monthly payment remains the same over the life of the mortgage. Shop around for different lenders to compare interest rates. You can usually obtain a lower interest rate by giving the lender points up front. A point is a certain percent of the mortgage price which you pay to the lender at closing. Depending on the amount of points you pay, your long-term interest rate will be lower. In determining whether or not you should pay points or a higher interest rate you should consider how long you intend to own the home. If you intend to only own the home for a few years, it may be more economical for you to pay a higher interest rate over paying points at closing.

Adjustable rate mortgages are also available. With an adjustable rate mortgage (ARM), a borrower can obtain a lower initial interest rate. As interest rates fluctuate, however, the interest rate the borrower must pay on the loan will change. ARMs vary considerably on their terms, how much the interest rate is allowed to fluctuate, and on what interest rate the ARM interest rate is based. An ARM should state when the interest rate can change (once a year, or some other specified time period), and have a ceiling as to how high the interest rate can go each period and overall. For example, it may not increase more than one or two percentage points each time period and will never go over a certain rate. This gives you a built-in guarantee that the interest rate will not fluctuate too greatly and will not rise too high. In addition, the mortgage should state on what the interest rate is based. Usually, the interest rate will be based on the U.S. Government Treasury Bill rate or on the prime rate of the Federal Reserve Bank or some other well-established interest rate, plus a number of points. This must be agreed upon by you and your lender.

A buy-down is another option for people who need lower mortgage payments the first few years of the mortgage but can then afford higher mortgage payments. With a buy-down, you pay a lower interest rate in the first few years, and then lock in a higher interest rate for the life of the mortgage. Typically, the borrower will have to pay points to obtain the lower interest rate, but the money needed to pay the points is built into the price of the home. The borrower is actually financing the points. The interest rate for the first couple of years is typically below market rates for conventional loans and the lock-in rate is typically at market rates or possibly slightly higher.

You will have to decide when to lock into an interest rate. Because interest rates fluctuate from day to day, you want to be ready for any changes and want to evaluate how much to risk waiting for the "perfect" interest rate. Usually, the mortgage company will not let you lock in a mortgage rate more than sixty days before the closing.

These are several of the financing options for residential loans. You should contact your lender to discuss other available financing structures that it may have available for buyers of residential property.

### Title Insurance

Title insurance protects you and your lender against defects in the condition of the title of the property and against other people claiming interests in the property. Before closing, the title insurance company reviews the title of the land to see if anyone else holds interest in the property. Most title insurance companies do not cover items that you had knowledge of at closing. Therefore, if you are aware of a defect you should disclose it to the title insurance company and determine what the seller needs to do to cure the defect.

If you are financing your purchase, your lender will usually want title insurance coverage to the extent of the mortgage debt on the property. You typically pay for this insurance at the closing.

You may also purchase title insurance for your own interest. Make sure you review the title commitment you receive before closing (including the preprinted language) to see what risks the title insurance company is insuring against.

Once you have closed on the property, review the policy the insurance company sends you to make sure it covers the same contingencies and risks as were set forth in the marked-up title commitment and what was agreed to at closing.

## Selling Your Home

There are numerous ways to sell your home and the method you choose can depend on the time you have to dedicate to selling it or your need for an expert to assist you. The method you choose can also affect the price you receive, the time it takes to sell the home, and, of course, the commission you have to pay.

### For Sale by Owner

One option is to sell a home without any professional assistance. There are businesses in some areas of the country which rent for sale signs, brochure boxes, open house signs, and sell the documents needed for a real estate sale, which are also available in many stationery stores. These companies do not assist you in selling the home, except to provide the needed materials. This option is attractive only to those people who have a lot of time to sell their home. One of the more difficult aspects of selling a home without the assistance of a service or realtor is determining the price. To feel comfortable with your price, a qualified appraisal can be obtained for a minimal fee. Also, the opinions of several real estate brokers may be obtained for free with no obligation to list.

### "For Sale By Owner" Services

Some areas of the country have "For Sale by Owner" services. They provide all the services a real estate agent would provide, including preparing the purchase agreement, doing a market analysis of the home, formulating a price, and assisting in the closing. These companies, however, do not actually show the home to prospective buyers. The owner of the home actually shows the house to a buyer. These services will charge a fee, but their rates are usually much lower than those of a real estate agent or broker. The commission varies; if the buyer is using an agent, the rate is higher. Again, you would have to dedicate more time to the sale of the home, but you would have the expertise of real estate business people with some experience to help assist in the sale.

### Using a Real Estate Agent, Broker, or Realty Company

Many people prefer to use the expertise of a realtor to help sell their homes. The best advice in looking for a realtor is to shop around and take your time. Find someone who is compatible with you and whom you feel you can trust. Ask friends and family members about realtors and realty companies they have dealt with. Do not sign anything until you feel you have a good fit with your realtor. The right realtor can make the difference in how smoothly the sale goes and how profitable the sale is. In most states, a salesperson (agent) must work under a real estate broker. Most states have training and licensing requirements for both agents and brokers.

Once you have decided on a real estate agent, the real estate agent will ask you to sign a listing agreement, which is an agency contract that outlines your duties and the real estate agent's duties in selling your home. The real estate agent is bound by this contract to act in the best interests of you, the seller. Many states require that a listing agreement be in writing.

A listing agreement will spell out which kind of agency arrangement exists between you and the agent:

- Exclusive right to sell/list. Typically, under an exclusive right to sell/list arrangement, during the term of the agreement the seller must give the agent her commission no matter who sells the property, even if it is the seller herself.

- Exclusive agency. Under an exclusive agency arrangement, you can only allow the listing agent to sell the property. If another agent sells the property, the first agent gets her commission. However, if you sell the property yourself no commission is due.

- Open listing agreement. Under a typical open listing agreement, the agent gets the commission only if she is the one who sells the property. The seller could have several different agents working on selling the property.

In reviewing a listing agreement you may want to require that the agent use her "best efforts" to sell the property, not just "cooperate" with you in selling the property. The agent will probably want the listing agreement to relieve the agent from liability if there is any damage or theft done to your property while she is showing your house. This can be negotiated.

## Information About the Property

The listing agreement gives detailed information about the property, such as the size of rooms, amenities, etc. Make sure this information is accurate since you may be responsible for any misstatements. This information may then, depending on your region and listing agreement, be put in the Multiple Listing Service (MLS), where realtors and other individuals in an area place descriptions of houses for sale.

## Showing the House

The listing agreement may specify special promotional devices that will be used, such as open houses and brochures, as well as when the agent can show the house or if the agent must give a telephone call before showing the house. You will also want to discuss whether or not there will be a key box to your house. A key box is obviously convenient because the agent can show the house at any time of the day that is convenient for the buyer; however, you should consider whether or not you want people going through your home when you are not at home.

## Commission Rate

The commission rate can be negotiated. Factors such as the estimated time it will take to sell the home as well as the price of the home should be considered when negotiating the commission rate. If the buyer has a real estate agent, that agent will typically receive 40 to 50 percent of the commission. Alternative forms of compensation for the realtor include an hourly rate or a flat fee. Discuss the options with the realtor. If she will not agree to consider your terms, you may want to look for another agent who will.

## Duration of the Listing Agreement

Typically the listing agreement is only in effect for a specified period, such as three months, six months, or one year. The agent will usually include a clause that if a prospective buyer becomes aware of the property while the listing agreement is in effect, but signs the contract for sale within a few months after expiration of the listing agreement, you still have to pay a commission to the agent. This clause is designed to protect the agent against a seller waiting until the listing agreement expires and then signing a contract.

## The "Successful Closing" Clause

You should be certain that a listing agreement clearly states that a commission is only owed upon the successful closing of a transaction to a buyer at the terms set out in the listing agreement. If this is not clear, a commission may be owed even if a buyer defaults.

## Signing a Residential Lease

Most people have, at some time, entered into a lease contract. Because a residential lease is a legally binding contract, it is important that you negotiate the terms and understand what obligations you have before you sign. A preprinted lease form does not mean that the terms cannot be altered.

Once you and the landlord have discussed the lease terms, be sure that they are all contained in the lease. Also, if the landlord is holding the property until your current lease terminates, have her confirm in writing that the apartment or house will be available on the agreed-upon date. You should receive a copy of all documents you sign. If you do change a term in a preprinted lease, both you and the landlord should initial the change. There are many terms you will want specified in the lease. One of the most important terms is the amount of rent. You will also want to specify how often, if ever, the lessor can increase the rent. You will also want to determine which day of the month rent is due and any late charges. The lease should also state whether the lessor or the renter is responsible for paying for sewer, garbage, electricity, heat, gas, and any other utilities. You will also want to cover the telephone system as well as the availability of cable TV.

You may also want to cover which party is responsible for maintenance of the property. If you are renting a house, you may be responsible for mowing the lawn and shoveling the walkway. You may wish to cover major cleaning, such as carpet and window cleaning, as well as cleaning when the renter leaves the apartment. A renter should also ask about decorating, whether the unit may be painted or wallpapered, and repair of nail holes. The renter may want to ask about the age of the appliances and possible replacement of the appliances, if the renter intends to live in the unit for several years, as well as scheduled maintenance of the appliances. Your negotiated agreement as to all of these items should be in the lease language.

The length of the lease is another essential term. You will want to discuss whether it will be a one-year, six-month, month-to-month, and so on, lease. If you do not stipulate the lease term, but the landlord accepts rent payments monthly, you will have created a month-to-month lease. You should also specify in the lease how far in advance you must give the landlord notice before terminating the lease, and vice versa. You may also want to include a clause which lets you terminate the lease if your job transfers you to a different city.

Most landlords require a damage deposit. Discuss how the damage deposit will be applied so that you may avoid unnecessary costs. Some landlords are more particular about the condition in which you must leave the apartment. If you receive your damage deposit after the lease expires, the terms of the lease may require that you receive interest on the amount of the deposit. You should also require that the lessor send your deposit to your new address within a couple of weeks of the lease's end.

The lessor may include a clause requiring you to sign an estoppel certificate; this will typically state that the you are in possession of the premises under a lease, that you have paid all rent due as of the date of the certificate, and that there is no default on the lease. The lessor will want to include this clause because often a prospective buyer of the property will request an estoppel certificate so that they know the condition of the tenancies. The lessor cannot force you to sign an estoppel certificate, unless you had previously agreed to do so.

A provision you may want to request be added to your lease is what is commonly referred to as a buy-build clause. This clause allows you to terminate the lease on a certain number of months notice if you either buy or build a home. You can negotiate the notice required. In addition, you may want to negotiate an option to renew at a preset rate. Keep in mind that if rental rates have dropped you don't have to exercise your option and can negotiate again with the landlord.

## Real Estate Taxes

Real estate taxes are typically calculated by determining the assessed value of property and multiplying that value against a tax rate. The tax rate is based on governmental budgets and is generally not subject to negotiation on the individual level. However, you do have some control over your property's assessed value.

In most states there are different property classifications depending on the use of the property. In addition, many states have some form of credit/exemption for property that is an owner's residence. You should review your tax statement to be certain that the classification is correct and if your property is your residence, that you are receiving the benefit of any credit/exemption if it is available. If you are in doubt, contact your city or county assessor to determine your classification and if inaccurate, what is necessary to change that classification.

In reviewing your property tax statement you should also review your property's assessed value. If this value appears high you may challenge this valuation. If you are not certain whether the value is correct you may want to talk to your neighbors, look at homes in your area that are comparable to your home, or talk to a local realtor to find out generally what is the fair market value of your property. In addition, you may also want to consider obtaining an appraisal. In many states there are several levels at which valuations can be contested: the county board, the court, or the abatement process. Each state varies the process that each of these involve, but there are usually strict time deadlines. If you think your property is overvalued, you should consider as a first step, talking to your local assessor. When you meet with her, bring evidence showing grounds for your argument. Many cases are settled by the assessor prior to going to the board or court. In some states you can challenge previous payments of real estate taxes if the property was overvalued. This process is sometimes referred to as abatement. If you think your property has been overvalued you should also consider contacting an attorney to determine what options are available to you.

## Conclusion

Real estate law, probably more than other areas of law, varies greatly by state and/or county. This chapter is a general overview of matters to consider. You should seek the advice of a competent attorney in the area of the country in which you are entering into a transaction in order to determine if your interests are being protected.

### Bibliography

Devine, George. *For Sale by Owner, 2d ed.* Berkeley, CA: Nolo Press, 1992.

Hinkel, Daniel F. *Practical Real Estate Law, 2d ed.* St. Paul, MN: West Publishing, 1994.

Jordan, Cora. *Neighbor Law, 2d ed.* Berkeley, CA: Nolo Press, 1995.

Steiner, Gerald F., and Martin M. Solomon. *Handbook of Condo Law: A Survival Manual.* Fort Lauderdale, FL: Reniets Press, 1994.

Warda, Mark. *How to Negotiate Real Estate Contracts.* Clearwater, FL: Sphinx Publishing, 1992.

Weaver, Jefferson H. *The Compact Guide to Property Law: A Civilized Approach.* St. Paul, MN: West Publishing, 1992.

### Organizational Resources

Most information can be obtained from the local Board of Realtors. Check the telephone directory. In addition, many realtors will be glad to provide a market analysis of a property in the hope of obtaining the listing.

---

**Laura J. Schoenbauer** practices real estate law extensively at Gray, Plant, Mooty, Mooty & Bennett P. A. in Minneapolis and has since 1987. She was admitted to the bar in Minnesota in 1987 after attending Mankato State University (B.S., *summa cum laude,* 1984) and the University of Minnesota (J.D., *magna cum laude,* 1987). She was the executive editor of the Law and Inequality Journal from 1986 to 1987. She is currently a member of the American Bar Association, Minnesota Bar Association, and the Hennepin County Bar Association.

Chapter 20

# Bankruptcy

Marcia S. Krieger

Chapter Outline

**Introduction**

**Definition of Bankruptcy**
Federal Law for Discharge or Reorganization of Debts • The Purpose
of Bankruptcy • Types of Bankruptcy • Qualifications for Filing •
Terms and Definitions

**How a Bankruptcy Is Initiated**
Voluntary Case • Involuntary Case

**When and Why to Get Bankruptcy Advice**

**Where to Get Bankruptcy Advice and What to Expect**
The Bankruptcy Attorney • Bankruptcy Mills

**How Bankruptcy Works**
Liquidation • Reorganization • Reaffirmation of Debts

**Duties of the Debtor**

**Rights and Responsibilities of the Creditor**

**Powers of the Trustee**

**Bankruptcy As a Last Resort**
Disadvantages • Alternatives

**Conclusion**

Introduction      What happens when you or your business cannot pay the bills? The dreaded remedy of bankruptcy, although a last resort, can provide much-needed relief. Since enactment of the Bankruptcy Code in 1978, over 8 million bankruptcy cases have been filed.[1] In 1993 alone, more than 875,000 cases were filed, most of which were filed for individual consumers.[2]

Each bankruptcy case affects not only the debtor who files, but family members, creditors, investors, and often individuals or entities who did business with the debtor prior to the bankruptcy. This chapter outlines the complex process of bankruptcy.

Definition of   **Federal Law for Discharge or Reorganization of Debts**
Bankruptcy      Although many states have procedures for liquidation of assets, repayment of creditors, or reorganization of debts, bankruptcy is governed by federal law, the U. S. Bankruptcy Code, also called the Code.

The Code, found in Title 11 of the U.S. Code, was enacted in 1978 and has since been amended several times, most recently in October 1994. It is divided into eight chapters; most are odd numbered. Chapters 1, 3, and 5 set out general provisions applicable to each type of bankruptcy relief. Chapters 7, 9, 11, 12, and 13 apply to specific types of bankruptcy relief.

Bankruptcy cases are administered by bankruptcy courts, which are a division of the U.S. District Court sitting in each state and territory of the United States. The Federal Rules of Bankruptcy Procedure and Local Rules of Bankruptcy Procedure are applicable in these courts.

### The Purpose of Bankruptcy

Bankruptcy law has two purposes—one for the individuals and businesses who seek bankruptcy protection (debtors) and one for the individuals or entities to whom the debtors are indebted (creditors).

For the debtor, the primary purpose of the Bankruptcy Code is to allow a "fresh start" in financial affairs. For some debtors, the fresh start means relief from burdensome or overwhelming financial obligations that existed prior to the bankruptcy. Relief from the debt obligations is known as a discharge.

Alternatively, for debtors who seek to reorganize or restructure but not to discharge their debts, the Code provides time and opportunity to regain financial solvency. A bankruptcy filing instantly freezes the creditors and prevents them from attempting to collect their claims. The Code also allows the debtor, in appropriate circumstances, to obtain additional credit, reject unfavorable contracts, and to sell or lease property for the purposes of restoring financial solvency.

For the creditor, the primary purpose of the Code is to provide for collection and liquidation of the debtor's nonexempt assets and for distribution of the proceeds in an orderly manner. Each creditor receives payment based upon the type of debt it holds. Creditors are grouped in classes; the Code sets out the order in which the classes are paid. The creditors in a class divide the funds for that class on a *pro rata* basis.

## Types of Bankruptcy

There are five chapters under which a bankruptcy may be initiated.

### Chapter 7

Chapter 7 is designed for individuals and businesses who cannot pay their debts from their current income. Chapter 7 provides for liquidation of the debtor's nonexempt assets. The individual is allowed to keep exempt property; the remaining property is collected and sold, and the proceeds are distributed to creditors by a trustee. An individual debtor receives a discharge which cancels the obligations on most remaining debts. Chapter 7 cases account for approximately 70 percent of all bankruptcy filings.

### Chapter 9

Chapter 9 provides for reorganization by insolvent municipal entities.

### Chapter 11

This type of bankruptcy allows a business or individual to reorganize. In Chapter 11, the business often continues to operate as a debtor-in-possession (DIP) under the supervision of the U.S. Trustee's Office or under the direction of a trustee. The debtor's objective is to propose a reorganization plan to repay creditors.

### Chapter 12

Chapter 12 allows family farmers who are individuals or specially qualified partnerships and corporations to reorganize. As in Chapter 11, the debtor's objective is to propose a plan to repay creditors. The plan is administered by a Chapter 12 trustee.

## Chapter 13

Chapter 13 was formerly referred to as the "wage-earner's plan." Chapter 13 allows individuals to propose a repayment plan to creditors (usually over a period of three to five years) which is funded from the debtor's income. The plan is administered by the Chapter 13 trustee. Chapter 13, unlike Chapter 7, allows debtors to keep their assets and pay their financial obligations over time.

### Qualifications for Filing

Subject to some limitations, any individual, corporation, partnership, limited partnership, or joint venture that resides in, has a business in, or owns property in the United States may seek bankruptcy protection. Except for municipalities, it is not necessary that the debtor seeking bankruptcy protection be insolvent or unable to pay debts to be eligible for bankruptcy protection. A debtor seeks bankruptcy relief by filing a petition in bankruptcy court.

### Terms and Definitions

The following terms have specific meanings in a bankruptcy context.

### Assets

Assets are property or property rights including personal property, real property, contracts, expectancies, entitlements, claims, and other legal or equitable interests.

### Automatic stay

A temporary injunction is imposed at the time of the filing of *any* bankruptcy case. This injunction prohibits creditors from seeking to collect on any debts incurred before the filing of the bankruptcy petition from the debtor or the property of the bankruptcy estate without permission of the bankruptcy court. This automatic stay prohibits creditors from telephoning, writing to collect debts, continuing or initiating lawsuits, continuing or initiating foreclosures, or repossessing property. In Chapters 12 and 13, the automatic stay also protects cosigners and comakers of the debtor on consumer debts. Violation of the automatic stay may subject the creditor to sanctions. Creditors may obtain relief from the automatic stay and act to collect on debts by obtaining permission from the bankruptcy court.

### Claim

A claim means one of two things. It is a right to payment regardless of whether the right is liquidated or unliquidated, contingent, matured or unmatured, disputed or undisputed, secured or unsecured. It is also a right to an equitable remedy. In a bankruptcy case, there are three types of claims—priority claims, secured claims, and unsecured claims. A claim is made against a bankruptcy estate when a creditor files proof of her claim with the court or in certain circumstances when the debtor has listed or "scheduled" a creditor and the creditor has no dispute as to the amount and the manner in which the debt has been identified.

## Confirmation

Confirmation is the bankruptcy court's approval of a debtor's proposed repayment or reorganization plan. The approval is granted according to the procedures specified for each of the reorganization Chapters 9, 11, 12, and 13. The confirmation order often includes detailed instructions about distribution of payments to creditors.

## Creditor

A creditor is an individual or entity with a claim against the debtor. In Chapter 7 cases, creditors may present only those claims that arose before the filing of the bankruptcy. In reorganization cases, under Chapters 9, 11, 12, and 13, creditors may also press claims against the debtor that arose during the bankruptcy case but prior to confirmation of a reorganization plan.

## Creditor with a priority claim

Certain claims are granted a priority status and are paid before other unsecured claims. Priority claims include certain taxes; debts for wages, salaries, or commissions; certain claims for contributions to employee benefit plans; certain claims of people engaged in production or raising of grain or engaged as a U.S. fisherman; and the administration costs of the bankruptcy estate.

## Creditor with a secured claim

A creditor holds a secured claim if the claim is secured by property in which the bankruptcy estate has an ownership interest. In other words, a claim is secured when the debtor pledges a piece of property (usually land, automobile, or goods) to the creditor to assure payment. The creditor may collect against this property (collateral) if the debtor fails to pay. The claim is secured *only* to the extent of the value of the collateral. The creditor has an unsecured claim, that is, merely a promise to repay, for the amount of the claim which exceeds the value of the collateral. A secured claim is paid by returning the collateral or its value to the creditor.

## Creditor with an unsecured claim

A creditor whose claim is neither secured by collateral nor is a priority claim is a creditor with an unsecured claim.

### Creditors committee

A group of creditors with unsecured claims (usually the twenty largest) acts to supervise and participate in a Chapter 11 case. This committee is appointed by the U.S. Trustee's Office and may hire legal counsel or other professionals whose fees are paid by the debtor-in-possession.

### Debtor

A debtor is a person for whom a case under the Bankruptcy Code has been commenced. All individuals, partnerships, or corporations who file a case under bankruptcy law or are the subject of an involuntary petition are called debtors.

### Debtor-in-possession

The debtor-in-possession is a debtor in a Chapter 11 case where no trustee has been appointed. Most Chapter 11 cases begin with a debtor-in-possession. A trustee is appointed by the bankruptcy court only in special circumstances. A debtor-in-possession has many of the same powers as a trustee and operates as a fiduciary for the benefit of creditors.

### Discharge

A discharge is the order entered in a bankruptcy case which relieves the debtor of the obligation to pay creditors. The debts that may be discharged vary from chapter to chapter of the Code.

### Estate

The bankruptcy estate comprises all of the property and rights of the debtor on the date of the bankruptcy filing. In a Chapter 7 case, the estate may also include property acquired by the debtor under a will or probate estate or by property settlement within 180 days after filing. In Chapter 9, 11, 12, and 13 cases, the estate also includes the property or rights acquired after the bankruptcy filing but before confirmation of a reorganization or repayment plan.

### Exemptions

Certain property of the debtor is not included as property of the bankruptcy estate and is termed "exempt." These exemptions are determined either by federal law or by state law if the state has elected not to utilize the federal bankruptcy exemptions. Exemptions usually include a specified amount of equity in a house, vehicle or vehicles, household goods, tools or equipment, and various other items of property that are considered minimal necessities.

## First meeting of creditors

A meeting of all creditors is called by the U.S. Trustee's Office, usually within sixty days after a bankruptcy filing. Notice is sent to all creditors who are listed in the debtor's schedules. Any creditor may attend and inquire about the debtor's financial condition or information contained in the Schedules or Statement of Affairs.

## No asset case

A case in which all of the debtor's property, if any, is exempt.

## Petition

The petition is the document that when filed with the appropriate filing fee, initiates a bankruptcy case. The petition can be either voluntary and signed by the debtor, or involuntarily executed and filed by creditors of the debtor.

## Schedules and Statement of Affairs

A debtor is required to list her debts and assets and certain other financial information on forms known as the Schedules and Statement of Affairs. The information provided on the Schedules and Statement of Affairs is sworn to by the debtor under penalty of perjury. A knowing omission or misrepresentation in the Schedules and Statement of Affairs is punishable as a federal crime. In addition, such misinformation can be grounds for denial of a debtor's discharge of debts in a Chapter 7 case.

## Secured claim

See *Creditor with a secured claim.*

## Unsecured claim

See *Creditor with an unsecured claim.*

## Voluntary Case

A debtor initiates a voluntary bankruptcy case by filing a Petition, Schedules and a Statement of Affairs, and a filing fee with the U.S. Bankruptcy Court. The filing should be made in the bankruptcy court in the state where the debtor has lived or has had a principal place of business for the greater portion of the six months prior the bankruptcy filing.

Upon filing, all collection action against the debtor is stopped by an automatic stay. The bankruptcy court will send a notice of the bankruptcy filing to each creditor listed by the debtor in the Schedules. This notice will contain information about the first meeting of

**How a Bankruptcy Is Initiated**

creditors, the appointment of a trustee, whether creditors should file Proofs of Claim with the court, and deadlines or dates that may affect the creditors' rights in the bankruptcy case.

### Involuntary case

Creditors may file an involuntary bankruptcy case against an individual or business who is generally not paying debts as they come due. An involuntary case requires the joint action of three or more creditors with noncontingent, undisputed, unsecured claims aggregating at least $5,000. If the debtor has fewer than twelve creditors (excluding employees or insiders), one creditor holding a current undisputed debt of at least $5,000 may file an involuntary petition. If the debtor is a partnership, a general partner can file an involuntary petition for the partnership.

## When and Why to Get Bankruptcy Advice

Bankruptcy law often appears complicated and unfamiliar, both to the layperson and to the attorney who does not routinely practice in this area. Familiarity with the Bankruptcy Code, bankruptcy procedure, and bankruptcy court is important in assessing the rights and alternatives available to debtors who are considering a bankruptcy filing, to creditors or investors of a debtor, or when current legal decisions may be affected by a future bankruptcy filing. It is advisable to obtain bankruptcy advice in the following circumstances:

1. When there are persistent or overwhelming financial problems. Both individuals and businesses may suffer from financial problems that they are unable to resolve. For an individual, financial problems may place stress on relationships, affect the ability to work at a job, and have other emotional and psychological effects. For a business, financial problems may affect a business' ability to develop or sell new products, retain valued employees, or simply to continue doing business.

   For an individual, there are certain "red flags" that indicate that financial problems are becoming so serious that the individual should obtain outside help or advice. These red flags include:

   - Inability to pay ongoing obligations (the individual may have to choose the bills she can afford to pay each month, or pay only part of the amounts due)

   - Receipt of "dunning" letters

   - Calls at home or at work from creditors demanding payment

- Being consistently behind in making house or car payments

- Initiation of a lawsuit for collection on a debt

- Initiation of foreclosure on the individual's residence

- Garnishment of wages

- Filing of a tax lien by the Internal Revenue Service or state or local tax authorities

- Closing of business for taxes owed

- Filing of an involuntary bankruptcy petition

The "red flags" for a business include:

- Inability to meet normal cash obligations

- Inability to take advantage of early payment or payment discounts or volume purchases

- Substitution of a promissory note for an account payable

- Giving a security interest to assure payment of an account payable

- Need for financing to maintain cash flow

- Inability to obtain a loan from a bank or lending institution

- Consideration of loans from private lenders at high interest rates or factoring of accounts receivable to generate cash

- Discounting of accounts receivable to accelerate collections

- Threats by creditors for appointment of a receiver, custodian, or creditors committee

- Threats of foreclosure against business assets

- Calls from creditors demanding payment

- Filing of an involuntary bankruptcy petition

2. As a creditor of or investor in a debtor. Someone who is owed money is often aware of a debtor's financial problems that delay or prevent repayment. The creditor may have tried to collect on the debt either by telephone call, letter, a lawsuit, or foreclosure of a security interest or lien. Some creditors, however, may be unaware of a debtor's financial problems until the creditor receives a notice from the bankruptcy court.

When a notice of bankruptcy is received, a creditor should consult with an attorney to determine available rights in the bankruptcy case. This consultation should not be delayed because there are short time limits for exercising certain rights.

Investors are frequently unaware of the financial problems in the entities in which they invest. Partners in a partnership or limited partnership, shareholders in a small or large corporation, or customers who have deposits with a business that goes into bankruptcy should also obtain bankruptcy advice if they receive notice or hear a news report of a bankruptcy filing.

3. When important legal decisions must be made and a future bankruptcy could impact those decisions. Though it is difficult to do, anticipating the effect of a bankruptcy filing is important in making certain legal decisions. Such anticipation may allow preventative planning and minimize the adverse effect of a bankruptcy upon an investor or other creditor. Three areas in which anticipation of bankruptcy is frequently important are divorces, making a loan, and selling of a business.

- *Divorce.* An individual who is involved in or anticipating a divorce should consider bankruptcy alternatives before executing a separation agreement or the entry of permanent orders. If a couple has substantial debts and both are unable to repay them, they may consider filing a joint bankruptcy petition before the divorce decree is entered. A joint bankruptcy filing before the divorce is finalized often saves spouses substantial expense and simplifies the divorce proceeding.

Bankruptcy strategies should also be considered where the assets and debts will not be equally distributed between the spouses, the spouses have substantially differing abilities to earn and repay debts, there is a high degree of animosity between the spouses, or one spouse is having personal or business financial problems. Consideration of bankruptcy alternatives in these contexts is preventative. A separation agreement or the permanent orders entered in a divorce may be upset by a subsequent bankruptcy filing. When a bankruptcy filing is likely, the client and the divorce attorney should consider the impact of a bankruptcy filing on the distribution of property, the repayment of marital debts and debts of one spouse to the other, characterization of obligations as property settlement, alimony or maintenance, and the availability of transfers made pursuant to a separation agreement or court order. For example, if one spouse assumes all of the debts and the other takes most of the marital property and the spouse with the debts files for bankruptcy within a year of the divorce settlement, property already transferred to the other spouse might be recoverable by the bankruptcy trustee into the bankruptcy estate. In addition, characterization of past divorce payments between former spouses can be important. Property settlement obligations are often discharged in bankruptcy; alimony and child support obligations are not.

- *Loans*. The possibility of a bankruptcy filing should also be considered any time a loan is made or credit extended. The lender should consider how it will be repaid in the event the borrower is unable to pay or files for bankruptcy.

- *Sale of a business*. Credit is often extended in the purchase or sale of a business. For example, the business owner will agree to accept payment of the purchase price over time. The seller of the business should consult with a bankruptcy attorney regarding the collectability of this obligation if the business fails or the buyer seeks bankruptcy protection.

## The Bankruptcy Attorney

Bankruptcy law is a specialty. The Bankruptcy Code is changed by Congress from time to time. Although many attorneys may have been involved in a bankruptcy case or two, a client who wants bankruptcy advice should consult an attorney who devotes a substantial portion of her practice to representation of debtors or creditors in bankruptcy cases, is familiar with the current version of the Code, and knows the practices and procedures of the particular bankruptcy court where the case is or may be filed.

Some states allow attorneys to advertise bankruptcy as a specialty or to be a certified specialist in bankruptcy. Other states do not allow attorneys to represent that they are specialists or certified in a particular area. Although certification, for example by the American Bankruptcy Institute or the Commercial Law League, may indicate that an attorney has a substantial knowledge of bankruptcy law, certification is not necessary to find a competent bankruptcy attorney.

**Where to Get Bankruptcy Advice and What to Expect**

The client should assess the attorney's familiarity with bankruptcy law. The client should ask the attorney to describe prior bankruptcy experience. Has the attorney handled primarily consumer bankruptcy cases? How many cases under Chapters 7, 11, and 13? How many business bankruptcies has the attorney handled? Does the attorney primarily represent creditors or debtors? What percentage of the attorney's practice involves bankruptcy issues? How long has the attorney practiced in the bankruptcy area? Does the attorney belong to professional organizations dealing with bankruptcy issues such as the American Bankruptcy Institute, the Commercial Law League, or sections or subsections of the local, state, or national bar association which deal with bankruptcy issues?

A bankruptcy specialist is likely to charge a higher hourly rate for consultation than an attorney who does not practice in the bankruptcy area. Ordinarily, a bankruptcy attorney bills strictly on an hourly basis; however, a flat fee is sometimes charged for representing debtors in Chapter 7 or 13 cases.

If the attorney represents a debtor, the attorney may require the client to pay all fees or post a substantial retainer before the bankruptcy petition will be filed. In a Chapter 9, 11, or 12 reorganization case, the attorney may request a substantial retainer because the court must approve the payment of all fees incurred after the bankruptcy filing. In a Chapter 13 case, the attorney's fees may be paid as part of the reorganization plan and distributed from the monthly payment made by the debtor to the Chapter 13 trustee.

## Bankruptcy Mills

Individuals who are considering a bankruptcy filing under Chapter 7 or 13 may save attorney fees by consulting with an attorney who runs a bankruptcy "mill." A bankruptcy mill is generally an office with one or two attorneys and a large staff of paralegals. A mill processes a high volume of consumer bankruptcy cases at a relatively low cost to each debtor. These attorneys frequently advertise in newspapers, telephone books, and on television. Most consultation with the client and preparation of bankruptcy documents is done by paralegals, rather than the attorney.

An individual might consider consulting with a bankruptcy mill if seeking to file under Chapter 7 or 13 and if the individual has:

- No business or partnership interests

- No business debts and has relatively few consumer debts

- Not transferred any property within the year before the filing

- No individuals or entities who are codebtors on any debt

- No student loans, tax debts, or debts arising from a divorce

Debtors who have any of these problems should consult a bankruptcy attorney rather than relying on a mill.

## Liquidation

How Bankruptcy Works

A bankruptcy liquidation or "straight bankruptcy" usually occurs under Chapter 7. Individuals, as well as partnerships and corporations, may elect to file under Chapter 7.

In a Chapter 7 case, a trustee is appointed to administer the estate and eventually distribute the assets to creditors. A trustee will review the Schedules and Statement of Affairs submitted by the debtor and conduct the first meeting of creditors. The trustee will then attempt to collect and liquidate the nonexempt assets of the bankruptcy estate. The trustee may offer the debtor an opportunity to buy nonexempt assets from the estate. This allows the debtor to retain her property while paying the value of that property to the trustee. The trustee may sell assets and may seek to avoid and recover transfers of assets made by the debtor prior to the bankruptcy filing using the trustee's strong-arm powers. (This is discussed in more detail below.) Once the trustee has collected and liquidated the estate's assets, the trustee will distribute the assets in accordance with the priorities set out in the Code.

Secured creditors will retain their liens against collateral securing the debt and hold an unsecured claim to the extent that the amount owed to them by the debtor exceeds the value of the collateral. The debtor may retain the collateral securing the debt if the debtor continues to pay the obligation and the debtor has no nonexempt equity in the collateral that could be used by the trustee to pay other creditors.

Funds of the estate are used first to pay priority claims in full and then distributed *pro rata* among unsecured claims.

## Debts That Are Not Dischargeable

If the debtor is an individual, the debtor will receive an order discharging all prepetition debts that are not specifically excepted from discharge by the Code. The Code provides that certain debts are not discharged. These include:

- Certain tax debts

- Debts in the nature of alimony, maintenance, and child support, and certain property obligations

- Certain debts for fines, penalties, or forfeiture

- Certain student loans

- Debts incurred when operating a motor vehicle while intoxicated

- Certain debts arising from associations with federal depository institutions

- Consumer debts owed to a single creditor and aggregating more than $500 for luxury goods or services incurred within forty days before the bankruptcy filing

- Debts for cash advances under an open-end credit plan aggregating more than $1,000 within twenty days before the date of filing

The Code also allows creditors to prevent the dischargeability of specific debts incurred for the following:

- Money, property, or services obtained by false pretenses, false representation, fraud, or fraudulent statements

- Fraud while acting in a fiduciary capacity, such as embezzlement or larceny

- Willful or malicious injury by the debtor to another entity or to the property of another entity

Complaints to determine the dischargeability of debts based on these three grounds and debts arising from property settlement must be filed within sixty days after the date set for the first meeting of creditors.

### Denial of Discharge

In addition, creditors may seek to have the bankruptcy court deny the debtor discharge of *all* debts if:

- The debtor has been granted a discharge within six years of the filing date of the petition.

- The debtor transferred, removed, destroyed, or mutilated property of the estate within the year before the date of the filing.

- The debtor transferred, removed, destroyed, or mutilated property of the estate after the date of the filing with the intent to hinder, delay, or defraud a creditor.

- The debtor concealed, destroyed, mutilated, falsified, or failed to keep or preserve records from which her financial condition or business transactions could be ascertained.

- The debtor knowingly and fraudulently made a false oath, or gave, offered, received, or attempted to obtain money, property, or a promise of money or property for acting or failing to act in the bankruptcy case or withheld recorded information from the trustee.

- The debtor has refused to obey lawful orders of the court or failed to answer a material question by the court.

## Reorganization

Four chapters of The Bankruptcy Code provide for reorganization of various entities. Chapter 9 provides for reorganization of insolvent municipalities, Chapter 11 for businesses, Chapter 12 for family farmers, and Chapter 13 for wage earners. Under all four chapters, the debtor is required to propose a reorganization or repayment plan that provides for payment to creditors in the priority required by the bankruptcy court. Each chapter has a specified time period over which the plan will operate. Each chapter provides for various voting rights and objection rights to be exercised by creditors. Each chapter requires that the plan be confirmed by the bankruptcy court. The scope of the discharge varies from chapter to chapter. It often requires substantial performance of the plan's terms. Exceptions from discharge can be asserted by creditors in limited circumstances. Creditors may have specific rights under each chapter; they may, for example, be able to participate on a creditors committee to assist in the formulation of the plan and administration of the estate.

## Reaffirmation of Debts

The Code does not prevent a debtor from voluntarily repaying any debt after filing for bankruptcy. An agreement to repay a debt, however, is not binding on the debtor or enforceable by a creditor unless the underlying debt is formally reaffirmed. The only way a debt can be formally reaffirmed is by the execution of a written agreement, which requires court approval under some circumstances.

**Duties of the Debtor**

The debtor receives bankruptcy court protection and a discharge in exchange for full and complete disclosure of financial affairs, turnover of property to the bankruptcy estate, and compliance with the Bankruptcy Code and bankruptcy court orders. If a debtor fails to perform the required duties, the debtor may lose an entitlement to discharge, have the case dismissed, or be subject to criminal sanctions.

**Rights and Responsibilities of the Creditor**

In a Chapter 7 case it is essential that the creditor file a proof of claim within the time limit set by the rules, or such claim may not be eligible for participation in the distribution from the estate. In Chapter 11 and 13 cases, some creditors may not be required to file a proof of claim if such creditors accept the debtor's classification and treatment of the claim. Creditors have the opportunity to attend the first meeting of creditors to ask questions of the debtor.

A creditor may obtain relief from the automatic stay for the following reasons: (1) for cause, including lack of adequate protection or (2) to act against the debtor's property, to foreclose, or seize the property, only if the debtor does not have equity in the property and the property is not necessary for an effective reorganization. The filing of a motion for relief from stay creates a contested matter to be resolved by the bankruptcy court. A preliminary hearing must be concluded no later than thirty days after the filing of the motion.

A creditor may contest the right of a debtor to receive a discharge of all debts in Chapter 7 or the right of a debtor to receive discharge of a particular debt in Chapters 7, 11, 12, or 13.

**Powers of the Trustee**

Under the Code, a trustee's primary obligation is to gather all of the debtor's assets or interests into the bankruptcy estate to be liquidated and distributed to creditors. In order to facilitate that obligation, the Code gives the trustee certain "strong-arm" powers to set aside and recover transfers or payments made by the debtor prior to the bankruptcy filing. These powers include the following:

1. Avoid and recover preferences. A preferential transfer is a prepetition voluntary or involuntary transfer of the debtor's property (or the debtor's interest in property) to a creditor made within a specific time prior to the bankruptcy filing, which allows the creditor to receive a greater percentage return on its claim than it would have received if the creditor had participated in the asset distribution under Chapter 7.

   There are certain exceptions to recovery of preferential transfers. A trustee may not recover a preferential payment by an individual debtor whose debts are primarily consumer debts if the transfers aggregate less than $600 to a particular creditor. The trustee may not recover payments made in the ordinary course of business, payments that are part of a substantially contemporaneous transaction, or certain other transfers given for new value or enabling loans.

2. Turnover. A trustee may seek turnover of the estate's property in the possession of the debtor or third parties.

3. Fraudulent transfers. A trustee may set aside a transfer of property or the debtor's interest in property, or an obligation undertaken by the debtor, if it occurred within one year prior to the bankruptcy and is a "fraudulent transfer." A fraudulent transfer is a transfer that was made with the actual intent to hinder, delay, or defraud creditors or a transfer for less than reasonably equivalent value by which the debtor became insolvent, was engaged in a business with too little capital, or purposely incurred the debt beyond her ability to pay. For example, the sale of property to a relative for less than market value six months prior to bankruptcy may be a fraudulent transfer.

4. Exercise of rights of creditors under state law. The trustee is also empowered to exercise the state law rights of a creditor on the date of the bankruptcy filing. One of the most frequently used state law remedies is the trustee's reliance upon fraudulent conveyance rights under state law.

## Disadvantages

Although the promise of a "fresh start" is alluring to a financially distressed debtor, it is a solution to financial problems that should be invoked with caution and restraint. Indeed, bankruptcy should be looked at as the debtor's last resort. Although there may be a variety of compelling reasons for a debtor to file for bankruptcy, there are a number of disadvantages and undesirable consequences to bankruptcy.

**Bankruptcy As a Last Resort**

1. Bankruptcy does not change the economic facts of life. While the Bankruptcy Code provides the legal tools to effect a fresh start, it cannot change the economic conditions that led to the bankruptcy filing in the first place. It does not provide the debtor with good financial judgment, control over expenditures, wise use of credit, or good management skills. All the legal gymnastics in the world cannot substitute for good financial judgment and practices that are necessary for a stable and successful financial turnaround.

2. Although bankruptcy has been and is used by many individuals, bankruptcy still carries a stigma.

3. A bankruptcy filing may impair a debtor's ability to obtain credit for up to ten years. The record of a bankruptcy filing will stay on a debtor's credit report for up to ten years. Some debtors may find that they can obtain new credit only at higher interest rates or on more severe terms within the ten-year period. Other debtors will find that they are unable to obtain credit at any cost.

4. There is a cost involved in the filing. Although a consumer bankruptcy under Chapter 7 or 13 might have a relatively small price tag in terms of attorney's fees, the debtor and her counsel should consider total cost of the bankruptcy filing, including the loss of exempt assets and potential litigation over discharge or asset recovery.

In a reorganization under Chapters 9, 11, and 12, the cost of professional fees for attorneys and accountants can be substantial. Most often some fees are paid by retainer before the filing of the bankruptcy case. In addition, if a creditors committee is appointed, the debtor is required to pay the fees for the professionals hired by the committee. If new lending is sought, lenders often require nonrefundable fees for loan investigation.

To debtors for whom bankruptcy is truly the last resort and to creditors who must be repaid from constantly dwindling assets, the substantial professional fees and administrative expenses may be a comparatively small price for the financial relief afforded.

## Alternatives

Before any bankruptcy filing is made, a potential debtor and counsel should evaluate alternatives to bankruptcy.

## For Individuals

Individuals may have a number of resources to which they can turn in order to avoid a bankruptcy filing. Some communities have nonprofit organizations that help debtors consolidate and repay debts, such as Consumer Credit Counseling. If such an organization is not available, the debtor might explore a debt consolidation loan with a friendly party or institution. A debt consolidation loan allows the debtor to pay off all debts in a lump amount. The debtor then has only one creditor (the friendly party or institution) to pay, often at an interest rate that is less than what is charged on individual debts. Debtors may also consider selling assets to pay debts, especially property that would not be exempt if a bankruptcy were filed. Finally, the debtor may engage in a "workout" by entering into independent payment arrangements with each creditor.

## For a Business

Depending upon the size of the business and the complexity of its financial affairs, a business has a number of alternatives to bankruptcy. A business may engage in a formal "workout" agreement with its lending institution(s) and major creditors and continue to operate. A business may decide, instead, to shut down, liquidate assets, and distribute the proceeds to creditors. A new buyer may be willing to take on certain debts or buy certain assets which can be used to retire debts. A business might obtain new sources of financing either through a lending institution or new investors. Finally, many states have procedures for receivership or liquidation for corporations and partnerships.

## Conclusion

Successful navigation through bankruptcy law and procedure generally requires the assistance of able and experienced bankruptcy counsel. A thorough and comprehensive analysis of the rights and remedies in bankruptcy, as well as the alternatives to bankruptcy, will help ensure that sound decisions and acceptable consequences can be obtained by both debtors and creditors.

## Notes

1. Bankruptcy statistical information prepared by the Administrative Office of the U.S. Courts, March 19, 1993.

2. News Release, Adminstrative Office of the U.S. Courts, June 1994. Data collected by statistics division.

## Bibliography*
*Directory of Bankruptcy Attorneys, 1994, 8th ed.* Englewood Cliffs, NJ: Prentice Hall, forthcoming. (Look for prior edition in the library).

Elias, Stephen, Albin Renauer, and Robin Leoard. *How to File for Bankruptcy, 5th ed*. Berkeley, CA: Nolo Press, 1995.

Fitzgerald, Judith K., and Ramona M. Arena. *Bankruptcy and Divorce: Support and Property Division, 2d ed*. New York: John Wiley & Sons, 1994.

Jurinski, James J. *Keys to Understanding Bankruptcy, 2d ed*. New York: Barron's, 1994.

LoPucki, Lynn M., and Ann T. Reilly, editors. *Law and Business Directory of Bankruptcy Attorneys*. Englewood Cliffs, NJ: Prentice Hall, 1988.

Sommer, Henry J. *Consumer Bankruptcy: The Complete Guide to Filing for Chapter 7 and Chapter 13 Personal Bankruptcy*. New York: John Wiley & Sons, 1994.

White, Darryl. *You and Your Credit: Tools for Understanding and Repairing Your Own Credit*. Forest Hills, NY: Pyramid Publishing, 1994.

---

**Marcia S. Krieger** is a U. S. Bankruptcy Judge for the District of Colorado. She graduated *summa cum laude* from Lewis and Clark College in Portland, Oregon. After graduate study at the Max Planck Institute in Munich, she earned her J.D. degree from the University of Colorado, Boulder. She specialized in commercial litigation and bankruptcy matters as a private attorney before being appointed as a bankruptcy judge.

---

*Books in bibliography are recommended by the editor, not by the contributing author.

Chapter 21

# Consumer Rights and Insurance

Julie A. Tigges

Chapter Outline

**Introduction**

**What Is a Contract?**

**Making a Purchase**

**Credit**

**Home Improvements**

**Possible Sources of Fraud**

**Auto Purchasing and Repair**

**Product Safety**

**Nutrition Labeling**

**Warranties: If It's Broke, Will You Fix It?**

**Protecting Your Credit Rating and Personal Privacy**

**Remedies**
Handling Your Own Complaint • The Court System

**Insurance**
Automobile Insurance • Life Insurance • Medical Insurance • Homeowner's Insurance • Liability Umbrella • Unemployment

**Conclusion**

**Introduction**

Every one of us has been a consumer at some point in our lives, whether we purchased a car or selected a day care center. Every one of us has also been unhappy with a purchase at some point, whether it was the car that seemed to break down every fifty miles, or the day care center that didn't seem to pay much attention to a child. Consumer law focuses on these types of personal and family-use purchases, providing consumers with legal remedies to problems. Due to the large number of consumer transactions occurring on a daily basis, consumer law is perhaps the most pervasive segment of the law with respect to our daily lives. While consumer law affects all people, women have very specific rights and concerns in certain consumer areas. Women make up the largest segment of consumers in our society, both because they make up a majority of the population and because they conduct most of the business transactions for a family. In each section below, broad aspects of consumer rights are explained; where applicable, special concerns for women are highlighted.

Historically, consumer rights were characterized by the Latin phrase *caveat emptor*, or "let the buyer beware." If a purchaser of a good or service was dissatisfied with her purchase, there was no remedy available to the purchaser, even if the product was defective or the seller was dishonest. It was the purchaser's responsibility to protect herself from inadequate products or services, either through careful inspection or through common sense. This regime, which favored the sellers of goods and services and provided little or no protection for consumers, slowly began to erode in the early twentieth century, evolving into a regulated system designed to protect consumers and prohibit dishonesty by sellers.

In the United States, the consumer movement culminated in the creation of several administrative bodies. Unlike most segments of the law, which are governed by previous court decisions, or *precedents*, consumer rights are largely regulated by statutes prescribed by administrative agencies. The "big three" of these agencies, the Food and Drug Administration (FDA), the Federal Trade Commission (FTC), and the Consumer Product Safety Commission (CPSC) were all created in the twentieth century as a response to the need for consumer protection. The FDA, which operates within the Department of Health and Human Services, regulates the safety of food, drugs, and cosmetics. The FTC ensures fair competition in the marketplace and scrutinizes advertising and pricing practices, ensuring that sellers are not dishonest with consumers. Finally, the CPSC evaluates the safety features of consumer products, insuring that the public is immune from hazardous products. In addition to statutory regulation, consumer law typically falls under the aegis of two broad segments of law: torts and contracts.

While federal agencies and courts of law provide protection against dishonesty and unfairness in consumer transactions, most problems can be avoided by taking proactive steps and becoming a good consumer, thus protecting yourself and your purchases. An informed consumer is a good consumer; this chapter seeks to inform, educate, and protect, providing for legal remedies only when necessary.

## What Is a Contract?

Contracts are a significant portion of the law, covering a wide variety of circumstances; because of the breadth of contract law, this section serves only as an introduction to the major elements of a contract. If you find yourself involved with a complicated contract, or a contract involving very large sums of money or substantial services, it is best to consult a lawyer about your specific contractual rights. Generally speaking, a contract is an agreement between two or more parties, in which a promise or something of value is exchanged for a return promise or something else of value. Each time we purchase something at a retail store, order a meal at a restaurant, or get our hair styled, we form a contract with the party supplying the goods or services in return for our payment. Contracts are also very important in insurance and warranties (described below). A contract may be oral or written, although certain circumstances dictate that the contract be written. To be enforceable, a contract must contain the elements of an offer, an acceptance, and consideration.

When one party creates the impression in another's mind that she would like to conduct business on certain terms, an offer is formed. The assent to these terms is known as the acceptance of the contract. For an offer to be valid, it must contain definite terms as to what is being transacted.

Offer and acceptance are best illustrated by the following example. Joanne is in need of a nanny to care for her two children while she works. She asks her neighbor Susan if she would be willing to care for the children for nine hours a day, between 8:00 A.M. and 5:00 P.M., at a pay of $10 an hour. This is an offer, the terms of which are nine hours of work per day at the pay of $10 an hour. Susan tells Joanne that she is willing to do the job as per the terms specified; this is an acceptance. If Susan tells Joanne that she will work for the specified hours, but requests a pay of $12 an hour, this is *not* an acceptance, as Susan is not assenting to the terms of Joanne's offer. Instead, this is a counteroffer, which vests Joanne with the right of acceptance.

A tricky area involving offer and acceptance is advertisements. What about an item advertised in the newspaper, for example, a sale on a dress for $50? You arrive at the store and realize that the sale was only on size fours! Is the ad really an offer to you, the consumer, and you simply have to show up to accept, to claim the merchandise? No—advertisements are not offers; instead, they are requests for offers. Thus, when a store advertises snow tires for $49.99, it is simply a request by the store for consumers to come to the store, pay $49.99 (the offer) in return for the sale of the tires (acceptance).

Acceptance does not always need to be in the form of an oral or written agreement to be valid, but may also be inferred from conduct of the assenting party. For example, if Joanne tells Susan that she will pay her $10 to walk her dog while she is on vacation, and Susan does not give an affirmative response to the offer, it is considered acceptance if Susan shows up and walks Joanne's dog. Joanne would owe Susan the $10.

Acceptance can also be manifested in the form of a request, along with some form of consideration, to keep an offer open to the assenting party for a specific period of time; this is known as an option contract. For example, if Joanne offers to sell her car to Susan for $500 on June 1, and Susan requests that Joanne keep her offer open until June 7 in exchange for $10, Susan has formed an option contract, the acceptance of which will be full payment on June 7.

The third element of a contract is known as consideration. Consideration is a promise or action which is given in exchange for a return promise and which represents a benefit to one party or a detriment to the other party. Consideration is the motive for the formation of the contract. In the nanny example above, Joanne's payment of $10 an hour is consideration for Susan's promise to perform as her nanny. Joanne suffers the detriment of losing $90 a day, but receives the benefit of Susan's services; likewise, Susan suffers the detriment of losing her free time, but receives a benefit of $90 per day. Consideration does not have to be equivalent to the promise being exchanged; thus, a payment of $1 can serve as adequate consideration for the purchase of a car.

Enforceable contracts may be oral or written, depending on the circumstances. Although all states recognize oral contracts, it is often advisable that the consumer get the contract in writing; in case of a problem, a written contract provides proof of the contractual terms, and the situation will not degenerate into a battle of "who said what." However, certain contracts must be in writing, governed by a rule known as the Statute of Frauds.

The three main forms of contracts that are required to be in writing are: a promise to pay for the debts of another party (suretyship), a promise that cannot be performed within one year from the date of contract, and any sale of goods over $500, including the sale of real property. In the realm of consumer law, the final type, sale of goods over $500, will be the most commonly experienced. For example, when you purchase a new car, the contract must be in writing.

Once a contract is formed between parties, each party must perform their respective promises under the terms of the contract. Each party may request changes to the contract's terms; this would form an offer, which the other party must accept to modify the contract. If one party fails to perform a requirement, it is considered a breach of the contract. In our example above, if Susan leaves the children at 2:00, then she has breached the contract with Joanne, failing to keep her part of the bargain. Failure to perform specific contractual requirements, however, is sometimes justifiable; for example, if a contract is formed under duress or unlawful coercion, or if terms were misrepresented by the other party, a contract may be void. Unfortunately, many suppliers of goods and services use such techniques on women, especially in areas that women are not deemed "qualified," such as auto sales or home repair. If you feel you that you entered into a contract under duress, or were the victim of dishonesty, it is best to contact an attorney to seek remedies for your problem.

## Making a Purchase

There are a few general rules that apply to all purchases of goods and services. Whether you are buying a car or an insurance policy, always comparison shop. Ask friends, relatives, and coworkers for recommendations and look for expert product comparison reports in publications such as *Consumer Reports*. Look for a company with a good reputation and plan ahead to take advantage of sales and special deals. Check with your local Better Business Bureau (BBB) or consumer protection office to find out about the company's complaint record and reputation. Make sure that there are no extra or "hidden" charges, such as delivery fees, installation charges, and service costs; if such costs exist, be sure that you are aware of them up front. There is nothing worse than buying a product and being hit with extra charges when the product is delivered. Read all pertinent contracts, including warranties, so that you understand what your rights and duties are under the agreement. Cross out those provisions you do not agree with, and initial these areas in the margin. *Never* sign a contract with blank spaces; fill them in with a line or write N/A (not applicable). Also, be wary of form or boilerplate contracts, generic contracts used by parties for a variety of situations. Many times, these contracts suffer from being either over- or under-inclusive in their terms. To protect yourself, read every item of a contract carefully. Keep all contracts in a safe place. Finally, ask the salesperson or service provider to explain the company's return and exchange policy. By keeping these simple hints in mind, you will probably protect yourself from most problems associated with consumer rights.

## Credit

At one point in each of our lives, we will apply for credit in one form or another. Credit is, in a broad sense, borrowing a certain amount of money for a specified time period and repaying the principal along with some form of interest. There are two broad forms of credit: mercantile credit, which covers bank and credit cards, and loan credit, which includes mortgages, auto, and other bank loans. This section is primarily concerned with the former; however, most of the rules involving credit are uniform and apply to both types. The administration of credit is largely governed by two government statutes: the Equal Credit Opportunity Act and the Truth in Lending Act.

Prior to 1974, there was rampant discrimination in the granting of credit. Companies supplying credit were allowed to discriminate based on gender and marital status. Thus, many single women, who would otherwise be eligible, were restricted in obtaining credit. In 1974, Congress passed the Equal Credit Opportunity Act, which banned all discrimination based on gender, race, and marital status. Thus, today, women are on level ground with men when applying for credit. While credit suppliers are no longer allowed to base the granting of credit on marital status, they can inquire into such status to ascertain their rights and remedies applicable to the extension of credit. The Act also provides that an applicant for credit must be notified within thirty days whether credit will be extended. If credit is not extended, the consumer is entitled to a statement of reasons from the creditor, and may have to contact a third-party credit agency (see below).

In 1968, as part of the first major consumer protection act, Congress passed the Truth in Lending Act (TILA). This Act provided for several consumer rights that are commonplace in today's business environment. First, the TILA requires that all companies providing credit must disclose the Annual Percentage Rate (APR), or the annual interest rate payable on credit. The APR can be variable; if this is the case, it is linked to some index, such as Treasury Bills, and varies with fluctuations in the index. Credit companies must make such disclosures to consumers prior to extending credit. The TILA regulates advertising by credit companies. For example, credit companies are disallowed from using "bait" advertising, which is advertising of low APR rates that are not available to most consumers, in the hopes of generating business. The TILA also allows for private legal actions by consumers against credit companies, in the event that the consumer is harmed by the credit company's actions. Finally, the TILA provides that, if a credit card is lost or stolen, the cardholder is only liable for $50 if the card is used by the thief; for your protection, it is best to notify the issuer of the card as soon as you become aware that the card is missing.

Because credit is such a pervasive part of most of our lives, in one form or another, it is important to keep several principles in mind when dealing with credit. Credit companies offer a wide variety of terms, such as APR, methods of calculating the balance subject to a finance charge, minimum monthly payments, and annual membership fees. When selecting credit, whether it be a credit card or a bank loan, compare the terms offered by several issuers to find the credit that best suits your needs.

If you get a divorce or your husband passes away, the Equal Credit Opportunity Act protects any credit you have; you do not have to reapply for credit in these situations unless you experience a drastic loss of income from your loss. Be aware, however, that credit companies are very lax about letting family members—such as ex-husbands—charge on the wife's card if the last names are the same. To protect yourself from the loss of credit by death or divorce, it is imperative that you obtain credit in your own name; this will insure that you have a credit history, which will be useful if you need to apply for new forms of credit (for example, a home mortgage). If you are married and cosign a credit application with your spouse, be aware that you are likely to be held responsible for any balances due on the credit account. Some states have "family expense" statutes, which provide that, even if the credit is not cosigned, either spouse is responsible for any credit debts incurred for family expenses. Finally, although they are long and tedious, always read credit disclosure statements, so that you are fully aware of your rights and responsibilities in holding credit. This disclosure, in effect, acts as the contract between you and the credit company.

Mercantile credit comes in two forms: credit cards, which are issued by merchants, and bank cards, which are issued by banks. You should keep a list of credit card numbers, expiration dates, and phone numbers of card issuers in a safe place, in the event that they are lost or stolen. When you make a purchase with a credit or bank card, never sign a blank credit receipt; draw a line through any blank spaces above the total when you sign the receipt.

When your monthly bill arrives, compare purchase receipts with the credit card bill, checking for any discrepancies. If there are any problems, write the card issuer promptly to report any questionable charges. Telephoning the card issuer to discuss the problem ***does not*** preserve your rights. Do not include written inquiries with your payment. Instead, check the billing statement for the correct address for any billing questions. The inquiry must be in writing and must be sent within sixty days to guarantee your rights.

If any of your credit cards are missing or stolen, report the loss as soon as possible to the card issuer. Check your credit card statement for a telephone number for reporting stolen credit cards. Follow up your phone calls with a letter to each card issuer. The letter should contain your card number, the date the card was stolen or lost, and the date you reported the loss. Unlike stolen or lost credit cards, for which you are only responsible for $50 in improper charges, if an automatic teller machine (ATM) card is lost or stolen, you could lose as much as $500 if the card issuer is not notified within two business days after you learn of the loss or theft.

If you use your credit card to purchase goods through the mail or over the phone, and the item is not received or your order was obtained through misrepresentation or fraud, you can get the charge removed from your credit card statement. You must notify the credit card company in writing, at the billing/inquiries address within sixty days after the charge first appeared on your bill.

## Home Improvements

Hiring a contractor to renovate your home, add a room, or make some other improvement can be a confusing maze of contracts, licenses, permits, and payment schedules. This is a common area where service providers sometimes try to take advantage of women. By keeping the basic tenets of contract law in mind, as well as common sense, you should be able to protect yourself against any dishonest behavior.

When you are looking to have work done, compare costs by getting more than one estimate or bid. Each estimate should be based on the same building specifications, materials, and time. This way, you will ensure that any comparison is a true "apples to apples" comparison. When you are looking for a contractor, check with state, county or local consumer protection agencies to see if any complaints have been filed against the contractor. Inquire about information on unresolved cases and how long a contracting company has been in business under its current name. Also, ask a potential contractor for a list of previous customers whom you could call to find out about work quality and if they would hire the contractor to perform future work.

Often, when you undertake any significant home improvement, a license or permit is required. Check with your local building inspections department to see if licensing and/or bonding are required in your area. If licensing is required, ask to see the contractor's license and bonding papers. If the work requires a building permit, the contractor should apply for it in his or her name. By keeping any permits under the contractor's name, you are not financially responsible in the event that the work does not pass inspection.

To protect yourself against potential problems with accidents and other small disasters, make sure your contractor has some common forms of insurance. Most contractors have liability and workers' compensation insurance to protect you from a lawsuit in the event of an accident to one of the workers. Make sure that your contractor is also insured against theft and negligence. You can request that the contractor carry a performance bond, which compensates you for completion of the work in the event that the contractor does not finish the project. Make sure that you are named as beneficiary to such a bond.

A written contract with a contractor should include the contractor's full name, address, phone number, and professional license number (when required), a thorough description of the work to be done, grade and quality of materials to be used, agreed-upon starting and completion dates, total cost, payment schedule, warranty, how debris will be removed, and any other information you have agreed upon. Also, it is good to include a recital of how changes to the contract will be made; this will ensure that you are aware of any modifications to the contract. When you sign a nonemergency home improvement contract in your home and in the presence of a contractor, (or contractor's representative), you have three business days in which to cancel the contract. The contractor must inform you of these cancellation rights and provide you with cancellation forms. If you decide to cancel, it is recommended that you send a notice of cancellation by express mail, which guarantees a return receipt. This cancellation is operative upon receipt by the contractor.

For a remodeling job involving many subcontractors and a substantial amount of money, you should protect yourself from liens against your home by subcontractors in case the contractor does not pay the subcontractors or suppliers. If state law permits, add a release-of-lien clause to the contract, which would place all liens on the contractor, place your payments in an escrow account until the work is completed, or provide for joint checks to be paid to the contractor and the subcontractor or supplier. If you cannot pay for a project without a loan, add a clause stating that the contract is only valid if financing is obtained. This clause will serve as a condition that must be met before the contract becomes valid.

Regarding contractual terms for payment, when signing a contract, limit your first payment to no more than 30 percent of the contract price. The remaining payments should depend on the progress of the work. Ten percent of the contract amount should be held back until the job is complete, and all problems, if any, are resolved. Some states have home improvement laws that specify the amount of deposit and payment schedule. Check with your state and local consumer protection offices to see if there is such a law in your community. Before making a final payment or signing a completion certificate, thoroughly inspect the contractor's work, and if you feel it is necessary, bring in an expert to assess the work; also, make sure that city inspectors approve the work. Finally, get lien releases from all subcontractors or suppliers, shielding yourself from contractual liability to these parties.

## Possible Sources of Fraud

As recently as twenty years ago, the majority of consumer purchasing was conducted at a retail outlet of some sort. With the rapid changes in communication and the rise in mail-order houses that we have experienced over the past two decades, home shopping via the telephone and postal service have begun to encroach on retail's domain. With the development of a worldwide computer network, purchasing items directly from television is on the horizon. While these methods of purchase are touted for their convenience, they also represent potential areas of danger for consumers.

If you intend to purchase items over the phone or through the mail, you should be aware of the potential dangers. Keep a complete record of your order, including the company's name, address, and telephone number, price of the items ordered, any handling or other charges, date of your order, and your method of payment. Keep copies of canceled checks and/or statements. If you are ordering by telephone, get the name of any company representatives with whom you speak. Your order should be shipped within thirty days after the company receives your completed order, unless another period is agreed upon when placing the order or is posted in an advertisement. If your order is delayed, a notice of delay should be sent to you within the promised shipping period, along with an option to cancel the order.

Postal regulations allow you to write a check payable to the sender, rather than the delivery company, for cash on delivery (COD) orders. If, after examining the merchandise, you feel that there has been misrepresentation or fraud, you can stop payment on the check and file a complaint with the U.S. Postal Inspector's Office.

Be extremely wary of certain types of mailings, which most often constitute mail fraud of some form. These include sweepstakes that require you to pay an entry fee or order a product, mailings that look like they are from government agencies, but are not, classified "employment" or "business opportunity" advertisements promising easy money for little work, and prize awards that ask for your credit card or bank account number. Usually, these forms of mail are scams designed to get you to pay a fee or purchase products in return for a job or prize. Often times, the fee or purchase costs you more than the value of the prize you receive. Remember, if it seems too good to be true ("You can win a Mexican holiday if you purchase some vitamins!"), it probably is.

If you feel that you have been a victim of mail fraud, contact your local postal inspector. The Postal Inspection Service has been enforcing the mail fraud statute since its passage in 1872. Postal inspectors are the experts in identifying questionable promotions offered through telemarketing or direct mail sales techniques.

Another technique of soliciting consumers which often leads to fraudulent results is the use of "900" numbers, which you must call to claim a prize or service. This is not to say that 900 numbers are bad; some offer useful services to consumers. If you are going to use a 900 number, keep several things in mind. There is a fee for every 900 number call; the cost varies from call to call, so be sure that you know the fee before you dial. Usually, there are two charges: a connection fee to make the call and a per-minute charge, based on the length of the call. If you have a billing problem and cannot resolve it through your local phone company, complain directly to the long-distance carrier involved. The following long distance companies have toll free numbers and 900 number complaint services: AT&T 800/222-0300; MCI 800/444-3333; Telesphere 800/346-6329; and US Sprint 800/366-0707.

If your problem is not resolved by contacting your local phone company, long distance carrier, service bureau, or information provider, you should contact the Federal Trade Commission or the Chief Postal Inspector, if you received a solicitation for the number in the mail.

If you suspect that other family members are using 900 numbers (this is especially prevalent among teenage boys calling "phone-sex" lines), and you cannot control their use, arrangements can be made with the local phone company so that 900 numbers cannot be dialed from your phone. There may be a fee for this service.

## Auto Purchasing and Repair

In today's mobile society, the automobile is as important as good credit; without either, it is hard to get around. We have all heard the horror stories about how auto salesmen and mechanics can be dishonest, especially with women. Many women have had to do a considerable amount of shopping around in order to find a reputable salesman or repair shop. By keeping a few pointers in mind when buying a car, or getting one fixed, you can avoid these problems.

Whether purchasing a new or used car, decide how much you are willing to spend. Talk to owners of similar vehicles to compare pricing. This way, when you go to the dealer, you can hold firm on a price and prohibit the possibility of being talked into paying more than you intend. Remember that when you purchase a car, it is probably covered by the Statute of Frauds, necessitating a written contract. This is especially important with regard to used cars. This contract will help in applying warranties and any relevant "lemon laws" (see below).

If you purchase a used car, you can either purchase from a dealer or from a private individual. If you purchase from a dealer, chances are the car will be more expensive; however, unlike buying from an individual, you usually receive some form of warranty from the dealer. In a private sale, check to be sure that the seller is the registered owner of the vehicle. Make sure you get the car's title and registration, bill of sale, and copies of all other financial transaction papers necessary to register the car in your name. As with all contracts, be sure to read all of the terms carefully. "Form" contracts are often used between private parties buying and selling an automobile; if you use a "form" contract, make sure that all of the contractual language is applicable to your situation.

Look for and read the *Buyer's Guide*, which must be displayed in the window of all used cars sold by dealers. The *Buyer's Guide* explains who must pay for repairs after purchase. It will tell you if there is a warranty on the car, what the warranty covers, and whether a service contract is available. Also, before purchasing a used car from either a dealer or a private party, have it inspected by a mechanic.

Almost every state has a "lemon law" which covers new, and sometimes used, cars. These laws allow the purchaser to get a refund or replacement if there are substantial problems with the purchased automobile and it cannot be repaired within a reasonable period of time or number of attempts. If you think that your car is a lemon, you should first contact state or local consumer protection agencies, which will be able to tell you what the law is for your locale. Each time you bring the car in to get repaired, give the dealer a list of symptoms. Make sure to get copies of all repair orders and repairs performed. Finally, contact the automobile manufacturer; in some states, this is required. A general summary of lemon laws is available by sending a self-addressed stamped envelope to the Center for Auto Safety, listed at the end of this chapter.

If you do not have enough money to purchase a car, or are unable to obtain or cannot afford payments for an auto loan from a bank, an additional option is to lease the automobile. By leasing an automobile, you contract with an independent third-party leasing company to pay lower monthly payments over an extended period of time. The difference between a lease and a loan, however, is that the leasing company owns the automobile; you must return it after the leasing period has expired. Leasing is, in essence, long-term renting for a specified period of time. The two types of lease agreements are "open-ended" and "closed-ended." In an "open-ended" lease, the periodic payments are lower; however, you are making payments based on an estimated value at the end of the leasing period. If the car is not worth as much as the estimated value due to depreciation, you must pay the difference to the leasing company. In a "closed-ended" lease agreement, by contrast, so long as the car is not seriously damaged, you are not responsible for its value at the end of the leasing period. Under the Federal Consumer Leasing Act, the leasing company must provide you with certain pieces of information when you apply for the lease, including: the initial payment; the number and amount of periodic payments; penalties, if any, for late payments; provisions if you wish to terminate the contract; an option to purchase the vehicle at the end of the leasing period, if applicable; and terms of payment if it is an "open-ended" lease. As with any contract, it is necessary to read and understand all the terms of a leasing contract.

If you find that your car needs repairs, you should first check the terms of your car's warranty. The warranty might require the dealer to perform routine maintenance and any necessary repairs in order to preserve the warranty. If you need major repairs, you should always get a second estimate, even if this involves towing your car to another shop.

Before having your car repaired, check the repair shop's complaint record with your state or local consumer protection office, or local Better Business Bureau. Some repair shops have mechanics certified by the National Institute for Automotive Service Excellence (ASE) to perform one or more types of services. Be aware, however, that repair shops can display the ASE sign even if they have just one mechanic certified in one tested specialty.

Before you leave the car, make sure you have a written estimate and that the work order reflects what you want done. Ask the mechanic to contact you before making repairs not covered in the work order. If additional work not covered in your estimate or contract is done without your permission, you don't have to pay for unapproved work; you have the right to have your bill adjusted.

## Product Safety

Product liability is a type of tort (see discussion of torts under insurance, below) which falls under strict liability. Thus, a company can be held liable for injuries resulting from its product, even if the company used the utmost care in designing and manufacturing the product. Product defects include construction and design defects. Construction defects are those which arise from the actual manufacture of the product; if, for example, a bolt is not inserted in a car, and the car breaks down because of this, it is a construction defect. Design defects, by contrast, are those which are attributed to the actual design of the product; nothing in its manufacture renders it harmful. In the 1970s, Ford Motor Company designed the Pinto with a gas tank behind the rear axle. When some Pintos were rear-ended, they would explode. Even though the cars were not manufactured poorly, they were defective as to their design.

Product safety has a special relevance for women. Probably more than any other class of citizens, women have been adversely affected by harmful products over the last three decades. Some of these products have included DES, an anti-miscarriage drug; silicone breast implants; intrauterine devices (IUDs); and tampons, which caused toxic shock syndrome. Because of the number of personal products women use in their daily lives, it is very important for all women to pay special heed to potential product defects. If you suspect that you might be using a product that is defective and may be causing you harm, you should contact an attorney.

Every year, in order to prevent injury to consumers, federal agencies recall or issue warnings about hundreds of products, including food, drugs, cars and other vehicles, home and garden products, appliances, and toys. Hazards might occur because of design flaws, production defects, new scientific information about dangers from materials previously thought safe, accidental contamination, tampering, unforeseen misuse of products, or failure to meet safety standards.

Consumers are critically important in these product safety efforts because they identify product safety problems and because they respond to the warnings and the recalls. In fact, product recalls and warnings can protect consumers only if consumers react to them. Yet only 2 to 50 percent of all consumers respond to recall notices. In addition to watching for product defects, you can prevent danger from harmful items by paying special heed to all safety warnings contained with a product. An ounce of prevention can easily prevent serious injury.

The U.S. Office of Consumer Affairs has prepared a leaflet that explains which federal agencies issue consumer product safety warnings and recalls, the types of products each of them covers, and how to let them know about product safety problems, or to find out about warnings or recalls they have announced. For a free copy, write to Recalls, Item 634X, Pueblo, CO 81009.

In most households, women still do most of the shopping and prepare most of the meals. They tend to be more concerned with diets and nutrition, not only for themselves, but for their families as well. Recently, the FDA has passed new requirements for food labeling. This new food label format offers more complete and accurate nutrition information than has ever been available. With the new labeling, it is easier to compare nutritional information on various products. Every nutrient must list the percentage of "Daily Value" contained in each serving. This serves to give the consumer information on how the specific product fits into an ideal day's worth of nutrients. One special warning when computing the nutrients and dietary components in a product; pay attention to serving size. It is great if dietary ice cream only lists 4 grams of fat per serving; however, if the serving size is one-fourth cup, the fat calories will load up fast.

## Nutrition Labeling

A warranty is a specific form of contract, providing for repair and/or replacement of a product should it break within a certain amount of time or if it is defective. The Magnuson-Moss Act of 1975 established minimum disclosure requirements for warranties: they must specify whether they are limited or full, and must present the terms of the warranty in clear language. It is important to note that warranties are not required by law; the disclosure requirements only pertain to express warranties distributed with the product. A warranty may also be implied if it is not included with a product. The most common implied warranty is one for merchantability, which implies that the product is adequate for the purposes for which the purchaser bought the product.

Warranties will typically include as their terms the name of the product, whether it is for replacement or repair of the product, whether the consumer must incur any expenses in getting a replacement or repair, what to do if a problem arises, and what the consumer's legal rights are under the warranty. Oftentimes, a manufacturer or retailer allows the consumer to purchase extended warranty coverage; this serves as insurance should the regular warranty expire. Since warranties are the last line of protection against harmful or poor products, it is important to ask yourself several questions when reviewing a warranty, ensuring that you get one that meets your needs:

## Warranties: If It's Broke, Will You Fix It?

- How long is the warranty and when does it start/end?

- What is covered? Which parts? What types of problems?

- Will the warranty pay for 100 percent of repair costs, or will it pay for parts, but not the labor to do the repairs? Will it pay for

testing the product before it is repaired? Will it pay for shipping? Will it provide for a "loaner"?

- What do you have to do and when? Are regular inspections or
maintenance required? Do you have to send the product out of
state for repairs?

- Is it a manufacturer's or retailer's warranty? How reliable are
they? How long have they been in business?

## Protecting Your Credit Rating and Personal Privacy

As we move further into the information age, where billions of
pieces of information can be stored on a diskette the size of a piece of
toast, we pay the price of decreased privacy. Every time you give out
personal information, it is stored and often disseminated to various
organizations. Thus, you must be careful to protect your privacy. When
you are filling out an application for credit, insurance, or a job, inquire
as to how the information you give about yourself will be used. Who
has access to it? Will the information be exchanged with other companies? How long will the information be kept? How often is it updated?
If you have a problem with how the information is being disseminated, you have a right to object.

The Medical Information Bureau (MIB) is a data bank used by
insurance companies. Medical and some nonmedical information about
you is collected from insurers and, with your authorization, shared
when you apply for individual life, health, or disability insurance. You
can obtain a copy of your MIB file from the Medical Information Bureau, listed at the end of this chapter. It is advisable to periodically
discuss your MIB file and other medical records with your doctor to
verify the accuracy of the file.

In 1970, Congress passed the Fair Credit Reporting Act, which
provides guidelines as to how credit bureaus can obtain and dissemi-
nate personal credit information on consumers. Credit bureaus keep
records about how you pay your bills and how much credit you have,
among other things. Specifically, the Act provides that credit bureaus
can share information on your credit history with businesses with
which you seek credit, employers, and insurance companies handling
your policy. Under the Act, most information about general credit
problems can remain on your record for seven years, while bankruptcies can remain for up to ten years.

Because of the possibility of adverse information which can affect
obtaining credit (e.g., mortgage, bank card), it is important to check
your credit report once a year, checking for inconsistencies. For a
small fee, you can obtain a copy of your credit record and the names

of companies that have asked for information about you. If you are denied credit based on information in your credit bureau files, there is no cost to obtain a copy of your credit report. The creditor will tell you which credit bureau to write or call.

If you find a mistake in your credit report, the credit bureau must check it and correct it for you. Any negative information that cannot be proven must be removed. In addition, you can add to your file a hundred-word statement of explanation for a credit problem. When you make a correction in your credit file, make sure the correction is made with all three credit bureaus (TRW, (800) 682-7654; Equifax, (800) 866-6520; and Trans Union (check your local phone book)).

If you find that you are having severe credit problems, you can seek assistance from the Consumer Credit Counseling Service (CCCS), a non-profit organization which provides money management techniques, debt-paying plans and educational programs. You can find the CCCS office nearest you by consulting the National Foundation for Consumer Credit, Inc., address at the end of this chapter. This service is especially helpful for women who, because of a marital or other relationship, never took care of paying bills, but have to now take care of their credit because of the relationship's termination. Other organizations offer credit counseling; some of these companies, however, charge exorbitant fees for doing little more than you could do yourself.

Once you have obtained credit, you are liable to the issuer of the credit for any moneys that you owe the company. If you consistently make late payments, the credit issuer (creditor) will usually notify a credit reporting agency, which will affect your personal credit negatively. If you do not pay a debt that you owe a creditor, you will usually be referred to a debt collection agency. If the nonpayment is for an automobile or household appliance, there is usually some caveat in the contract which allows the creditor to repossess the item; they must, however, give some form of notice and cannot seize the item "out of the blue."

Under the Fair Debt Collection Practices Act, debt collectors must observe several rules, governed by the FTC, when attempting to collect a debt. A debt collector cannot contact a consumer at an unusual time or place, unless the consumer has give permission to do so. If the consumer has contracted an attorney to handle credit problems, and the debt collector is aware of this, the debt collector must contact the attorney. Finally, if the consumer requests that the debt collector discontinue all contact, the debt collector must honor this request, except to notify the consumer of any legal remedies that the creditor is seeking against the consumer.

Within five days of the initial communication with the consumer, the debt collector must, unless it was contained in the initial communication, notify the consumer in writing of the nature of the credit action, including the amount of debt and the name of the creditor. If the consumer disputes this claim within thirty days, the debt collector must obtain verification of the debt owed and cannot attempt to collect the debt during this time. If, however, the consumer does not respond within thirty days, the claim is deemed valid and the debt collector may attempt to collect the debt, within the parameters discussed below.

When contacting the consumer, the debt collector cannot engage in harassing behavior (e.g., threats, profanity, telephoning continuously, releasing name of consumer to persons other than credit agencies), and cannot mislead the consumer (e.g., imply that legal action that cannot be taken will be sought, such as taking custody of children). If a debt collector engages in such conduct, you should contact the state attorney general's office. Dealing with a debt collector can be a frightening experience; by understanding your rights, you can ensure that the experience is handled in a professional and civil manner.

## Remedies    Handling Your Own Complaint

As a consumer, you have a right to expect quality products and services at fair prices. If something goes wrong, there are things that you can do to resolve the problem. Here are some suggestions for handling your own complaint.

*Describe the problem:* When you complain, be sure to describe the problem, what (if anything) you have done already to try to resolve it and what you expect as a fair solution. Do you want your money back? Would you like the product repaired? Do you want to exchange the product?

*Go back to where you made the purchase:* Contact the business that sold you the item or performed the service. Calmly and accurately explain the problem and what action you have taken. If a salesperson is not helpful, ask for a supervisor or manager and restate your case. Most consumer problems are resolved at this level. Keep a record of your efforts and include notes about whom you spoke with and what was done about the problem.

*Don't give up:* If you are not satisfied with the response at the local level, don't give up. Call the company or write a letter to the person responsible for consumer complaints at the company's headquarters. Many companies have toll-free telephone numbers. Often, these "800" numbers are printed on product packaging. Check your local library for a directory of toll-free numbers of national companies or call (800) 555-1212 to get the company's toll-free number.

If talking with a salesperson or higher-level company representative does not resolve your problem, you will need to write a letter to the company to resolve your complaint. The following books, located in the reference section of your local library, might help you locate company addresses and brand name information: *Standard & Poor's Register of Corporations, Directors and Executives; Standard Directory of Advertisers; Thomas Register of American Manufacturers; Trade Names Directory;* and *Dun & Bradstreet Directory.* A sample complaint letter follows this chapter.

## The Court System

Often, a problem can be remedied quickly with a phone call or a letter; more complex complaints may require the assistance of a lawyer or consumer advocacy group.

*Small Claims Courts* are designed to resolve disputes involving claims for small debts and accounts. While the maximum amounts that can be claimed or awarded vary from state to state, actual court procedures generally are simple, inexpensive, and quick. Court fees are minimal, and you can often get the court filing fee back if you win your case. Generally you do not need a lawyer; in fact, some states do not permit lawyers in small claims court. If the party that you are bringing suit against brings a lawyer, do not be intimidated. The court is informal, and most judges make allowances for consumers who appear without lawyers. Even though the court is informal, the ruling must be followed, just like the ruling of any other court.

If the party bringing suit wins the case, the party who lost often will follow the court's decision without further legal action. Sometimes, however, the losing party does not obey the court's decision. If this occurs, the winning party can go back to court and ask for a court order to be "enforced." The court could, depending on local laws, for example, order property to be taken by law enforcement officials and sold, with the proceeds awarded to the winning party, up to the amount owed. Alternatively, the court may order the losing party's employer to garnish or deduct money from each paycheck and give it to the winner of the lawsuit.

To get information about local small claims courts and their procedures, check your local telephone book under the municipal, county, or state government headings. When you contact the court, ask the clerk how to use the small claims court system. To better understand the process, sit in on a small claims court session before taking your case to court. Many small claims courts have created alternative dispute resolution (ADR) programs to help citizens resolve their disputes. The three most common forms of ADR are negotiation, mediation, and arbitration. Negotiation takes place between two attorneys representing their respective clients. In a negotiation, the attorneys, through guidelines set by their clients, seek to reach an agreeable settlement.

Mediation and arbitration are more formal, in that they involve the parties and a neutral third party, who attempts to elicit an agreement from the parties. Of the two, mediation is less formal; decisions are not binding and the mediator acts only as a facilitator of discussion. In arbitration, the parties often agree to submit to a ruling of the arbitrator, thus creating a binding decision. These dispute resolution processes often simplify the process.

As to the success of ADR, research indicates that if both parties attend a mediation session, an agreement is reached 85 to 90 percent of the time. Just as importantly, researchers learned that six months after the session, 85 percent of the agreements formed in mediation were "substantially fulfilled."

For additional information about alternative dispute resolution, contact the American Bar Association, listed at the end of this chapter.

*Legal Aid Offices* help individuals who cannot afford to hire private lawyers. There are more than one thousand Legal Aid offices across the country, staffed by lawyers, paralegals, and law students. Each Legal Aid office offers free legal services to people who financially qualify. Funding is provided by a variety of sources, including federal, state, and local governments and private donations. Law schools also conduct clinics in which law students, as part of their training, assist practicing lawyers with these cases.

Legal Aid offices generally offer legal assistance with such problems as landlord-tenant disputes, credit, utilities, family issues (e.g., adoption and divorce), social security, welfare, unemployment, and workers' compensation. Each Legal Aid office has its own board of directors which determines the priorities of the office and the types of cases handled by the office. If the Legal Aid office in your area does not handle your situation, it should be able to refer you to other local, state, or national organizations that can provide advice or assistance. Check the telephone directory or call your local consumer protection agency to find the address and telephone number of the Legal Aid office near you. To obtain a directory of Legal Aid Offices around the country, contact the National Legal Aid and Defender Association, listed at the end of this chapter. (See also chapter 1.)

## Insurance

Insurance is the mechanism by which we assess and protect against risk. The risk of liability is one of these risks, and to best understand it, it is necessary to understand the concept of a tort.

A tort is defined as a wrongful act, other than a breach of contract, which results in injury to person or property, and for which a civil action can be brought against the offending party. Liability for torts is divided into two broad categories: strict liability and negligence. To prove strict liability, one only needs to show that an injury occurred, regardless of fault. Thus, even if a person did not intend to harm another, she would be liable. Torts may be intentional, such as assault and battery, trespass, false imprisonment, and defamation, or unintentional, as in product liability, which was discussed previously.

The standard for negligence does not look solely at the fact that an injury occurred in determining fault; instead it focuses on the conduct of the person causing the injury. Negligence occurs when a person does not act as a "reasonable person" would have acted under similar circumstances. Examples of negligence include auto accidents, property damage, and a physician's malpractice.

Once a person proves that a tort has been committed, she is able to recover damages, which are established to make the injured party "whole." There are two types of damages for which recovery can be sought: compensatory and punitive. Compensatory damages are those which directly compensate the injured party for harms incurred. They include special, or pecuniary, damages, which have a definite monetary value (e.g., loss of job, loss of a limb, physical impairment), and general damages, which are losses for which it is more difficult to attach a monetary value (e.g., pain and suffering, emotional harm). Punitive damages are designed to punish the party causing the damage and deter similar behavior; for this reason, they are generally limited to cases of strict liability.

When a person sues another for tort liability, there are two other factors which courts look at to determine damages. Comparative fault looks at the conduct of the injured party, determining if she contributed to the injury; if the court finds that she did, recoverable damages are reduced by the percentage that this party is culpable. Comparative fault has been accepted by most states. Joint and several liability is applicable when there is more than one party that caused the injury; it allows the injured party to recover the entire settlement from either of the two parties, or to recover from each party the amount that she was culpable.

Torts have become a familiar news item lately, as both state and national legislatures move for "tort reform." Proponents of reform include corporations, insurance companies, and manufacturers. They argue that the tort system needs reform, because court costs for civil liability claims (largely made up of torts) are larger in the United States than in any country in the world. Specific arguments include revising joint and several liability so that a party is only accountable for her own percentage of guilt in computing damages, putting a cap on general damages, as they are difficult to compute and very subjective, and developing stricter standards for collecting punitive damages. Although these proposals sound good on their face, they could have potentially detrimental effects on consumer rights. For example, damages could be lessened in product liability cases, which could lead to companies not taking as much care to keep potentially harmful products off the market. Also, many times emotional damages exact a greater toll on an individual than actual physical harm; capping these damages would deny a major source of recovery for those who are harmed.

Insurance is designed as a hedge against various forms of risk. Some types are designed to keep a person, to the best extent possible, out of the torts arena, insulating her from liability. To do this, insurance companies assess the risk of an individual for a certain type of harm. The individual pays a premium, which is pooled with all the premiums collected for the specific type of insurance by the company, spreading the risk among a class of individuals. When a person is injured, she files a claim with her insurance company, which then reimburses her according to the terms of the policy.

### Automobile Insurance

Auto insurance protects you against damage you cause to another, including personal injury, as well as damage caused to you by another driver. It may also protect you against damage that you cause yourself if you were, for example, to lose control of your car because of weather conditions and hit a tree. In most states the insurer determines parties at fault before reimbursement; if another person caused your accident, their insurance company reimburses you. Several states have adopted a regime of "no fault" insurance, which provides that your insurance company will reimburse you no matter who caused the loss (damage). Your insurance company can then seek recovery from the person who caused the damage (but not from you). Many states also have a provision that premiums will rise with "chargeable" accidents, i.e., when you are at fault, as you will be assessed as a riskier individual.

### Life Insurance

There are several types of life insurance, and some are worth consideration. All forms of life insurance are bought by paying premiums, usually on a yearly basis. Sometimes a medical examination is required for certain kinds of insurance.

Whole life insurance provides coverage for the entire life of the insured in exchange for a series of equal premiums paid over the life of the insured. The owner can terminate a whole life policy at any time and receive the "cash surrender value" or can continue the policy in force and borrow against the cash surrender value. The cash surrender value of a life insurance policy is an amount roughly equal to the premiums paid, plus interest on them since their payment, less administrative costs.

Term life insurance, by contrast, provides that the company will pay the face amount if the insured dies within the "term," a stated number of years, usually between one and five. The price of a term life insurance policy is ordinarily a single premium paid at the beginning of the term. The premiums for term policies are often lower than the premiums for the same face amount of whole life insurance because the policy, and therefore the risk, is for a relatively short term, and because the policy has no cash surrender value, nor any loan value.

Mortgage insurance, eagerly marketed by nearly every mortgage company, pays the amount remaining on the mortgage if the mortgagor dies.

There are other forms of life insurance, but a complete discussion is beyond the scope of this article. There are many books that deal just with insurance.

## Medical Insurance

Medical insurance is frequently paid all or partially by a person's employer. If you are self-employed or unemployed, you may prefer to carry individual coverage. A number of companies do make this kind of insurance available, particularly HMOs (health maintenance organizations), but they tend to be expensive. As with any insurance you should be very sure what your insurance covers and what part of your care you must pay for.

## Homeowner's Insurance

Homeowner's insurance protects your residence and belongings against fire, theft, and other disasters. Some policies exclude flooding or other natural phenomena (for example, it is very expensive to have insurance against earthquake damage in California). Homeowner's insurance is usually offered for either the actual cash value or the replacement value of your property. Although actual cash value insurance is less expensive, it only reimburses you for the cash value of your property, minus depreciation. If you have an older house, this depreciation can be considerable, making replacement value the better policy. If you own expensive luxury items, such as art or jewelry, you will have to obtain additional coverage, known as a "rider," to your homeowner's insurance. Finally, you do not have to be a homeowner to have insurance for your property; renter's and condominium owner's insurance is also available.

## Liability Umbrella

Most companies offer a special "umbrella" policy for those who insure both home and car with the same company. This is a relatively inexpensive policy that provides additional liability coverage, generally

$1 to $3 million, after the liability provisions of the other policy is exhausted. For example, if your teenager gets drunk at a party, gets behind the wheel of a car, and kills another motorist or pedestrian, your vehicle liability policy will probably not cover the damages. An umbrella policy will.

## Unemployment

Unemployment insurance is a state-regulated mechanism to compensate people while they are out of work. While you are employed, your employer pays into a pool from which unemployment compensation is drawn. Although the specific mechanism varies from state to state, there are general requirements that must be fulfilled to receive unemployment compensation. Benefits are not paid if you were fired for serious misconduct on the job (e.g., you were embezzling), or if you quit without good cause. You must have worked a requisite number of hours or earned a minimum amount over a specified period. Finally, you must apply with your local unemployment office and actively be seeking work; you do not have to, however, take a job for which you are seriously overqualified. To receive unemployment benefits, or to find out how the system operates in your state, contact your local unemployment office.

Insurance is a unique field in that it operates an almost-sanctioned form of discrimination; people are pooled in groups, based on age, gender, race, and marital status, allowing the insurance companies to determine a broad-based policy of insurability based on these classes. This is most evident in auto, health, disability, and life insurance. With auto and life insurance, women tend to be treated better than men, as they typically have better driving records and live longer, usually out-surviving their spouses. On the other hand, with disability and health insurance, women tend to be treated as a riskier class than men, especially when they are of childbearing age.

One recent disturbing trend has health and life insurers denying coverage for battered women. The insurance companies justify this exclusion based on the high risk of injury to these women. Also, it is often difficult to get health insurance if you have serious pre-existing medical conditions, especially AIDS. Various health insurance reform proposals are calling for an elimination of such exclusionary practices. Other forms of insurance, including homeowners, Medicare, and unemployment, do not tend to discriminate based on any broad class.

This discrimination is allowable except for two circumstances. Employers cannot charge employees different insurance rates based on gender. Also, some states have statutes that bar any form of gender-based pricing. For example, Montana disallows gender-based pricing on any form of insurance. Several other states, including Michigan, Massachusetts, and New Jersey, bar gender-based pricing in auto insurance.

In examining which insurance policy is best for you, it is not only necessary to examine the types of coverage available; it is also essential to look at ways to mitigate or avoid situations where insurance is needed, saving both money and time. For example, to help avoid costly auto accidents, you should maintain your automobile in good condition and obey speed limits; to avoid high health costs, you should monitor your diet and exercise regularly. This type of behavior may avoid having to make claims on insurance policies, and it might also be rewarding in the form of reduced premiums for good health or a good driving record.

It is also essential to measure your exposure to certain risks, which will help you determine what type of insurance you need. Is there a good chance you will need serious health care in the next couple of years? Do you drive an expensive automobile which is vulnerable to theft? Do you live in a geographic area susceptible to earthquakes or tornadoes, exposing your home to risk? Do you have trouble maintaining a savings account, which would make a whole life insurance policy a good option? When assessing your risk, keep in mind that liability awards for serious tort actions tend to be rather high with respect to average salaries. Make sure you are adequately covered in the case of a serious accident, but not so much that you are wasting money. Finally, once you have determined the type of coverage you really need, you must determine how much coverage you need. Most insurance policies operate on a diminishing scale of payment: as the amount of coverage is increased, the premium paid per $X of coverage generally decreases.

Remember, an insurance agreement is a contract. The specific coverages described in the policy are the terms of the contract. Some forms of insurance, especially homeowner's, cover a certain class of risks; if you want additional coverage, you must have a "rider" attached to the contract, adding and amending standard coverage. Insurance contracts also contain specifics as to your responsibilities should coverage become necessary. These responsibilities usually include how and when the insurance company must be notified of a claim.

Since your premiums and coverage are based on information you provide, you must be honest in supplying information; an insurance contract can be rendered void if it is discovered that the insured was dishonest as to material facts covered by the policy. One term which you may wish to have included is a waiver of payment clause, which allows a waiver of premium payments in the event that you are injured. Also, make sure that the contract does allow a grace period for late payments, so that you do not jeopardize your policy if you are unable to pay your premium on time. As with all contracts, make sure to read all of the terms *very* carefully; your life or property could depend on it.

## Conclusion

As you can see, your rights and remedies as a consumer are wide and varied. Although protection exists in the form of courts and statutes, the best protection is common sense and knowledge. If you are a smart consumer, you will not face many problems. Thus, as in most aspects of life, education is the key to protection of yourself, your family, and your property.

(Your address)
(Your city, state, zip code)
(Date)


(Name of Contact Person)
(Title)
(Company Name)
(Street Address)
(City, State, Zip Code)


(Dear Contact Person):

On **(date)**, I purchased **(or had repaired)** a **(name of product with serial or model number or service performed)**. I made this purchase at **(location, date, and other important details of the transaction)**.

Unfortunately, your product **(or service)** has not performed well **(or the service was inadequate)** because **(state the problem)**.

Therefore, to resolve this problem, I would appreciate **(state specific action desired)**. Enclosed are copies of my records **(receipts, warranties, canceled checks, contracts, model and serial numbers, and any other documents)**.

I look forward to your reply and a resolution to my problem, and will wait **(set a time limit)** before seeking third-party assistance. Please contact me at the above address or by phone at (work/home phone number).

Sincerely,


(Your Name)
(Account Number if applicable)

*A Model
Complaint Letter*

## Bibliography

Abromovitz, Les. *Family Insurance Handbook: The Complete Guide for the 1990s*. Blue Ridge Summit, PA: Liberty Hall Press, 1990.

Brownlie, William D., and Jefferey L. Seglin. *The Life Insurance Buyer's Guide*. New York: McGraw-Hill, 1989.

Consumer's Resource Handbook, U. S. Office of Consumer Affairs

Epstein, David G. *Consumer Protection in a Nutshell*. St. Paul: West Publishing, 1976.

"Equal Credit Opportunity Act of 1974", 15 U.S.C. §1691

"Fair Credit Reporting Act of 1970," 15 U.S.C. §1681

Foehner, Charlotte, and Carol Cozart. *The Widow's Handbook: A Guide for the Living*. Golden, CO: Fulcrum Publishing, 1988.

Hogue, Kathleen, Cheryl Jensen, and Kathleen McClung Urban. *The Complete Guide to Health Insurance: How to Beat the High Cost of Being Sick*. New York: Walker and Co., 1988.

Horvitz, Simeon I., J.D. *Legal Protection for Today's Consumer*. Dubuque, IA: Kendall/Hunt Publishing Co., 1980.

Nader, Ralph, and Wesley J. Smith. *Winning the Insurance Game*. New York: Doubleday, 1993.

## Organizational Resources

Alliance Against Fraud in Telemarketing (AAFT)
c/o National Consumers League
815 15th Street, N.W., Suite 928-N
Washington, DC 20005
(202) 639-8140
(202) 347-0646 (fax)

American Bar Association
1800 M Street, NW
Washington, DC, 20036
(202) 331-2258

American Council on Consumer Interests (ACCI)
240 Stanley Hall
University of Missouri—Columbia
Columbia, MO 65211
(314) 882-3817
(314) 884-4807 (fax)

Auto Safety Hotline
National Highway Traffic Safety Administration
Department of Transportation
Washington, DC 20590
(202) 366-0123
(202) 366-7800 (TDD)
(800) 424-9393 (toll free outside DC)
(800) 424-9153 (toll free TDD outside DC)

Bankcard Holders of America (BHA)
560 Herndon Parkway, Suite 120
Herndon, VA 22070
(703) 481-1110
(703) 481-6037 (fax)

Call for Action
3400 Idaho Avenue, N.W.
Suite 101
Washington, DC 20016
(202) 537-0585
(202) 244-4881 (fax)

Center for Auto Safety (CAS)
2001 S Street, N.W., Suite 410
Washington, DC 20009
(202) 328-7700

Center for Science in the Public Interest (CSPI)
1875 Connecticut Avenue, N.W.
Suite 300
Washington, DC 20009
(202) 332-9110
(202) 265-4954 (fax)

Citizen Action
1120 19th Street, N.W., Suite 630
Washington, DC 20036
(202) 775-1580
(202) 296-4054 (fax)

COCO (Congress of Consumer Organizations)
P.O. Box 158
Newton Center, MA 02150
(617) 552-8184

Community Nutrition Institute (CNI)
2001 S Street, N.W., Suite 530
Washington, DC 20009
(202) 462-4700
(202) 462-5241 (fax)

Congress Watch
215 Pennsylvania Avenue, S.E.
Washington, DC 20003
(202) 546-4996
(202) 547-7392 (fax)

Consumer Action (CA)
116 New Montgomery, Suite 233
San Francisco, CA 94105
(415) 777-9635 (consumer complaint hotline, 10 A.M.–3 P.M., PST)
(415) 777-5267 (fax)

Consumer Alert
2700 South Quincy Street
Suite 210
Arlington, VA 22206
(703) 845-8802
(703) 845-8920 (fax)

Consumer Federation of America (CFA)
1424 16th Street, N.W., Suite 604
Washington, DC 20036
(202) 387-6121
(202) 265-7989 (fax)

Consumer Insurance Interest Group
9321 Millbranch Place
Fairfax, VA 22031
(703) 836-9340

Consumers for World Trade (CWT)
2000 L Street, N.W., Suite 200
Washington, DC 20036
(202) 785-4835
(202) 416-1734 (fax)

Consumers Union of U.S., Inc. (CU)
101 Truman Avenue
Yonkers, NY 10703-1057
(914) 378-2000
(914) 378-2900 (fax)

Council of Better Business Bureaus, Inc. (CBBB)
National Headquarters
4200 Wilson Boulevard
Arlington, VA 22203
(703) 276-0100

Federal Communications Commission
1919 M Street, NW
Washington, DC, 20554

Federal Trade Commission
6th and Pennsylvania Aves, NW
Washington, DC 20580

Insurance Information Institute
110 William Street
New York, NY 10038
(800) 221-4954

Mail Preference Service
P.O. Box 3861
Grand Central Station
New York, NY 10163

Medical Information Bureau
P.O. Box 105, Essex Station
Boston, MA 02112

National Association of Consumer
   Agency Administrators (NACAA)
1010 Vermont Avenue, N.W.
Suite 514
Washington, DC 20005
(202) 347-7395
(202) 347-2563 (fax)

National Coalition for Consumer
   Education (NCCE)
434 Main Street, Suite 201
Chatham, NJ 07928
(201) 635-1916
(201) 635-9526 (fax)

National Consumers League (NCL)
815 15th Street, N.W., Suite 928-N
Washington, DC 20005
(202) 639-8140
(202) 737-2164 (fax)

National Foundation for Consumer
   Credit, Inc. (NFCC)
8611 2nd Avenue, Suite 100
Silver Spring, MD 20910
(301) 589-5600
(800) 388-2227 (toll free)
(301) 495-5623 (fax)

National Fraud Information Center
   (NFIC)
c/o National Consumers League
815 15th Street, N.W., Suite 928-N
Washington, DC 20005
(800) 876-7060 (toll free—TDD
   available)
(202) 347-0646 (fax)

National Institute for Consumer
   Education (NICE)
207 Rackham Building
College of Education
Eastern Michigan University
Ypsilanti, MI 48197
(313) 487-2292
(313) 487-7153 (fax)

National Insurance Consumer Organization (NICO)
P.O. Box 15492
Alexandria, VA 22309
(703) 549-8050

National Legal Aid and Defender
   Association
1625 K Street, NW
8th Floor
Washington, DC 20006
(202) 452-0620

Product Safety Hotline
U.S. Consumer Product Safety
   Commission
Washington, DC 20207
(800) 638-CPSC (toll free)
(800) 492-8104 (toll free TDD in
   MD)
(800) 638-8270 (toll free TDD outside MD)

Public Citizen, Inc.
2000 P Street, N.W.
Washington, DC 20036
(202) 833-3000

Telephone Preference Service
6 East 43rd Street
New York, NY 10017

U.S. Postal Service
Chief Postal Inspector
Washington, DC 20260

U.S. Public Interest Research
   Group (U.S. PIRG)
215 Pennsylvania Avenue, S.E.
Washington, DC 20003
(202) 546-9707

**Julie A. Tigges** received her J. D. in 1985 from the University of Iowa College of Law. She was law clerk to the Honorable Myron H. Bright, Senior Circuit Judge for the Eighth Circuit Court of Appeals. Subsequently, she practiced law in Washington, D.C. for several years. Upon moving to Minneapolis in 1990, she clerked for the Honorable James B. Loken, Circuit Judge for the Eighth Circuit Court of Appeals. Currently she cares for her infant twins, Kyra and Zachary.

Chapter 22

# *Retirement Planning*

Anne E. Moss

Chapter Outline

What income will you have to live on when you retire? If you are one of the lucky few, you will have income from social security, a pension, *and* savings. Most people are unable to save enough on their own to see themselves through old age, with the result that social security and an employer-sponsored pension plan are more likely to be the primary sources of their retirement income. But even these benefits are not assured, for women in particular.

Women, on the average, receive lower pension benefits ($5,432 per year) than men ($10,031 per year), according to the Census Bureau in *Current Population Survey,* published in 1993. One reason is that the jobs in which women are characteristically employed—jobs in the service industry or in small firms—often have few or no benefits. Another obstacle to accumulating retirement benefits is the fact that women, in order to care for children or relatives, tend to move in and out of the workforce or accept flexible work arrangements, typically with less pay and fewer, if any, benefits.

Married women may take it for granted that they can count on a husband's retirement benefits. With many couples, the perhaps unspoken assumption is that the husband's benefits will be enough for both of them. But women tend to outlive their husbands, and a husband's death may mean a drastic reduction in the wife's retirement income. Almost four times more widows live in poverty than do wives of the same age. More than half of the widows who are poor were not poor before the death of their husbands.

Likewise, a couple's divorce can mean an impoverished retirement for a wife. One study shows that half of divorced women age sixty-two and over have an income of only a little more than $9,000 a year.[1]

It is important that you start examining your retirement income as early as possible. Where is it likely to come from, and how much in benefits can you expect? Investigating your rights and options in advance will help ensure you will receive all the benefits you expected and to which you are entitled.

This chapter discusses your rights under social security, private pension plans, and individual retirement accounts. It also advises how pension rights may be protected in a divorce.

## Introduction

## Social Security

Social security pays benefits to retired and disabled workers and their families. It also pays benefits to surviving family members of deceased workers.

### How Benefits Are Earned
#### Retirement

If you are a worker who was born after 1928, you need forty "quarters" of credit to be entitled to a social security benefit at retirement.

(You need fewer quarters if you were born in 1928 or earlier.) You receive the quarters of credit when you earn wages. For example, if you worked in a job covered by social security in 1994, you will receive one quarter of credit if you earned at least $620, up to a maximum of four quarters if you earned at least $2,480 during the calendar year. The amount of money you need to earn for one quarter of credit increases each year.

### Disability

The number of quarters of credit you must have accumulated to collect a disability benefit is determined by your age at the time you become disabled. You probably will not need as many quarters of credit to collect a disability benefit as you would need to receive a retirement benefit. But there is an additional requirement that you have at least five years of work in the ten-year period immediately preceding your disability (that is, twenty quarters of service within the last forty-quarter period). This "recency-of-work" test can be a hardship for a woman who takes more than five years out of the workforce to care for her children and then becomes disabled while still off the job or soon after returning to work.

### Creditable Earnings

You may notice that your W-2 form—the wage statement that your employer gives you at the end of the year to file with your income tax form—has a box called "social security wages." This figure shows how much of your annual wages will be counted toward your quarters of credit and the amount of your social security benefit (except for any tips you may have received, which are shown in a different box).

Another box on the W-2 form indicates "social security tax withheld." This is the amount of money you paid in to social security, equal to 6.2 percent of your social security wages and tips. (Another 1.45 percent is paid in for Medicare.) In 1994, a worker must pay social security taxes on wages up to a maximum of $60,600. (Medicare taxes are paid on all wages.) Your employer is required to pay an equal amount of taxes on your behalf. If you are self-employed, you will be paying a higher amount of social security taxes than an employee, approximately equal to the employer's plus the employee's contribution.

### How Benefits Are Calculated

The amount of your worker's benefit is calculated based on your average earnings in your thirty-five highest years of social security-covered earnings (even if you had zero earnings in some of those years). If you were born in 1928 or earlier, your benefit will be based on your average earnings over a smaller number of years, with the exact number of years determined by the year in which you were born. The earnings that are used to calculate your benefit are "indexed," or adjusted upward, to reflect the average national increase in wages that has taken place since the years in which you had those earnings. Contrary to popular belief, benefits are *not* based on the taxes that you and your employer pay in.

Benefits in 1993 averaged $7,836 a year for a retired worker. Social security benefits receive cost-of-living increases annually.

To have an idea of what your benefit is likely to be, you can request a free personal earnings statement from the Social Security Administration. This statement will give you not only an estimate of your benefit at retirement, but will also show your past earnings covered by social security. You should make sure that all your earnings have been properly credited to your social security number. Slip-ups can occur and, occasionally, it happens that one person's earnings are accidentally reported under someone else's number. It's a good idea to ask for a statement every two years or so. If you find an error, be sure to contact the Social Security Administration immediately. The toll-free number is 1-800-772-1213.

## Who May Collect Benefits

Workers and their family members are eligible to collect a variety of benefits.

### Workers

Full monthly retirement benefits can be paid to a retired worker at age sixty-five, if he or she was born prior to 1938. For workers born in 1938 or later, the "normal" retirement age, that is, the age for a full benefit, is more than age sixty-five, but varies depending on the year of birth, ranging up to age sixty-seven for workers born in 1960 and after.

Monthly benefits are payable as early as age sixty-two, but they will be reduced for early retirement. The exact amount of the reduction, which is permanent, depends on how many months that you are away from your normal retirement age when you start collecting. For example, the reduction at age sixty-two would be 20 percent if you were born in 1937, or 30 percent if you were born in 1960.

Benefits are payable at any age, with no reduction for being under the normal retirement age, to a worker who becomes disabled. To meet the medical requirement for a social security disability benefit, a worker must have a mental or physical disability that is expected to last as least twelve months or result in death.

## Spouse and Children

If your husband collects social security worker benefits at retirement or upon becoming disabled, you as his wife will also be able to collect when you become age sixty-two. Your benefit will be equal to about one-half of his full benefit if you start collecting at your normal retirement age, but a lesser amount if you start collecting earlier. For example, the maximum reduction, applicable if you start collecting at age sixty-two, will range from 25 to 35 percent, depending on how many months you are away from normal retirement age.

A spouse of any age who has in her care the worker's child or children under age sixteen (or disabled prior to age twenty-two) may collect benefits when the worker starts collecting. Children of the retired or disabled worker may collect benefits up to age eighteen; or age nineteen, if the child is a full-time student in an elementary or secondary school; or until the child recovers from the disability. Children and eligible spouses caring for minor children receive 50 percent benefits.

If a spouse is also eligible for a social security benefit through her own work, she cannot collect both her spouse's and her own worker benefits in full. (See below, Other Rules That May Affect Benefits.)

## Survivor Benefits

A widow (or widower) may begin collecting reduced benefits starting at age sixty, or fifty if she is disabled. Full benefits are payable if the survivor waits until age sixty-five (or whatever is her normal retirement age). The full widow's benefit is equal to 100 percent of the benefit the retiree was collecting. The maximum reduction, if you start receiving benefits as early as age sixty, or fifty, in case of disability, is 28.5 percent.

A surviving spouse who has in her care the worker's child, who is under age sixteen or disabled prior to age twenty-two, may also receive a "mother's" (or "father's") benefit until remarriage, or the child reaches age sixteen or recovers from the disability. Children may also receive benefits until they marry, attain age eighteen (age nineteen, if a full-time elementary or secondary school student), or recover from the disability. Surviving spouse and children's benefits are each equal to 75 percent of the retiree's benefit.

The widow's remarriage prior to age sixty will terminate her widow's benefits, although benefits can be restored if the new marriage ends. Remarriage of a surviving mother or father at any age terminates benefits. An individual who loses benefits due to remarriage may become eligible for spouse benefits if and when the new husband or wife receives social security benefits.

## Divorced Spouse

A divorced wife who was married at least ten years to the worker may start collecting divorced wife benefits when both she and the worker are at least age sixty-two. No benefits are payable if you were married fewer than ten years. Your former husband need not actually be collecting benefits himself, but if he is not yet receiving benefits, then there are two additional requirements that must be met before you can receive a divorced spouse benefit. One is that your former husband must be "eligible" for retirement benefits, meaning that he has earned the required number of credits and is himself at least age sixty-two. The other is that you must have been divorced at least two years before you may collect.

After the worker's death, the divorced widow may collect benefits as early as age sixty, or fifty if she is disabled.

Benefits paid to divorced wives and widows are calculated the same way as benefits paid to spouses who are not divorced. Your former husband's remarriage will not affect the amount of your benefits. Both you and his current spouse can collect full benefits at the same time, unless the Family Maximum Rule applies (see below).

If you are a divorced wife, your eligibility for benefits terminates if you remarry at any age. If you are a divorced widow, your right to benefits ends if you remarry prior to age sixty. If you lose benefits due to remarriage in either situation, your benefits will be restored if your subsequent marriage ends.

## Other Rules That May Affect Benefits

Your remarriage is not the only event that can result in your receiving less in benefits than you had counted on. The following rules affect all social security recipients.

### The Dual Entitlement Rule

Even if an individual is technically eligible to receive two social security benefits, she may receive only the larger amount. This is known as the "dual entitlement rule." For example, if you have a social security worker benefit through your own employment and are also eligible for benefits as a spouse (whether married or divorced), then you should expect to receive an amount equal to the larger of the two benefits, but not both benefits in full. (The same rule will apply to your husband if he is eligible to collect both a worker benefit and a spouse benefit.)

### The Earnings Test

If you go back to work after your retirement, your benefits may be reduced in any year that your earnings exceed a certain amount, a rule known as the "earnings test." In 1994, a social security recipient's benefits for that year would be reduced $1 for every $2 she earns over

$8,040 if she is under age sixty-five, or reduced $1 for every $3 she earns over $11,160 if she is between age sixty-five and seventy. The earnings test does not apply to anyone who is age seventy or over.

Keep in mind that if you do go back to work after retirement, you and your employer are still required to pay social security taxes on your earnings, whether or not the earnings are high enough to cause a reduction in your benefits under the earnings test.

### The Family Maximum Rule

This rule provides that only a certain maximum total amount of benefits is payable on the earnings record of a wage-earner. The maximum amount paid to any one family is calculated according to a formula based on the worker's full retirement benefit (even if the worker's benefit is reduced for early retirement). For example, if the worker's full individual benefit is $495 per month, the maximum amount of total benefits payable to that individual and his or her family is $743 per month. Benefits payable to a divorced spouse, however, generally do not count toward the maximum.

Once the total amount of benefits being paid to the retiree and family members has been reached, each family member—except for the retired worker and the divorced spouse—will have his or her benefits reduced proportionately.

### Applying for Benefits

You should usually apply for benefits at least three months before you expect to retire. This allows plenty of time for the Social Security Administration to process your application. You can apply in person, by visiting your local Social Security office, or by telephone. The toll-free number is (800) 772-1213.

### How to Appeal Social Security's Decision

If you disagree with all or a part of Social Security's decision about your claim for benefits, you have the right to appeal. Usually, you will receive written notice of your appeal rights when you receive the agency's decision. You have sixty days from the date you receive the initial decision to ask for a reconsideration by Social Security. If you are not satisfied with the results of the reconsideration of your claim, then you may ask for a hearing before an administrative law judge. If necessary, you may then ask for a review by the Appeals Council, and finally, you may file a lawsuit against the Social Security Administration in federal district court.

You are not required to have a lawyer at any stage of the appeal, but you should at least consult a lawyer if you plan to ask for an administrative hearing.

## Taxes

Once you begin receiving your social security benefits, you may be required to pay taxes on them, depending on the size of your income. You may have to pay taxes on as much as 85 percent of your benefits, if the total of all your income is over $34,000 ($44,000 for a married couple). You will be taxed on up to 50 percent of your benefits if your income is between $25,000 and $34,000 ($32,000 to $44,000 for a married couple). You owe no taxes on your benefits if your income is under these limits.

## Private Employer Retirement Plans

About half the private sector workforce is covered by employer-sponsored pension and retirement plans. These plans form an important part of your retirement. Although employers are not required to have plans, the plans that do exist must meet certain minimum standards required by federal law.

The Employee Retirement Income Security Act (known as ERISA), enacted in 1974, gives specific rights to individuals working under pension plans, and establishes various protections for employees against pension fund mismanagement. It also establishes a federal pension insurance program. ERISA applies to most pension and retirement plans sponsored by businesses of all sizes (regardless of the number of employees), nonprofit organizations, and private colleges and universities, among others. The law does not generally apply to plans sponsored by religious organizations.

## Types of Plans

There are two main types of pension and retirement plans: the defined benefit plan and the defined contribution plan. Most private sector plans, whether defined benefit or defined contribution, are primarily employer-paid (with one major exception—the 401(k) plan—described below). Either type of plan, however, may also provide for the employee to contribute.

The *defined benefit plan* promises an employee a specific amount of money at retirement based on her average earnings and years of work. If you participate in this type of plan, and you ask your "plan administrator" how much in benefits you have earned thus far, you will probably be told that you have earned a certain amount per month payable starting at retirement age. Employees do not have their own individual accounts under these plans as they do with defined contribution plans.

Under a *defined contribution plan,* employees have separate accounts into which an employer, and sometimes the employee, contributes money each year, usually a certain percentage of pay. Under this type of plan, you will not know what your benefits will be until you actually retire. What you eventually receive from the plan will depend on how much money is in your account at the time funds are paid out to you, which in turn depends upon how much was put in and how well the money was invested over the years. Some defined contribution plans pay benefits in the form of a lifetime monthly pension, while other plans pay lump sums rather than pensions.

The most common type of nonpension plan is a 401(k) plan. This plan usually depends on the employee to put money into the program voluntarily on a tax-deferred basis (meaning that you do not pay tax on the money you contribute until the funds are withdrawn at retirement). The employer may contribute money also, usually on a matching basis, up to a certain amount. Generally, this type of plan is most useful to the employee who can afford to put aside her own money for retirement.

A 401(k) plan is typical of the type of retirement plan that permits the employee to withdraw her funds in a lump sum when she leaves the job. Some of these plans also allow an employee to borrow against the money that she has contributed.

Other types of defined contribution plans include profit-sharing plans and employee stock ownership plans (ESOPs). Under a profit-sharing plan, the employer pays into the plan a certain percentage of pay annually for each employee. The yearly percentage may vary according to how profitable the company is from year to year. If profits are down, there may be no employer contribution for the year.

Under an employee stock ownership plan, employees accumulate company stock in their retirement plans. The amount of retirement benefits would then depend on the value of the stock at the time you withdraw your funds.

Small firms are more likely to have defined contribution plans, especially 401(k) plans. Large corporations often have a defined contribution plan (or plans) in addition to a basic defined benefit pension plan.

## How Benefits Are Earned

In general, a plan must allow an employee to become a plan member (that is, a participant) once she has worked at least a thousand hours (approximately equal to working forty hours a week for six months or twenty hours a week for one year). Once you become a member of the plan, you start to accumulate benefits every year that you work at least a thousand hours. You will receive these "accrued" benefits at retirement if you work long enough to become "vested."

A pension or retirement plan generally must allow a worker to earn the right to a benefit, or "vest," after five years of service. Being vested means you have the right to receive a monthly pension or retirement benefit starting at retirement age, even if you leave the company long before that date. Some plans allow workers to vest gradually, for example, 20 percent after three years, with the percentage increasing each year, reaching 100 percent vesting after seven years. Being 20 percent vested, for example, means that you have a vested right to 20 percent of the benefits you have accrued thus far. Certain small plans are required by law to allow workers to vest more quickly, 100 percent after three years or gradually over a two- to-six-year period.

Certain types of plans, known as multiemployer plans, are still permitted to require ten years of work for vesting. These are plans that cover employees working under a union collective-bargaining contract made with several employers.Usually, you must work at least a thousand hours in a year to get credit toward being vested, but individual plans may have slightly different ways to count service.

## When Benefits Are Paid

A typical pension plan pays monthly benefits to the employee starting at retirement age and continuing for life. If your company tells you how much your benefits will be, the amount is usually stated as benefits payable at age sixty-five. But most plans also have an early retirement age, such as age fifty-five or fifty.

As mentioned previously, many defined contribution plans will pay benefits as soon as an employee terminates employment. You still may have to wait a number of months to receive your benefits—refer to your plan booklet for the rules on getting your benefits.

## How Benefits Are Calculated

Most pension plans have a benefit formula that gives you a certain percentage of your final earnings (such as your average earnings for the last five years) multiplied by the number of years you have worked. If your plan is a defined contribution plan, the amount of your benefits will depend on how much is in your account at retirement.

If you start receiving your pension prior to age sixty-five, as most people do, your monthly benefit may be reduced to take into account that your pension is being paid over more years. For example, if you start collecting benefits at age fifty-five, your monthly amount might be only half as much as if you waited to start collecting at age sixty-five.

On the other hand, a number of large companies that want to encourage older, more expensive employees to retire often pay full pensions to employees who are younger than sixty-five. For example, they may pay full pensions to certain long-service employees with twenty or thirty years of service, or whose age and years of service add up to a certain number, such as seventy-five or eighty.

Companies once were permitted to freeze workers' pensions at age sixty-five, another practice designed to encourage older employees to leave. In other words, a worker would find that her pension benefit remained the same, even if she worked well past age sixty-five. Amendments to the age discrimination laws now prohibit this practice. A plan may, however, provide that your benefit will not increase once you have worked a certain maximum number of years under the plan, such as thirty or thirty-five, as long as the "freeze"" is not tied to a specific age.

One other point that you should keep in mind, if you are trying to decide when to retire, is that the vast majority of pension plans do not have cost of living adjustments. Consequently, the amount of your basic monthly pension on the day you retire is likely to be exactly the same for the rest of your life, which may easily extend another twenty or thirty years.

## Other Factors That May Affect Benefits
### Job Loss

If you lose your job, then the plan must still pay you any vested benefits, though no earlier than at the retirement age stated in the plan rules.

### Sale of the Company

If your company or division is sold, the benefits you have already earned must be preserved. The arrangements made between the buying and selling companies will determine who will be paying you the benefits earned from the old company. If the new company has its own plan, it is possible that the company will assume responsibility for paying to the "acquired" employees the benefits they had already earned, in addition to the benefits they earn under the new plan.

Although a new employer cannot take away any benefits you have already earned, the employer *can* provide that, in the future, you will be earning benefits at a lower rate, meaning that your benefits will not be increasing as much as if you had been able to continue working under the old plan.

### Plan Termination

If your employer intends to "terminate" or stop the company pension or retirement plan, you must be given advance written notice that the plan will be ending. Plan termination is most likely to occur if your company goes out of business, but also may happen if your employer simply decides not to operate the plan any more.

Usually, when a company terminates a plan, it buys an annuity (that is, a pension) from an insurance company for each person who worked under the plan. At the time your plan is terminated, you are told the name and address of the insurance company handling your benefits. When you reach retirement age, you apply to the insurance company for your benefit. The insurance company uses the rules in effect when your plan terminated in determining who is entitled to a pension and how much those benefits are.

If your plan terminates without enough money to pay the promised benefits (which is unusual), then the federal government's pension insurance program, which is run by the Pension Benefit Guaranty Corporation (PBGC), will take over the plan and pay benefits according to the plan provisions. *But* 401(k) and other defined contribution plans are not covered by this insurance. (Note: These are not the only exclusions.) For more information about the pension insurance program, read *Your Guaranteed Pension* (see Bibliography).

## Benefit Payment Options
### Protections for Spouses

If you are married when you start receiving your pension, your monthly pension is likely to be reduced to pay for a survivor pension for your spouse, known as the "joint and survivor" option.

*Spousal consent rule.* If you do not want this survivor pension paid to your husband, then you and your husband must both sign a form provided by the plan to waive this benefit. For example, you would need your husband's signature if you want to provide a survivor benefit for a child or to take your benefit as a pension for your life only or to collect benefits as a lump sum.

The same rule applies to your husband if he is covered by a pension at work—he must have *your* written consent before signing away your survivor's pension.

There is one important exception to the consent rule. If your husband (or you) has a 401(k) or other nonpension plan, such as a profit-sharing plan, you as the surviving spouse will be entitled to receive 100 percent of his benefits if he dies while the money is still in his account, unless you give your written consent for someone else to be the beneficiary. These plans, however, typically permit employees to withdraw their benefits when they leave their job. In this situation, your husband is not required to obtain your consent to withdraw his benefits and, once the money is withdrawn, you have no claim to a survivor benefit from the plan.

*How a survivor benefit is calculated.* The joint and survivor option works as follows. Assume that your husband has earned a pension of $1,000 a month, if paid for his life only. Accepting the joint and survivor option rather than the single-life pension might require him to take a pension reduced to $900 a month. After his death, your survivor pension would be 50 percent of that reduced pension, or $450 a month for the rest of your life. The calculation depends on your age compared to his. If you are much younger than your husband, he would probably be required to take a greater reduction in his monthly benefit, to take into account the fact that you would likely outlive him by more years, meaning that the pension would have to be paid over a longer period.

A pension plan must also provide a preretirement survivor benefit to a surviving spouse if the vested employee dies before retirement. If the employee lives to retirement, he may be required to accept a small reduction in his pension to pay for this preretirement protection. This survivor benefit may also be waived with spousal consent, if the employee does not want the eventual reduction. A number of plans provide this benefit at no cost to the employee.

*Other family members.* Although plans are required by law to provide benefits for a surviving spouse, they are not required to provide survivor benefits for any other family member or individual. Many plans, however, do allow an employee to provide for a child or a parent.

### Other Options

In general, a plan that is considered a pension plan is not required to provide any method of payment other than a joint and survivor pension or a single-life pension. But many plans also offer benefits in the form of a lump sum.

Another common option is a "life and ten-year certain" pension. This means that the pension is paid for your lifetime, but if you die within ten years after retirement, your designated beneficiary will receive the balance of the ten-year payments. Thus, if you die eight years after retirement, your beneficiary would receive benefits for two more years, but if you die after eleven years, no more benefits would be payable.

### Applying for Benefits

Contact your personnel office when you are ready to file for benefits. Technically, the plan administrator is in charge of paying benefits. Your personnel office can probably tell you where to send your application and what documents you need in order to apply for benefits. Within ninety days after you file, the plan must tell you whether or not you qualify for benefits. If your claim is denied, the plan must explain to you in writing and in detail why the claim was denied.

### Appealing the Plan's Decision

If you are denied pension benefits or if you disagree with some aspect of a plan's decision, you have the right to request a review by plan officials, and you must be given at least sixty days following the initial denial to file this appeal. Your plan booklet should describe how to appeal this decision. These rules about appeal rights apply to spouses as well as employees. Contact the plan administrator promptly if you have a disagreement. If you wait too long, the plan may be able to say that you have given up your right to appeal.

Once you have asked for a review, the plan must make a decision on your appeal within sixty days of the date of filing the appeal, unless it notifies you in writing that there will be a delay beyond the sixty days. In that case, the plan may take up to 120 days, or longer if the review is to be made by a plan committee or a board of trustees that meets only quarterly.

You also have the right to sue the plan in state or federal court (the proper court being determined by the nature of the claim you are making). If you win your case, the plan may be required by the judge to pay your attorneys' fees.

In general, however, you must pursue your claim through the plan's claims review procedures before going to court. You are not required to have a lawyer at any stage of the appeal, but you may want to at least consult a lawyer. The law says that you cannot be fired or otherwise retaliated against by your employer, a plan official, or another individual in order to prevent you from exercising your rights under a plan.

## Taxes

Although you do not have to pay taxes on your pension benefits while they are accumulating in the plan, you will have to pay taxes on the benefits paid out to you (with certain exceptions, such as money that represents contributions you were required by the plan to make, on which you will already have been taxed). If your plan pays you benefits in a lump sum before you are age fifty-nine and one-half, your employer is required to withhold 20 percent of your benefits for an excise tax. You will also have to pay income tax on the entire amount. To avoid paying so much in taxes, it usually makes the most sense to have the plan transfer your lump sum directly to your Individual Retirement Account.

## For More Information

Under ERISA, every pension and retirement plan has a designated *plan administrator,* the person in charge of the day-to-day operation of the plan. By law, a plan participant is entitled to receive certain information about the plan rules and her own benefits from the plan administrator. The documents you are entitled to receive include:

- The *Summary Plan Description* (SPD) highlights information about your plan, such as how you earn benefits, how benefits are figured, and when you can start collecting them. It also should explain how to apply for benefits and how to appeal a negative decision. You should be given this booklet automatically when you become a member of the plan. If not, however, you should request it in writing.

- The *Plan Document* is the full, official set of rules applicable to the plan. You may be charged a copying fee of up to 25 cents a page for this document.

- The *Annual Financial Report* will show you where the plan money was invested on the date of the report, and what the rate of return was for that year. Plans are supposed to give out a summary of this report automatically each year, but you are also allowed to ask for the full report.

- The *Individual Benefit Statement* should tell you whether you are vested under your plan and how much in benefits you have earned thus far, if you stopped working as of the date of the statement and then collected your benefits at age sixty-five. It also may show your projected benefits, that is, an estimate of how much in benefits you might accumulate if you stay on the job until age sixty-five. If you are trying to plan for retirement, be sure you understand which figures show the benefits you have already earned versus the benefits you might earn in the future. You have the right to receive this statement once a year, upon written request, and it is a good idea to ask for one each year just to stay informed about your benefits. Many larger companies distribute these statements automatically each year to every employee.

## Individual Retirement Accounts

If you have earnings from employment, you are eligible to pay money into an Individual Retirement Account (IRA). An IRA is a way to save for retirement while saving on taxes at the same time. You may set up an IRA at almost any bank or financial institution.

You may contribute up to $2,000 a year into an IRA, or an amount equal to your earnings for that year, if less than $2,000. The money you put in will be deductible, that is, subtracted from your taxable income for that year, *if* neither you nor your spouse was covered by an employer-sponsored pension or retirement plan during the year and did not have income over a certain amount.

If one spouse has earnings, but the other has no earnings (or only negligible earnings—under $250), then together they may contribute up to a total of $2250 to two IRAs, with no more than $2,000 going to a single account.

## Nondeductible IRA

If either spouse was covered by a pension or retirement plan in the year for which you are making a contribution, *and* your gross income as a couple exceeds $50,000, your contribution will not be tax deductible. If your total income is between $40,000 and $50,000, your contribution will be partially deductible. The contribution is fully deductible if your income is under $40,000. The fact that either spouse worked under a pension plan in a previous year or is *receiving* benefits from a plan does not count as being "covered" by a pension plan during the year for which you are making IRA contributions.

If you are single and covered by a pension plan, your IRA contribution is nondeductible if your income is over $35,000, but partially deductible if your income is between $25,000 and $35,000, and fully deductible if under $25,000. Note that the rule about deductibility depends on your *income* from all sources, not just your earnings.

Whether your contribution is deductible or not, keep in mind that an IRA can still be a good idea because you do not pay taxes on the interest your money is earning each year, regardless of your income, until you withdraw the money at retirement.

## Rollovers to IRAs

You also may use an IRA to receive funds from a pension plan if you are entitled to a lump sum known as a "qualified distribution." The money that you "roll over" from the plan to the IRA or that is transferred directly into the IRA from the plan by your employer, does not count as part of the $2,000 personal contribution you may otherwise be eligible to make.

A surviving spouse who receives benefits in a lump sum from her husband's pension plan is also eligible to roll over these funds to an IRA, with certain exceptions. A divorced spouse who receives her share of the pension in a lump sum under what is known as a "qualified domestic relations order," is similarly eligible to transfer the amount to an IRA.

## Taxes

When you withdraw your IRA money at retirement, it will be taxable, except for any nondeductible contributions you have made. The Internal Revenue Service has special rules about how to figure the taxes.

You may start withdrawing your IRA money without tax penalty when you are age fifty-nine and one-half, or at any time before that if you become disabled or you withdraw the money in regular installments over your life. Thus, for example, if you became disabled at age forty-five, you could withdraw your IRA funds without paying a penalty tax. The penalty tax is intended to discourage people from spending their retirement money before they retire. Regardless of your age when you start drawing your money you will, of course, have to pay regular income tax on any deductible funds you receive.

### Beneficiaries

The owner of an IRA may choose anyone as the beneficiary to receive his or her account after death. There is no legal requirement that a person designate a spouse as beneficiary.

### For More Information

To find out more about the rules for IRAs, see Publication No. 590—*Individual Retirement Arrangements,* available free from the Internal Revenue Service, by calling 1-800-829-3676. Because the rules for IRAs can be somewhat technical, you should be sure to consult this booklet, or the IRS directly, if you are setting up an IRA for the first time or you expect to have money transferred from an employer pension plan into an IRA.

## Your Rights at Divorce

In every state a pension earned during the marriage is treated as a marital asset divisible at divorce, and may be divided along with the couple's other property. The pension, especially if it was earned over a long career, may well be the couple's largest asset, second only to the house. The principle behind pension-sharing is that the pension was being earned during the marriage and represents money that the couple could have spent on something else if it had not gone into retirement.

If you are divorcing and your husband has a pension that includes his years of work during the marriage, you should be sure that your divorce decree or settlement addresses your pension rights. Your rights are likely to depend on what your divorce decree says concerning the pension. With the exception of social security, benefits are not provided automatically by a pension plan to a former spouse. It is important that the attorney handling your divorce have information about the pension and use it to negotiate a share for you or ask the court to award you a share.

Nearly every type of pension and retirement benefit may be treated as a marital asset upon divorce. These include private pensions, federal and state government retirement benefits, military retired pay, and individual retirement accounts.

When a court is dividing up marital property or a couple is negotiating a property settlement, it is typical to treat as marital property that portion of the pension earned during the marriage. Then the marital portion of the pension is divided up the way that the other marital property is divided, often with one-half going to each party.

In some cases, the wife—if she is the "nonemployee spouse" for pension division purposes—will agree to take other marital property, such as the house, in exchange for what would have been her share of the pension. If both husband and wife each have a pension of approximately equal value, they might decide that each will just keep his or her own pension.

If you are to receive part of the pension itself, it is likely that you can have your share of the pension paid to you directly from the plan. This must be done by having a carefully written "court order" telling the plan to pay you. A court-approved property settlement which includes a provision for dividing the pension can often be used for this purpose if its provisions meet the plan's requirements for such orders. This special type of court order or court-approved property settlement is known as a Qualified Domestic Relations Order (QDRO) when it is directed at a private pension plan, but may be called by another name if it is applied to a different type of pension plan, such as one provided through the federal government.

If you will be claiming a share of the pension from your marriage, be sure to find out what will happen to your benefits if your former husband dies before you. Ask your attorney whether you should also be provided survivor pension rights through the court order. You also will want to make sure that your rights are protected in case your former husband dies before retirement or remarries.

Once you have your QDRO or similar order issued by the divorce court, your attorney should send it to the pension plan for approval. The order should be sent to the plan as soon as possible after it is issued, even if your husband is not expected to retire soon. This will ensure that you do not lose benefits if your husband suddenly dies or leaves his job.

## Conclusion

Employer-sponsored pension benefits can provide a significant source of retirement income if you know the rules for accessing them. But sound planning for retirement means learning about your legal rights long *before* you reach retirement age or find yourself suddenly widowed or divorced.

## Notes

1. Crown, Mutschler, et al., *The Economic Status of Older Divorced Women,* Policy Center on Aging, Brandeis University, 1993.

## Bibliography

(Publications are free except where noted.)

American Association of Retired Persons, A *Woman's Guide To Pension Rights,* American Association of Retired Persons, 1993. Order No. D 12258. Women's rights under private pension plans.

————, *Guide To Understanding Your Pension Plan,* American Association of Retired Persons, 1989. Order No. D 13533. How to read your pension summary plan description.

————, *Women, Pensions & Divorce (Small Reforms That Could Make a Big Difference),* American Association of Retired Persons, 1993. Order No. D 14956. Analysis of state domestic relations laws and federal retirement systems as they affect the pension rights of divorcing spouses; proposals for reform.

Internal Revenue Service, *Individual Retirement Arrangements,* Pub. 590, Internal Revenue Service, 1994. Describes the rules for Individual Retirement Accounts.

————, *Looking Out For No. 2: A Married Couple's Guide To Understanding Your Choices At Retirement From A Defined Benefit Plan,* Pub. 1566, Internal Revenue Service, 1993. Benefits for surviving spouses under defined benefit plans.

————, *Pension and Annuity Income,* Pub. 575, Internal Revenue Service, 1994. Describes the rules for taxation of pension benefits.

————, *Social Security Benefits and Equivalent Railroad Retirement Benefits,* Pub. 915, Internal Revenue Service, 1994. Taxation of social security and Railroad Tier 1 benefits.

————, *Your Pension,* U.S. Government Printing Office, 1988, No. 068000-00002-5. Charge. An individual's basic rights under a pension plan.

Leonard, Francis. *Money and the Mature Woman: How to Hold onto Your Income, Keep your Home, Plan Your Estate.* Reading, MA: Addison-Wesley, Inc., 1993. charge

Martindale, Judith A., and Mary J. Moses. *Creating Your Own Future: A Woman's Guide to Retirement Planning.* Naperville, IL: Sourcebooks, Inc., 1990. charge

Matthews, Joseph L., *Beat the Nursing Home Trap: A Consumer's Guide to Choosing and Financing Long-Term Care.* Berkeley, CA: Nolo Press, 1993. charge

Matthews, Joseph L. with Dorothy Matthews Berman. *Social Security, Medicare, and Pension: The Sourcebook for Older Americans, 5th ed.* Berkeley, CA: Nolo Press, 1993. charge

Moss, Anne E., *Your Pension Rights At Divorce: What Women Need To Know,* Pension Rights Center, Washington, DC., 1995. Charge. Rules for collecting pensions from various retirement systems, such as private pensions, federal government retirement systems; impact of state domestic relations laws.

Pension Benefit Guaranty Corporation, *Your Guaranteed Pension,* Pension Benefit Guaranty Corporation, 1990. Benefits insured by the federal government when a pension plan terminates.

Patterson, Martha P. *The Working Woman's Guide to Retirement Planning: Saving and Investing NOW for a Secure Future.* Englewood Cliffs, NJ: Prentice-Hall, 1993. charge

Sinclair, Carole. *When Women Retire: The Problems They Face and How to Solve Them.* New York: Crown Publishing Group, 1992. charge

Social Security Administration, *A Pension From Work Not Covered By Social Security,* Social Security Administration, 1994, Pub. No. 0510045. Fact sheet describing the windfall penalty applicable to social security retired workers who also have government pensions.

————, *Government Pension Offset,* Social Security Administration, 1994, Pub. No. 0510007. Fact sheet describing the government pension offset applicable to social security spouse benefits.

————, *Social Security Handbook 1993,* U.S. Government Printing Office, SSA Pub. No. 65-008. $20.00. Describes rules for collecting social security benefits.

U.S. Department of Labor, *How To File A Claim For Your Benefits,* U.S. Department of Labor, 1989. How to file a claim and your right to appeal if your claim is denied.

————, *How to Obtain Employee Benefit Documents From the Labor Department,* U.S. Department of Labor, 1990. Describes what pension documents are available and how to request them.

U.S. Office of Personnel Management, *Handbook For Attorneys on Court-ordered Retirement and Health Benefits Under the Civil Service Retirement System, the Federal Employees Retirement System and the Federal Employees Health Benefits Program, U.S.* Government Printing Office, 1995. Pub. No. S/N/006-000-01377-5. Charge. Contains the regulations applicable to pension orders and health benefits for former spouses of federal civilian employees. Model paragraphs for court orders are included on a computer disk

Pension Rights Center, *Can You Count On Getting A Pension?,* Pension Rights Center, 1990. $3.00. Summary of vesting rules for company and union pension plans.

————, *Where to Look for Help With a Pension Problem,* Pension Rights Center, 1993 (includes 1994 update). Charge. Lists government agencies and private organizations that answer pension questions; legal programs that provide referrals and assistance.

## Organizational Resources

### Federal Agencies:

Internal Revenue Service
1111 Constitution Avenue, NW
Washington, DC 20224
*The IRS Employee Plans Technical and Actuarial Division, Room 6526, answers questions about the interpretation of specific provisions of the private pension law, (202) 622-7074*

*Publications, which are usually updated annually, may be ordered by calling (800) 829-3676.*

Pension Benefit Guaranty Corporation
1200 K Street, NW
Washington, DC 20005
(202) 326-4000
*The PBGC is a federal government agency insuring certain pension benefits for many company and union defined benefit plans. If you are concerned that your plan may stop, or it is in the process of terminating, contact the Case Operations and Compliance Department at the above telephone number.*

*To receive free publications, write to the above address.*

Social Security Administration
(800) 772-1213
*The Social Security Administration provides services through local offices and teleservice centers. To locate the nearest office, see the U.S. Government pages of your telephone book. By calling the above toll-free number, however, you can request publications or benefit statements, or make an application.*

U.S. Department of Labor
Pension and Welfare Benefits Administration
200 Constitution Ave., NW
Washington, DC. 20210
*The Division of Technical Assistance and Inquiries gives general information about rights under federal laws applicable to private pension plans. Telephone callers must listen to a number of recorded messages before speaking to a pension benefits adviser, (202) 219-8776. Copies of summary plan descriptions and annual financial reports are available from the Public Disclosure Room, (202) 219-8771.*

*Publications are available by writing the Division of Public Affairs, Room N-5656 at the above address.*

### Nonprofit Organizations:

American Association of Retired Persons
601 E Street, NW
Washington, DC 20049
(202) 434-2277
*The Worker Equity Section of AARP gives information on federal*

*laws applicable to private pension plans. Write to Room A5520 at the above address.*

*The AARP Women's Initiative works to ensure that the economic, social, health, and long-term care needs of mid-life and older women*

*are met. It advocates and supports
policies, programs, and legislation
that improves the status of women
today and in the future.*

*To order publications, write
to AARP Fulfillment at the above
address.*

Association of Retired Americans
Lincoln Center
1660 Lincoln Street, Suite 2240
Denver, CO 80264

International Society of Preretirement Planners
c/o L. Malcolm Rodman, CAE
11312 Old Club Road
Rockville, MD 20852
(301) 881-4113
(800) 327-ISPP

National Institute on Age, Work
    and Retirement
c/o National Council of Aging
600 Maryland Avenue SW,
West Wing 100
Washington, DC 20024
(202) 479-1200

Older Women's League
666 11th St., NW, Suite 700
Washington, DC 20001
(202) 783-6686
*OWL is a national grassroots
membership organization focused
exclusively on women as they age.
To receive a list of publications, including several on pensions and
health insurance, send a self-addressed stamped envelope to the
address above.*

Pension Rights Center
918 16th St., NW, Suite 704
Washington, DC 20006
(202) 296-3776
*The Pension Rights Center is a pub-
lic interest group organized to protect and promote the pension rights
of workers, retirees, and their
families. The Center's Women's
Pension Project is committed to en-
hancing the economic security of
older women. It also targets inequities in the nation's pension programs, provides policy makers with
reasoned analyses of pension issues, proposes workable solutions
to pension problems, and provides
technical assistance to women's
and retiree groups.*

Women's Pension Policy Consortium
918 16th St., NW, Suite 704
Washington, DC 20036
*The Women's Pension Policy Con-
sortium is a coalition of three organizations, the Pension Rights
Center, the Older Women's League,
and the National Senior Citizens
Law Center, established to encourage companies to expand pension
coverage for women and alert the
public to inequities jeopardizing
women's retirement security.*

*The Consortium has recently
initiated a "Pensions Not Posies"
campaign to boost public awareness
of the critical link between pensions
and the prevention of poverty in
later years, and to increase women's
access to adequate pension benefits.
To receive a copy of campaign materials, send $1.00 and a stamped,
self-addressed business-size envelope to the above address.*

**Anne E. Moss** is an attorney with the firm of Fierst & Moss, P.C., of Washington, D.C., where she concentrates on pensions and domestic relations. She previously served as the Deputy Director of the Pension Rights Center, a Washington D.C.–based advocacy organization. She is the author of *Your Pension Rights at Divorce: What Women Need to Know* (Pension Rights Center, 1995) and has frequently testified before Congress on pension reform for women.

Chapter 23

# *Estate Planning*

Amy Morris Hess

### Chapter Outline

**Introduction**

**Property and Family Considerations**
Wills • Intestacy • Lifetime Transactions That Result in Property Transfer at Death (Testamentary Substitutes)

**Mechanics of Transfer: Procedures for the Administration of Estates**
Probate

**Dealing With Dying and Death**
Living Wills • Durable Powers of Attorney for Health Care • A Word About Organ Donation

**Tax Considerations**
Gift Taxes: Federal Gift Tax • State Gift Taxes • Death Taxes: Federal Estate Tax • State Death Taxes

**Further Reading**

## Introduction

Estate planning is the process by which people provide for the orderly acquisition, management, and disposition of material wealth. It deals not only with planning and writing wills, but also with acquiring and managing property during life, and with gift giving. During the last ten years, estate planning has begun also to include end-of-life planning, such as writing health care directives which specify the sorts of medical care an individual wishes to receive if she is terminally ill and incapable of speaking for herself. It may also include planning for organ donation after death.

The legal aspects of estate planning are rather complex because they are affected by both state and federal laws. Frequently in these days of high mobility, the estate of one individual will involve the laws of several states, which may not be uniform. In addition, several substantive areas of the law may be involved, including property, decedents' estates, trusts, taxation, and health care law. Furthermore, the laws relevant to estate planning change frequently. Thus, even a person of relatively modest means may find that planning her estate entirely without the help of an attorney is impossible.

However, estate planning is also an area of the law which offers great opportunity to tailor the plan to suit individual needs and preferences, provided the legal ramifications of each possible alternative are clearly understood. Thus, a knowledgeable consumer will be in a particularly good position to get exactly what she wants in this area of the law, by knowing what to ask for.

## Property and Family Considerations

## Wills

### What Is a Will?

A will is a written document in which a person directs how and to whom her property is to be distributed after her death. A will does not take effect until the person whose will it is (the testator) dies; a will may be changed, or amended, as often as the testator wishes during her life. An amendment to a will is called a codicil.

In most states, any person who is over the age of eighteen years and of sound mind may make a will or a codicil. No special language must be used to write an effective will, but the words used must show clearly that the testator intends the document to dispose of her property after her death and not before. In other words, the document must clearly be a *will*, and not something else, such as a deed which a property owner could use to dispose of property *during* her lifetime.

### Execution, or Signing Ceremony

Execution is the legal term for the signing of a document. All states have fairly strict statutory requirements concerning the procedure by which wills are executed. The requirements for the proper execution of a will are called "testamentary formalities." The most common of these requirements are that the testator whose will it is sign the will in the presence of several witnesses, usually two but sometimes more, to whom the testator declares that the document is her will and that she would like them to sign as witnesses. The witnesses then each sign in the presence of the testator and of the other witness or witnesses. The act of the witnesses in signing is called attestation. In some states, anyone over the age of eighteen and of sound mind may be a witness. However, in a fairly substantial number of states, a person who is "interested" in the testator's estate may not be a witness. The word "interested" generally refers to anyone who is a beneficiary under the will and sometimes also includes spouses of beneficiaries.

Witnesses are important because, before the will can take effect, a court proceeding (probate) must take place. During the probate proceeding, the testamentary formalities required by the particular state where the probate takes place must be proven to have been complied with when the will was executed. Usually, the witnesses testify that these formalities did indeed take place.

Testamentary formalities are strictly enforced, because they are designed to protect the testator, who is dead when the probate takes place, from those who might try by fraud or other nefarious means to have a document admitted to probate that is not the true will of the testator. If the testamentary formalities are not proven to have occurred when the will was executed, the judge generally is without power to admit the will to probate even though there is ample evidence that the document does, in fact, embody the testator's wishes concerning the disposition of her property. A will that is not admitted to probate has no effect, and the testator's property will be distributed as if she had died without writing a will.

Testamentary formalities vary from state to state. Although most states allow probate of a will executed in another state, the safest course to follow is to have your will reviewed by a lawyer when you move to a new state, to make sure it can be probated there if you die there.

There is a widespread belief today that probate is a highly complex, time-consuming, and expensive procedure, which ought to be avoided at all cost. Part of the reason for this belief is a confusion concerning the meaning of the word probate. Technically, probate refers only to the court proceeding in which a will is proved to be the true last will and testament of the decedent. This is the only sense in which it is used in this chapter. However, since the same court usually hears the probate proceeding and oversees estate administration and is often called the probate court, the entire process of administration is sometimes colloquially referred to as probate.

In most cases, the probate of the will is an inexpensive and quick proceeding, which may not even require a formal hearing before a judge. For a description of the typical probate proceeding, see chapter 24. Administration of the estate, on the other hand, may take some time, even a few years in some cases. (A description of the administration of an estate can be found in chapter 24.) However, readers should remember two points concerning probate and administration when deciding whether to write a will: First, not all estates require lengthy administration, even though they involve the probate of a will. Second, a will is often the simplest and least costly way for an individual to dispose of her property after death. And in order to be effective to dispose of the testator's property, the will must be probated.

Of course, some individuals may have good reasons to provide for the disposition of their property after death other than by means of a will. These reasons and several of the other means of disposing of property after the death of the owner will be discussed in greater detail.

## Unwitnessed Wills

Some states have laws allowing wills to be probated that are written entirely in the testator's handwriting and are dated, even though they are not witnessed and do not comply with the testamentary formalities. This seems to be an area of the law in which state legislatures make rapid changes. Therefore, before deciding to write out your will in this way, you should find out the details of the current law in your state. However, a few generalizations can be made about the law in those states which allow unwitnessed wills to be probated.

An unwitnessed will written entirely in the handwriting of the testator is called a "holograph" or a "holographic will." Those states which allow holographs to be probated usually require that, before the will may be declared valid, at least two people must appear at the probate proceeding to testify that the handwriting is that of the testator. Because a holograph is not witnessed at the time it is signed, there is a greater chance for fraud. Therefore, judges tend to be somewhat wary of admitting holographic wills to probate unless the evidence in favor of the will's validity is beyond question. Furthermore, the statutes concerning admission of holographic wills are generally read quite narrowly. Thus, "entirely in the handwriting of the testator" means literally what it says; wills that are typewritten by the testator, wills dictated by the testator to another, and wills that consist of a printed form on which blank spaces have been filled in are *not* holographic wills and cannot be admitted to probate unless they are witnessed and the testamentary formalities are complied with.

## A Note About "Homemade" Wills

You may write your own will without consulting an attorney. However, you should bear in mind three points before deciding to write your own will: First, unless the will you write is a holographic will and you live in a state that recognizes the validity of unwitnessed holographic wills, you must comply with the testamentary formalities described in the section on execution, including having the will witnessed by the number of witnesses required in the state where the will is to be probated. Second, legal language tends to be quite precise, and this is especially true with respect to the language used to direct the disposition of property in a will. If you write a will in your own words, you run the risk of writing something which, although it seems quite clear to you, is capable of several legal interpretations. An ambiguous will can be probated. However, before your property can be distributed, your beneficiaries may be required to engage in a lawsuit called a "construction proceeding" to have a court determine what your will means. Obviously, this litigation could cost substantially more in time and money than having the will drawn up by an attorney. Third, in writing your own will you may fail to consider the effect of future factual changes that an attorney is trained to plan for.

## Why Should I Have a Will?

*Transfer of Property at Death:* A will is the only effective means of directing to whom and under what conditions your property will pass after your death. If you do not leave a will, any property you own on the date you die will be distributed in accordance with the laws of "intestate succession."

Perhaps, then, the most important reason to leave a will is to direct that some or all of your property pass to someone other than the person to whom it would pass under the laws of intestate succession. In most states, when a married person with children dies, her property is divided among the surviving spouse and children. Many people would prefer that all their property pass to the surviving spouse.

There are various reasons for this: If you are a married woman with grown children, you might leave all your money and property to your husband because you believe that your children are now capable of providing for themselves while your husband, who is now getting older and perhaps living on a fixed income such as a pension, could use your assets to pay for increased medical costs or other living expenses. On the other hand, if your children are young, you might want a part of your assets to be used for their benefit, such as to help raise them, or to pay for their education, or for summer vacations. However, you would want your husband to manage the money and property for them because they are not old enough to handle it wisely themselves. In the second situation, you would want to leave all or part of your property to your husband "as trustee" for the benefit of your children. The point here is that if you want your husband to have control over that portion of your money and property that you intend to be used for your children's benefit, you must write a will. If you die without writing a will, a portion of the money and property you own at your death will automatically belong to your children under the laws of intestate succession.

Similarly, if you are a single parent of young children, you must write a will to designate the person who will manage your property for the benefit of your children after your death.

Other, similar reasons for writing a will are as follows:

1. To provide that specific assets go to specific persons.

2. To make a deliberately unequal distribution among close relatives, such as children, because their personal financial resources are unequal, or you have provided for them unequally before and now wish to give more to the one who got less earlier, or because one is handicapped.

3. To leave property to a relative who would not receive the property under the laws of intestate succession, for example, a sister, brother, or parent if you are a married person with children; or to a friend; or to make a contribution to charity.

The laws of intestate succession are written and interpreted exclusively in terms of traditional family relationships. Therefore, if you are not legally married to your life partner, he or she will not receive any part of your property as your "surviving spouse" under the laws of intestate succession. You must write a will in order to give your property to that person at your death.

## Appointment of Executor

Another reason to write a will is to specify your personal representatives, that is, those who will carry out your wishes. The personal representative is the person responsible for finding all of the property, inventorying it, selling any that might need to be sold to raise money for debts, expenses, and taxes, and distributing the rest among the persons entitled to receive it under the deceased person's will or under the laws of intestate succession. (See chapter 24, "The Legal Aspects of a Death.")

A personal representative named in a will is generally called an executor. If a person dies without a will, the law of the state of her domicile (permanent home) at the time of death will determine who her personal representative will be. The person designated by state law to be a personal representative is often called an administrator and is generally a close relative; for example, surviving spouse, child, etc. By writing a will the property owner can choose the person she thinks will do the job best, or can choose more than one in which case they would act jointly.

It will be extremely helpful to the executor(s) if you create a file folder containing a copy of the will, a list of property owned, bank and brokerage accounts, and a record of where all safety deposit boxes are located. These documents should also be kept in the safety deposit box as a backup.

In most cases, anyone over the age of eighteen years and of sound mind may act as executor. In addition, some banks and trust companies licensed to do business in the state of the deceased person's domicile may also act as executors. Some states require that at least one executor be a resident of that state. The laws of those states generally give the probate court judge authority to appoint a resident executor in the event none is named by the testator in her will.

Executors generally receive compensation for their work (commissions). The money to pay these commissions comes out of the estate assets of the deceased person. In a few states, the amount of these commissions is set by statute, but in most states it is set by the judge of the probate court that oversees administration of the estate. Most banks and trust companies have printed schedules of the commissions they charge to serve as executors, and these schedules are generally respected by the probate court. Commissions are generally figured in terms of a percentage of the value of the estate assets, but the percentage may vary with the extent and difficulty of the work the executor must do to complete the administration of the particular estate.

You may specify in your will the amount of the commissions to be paid to your executor, and this specification will generally be respected by the probate court. However, no one is required to serve as executor simply because he, she, or it is nominated in another person's will. Therefore, before you write a will nominating someone, you should ask your nominee whether he, she or it will be willing to act as executor for the commission you want your estate to pay. If the person has never been an executor before, it might also be wise to review with her the duties of the executor. Anyone may serve as executor without compensation if she chooses to do so. Close relatives of the deceased person often do.

## Provision for the Care of Children and Other Dependent Relatives (Guardians and Trustees)

A third reason for writing a will is to provide for the care of minor children and the management of property to be distributed to children and other people who might be unable to handle it themselves.

In most states, a parent who dies leaving orphaned minor children (that is, the second parent to die) may designate someone (a guardian of the person) to raise and care for the children until they attain the age of majority, currently age eighteen in most states. The duties of a guardian of the person are different from those of a guardian of the property, discussed below. The same person might but need not be guardian both of the person and of the property of a particular child. A guardian of the person is responsible for the physical custody and upbringing of the child, while a guardian of the property is responsible for managing the property owned by the child.

In some states, the parent's designation of a guardian is binding; in others, the court may designate someone other than the person named by the parent upon a showing that the best interests of the child require it to do so. In a number of states, the court may consider the personal preference of a child over a certain age, usually fourteen. If the parent dies without having made such a designation, the court will appoint a guardian.

The designation of a trustee to manage property for those who cannot handle it themselves is one of the most important things that can be done in a will. The decedent's property will not be held in trust for a beneficiary, even a minor child, unless it is specifically placed in trust by the terms of the will. Since, in most states, any contract made during minority may be disaffirmed by the minor upon attaining majority, property given to a minor child will have to be handled by an adult until the child reaches eighteen if she is to receive the economic benefits of it. In any event, entrusting substantial sums of money or other valuable property to a child is obviously undesirable.

If property passes outright to a minor under a will or by intestate succession, an adult may be appointed by the appropriate court to handle the property (a guardian of the property). In most states, the guardian may serve only until the minor reaches eighteen and will have relatively little discretion concerning use and investment of the money or property. Generally, state law requires the guardian to get prior court approval before expending the funds on the child's behalf. Like executors and administrators, guardians of the property are entitled to compensation (commissions) for their services. In some states, these commissions are prescribed by state law; in others, the law requires the court to set the amount of the commission.

Substantially greater flexibility can be achieved by directing in the will that the property be held in trust by a named trustee who will manage the property of the child. A trust is a device by which legal title to property is transferred to one person (the trustee), who must manage the property for the benefit of another (the beneficiary) upon specific terms set out by the testator in her will. The property can be held in trust for longer than it would be possible for a court-appointed guardian of the property to hold it. Indeed, it can remain in trust for the entire lifetime of the beneficiary. The trustee can also be given wide latitude in determining how the trust fund will be used for the benefit of the minor. Conversely, the testator may narrowly circumscribe the uses to which the trust fund may be put; for example, the trustee could be required to use the trust fund only for the beneficiary's education. Thus, the express directions of the testator concerning the operation of the trust are generally enforceable in court against the trustee by the beneficiary.

Furthermore, since an adult can be the beneficiary of a trust, trusts are often used to provide for management of property for the benefit of adults who are unable or simply unwilling to handle it themselves due to advanced age, physical or mental impairment, lack of financial expertise, or lack of interest.

In general, the rules concerning nomination and compensation of trustees are the same as those concerning nomination and compensation of executors. Any person over the age of majority and of sound mind can be a trustee, and certain banks and trust companies can be trustees as well. The trustees ordinarily receive compensation for their services, called commissions. These commissions are usually payable annually and are determined principally by the value of the property held in trust, the amount of income it earns during the year, and the amount of work the trustee must do to comply with the terms of the trust. In some states, commissions are set by statute; in others, they are set by the probate court. Banks and trust companies generally have a set schedule of commissions which will be respected by the court.

As in the case with executors, a trustee's commission may be set by the testator in the will, and this direction will generally be respected by the court. However, as is also the case with executors, no one is required to serve as trustee merely because of the testator's nomination. Therefore, you would be wise to ask if your nominee will be willing to serve before you include his, her, or its name in the will. A trustee may consent to serve without compensation, and close relatives of the testator often do.

More than one trustee may be appointed to administer a trust. Testators commonly appoint two or more, each of whom has a different area of knowledge, to serve jointly. For example, you might appoint a bank for its knowledge of financial matters to serve jointly with a close relative who is personally acquainted with the beneficiary and knows her particular needs.

In a number of states, property may be left in a will to a custodian under the state's version of the uniform gifts to minors acts. A custodianship is another statutory means of providing adult management of property intended to be used for the benefit of a minor. A custodian has somewhat more discretion in managing the property than has a guardian of the property, but somewhat less than a trustee.

## If I Already Have a Will, When Should I Think About Writing a New One?

Once you have executed a will, you should reread it at least once every three years, to be sure that it still embodies your wishes, even if no major changes have taken place in your family situation. Each time you do one of these periodic reviews, you should make a list of your assets with their approximate current values. This will encourage you to consider whether the distribution of your assets should change because their relative values have changed. It will also enable you to determine whether your estate has gotten large enough so that transfer taxes may be due at your death. (For a description of federal and state gift and death taxes, see the last portion of this chapter.)

You may wish to check with your lawyer while you are doing your periodic review to see if your will should be changed because of changes in the federal or state tax laws, or in the state laws concerning decedents' estates. We cannot emphasize often enough that the laws relevant to estate planning are constantly changing. This chapter can provide you with knowledge of general trends and with some guidance as to the questions that you might ask concerning the state and federal laws relevant to your particular estate, but it cannot completely substitute for accurate, up-to-the-minute knowledge of the laws themselves.

In addition to these periodic reviews, you should consider rewriting your will if any one of the following events occurs:

1. Your marital status changes;

2. You give birth to a child or adopt one;

3. You move to a new state; or

4. The value of your assets increase substantially.

In the paragraphs that follow, we will explore the reasons why these changes might cause you to change your will.

*Your Marital Status Changes:* If you marry, you might want to leave much of your property to your new husband. Conversely, if you become divorced, you would probably want to delete your former husband from your will. A number of states have statutes that treat as revoked any part of a will that leaves property to a former spouse and was written before the divorce occurred. The effect of the statute will be that the former spouse will not receive the property. However, the identity of the beneficiary who will receive it instead will depend on the particular state statute and the wording of the will. Should you become divorced and still want to leave property to your former husband, you must write a new will after you and he are divorced to provide for him.

In the special case in which you do *not* want your new husband to receive your property after your death, merely writing a will may not be sufficient. This is because most states allow a surviving spouse to receive a certain share of the deceased spouse's property by filing an "election against the will" (see the section on statutory share). The only way to obtain the result you desire in such a case may be to enter into a prenuptial agreement with your prospective husband before you are married. In a prenuptial agreement, each party agrees not to demand a greater share of the other's estate than is left to her/him in the will.

Readers should bear in mind that these rules do not apply to changes in relationships between people who live together but are not legally married. Therefore, if you want to leave property to a life partner who is not legally your husband under state law, you must provide for that person in your will. Conversely, if you terminate such a relationship and no longer wish the former partner to receive property, you must write a new will to omit the former partner from your will and leave your property to someone else.

*You Give Birth to a Child or Adopt One:* Rewriting your will when a child is born may still be desirable for a number of reasons.

First, a number of states have statutes that will allow the child to take her intestate share of your estate unless some language in your will shows that you intended to disinherit the child. Ordinarily, a will written before a child was born will give no indication of how the testator would have wanted the property distributed if a child were born.

Second, your will should designate a guardian of the person for the child in the event you and your husband die simultaneously (for example, as the result of an airplane crash) or he dies and you die very shortly thereafter without having had time to write a new will.

Third, your will should provide for a trustee of your property for the child's benefit, if you are going to leave property to the child.

Fourth, if you adopt a child, in most states the child will be treated the same way as a child who was born to you for purposes of interpreting your will, unless you specifically provide otherwise. Thus, anytime you use the word "children" to describe a group of beneficiaries, in most states the adopted child will receive a share of the property. This will likely be the result you intend in most cases. However, you should check to be sure that adopted children do, in fact, share in such a gift in the state where your will will be probated, as the rule is not uniform in all states. Furthermore, if the adopted child is your husband's child by a previous marriage, you may not wish the child to share equally with your own children. In that case you should provide explicitly in a new will or a codicil to your old will for how this adopted child is to be treated in the division of your assets.

*You move to a new state:* Since the laws concerning testamentary formalities, intestate succession, and the interpretation of language used in wills is not uniform among the fifty states, you should check with a lawyer to be sure your will can be probated in the new state and that it will be interpreted the same way in the new state as it would have been in the state you lived in when you executed it.

*There Is A Substantial Increase in the Value of Your Assets:* One of the most important reasons to review your will when your assets become substantially more valuable is that your estate may now be large enough to cause transfer taxes to be due at your death. If this is the case, you may wish to consult a lawyer to find out about ways of rewriting your will or making transfers during your life that will reduce the total taxes to be paid. Other reasons to consider in these circumstances include placing property in trust for a beneficiary, changing the designated trustee from an individual to a bank to assure expert investment management of the larger trust fund, or adding gifts to new beneficiaries to whom you could not have afforded to leave property when your estate was smaller.

## What Are the Rights of One Spouse in the Property Owned by Another?

Historically, governments have granted to a surviving spouse certain rights in the estate of the deceased spouse which cannot be defeated by the provisions of the deceased spouse's will. Their purpose is to provide for the support of the survivor. The most common of these are dower and curtesy, statutory share, family support allowance, and homestead allowance.

In other words, in most states, completely disinheriting your spouse is impossible. As a general rule, no similar restrictions apply to disinheriting a child, except that the number of dependent children a person had at the time of death is often taken into consideration in determining the amount of the support allowance.

*Dower and Curtesy:* Dower and curtesy are the oldest of these spousal property rights, having their origins in feudal land ownership laws of medieval England. Originally, dower referred to a surviving wife's right upon the death of her husband to a one-third interest for life in all real property owned outright by her husband at any time during their marriage.

Curtesy referred to a surviving husband's interest for life in all real property owned by his deceased wife at any time during their marriage provided they had a child born alive.

Today, dower and curtesy have been abolished in many states. In others, although the terms dower and curtesy may still be used, the rights of the survivor have been extended to include personal property, and have become outright interests instead of life interests.

*Statutory Share:* In most states today, a surviving spouse has the right to elect to take a fraction, usually one third, but sometimes one half, of her deceased spouse's estate in lieu of what the deceased spouse leaves the survivor by will. The election is made by filing a paper with the probate court.

To give an example: Suppose you are a married woman living in a state in which the elective share is one third of the decedent's estate. Your husband dies owning property worth $600,000. In his will, he left you property worth $50,000 and left the rest of his property to his brothers and sisters. Since one third of $600,000 is $200,000, you would be entitled to file a paper "electing against the will," and the probate court would direct the executor of your husband's estate to distribute $200,000 worth of your husband's property to you and the remaining $400,000 to your husband's siblings.

In some states, the election applies only to property owned outright by the deceased spouse at the time of death. In those states, the first spouse to die can render the election worthless and successfully disinherit the survivor by giving away all of the property during her lifetime. In our example in the preceding paragraph, suppose your husband had owned $600,000 worth of property, but one year before his death, he gave his sister a gift of $300,000 worth of property. Now, when he dies, his estate is worth only $300,000. Since your right of election apples only to those assets he still owned at death, you will now receive only $100,000 (one third of the $300,000 left in your husband's estate) when you elect against the will. His sister will be allowed to keep all of the $300,000 your husband gave her the year before his death.

The laws of a growing number of states include certain lifetime transfers in the property to which the election applies, such as transfers made shortly before death (usually within two years before death) and transfers in which the deceased spouse retained some interest in the property, such as the power to revoke the transfer or the right to receive the income from the property. To continue our example, in a state that follows this rule, because your husband made the $300,000 gift to his sister one year before he died, it would be added to the assets remaining in his estate for purposes of determining the amount of property you would be entitled to if you elected against his will. Thus, you would once again be entitled to $200,000 worth of property, or one third of $600,000. Since the gift to your sister-in-law is equal in value to one half of all the property to which your election applies, the probate court would probably be required by state law to direct the executor of your husband's estate to pay one half of your share, or $100,000, out of estate assets, and to direct your sister-in-law to give you the other $100,000.

In other states, the law requires that the deceased spouse's lifetime gifts be included in the pool of property to which the surviving spouse's election applies if the survivor can show that the deceased spouse made the gift for the purpose of defrauding the survivor of the property. Thus, in our example, if you can show in court that the transfer to your sister-in-law was a sham, that your husband still had all the rights of an owner with respect to the property until he died and that he transferred title to the property into his sister's name only so that you would not be able to obtain it after his death, your right to elect may again entitle you to $200,000 worth of property because the gift to your sister-in-law would be considered a "fraud on the statutory share."

*Support Allowance and Homestead Rights:* These rights are designed for the maintenance of the family while the property constituting the estate of the deceased spouse is in administration. Often, particularly in smaller estates, during the early stages of administration, property may not be distributed to the beneficiaries without a court order, because it cannot be ascertained immediately how much will be needed to pay the decedent's debts, estate administration expenses, and taxes. The probate court is therefore given authority to allow payment of a monthly allowance out of the estate to the surviving spouse to support her and any dependent children for a specified length of time, usually a year. Often, the surviving spouse is also entitled to receive a specified amount of property, called exempt property, and to live in the family home for a specified time. This last right is often called the "homestead" right, although the reader should be aware that it is not necessarily the same right as the homestead right referred to in the bankruptcy laws and the real estate and divorce laws of a number of states (for information on *those* laws see the relevant chapters). The support allowances and homestead rights usually have priority over the rights of the deceased spouse's creditors and are in addition to the surviving spouse's rights under the will, the intestacy laws, and the statutory elective share.

## Intestacy
### To Whom Does Property Go If the Owner Does Not Leave a Will?

A person who dies without a will is called an intestate decedent, and such a person's property is distributed according to the laws of intestate succession. Each state has its own law of intestate succession. Usually the intestate succession law of the state where the person was domiciled at death governs the distribution, except that if one dies owning real estate or tangible personal property in another state, the law of that state will govern the distribution of that property.

Although the laws of intestate succession vary from state to state, these laws are quite similar and generally follow this basic format:

If an intestate decedent was married and had children, half of the property is distributed to the surviving spouse and half to the children. In some states, if there is more than one child, the spouse receives one third, and the children receive two thirds. If there is a surviving spouse but no children, the spouse may receive all the property, but in a number of states, the property is divided between the surviving spouse and the deceased spouse's parents. If there is no surviving spouse, the children generally receive all the property; if any child has predeceased the parent, that child's children (the decedent's grandchildren) receive the child's share.

Children will receive their shares even though they are adults and financially independent when one of their parents dies intestate, and even though some other person, such as the decedent's spouse, needs the property more. And a person who was not legally married to the decedent will not receive the surviving spouse's share under the laws of intestacy, since the word "spouse" is always given its traditional meaning in this body of law. As was noted earlier in this chapter, these are good reasons to write a will. If a person leaves a validly executed will, the property will always pass to those named in the will, rather than those who are named in the laws of intestate succession.

If an intestate decedent leaves neither spouse, children, nor descendants of children, the property will generally be distributed to the decedent's parents, or if they are dead, the decedent's brothers and sisters and their descendants.

In most states, the law provides for distribution to more remote relatives if the decedent left no close relatives. Ultimately, however, all states provide that the property will become the property of the state if a person who dies intestate leaves no relative within a stated degree of kinship. This is called the law of escheat.

At one time, each state had one set of rules governing intestate succession to real estate and a different set of rules governing intestate succession to personal property. This is no longer generally the case, although some states may preserve the distinction for some purposes. In those states that do, real estate will generally pass directly to the children of the intestate decedent even if her spouse is alive. The property will, however, generally be subject to the spouse's dower or curtesy rights. Thus, in such a state, if the legal title to the family home were in a husband's name alone, and he died survived by his wife and children, the home would pass to the children, subject to the wife's dower rights.

## Lifetime Transactions That Result in Property Transfer at Death (Testamentary Substitutes)

There are a number of fairly common property transactions that people enter into during their lives that result in automatic transfer of property to someone else upon their deaths. Since a will disposes only of property not otherwise disposed of during the testator's life, the property acquired in these transactions will be disposed of in accordance with the specific provisions of the contract, deed, or other document executed in connection with the transaction, rather than by the terms of the testator's will.

In this section, we will discuss three of the most common types of property in this category: life insurance, jointly owned property, and living trusts. Another common type of property that also belongs in this group is employer-created retirement benefits, such as pensions, and the related benefits payable to an employee's survivors after the employee's death. These benefits are discussed in the previous chapter.

Among the principal advantages to the transactions discussed in this section are that the property is not part of the deceased's estate for administration purposes, and the documents creating the interests do not have to be probated. A probated will is a matter of public record that anyone may read at the county courthouse. Thus these lifetime transactions have two advantages: They expedite receipt of the property by the survivors, and they allow the family to keep its financial affairs private.

*Life Insurance:* A life insurance policy is a contract whereby the insurance company agrees to pay a stated sum, usually called the face amount, to a designated beneficiary upon the death of the insured person in exchange for a payment or a series of payments of money called premiums paid during the insured person's life.

Usually the insured person is also the owner of the policy, but the owner may be another person. The owner has a number of contract rights, such as the right to borrow against the policy, change the beneficiary, cancel the policy, direct that the proceeds be paid to the beneficiary in installments rather than in one lump sum, and transfer ownership of the policy to someone else.

Upon the death of the insured person, the proceeds are paid directly to the named beneficiary. They need not be held by the personal representative of the decedent's estate subject to administration.

Many kinds of life insurance are available, and each provides the owner with a different set of rights. You should understand exactly which rights you are buying for yourself and your family in each policy that you select. The difference between whole life insurance and term life insurance is one of the most common of these distinctions. See chapter 21, "Consumer Rights and Insurance." Basically, however, whole life insurance provides coverage for the entire life of the insured in exchange for a series of equal premiums paid over the life of the insured. The owner can terminate a whole life policy at any time and receive the "cash surrender value" or can continue the policy in force and borrow against the cash surrender value. The cash surrender value of a life insurance policy is an amount roughly equal to the premiums paid, plus interest on them since their payment, less administrative costs.

Term life insurance, on the other hand, provides that the company will pay the face amount if the insured dies within the "term," a stated number of years, usually between one and five. The price of a term life insurance policy is ordinarily a single premium paid at the beginning of the term. The premiums for term policies are often lower than the premiums for the same face amount of whole life insurance because the policy, and therefore the risk, is for a relatively short term, and because the policy has no cash surrender value nor any loan value.

*Jointly Owned Property:* Married couples commonly take title to their major assets (the family home, checking and savings accounts, and often stocks and other securities) in the names of both spouses as joint tenants with right of survivorship. At the death of the first spouse, jointly held property becomes the sole property of the surviving spouse, regardless of the provisions of the will of the deceased spouse. These assets do not have to go through administration in the estate.

Of course, wives and husbands are not required to own their property as joint tenants with right of survivorship. They are free to decide for themselves how to own each asset, and they could own some or all of the family property individually, or as tenants in common, rather than as joint tenants with right of survivorship.

In deciding how to take title to any particular asset, you should be sure you understand exactly what the words "joint tenancy" mean in the state whose law will govern the transaction. In some states, a joint tenancy has no survivorship feature unless the words "with the right of survivorship" or a similar phrase is used. Thus half the property might be subject to the terms of the will of the first spouse to die. In some states, a joint tenancy with right of survivorship in certain bank accounts and savings accounts may be considered for convenience only and will not automatically create survivorship rights in the survivor, especially if the first spouse to die has made all the deposits into the account.

The difference between joint tenancies with right of survivorship and tenancies in common is also important. A tenancy in common is a form of co-ownership that allows each tenant to dispose of her share of the property during life without the consent of the other, and to dispose of that share at death by will. Tenancies in common have no survivorship feature.

Some states allow spouses to own real estate in a special kind of joint tenancy called a tenancy by the entirety. The rights of the surviving spouse at the death of the first spouse are essentially the same whether the spouses owned the property as tenants by the entirety or as joint tenants with rights of survivorship. However, the spouses' rights are somewhat different during life. If they own property as joint tenants, either spouse may generally dispose of her/his half of the property without the consent of the other. The transfer of half the property destroys the survivorship feature. Further, the creditors of one spouse can bring a lawsuit called a partition proceeding to have the debtor spouse's half of the property transferred to them to satisfy the debts due. If the property cannot be easily divided in half, the judge in the partition proceeding generally has power to require the entire property to be sold. On the other hand, if the spouses owned the property as tenants by the entirety, neither could convey her/his half of the property without the consent of the other, and the property could not be partitioned or sold to satisfy the creditors of one spouse.

Joint tenancies with or without right of survivorship and tenancies in common may be created between people who are related but are not spouses (for example, sister and brother, or parent and child), between people who are unrelated, and between more than two people.

Joint tenancies, particularly joint bank accounts, often are suggested as a means to permit a younger family member to manage property or money for an older family member. For example, an older person might create such joint account with a child or a niece or nephew as the other tenant, assuming that the younger person will manage the money for the older person's benefit but will make no claim on the balance in the account when the older person dies. This method of obtaining financial management is ill advised because the first tenant to die has no way to force the survivor to turn over the balance of the account to the personal representative of the deceased tenant's estate. A court might find that the account was for convenience only and require the survivor to relinquish the balance, but the modern trend is to assume that the property owner used the words "joint tenants" intentionally and that she wanted the account balance to belong to the surviving tenant at her death. Joint tenancies should never be used *unless* the person who will contribute most or all of the property to the tenancy actually desires to convey a survivorship interest to the other tenant. The best methods of securing financial management of assets are to create a revocable living trust, which is discussed in the next section of this chapter, or to execute a durable power of attorney for property management.

*Living Trusts:* As was noted earlier in this chapter, a trust is a highly useful means of transferring property.

In our earlier discussion, we dealt with trusts created in a will (testamentary trusts). A trust may also be created by transferring property to a trustee during the owner's lifetime. Such trusts are called living trusts, or *inter vivos* trusts. The terms of a living trust are usually written in a document called a trust instrument or trust agreement signed by the property owner (grantor or settlor) and the trustee. All comments concerning trustees and beneficiaries of testamentary trusts in our earlier discussion are also true of trustees and beneficiaries of living trusts.

Living trusts may be either revocable or irrevocable, and may last for either a stated term of years or until the death of a certain named person.

If a trust is revocable, the settlor may revoke it entirely or in part and take back the property. In most states, the settlor may also change the terms of a revocable trust. An irrevocable trust is one that cannot be changed, nor can the property be taken back. Under the law of most states, a trust is irrevocable unless the settlor expressly reserves the right to revoke it as part of the provisions of the trust agreement.

*Use of Trusts as "Will Substitutes":* Because a trust may continue beyond the death of the settlor, people with moderate to large estates commonly put much of their property in revocable living trusts. The trust agreement provides that the property owner receive the income for life and that, upon her death, the property continue in trust for others. A common disposition after the settlor's death provides for income to be paid to the settlor's spouse for life together with so much of the principal property as he might need for support and health expenditures in excess of the income, and for the remainder of the principal to be distributed to the children at the spouse's death. Provisions for retention in trust of property that might otherwise pass to a minor child are also included.

The advantage to the living trust is that, like life insurance and jointly held property, these assets avoid administration, and the trust assures privacy, since the trust agreement need not be probated.

A common estate-planning device combines life insurance and a living trust to create what is called a revocable unfunded life insurance trust. The terms of such a trust can be varied to meet the needs of the individual settlor. The general format is as follows: The settlor creates a revocable trust and makes the trustee the beneficiary of life insurance on the settlor's life. The settlor continues to own the policies and, usually, to pay the premiums during her life. The trust agreement directs the trustee to pay any income to the settlor during her life, and then to collect the proceeds at death and manage them in accordance with the terms of the trust agreement, usually for the benefit of the spouse and children of the settlor. For example, the trust agreement might provide that after the death of the settlor, the trustee should invest the life insurance proceeds and pay the income from the investment to the settlor's surviving spouse for life. After the spouse's death, the trustee might be directed in the trust instrument to divide up the principal (the investment) among the settlor's children.

*Lifetime Uses:* Trusts are sometimes created for benefits the settlor may enjoy during her life. The principal lifetime benefit of a trust is property management. Trusts are often created to shift responsibility to the trustee for the day-to-day management and investment decisions which a property owner must make, such as checking that dividends, interest, or rent are paid on time and deciding when and upon what terms to sell and purchase such assets as stocks, bonds, and real estate. A property owner might decide to shift this burden for a number of reasons, including lack of financial expertise or interest, preoccupation with other family or business matters, ill health, or advancing age.

### Is It Always Better to Have a Living Trust Instead of a Will?

A living trust may be desirable in many estate plans but it is not the best plan in all cases.

The major advantages of using a living trust instead of a will to transfer property after the death of the settlor are (1) privacy, because the trust agreement does not have to be probated; and (2) speed, because the trustee simply continues to manage the property for the designated beneficiaries without having to wait while the deceased settlor's estate goes through the procedures of administration. In some cases, using a trust may also save money, because, as will be seen in the section on probate, some states have probate court fees (sometimes called probate taxes) based upon the amount of property passing under a will (but not under a living trust), and in a few special circumstances the probate proceeding itself may be complicated or costly. However, there are also situations in which the living trust may be the more expensive or time-consuming alternative, and having a will is preferable.

The most common such situation is that of the estate which is small enough and involves beneficiaries capable enough so that no asset management is really necessary after the death of the settlor. Trustees are entitled to commissions. Paying commissions is an unnecessary expense when the trustee's services are not needed, especially if, because of the particular provisions of the state's law, the probate fees or taxes are less than the trustee's commissions would be, and the settlor's will is very unlikely to require a costly or complicated probate proceeding.

Essentially, two categories of wills might require costly or lengthy probate: (1) those which might be contested because of unusual provisions or disharmony among family members; and (2) those for which state law will require a more formal probate proceeding than is ordinarily necessary because some of the decedent's intestate beneficiaries (those who would receive the decedent's property if she died without a will) are minors; for example, if the decedent is survived by minor children.

Thus, a woman who wishes to manage her own affairs while she is alive and plans to leave all her property outright to her adult children when she dies is probably better off writing a will rather than creating a living trust. On the other hand, a woman who wants to employ a trustee to manage her assets during her life and will leave the property in trust for her minor grandchildren after she dies is probably better off creating a living trust. A woman who prefers to manage her property herself during her life, but expects to leave it in trust for her minor children at her death, might be better off with a will or a living trust depending upon the particular state laws likely to govern the probate of her will and the administration of her estate, the extent of her assets, and her particular family situation.

A woman who presently wishes to manage her own assets might still wish to consider creating a living trust to provide a smooth transition to professional management should she ever become incapable of managing her affairs personally. Such incapacity might occur as the result of a debilitating physical illness, such as cancer or heart disease, or because of a disease that directly affects mental ability, such as a stroke or Alzheimer's disease. Advance planning is important here because once you are mentally or physically incapable of handling your financial affairs you are also likely to be incapable of creating a trust.

Women who have estates that are large enough to justify professional financial management but who wish to handle their own affairs as long as they are able should consider creating what some estate planners call a "trigger trust." A trigger trust is a revocable living trust in which the property owner names herself as the trustee initially, but provides for a professional trustee to take over when she can no longer handle the job. The trust agreement contains a procedure (the trigger) for determining when the property owner is no longer capable of managing the trust property herself and the successor trustee must take over. The usual procedure requires the property owner's personal physician and at least one other medical doctor to certify that the property owner is no longer capable of handling financial matters. However, you can specify a different procedure in the trust agreement if you prefer.

A woman whose estate is small enough so that professional management is undesirable even when she can no longer handle her own finances might prefer to execute a durable power of attorney for financial management instead of a trigger trust. Durable powers are described in the next section of this chapter.

If a person becomes incapable of handling financial matters and has neither created a living trust nor executed a durable power of attorney, the law does provide a procedure for appointing someone to manage the incompetent person's property. The property manager in that case is appointed by the probate court of the county where the incompetent person lives and is usually called a conservator, or sometimes a committee or a guardian. While having a conservator is obviously useful if the property owner has made no advance provision for her own incompetence, it is less desirable than either a living trust or a durable power of attorney for several reasons: First, appointment of a conservator requires a court proceeding. This exposes the property owner to the embarrassment of being publicly determined to be incapable of managing her own affairs, and puts the family to the expense of paying court fees and hiring an attorney to handle the litigation. Second, the probate court judge makes the final decision of who should be the conservator. If the property owner plans ahead, she can appoint the successor trustee or the agent under the durable power of attorney herself. Third, a conservator is subject to the continuing supervision of the probate court judge and must file periodic reports concerning management of the incompetent person's property and financial affairs. Therefore, the incompetent person's affairs become a matter of public record. Living trusts and durable powers of attorney are handled privately.

## A Note About Durable Powers of Attorney

As human beings live longer, we are becoming increasingly likely to live beyond our ability to manage daily financial matters. Some older people find that they tire so easily that making weekly trips to the bank and the supermarket becomes a chore. Others are hampered by diseases that affect their mental capacity, such as a stroke or Alzheimer's disease. Even if your estate is not very large nor your financial affairs complex enough for you to want to create any of the types of revocable living trusts described in the previous section, you would still be well advised to plan while you are competent for the possibility that you may someday find yourself unable to handle everyday transactions.

The simplest method for solving this problem is to execute a durable power of attorney for financial management. A power of attorney is a document in which a property owner designates someone else to handle her financial affairs for her. The property owner is called the "principal" and the designated person is called the "agent" or the "attorney-in-fact." A power of attorney can give an agent authority to transact all of the principal's business, in which case it is called a "general" power of attorney, or it can give the agent authority to represent the principal only in specific matters, in which case it is called a "special" power of attorney. You may already be familiar with special powers of attorney if you have given someone such as your spouse or a real estate agent authority to sign papers on your behalf in the purchase or sale of a home because, for example, the closing was scheduled to take place at an inconvenient time or at a considerable distance from your present home.

A power of attorney is "durable" if it continues after the principal becomes mentally or physically incompetent to handle her own affairs. At common law, an agent could not act for an incompetent principal because the law required the principal to be able to supervise the acts of the agent and approve ("ratify") the agent's transactions. Responding to pressure from citizens who wanted to be able to delegate authority to an agent to handle their finances when they could not do so themselves, most states have now passed statutes that permit a power of attorney to continue after the principal is incompetent, provided the power of attorney contains a provision stating that it is durable. Some states even recognize "standby" durable powers of attorney. These are powers of attorney that are not valid *until* the principal is certified by a medical doctor to be incompetent. Even if you live in a state that does not recognize standby durable powers of attorney, you can still manage your own affairs so long as you are capable even after you have given someone your durable power of attorney because the principal can always act for herself if she chooses to do so.

The agent appointed under a durable power of attorney usually is a close family member of the principal, such as a spouse or a child.

Like trustees, agents are fiduciaries, which means that they occupy a position of trust toward the principal and can be sued by the principal for failure to act in the principal's best interest. Unlike a trustee, however, an agent under a durable power of attorney does not ordinarily receive commissions.

A durable power of attorney is revocable at any time as long as the principal is competent.

Forms of durable powers of attorney are often printed in magazines and newspapers. Although these are useful as examples of what a durable power of attorney looks like, readers would be well advised not to simply fill in the blanks on these forms and sign them. Law books are replete with lawsuits that arose because a property owner used one of these forms and inadvertently gave the agent a power that the agent was not intended to have, or failed to include a power that the agent should have had. Even general durable powers of attorney can be tailored to answer the needs of an individual property owner. To avoid unintended results and needless expensive litigation, you should have a durable power of attorney drafted by a lawyer.

Unlike a revocable living trust, a durable power of attorney cannot provide for property distribution after the death of the principal. In fact, it terminates upon the death of the principal. Therefore, a property owner who decides to use a durable power of attorney for property management during life, must execute a will to dispose of her property after her death.

## Mechanics of Transfer: Procedures for the Administration of Estates

### Probate

The probate proceeding is conducted in the probate court for the county where the decedent was domiciled; that is, where she made her permanent home at the date of her death. Sometimes additional probate proceedings, called ancillary probate proceedings, are required in each additional state where the decedent owned real estate or tangible personal property that passes by the terms of her will.

Many states have a probate court fee (sometimes called a probate tax), which must be paid before the probate proceeding may be commenced. The probate fees of most states are based upon the total value of all the property that will pass to the beneficiaries under the will.

There are two kinds of probate in many states, common form, or informal, probate and solemn form, or formal, probate. Common form probate is a simple, short proceeding, usually held before the probate clerk, rather than the judge. In the common form proceeding, it is usually unnecessary for the beneficiaries named in the will or the intestate beneficiaries to receive formal notice of the hearing. Wills admitted to probate in common form have the same legal force as those admitted to probate in solemn form, except that the former are subject in most states to contest and revocation of probate by a proceeding in solemn form brought within a statutory length of time, usually one year, but sometimes longer.

A solemn form probate proceeding is a formal court hearing before a judge and, often, a jury. Legal notice of the hearing must be given to all interested parties who could come in to contest the validity of the will, usually the potential intestate beneficiaries and all beneficiaries under earlier known wills of the testator. Solemn form probate is generally not used except in cases of contest, due to the additional delay and expense of a formal trial. Will contests are relatively rare, and most wills are probated without formal litigation.

In some states, somewhat more formal procedures (though not necessarily solemn form probate) are required when minors might receive some of the testator's property, either under the will or under the laws of intestate succession if the will were denied probate. The laws of those states generally require a guardian *ad litem* to be appointed to represent the minors' interests during the probate proceeding. The guardian *ad litem* will be a lawyer chosen by the probate court judge. The guardian *ad litem* is entitled to a fee, which is payable out of estate assets.

The inquiry in all probate proceedings is the same: Is the document under examination the true last will and testament of the testator? Testimony will be heard as to whether the testator was of sound mind, was over the age of eighteen, and intended that this writing dispose of her property after her death, and whether the testamentary formalities were complied with. If all requirements are met, the will is "admitted to probate," that is, declared to be the true last will and testament of the testator.

Many states today have statutes allowing for what is referred to as a self-proved will. This is a will to which an affidavit is attached during the life of the testator, usually at the time the will is executed, which states that the testator is of sound mind, over the age of eighteen years, and intends the document to be her will, and that all of the testamentary formalities of execution were complied with. The affidavit is signed and sworn to before a notary public by the testator and the witnesses. In most states that have such a statute, a self-proved will can be admitted to common form probate without the witnesses testifying.

The fact that a witness dies before the testator and is therefore unable to testify is not fatal to probate. Others present at the execution ceremony but who did not sign as witnesses may testify at a probate proceeding.

The reader has probably noticed that nowhere in this section is there any mention of the family gathering at the decedent's lawyer's office for a reading of the will. The reason for this omission is simple: In modern practice, wills are almost never formally read in this manner. Although it might be an efficient way of acquainting all family members with the terms of the will, a reading is certainly not required by law.

## Dealing With Dying and Death

During the last decade, people have become increasingly concerned with assuring that their physicians and family members will know and respect their wishes about being kept alive when they are near death and no longer able to state their desires themselves. You have undoubtedly heard friends and family members speak of being permitted to die with dignity, of not wishing to prolong death, or of not wanting to be kept alive when they are vegetables. These statements are reactions to the fact that health care professionals are capable today of keeping patients physically alive for long periods of time when the patients are unconscious and are unlikely ever to resume normal lives or even to regain consciousness.

Writing down your wishes on this subject is important. This is because many health care professionals justifiably fear that they will be accused of malpractice or even homicide if they permit a patient to die whom they could have saved, unless they have clear directions from the patient not to continue life support under certain circumstances. Therefore, without such instructions in writing from you, the doctors attending you when you are near death and unable to speak for yourself may not follow your family's instructions to end life support. In order to carry out your wishes, your family may be forced to go to court and obtain an order from a judge requiring the doctor to remove machines such as respirators that are keeping you alive.

Laws in many states today permit you to sign two documents expressing your wishes concerning death and dying. These laws provide that a health care professional who carries out the wishes expressed in these documents cannot be criminally prosecuted for killing the patient nor sued for malpractice by the family when the patient dies. The documents are called different names in different states but the most common names for them are a "living will" and a "durable power of attorney for health care."

### Living Wills

A living will is a document that states a person's wishes concerning termination of life support, to be carried out if she is terminally ill and unconscious or otherwise unable to communicate her wishes directly to her doctor. Usually, the living will states that it is to be followed only when the signer has no reasonable hope of recovery and treatment is likely only to prolong the dying process.

A living will is not really a will at all: It does not dispose of any property nor does it appoint an executor to carry out the instructions it contains. Furthermore, it does not have to be signed in accordance with the formal execution ceremony that is required for wills. However, most states' laws do require a different set of formalities to be followed in signing a living will in order for the living will to be valid. In most states, for example, a living will must be signed in the presence of witnesses and the signatures of the person signing the living will and of the witnesses must be notarized. Most states also prohibit certain people from acting as witnesses to a living will, most commonly, the signer's attending physician and the physician's employees as well as employees of the hospital where the signer is being treated. In addition, many states have laws that provide a statutory form of living will. Although these laws also often provide that other forms are valid if they are signed in accordance with the proper formalities, this area of the law is so new that the laws of the states still differ fairly widely on many aspects of living wills. Therefore, readers should consult an attorney familiar will the law of the state where they live before executing a living will. If you use a form that you find in a magazine written for nonlawyers, you run the risk that a doctor may question its validity and refuse to follow the wishes you express in it. Thus, your family may have to get a court order to terminate any life support procedures that are being performed for you, which is exactly the result that you were trying to avoid by signing a living will.

The laws of the different states differ sharply on two matters: First, whether a living will can be followed *only* when the patient is terminally ill or is also valid when the patient is in a persistent vegetative state; and second, whether a living will may authorize *only* the termination of life support procedures or may also authorize stopping artificial administration of food and water.

The difference between a terminal illness and a persistent vegetative state is that a terminally ill patient is likely to die of her illness within a relatively short period of time while a patient in a persistent vegetative state is in an irreversible coma and has no voluntary (conscious) brain function, but can be kept alive for many years. If you do not wish to be kept alive in a persistent vegetative state, it is important to express this wish clearly in your living will.

Life support procedures are those that assist your body in performing vital functions such as breathing. Artificial administration of food and water, on the other hand, does not assist the body to do anything, it simply provides food and water in a form that the patient can digest so that she will not starve to death or die of thirst. Because a patient may not be able to eat and drink on her own even though her body is still able to perform vital functions such as breathing and digestion, removing artificial feeding and watering is much more controversial than stopping medication or even removing life support procedures. Removal of food and water looks more like homicide to many people than do the other actions. Nevertheless, many people do not wish to be kept alive in a persistent vegetative state even if that means that feeding and water tubes must be removed. If you hold this belief, it is important to express your wishes concerning food and water clearly in your living will.

### Durable Powers of Attorney for Health Care

A durable power of attorney for health care is a document in which you designate another person to make health care decisions for you. Durable powers of attorney for health care bear a closer resemblance to durable powers of attorney for financial management (discussed in this chapter at pages 444–46) than living wills bear to wills.

The person executing a durable power of attorney for health care is usually called the "principal" and the person who will carry out the principal's wishes under the power of attorney is the "agent." Some states, however, call the agent a "proxy," and the document itself is called a "health care directive." Like a durable power of attorney for financial management, a durable power of attorney for health care continues to be effective even when the principal is unconscious or otherwise unable to make decisions.

The agent named in a durable power of attorney for health care is authorized to make decisions about which medical procedures may or may not be performed upon the principal if the principal is unconscious or otherwise mentally incapable of making such decisions herself. Typically, the agent is authorized to make end-of-life decisions similar to those that might be covered by a living will, such as whether to remove artificial life support or to stop artificial feeding. However, the agent under a durable power of attorney for health care generally is given broad authority to make all health care decisions that must be made while the principal is incapable of deciding for herself. A principal who is capable of making decisions generally may override the decisions of her health care agent.

Like a living will, a durable power of attorney must be executed following certain formalities listed in a state statute, and is invalid if the formalities are not observed. In addition, most states have statutes restricting who can act as an agent under a durable power of attorney for health care and some states provide statutory forms of durable power of attorney for health care. Anyone wishing to sign a durable power of attorney for health care would be wise to ask an attorney to prepare it, rather than resorting to a form printed in a magazine or a book, in order to assure that the relevant state statutes will be complied with.

In deciding whom to give a power of attorney for health care, readers should remember that no one is required to act as an agent just because she is nominated to do so. Therefore, readers should ask the person they wish to name as agent whether she will be willing to make these difficult and emotional decisions concerning the end of life if called upon to do so.

## Should I Sign Both a Living Will and a Durable Power of Attorney for Health Care?

The answer to this question is definitely "Yes." You should sign both documents for several reasons: First, the law in this area is still developing and is not uniform in all states. The law of the state where you are located when treatment decisions must be made will determine the rights and responsibilities of the health care professionals who are administering your treatment. This will not necessarily be the state in which you live because you might suddenly become ill while you are visiting family members or friends in another state, or while you are away from home on business, or while traveling between two destinations in a state with which you have no connection. Signing both a living will and a durable power of attorney for health care assures you the maximum chance that your wishes will be carried out, in case one or both of your documents does not meet the legal requirements of the state where you are ill, or in case that state recognizes the validity of only one of these documents and not the other.

Second, a living will has a more limited use than a durable power of attorney for health care. Living wills state the patient's wishes concerning termination of life support only and can only communicate the patient's wishes about conditions that the patient knew about when she signed the living will. An agent acting under a durable power of attorney for health care, on the other hand, can be given the authority to make all medical decisions that arise while the patient is unable to decide for herself.

## Suppose I Change My Mind About the Contents of My Living Will or My Durable Power of Attorney for Health Care?

Living wills and durable powers of attorney for health care are easy to revoke in most states. They generally can be revoked orally at any time, even when the patient is terminally ill, so long as she is capable of making decisions and communicating them to her health care providers. In addition, most state statutes governing living wills and durable powers of attorney provide that they can be revoked in writing at any time. Generally, if a person has executed more than one living will or durable power of attorney for health care, the document bearing the later date controls, even if the older document has not been expressly revoked. Some states have statutes providing for the automatic expiration of these documents after a certain number of years. In these states, living wills and durable powers of attorney must be renewed periodically to remain valid.

### A Word About Organ Donation

Many people want to leave their bodies to be used in scientific research after their deaths or wish that certain of their organs, such as their eyes or their kidneys, be given after their deaths to a living person who needs them to replace her own damaged or defective organs.

Most states today have a statute setting out the procedure for making these wishes known. Some states even permit licensed drivers to note on their driver's licenses that they wish to donate certain organs for medical or scientific use. In addition, in many states, a person who executes a living will or a durable power of attorney for health care can add her wishes concerning organ donation to either of these documents. Last, writing down your wishes about the use of your body or any of your organs after your death and giving these written instructions concerning organ donation to a close family member is usually an effective way to make your preferences on this subject known. Unlike the other documents discussed in this chapter, written instructions concerning organ donation generally do not have to meet statutory formalities. This is because a person's body is generally deemed by the law to belong to the person's family after she dies, and the family is free to dispose of the body as they wish.

If you do wish to make your preferences concerning disposition of your body known to your family and the health care professionals who treat you during your last illness, putting this information in a will is not advisable. This is because organs often must be removed from the body promptly after death in order to be useful to another person. Your will may not be read for several days after your death— indeed, it is unlikely to be read until after your funeral—and it may not be probated for weeks after that. Thus, putting this information in your will may make carrying out your wishes concerning organ donation impossible. The person who is in the best position to fulfill your desires in this regard is the family member most likely to be charged with making your funeral arrangements.

## Tax Considerations

### Gift Taxes: Federal Gift Tax
#### What Property Is Taxed?

The federal tax laws impose a gift tax on each lifetime transfer of property in which the giver receives from the beneficiary less than the full value (in money or other property) of the property transferred. For example, a "sale" of land worth $20,000 to one's son for $10 is not a sale but, rather, a gift of $19,990 worth of property. The tax is imposed on all types of property, including real estate, tangible personal property such as jewelry or furniture, and intangible personal property such as stocks and bonds, savings accounts, and life insurance policies.

*Annual Exclusion from Tax:* Each person may give up to $10,000 per year to as many beneficiaries as she wishes without incurring gift tax. Thus, in the example in the preceding section the total gift was $19,990, but if the mother had made no other gifts to that son that year, she would be entitled to exclude $10,000 of the gift and pay tax on only $9,990. She could also give up to $10,000 each to as many other people as she wished this year without incurring gift tax.

It seems appropriate to insert a warning at this point: The federal tax laws, like any other federal statutes, can be changed by Congress at any time, and in fact are amended quite frequently. Thus, although this chapter accurately reflects the state of the law as it existed at the time the chapter was written, it could suddenly become outdated by an act of Congress. Therefore, before doing any actual estate planning, you must check that the law has not changed.

*Split Gifts:* A married person may agree to treat one half of the gifts made by her spouse as her own gifts for gift tax purposes. Thus, the mother in our previous example and her husband could elect to treat the gift for tax purposes as if each of them had made a gift of $9,995 to the son. Since each of them may exclude the first $10,000 of gifts to any beneficiary, the effect of this gift splitting is to allow the entire transfer to escape federal gift tax.

*Marital Deduction:* A married person may make unlimited gifts to her spouse without incurring federal gift tax.

The federal tax laws treat legally married people as "married." Therefore, gifts made to a life partner to whom you are not legally married are fully taxable, except, of course, for the $10,000 annual exclusion.

## How Is the Tax Computed?

Federal gift tax is computed annually on the total amount of gifts made in that year in excess of $10,000 per beneficiary. The tax is cumulative; that is, in the second year in which one makes gifts, one computes the tax by adding the two years' gifts together, determining the tax on the total, and subtracting the tax on the first year's gifts. This has the effect of taxing succeeding years' gifts at higher tax rates.

The federal estate and gift taxes are unified, which means that the rates for both taxes are the same. The federal gift and estate tax rates are graduated like the federal income tax rates. Presently, they run from 18 percent on transfers under $10,000 to 50 percent on those over $2.5 million.

Unification of the federal estate and gift taxes also includes a "unified credit," which can be used against the two taxes. The unified credit has the effect of allowing each person to transfer a certain amount of property tax-free either during life, at death, or partly at each time, in addition to the $10,000 per year per beneficiary. The total amount of property that a person may transfer tax-free is currently $600,000. However, the unified credit also has the effect of eliminating the lowest brackets on the tax rate schedule. Thus, the first dollar of gifts that you make after the $600,000 of tax-free gifts is taxed at 37 percent, the current rate on gifts of between $500,000 and $750,000, and not at 18 percent.

The way these tax provisions work can be illustrated as follows:

Suppose you have assets with a total fair market value of $800,000 and make a gift worth $100,000 to your daughter in 1995, and you and your husband elect to treat the gift as a split gift. The federal gift tax would be figured as follows: First, you and your husband would each be considered to have made a gift of $50,000 worth of property, one half of the gift, by virtue of the split gift election. Each of you may subtract one annual exclusion of $10,000, so you would therefore each have made taxable gift of $40,000. If neither of you had ever made any taxable gifts before, you would each have all of your unified credit available. Since the unified credit allows each of you to transfer $600,000 tax-free, neither of you would pay any gift tax in 1995. Now, suppose you were to die in 1996. At your death, you still owned the rest of your assets and they still had a fair market value of $700,000. In your will, you leave all these assets to your children. Since you have used up $40,000 of your unified credit by making the gift of $40,000 in 1995, your estate will escape estate tax on $560,000 (that is, the $600,000 total unified credit less the $40,000 prior gift). The estate will owe tax on the remaining $140,000 worth of property. At the rates in effect when this chapter was written, the estate tax liability would be approximately $53,000.

You may use as much of the unified credit as you wish to give property tax-free during your lifetime, or, if you prefer, you may refrain from making gifts entirely during your lifetime and the entire amount of the unified credit will be available at your death.

### State Gift Taxes

Some states' gift taxes are assessed approximately the same way as the federal gift tax. A few have a gift tax that is assessed the way the inheritance tax is assessed. Inheritance taxes are discussed in greater detail below. Basically, a gift tax that is assessed in the way that an inheritance tax is assessed would involve varying rates and exemptions, depending on the familial relationship between each beneficiary and the giver. Such a gift tax is not ordinarily cumulative from year to year. Some states have no gift tax.

## Death Taxes: Federal Estate Tax
### What Property Is Taxed?

The federal tax laws require that estate tax be paid on the total fair market value of all property in which the decedent had an interest, to the extent of her interest on the date of her death. As was noted in the discussion of estate administration, the term fair market value means the price that an item of property would sell for on the market in a transaction between a willing buyer and a willing seller. As with the federal gift tax, the federal estate tax is imposed on both real estate and personal property and on both tangible items, such as jewelry and furniture, and intangible items, such as stocks and bonds, savings accounts, and life insurance policies. Furthermore, the federal estate tax is assessed not only on property that is administered as part of the decedent's estate and that passes under her will or by the law of intestate succession, but also on certain property in which the decedent had an interest during her life and which passes to another at her death by the terms of some other instrument. For example, the property in a revocable living trust created by the decedent, and life insurance on her life that the decedent owned, are subject to federal estate tax at the decedent's death.

The tax is paid out of the estate, usually by the personal representative.

The reader will undoubtedly notice the number of times that the phrase "under current law" appears in the discussion of federal estate tax. The warning given in the section on the federal gift tax is important enough to bear repeating here: The federal estate tax can be changed by Congress at any time. It has, in fact, undergone four fairly substantial revisions within the last twenty years. Therefore, it would be unwise to treat the statements made in this chapter as any more than a guide. Before doing any actual estate planning, the reader should consult an attorney to find out the current specific provisions of the law.

There are special rules governing the federal estate taxation of a number of types of property. Among the most commonly encountered of these special categories of property are jointly held property, life insurance, and family-run farms.

The rules concerning estate taxation of *jointly held property* are rather complex. Therefore, the following is necessarily an oversimplification designed to summarize the general rules.

Property held in a tenancy in common or in a joint tenancy without right of survivorship is taxed in the estate of a decedent only to the extent of the fractional interest the decedent had during life. Thus, if a person owns property as an equal tenant in common with her brother and sister, when she dies only one third of the fair market value of the property is taxable.

On the other hand, if the property is held in joint tenancy with right of survivorship, the estate of the first tenant to die is generally taxed on that portion of the fair market value of the property that corresponds to the portion of the purchase price paid by the deceased tenant. Thus, if the decedent in the previous example owned the property as a joint tenant with right of survivorship with her brother and sister, and paid one third of the price when they bought it, one third of the fair market value at her death would be subject to estate tax. If she paid for the whole property, however, the whole property is subject to federal estate tax at her death.

A special rule covers situations in which the only two joint tenants with right of survivorship are husband and wife. In that event, not more than one half of the property will be taxed to the estate of the first spouse to die even if she paid the entire purchase price for the property. This rule also applies to tenancies by the entirety.

Naturally, the entire property will be subject to federal estate tax in the estate of the survivor, because the property will have been solely owned by that person at the time of his or her death.

*Life insurance* is generally taxed to the owner of the policy at her death, regardless of whether the owner is also the insured, unless the proceeds are payable to the estate of the insured. Thus if a person died owning a policy of insurance on her own life, the proceeds would be subject to federal estate tax at her death no matter who the beneficiary was. On the other hand, if her husband owned the policy, the proceeds would be subject to federal estate tax on the insured's death only if the beneficiary of the policy was the insured's estate. If the beneficiary was anyone else, such as her husband or children, the proceeds would not be taxable in the insured's estate.

If the owner of a policy dies before the insured, an amount roughly equal to the cash surrender value of the policy will be subject to estate tax at the owner's death.

As a general rule for federal estate tax purposes, all property is valued at its "highest and best use" fair market value, rather than at its fair market value for the use to which it is actually put by the decedent and his or her family. Thus, if a decedent owned farmland that would have a higher fair market value for sale to a developer to build residential housing, under the general rules of valuation the farmland would be taxed at its development value, rather than at its value as a farm, even though the decedent farmed the land and the beneficiaries intended to continue to do so when they inherited it.

To reduce the hardship this causes to farm families, Congress passed an amendment to the federal estate tax laws in 1976 which allows the personal representative of a decedent who owned a working farm to elect to have it valued for estate tax purposes at its farm value, even if that is lower than its highest and best value, under certain conditions. Again, as with much of the tax law, the rules are too lengthy and technical to admit of complete explanation here. Basically, however, the election is available only if the farm makes up the major part of the decedent's estate, the decedent or a member of her immediate family has been active in the operation of the farm for a certain number of years immediately prior to the decedent's death, and a member of the decedent's family continues to run the farm as a farm for a certain number of years after the decedent's death. The special use valuation cannot be used, under current law, to reduce the value of the farm by more than $750,000 below its highest and best use fair market value. If the family sells the farm, even to another farmer, within a certain number of years after the death of the decedent, all or part of the estate tax saved may become due and payable.

## Can the Federal Estate Tax Be Avoided by Making Transfers During Life?

The answer to this question is, "Yes and no." Since the federal estate tax is payable only on property in which the decedent had an interest at the time of death, any property that is completely disposed of during life will not be taxed at death. However, any transfer that does result in complete disposition during life will be a taxable gift under the federal gift tax, unless the person who receives the property pays the transferor the full fair market value for the property. The gift tax rates and the estate tax rates are the same. Thus, the tax on the property will be the same whether it is subject to gift tax or to estate tax. However, the fair market value of the property for gift tax purposes is determined as of the date of the gift. If the property increases in value after the gift is made, the result of the gift will be to save the tax on the increase in value between the date of the gift and the date of the transferor's death.

Perhaps an illustration will make this clearer: Suppose you make a gift of property worth $200,000 in 1995, and then die in 1998, when the property is worth $300,000. The federal gift tax would be assessed in 1995 on $200,000, that is, on the fair market value of the property on the date the gift was made. At your death, in 1998, this property would not be subject to estate tax at all, since the property would then belong not to you, but to the person you gave it to in 1995. On the other hand, if you had kept the property until your death in 1998 and left it in your will to the same beneficiary (or that beneficiary received it under the laws of intestate succession), the property would be valued at $300,000 for federal estate tax purposes, since that is its fair market value on the date of your death, and federal estate tax would be assessed at that time.

In order to prevent tax avoidance, Congress and the courts have adopted very strict definitions of the terms "completely disposed of" and "interest" to determine whether the property should be taxed as a gift during the life of the giver, or should be included in her estate and subjected to federal estate tax. The retention of any rights in transferred property may cause the property to be fully taxable at the transferor's death, even though she would not ordinarily be thought of by a layperson as the owner of the property. Examples of rights or interests that will result in the federal estate taxation of transferred property are as follows: the right to revoke the transfer; the right to change the terms of the transfer, such as the right to modify the terms of a trust agreement; and the right to use the property or to receive the income from it during life, even though the rights to the property after the transferor's death are irrevocably transferred during her life.

### The Marital Deduction:
### Special Treatment for Property Transferred to a Spouse

Under current law, all property that a decedent leaves to his or her surviving spouse is relieved of federal estate tax. In other words, if you leave all your property to your husband, there will be no federal estate tax due at your death, no matter how much property you own at your death. The property may pass to the spouse by the decedent's will, under the law of intestate succession, or by virtue of the terms of a lifetime transaction such as the survivorship provisions of a joint tenancy. The property may pass to the surviving spouse outright or it may be held in any one of several qualifying trust arrangements. Again, you must be legally married to take advantage of this deduction.

### How Is the Tax Computed?

As was stated in the discussion of the gift tax, the federal estate and gift taxes are unified. Because of unification, the actual computation of the estate tax is rather complex. The law requires that an estate tax be computed on the total of the taxable estate plus all gifts made during life to arrive at the estate tax due. The gift tax previously paid is then subtracted from the amount of estate tax computed in the first part of the calculation. The taxable estate is the total of the fair market values of all the interests in property the decedent owned at death, less certain debts, and expenses such as mortgages and medical bills of her last illness, executors' commissions, probate filing fees, etc., and deductions for charity and for property passing to a surviving spouse. There are credits against the federal tax for state death taxes and the unified credit.

## State Death Taxes
### Estate Tax

Many states have an estate tax that is computed roughly the same way as the federal estate tax. The interests in property that are subject to tax, and the method of valuing them, may differ, as may the amount of allowable deductions and credits. Thus, for example, a state might allow more or less property to pass free of state estate tax than passes tax-free by virtue of the federal estate tax unified credit, and it might allow a marital deduction for a certain fraction of the estate passing to the surviving spouse but tax the excess.

### Inheritance Tax

The total tax base of a state inheritance tax is generally the same as that of a state estate tax, that is, all the interests in property that pass to others by virtue of the decedent's death.

The main difference between an estate tax and an inheritance tax is in the way they are computed. The inheritance tax is computed separately on the total property passing to each beneficiary, less certain debts and expenses allocable to the beneficiary's interest. The rates of tax and the amount of property that passes free of tax depend on the relationship of the beneficiary to the decedent. In general, the decedent's spouse and children enjoy the highest exemptions and the lowest rates of tax; the exemptions get lower and the rates higher as the familial relationship between the decedent and the beneficiary gets more remote. Each beneficiary is responsible for paying inheritance tax on the property she receives.

## Further Reading

The best source of additional material on the topics considered in this chapter is your local or state bar association. Many have pamphlets on such topics as Wills, Estate Administration, the Laws of Intestate Succession, and Estate Taxation, which they will provide free or at a nominal charge to the public.

### Bibliography

See previous chapter for additional listings.

Clifford, Denis. *Make Your Own Living Trust.* Berkeley, CA: Nolo Press, 1995.

Clifford, Denis, and Cora Jordan. *Plan Your Estate, 3d ed.* Berkeley, CA: Nolo Press, 1995.

Duff, Richard W. *Preserving Family Wealth Using Tax Magic.* New York: Berkley Publishing Group, 1995.

Doukas, David J., and William Reichel. *Planning for Uncertainty: A Guide to Living Wills and Other Advance Directives for Health Care.* Baltimore: Johns Hopkins University Press, 1993.

Matthews, Joseph. *Savvy Legal Planning Over 50*. Berkeley, CA: Nolo Press, 1995.

Phillips, David T., and Bill S. Wolfkiel. *Estate Planning Made Easy: Your Step-by-Step Guide to Protecting Your Family, Safeguarding Your Assets and Minimizing the Tax Bite*. Chicago: Dearborn Financial Publishing, Inc., 1994.

Prestopino, Chris J. *Estate Planning and Taxation, 1995*. Dubuque, IA: Kendall Hunt Publishing, 1994.

## Organizational Resources

American Association of Retired Persons (AARP)
601 E Street NW
Washington, D.C. 20049
(202) 434-2277

National Association of Estate Planning Councils
98 Dennis Drive
Lexington, KY 40503
(606) 276-4659
*Over 200 local groups made up of professionals—attorneys, CPAs, trust officers, and life underwriters.*

---

**Amy Morris Hess** is a professor of law at the University of Tennessee College of Law in Knoxville, Tennessee, where she has taught estate planning, wills and trusts, and taxation for the last fifteen years. Before beginning to teach, Hess practiced primarily in the field of estate planning in New York and Charlottesville, Virginia. She is co-author of a textbook on estate planning and administration and is an articles editor of *The Real Property, Probate and Trust Journal*, published by the American Bar Association.

Chapter 24

# *The Legal Aspects of a Death*

Constance Hauver

**Introduction**

Although this chapter is designed to assist an individual in dealing with the legal problems resulting from the death of another, it would be useful to review this material in advance of the need to use it. It is, for example, difficult for a widow to deal with the financial and legal aspects of her husband's estate if she has not met his advisors, does not know the location of legal documents, or has no familiarity with the assets involved. The traumatic period surrounding the death of a close friend or member of the family is not an ideal time to absorb new information.

The death of a husband, lover, parent, child, friend, or business partner could involve a woman in settling an estate. There are a number of tax and state law benefits that apply only to a surviving spouse, but the discussion in this chapter will otherwise be generally applicable to anyone in charge of handling a deceased person's estate.

There are few legal or financial actions that must be taken immediately after a person dies. In fact, it is wise to take time to understand the process of administering an estate and to learn about the assets involved before taking any significant steps that would change those assets. The first steps in the legal and financial areas will involve a determination of the need for professional help—lawyers, accountants, bank trust officers—and identification of the proper people to fill such needs, if they exist, and a determination of the composition and size of the estate and the means to protect it.

**Funeral and Burial Arrangements**

If an individual dies at home, certain legal requirements must be met. If the individual was under a doctor's care, the doctor may be permitted to pronounce the person dead and release the body to a funeral home. If there was no attending physician, the coroner's office should be contacted to determine the required procedures.

Funeral and burial arrangements will need to be made immediately. These may have been preplanned and prepaid by the person who has died (the decedent). Although describing all of the alternatives available for funeral and burial arrangements is beyond the scope of this book, it is important to note that these arrangements will most likely involve the signing of contracts that incur financial obligations. You will need to understand the extent of those obligations before undertaking them.

Funeral expenses are generally one of the first claims against an estate and are paid before family members are entitled to benefits. If funeral arrangements were not made in advance, you may need to make decisions about purchasing funeral goods and services while experiencing intense grief, time constraints, and family differences regarding disposition of the body, type of funeral or memorial service, and place of burial. Funerals can be expensive, and it is easy to be persuaded to buy more than one intends. Some states have organizations that assist people who want to limit the cost by providing simple alternatives to the more costly products sold by funeral homes.[1]

The federal Funeral Industry Practices Regulation, adopted by the Federal Trade Commission in 1984, makes it easier for you to select only the goods and services you want or need and to pay for only those you select.[2] This regulation requires disclosure of the funeral provider's practices and fees. A state may apply for exemption from this federal regulation if the state has similar requirements regarding funeral industry practices that provide as good or better protection than the federal regulation.[3]

As required by the Funeral Industry Practices Regulation, a funeral provider may quote prices over the telephone. If you inquire in person about funeral arrangements, the funeral provider must supply a general price list. This list, which you can keep, contains the cost of each individual funeral item and service offered. You can use this information to help select the funeral provider and funeral items you want, need, and are able to afford.

The price list also discloses important legal rights and requirements regarding funeral arrangements. It must include information on embalming, cash advance sales (such as newspaper notices or flowers), caskets for cremation, and required purchases.

Certain services, such as cash advance items, are paid by the funeral provider on your behalf. These may include, if you order them, honoraria to clergy, limousines, funeral escorts, memorial cards, newspaper obituary notices, musicians' fees, flowers, and copies of the death certificate. In some cases, the funeral provider will charge you a service fee in addition to the actual cost of these items.

You will need certified copies of the death certificate for many purposes in administering the estate—for example, to file claims for life insurance proceeds, social security benefits, and retirement benefits, as well as to clear title to any joint bank accounts or jointly held real estate. The funeral provider can order these for you—or you can obtain them yourself from your state's vital statistics or health agency, but this may take a week or so longer.

It may be important not to make too many changes too quickly. However, certain matters must be attended to or value could be lost. It will be important to determine, if you do not already know, what periodic payments must be made to preserve assets and/or protect them. Did the decedent have outstanding loans or debts for payment of a home or car? Credit card balances? Are liability and casualty insurance in effect and, if so, when is the next payment due? Did the

## Maintaining the Status Quo

decedent's health insurance policy cover any dependents or related family members and, if so, do they have continuing health insurance coverage? Are income taxes due—or estimated payments on next year's taxes? The first task is to determine what payments need to be made. The second task is to make provision for payment consistent with rights of creditors in the estate.

## Settling the Estate

The major burden of settling a husband's estate usually falls on his wife. A daughter may be responsible for her parents' estates and a mother for her child's. If you are the person responsible, you may want to hire professionals to undertake some or all of the complex procedures involved in estate settlement. But even so, you alone may be the only person who can assist your attorney or bank trust department in locating important papers, determining the validity of creditors' claims, and making sure the decedent's estate is distributed as she wished.

If the decedent died without a will (intestate), it will still be necessary to follow most of the estate settlement procedures to ensure that you determine what assets she had, settle any debts, pay taxes, and ultimately distribute the remainder of the estate. See chapter 23 for information on wills, trusts, jointly held property, distribution of an estate, and the estate as an economic entity.

## Estate Settlement Overview

We are assuming here that the decedent left an estate of some sort and that you will become involved in helping settle it. If you are the surviving spouse, then even though a bank, friend, or other relative might have been named personal representative of the estate, you should be aware of the overall process—what is expected and when. If you have been named as the personal representative, you have even more need to understand the steps and terminology. But even if you have taken on much of the burden, an attorney can help direct and review the work you have done, to make sure it complies with the applicable laws. And, in states where the attorney's fee for estate settlement is a percentage of the estate, letting her do most of the work makes good sense.

The following explanations are designed to familiarize you with the terminology you will encounter; this will be useful particularly if you choose to take part in the estate settlement and do some of these steps yourself. In some cases you can help close the estate sooner and save yourself money by doing some of the groundwork for your attorney. Ask how you can help and what is required. The procedures we outline are not all-inclusive. Each state has different laws, which may require either more or fewer steps, depending on the size and complexity of the estate. Your attorney will guide you. The most common estate settle-ment task a family member performs is to locate and describe all the decedent's assets. Inventory worksheets for the estate's assets and liabili-ties are provided at the end of this chapter.

## The Executor, Administrator, or Personal Representative

For guidance in settling an estate, it is common to hire a lawyer or the services of a bank trust department. Check the decedent's will to see if it specifies a particular bank or person to act as personal repre-sentative. You may need to coordinate your choice of legal assistance with what is specified in the will.

The terminology used in legal documents may differ from state to state. For example, you may see the word "executor" to designate a male person who is responsible for carrying out the terms of the will while a woman is referred to as the "executrix." When there is no will, the re-sponsible male person may be called an administrator and the female an administratrix. To simplify, some states use the term personal represen-tative for either sex, and whether or not the decedent left a will, and for simplicity we will use this term. The deceased person is often termed the decedent. Legal documents are also extensively enumerated or contain paragraph designations. This is to help locate a particular word or point that may need to be discussed or questioned.

### Duties of the Personal Representative

The personal representative has four major areas of responsibility in settling the decedent's estate:

1. Inventorying and safeguarding the assets

2. Overseeing and managing the estate while settlement procedures are ongoing

3. Paying taxes and debts

4. Accounting for and distributing the assets to the proper beneficiaries

The personal representative is legally responsible for seeing that the estate settlement procedures are completed. There can be co-personal representatives such as an individual and a bank who work together on an estate. The personal representative need not perform the tasks alone and may hire an accountant, attorney, and other pro-fessionals, who are all entitled to reasonable fees and, in some states, may receive a percentage of the value of the assets. You may be able to contract and pay an hourly rate instead.

## Estate Settlement Steps

Estate settlement is sometimes called estate administration. The personal representative's major responsibilities have been grouped here into five areas, each followed by a list of specific tasks. The order may be varied and some steps may not be required, depending on state laws and guidance from your attorney. The personal representative is ultimately responsible for seeing that, when appropriate, these steps are accomplished.

### 1. Getting Organized and Getting Information

*Make funeral arrangements,* if these have not already been completed. Sometimes the decedent has specified what she wants in the will or a written memorandum.

*Retain an attorney.* (See chapters 1 and 23 for guidance.) Be sure to find out whether the attorney's fees are set by law as a percentage of the estate. In some states, the fees an attorney will charge for handling an estate are set by law, based on the size of the estate. In many states, however, attorneys' fees can be negotiated on a contract basis.

*Locate the will, life insurance policies, and any trust agreements* describing trusts that the decedent created or in which she had any interest by searching desks, cabinets, closets, safe deposit boxes (requires the decedent's and the bank's keys), office files and drawers—any places the decedent might have stored private papers. If you or an attorney can't locate the will in any of the logical places, then it is possible that there is no will or that the will is lost. Contact the decedent's attorney, who may know when the will was written and who may have a copy, if not the original. The original must be filed with the probate court, often within a few days after the death. The person or institution in possession of the will has the obligation to file it with the court.

*Protect assets.* Determine whether the decedent had assets that need immediate protection (such as livestock, crops, pets, or perishables) and take steps to provide care and security. In an emergency, the probate court can appoint a temporary special administrator to perform these functions if necessary, or you can ask a family member or friend to help.

*Apply to (petition) the probate court* to admit the will to probate and ask that the named personal representative be appointed. Usually your attorney does this for you, but you may apply yourself if you are the person designated as the personal representative in the will, or if you have priority for appointment under state law if there is no will. The court will respond with a special document called "letters testamentary," which gives the personal representative authority to begin settling the estate. Ask the attorney if the will can be informally probated, or if you can use any simplified estate settlement procedures to avoid the need for a court hearing. For more details on the probate process, see chapter 23.

Probate is the procedure or process by which specialized courts prove that the written will of the decedent is valid, before authorizing the distribution of a deceased person's property according to the will's provisions. It is this court that also appoints the personal representative as the person or institution with the power and responsibility for administering the estate. The mere word probate can conjure up images of an expensive process and high attorney's fees. The cost of settling an estate is not generally attributable to probate (or title transfer) itself but, especially in complex estates, to the determination and minimization of tax liabilities and distribution of the estate. However, in some states, especially those that have not adopted the Uniform Probate Code,[4] attorneys' fees and personal representative's fees may be based on the size of the estate which, in a large but uncomplicated estate, can result in high fees disproportionate to the work done. (See also chapter 23.)

*Note quantities of expendable or consumable assets*, such as animals and their food supplies, or crops.

*Immediately begin keeping detailed records* of all expenses and income regarding the estate. Keep all receipts. You will need this record to prepare the estate's income and estate tax returns, to provide an accounting to the estate's beneficiaries, and to close the estate.

*Obtain as many copies of the death certificate* as may be needed to be used in filing life insurance claims and to facilitate transfer of assets. You will likely need a death certificate for each different insurance company insuring the decedent and one for each asset held in joint tenancy (for example, home, stock—one for each company, automobile, bank accounts). Some funeral providers will order the copies for you, sometimes at a small additional charge. Or you can apply in person to the appropriate state agency, such as the bureau of vital statistics (it may take several weeks) and pay a fee for each certified copy. You can always obtain additional copies after the initial order, if needed.

*Find out if checking accounts are still open* so you can have access to funds if needed. If they are accounts held jointly with you, change them to your name. You may have to provide a death certificate to do this, and in some states you may need an inheritance tax clearance. If the account is not jointly held, find out what documents you need to change them to the name of the estate, with you—as personal representative—as signatory, so that you have access to the account. The bank or other institution in which the account is located will be able to help you meet these requirements. If you use funds in your joint accounts to pay estate bills, you should be reimbursed by the estate.

*Establish an estate account;* this is a separate checking account to receive funds earned by the decedent before death but not received until after death and to receive estate income. It is also used to pay estate expenses. If all income of the estate goes through this account and all bills are paid from it, you will have an easy and accurate method of accounting for estate transactions. You will need a separate taxpayer identification number (rather than your own Social Security number) for this account. You can apply for a taxpayer identification number using a Federal IRS form SS-4. (This identification number will be needed for paying estate taxes, so you will need to apply for one eventually in any event.) Ask your attorney, accountant, or the bank trust department for help.

*Determine the present and near-future cash needs* of the decedent's spouse. In some cases, the estate's attorney can help the surviving spouse apply for an immediate living allowance from the assets of the estate while the estate is being settled. Dependent children may also be entitled to a living allowance during this period.

*Locate birth certificates for each member of the family* (including the decedent), any military documents, the decedent's marriage certificate, any divorce or annulment records, Social Security numbers for each family member and beneficiary, and income tax records of the decedent for the past three years. Some of these will be needed to file claims for Social Security and veterans' benefits.

*File claims for life insurance benefits.* Look for life insurance policies among the decedent's important papers. If you cannot find them, look in the decedent's checkbook to see to which insurance companies the decedent made payments. If the decedent was still employed, call his or her supervisor or the personnel office to ask if the company had insurance on the decedent's life. Some people have life, health, auto, and homeowner's insurance coverage with the same company.

Once you have determined which policies covered the decedent's life, you can call the insurance companies to obtain claim forms. The claim form must be signed and submitted to the insurance company by the beneficiary named on the policy or by the personal representative if the insured's estate is the beneficiary. The insurance company will want the policy and a certified copy of the death certificate along with the claim form. Make a copy of the policy before mailing for your own file. If you cannot locate the policy, you must contact the insurance company and request a "lost policy form." Then complete the lost policy form and submit it along with the death certificate. Remember: *Life insurance proceeds are not automatically paid following a death. You must file a claim for them.* See sample letter at end of chapter.

If your state law provides for interest to be paid on the insurance proceeds from the date of death until the payment is made to the beneficiaries, make reference to that statute in your letter sending in the policy and claim form. If premiums were prepaid on any life insurance policy, ask for reimbursement.

Even if the death was a suicide, you may still have a claim in some states. If the policy was in effect for the minimum time required by your state law, you may be eligible for benefits, unless the policy specifically states that no benefits will be paid in the event of a suicide. The major insurance companies usually require that the policy be in effect for a year or more. Some state laws require less time. Be aware that in suicide deaths, no accidental death benefits are ever paid. Some persons may have separate accidental death and dismemberment or accident policies; these benefits are payable only in case of an accident, not for death by illness or suicide.

You will need an explanation of the payout for estate settlement purposes. Depending on the type of life insurance, the amount of payment may include the death benefits, or "face amount," plus credit for unused premiums, accumulated dividends and possibly interest on the proceeds from the date of death to the date of payment, less deductions for outstanding loans. The form 712 that the insurance company will provide will itemize these amounts.

*Determine if the decedent had a pension.* A pension refers to a special type of employee benefit account to which the decedent and/or his or her employer may have made regular contributions. This money is to be invested, then in the future paid out as a retirement or disability benefit. The decedent may have had one through her employer or a labor organization. Depending on several conditions, the spouse of the decedent may or may not be eligible for survivor benefits.

- Did the decedent participate in a pension fund? First, ask the employer (or former employer). If the decedent belonged to a labor organization, look in the yellow pages and call or write them. Ask how you might apply for survivor benefits.

- Is the surviving spouse or other beneficiary eligible for any survivor pension benefits? Many employees, in anticipation of larger pension checks, choose to waive the option for survivor benefits if they should die. As of August 1984, however, an employee may no longer waive the survivor benefit for a surviving spouse without the spouse's written consent.[5]

- How much will the survivor benefits be? If they are available at all, they will be smaller than the amount that would have been payable to the decedent.

- When will they begin? They may not begin until the decedent would have been sixty-two, or at retirement age for that particular pension.

- How long will they continue?

- How frequently are cost-of-living increases applied?

*Determine whether or not the decedent owned an annuity.* An annuity is a contract that guarantees a series of agreed-upon payments at some future time—typically at retirement—to an individual, called an annuitant. Insurance companies sell annuities and some employers have annuity programs. Check with the decedent's employer, stockbroker, and insurance agent to see if any annuities were purchased.

Call the decedent's employer or the insurance company for information about how to apply for survivor annuity benefits. When you apply, you will need a copy of the death certificate and Social Security numbers for the decedent and the beneficiary. Be sure to get a written explanation of the estimated benefit calculations for any beneficiary.

Under the Civil Service Retirement System for survivors of federal government employees, it can take months to receive the first annuity payment. Special conditions apply for children over eighteen to qualify for benefits. If the amount of payment is different from what you expected, photocopy the check and deposit it to your account. *Do not return the check*. Returning the undeposited check just causes confusion. The system is huge and it takes time to process thousands of claims. If you were overpaid, the government will let you know; be prepared to write a personal check to return the amount of overpayment at their request. If you feel you were undercompensated, it is up to you to write a letter requesting an adjustment. Include your reference or claim number, the amount you feel you are entitled to, along with clearly stated reasons, and list the dates and amounts of each check received. Photocopy all checks and keep careful records for tax purposes and to document any adjustments you request.

*Determine if Veterans Administration benefits are available.* Survivors and dependents of veterans may be eligible for certain Veterans Administration (VA) benefits. The benefits usually include burial in a national cemetery, payments toward burial expenses, a headstone or marker, and an American flag to drape the casket. There are 110 national cemeteries, and the VA may pay for transportation of the decedent to the cemetery nearest his last place of residence. There is no charge for burial of a deceased veteran in a national cemetery. If a qualified deceased veteran has already been interred in a private cemetery, either by preference or because the funeral provider wasn't aware of or did not advise you of the national cemetery alternative, you can still apply for burial reimbursement and other benefits. Your application must be made within two years of the date of death.

Other benefits include educational assistance for dependents, dependency and indemnity compensation (DIC), and nonservice-connected death pensions. In some cases medical care is available to the surviving spouse or child. Divorced widows may also apply for benefits.

*How to apply for benefits.* In every telephone directory there is a toll-free number listed for the Veterans Administration assistance in your state. They will send you a packet of instructions and forms you need to complete in applying for benefits. Or you can apply in person at any VA office. If you live in a rural area or small town, telephone or visit your local Disabled American Veterans (DAV) or Veterans of Foreign Wars (VFW) office. These service organizations can help you apply for widow's benefits if you are the surviving widow.

If you apply in person, you will need the following documents:

- Certified copy of the decedent's death certificate

- Military records, especially the *Form DD 214,* the *Certificate of Release* or *Discharge from Active Duty* (also called separation papers)

- Certified copy of the decedent's marriage license if the applicant is the surviving spouse (if you need a certified copy, just write or visit the county clerk's office where the marriage license was issued and pay for a copy)

- Certified copy of birth certificate for each child

- Divorce or annulment agreements, if applicable

- Social Security number of decedent and of you

- Name and address of any guardian for minors (children under legal age)

- Name and address of personal representative, if any, appointed by the court to settle the estate of the decedent

*Apply for Social Security benefits, if applicable.*

*Review the decedent's health insurance coverage.* Determine if there is a time limit for filing claims for benefits.

*Ask the decedent's home and auto insurance agents* to check the decedent's insurance coverage for mortgage insurance (home insurance policy) and accidental death and dismemberment benefits (auto insurance policy). Mortgage insurance may also have been purchased from the lender who financed the purchase of the decedent's home. Change the name of the policyholder as needed.

*Review credit and bank cards for any insurance* on outstanding credit card balances. If there is none, you may decide to pay valid charges as usual or write to the creditor explaining the death and requesting a delay, or arrange for lower payments until the estate is settled. Some companies automatically cover accidental death if the decedent was traveling when she died and bought her ticket by credit card.

*Locate and begin to inventory assets* by describing physical (tangible) assets or by collecting documents. These assets or documents should include all bank accounts, stocks, bonds, life insurance policies, annuity or pension accounts, ownership of business interests, partnership agreements, real estate deeds and abstract descriptions, lease contracts, collections of coins or stamps, and titles to personal property such as automobiles. Reviewing the sources of income on the decedent's most recent income tax return is a useful way to make certain you have located all assets.

*Get current addresses and Social Security numbers* of all heirs and persons who will receive property or cash from the estate.

*Value each asset* as of the date of death, or, if you are required to pay federal estate taxes, then on another allowable date called the "alternate valuation date," which is usually six months after the date of death.[6] In calculating these valuations, you may encounter the following terms:

- Fair market value. For valuation purposes, this is the price at which the property would change hands between a willing buyer and seller in a free and open market.

- Tangible Personal Property. A qualified personal property appraiser can help you arrive at the appropriate values. The fair market value is used for silver, antiques, jewelry, furs, art, coins, and other collectibles. Auction value may be more appropriate for less unique furniture and furnishings.

- Real estate valuation. Have property appraised by a real estate agent or appraiser.

- Oil, gas, and mineral interests. Ask your attorney or bank trust department for expert appraisals on these properties.

- Farm estates. Since 1981 farms or other businesses considered major assets may be valued at "current use"—meaning the use to which they were put during the decedent's lifetime—providing they remain in the family. There are several special rules and conditions for using the current-use valuation; for example, you can prevent farmland next to a town from being valued as if it were to be a shopping center or at "highest and best use." Consult with your attorney.

- Stocks and bonds. Prices for these securities on the date of death, or on the alternate valuation date, can be found in the financial section of the newspaper. The mean or average between the high and low values on the date of death (or alternate valuation date) apply. Check at the library to obtain the newspaper reporting stock values on the valuation date or ask your broker to determine these values.

- Autos. At the library, consult the CPI Value Guide, the NADA Official Used Car Guide or the Kelly Blue Book.

- Business interests. The bank trust department or your attorney will assist in reviewing the terms of business or partnership agreements, value of the decedent's share and the estate's rights.

## 2. Managing the Estate

The personal representative has a fiduciary obligation, or position of trust, in managing the property and financial affairs of the decedent for the benefit of others. The personal representative is not to favor the interests of one party over another, is not to put her own interests in conflict with those of the estate, and is to administer the estate carefully and prudently.

The personal representative must keep records and make reports or accountings to interested parties.

*Recordkeeping.* Continue careful accounting for all income and expenses pertaining to the estate, including income in respect of the decedent (income earned before death, but not paid until after death).

*Inventory.* Within about three months, or at specified times, prepare an inventory of assets (noting changes in live assets such as livestock and crops) and a detailed accounting of estate transactions. Consult with your attorney as to whether the inventory or accountings need to be filed with the court.

*Accounting.* Periodically submit to the beneficiaries a report and detailed accounting of estate transactions.

*Insurance.* Examine all insurance documents as to adequacy of property insurance coverage and status of taxes and assessments.

*Property.* Make sure taxes and assessments are paid in a timely manner. Collect rents, obtain tenants, make repairs—be the rental property manager. Arrange for management of "live" assets such as animals and crops.

*Title transfer.* Have the names on all stocks and bonds changed to the designated personal representative, and arrange for collection of dividends and interest. Usually a stockbroker is involved, and you will need to provide her with certified copies of the death certificate or certified copies of the letters testementary, and properly executed stock powers. An alternative is to send the stock certificates and proper documentation (death certificate or letters testamentary and stock power) directly to the stock transfer agent of the company involved. This, however, takes time, research, and knowledge as to proper execution of a stock power. Assets that are owned in "joint tenancy"[7] should be retitled in the name of the surviving joint tenant. In some states, with respect to real estate owned in joint tenancy, the mere recording of a certified copy of the death certificate of one joint tenant will clear title to the real estate in the surviving joint tenant.

*Investments*. Review all investments for safety versus risk and make changes as necessary. For example, some stocks may be speculative and unsuitable for estate investment. Consult a stockbroker for advice, but beware of sales pitches for other stocks.

*IRAs*. Notify managers of IRA and other retirement funds in the decedent's name of the death so the account can be transferred to the beneficiary designated.

## 3. Determining Debts and Claims Against the Estate

In addition to assets, the estate usually has debts—funeral expenses, medical bills, and balances on mortgages and loans. The personal representative is responsible for determining the validity (truthfulness) of claims against the estate and for paying estate debts. You may wish to ask your estate attorney to do any or all of the tasks below.

*Bills*. Determine current bills—such as rent, utilities, medical, credit card balances—and arrange to pay them if the estate has the funds to do so. If there are not enough funds to pay all bills and debts, you should consult with your attorney. Certain claims against an estate have priority and paying one creditor at the expense of another may result in your being held personally liable for the loss.

*Death notices*. Publish required notice of death to creditors. This is usually done in the local newspapers. In most states, this allows creditors about four months in which to file claims. Publication is not required in all states, but, if a notice is not published, the risk is that creditors could have up to one year or longer to file claims.

*Estate expenses*. Keep track of estate administration expenses that may be deductible on estate or income tax returns, such as legal and accounting fees for work done to settle the estate. These may still be deductible even though the Tax Reform Act of 1986 sharply curtailed available income tax deductions.

## 4. Filing Returns and Paying Estate Taxes

Estate, inheritance, or fiduciary taxes to be paid on the decedent's estate are usually calculated by the estate's attorney or an accountant working with your attorney. The federal estate and state estate and inheritance taxes are commonly called "death taxes." Additionally, "fiduciary income taxes" may have to be paid on income earned by the estate during its administration. Death taxes and fiduciary income taxes are perhaps the most distressing aspect of estate settlement. These taxes are complex, and you would be well advised to ask for assistance in meeting these responsibilities. See the previous chapter.

By the time taxes are due, the estate assets have been valued, most administration expenses have been recorded and debts have been determined. It is advisable to employ either an estate attorney or tax accountant experienced in filing these returns to work with you. If the attorney or accountant is retained soon after the death, she will alert you to time deadlines for filing the tax returns and the information needed to prepare the returns so that you can be gathering and organizing this information as you proceed through the estate's administration.

Listed below are the types of tax returns involved in estate settlement and the procedures that the estate's attorney or accountant will most likely perform. The estate may have to pay several different taxes following the death, depending on federal and state laws.

If you are the surviving spouse, continue to file your U.S. *Individual Income Tax Return* (Form 1040) as usual, showing your income and deductions for the entire year, but showing your late husband's income and deductions only until the date of his death. This will be your husband's "final income tax return." As a surviving spouse, you may file a joint return for the year of death and be entitled to special benefits for the two following years, if you meet the IRS requirements for qualifying widows. If you are not the surviving spouse, you will need to see that the final form 1040 is filed for the decedent including on it all income received by the decedent in the year of death but prior to death.

The *Fiduciary Income Tax Return* (Form 1041) is usually filed if the gross income of the estate is $600 or more during the taxable year (at the time of this writing). Income earned before death, but not received until after death, is called "income in respect of a decedent." For tax purposes, you may think of the decedent's income that arrived after death as "estate income." This income is reported on the estate's income tax return, Form 1041, not on the decedent's personal Form 1040. It is as though the decedent became two tax-paying entities in the year of death—the first (while alive) filing a 1040 (or a joint 1040 if there is a surviving spouse) and the second (the estate) filing a 1041 and recording income and expenses realized after the decedent's death. This splits the income into two parts, which may or may not result in a lower tax bill. The fiduciary return, Form 1041, is used to pay income taxes for the estate. In some cases where the estate is open for more than one year, a fiduciary return is filed each year.

The *United States Estate Tax Return* (Form 706) is not filed for every estate, but only when the gross estate is worth more than $600,000. This return is due within nine months after death, unless an extension is granted. The estate tax is imposed on the estate—not on the estate's beneficiaries—and the tax is paid before the estate assets are transferred to heirs and beneficiaries. The estate tax is calculated on both the assets of the estate and certain gifts made to beneficiaries before death. First, a total dollar value is determined for the deceased's gross estate, including taxable gifts. Then allowable deductions (debts, expenses, losses, marital transfers, and charitable contributions) are taken to leave the *taxable estate*. Taxes are assessed against the taxable estate. The taxable estate may include the value of joint tenancy property (one-half the value if owned by husband and wife or the percentage of the value contributed by the decedent if the joint owner is not the decedent's spouse). Life insurance proceeds are also included in the taxable estate if the decedent had any rights in or to the policy at death.

A *federal gift tax* may be levied on gifts that exceed the current annual excludable limit of $10,000 which may be given each year to as many people as the donor (person making the gift) wishes. Such gifts in excess of the $10,000 which also do not qualify for the marital (gifts to a spouse) or charitable (gifts to qualified charities) deductions are referred to as taxable gifts. Twenty-five percent of the states have a *gift tax* and 60 percent of the states levy an *inheritance tax*.

While estate assets must be valued for tax purposes, the estate can utilize exemptions and deductions to reduce the overall tax bill. Minimizing taxes is not only appropriate but a responsibility of the personal representative, with the help of your accountant and attorney. Two major tax savings can be realized by using the unified tax credit and the marital deduction.

## Unified Tax Credit

In the past, a vast number of estates, including estates of people of modest means, were burdened with the requirement of paying federal estate taxes. To alleviate this problem, especially for the surviving spouse, a federal law enacted in 1976 provides that a "unified tax credit" is allowed for each person's estate. In effect, this means that the estate tax will be lower because part of the estate is not taxed. You get a "credit" on your tax bill. The tax credit on the estate and the tax credit on gifts are combined or "unified."

The unified tax credit applies to and protects $600,000 of the decedent's estate. That is, there would not be a tax on the first $600,000 of the taxable estate. You should not even have to file this tax return (Form 706) if the decedent's gross estate was less than $600,000. However, if the taxable estate were worth more than $600,000, say as much as $750,000, then the estate might be liable for taxes on $150,000. (See also chapter 23.)

## Marital Deduction

The next most important tax savings, if the decedent left a surviving spouse, is the "unlimited marital deduction," which allows an estate to deduct all of the portion of the estate that is given outright to the surviving spouse under the will or under state law—thus possibly saving the estate from any federal estate tax bill. Some trusts will also qualify for the marital deduction. However, there are qualifying circumstances that must be met. Ask your attorney or accountant to explain in detail. Also, in some cases maximum use of the marital deduction may not be in the future heirs' best interests as maximizing the marital deduction may diminish or eliminate the tax benefit of the unified credit to the decedent's estate. This varies with each individual estate plan and must be carefully considered with guidance from your tax accountant or estate planner.

Consult with your attorney for specific guidance regarding your tax liabilities. Keep in mind that the taxes are paid only when base levels are exceeded.

| Taxes Payable After Death (Death Taxes or Unified Transfer Taxes) | | | |
|---|---|---|---|
| **Decedent** | **Estate Tax** | **Inheritance Tax*** | **Fiduciary Income Tax** |
| Form to use | U.S. Estate Tax Return 706 | State Forms | Fiduciary Income Tax Return 1041 |
| Paid to | Federal government | State government | Federal government and state (if applicable) |
| Based on | Both the estate and inheritance tax are each calculated on the value of the gross estate, which may include jointly owned property and gifts. | | Income received on probate assets are earned by the estate after death. |
| Reason levied | Paid on right to transfer wealth. | Paid on right to receive wealth. | Paid on income earned in respect of the decedent and income earned by estate. |
| *Note: 60% of states have an inheritance tax and 25% of states have a gift tax. | | | |

*Taxes Payable After Death*

## Tax Filing And Tax Paying Duties

The following checklist outlines the tax filing and tax paying duties of the estate's personal representative. The personal representative is legally responsible for paying the estate taxes, but should be able to delegate the preparation tasks to an attorney or accountant. The list below is provided to help the personal representative understand the steps that are required.

- Apply for a tax identification number using Federal IRS Form SS-4, *Application for Employer Identification Number.* This is required because the estate is considered to be a different taxpayer than the decedent.

- File a written notice with the IRS (Form 56) of the person named to act in a fiduciary capacity, that is, the personal representative.

- Complete the final 1040 tax return for the decedent and file by the required deadline date.

- Prepare and file the applicable state income tax return.

- Determine the proper valuation date (for assets for federal estate tax purposes).

- Determine whether estate administration expenses should be deducted from the 1041 income tax or on the 706 estate tax return. Ask your tax accountant for guidance.

- Determine which funds will be used to pay taxes.

- If necessary, complete and file estate tax return, Form 706, which is due nine months after death. Include a copy of the will (if there was one), a death certificate, and Form 712, *Life Insurance Statement,* to be obtained from and completed by the life insurance companies for each policy listed on the estate tax return. Copies of other documents may be requred, depending on the nature of estate assets.

- File state estate tax returns, as required.

- Estate and fiduciary income taxes must be paid when the returns are filed. You may need to apply for an extension of time to pay or arrange for installment payments. The 1986 Tax Reform Act requires some estates to make estimated quarterly payments of income taxes.

- Pay personal property or real estate taxes (if any).

The personal representative must also provide an explanation of "income tax basis" to beneficiaries receiving noncash assets, so that these beneficiaries have the tax information needed when the assets are resold. For example, suppose Denise is the beneficiary of the family summer cottage, which her parents bought in 1955 for $11,000 and which for estate tax purposes in 1995 was valued at $89,000. If ten years later Denise decided to sell the cottage for $95,000, her capital gain would generally be calculated on the basis of $89,000, not on the decedent's original purchase price. "Basis" is the term that describes the recently determined value of the inherited property.

## 5. Paying Claims, Settling Debts, Accounting for and Distributing the Estate

While the estate settlement procedures are ongoing, the personal representative may make a partial distribution of assets to the beneficiaries, if there are enough assets remaining to pay taxes and debts. It isn't necessary to wait until the estate is closed. The exact order of distribution may vary, according to state law. Generally, funeral costs are paid before debts and taxes, with the "residuary estate" (what remains) being distributed to beneficiaries and heirs last.

With few exceptions, a decedent can leave her property to whomever she chooses and in different forms—outright or in trust. A major exception to this rule is created by laws in the various states which protect the surviving spouse. In non-community property[8] states a surviving spouse has the right to up to one-half of the decedent's estate. This fraction may differ from state to state. If that value of the estate is not provided to the surviving spouse by the decedent's will or other type of disposition (such as passage of joint tenancy property to the surviving spouse), the surviving spouse has the right to "elect to take against the will"—to obtain the protected share. While the right to the share is given by state law, it is not automatic and the right must be exercised if appropriate—usually by filing a document with the probate court within a specified time—often no more than six months after death. In most states children of the decedent do not have such protected rights and can be disinherited by the will of the parent. For a more detailed description of the disposition of estates, see chapter 23.

When administration is complete, the personal representative must file with the court or give the beneficiaries a final accounting for all income and expenses and of the administration of the estate. If formal proceedings for closing the estate are required, the court will issue a decree that approves the accounting and proposed distribution and discharges the personal representative. In informal proceedings, the personal representative or the attorney may file a closing statement, signed by the personal representative, that the estate has been fully administered.

Settling an estate can be an extremely complex, time-consuming, and legally specific process. It may require your attention for at least one year, sometimes two or more. Hiring professionals, understanding some of what they do, and overseeing the administration of the decedent's estate will protect and preserve the assets the beneficiaries are to receive.

---

June 30, 1995



New York Insurance Company
Claims Department
Street Address
City, State, Zip

Reference: Policy No. 12345-XYZ

Dear Claims Adjuster:

My late husband, John Doe, died on June 1, 1995. I am filing a claim for the life insurance benefits as described on Policy No. 12345-XYZ.

I am enclosing the policy and a certified copy of the death certificate. Please explain in detail how you determine the amount of payment and enclose form 712. I will appreciate your prompt attention to my request.

Sincerely,



your signature
your typewritten name

Enclosures

---

*Sample Letter for Filing a Claim for Life Insurance Benefits*

## Estate Assets Worksheet

**Cash**  (bank, credit union, savings & loan, checking, money market, CDs, Christmas club, etc.)

| Financial Institution Name/Phone | Type of Account | Account No. | Ownership Sole—Joint | Amount |
|---|---|---|---|---|
| _____ | _____ | _____ | _____ | $_____ |
| _____ | _____ | _____ | _____ | $_____ |
| _____ | _____ | _____ | _____ | $_____ |
| _____ | _____ | _____ | _____ | $_____ |
| _____ | _____ | _____ | _____ | $_____ |
| | | | **Total Value** | $_____ |

### Life Insurance

| Company Name/Phone | Policy No. | Beneficiary(ies) | Cash Value* | Face Amount |
|---|---|---|---|---|
| _____ | _____ | _____ | $_____ | $_____ |
| _____ | _____ | _____ | $_____ | $_____ |
| _____ | _____ | _____ | $_____ | $_____ |
| _____ | _____ | _____ | $_____ | $_____ |
| _____ | _____ | _____ | $_____ | $_____ |
| | | | **Total Value** | $_____ |

*(accumulated dividends, credit for unused premiums, etc.)

### Real Estate

| Description & Location | Purchase Date—Price | Ownership Sole—Joint | Appraised Value |
|---|---|---|---|
| _____ | _____ | _____ | $_____ |
| _____ | _____ | _____ | $_____ |
| _____ | _____ | _____ | $_____ |
| _____ | _____ | _____ | $_____ |
| _____ | _____ | _____ | $_____ |
| | | **Total Value** | $_____ |

### Securities—Stocks, Bonds, Mutual Funds, Unit Trusts, Government Securities

| Institution–Broker Name/Phone | Account No. | Ownership Sole—Joint | Value at Death or Alternate Date |
|---|---|---|---|
| _____ | _____ | _____ | $_____ |
| _____ | _____ | _____ | $_____ |
| _____ | _____ | _____ | $_____ |
| _____ | _____ | _____ | $_____ |
| _____ | _____ | _____ | $_____ |
| | | **Total Value** | $_____ |

## Pensions, Annuities, Retirement Plans, Profit Sharing, IRAs, KEOGHs

| Description & Location (firm name) | Account No. | Value of Survivor Benefits (if any) |
|---|---|---|
| _____ | _____ | $_____ |
| _____ | _____ | $_____ |
| _____ | _____ | $_____ |
| _____ | _____ | $_____ |
| _____ | _____ | $_____ |
| | **Total Value** | $_____ |

## Business Interests (corporations, partnerships, sole proprietorships)

| Firm Name/Address/Phone | Type of Business | Cost Basis | Appraised Value |
|---|---|---|---|
| _____ | _____ | $_____ | $_____ |
| _____ | _____ | $_____ | $_____ |
| _____ | _____ | $_____ | $_____ |
| _____ | _____ | $_____ | $_____ |
| _____ | _____ | $_____ | $_____ |
| | | **Total Value** | $_____ |

## Debts Due The Estate (notes, mortgages, royalties, patents, etc.)

| Name of Person/ Firm Owing | Address/Phone | Ownership Sole—Joint | Date Due | Amount |
|---|---|---|---|---|
| _____ | _____ | _____ | _____ | $_____ |
| _____ | _____ | _____ | _____ | $_____ |
| _____ | _____ | _____ | _____ | $_____ |
| _____ | _____ | _____ | _____ | $_____ |
| _____ | _____ | _____ | _____ | $_____ |
| | | | **Total Value** | $_____ |

## Personal Property (collections such as coins, guns, stamps, vehicles, art, furniture, etc.)

| Description | Location | Approximate Current Value |
|---|---|---|
| _____ | _____ | $_____ |
| _____ | _____ | $_____ |
| _____ | _____ | $_____ |
| _____ | _____ | $_____ |
| _____ | _____ | $_____ |
| | **Total Value** | $_____ |

| | | |
|---|---|---|
| | **Total of All Assets** | $_____ |

## Notes

1. For example, in Denver, Colorado, The Rocky Mountain Memorial Society, a nonprofit consumer organization, helps its members in arranging low cost, prearranged mortuary services.
2. Code of Federal Regulations, Title 16, Part 453.
3. Id. at § 453.9.
4. The Uniform Probate Code was designed to simplify the probate process and minimize its cost. Unfortunately, it has been adopted by only a minority of states and uniformity in even those has not been achieved as many states have modified certain of the Code's provisions and/or have failed to adopt uniform amendments to the Code as they have been added. The states that have adopted the Uniform Probate Code are Alaska, Arizona, Colorado, Florida, Hawaii, Idaho, Maine, Michigan, Minnesota, Montana, Nebraska, New Mexico, North Dakota, South Carolina, South Dakota (but only in part), and Utah. The adoption process is an evolving one. Some states have adopted only parts of the Code and others have adopted the Code with substantial modifications. Alabama used the Code as a guide in drafting its own probate code.
5. The Retirement Equity Act of 1984 provided protection of an employee's retirement benefits for the nonparticipating spouse by requiring the written consent of the spouse to waive the joint and survivor annuity form of payout. Any waiver by a spouse must show the spouse knew of and understood what she was waiving, must be in writing and notarized or witnessed by the employee benefit plan's administrator.
6. If estate taxes are payable, the estate has the option of valuing the estate assets on date of death or on the "alternate valuation date" which is six months after date of death. If the alternate valuation date is used, any assets sold or distributed prior to the alternate valuation date must be valued as of the date of sale or distribution.
7. Joint tenancy with right of survivorship is a unique form of ownership of assets among two or more persons. Each tenant has equal rights in the ownership of the asset and the surviving joint tenant or tenants automatically become the owners of the share of the deceased joint tenant. The joint tenancy form of ownership can apply to ownership of real property and personal property. Each state has its own requirements for establishing joint tenancies. In most states, to establish a joint tenancy in real estate takes express language on the deed creating the tenancy stating that the grantees take the property "not as tenants in common but as joint tenants." In some estates, with respect to bank accounts, two or more names on the account alone will create a joint tenancy. With most other types of assets, express language of joint tenancy is

required to create such a tenancy. Ownership of assets as tenants in common does not have the right of survivorship and the deceased tenant's percentage of ownership passes in accordance with the terms of the decedent's will.

8. Most states are "non-community property" states. Community property states include Arizona, California, Idaho, Louisiana, Nevada, New Mexico, Texas, and Washington. In addition, Wisconsin has enacted the Marital Property Act, effective January 1, 1986, which created community property rights in spouses. Essentially, community property states treat income earned by either spouse during a marriage as community property in which both spouses have equal rights. These rights include the right of each spouse to dispose of one-half of the community property at death. In community property states, separate property is property brought into the marriage or acquired after the marriage by gift or inheritance. In non-community property states, income earned by a spouse belongs to the spouse who earns it. Assets acquired with such earnings are separate property and subject to disposition by the owner of them. Casner, *Estate Planning,* Sec.10.31.1.

## Bibliography

Much of this chapter borrowed very heavily, with permission, from chapters in *The Widow's Handbook* by Charlotte Foehner and Carol Cozart, published by Fulcrum, Inc.

Foehner, Charlotte, and Carol Cozart. *The Widow's Handbook: A Guide for Living.* Golden, CO: Fulcrum Publishing, 1988.

Kubler-Ross, Elisabeth. *On Death and Dying.* New York: Macmillan Publishing, Inc., 1970. The classic study of death, dying, and bereavement.

Houlbrooke, Ralph, ed. *Death, Ritual, and Bereavement.* New York: Routledge, 1989.

Norrgard, Lee E., and Jo DeMars. *Making End-of-Life Decisions,* Santa Barbara, CA: ABC-Clio, 1992.

## Organizational Resources

A number of organizations provide emotional support for people who have lost a loved one, particularly a spouse or a child. Other groups provide assistance for people with terminal illnesses and their families. Contact your local library to obtain listings of these. The organizations below are national and provide advice, support, and referrals.

American Association of Retired Persons (AARP)
Widowed Person's Service
601 E Street NW
Washington, DC 20049
(202) 434-2277

Funeral Service Consumer Arbitration Program
P.O. Box 27641
Milwaukee, WI 53227
(414) 541-7925
(800) 662-7666
*Promotes arbitration of disputes between customers and funeral directors or funeral homes.*

National Sudden Infant Death Foundation
8200 Professional Place, Suite 104
Landover, MD 20785
(301) 459-3388
(800) 221-SIDS

Older Women's League
730 11th Street NW, Suite 300
Washington, DC 20001
(202) 783-6686

---

**Constance Hauver,** now retired, practiced law for twenty-four years with a large Denver law firm and was a partner for nineteen of those years. She specialized in the areas of tax, estate planning, and estate administration. She served as president of the Rocky Mountain Estate Planning Council and as chair of the Probate and Trust Law Section of the Colorado Bar Association.

Chapter 25

# Legal Issues for Refugee Women

Karen Musalo

Chapter Outline

**Introduction**

**Historical Origins and Current Definition of Refugee in U.S. Law**

**Difficulties in Establishing Eligibility**

**The Canadian Approach**

**Recommendations for the United States**

In greater numbers than ever before, people from all parts of the world are fleeing their home countries as a result of war or oppression, and are seeking refuge in other countries. The United Nations High Commissioner for Refugees (UNHCR), the international organization charged with refugee protection, recently issued a report putting the number of refugees at an all-time high of 44 million people. A majority of the world's refugees are women, who face special problems in their search for protection and safety. It is only recently that international organizations and state governments have begun to recognize and address the unique problems confronting women refugees.

**Introduction**

This chapter provides an historical overview of international and domestic refugee law, and will explain the special issues implicated in women's claims for asylum. It will discuss recent changes which have more favorably addressed the situation of women, and will make recommendations for modifications in U.S. policy which would result in fairer treatment of females seeking asylum.

## Historical Origins and Current Definition of Refugee in U.S. Law

After World War II, with its massive displacement of people, the international community came together and developed two international refugee agreements: the United Nations Convention Relating to the Status of Refugees (the Convention); and the United Nations Protocol Relating to the Status of Refugees (Protocol). The United States, along with many other nations, signed the Convention and/or the Protocol, agreeing to accept the definition of refugee contained in these treaties.

The U.S. definition of refugee, which is almost identical to the definition in the Convention and Protocol, is contained in a law known as the Refugee Act, enacted by Congress in 1980. The Refugee Act defines a refugee as a person who has been persecuted in the past, or who has a "well-founded fear" of being persecuted in the future "on account of" race, religion, nationality, political opinion, or membership in a particular social group (these five categories are often referred to as "enumerated grounds"). The "on account of" language requires the showing of a causal connection between the persecution and the enumerated grounds. In other words, it is not enough to have been persecuted or to have a well-founded fear of future persecution; in order to present a successful claim for asylum, the applicant must show that she was persecuted *because of* her race, religion, nationality, political opinion, or membership in a particular social group.

## Difficulties in Establishing Eligibility

Women seeking asylum have faced difficulties relating to both parts of the refugee definition—proof that the harm they have suffered is persecution, and proof that the harm is linked to the five statutory grounds. Decision makers have been slow to recognize that the types of harms from which women suffer are "persecution" within the meaning of the law. Although there is no universally accepted definition of persecution, it is generally acknowledged that a threat to a person's life or freedom is persecution. It is less clear, however, whether other harms that are particular to women are also persecution. Harms specific to women include rape and other forms of sexual violence, infanticide, genital mutilation, bride burning, domestic violence, forced abortion, and compulsory sterilization. Women also suffer harm in the form of institutionalized discrimination, which limits their ability to pursue an education, or choose a profession, or to earn a livelihood.

Even in cases where women have been successful in establishing that the type of harm they suffered is persecution, they have often lost their claims because the decision makers have declined to find that it was linked to their race, religion, nationality, political opinion, or membership in a particular social group. A 1987 U.S. federal court case is illustrative of this problem. The case involved a young Salvadoran woman, who went to visit her uncle, who was involved in an agricultural cooperative. During the visit, three unknown individuals came to the house, executed her uncle and male cousins, and raped her and her female cousins, threatening to kill them unless they fled immediately. The woman fled to the United States, where she applied for refugee status. She was denied asylum because the judges said that the harm she had suffered was not connected to her race, religion, nationality, political opinion, or social group membership. In the opinion of the judges, the woman just happened to be in the wrong place at the wrong time, and therefore was not entitled to refugee status.

## The Canadian Approach

Canada has taken the lead in developing an innovative and compassionate approach to addressing the claims of women refugees. In March of 1993, the Chairperson of the Canadian Refugee Board, Murjehan Mawani, issued Guidelines to be applied in the cases of women refugee claimants. Reportedly, the case of a twenty-four-year-old Saudi woman who had been beaten and stoned in her native country for refusing to wear a veil brought the issue of women asylum applicants to a head in Canada. The woman was initially denied refugee status, but the denial was later withdrawn.

The Canadian Guidelines present a more enlightened approach both in determining whether the feared harm is persecution, and whether it can be linked to one of the enumerated grounds.

1. Is the harm persecution?

   In determining whether the harm is persecution, the Guidelines encourage the use of international human rights standards as a point of reference. There are many international treaties and covenants which provide such a framework, including the Universal Declaration of Human Rights, the International Covenant on Economic Social and Cultural Rights, the International Covenant on Civil and Political Rights, the Convention on the Elimination of All Forms of Discrimination Against Women, the Convention on the Political Rights of Women, and the Convention on the Nationality of Married Women.

The use of these and other international standards is extremely useful, and results in increased protection of women. The harm suffered by a woman will be considered to be persecution if it constitutes a serious violation of a fundamental human right. When analyzed in this context, practices such as genital mutilation or bride burning will more clearly be characterized as persecution. National laws or policies that result in discrimination and interference with the ability to lead a productive life will also be more clearly identifiable as persecution when viewed through the lens of international human rights norms.

2. Is the harm on account of race, religion, nationality, political opinion, or membership in a particular social group?

The Guidelines provide a generous framework also in determining whether the persecution is on account of an enumerated ground. Furthermore, they use the "membership in a particular social group" ground almost as a safety net for providing protection to women whose claims might not easily fit within the other grounds.

For example, women who are subject to domestic violence in a country that denies them protection, would be considered to be a "social group." In line with this type of analysis, a woman who suffered beatings at the hands of her husband, and who had no legal recourse, could raise a successful claim for refugee status. The Saudi woman, mentioned above, who suffered beatings and stonings for not wearing a veil, could also raise a successful claim based on social group. Women who suffer severe discrimination by virtue of being women would also be able to raise social group claims.

3. Other Important Aspects of the Canadian Guidelines:

Decision makers in refugee cases are often reluctant to apply the law in a way which might open the metaphorical "gates" of a country to large numbers of refugees. Fear of the "floodgates" has often led to a fairly restrictive interpretation of the law. This can be especially true in the case of women asylum seekers. Decision makers are reluctant to grant asylum to a woman who suffers from a type of harm which all the women in that society face. An example would be the reluctance to grant refugee status to a woman who did not want to submit to genital mutilation. Theoretically, if that particular woman is granted refugee status, then all women from that country would likewise qualify. The Canadian Guidelines make the point that regardless of the size of the potential refugee group, the law is to be fairly and impartially applied. This is an important principle, even though the reality is that not all the women from that country would make the choice to flee their home country and seek asylum in Canada or the United States. Therefore a grant of asylum to a particular woman does not in reality open the country to hundreds of thousands of similar claims.

Another important factor addressed by the Canadian Guidelines is the need for enhanced sensitivity in dealing with women refugees. Asylum seekers are required to recount the facts of their cases to judges or other adjudicators. If their testimony is consistent, specific, and detailed, they will be found to be credible, that is, believable.

For cultural as well as psychological reasons, women applicants may find it difficult to tell their stories to male adjudicators. This reluctance is certainly heightened where the persecution consisted of rape or other sexual assault. The shame which attaches to such experiences may make it extremely difficult for an asylum seeker to recount it. In addition, women claimants who have been the victims of sexual violence may suffer from rape trauma syndrome, and may require an extremely sensitive approach.

The Canadian Guidelines make a number of recommendations to address these issues, including the use of adjudicators specially trained in dealing with violence against women, the option of giving testimony in written rather than oral form, and the option of providing the testimony by videotape in a safe, secure environment. These recommendations are quite a move in the right direction given the reported incidents of insensitivity on the part of male decision makers.

## Recommendations for the United States

In periods of economic downturn, public sentiment generally has turned against immigrants and refugees. At the time of this chapter's writing, a worldwide recession has resulted in a shrinking welcome for refugees globally. In the United States this restrictionist attitude has been evidenced in a flurry of congressional activity to amend the Refugee Act in a way that cuts back on its protections.

In such a climate, it is a formidable task to argue not only against such cutbacks—but for an expansion of protections. Yet that is the struggle women refugee advocates have undertaken. Refugee lawyers have developed proposed guidelines for modifying the U.S. approach to dealing with the claims of women asylum seekers. The guidelines were intended to bring the United States more into line with the approach taken by Canada. In May 1995, the U.S. Immigration and Naturalization Service has adopted what it calls "considerations" (rather than guidelines) for gender-related asylum claims, adopting many of the concepts proposed by refugee advocates.

Thus, even in light of the shrinking welcome extended to refugees, there is reason for a measure of optimism regarding women asylum seekers. Women are making their voices heard all around the world on issues of refugee and human rights, and hopefully it will be impossible for the United States to ignore the stories they are telling.

## Organizational Resources

American Friends Service Committee
Immigration Law Enforcement
  Monitoring Project
5711 Harrisburg Boulevard
Houston, TX 77011
(713) 926-2799

Ayuda, Inc.
1736 Columbia Road NW
Washington, DC 20009
(202) 387-4848

Asian Immigrant Women Advocates
310 8th Street, Suite 301
Oakland, CA 94607
(510) 268-0192

Asian Law Caucus
468 Bush Street, 3d Floor
San Francisco, CA 94108
(415) 391-1655

California Women's Law Center
The Civil Rights of Women:
  Focus on Immigrant Women
6024 Wilshire Boulevard
Los Angeles, CA 90036
(213) 935-4101

Center for Immigrants' Rights
48 St. Mark's Place
New York, NY 10003
(212) 505-6890

Chinese Staff and Workers' Association, Inc.
15 Catherine Street, 2d Floor Rear
New York, NY 10038
(212) 619-7979

Coalition for Humane Immigrant
  Rights of Los Angeles
1521 Wilshire Boulevard
Los Angeles, CA 90017
(213) 353-1333

Coalition for Immigrant and
  Refugee Rights and Services
Immigrant Women's Task Force
955 Market Street, Suite 1108
San Francisco, CA 94103
(415) 243-8215

Federation for American Immigration
  Reform
1666 Connecticut Avenue, NW
Suite 400
Washington, DC 20009
(202) 328-7004

Filipina Girls Development Program
Filipinos for Affirmative Action
3982 Homer Street
Union City, CA 94587
(510) 487-8552

Fund for New Citizens
c/o Taym Higashi
The New York Community Trust
2 Park Avenue
New York, NY 10016-9385

GABRIELA Network
P.O. Box 703
Times Square Station
New York, NY 10036
(212) 592-3507

Grantmakers Concerned with Immigrants and Refugees Rights
c/o Antonio Maciel
Joyce Mertz-Gilmore Foundation
218 East 18th Street
New York, NY 10003
(212) 777-5226

Immigrant Workers' Resource
Center
25 West Street
Boston, MA 02111
(617) 542-3342

La Mujer Obrera Program
Centro Obrero, Inc.
P.O Box 2975
El Paso, TX 79923
(915) 533-9710

Lucy Parsons Project
The Funding Exchange
666 Broadway, #500
New York, NY 10012
(212) 529-5300

Manavi
P.O. Box 614
Bloomfield, NJ 07003
(908) 687-2662

Mexican American Legal Defense
and Education Fund
182 Second Street, 2nd Floor
San Francisco, CA 94105
(415) 548-8235

Mujeres Unidas y Activas
955 Market Street, Suite 1108
San Francisco, CA 94103
(415) 243-8215

National Coalition of Advocates for
Students
Clearinghouse for Immigrant Information
100 Boylston Street, Suite 737
Boston, MA 02116
(617) 357-8507
(800) 441-7192

National Immigration Forum
220 I Street, NE, Suite 220
Washington, DC 20002
(202) 544-0004

National Immigration Project of
the National Lawyers' Guild
14 Beacon Street, Suite 506
Boston, MA 02108
(617) 227-9727

Refugee Women in Development
1735 Eye Street, NW, Suite 501
Washington, DC 20006
(202) 289-1104

Sakhi for South Asian Women
P.O. Box 20208
Greeley Square Station
New York, NY 10001
(212) 714-9153

Sepa Mujer
91 North Franklyn Steet, Suite 211
Hempstead, NY 11550
(516) 489-8330

Women Refugees Project
Harvard Immigration and Refugee
Program
Cambridge and Somerville Legal
Services
432 Columbia Street, Suite 16
Cambridge, MA 02141
(617) 494-1936, ext. 134

Women's Commission for Refugee
   Women and Children
122 East 42nd Street, 12th Floor
New York, NY 10168-1289
(212) 551-3086

---

**Karen Musalo** received her B.A. in Comparative Literature from Brooklyn College, New York, and her J. D. from Boalt Hall School of Law in 1981. Her interest in immigration and refugee issues led her to work as staff attorney at the Father Moriarty Central American Refugee Center in the Mission District of San Francisco, and then as Director of the Refugee/Human Rights Clinic at the University of San Francisco School of Law. She is currently acting director of the International Human Rights Law Clinic at American University. Professor Musalo has been responsible for a number of innovative developments in the refugee field. She pioneered the use of psychological and anthropological expert witness testimony in political asylum hearings and has successfully litigated refugee cases at the Ninth Circuit Court of Appeals. She is a frequent speaker at national conferences and spends much of her time engaged in pro bono work on refugee and human rights issues. She has recently traveled to the former Yugoslavia, Chiapas (Mexico), and Guatemala on human rights projects.

# Postscript:
# The World, Women, and Law

## Marsha Freeman

In the United States, as everywhere else in the world, the legal system is a reflection of the culture that creates it. Laws define relationships between women and men, between citizens and their governments, between people and property, in ways that reflect people's understanding of these relationships and meet people's cultural expectations of what the relationships should be. Family laws in the United States, for example, have always reflected the dominant cultural understanding of what family life should be. Until the late nineteenth century, married women could not own property. Well into the twentieth century laws reflected and courts acted on the assumption that fathers as heads of families always should get custody of children. Until the law reforms of the 1970s, property division upon divorce reflected the assumption that women's lives were property of the marriage and that their labor to build family assets could not be valued outside the marriage.

The legal reflection of culture is not a mirror image, however. Because changing the law is cumbersome and the consequences cannot be predicted with precision, the legal system does not exactly match cultural reality at any given time. Sometimes the law is ahead of the culture, reflecting hopes or attempting to redress unfairness in ways that are not universally accepted. Sometimes it is behind, because lawmakers do not always have a full picture. For example, no-fault divorce, intended to simplify and de-escalate a generally difficult personal process and fairly distribute marital property, resulted in some cases in unwanted dissolutions and unanticipated impoverishment because the laws and the courts did not realistically acknowledge women's low economic status and expectations. At the same time, no-fault divorce came only after at least a decade of increasing educational and employment opportunity that gave some women the personal power to leave miserable marriages that were legally difficult to dissolve. To this day lawmakers, judges, and advocates struggle continually with revising and interpreting family laws to fairly balance the economic interests and emotional welfare of ex-spouses and children, reacting to constant changes in economic reality and in the relationships between men and women and their children.

Throughout the world legal systems reflect the cultural realities and expectations that define women's place. Laws allocate power in families and societies, by allocation of economic rights and responsibilities and of decision making powers. Many women in the world still have limited legal capacity, which defines a person as a full adult for legal purposes—capable of making contracts, owning and managing property, suing and being sued, testifying in court. And where a woman is not recognized fully as an adult in her society, her options are limited and she becomes a captive of her father, husband, or son. She has little say in where the family lives or other major decisions. She may have to get her husband's permission to obtain birth control and may be pressured to have more children than she wants. And with limited access to property or credit, and little education, leaving may be impossible.

The achievement of equality for women ultimately rests on their recognition in law and culture as fully contributing adults. The pace of that recognition has been slow. But it has been increasing, and women have learned a great deal about making change for themselves.

In many societies men still are solely recognized as heads of household, making all economic decisions and holding more power to dissolve the marriage than their wives. In African customary law, which governs the personal relationships of millions of women in sub-Saharan Africa, wives have no right to any of the property accumulated by the couple during the marriage, women—including widows—do not inherit, and usually the husband and his family have primary unquestioned rights to custody of children upon dissolution of the marriage. Under most interpretations of Islamic law, which governs the lives of about one billion people in the world, husbands have responsibility for maintaining the household and make all economic decisions. They also can divorce readily, simply by stating a renunciation of the marriage before witnesses, while women must make a case for divorce before a religious court. In many Latin American countries the grounds for divorce are simpler for husbands than for wives. And in many countries the legal age of marriage is lower for girls than for boys, reflecting an assumption that girls do not have to finish their education and resulting in a lifelong imbalance of power between the spouses.

We commonly think that in the industrialized world things are better for women. But the question is one only of degree. Old assumptions about roles and responsibilities die hard. European countries with very progressive parental leave laws find that most leave still is taken by women rather than men; Sweden, which has had the most liberal leave laws, recently passed a law requiring men to take parental leave. Most European countries are only now coming to grips with the fact that domestic abuse exists in their culture, and recognition of sexual harassment as a discrimination claim is in its infancy. Japan introduced a law several years ago prohibiting sex discrimination in employment, but the enforcement provisions were extremely weak, providing for mediation rather than penalties. Even this weak law went unenforced until a group of women, calling themselves A Letter From Japanese Women Circle, forced mediation of their claims in 1995 after a long battle. And in the United States, the financial and emotional cost of bringing an employment discrimination claim can defeat even the strongest woman.

What has changed in the world is that women have learned how to define their rights and to claim them, and they have made things happen. Test cases, which we in the United States recognize as a major method of claiming rights, are being used in some other common law countries. In Botswana in 1990, for example, Unity Dow, a young Botswana lawyer who is married to a foreigner, successfully challenged the nationality law that denied her rights to pass on her citizenship to her children—a terribly important issue because it placed in question her children's rights to travel with her and to reside in the country with her. Similar cases are under way in Sri Lanka. In India, a human rights lawyer has brought a case to force the government to live up to international obligations concerning women's rights that it has undertaken on paper but not delivered in fact. In Malaysia, a woman successfully sued to prohibit her husband from taking another wife, which has been allowed under Islamic law but can be unfair to prior wives. In Tanzania, a woman successfully sued in 1990 *(Ephraim v. Pastory,* High Court, Mwanza, Tanzania) to change customary law that had denied women the right to inherit and sell certain kinds of property.

Women also have made major progress using advocacy methods to change laws and policies. Women's advocacy helped change laws in many Latin American countries so that men are no longer designated the sole head of household. In Tunisia, where the family law code adopted at independence had eliminated many of the inequities of traditional Islamic law, women recently have been successful in moving the government to address domestic violence, which is rarely recognized publicly as an issue in Islamic countries.

Women's participation in independence and human rights struggles has given them the opportunity to make major progress in changing systems when the struggles succeed and provide new beginnings. In Zimbabwe (formerly Rhodesia), women's contribution as soldiers and front-line supporters in the eight-year guerrilla war of independence was recognized by a revolutionary change in the law, the Legal Age of Majority Act (1982), that grants them full recognition as adults at age eighteen regardless of any provisions of African custom and tradition. In Brazil, women's organization to support democracy during the military regime gave them the skills and credibility to participate effectively in the drafting of a new democratic constitution, resulting in many explicit equality provisions. In South Africa, women's participation in the anti-apartheid struggle has given them a significant voice in the design of the interim constitution and in the new permanent constitution currently being drafted. The Speaker of the new Parliament is a woman who spent years in exile with the African National Congress and is a vigorous champion of women's rights.

In each of these cases, progress toward equality is directly related to recognition of women's abilities and responsibilities. What women in the United States have in common with women everywhere is the need to be recognized in law and in the culture as fully able and fully responsible adults. The question is not our capabilities; the question is acknowledging them.

Legal and cultural recognition of women's full capacities as adults is central to their lives no matter where they live and who they are. The necessity of recognizing and pursuing equality is not a Western or elitist idea. It is a fundamental and universal human rights issue, defined and accepted by women from every region of the world. It is included in every major human rights document and is stated in detail in an international treaty drafted and adopted by the United Nations in 1979, the Convention on the Elimination of All Forms of Discrimination Against Women. This Women's Convention, or CEDAW, as it is variously called, is a brief document that states clearly the premises of equality in education, health, employment, family law, social welfare benefits, and political participation. It includes provisions on sex stereotyping, changing culture, and affirmative action. It is, in short, an international bill of rights for women that suggests some very creative possibilities.

As of September 1995 the Women's Convention had been ratified by 147 countries, making it a near-universal standard of equality. All the countries of Latin America and about half of Africa and Asia have ratified it. No country entirely lives up to its provisions, but ratification only means that a government agrees to try. The United States is closer than most countries to meeting the standards of equality in the Women's Convention, but it has not ratified it. In a close race with time and the vagaries of the U.S. political situation, advocates lost on ratification at the very end of the 1994 Congressional session.

Why is ratification of this treaty important in a country that already lives up to most of its provisions? All the industrialized countries of the world, except Switzerland, have ratified it. Most of them have good to excellent records on equality issues. But by ratifying, a government goes on record as being willing to be held accountable by its citizens as well as by the world. It underscores a dedication to the essential democratic principle that a government owes its citizens both the effort to build a fair society and the willingness to have its actions examined.

In many countries the Women's Convention has provided a framework and an important tool for advocacy. Women have been able to point to the provisions of the Convention, as a basic standard of equality, to make their case for changes in statutes and for reallocation of funds. While in common law countries a treaty does not automatically become law—and it would not in the United States because the ratification documents would explicitly state that it is not law—the Convention and its principles have been invoked successfully in test cases, as a guide to interpretation of constitutions and statutes.

The Women's Convention does not include strong enforcement provisions. In fact, no human rights treaty is enforceable in the sense in which Americans understand enforcement. One cannot readily take a country to court over violations of human rights treaties; the real enforcement of human rights standards is in the court of international and national public opinion, and it is surprisingly effective given that countries cannot be sent to jail. But the Women's Convention does include a requirement that ratifying countries provide reports to a special UN Committee on Elimination of Discrimination Against Women. In many countries women have used this reporting requirement to remind governments that they are being held accountable, both by becoming involved in or monitoring the preparation of the country report and by providing the UN Committee with additional information that the government may not want to release.

American women have a history of organizing effectively to obtain their rights and to change both culture and law. Organizing to become involved in or to monitor the preparation of a report—essentially to watchdog the process—will not be difficult. Publicizing the existence of the international obligation to provide for equality and the degree to which we live up to it also will call on skills that Americans have developed through many years of civic involvement.

Ratification of the Women's Convention would provide a new meeting point for all those who care about women's lives and a new opportunity to hold the government accountable to the governed. And it would give American women a new sense of their belonging in the world, sharing an enterprise with women from every part of the globe.

---

**Marsha Freeman** is the Director of the International Women's Rights Action Watch project, which is based at the Humphrey Institute of Public Affairs, University of Minnesota. The IWRAW project is a women's human rights resource and communication center, focusing on implementation of the Convention on the Elimination of All Forms of Discrimination Against Women, an international treaty ratified by 147 countries. The project serves a global network of over five thousand individuals and groups concerned with women's human rights and monitors developments concerning women throughout the world and in the United Nations human rights bodies. Freeman has also served as Reporter for the Minnesota Supreme Court Task Force for Gender Fairness in the Courts and works closely with other lawyers in the international human rights community. She holds a Ph.D. in English and American Literature from the University of Pennsylvania and a J.D. from the University of Minnesota.

# Glossary

**Adoption**  Legal process that terminates natural parents' rights and duties toward their child and in turn, places those rights and duties with adoptive parents.

**Affirmative action**  Programs designed to remedy discriminatory practices toward minority group members.

**Agent**  A person authorized to act for another.

**Alimony**  The support of one spouse by the other spouse after divorce. Alimony may also be temporary, awarded during the pendency of the divorce proceeding.

**Allegation**  Assertion, claim or statement of what a party to a lawsuit expects to prove.

**Asylum**  A place of refuge or protection, including a foreign country for persons fleeing their native land.

**Capacity**  The ability to understand the nature and effects of one's acts.

**Child abuse**  Any form of cruelty to a child's well-being; also used to describe a sexual attack which may or may not amount to rape.

**Child support**    The parents' legal obligation to contribute to the economic maintenance of their children, enforceable in both civil and criminal contexts.

**Civil action or suit**    Any lawsuit that deals with private rights; any court proceeding other than a criminal one.

**Common law**    It is distinguished from those statutes enacted by legislative bodies. It is the body of principles and rules derived from the statutory and case law background of England and is recognized and enforced by court judgments.

**Competent**    Qualified; having sufficient ability or authority for the task at hand.

**Creditor**    One to whom money is due.

**Custody**    The care and control of a thing or person. Child custody may be awarded by a court to one or both of the parents in a divorce proceeding.

**Damages**    Monetary compensation that may be recovered in court by any person who has suffered loss, detriment, or injury through the unlawful act or omission of another.

**Debtor**    One who owes payment.

**Decedent**    A deceased person.

**Defendant**    The party against whom relief is sought in a civil lawsuit; the accused in a criminal case.

**Delinquency**    Refers to an illegal act by a juvenile.

**Disability**    Physical or mental impairment that results in the inability to perform an act.

**Discrimination**    Unfair treatment because of some characteristic which is not relevant to the issue at hand; for example, an employment decision based on race, age, sex, nationality or religion.

**Due process**    A constitutional safeguard that guarantees fundamental fairness. More specifically, the opportunity to be heard and protect one's rights before a court having the power to hear and determine those rights.

**Equitable**    Just or fair.

**Estate** The total property of any kind that is owned by a deceased person.

**Euthanasia** Painlessly putting to death persons suffering from incurable and distressing disease as an act of mercy.

**Gift** A voluntary transfer of property to another made without compensation.

**Good cause** A legally sufficient reason. It is a relative concept and depends upon the circumstances of the individual case.

**Good faith** An honest belief or intention. An abstract concept, it has no technical or statutory definition.

**Guardian** Someone ordered by a court to care for a person, including the management of her property and other rights, who, because of insufficient age, inability to understand or control her actions, is considered incapable of administering her own affairs. This person is called a "ward."

**Informed consent** A person's agreement to allow something to happen (usually a medical procedure) that is based on a full disclosure of facts needed to make the decision intelligently.

**Irreconcilable differences** A no-fault basis for divorce in many states.

**Jurisdiction** Generally, it is the authority by which courts decide cases; often refers to the geographic area or types of cases over which a court has power.

**Juvenile** A person who is younger than the age at which she is treated as an adult for purposes of criminal law. This age may differ from state to state.

**Liability** Any debt, obligation, duty, or responsibility.

**License** The permission by competent authority to do an act which, without such permission, would be unlawful. For example, states grant professionals such as doctors, lawyers, and dentists licenses to practice their profession.

**Living will** A written directive regarding the administration or withdrawal of life-sustaining medical treatment under certain conditions.

| | |
|---|---|
| **Maintenance** | The furnishing of financial support for another person, usually a spouse or child. |
| **Malpractice** | Professional misconduct or unreasonable lack of skill. Malpractice is a variety of tort, most often brought against doctors and lawyers. |
| **Miranda rights** | Refers to the warning that the police must give upon arrest: the right to remain silent, that any statement may be used as evidence in a court of law, the right to have an attorney present and if the arrested individual cannot afford an attorney, one will be appointed for her. |
| **Negligence** | The failure to use the same degree of care as a reasonably prudent and careful person would use under similar circumstances. Proof of negligence is usually required for an injured person to recover money damages in a court of law. |
| **No-fault divorce** | Popular name for a type of divorce available in many states in which a marriage can be ended on a mere allegation that it has "irretrievably" broken down or because of "irreconcilable" differences between the spouses. Fault on the part of either spouse need not be shown. |
| **No-fault insurance** | A type of car insurance in which each person's own insurance company pays for injury or damage up to a certain limit no matter who was actually at fault. |
| **Palimony** | "Alimony" for unmarried cohabitants who separate. |
| **Parental rights** | The totality of rights of parents over and in connection with their children, including, for example, custody and companionship, the right to discipline and give moral guidance, and the right to manage a minor's earnings and property. |
| **Pension** | Retirement benefit paid regularly, with the amount based generally on length of employment and amount of wages. |
| **Plaintiff** | A person who brings a civil lawsuit; the party who sues. |
| **Plea** | A response or answer in court. In a criminal proceeding, a plea is the defendant's response to the charge. |

**Power of attorney**    A document authorizing another to act as one's agent or attorney. Such power may be either general (for all purposes) or special (for a specific purpose).

**Premarital agreement**    Contract signed by a couple before they marry to determine their property rights and/or those of their children.

**Principal**    Someone who permits or directs another to act for her benefit, subject to her direction and control.

**Privilege**    Refers to those statements made by certain persons within a protected relationship which the law protects from forced disclosure. Privileged communications exist, for example, between attorney and client, and physician and patient.

**Pro bono**    Literally means "for the good." This term is used to describe legal services that are provided free of charge to the client.

**Probate**    Court proceeding by which an estate is administered.

**Product liability**    A tort which makes a manufacturer legally liable for a product in a defective condition that makes it unreasonably dangerous to the user.

**Prosecutor**    The attorney who conducts criminal prosecutions on behalf of the government.

**Punitive damages**    Awarded and are in addition to those money damages that may compensate an individual for her injuries to punish outrageous conduct.

**Restraining order**    A court order that forbids the defendant from doing the threatened act until a hearing can be held.

**Retainer**    The fee a client pays to an attorney to represent her. Generally, a retainer is a fixed sum paid at the beginning of the lawyer/client relationship. The attorney then bills her fees and costs against the retainer as services are rendered. Any money left after the matter is completed is returned to the client.

**Revocation**    The cancellation or destruction of a power or thing within a person's control.

**Sexual assault**   The crime of touching the genitals without consent.

**Sexual harassment**   A type of unlawful sex discrimination in which an unwelcome sexual advance occurs in the workplace, sex is a term or condition of employment, or a hostile work environment is created for women.

**Statute**   A law passed by the legislature.

**Statute of limitations**   A law setting a time limit for bringing certain types of lawsuits and criminal charges.

**Summons**   Document used to begin a civil lawsuit. It requires the sheriff or other designated officer to notify the person named that a lawsuit has been commenced against her in the court from where the summons issues.

**Tort**   A private wrong or injury, other than a breach of contract, for which a remedy is available in the form of a lawsuit for money damages.

**Trust**   An arrangement in which property is transferred and administered by a trustee for another's benefit.

**Visitation**   In a divorce or custody proceeding, the permission granted to parents to visit their children.

**Waiver**   The intentional or voluntary relinquishment of a known right.

**Warranty**   A promise that certain facts are true as represented and that they will remain so, subject to any specified limitations. In sales of goods, the seller gives an implied warranty of merchantability which is a promise that the goods sold are fit for the general purpose for which they are sold.

**Will**   An instrument, usually a document, by which a person disposes of her property, to take effect after her death.

**Workers' Compensation**   The system of state law that provides for fixed monetary awards to employees in case of employment-related accidents and diseases without proof of negligence.

# General Resources

## Bibliography

DiMona, Lisa, and Constance Herndon. *1995 Information Please Women's Sourcebook*. Boston: Houghton Mifflin, 1994.
Easy to use and concise, this reference covers education, work, health, child care, safety, sexuality and relationships, retirement years, politics, and the family.

Women's Action Coalition. *WAC Stats: The Facts About Women*. New York: The Free Press, 1994.
Facts and figures about women in categories from art and cosmetics, to violence and work.

## Organizations

ACLU—Women's Rights Project
American Civil Liberties Union
132 W. 43rd Street
New York, NY 10036
(212) 944-9800

The Arthur and Elizabeth Schlesinger Library
Radcliffe College
10 Garden Street
Cambridge, MA 02138
(617) 495-8647

Center for Law and Education
Larsen Hall, 6th Floor
14 Appian Way
Cambridge, MA 02138
(617) 495-4666

Center for the Study of Family Policy
The City University of New York
Hunter College
Room E1209C, East Building
695 Park Avenue
New York, NY 10021-5085
(212) 772-4450

Center for Women's Global Leadership, Rutgers University
Douglass College
27 Clifton Avenue
New Brunswick, NJ 08903
(908) 932-8782

National Center on Women and
Family Law
499 Broadway, Room 422
New York, NY 10003
(212) 674-8200

National Lawyers' Guild
55 Sixth Avenue, 3rd Floor
New York, NY 10013
(212) 966-5000

National Organization for Women
1000 16th Street, NW, Suite 700
Washington, DC 20036
(202) 331-0066

National Women's Law Center
1616 P. Street NW
Washington, DC 20036
(202) 328-5160

NOW Legal Defense and Education
Fund
99 Hudson Street, 12th Floor
New York, NY 10013
*Write to the Intake Department for assistance.*

Older Women's League
730 11th Street NW, Suite 300
Washington, DC 20001
(202) 783-6686

Southwest Institute for Research
on Women
University of Arizona
Douglass Building, Room 102,
Garden Level
Tucson, AZ 85721
(602) 621-7338

Women's Educational and Industrial
Union
356 Boylston Street
Boston, MA 02116
(617) 536-5651

Women In Transition
125 S. Ninth Stret, Suite 502
Phildelphia, PA 19107
(215) 922-7177

Women's Law Project
125 S. Ninth Street, Suite 401
Philadelphia, PA 19107
(215) 928-9801

Women's Legal Defense Fund
1875 Connecticut Avenue NW
Suite 710
Washington, DC 20210
(202) 986-2600

United Nations Development
Fund for Women
304 E. 45th Street, 6th Floor
New York, NY 10017
(212) 906-6400
*Autonomous fund affiliated with United Nations and concerned with women in developing countries.*

# Index